Jen P.

CIVICS
RESPONSIBILITIES AND CITIZENSHIP

★ ★

CIVICS

RESPONSIBILITIES AND CITIZENSHIP

DAVID C. SAFFELL, Ph.D.
Chair, Department of History and Political Science
Ohio Northern University
Ada, Ohio

GLENCOE

Macmillan/McGraw-Hill

Lake Forest, Illinois
Columbus, Ohio
Mission Hills, California
Peoria, Illinois

* *

Send all inquiries to:
GLENCOE DIVISION
Macmillan/McGraw-Hill
936 Eastwind Drive
Westerville, OH 43081

ISBN 0-02-652960-2

Printed in the United States of America.

2 3 4 5 6 7 8 9 10   AGH   99 98 97 96 95 94 93 92

Cover/Paper Sculpture: Eileen Mueller Neill
Interior Design: Design Associates, Inc.

* *

About the Author . . .

David C. Saffell teaches courses in national, state, and local government and politics at Ohio Northern University in Ada, Ohio, where he is also chair of the Social Sciences Division. He is a graduate of Baldwin-Wallace College and holds master's and doctoral degrees in Political Science from the University of Minnesota. Professor Saffell has taught for over twenty-five years at various colleges in Minnesota and Ohio. Among his various publications are *Essentials of American Government: Change and Continuity* and *State and Local Government: Politics and Public Policy*.

Reviewers and Consultants

Francis Bryant
Teacher, Social Studies Department
Millbrook High School
Raleigh, North Carolina

Terrence Bumgardner
Teacher, Social Studies Department
Carver High School
Chicago, Illinois

Roy Erickson
Social Studies K-12 Coordinator
San Juan Unified School District
Carmichael, California

Helen Richardson
Executive Director Secondary Curriculum
Fulton County Board of Education
Atlanta, Georgia

Denny Schillings
Teacher, Social Studies Department
Homewood-Flossmoor High School
Flossmoor, Illinois

Michael A. Solliday, Ph.D.
Department of Curriculum and Instruction
Southern Illinois University
Carbondale, Illinois

John Soper
Social Studies Curriculum Coordinator
Webster School District
Webster, New York

Warren Tracy
Director of Social Studies
Duval County School District
Jacksonville, Florida

HOW TO USE THIS BOOK

You will get a lot more out of *Civics: Responsibilities and Citizenship* if you know what it contains, how it is organized, and where to find particular information. Let's start with the Table of Contents. This is your key to the book. It tells you what subjects are discussed in the book and where they can be found. It indicates, for example, that the Bill of Rights is covered in Chapter 4. As you can see, the book is divided into eight units, or parts, and 24 chapters.

Once you get into the book, you will find that each unit begins with a section of the Bill of Rights or a later amendment to the Constitution. This quotation sets the theme for the unit. The First Amendment is the theme of Unit 1.

Each chapter begins with a list of objectives. These provide a preview of the important points discussed in the chapter. Within each chapter you will find several special features that are designed to give you background on people and events, and documents that have had a significant influence on American society.

★ **American Profiles** presents the stories of individuals or groups who have served their communities or their country.
★ **Great American Documents** contains original passages from important documents in American political life.
★ **Legal Landmarks** discusses major court decisions. It gives you the history of each case and explains the decision.

★ **Issues of Our Time** focuses on the political, economic, and social issues that you hear about on the evening news.

Two other features are more practical:
★ **Citizenship Skills** provides step-by-step guides to important functions of citizenship, such as "How to Register to Vote," and reviews basic skills of social studies.
★ **Careers** describes jobs in the fields of public and community service.

Each chapter ends with a two-page Chapter Review. This summarizes the main points of the chapter and gives you an opportunity to find out whether you have mastered the vocabulary and the information in the chapter. It also challenges you to think about the ideas presented in the chapter.

Each unit of the book also ends with a two-page review. The first page reviews the material covered in the unit. The second page, **Closeup**, focuses on a subject related to the unit.

The back of the book contains several useful sections. There are maps of the United States and the world, charts of the Presidents and the states, the full text of the Declaration of Independence, the Constitution of the United States, and other important documents. The Glossary explains the civics terms used in this book. The Index tells you where to find specific information in the book.

CONTENTS

UNIT 8   The United States and the World 498

MAPS

CHARTS, TABLES, AND GRAPHS

*C*ongress shall make no law respecting an establishment of religion, or prohibiting the free exercise thereof; of abridging the freedom of speech, or of the press; or the right of the people peaceably to assemble, and to petition the government for a redress of grievances.

— FIRST AMENDMENT

Foundations of American Citizenship

As Americans, we tend to take our freedom for granted. We think of free speech and freedom of religion as our normal rights. But every day, in some parts of the world, people fight, die, go to jail, or leave their homelands so that they can enjoy these precious freedoms.

* * * * *

CHAPTERS IN THIS UNIT

★ ★

What Is Civics?

OBJECTIVES

After you have studied this chapter, you will be able to:

★ Explain the function and purpose of government.

★ Explain the difference between dictatorships and democratic governments.

★ Distinguish between citizens by birth, aliens, and naturalized citizens.

★ Summarize the process of becoming a naturalized citizen.

★ Discuss the important role of immigration in the history of the United States.

★ Describe major shifts in the population of the United States since the Civil War.

SECTIONS

1 Government of the People, by the People, for the People
2 We the People
3 Who Are Americans?

INTRODUCTION

The citizens of Athens in ancient Greece had an odd custom. Once a year they met to decide whether to hold an ostracism, which was like an election in reverse. The citizens would write the name of any Athenian they considered too powerful on *ostraka*, broken pieces of pottery. Anyone who received a certain number of votes had to leave town. The system enabled Athenians to get rid of dangerous individuals who might take over the government and abuse the rights of citizens.

Voting on ostracism was one of the responsibilities of Athenian citizens. The requirements of citizenship have changed greatly since that time. Today, citizens protect their rights by voting for the people they want as their leaders. One thing has not changed, however. With the rights of citizenship come certain responsibilities.

To fulfill our responsibilities as American citizens requires study and thought. We must learn how our government works, how it affects our lives, and how we can make it better. We must also be well informed about the major issues facing our communities.

That is why civics, the study of citizenship and government, is so important. People who know the facts and understand the political process are more likely to elect good leaders. In the words of one political observer, "People usually get the government they deserve."

SECTION 1

Government of the People, by the People, for the People

★ ★

VOCABULARY

civics	dictatorship
citizen	democracy
government	representative

The word *civics* comes from the Latin word *civis*, meaning "citizen." In ancient Rome, where the word was first used, only wealthy landowners were allowed to be citizens. As such, they enjoyed special privileges that the common people did not share. Today the word **citizen** applies to most people. It means being a member of a community with a government and laws. Wealth and property are no longer requirements for citizenship.

Being a citizen means much more than just living in a country. American citizens who live in foreign countries are still citizens of the United States. Similarly, many foreigners living in this country remain citizens of their own countries.

Being a citizen means being a part of a country or community in many ways. It usually means sharing a common history, common customs, and common values. It means agreeing to abide by a set of rules and to accept the authority of your government.

Government, the power or authority that rules a country, is an essential part of every nation and of many communities. It provides

These new Americans wait to take the oath of citizenship. In the background loom the Presidential heads of Mount Rushmore.

nations be settled? Disputes between individuals, for example, might have to be settled by fighting or arguing. The stronger or smarter person—not necessarily the "right" person—would most likely win. Rules help protect us from others, bring order to our lives, and help us live together peacefully.

Without government, imagine how much more difficult your lives would be in other ways as well. Getting from one place to another would be difficult because there would be few roads. Those that did exist would be owned by people who could afford to build them. If you wanted to use one of these private roads, you would probably have to pay a toll to the road's owner.

Every society needs rules and some form of government. It is likely that people learned this lesson very early. The earliest writings known—from the ancient Sumerians—show that people had set up formal governments more than 5,000 years ago.

What Governments Do

Ancient governments served much the same purposes that modern governments serve today. The most important purpose of a government is to provide laws, or rules of conduct. These laws help prevent conflicts between individuals, groups, or nations and help settle any conflicts that do occur. By using laws, a government establishes order and provides security for its citizens.

Governments not only make laws, but also make sure that people obey the laws. Almost every country in history, for example, has

the stability that makes so many things we take for granted possible. A government makes laws, provides services, and keeps order, forming the framework for citizenship.

Why We Need Government

To understand why having a government is important, imagine living without one. Without government, how would disagreements between individuals, groups, or

Building and maintaining the roads is an important service of government. As communities grow, highways may need to be widened to keep up with the increasing traffic.

had laws against stealing. When people know that they will be punished if they take someone else's property, they are less likely to steal.

In general, conflicts are settled by judges and courts, which are a part of government. If one person accuses another of stealing, but the accused person denies the charge, a court determines who is telling the truth. Then, an appropriate punishment, if necessary, is ordered by the judge.

In addition to providing and enforcing laws, governments serve many other purposes. They set up armed services, police forces, and fire departments to protect their citizens. They provide services, such as education, health facilities, and road construction, that most individuals would not be able to provide for themselves. Governments also plan for the future of their country by setting goals, making budgets, and cooperating with other governments.

Levels of Government

Many levels of government exist, each representing a particular collection of people. Each of the 50 states in the United States has its own government; so do most counties, cities, and towns. The students in your school may have their own "student government" to plan activities and suggest changes in school policy.

Although each of these is a government, when most people talk about "the government" they are talking about the *national* government—the government of an entire country. A national government is different

from other levels of government in two important ways.

First, a national government has the highest level of authority over its citizens. A student government, for example, cannot take any actions that go against the policies of the school principal or board of education. In the same way, a city or state government cannot make any laws that would go against the laws of the national government. The national government, however, has the power to make whatever laws it feels would benefit the country. Second, a national government provides the basic framework for our feelings of citizenship.

Being a citizen of a nation means that you share a history and a set of beliefs with the rest of that country's citizens. Americans, for example, share the ideals of individual rights and equality of opportunity. These ideals are expressed in many of our nation's most important documents, and time and again Americans have fought to uphold these ideals. The shared beliefs and history are a part of the heritage of all American citizens, whether they were born here or became citizens after settling here.

Teaching

Have you ever thought about what it is like to be a teacher? Your teacher's job is to help you learn about different subjects and also how to think well. In elementary school, teachers spend all day with the same group of students, teaching them several subjects, such as reading, writing, and arithmetic. In junior high and high school, teachers do just the opposite. They teach the same subject—social studies, for example—to different groups of students all day long.

Teachers also spend a great deal of time outside the classroom working at their jobs. They prepare lesson plans, grade exams and papers, take courses, attend meetings, confer with parents, or help with after-school activities. Teachers who work in colleges and universities also specialize in one subject.

Vocational teachers are another type of teacher. They often work for vocational schools or for labor unions, teaching students how to perform a

specific skill, such as repairing cars or operating a computer.

To become a teacher, you usually must be a college graduate. Many schools require advanced degrees as well. Public school teachers must take education courses in addition to courses in their subject area. To be a good teacher, a person must like chil-

dren or young adults and must have a great deal of patience.

Using Your Skills
1. How is teaching in an elementary school different from teaching in a high school or college?
2. What do you think are some of the rewards and some of the disadvantages of teaching?

Types of Government

There are more than 170 countries in the world today. Each has its own history and beliefs, and each has a government that is at least slightly different from the governments of other nations. Not all countries are governed in the same way as the United States. In many countries, the power of the national government is in the hands of a very small group of people—or sometimes of just a single person.

A government that is controlled by one person, or by a small group of people, is called a **dictatorship**. The leaders of a dictatorship have complete control over the laws and government of the country, and thus over the lives of its citizens. Often, the citizens of a dictatorship may be told where they must live, what kind of work they must do, and what political beliefs they must have. They may not be allowed to travel to other countries, or even within their own country.

Kinds of Democracy

The government set up by the ancient Athenians was a "direct democracy," in which every citizen participated directly in the government. When laws needed to be made or leaders chosen, the citizens of Athens would meet to debate and vote on every issue.

Because modern countries are generally much larger than ancient Athens, direct democracy is no longer a practical way to run a national government. (Imagine if some 250 million American citizens had to vote on every new law!) Instead, in many countries, including the United States, citizens elect **representatives** to act on their behalf. In a representative democracy, the work of government is carried on by the citizens' representatives.

In large, modern nations, a government of elected representatives can work more efficiently than a direct democracy. Nevertheless, the power to govern still comes from the citizens. In a representative democracy, the citizens are the final source of authority.

Adolph Hitler ruled Germany as a dictator from 1933 to 1945. Why do you think dictators need large armies?

Throughout the ages, there have been many dictatorships. History is filled with the names of kings, conquerors, and other powerful leaders who controlled their countries completely and often ruled by force. But more than 2,000 years ago, in ancient Greece, the citizens of the city of Athens established a different type of government. Instead of being ruled by a dictator, they created a system called **democracy**. In a democracy, the citizens hold the power to rule and decide what laws will be made.

When the United States was smaller, many community issues were discussed and voted on directly by citizens in town meetings.

SCHENCK, SKOKIE, AND FREE SPEECH

What are the limits of free speech? This question comes up again and again in the United States. Americans have long agreed that the limits must be very broad to ensure true liberty and democracy. Free speech, however, does have some limits. From time to time, a situation arises that tests where the courts and the people feel the boundaries should be.

Schenck v. *the United States* is one of the most famous free speech cases ever to reach the U.S. Supreme Court. In that case, a socialist named Charles T. Schenck was convicted of violating the Espionage Act of 1917. He had passed out leaflets to World War I recruits, urging them to resist the military draft. Schenck's attorneys contended that his conviction was unconstitutional because it violated the First Amendment protection of free speech.

In a landmark opinion upholding Schenck's conviction, Justice Oliver Wendell Holmes ruled that Schenck was not within his rights. The leaflets, he said, posed a "clear and present danger" of causing a criminal action (draft resistance). Holmes cited a now-famous example: "The most stringent protection of free speech would not protect a man falsely shouting fire in a theatre and causing a panic."

The Skokie case is much more complicated. It began in 1976 when a small neo-Nazi organization, the National Socialist Party of America (NSPA), was not allowed to hold a rally in a Chicago park. The group, which preached hatred of blacks, Jews, and Hispanics, decided to hold its demonstration in the Chicago suburb of Skokie, Illinois, instead.

Skokie had a large Jewish population, including several survivors of the Nazi Holocaust. The idea of neo-Nazis parading the Nazi swastika and shouting anti-Jewish slogans caused a furor in the town.

Skokie passed several laws banning military uniforms, "symbols offensive to the community," and literature containing false charges

against any group. The American Civil Liberties Union (ACLU), a legal organization that defends Americans' Constitutional rights, defended the neo-Nazis and their leader, Frank Collin.

Feelings ran very high. The citizens of Skokie felt they had a right not to be subjected to the NSPA's hatred. The ACLU defended the group's right to exercise free speech, no matter how offensive the message. There were four lawsuits; all were decided in favor of Collin. The court ruled that the laws passed by Skokie were unconstitutional violations of free speech.

Although Collin won the right to parade in Skokie, he decided to hold the rally in front of the federal courthouse in Chicago. About 20 NSPA members marched for half an hour, surrounded by Chicago police officers protecting them.

Using Your Skills

1. What was the major difference between the Schenck case and the Skokie case?
2. Do you think the ACLU was right to defend the neo-Nazis? Why or why not?
3. Why do you think the court found the Skokie laws unconstitutional?

Democracy in America

The United States government is one of the oldest democracies in the world. For over 200 years, the people of the United States have used their power and authority to influence their government. They have done this in various ways.

Each American citizen has the right to elect representatives to the national government, including Senators, members of the House of Representatives, a President, and a Vice President. As representatives of the people, these leaders have the responsibility to listen to the opinions of voters, whether expressed in person, by mail, by phone, or through public opinion polls.

Americans also have other ways to make themselves heard and influence their government. By joining a political party, they can help decide who will run for office and help plan for the country's future. Or, by joining with other citizens who share similar viewpoints about a particular issue (such as health care or gun control), they can get the government and other Americans to listen to their point of view.

Abraham Lincoln, America's sixteenth President, described the United States as "government of the people, by the people, for the people." His words make three important points about American democracy. First, Lincoln was saying that the power of the government comes from the people. Second, the American people themselves, acting through their representatives, run their government. And third, the purpose of the government is to make the United States a better place for the people who live there.

By obtaining information about a party's stand on issues, Americans can better choose representatives to act on their behalf when they vote in elections.

SECTION REVIEW

Define the Words

civics   dictatorship
citizen   democracy
government   representative

Check the Facts
1. What are the purposes of governments?
2. Explain the difference between a dictatorship and a democracy.
3. Explain the difference between direct democracy and representative democracy.

Think About the Ideas
4. *Assess.* Why is it important for the citizens of a nation to identify with a shared history and set of beliefs and ideals?

★ ★

SECTION 2

We The People

★ ★

VOCABULARY

alien	deport
immigrant	naturalization

The Constitution of the United States, the document that set up the government we have today, begins with the phrase "We, the people." With those words, the people of the original 13 American states took on the rights and responsibilities of citizens.

In 1787, the year the Constitution was signed, there were fewer than 4 million people in the United States. By 1800—less than 13 years later—there were already four new states, and the population of the country was well over 5 million. This remarkable growth has continued ever since. Today, our 50 states contain about 250 million people.

Which of these people are United States citizens? How can someone who is not a citizen become one? These have been important questions throughout the nation's history. The answers have affected the way our country is today and will affect our future.

Some of the answers have been determined by established customs—unwritten rules observed by all nations. Others have come from specific laws passed by the government. Although the answers have changed over the years, the essential question—who is a citizen?—remains important. United States citizenship is a prize that is sought by many, but given to only a few.

Citizenship by Birth

With very few exceptions, anyone born within the borders of the United States automatically becomes an American citizen. For purposes of citizenship, "the United States" includes not only the 50 states and the District of Columbia, but also American territories such as Guam and Puerto Rico.

If citizens of another country give birth to a child while they are in the United States, that child is considered a citizen. (The citizenship of the parents does not change, however.)

An exception to this rule is made for children born to official representatives of a foreign government living in the United States. Those children are considered citizens of their parents' country, even though they are born here.

A child whose parents are both United States citizens is automatically a U.S. citizen, no matter where he or she is born. The issue is more complicated, however, if only one parent is a U.S. citizen and the child is born outside the United States. Such children are usually considered U.S. citizens. At the same time, they may be considered citizens of the country where they were born. A child in this situation is said to have *dual citizenship*, that is, citizenship in two countries.

Noncitizens

Many people in the United States have come here from other countries. Those who have not become citizens are referred to as **aliens**, another word for noncitizens.

In the early 1900's, most of the immigrants to the United States had to pass through the processing center on Ellis Island in New York harbor.

Some aliens intend to stay in the United States for a short period of time, perhaps as tourists or as guests. They may have come to go to school or to learn skills that they can use when they return to their homelands.

Other aliens, however, come to the United States with the intention of living here permanently. These people are **immigrants**.

Not everyone who wishes to move to the United States can do so. For many years, the United States has restricted the number of immigrants. Any foreigner who wishes to spend more than a short time in this country must apply to the U.S. government for permission.

People who fall into special categories— for example, relatives of U.S. citizens, or people who have special occupational skills— are given preference in the selection process.

Most people who do not fall into one of these categories are denied permission to immigrate. Millions of people apply each year, but only a few hundred thousand are granted permission.

ILLEGAL ALIENS Despite the government's restrictions, an increasing number of aliens are living in this country illegally. Some are people who were refused permission to immigrate; others never applied for permission because they knew they would be turned down.

These illegal aliens come to the United States in a variety of ways. A few enter the country as temporary visitors, but then fail to leave. Others risk capture and arrest by sneaking across the borders of the United States. Although no one knows exactly how many illegal aliens there are in this country, some experts believe the number may be as high as 10 million.

Illegal aliens often have a difficult time in the United States. Many have no friends or family here, no place to live, and no sure way to earn money. It is against the law to hire illegal aliens. For all of them, even those with family or friends, each day is spent in fear of being discovered by government officials. Any aliens who are found to be here illegally are **deported**, or sent back to their own country.

LEGAL ALIENS Aliens who have entered the United States legally have a much easier time. Their lives, in fact, are not very different from the lives of U.S. citizens. Legal aliens may hold jobs, own property, attend school, and travel throughout the United States. They must obey the laws of the United States and pay taxes, just as U.S. citizens must.

There are, however, some things that aliens are not permitted to do. They may not vote in any political elections or run for political office. They may not work in most government jobs. The laws of some states also prohibit them from working in certain jobs such as public school teaching. And unlike United States citizens, aliens must carry identification cards at all times.

Some immigrants to the United States live their entire lives here as aliens, remaining citizens of their homeland. Others, however, decide to change their citizenship and become United States citizens.

Today, people continue to come to the United States as immigrants. Some of the people in this photograph may eventually become American citizens.

Carl Schurz: An Immigrant Patriot

Carl Schurz came to the United States in 1852, when he was 21. Like many immigrants from Germany, Schurz settled in Wisconsin. He quickly learned English and became an American citizen.

Schurz soon took up the antislavery cause, and in 1860 he worked in Abraham Lincoln's presidential campaign. Over the next four decades he was a U.S. minister to Spain, a Union general in the Civil War, a U.S. Senator, a U.S. Secretary of the Interior, an author, and a journalist. In almost every post, Schurz was ahead of his time, and his ideas helped shape American political thought.

After the Civil War, while reporting on conditions in the South, he advocated giving freed slaves the right to vote. That idea became law with the Fifteenth Amendment to the Constitution in 1870. As a U.S. Senator, Schurz was a tireless crusader against political corruption. As Secretary of the Interior in the 1870's, he sought better treatment of the American Indians. He began hiring and promoting government employees on the basis of merit long before Civil Service reform. He also favored protecting federal lands in a national park system.

As a journalist in the 1880's and 1890's, Schurz continued his battle against political corruption and strongly opposed the American policy that led to the Spanish-American War. Schurz's courage and vision place him in the front ranks of the immigrants who helped make America great.

Using Your Skills
1. What government posts did Schurz hold? What were some contributions he made while serving in them?
2. Identify at least two other immigrants to the United States, and describe their contributions to American life.

Naturalization

The process by which aliens become citizens is called **naturalization**. It is a long process, involving several years and many steps. Only aliens who have entered the United States legally may become naturalized citizens.

The first step toward naturalization is to file a Declaration of Intention with the immigration authorities. An immigrant may do this any time after entering the United States. The Declaration states that the immigrant intends to become a U.S. citizen. Filing this form is not required by law, but many employers will not hire aliens without it.

Most immigrants must live in the United States for five years before they can take the next step toward naturalization. (There are exceptions to this rule; for instance, those who are married to U.S. citizens must wait only three years.) During this time, many immigrants take special classes to prepare for citizenship. They study the English language, American history, and civics. Before they may become citizens, immigrants must demonstrate basic knowledge in all these areas.

After the waiting period, an immigrant may file an application for naturalization. Applicants must be at least 18 years old. A government agency called the Immigration and Naturalization Service reviews this application to make sure the information on it is true and complete. This review process often takes several months.

If the application is approved, the immigrant will be given an appointment to meet with an immigration examiner. The examiner's job is to decide whether the immigrant is qualified to become a United States citizen. The examiner determines this by asking the immigrant a series of questions about American history, American government, and his or her reasons for wanting to become an American citizen. The immigrant must answer these questions correctly, in simple English.

If the examiner is satisfied that the immigrant is ready to become a citizen, the only remaining step is a brief court appearance. In court, the immigrant is asked to take an oath of loyalty to the United States. After taking this oath, the immigrant is officially declared to be a U.S. citizen, with all the rights and responsibilities that go along with citizenship. If the immigrant has children under 18, those children automatically become naturalized citizens as well.

LOSS OF CITIZENSHIP American citizens, whether by birth or naturalization, are U.S. citizens for life. Even if they move to another country, they remain citizens of the United States.

All new citizens of the United States must take the citizenship oath.

OATH OF ALLEGIANCE TO THE UNITED STATES

I hereby declare, on oath, that I absolutely and entirely renounce and abjure all allegiance and fidelity to any foreign prince, potentate, state, or sovereignty, to whom or which I have heretofore been a subject or citizen; that I will support and defend the Constitution and laws of the United States of America against all enemies, foreign and domestic; that I will bear true faith and allegiance to the same; that I will bear arms on behalf of the United States when required by law; that I will perform noncombatant service in the armed forces of the United States when required by law; that I will perform work of national importance under civilian direction when required by law; and that I take this obligation freely without any mental reservation or purpose of evasion; so help me God.

Virtually the only way to lose United States citizenship is to become a naturalized citizen of another country. This is because the United States does not want its citizens to divide their loyalty between two governments. (An exception is made for those who were born into dual citizenship, since they were not given a choice.)

In the past, people sometimes lost their citizenship for other reasons, such as threatening to overthrow the U.S. government or serving in the armed forces of a foreign country. But later court decisions cast doubt on the legality of taking away citizenship for reasons like these. Therefore, no matter what crimes they commit, or how disloyal they may seem to be, most U.S. citizens can count on keeping their citizenship forever.

SECTION REVIEW

Define the Words

alien

immigrant

deport

naturalization

Check the Facts

1. In what ways can a person become a United States citizen?
2. What rights do U.S. citizens have that legal aliens do not have?
3. What is the only reason for which a U.S. citizen is likely to lose citizenship?

Think About the Ideas

4. *Evaluate.* Why do you think so many aliens come to the United States illegally?
5. *Speculate.* How might the feelings about citizenship be different in people who are born citizens and in those who earn their citizenship?

★ ★

SECTION 3

Who Are Americans?

★ ★

VOCABULARY

census   refugee

quota   migration

One of the duties of the U.S. government, as specified in the Constitution, is to keep an accurate count of the people living here. This includes both citizens and noncitizens. To do this, the government set up a process for counting population called the **census**. The government agency that does this job is called the Census Bureau. Since the first U.S. census, taken in 1790, the Census Bureau has counted the nation's population every 10 years.

From the very beginning, the government's census takers have done more than simply count people. They have also asked a variety of questions—in person or by mail—to get more information about the people who make up our country. These questions are concerned with people's place of residence, their work, their income, and many other things. After reviewing the answers to these questions, the Census Bureau is able to provide a snapshot—a group portrait—of what America looks like every 10 years. Not surprisingly, the portrait has gone through many changes.

The First Census

When the United States became a nation in 1787, it was the first government in the world to require that its population be counted every 10 years. The first counting or census, which took place in 1790, was very difficult.

Although the United States consisted of only 18 states at that time, its people were scattered from Maine to Georgia and as far west as Kentucky. There were few roads, and people lived far apart. U.S. marshals were assigned to ride from farm to farm taking the census.

The poorly trained marshals made many mistakes in their hand-written records, and they didn't find everyone. But they did manage to count 3.9 million Americans. The first census cost the nation $45,000—or about one cent per person counted.

Census taker today.

A Nation of Immigrants

The Latin phrase "E pluribus unum" is found on the backs of all American coins. The meaning of this phrase, "Out of many, one," reminds us that the United States is a nation made up of many kinds of people—people with different languages, backgrounds, beliefs, and cultures.

Because of its heritage, the United States is often called "a nation of immigrants." Every American, even those born here, is descended from someone who came to this country from somewhere else.

Even the first Americans—the American Indians, or Native Americans as they are sometimes called—were immigrants. There is evidence that they came to America from Asia many thousands of years ago. They made the journey on foot, traveling over a land bridge between Siberia and Alaska that no longer exists.

EARLY EUROPEAN SETTLERS The first Europeans to settle permanently in North America were from Spain. Throughout the 1500's, the search for gold and riches brought Spanish explorers and adventurers into what is now the southern and western United States. Spanish influence is still evident in states such as Florida, Texas, and California.

Beginning in the 1600's, people from France and England began coming here as well. The French settled primarily in Canada, but they also occupied a large area around the Mississippi River. Much later, a group of French settlers moved from Canada to the state of Louisiana, where their language and culture still thrive in the area around New Orleans.

English immigrants settled mainly along the east coast of North America, where their settlements formed the backbone of the origi-

This 1871 cartoon shows people from all over the world entering the United States. According to the cartoonist, what attracted these people to this country?

nal 13 colonies. During the late 1600's and the 1700's, these English settlers were joined by immigrants from Germany, Holland, Ireland, Scotland, and Sweden.

Another group of immigrants who arrived during this time were black Africans. Unlike other immigrant groups, however, these people did not come willingly. Thousands of black Africans were forced to come here as slaves. Once here, they lived and worked on plantations in what is now the southern United States.

By 1776, when the 13 English colonies officially became the United States of America, only 60 percent of the citizens in those states were of English descent. The way these early U.S. citizens ate, dressed, spoke, and led their lives was influenced by the cultures of many different lands. Over the next 75 years, as the United States expanded to the west, the cultures of the continent's earlier inhabitants—Spanish, French, and American Indian—entered the mix as well.

THE GREAT IMMIGRATION As the young nation grew, it became known throughout Europe as a land of promise. Poor and oppressed people from Germany, England, and Ireland flocked to the United States in search of freedom and opportunity. The flood of immigrants grew from 600,000 in the 1830's to more than 2 million in the 1850's. Between 1860 and 1890, more than 10 million more Europeans—many of them from Norway, Sweden, and Denmark—came to America.

In the early days, most Americans had welcomed the new arrivals. There was plenty of space and much work to be done. By the mid-1800's, however, many Americans began to worry that their land and jobs were being taken away by immigrants. As a result, in 1882 the U.S. government passed the first of several laws to restrict the number of immigrants who could enter the country.

Despite these restrictions, another flood of immigrants began just a few years later. Between 1890 and 1930, about 22 million

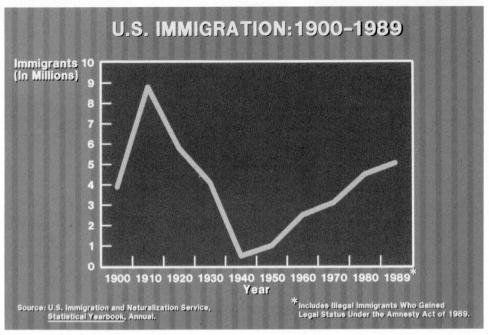

U.S. IMMIGRATION:1900–1989

Immigrants (In Millions)

Year

Source: U.S. Immigration and Naturalization Service, Statistical Yearbook, Annual.

*Includes Illegal Immigrants Who Gained Legal Status Under the Amnesty Act of 1989.

The graph shows the number of people who arrived in the United States as immigrants between 1900 and 1989. How did immigration change between 1940 and 1980?

people entered the United States. Most of these new immigrants came from central and eastern Europe, from countries such as Greece, Poland, and Russia. This new flood of immigrants was slowed only after the U.S. government passed new immigration laws in the 1920's. For the first time, these laws set **quotas**, or numerical limits, on the number of people who could enter the United States each year.

IMMIGRATION TODAY Although immigration laws have changed since the 1920's, the quotas still exist. According to current quotas, only 270,000 immigrants are allowed to enter the United States each year. In most cases, only 20,000 of those people may come from any one country.

The major exception to this rule involves **refugees**—people who have lost their homes because of war, famine, or political oppression. The United States has opened its doors to refugees many times during this century. One large group of refugees has come from southeast Asia, particularly from the countries of Vietnam and Cambodia. More

recently, hundreds of thousands of refugees have poured in from the troubled countries of Central America.

For many years, the United States was referred to as a "melting pot." This meant a place where people from many backgrounds and cultures blended into a new kind of person—an American. Today, however, most people realize that there is no such thing as a typical American. Americans come in all shapes, colors, and sizes. They hold a variety of views and beliefs. And they all have something special to contribute to the country.

Population Growth

The growth of America's population was not due entirely to immigration. Even before the first great flood of immigrants began, the number of Americans had increased from nearly 4 million in 1790 to more than 12 million in 1830. Much of this growth was simply the result of Americans having many children.

In the 100 years between 1830 and 1930, the nation's population grew almost 10 times larger, from about 12 million to about 120 million. Surprisingly, fewer than 40 million of these new Americans were immigrants. Instead, the leap in population was once again due primarily to a natural increase. Immigrant Americans, like the Americans who were here before them, tended to have large families. With more Americans having large families, the birthrate was high and the population grew rapidly.

One reason for this high birthrate is quite simple: during our country's earlier years, American families needed as much help as possible to survive. This was especially true on farms, where much of the American population lived. In the days before modern machines and appliances, the work of maintaining a home and family and earning a living was difficult and time-consuming. Children were needed to do household chores, work on family farms, and bring in additional money from outside jobs.

As modern life became more automated, and fewer people lived on farms, large families became less important. As a result, America's birthrate has dropped steadily throughout the 1900's. From 1930 to 1990, the country's population increased from 123 million to 251 million. Although the population nearly doubled in those 60 years, the rate of increase was the slowest in our nation's history.

Population Shifts

As the American population has grown, it has also moved around a number of times during our history. The first great shift in population came in the mid-1800's, when Americans began to move from rural areas to cities. The main reason for the move was employment: in the cities, jobs could easily be found in manufacturing, transportation, sales, and services. Also, as cities began to grow, they became exciting centers of art, music, and fashion. For more than 100 years, small towns throughout rural America steadily became smaller as cities became larger.

Shortly after this first shift in population began, another started. Freed from slavery after the Civil War, American blacks were seeking jobs, respect, and a new way of life. Like many American whites, they also headed for the cities, most of which were located in the northern part of the country. The result was a **migration**, or mass movement, of southern blacks to the northern states. This migration began in the late 1800's and lasted well into this century.

Another important population shift in the United States began taking place in the 1970's with a migration to the western and southern parts of the country. These regions were growing while the older, industrial areas in the North and East were losing population. Many people began to leave the crowded, industrial northeast for warmer, more spacious parts of the country. States such as Arizona, Nevada, and New Mexico have grown tremendously. For many years, the state with the largest population was New York; that honor now belongs to California.

Cities have also been losing population. Residential areas of New York, Chicago, Detroit, and many other cities of the Northeast or Midwest have deteriorated. It is often difficult to find decent housing at affordable prices in cities. So for many years, people have been moving outward from the centers of these cities to the surrounding areas, or suburbs. These suburbs, in turn, have spread out in ever-larger rings around the cities. As a result, most of the northeastern United States has turned into a single, large, dense metropolitan—or city and suburb—area.

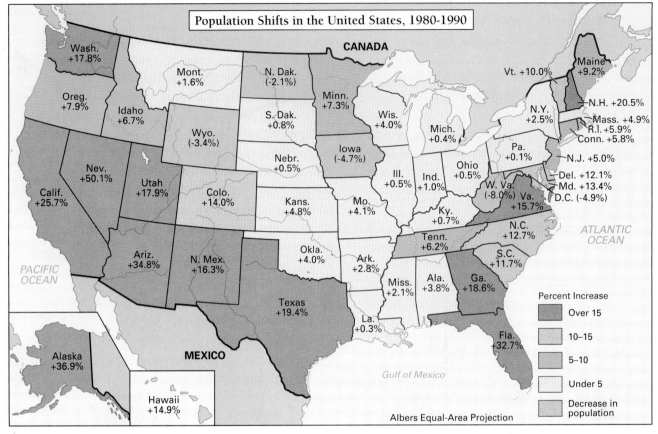

Population Shifts in the United States, 1980-1990

CANADA

Wash. +17.8%
Mont. +1.6%
N. Dak. (-2.1%)
Vt. +10.0%
Maine +9.2%
Oreg. +7.9%
Idaho +6.7%
Minn. +7.3%
N.H. +20.5%
N.Y. +2.5%
Mass. +4.9%
Wyo. (-3.4%)
S. Dak. +0.8%
Wis. +4.0%
Mich. +0.4%
R.I. +5.9%
Conn. +5.8%
Nev. +50.1%
Utah +17.9%
Nebr. +0.5%
Iowa (-4.7%)
Pa. +0.1%
N.J. +5.0%
Calif. +25.7%
Colo. +14.0%
Kans. +4.8%
Ill. +0.5%
Ind. +1.0%
Ohio +0.5%
W. Va. (-8.0%)
Del. +12.1%
Md. +13.4%
Va. +15.7%
D.C. (-4.9%)
Mo. +4.1%
Ky. +0.7%
N.C. +12.7%
Ariz. +34.8%
N. Mex. +16.3%
Okla. +4.0%
Ark. +2.8%
Tenn. +6.2%
S.C. +11.7%
PACIFIC OCEAN
Texas +19.4%
Miss. +2.1%
Ala. +3.8%
Ga. +18.6%
ATLANTIC OCEAN
La. +0.3%
Fla. +32.7%
Alaska +36.9%
MEXICO
Gulf of Mexico
Hawaii +14.9%
Albers Equal-Area Projection

Percent Increase
- Over 15
- 10–15
- 5–10
- Under 5
- Decrease in population

The map shows recent population shifts in the United States. Which regions have shown the greatest increase in population since 1990?

A CHANGING NATION Census Bureau information has revealed other ways in which the nation's population is changing. Since most Americans are living longer than they used to, there are more old and retired Americans than ever before. More women are taking jobs outside the home, and 25 percent of all small businesses are now owned by women.

The picture we see is of a growing, changing America. It is a country where people refuse to stand still and where new ideas constantly come into view. As we move toward the census in the year 2000, Americans will continue to look for new challenges, find new roles, and search for better ways of living.

SECTION REVIEW

Define the Words

census   refugee

quota   migration

Check the Facts

1. What is the purpose of the census?
2. Why did the U.S. government begin to restrict immigration in the late 1800's?
3. What were the reasons for the rapid growth of America's population?
4. In what way are refugees different from other immigrants to the United States?

Think About the Ideas

5. *Evaluate.* What effect have recent population shifts had on the different regions of the United States?

CITIZENSHIP SKILLS

How to Interpret Photographs

You can learn a lot from a photograph—or any other kind of illustration—if you examine it carefully. First look at a picture as a whole, then study its details. The details often provide important information about the subject and can help you understand what the photographer was trying to say.

You have read about the many groups of immigrants who came to the United States in the early 1900's. The photograph below shows a group of Europeans who have just arrived at the immigration center at Ellis Island in New York City. Study the photograph and answer the questions.

Using Your Skills

1. What can you tell about the people in the photograph?
2. Would you guess that the immigrants shown in the photograph came from a city or from a rural area? Why?
3. Do you think the people in the photograph are well to do? What details in the photograph make you think so?
4. How would you describe the expression or mood of the group?

CHAPTER 1 REVIEW

★ ★

MAIN POINTS

★ A citizen is a member of a community with a government and laws.

★ Governments serve many purposes. They help protect people and establish order by providing laws. They also provide services and set goals for the future.

★ Nations, states, counties, cities, and towns all represent different groups of people and different levels of government. The national government, however, has final authority.

★ Many countries have had a form of government called dictatorship, in which one person or a small group of people has complete control. Other countries have had a democracy, in which the citizens hold the power to rule.

★ People are citizens by birth or by naturalization. To become a naturalized citizen, an alien must be here legally and must complete certain steps.

★ The United States is a nation of immigrants. As the flood of immigrants increased, the government placed restrictions on the number that could come.

★ Various population shifts have changed the face of America. These shifts include the movement from farm areas to cities, the movement of blacks from the South to northern cities, and the movement of people from the North and East to the South and West and from the cities to the suburbs.

WORDS IN REVIEW

Choose the word or phrase from the list below that best completes each sentence. Write the missing words on a separate sheet of paper.

government   democracy
dictatorship   representative
alien   deport
immigrant   naturalization
census   refugee

1. Anyone who lives in this country but is not a citizen is a(n) _____.

2. The woman was elected by the citizens of her town as a(n) _____ to the state government.

3. In the _____, the leader ruled his people with an iron fist and tolerated absolutely no opposition to his authority.

4. The man had fled a civil war in his country and was considered a(n) _____ in this country.

5. The government was a(n) _____, in which everyone over 18 years of age could vote to elect leaders.

6. The government agreed to take a(n) _____ every 10 years to count the population.

7. The newly independent country established a(n) _____ to run the country and make laws.

8. The officials decided to _____ the man because he was not a citizen and he had come here illegally.

9. Because the woman had arrived in the country legally to become a citizen, she was considered a(n) _____.

10. _____ is the process by which a person not born a citizen can become one.

FACTS IN REVIEW

1. Explain why governments are necessary.

2. List at least three levels of government.

CHAPTER 1 REVIEW

3. What is the difference between a direct democracy and a representative democracy?

4. In what ways can a person become a citizen of the United States?

5. Explain the naturalization process.

6. How can American citizens lose their citizenship?

7. List at least three early groups of immigrants to America.

8. How did the U.S. government limit immigration?

9. What accounts for the enormous population growth of the United States after 1830?

10. List three important population shifts that have occurred since the mid-1800's.

THINKING ABOUT CIVICS

1. *Evaluate*. Do you think citizenship is as important in other countries as it is in the United States? Why or why not?

2. *Analyze*. The character of the United States is based, in part, on its multicultural heritage. How do you think the country would be different without this heritage?

3. *Evaluate*. Do you think United States citizens should have a more direct say in their government? Why or why not?

DEBATING IMMIGRATION QUOTAS

Various restrictions have been placed on immigration since the late 1800's. Since the 1920's, immigration quotas have further limited the numbers of immigrants allowed to enter the country. Prepare arguments, pro or con, for a class debate on the following statement: quotas and other restrictions on immigration should be eliminated.

WRITING ABOUT DEMOCRACY

Several countries in Eastern Europe, such as Poland, Hungary, and Romania, recently have broken away from the control of the Soviet Union. Many people in those countries have never had any experience living in a democracy. They are in the process of setting up new governments in their countries. Write a letter to your pen pal in Budapest, Hungary, explaining how life will be different with a democratic government than it was in a dictatorship. Describe the most important aspects of democracy, such as open elections and a free press.

INTERPRETING A MAP

Look at the map on page 40. Which two states showed a decrease in population during these years? Which states had almost no change in population (plus or minus 1 percent)? Which states showed an increase in population of more than 20 percent? What factors do you think influenced the great population growth in those states? Make a general statement about the pattern of population growth in the United States, 1980—1988.

FOCUSING ON YOUR COMMUNITY

Investigate the different groups of people who make up your community. What immigrant groups originally settled there? How has the character of the population changed over the years? Have there been any significant population shifts in the community? Interview some elderly citizens about the changes they have observed in the community over time. Prepare an informal report for your class on the character of your community and how it has changed.

Roots of American Democracy

OBJECTIVES

After you have studied this chapter, you will be able to:

★ Tell how the colonists drew on their English heritage in building their systems of government.

★ Describe some early forms of colonial government.

★ Discuss how the ideas of Rousseau and Locke influenced the thinking of American colonists.

★ Explain why the colonists decided to declare their independence from Great Britain.

★ Identify the Articles of Confederation and list some of its problems.

SECTIONS

1 Our English Heritage
2 The Colonial Experience
3 Toward Independence
4 The Nation's First Governments

INTRODUCTION

The writers of the U.S. Constitution did not invent democracy. Democratic governments existed in ancient Greece and Rome. But American colonists had a closer and more recent model to follow. Many colonists had come from England, and their ideas about government were based on the English system.

The story of English democracy began in the Middle Ages during the rule of King John. As was the custom, the king made large grants of land to nobles, who pledged to obey him and serve him faithfully. This meant supplying armies and equipment and paying taxes to help King John support his wars. Nobles who failed in their duties were punished severely. In 1215, the nobles rebelled. They felt that the king did not respect their rights as nobles and his taxes were making them poor. They forced him to sign an agreement, called the Magna Carta (or Great Charter). An important part of this document was a list of the nobles' rights.

The document established a principle that had far-reaching effects. In signing it, the king admitted that his power had certain limits and that he, too, had to obey the laws.

King John was forced by the nobles to sign the Magna Carta. Why did the nobles draw up the Magna Carta?

★ ★

SECTION 1
Our English Heritage

★ ★

VOCABULARY

Parliament	precedent
legislature	common law

Henry III, the king who followed John on the English throne, met on a fairly regular basis with a group of nobles and church officials. They advised the king and helped govern the realm. The group's meetings were called parliaments, from the French word *parler*, meaning "to talk." Over the years this advisory group grew in size and power.

By the late 1300's, **Parliament** had developed into a **legislature**. A legislature is a group of people who make laws for a state or country. The king still ruled England, but Parliament had taken over most of the day-to-day work of governing.

Although Parliament began as a single group, it eventually split into two parts, or "houses." The upper house, called the House of Lords, grew out of the group of nobles who had once advised King Henry. The lower house, called the House of Commons, was made up of representatives of towns and counties. This arrangement divided the governing power between the two houses of Parliament.

The Glorious Revolution

The role of Parliament changed again in the late 1600's, with an event called the Glorious Revolution. During the rule of King James II, England went through a period of great unrest. In 1688, Parliament removed King James from power and offered his throne to a new pair of rulers, William and Mary.

In doing so, Parliament demonstrated that its power was now greater than that of the king. The idea of government in England had become very different. No longer did Parliament's right to govern come directly from a king or queen. From that time on, Parliament's power would come from English citizens, and no ruler's power could be greater than that of the legislature.

The British House of Commons served as a model for representative government in the American colonies.

To make sure that no king or queen would ever question the legislature's right to govern, Parliament drew up a Bill of Rights in 1689. This English Bill of Rights gave Parliament the sole power to make laws, to raise taxes, and to control the nation's army. It also set up a system of elections by which representatives to Parliament would be chosen.

Unwritten Constitution

As you will discover in Chapter 3, the government of the United States was carefully planned by the framers of the U.S. Constitution. They spent many days discussing the way the government would be organized and how it would work. After they reached agreement, the plan was put in writing as a guide for future generations.

The government of England was never planned in this way, and its rules were never written down. There were, of course, many written documents that helped to shape the government—among them, the Magna Carta and the English Bill of Rights. But no one document contained a master plan for government. For this reason, England is said to have an unwritten constitution.

Common Law

Just as a constitution can be unwritten, the day-to-day laws people live by can be unwritten as well. If enough people follow a certain "law," then that law exists, even if no legislature ever voted on it or wrote it down.

In England's earliest days, there were no laws as we know them today. The king could make rules and could change them whenever he chose. The power to decide who was guilty or innocent also lay entirely with the king or with those he chose to serve him.

It's hard to believe that a hat could get someone into trouble, but that is what happened to William Penn.

In the 1600's, ordinary citizens were expected to remove their hats as a sign of respect in the presence of their "betters." Penn, however, was a Quaker, and he did not believe government officials or even members of royalty were his betters. For Quakers, all people were equals in the eyes of God.

In 1670, Penn was brought to trial for preaching an unlawful religion. When he refused to remove his hat in court, the judge fined him five pounds. The jury found Penn not guilty of the preaching charge, but the judge sent him to jail because he refused to pay the hat fine.

Some years later, Penn founded the colony of Pennsylvania. There, citizens could practice whatever religions they pleased—even if it meant keeping their hats on.

Over the centuries, however, a system of courts began to develop, and the courts' decisions became the basis of a system of law. When early judges were asked to decide a case, they would look for a **precedent**—a ruling in an earlier case that was similar. If someone was accused of breaking a contract, for example, the judge would try to find out whether anyone had ever been accused of breaking a similar contract. The judge would then find out whether that person had been found guilty, and, if so, what the punishment had been. The judge would then try to make a similar ruling in this case.

This system of law, based on precedent, is known as **common law**. An important aspect of common law was that it was consistent. That meant that in similar circumstances, the law would produce similar results. This was very different from the situation in the days before the Magna Carta. Then, a king's mood might have been the most important factor in deciding whether someone was guilty and what the punishment would be.

Like England's system of government, the system of common law came about without being planned. And because it worked well, it remained in place for many more centuries. Today our laws about property, contracts, and personal injury are based on English common law.

This, then, was the English citizen's heritage. It included the idea that the ruler is not above the law, that people should have a voice in their government, and that citizens have basic rights that are protected by law. This heritage also included a consistent system of common law and a legislature made up of representatives of different groups of English citizens. These ideas took root in a new land when the English established colonies in America.

SECTION REVIEW

Define the Words

Parliament	precedent
legislature	common law

Check the Facts
1. Identify the Magna Carta and the English Bill of Rights.
2. Explain what is meant by an unwritten constitution.
3. How did the government of England change after the Glorious Revolution?

Think About the Ideas
4. *Summarize.* How can laws exist without a legislature to make them?

The system of common law that developed in England became the basis of our laws about property, contracts, and personal injury.

The Colonial Experience

VOCABULARY

colony	compact
colonists	town meeting

A **colony** is a group of people in one place who are ruled by the government of another place. When English citizens left their own country to settle in America, they became **colonists**. They lived in America, but they were still under the rule of Parliament.

For most practical purposes, however, the colonists were beyond the reach of their home government. If colonists committed crimes, there were no English police to arrest them and no English courts to try them. If Parliament was considering a new law, there was no easy way for American colonists to express their opinion about it.

England was, after all, about 3,000 miles away. There were no airplanes, telephones, or radios. The only way to send messages between America and England was by sailing ship. Making that trip across the Atlantic could take as long as two months.

For these reasons, the English colonists in America could not depend on Parliament to meet their needs. They had to learn to govern themselves.

The House of Burgesses

In 1607, a group of English colonists arrived in what is now the state of Virginia. They founded Jamestown, which became the first permanent English settlement in North America. These early colonists had to struggle to survive in a strange land. They tried raising a variety of crops, often without success. They suffered from hunger and from various diseases, including malaria. At the same time, they had to fight off attacks by the American Indians, on whose lands they had built Jamestown.

Which of the 13 colonies were most isolated by geography?

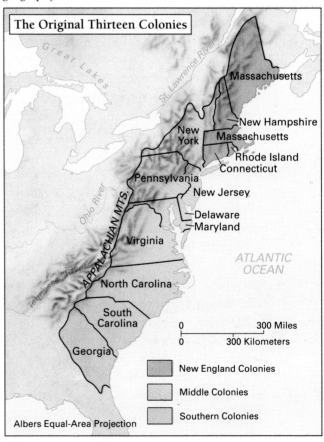

The Original Thirteen Colonies

Albers Equal-Area Projection

In 1619, the people of Jamestown took steps to deal with these pressing problems. Colonists from each town or plantation chose two representatives (called burgesses) to meet with the colony's governor. These 22 representatives formed the Jamestown House of Burgesses. It had very little power and solved few of Jamestown's problems. But this early attempt at representative government made history as the first legislature in colonial America.

The Mayflower Compact

In 1620, shortly after the House of Burgesses was formed, a new group of colonists arrived in America. They came ashore hundreds of miles north of Virginia and built a settlement called Plymouth. Today, this area is in the state of Massachusetts, part of New England.

Unlike the colonists of Jamestown, the Plymouth settlers drew up a plan for government to direct the colony. Even before their ship, *The Mayflower*, reached America, 41 of its passengers wrote and signed a document called the Mayflower Compact.

A **compact** is an agreement, or contract, made among a group of people. The Mayflower Compact said that the government would make "just and equal laws" for the good of the community. The signers pledged to obey those laws. The compact set up a direct democracy, in which all men would vote and the majority would rule. (As was true almost everywhere at this time, only adult males were allowed to vote.)

The Mayflower Compact established a tradition of direct democracy that remained strong in New England. Throughout the colonial period—and to this day—many communities in the New England states held **town meetings**. At these meetings, the town's citizens gathered to discuss and vote on the issues that mattered to them.

OTHER COLONIAL GOVERNMENTS The success of Jamestown and Plymouth led to the formation of other English settlements in America. By 1733, these settlements had grown into 13 colonies, from Massachusetts in the north to Georgia in the south. Following the examples of the House of Burgesses and the Mayflower Compact, each new colony set up its own government.

Although there were differences among the colonial governments, there were many similarities as well. Each colony had a governor, who in some cases was elected by the colonists and in other cases was appointed by the English king.

Each colony also had a legislature. Many of the colonial legislatures were modeled after the English Parliament, with an upper house and a lower house. The members of the upper house were most often appointed by the governor, but the members of the lower house were generally elected by the colonists themselves.

British or American?

As years passed, the colonial governments took on more power and responsibility. Although the Parliament paid little attention to what went on in America, the colonists continued to think of themselves as British citizens. (Their home country was renamed Great Britain in 1707.)

But although they remained officially British, the colonists were living as Americans. They built towns and roads; they organized

Shipping was an important activity in Boston and in other colonial cities.

their own churches, schools, hospitals, and fire departments. They built a thriving economy and learned that they could work out their own problems, without help from Britain.

At first, the British government was content to leave the American colonists alone. But as the colonies became more successful, Great Britain began to see them as a possible source of great wealth. In the mid-1700's, the actions of Parliament led to a series of events that made some colonists see themselves, for the first time, as Americans.

SECTION REVIEW

Define the Words
colony   compact
colonists   town meeting

Check the Facts
1. Name the first two permanent English settlements in America.
2. How were each of these settlements governed?
3. Explain why the colonists began to think of themselves as Americans.

Think About the Ideas
4. *Apply/Analyze.* Draw up a list of tasks and problems that a colonial government might have faced. In what ways are they different from the issues facing state governments today?

SECTION 3

Toward Independence

★ ★

VOCABULARY

mercantilism	delegate
boycott	congress
repeal	independence

During the 1600's and 1700's, the government of Great Britain followed a policy called mercantilism. **Mercantilism** is the theory that a country should sell more goods to other countries than it buys. The British believed that this policy would bring wealth into their country. This wealth would be used to develop the nation's industries and its navy.

For its policy of mercantilism to be successful, Britain needed a source of cheap materials with which to manufacture goods. It viewed America, with its fertile farmland and abundant minerals, as a good source. So after virtually ignoring the American colonies for many years, the British government began to realize how valuable those colonies could be.

Taxes

After 1760, when George III took the throne, British policy was to squeeze as much wealth as possible out of America. Parliament passed a series of laws that required the American colonies to sell raw materials, such as cotton and lumber, to Britain at low prices. The colonists also had to buy British products at high prices. Colonial businesses suffered as a result.

The situation became worse after 1763. Britain had fought a long, expensive war with France and had gone into debt. As the war's victor, Britain won control of France's North American territory. To pay its debts, Britain began to place heavy taxes on the American colonies. In 1765, for example, Parliament passed the Stamp Act, which required colonists to attach expensive tax stamps to newspapers and legal documents.

The colonists grew angry about the way the British government was treating them. Since the colonists could not send representatives to Parliament—as people living in Great Britain could—they felt that Parliament had no right to tax them. They summed up their feelings with the slogan "No taxation without representation!"

The colonists had to pay a tax on newspapers, legal documents, and every other sheet of paper they used. Stamps, such as those shown here, were affixed to the paper when the tax had been paid.

Librarians Help People

You probably think librarians have rather dull jobs shuffling dusty books all day. Not true. Take a look around your own public library. The reference librarian is helping a high school student find information for a report on ancient Mesopotamia, while workers at the circulation desk are helping people check out books, records, and videotapes.

If you want to become a librarian, you can choose among many library specialties. The school librarians teach children how to use the library and find information. Special collections librarians work in libraries devoted to a specific field, such as medicine. Classifiers and catalogers are specialists who work primarily with books—numbering, cataloging, and shelving them. Audiovisual librarians handle films, videotapes,

slides, and the equipment used to show these materials.

No matter what their specialty, all librarians must graduate from college and take a year or more of graduate courses in library science.

Using Your Skills
1. What is the difference between a school librarian and a special collections librarian?
2. What special personality traits do you think you should possess to be a good librarian?

Besides making protests, many colonists took action by **boycotting**, or refusing to buy, all British goods. Colonists began to take pride in wearing clothing made entirely of American cloth.

The boycott had its intended effect; Parliament **repealed**, or canceled, the Stamp Act and other tax laws. But the situation became worse. To demonstrate to the colonies that it was still in control, Parliament passed a new series of laws, which Americans called the Intolerable Acts. These laws placed restrictions on some of the colonists' rights—among them, the right to trial by jury. The Intolerable Acts also allowed British soldiers to search colonists' homes, even to move into their homes.

The First Continental Congress

The governments of the colonies banded together to fight the Intolerable Acts. In September of 1774, 12 of the 13 colonies sent **delegates**, or representatives, to a meeting in Philadelphia. The meeting became known as the First Continental Congress. (A **congress** is a formal meeting at which delegates discuss matters of common concern.)

The First Continental Congress lasted seven weeks. During that time, the delegates sent a document to King George III demanding that the rights of the colonists be restored. They also made plans to extend the boycott of British goods. When the Congress ended, the delegates vowed to hold another meeting if King George did not meet their demands by the following year.

Not only did King George refuse to meet their demands, but he also refused to allow any further protests against his government. He decided that it was time to use force against the colonists. In 1775, there were two battles between British and colonial soldiers in Massachusetts, at Lexington and Concord.

Until this time, most colonists still thought of themselves as loyal citizens of Great Britain. But now, with British soldiers shooting at Americans, many colonists began to doubt their attachment to Britain. More and more people began talking about "independence."

THE PUSH FOR INDEPENDENCE Independence means self-reliance and freedom from outside control. When applied to a country, it also means self-government.

Independence was not a new idea in the colonies. Patriots such as Samuel Adams, a Massachusetts political leader, had long insisted that the American colonies should break away from Great Britain. But after the battles of Lexington and Concord, the idea of independence was being supported by a broader group of colonial leaders. One of these was Benjamin Franklin, who had traveled to England as a representative of the colonies. He spent 16 years there, trying to iron out the differences between the colonies and Great Britain. In 1775, however, he returned to America, convinced that independence was the only answer.

Franklin and other colonial leaders formed the Second Continental Congress, which met in Philadelphia in May of 1775. Not every member of the Congress agreed that independence was a good idea. Some believed that the colonists could never win a war with Great Britain. Others still felt great loyalty to their home country. The Congress spent many months debating the proposal.

The Second Continental Congress appointed a committee to draft a statement announcing the independence of the colonies from Great Britain.

WASHINGTON'S LETTER TO THE NEWPORT CONGREGATION

Throughout their long history, the Jews have suffered persecution because of their religious beliefs. They have been tortured, exiled, killed, or forced to adopt other religions. That was why Newport, Rhode Island, must have seemed like a paradise on earth to the first few Jewish settlers who arrived there in the 1650's. It was a place where they could live and practice their religion openly and without fear.

Roger Williams founded the colony of Rhode Island in 1635 to escape from the religious intolerance of the Puritans in the Massachusetts Bay Colony. From the first, the laws of Rhode Island decreed freedom of religion for all. In that atmosphere, Newport's Jewish community thrived and contributed much to the social, business, and cultural life of the town. In 1759, the Jewish residents laid the cornerstone for the Touro Synagogue, now the oldest synagogue in the United States.

During the Revolutionary War, Newport's Jewish citizens supported the colonial cause wholeheartedly. Many fought in the Continental Army, and others gave money, arms, and supplies to support the war. George Washington was their hero, and when he became the nation's President, he visited the Jewish war veterans of Newport.

The members of this Synagogue, Congregation Yeshaut Israel, sent Washington a letter. It expressed their gratitude for living under a government in which people from all religious and national backgrounds had equal rights of citizenship.

President Washington was in complete agreement with the Jewish congregation. Replying in a letter to "the Hebrew Congregation in Newport, Rhode Island," he wrote that in the United States:

All possess alike liberty of conscience and immunities [protection] of citizenship. It is now no more that toleration [allowing other people's beliefs] is spoken of, as if it was the indulgence [favor] of one class of people, that another enjoyed the exercise of their inherent natural rights. For happily, the Government of the United States, which gives to bigotry [intolerance] no sanction [approval], to persecution no assistance requires only that they who live under its protection should demean [conduct] themselves as good citizens.

In the flowery language of the time, Washington was saying that in the United States all citizens enjoyed certain basic rights. These rights did not depend on the goodwill of one group. They were unconditional and would be protected by the government.

Using Your Skills

1. Why did Jewish colonists settle in Newport, Rhode Island?
2. Compare Washington's letter with the First Amendment to the Constitution. Do they deal with the same questions?

By 1776, however, more than half of the delegates had been persuaded that the colonies must become independent. The Congress appointed a committee to write a document that would officially announce America's independence from Great Britain.

The Declaration of Independence

Although the task of writing the document was assigned to a committee, the work was done almost entirely by one man—Thomas Jefferson. His Declaration of Independence was much more than an announcement. It was a passionate explanation of why Americans had the *right* to be independent. The second paragraph of the Declaration began this way:

> *We hold these truths to be self-evident, that all men are created equal, that they are endowed by their Creator with certain unalienable Rights, that among these are Life, Liberty, and the pursuit of Happiness.*

Most of these ideas did not originate with Jefferson. The idea that all people are equal—that no one person is born with the right to have power over another—came from a French philosopher named Jean-Jacques Rousseau.

The idea that people have certain natural rights—rights that no government may interfere with—came from an English philosopher named John Locke. Locke had defined those rights as "life, liberty, and property." Jefferson added "the pursuit of happiness." Locke also said that all governments were based on a social compact, an agreement between the people and the rulers. In return for the government's protection of their lives, property, and rights, the people gave up some of their freedom.

The Declaration of Independence argued that the British government did not look after the interests of the colonists or protect their rights. For this reason, the British government was no longer the rightful government of the colonies.

Congress approved the Declaration of Independence on July 4, 1776. The American colonies were now independent states—at least in theory. But their war with Great Britain had just begun, and they would not be truly independent until the fighting was over.

Thomas Jefferson wrote the Declaration of Independence in 1776. In 1800, he was elected President of the United States.

SECTION REVIEW

Define the Words

mercantilism	delegate
boycott	congress
repeal	independence

Check the Facts
1. Name three actions taken by the British government that angered the American colonists.
2. Identify the First Continental Congress, the Second Continental Congress, and the Declaration of Independence.
3. How did Britain's policy of mercantilism affect its relationship with the colonies?

Think About the Ideas
4. *Compare/Contrast.* How did the attitudes of the delegates to the First Continental Congress and the Second Continental Congress differ?

LEGAL LANDMARKS

TINKER V. DES MOINES INDEPENDENT COMMUNITY SCHOOL DISTRICT

We all know that the First Amendment to the Constitution protects the right to speak and write freely about public issues. But over the years, judicial opinion has extended the amendment to cover freedom of expression as well. This "expression" has included protest signs, advertising, clothing, and even obscenity.

In 1969, the U.S. Supreme Court ruled, in the case of *Tinker* v. *the Des Moines Independent Community School District*, that freedom of speech also applies to symbols. It also ruled that the right to free speech belongs to children as well as adults.

The Tinker case began in 1965, when America was becoming involved in the Vietnam War. At the time, many Americans supported the government's efforts to halt communism in Vietnam. Others felt that the United States was simply interfering in another nation's civil war. Feelings ran high on both sides.

In December, a group in Des Moines, Iowa, decided to wear black arm bands. The Des Moines School Board learned that some students were planning to wear the arm bands to school, and fearing disruption of classes, it voted to ban the arm bands. Any students who wore them on the school grounds would be suspended.

The school board subsequently suspended five students. Three of them, Mary Beth Tinker, 13, her brother John, 15, and Christopher Eckhart, 16, took the school board to court. They charged that it had violated their right to free speech. When the case finally reached the Supreme Court, lawyers for the students argued that the arm bands were a form of "symbolic speech." The lawyers pointed out that similar symbols, such as political campaign buttons, were allowed.

The school board's lawyer countered that the school had the right to make rules to ensure dis-

cipline and order. The board was afraid the arm bands would disrupt classes and might even lead to fights between pro- and antiwar students.

The Supreme Court voted 7 to 2 in favor of the students. The arm bands were a form of speech, it decided, and therefore protected by the Constitution. The court also ruled there was no evidence that the arm bands had caused any disturbance.

On the issue of whether free speech applied to children, Justice Abe Fortas said: "It can hardly be argued that either students or teachers shed their constitutional rights to freedom of speech or expression at the schoolhouse gate."

Using Your Skills
1. Why did the students' lawyers argue that the arm bands were protected by the First Amendment?
2. Do you think you enjoy freedom of speech in your school? Why or why not?

SECTION 4

The Nation's First Governments

VOCABULARY

interpret	ratify
confederation	amend

When the Continental Congress approved the Declaration of Independence, it took a giant step into the unknown. Once the colonies had thrown off the British government, what would they replace it with?

Patrick Henry, a leader in the movement for American independence, was delegate to the Continental Congress and the first governor of the state of Virginia.

The Declaration of Independence did not declare America to be a single country. The 13 colonies, in fact, became 13 separate countries, each with its own government and laws. They called themselves "states."

At the time, the idea of separate, independent states appealed to most Americans. The citizens of South Carolina, for example, felt that they had little in common with the citizens of Connecticut. After having their local interests neglected by the British government, few Americans were interested in creating a large central government of their own.

Statehood

Each new American state immediately confirmed its independence from Britain (and from the other states) by writing its own constitution. Unlike Britain's constitution, which was unwritten and largely unplanned, these state constitutions were detailed, written documents.

Each state's constitution set up a government similar to the colonial government that had come before it. Each state had a legislature, and most of these legislatures had two houses. The job of the legislature was to pass laws that the state and its citizens would live by.

Each state also had a governor, who was either chosen by the legislature or elected by the citizens. The governor's job was to carry out laws passed by the legislature.

Finally, each state had a system of courts. The job of the courts was to **interpret** the laws—to decide what the laws meant and how they applied to each new situation.

Many state constitutions also included a bill of rights, which guaranteed certain basic freedoms to the state's citizens. Many of these rights, such as trial by jury and protection of personal property, can be traced back to the Magna Carta.

Confederation

Although each state was well prepared and eager to govern itself, there were some things that a state could not do on its own. It could not raise and maintain a large army, for example. The war against Great Britain could never have been won by 13 small state armies. A single, strong army under central control was necessary.

For this and other reasons, the Second Continental Congress made plans for "a firm league of friendship" among the states. In 1777, the congress detailed these plans in a document called the Articles of Confederation.

A **confederation** is a group of individuals (or, in this case, individual governments) who band together for a common purpose. The Articles of Confederation did not unite the states into a single country. Instead, they established a system by which the independent states could cooperate with each other.

The Articles set up a one-house legislature called Congress, in which each state was given one vote. Congress was given a few, very limited powers. Among these was the power to control the army and to deal with foreign countries on behalf of the states.

Because of their bad experiences with the British government, the states refused to let Congress have two very important powers.

Congress had no power to tax and no power to enforce its laws. The Articles allowed Congress to ask the states for money, but not to demand it. Congress could not, in fact, require the states to do anything.

WEAKNESSES By 1781, all 13 states had **ratified**, or voted approval of, the Articles of Confederation. Within the next few years, however, it became clear that the Articles had serious problems.

To begin with, Congress could not pass a law unless nine states voted in favor of it. Any attempt to **amend**, or change, the Articles required a unanimous vote of all 13 states. These strict voting requirements made it difficult for Congress to accomplish anything.

Even when Congress managed to pass laws, it could not enforce them. Unlike the state constitutions, the Articles did not provide for a governor or for courts. If a state decided to ignore a law made by Congress, Congress could do nothing about it.

In the Articles of Confederation, why was Congress denied the power to tax the American people?

WEAKNESSES OF THE ARTICLES OF CONFEDERATION

Lack of power and money
- ★ Congress had no power to collect taxes.
- ★ Congress had no power to regulate trade.
- ★ Congress had no power to enforce its laws.

Lack of central power to direct policy and settle disputes
- ★ There was no single leader or group to direct government policy.
- ★ There was no national court system.

Rules too rigid
- ★ Congress could not pass laws without the approval of 9 states.
- ★ The articles could not be changed without the agreement of all 13 states.

The weaknesses of the Articles had severe consequences. Unable to collect taxes, Congress had to borrow money to pay for the war against Britain. It accumulated a debt that would take years to repay.

Congress also allowed the states to fall into debt. Conducting business was difficult during the war against Britain. To make up for lost income, each state placed heavy taxes on goods from other states and countries. Soon, every state was taxing its trade with almost every other state, and some foreign countries were refusing to trade with the American states at all. Congress could do nothing to remedy the problem.

Shays's Rebellion

The burden of taxes again fell on American citizens, as it had before independence. In 1786, a Massachusetts citizen named Daniel Shays finally decided he had had enough.

Although Daniel Shays and his supporters were driven back by the militia, their march on this Massachusetts courthouse brought sweeping changes.

Shays was a farmer who, like many other Americans, had fallen into debt because of heavy state taxes. Now the Massachusetts courts were threatening to take his farm away as payment for his debts. Shays felt that the state had no right to punish him for a problem the state had created. Many other people in Shays's situation agreed.

A group of 1,200 farmers, led by Shays, marched on a Massachusetts courthouse. Fearing a riot, the governor ordered state troops to break up the march. Shays and his followers were defeated, but word of the rebellion spread throughout the 13 states. Americans began to fear that there would be more violent incidents.

It had been clear for some time that the states needed to set up a stronger central government. Now they had a reason for immediate action. In 1787, 12 of the states agreed to send delegates to a meeting in Philadelphia.

The purpose of the meeting was to make major changes in the Articles of Confederation. At the time, however, no one realized quite how sweeping those changes would be.

SECTION REVIEW

Define the Words

interpret   ratify

confederation   amend

Check the Facts

1. Name two powers given to Congress under the Articles of Confederation.
2. Name two powers denied to Congress under the Articles of Confederation.
3. What were the major problems with the Articles of Confederation?

Think About the Ideas

4. *Analyze.* Why were Americans afraid to set up a strong central government?

CITIZENSHIP SKILLS

How to Volunteer for Community Service

A volunteer is someone who provides a service to the community without getting paid. Perhaps you have been a Boy Scout or Girl Scout or a member of 4-H. Maybe you have helped out with a school food drive or worked with students in the library. Or, perhaps you have helped out at your church or synagogue. Then you already have some volunteer experience.

In high school, you may have an opportunity to join an Interact Club. These are Rotary Club affiliates whose members carry out many volunteer projects to help the community. They may shovel snow for senior citizens, or run a car wash to raise money for a charity.

You do not have to belong to an organization to be a volunteer, however. There are opportunities to do volunteer work all around you.

★ **Local hospitals.** In nearly every hospital, volunteers visit patients and perform services to make their stay more pleasant. Some hospitals have volunteer pro-

grams for teens. This enables students to become familiar with hospital work to see if they want to pursue a medical career.

★ **Volunteer fire departments and rescue squads.** Volunteers usually start in their mid- or late teens to learn the skills they need to become fire fighters. Being a volunteer fire fighter is one of the most important jobs you can do for your community.

★ **Libraries.** Public libraries often use teenage volunteers to help shelve books, work with students, and help at the circulation desk.

★ **Nursing homes and day-care centers.** Like hospitals, these are two very good places to learn care-

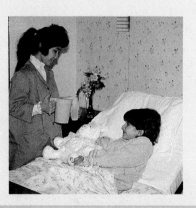

giving skills that you can use in many careers such as medicine, nursing, teaching, and child care. Many elderly people in nursing homes have no family to visit them. By volunteering at a nursing home, you can help brighten their days.

★ **Schools.** Many schools have programs in which older students tutor younger ones. If you are very good at one or two subjects, inquire at your school office to see if you can tutor someone else in those subjects.

To volunteer for any of these jobs, look up the organization in your telephone directory, and call. If one agency cannot use your help, try another. There is always a need for volunteers.

Using Your Skills
1. Why do you think volunteer work is an important way to practice good citizenship?
2. What kind of volunteer work would you like to do? Why?

CHAPTER 2 REVIEW

★ ★

MAIN POINTS

★ The English colonists who settled in North America brought with them ideas about the importance of law, representative government, and the basic rights of citizens.

★ The colonists could not depend on Parliament to meet their needs. They had to develop their own systems of government.

★ The Jamestown House of Burgesses and the Mayflower Compact established the principle of representative democracy in the American colonies.

★ The colonists continued to think of themselves as British, but conflicts with the British over taxes and colonists' rights increased.

★ The First Continental Congress protested the Intolerable Acts and demanded that the rights of colonists be restored.

★ The battles of Lexington and Concord caused many Americans to reconsider their ties to Britain. In July 1776, the Second Continental Congress issued the Declaration of Independence.

★ The 13 colonies became independent states, each with its own constitution. The states agreed to a plan, called the Articles of Confederation, that set up a government of the United States.

★ This new government had very little power. It could pass laws, but it had no means of enforcing them.

★ Shays's Rebellion worried many Americans. They knew their government did not have the power to maintain order. Many wanted a stronger central government.

WORDS IN REVIEW

Choose the word or phrase from the list below that best completes each sentence. Write the missing words on a separate sheet of paper.

delegate   colony
boycott   legislature
repeal   independence
amend   confederation

1. The club members chose a(n) _____ to represent them at the annual meeting.

2. The coach agreed to _____ the rules of the game to permit boys and girls to play.

3. In 1607, a group of settlers established a(n)_____ at Jamestown.

4. The colonies declared their _____ from Great Britain on July 4, 1776.

5. The legislature voted to _____ the tax, because the citizens felt it was unfair.

6. To protest unfair taxation, angry colonists decided to _____ British goods.

7. Each new colony had a governor and a(n) _____ to make laws.

8. _____ has two houses, the House of Commons and the House of Lords.

9. _____ is based on precedent and is often unwritten.

10. In Philadelphia, the state delegates voted to form a union or _____.

FACTS IN REVIEW

1. Name some aspects of our system of government that can be traced back to America's English heritage.

CHAPTER 2 REVIEW

* *

2. Explain what is meant by common law.

3. Give two reasons why the colonists could not depend on Parliament to meet their needs.

4. Each of the 13 colonies set up its own government. In what ways were these governments similar? In what ways were they different?

5. How did Britain's mercantilist policy affect the American colonies?

6. Why did American colonists protest against British taxes?

7. How did Parliament react to the colonial boycott of British goods?

8. Name two philosophers whose ideas influenced Thomas Jefferson in the writing of the Declaration of Independence. What ideas did he take from each?

9. What was the purpose of the Articles of Confederation?

10. What was Shays's Rebellion?

THINKING ABOUT THE ROOTS OF DEMOCRACY

1. *Analyze.* Although common law was part of their English heritage, the colonists decided to write down their laws. Why do you think they chose to have written laws?

2. *Evaluate.* Do you think the colonists could have settled their differences with the British in 1776? Explain your answer.

3. *Analyze.* The Articles of Confederation denied Congress the power to collect taxes. Could a government survive without this power? Why or why not?

WRITING ABOUT INDEPENDENCE

The year is 1776, and you are a young patriot living in the colonies. You believe the colonies should be independent. Your parents, however, are loyal supporters of the British government and disagree with your point of view.

Write a letter to your parents explaining why you favor independence. Support your view with reasons and examples from the textbook. Remember, you want to convince your parents that your position is practical and well thought out.

INTERPRETING A HISTORICAL MAP

Look at the map of colonial America on page 49. How are the colonies arranged? What do you think was the effect of vast distances between the colonies? What problems may have been created as a result of natural barriers? What effect might barriers and distance have had on efforts to unite the colonies?

FOCUSING ON YOUR COMMUNITY

Investigate the early history of your community. Find out when your town or city was founded and why it was founded. Who were the first people to settle there? Who were the early leaders? What type of government did the community have? How did the government grow and change over the years? Prepare an informal talk for your class on the early government of your community.

UNIT 1 REVIEW

★ ★

ESSAY QUESTIONS

The following questions are based on material in Unit 1. Answer each question with two or three written paragraphs. Be sure to give specific reasons to support your answers.

1. The idea of democracy began with the Greeks more than 2,000 years ago. Why do you think there have been so few democratic governments in years since then?

2. Before the Revolution, each of the 13 colonies was independent and self-sufficient. What effect do you think this had on the form of government established under the Articles of Confederation?

3. In recent years, many countries have become independent and have set up new governments. What factors do you think influence the form of government a new state chooses?

CONNECTING CIVICS AND ART

Art often has symbolic meaning—that is, it represents the artist's feelings or beliefs about something. Some artists have created works that express their feelings about democracy and free-dom. Be prepared to discuss the following: how could an artist express feelings about democracy and freedom? What types of images could an artist use to represent these ideas? What specific images do most people associate with the United States? What do these images symbolize? What effect do these images have on people who see them?

ANALYZING VISUALS

Immigration to this country has changed a great deal during the nation's history. The following table shows the numbers of immigrants who have come from Europe, Asia, Africa, and the Americas in the last 100 years. Use this table to help you answer the following questions.

1. Which immigrant groups have declined since 1970?

2. Which immigrant groups have grown in size since 1970?

3. During which period did the largest number of immigrants come to the United States?

4. What effects might the changing nature of America's immigrants have on the nation?

YEARS

SOURCE	1891-1910	1911-1930	1931-1950	1951-1970	1971-1988
Europe	11,611,392	6,785,081	968,713	2,449,219	1,343,554
Asia	398,405	359,295	53,623	580,891	3,708,036
Latin America	218,323	993,687	236,596	1,922,056	3,590,853
Africa	7,718	14,729	9,117	43,046	202,390
Canada	182,537	1,666,700	278,245	791,262	283,941

CLOSEUP ON THE AMERICAN FLAG

For Americans, the flag has always had a special meaning. It is a symbol of our nation's freedom and democracy.

The Continental Congress adopted the earliest version of the American flag on June 14, 1777. In 1916, June 14 was designated as Flag Day, a day of national observance. Flag Day became a national holiday in 1949.

Over the years, Americans have developed rituals concerning the flag. Congress adopted the American Legion Flag Code in 1942. That code spells out how the flag is to be handled. It also tells how the flag should be destroyed— by burning— when it becomes old and tattered. American school children have been reciting the Pledge of Allegiance since 1892. In 1988, George Bush brought the "Pledge" into the Presidential campaign by having it recited at Republican gatherings as a show of patriotism.

American poets, such as Ralph Waldo Emerson, Walt Whitman, and John Greenleaf Whittier, have all written tributes to the flag. In his poem "Barbara Fritchie," Whittier tells of a confrontation during the Civil War between the Confederate general Stonewall Jackson and an elderly woman in Maryland. As Jackson's men marched through the Northern town, Barbara Fritchie was defiantly waving the American flag from her bedroom window. She shouted:

> Shoot if you must, this old gray head,
> But spare your country's flag.

Her act of bravery and loyalty to the Union so moved Jackson that he told his men:

> Who touches a hair on yon gray head dies like a dog! March on.

The flag has also been memorialized in many patriotic songs such as "You're A Grand Old Flag," "Rally Round the Flag, Boys," and "Marching through Georgia." Congress adopted "The Star-Spangled Banner" as the national anthem in 1931. In 1987, Congress designated John Phillip Sousa's "The Stars and Stripes Forever" as the national march.

In 1989, the flag became the subject of a heated debate.

The U.S. Supreme Court ruled that burning the flag as an act of political protest was protected by the First Amendment right to freedom of expression. That decision caused waves of indignation across the land. Many Americans felt that since the flag represented America, the nation itself was under attack. Others, however, believed that the Supreme Court decision was a victory for the very ideals on which America was built.

Reaction to the Supreme Court's decision led Congress to pass a federal law outlawing flag burning. Within days after the new law took effect two groups of protesters burned American flags. This brought about a second Supreme Court case in 1990. Once again the U.S. Supreme Court ruled that flag burning as an act of political protest was protected by the First Amendment.

1. Why did the Supreme Court rule that it was unconstitutional to make laws prohibiting protesters from burning the American flag?

2. What is the difference between burning an old, torn American flag to destroy it and burning the flag as a political protest?

... *N*o State shall make or enforce any law which shall abridge the privileges or immunities of citizens of the United States, nor shall any State deprive any person of life, liberty or property, without due process of law; nor deny to any person within its jurisdiction the equal protection of the laws.

—FOURTEENTH AMENDMENT

* *

Blueprint for a New Nation

This nation was founded on the belief that all
people are created equal. The purpose of the
Fourteenth Amendment, added to the Constitution
after the Civil War, was to ensure that all citizens
of the United States would be treated equally
under the law. The amendment extended the protection of the Bill of Rights to all Americans.

* * * * *

CHAPTERS IN THIS UNIT

The Constitution

OBJECTIVES

After you have studied this chapter, you will be able to:

★ Describe the main conflicts and compromises of the Constitutional Convention.

★ Summarize the arguments of those supporting and those opposed to ratification of the Constitution.

★ Identify the three branches of government and discuss their functions.

★ Explain how the system of checks and balances works in the federal government.

★ Discuss the four underlying principles of the Constitution.

★ Explain the two ways in which the Constitution can be changed.

SECTIONS

1 The Road to the Constitution
2 The Constitution
3 Underlying Principles
4 A Living Constitution

INTRODUCTION

Throughout the long, hot summer months of 1787, a group of men held secret meetings in Philadelphia. This was where the nation's independence had been born 11 years before. Someone overhearing these men might have thought that they were plotting revolution. In a sense they were. They were planning to replace the nation's government under the Articles of Confederation.

Unhindered by outside influence, the men grappled with ideas for creating a new government. This government would have to be strong enough to govern the nation but still protect the rights of the people. When they emerged from their secrecy in September, the men had worked out a plan for a new government. It was all written down in a document they called the Constitution. Although their task was finished, more conflict lay ahead. The Constitution had to be accepted by the states and by the people.

★ ★

SECTION 1

The Road to the Constitution

★ ★

VOCABULARY

federal system	Electoral
compromise	College
export	Anti-Federalist
	Federalist

Ten years of living under the Articles of Confederation had shown Americans that the loose association of 13 independent states was not working. Many Americans became convinced that they needed a stronger central government. But few agreed on how that government should be set up, or what powers it should have.

Some people thought that the 13 states should be combined into one large state with one central government. Others felt that the states should keep as much power as possible for themselves. These people favored a **federal system**, in which the power to govern would be divided between a national government and the states.

The Constitutional Convention

Beginning on May 25, 1787, 55 delegates, or representatives, from 12 states met in Philadelphia. Rhode Island, the thirteenth state, was opposed to a stronger central government and did not send any delegates.

DELEGATES TO THE CONSTITUTIONAL CONVENTION

DELEGATE	STATE	AGE	OCCUPATION
Abraham Baldwin	Georgia	33	lawyer, minister
Richard Bassett	Delaware	42	lawyer
Gunning Bedford	Delaware	40	lawyer
John Blair	Virginia	55	lawyer, legislator
William Blount	North Carolina	43	planter, politician
David Brearley	New Jersey	42	judge
Jacob Broom	Delaware	35	politician
Pierce Butler	South Carolina	43	planter, politician
Daniel Carroll	Maryland	57	planter, politician
George Clymer	Pennsylvania	48	merchant, statesman
William R. Davie	North Carolina	31	lawyer, politician
Jonathan Dayton	New Jersey	27	lawyer
John Dickinson	Delaware	55	lawyer, statesman
Oliver Ellsworth	Connecticut	42	lawyer, politician
William Few	Georgia	39	lawyer, politician
Thomas Fitzsimons	Pennsylvania	46	businessman
Benjamin Franklin	Pennsylvania	81	scientist, editor, diplomat
Elbridge Gerry	Massachusetts	43	merchant, politician
Nicholas Gilman	New Hampshire	32	merchant
Nathaniel Gorham	Massachusetts	49	merchant
Alexander Hamilton	New York	30	lawyer, statesman
William Houston	New Jersey	41	lawyer, educator, politician
William C. Houston	Georgia	46	lawyer, politician
Jared Ingersoll	Pennsylvania	38	lawyer, politician
Daniel Jenifer	Maryland	64	planter, politician
William S. Johnson	Connecticut	60	lawyer, politician
Rufus King	Massachusetts	32	lawyer, statesman
John Langdon	New Hampshire	46	merchant
John Lansing	New Jersey	33	lawyer, politician
William Livingston	New Jersey	64	lawyer, writer
James McClurg	Virginia	41	physician
James McHenry	Maryland	34	physician
James Madison	Virginia	36	lawyer, statesman
Alexander Martin	North Carolina	47	merchant, lawyer, politician
Luther Martin	Maryland	39	lawyer
George Mason	Virginia	62	lawyer, statesman
John Mercer	Maryland	28	lawyer
Thomas Mifflin	Pennsylvania	43	merchant, general, statesman
Gouverneur Morris	Pennsylvania	35	lawyer, statesman
Robert Morris	Pennsylvania	53	financier, statesman
William Paterson	New Jersey	43	lawyer

DELEGATES TO THE CONSTITUTIONAL CONVENTION — continued

DELEGATE	STATE	AGE	OCCUPATION
William Pierce	Georgia	47	merchant, politician
Charles Pinckney	South Carolina	30	lawyer, planter
Charles C. Pinckney	South Carolina	41	general, lawyer, politician
Edmund Randolph	Virginia	34	lawyer, politician
George Read	Delaware	54	lawyer, politician
John Rutledge	South Carolina	48	judge, politician
Roger Sherman	Connecticut	66	lawyer, statesman
Richard D. Spaight	North Carolina	29	planter, politician
Caleb Strong	Massachusetts	42	lawyer
George Washington	Virginia	55	planter, general
Hugh Williamson	North Carolina	52	physician
James Wilson	Pennsylvania	45	lawyer, statesman
George Wythe	Virginia	61	lawyer, educator
Robert Yates	New York	30	judge

USA Freedom 1787-1987, Vol. 2, No. 1, 1986, USA TODAY, Gonnett Co., Inc.
Life, Constitution issue, 1987.
Encyclopedia of American History, Morris

What was the most common occupation of the delegates to the Constitutional Convention?

The delegates had assembled to revise the Articles of Confederation. Within a few days, however, they agreed that the Articles were not worth saving.

What they decided to do instead was to write a new document—a constitution—that would set up an entirely new central government. As a result of that decision, the meeting in Philadelphia became known as the Constitutional Convention.

The delegates to the Constitutional Convention were not a typical group of American citizens. Although America's population included people of many backgrounds, occupations, and ages, the delegates were all very similar. To begin with, all were white men. Although most Americans were farmers and laborers, all of the delegates were professionals and businesspeople. They were also unusually young—more than half were under age 40.

However, the delegates had two important qualities that made them well suited for writing a constitution: education and experience. At a time when few Americans had any formal schooling, the delegates were well read in politics, philosophy, and economics. About half of the delegates were college graduates. Most of the delegates also had experience in government. Many had been active in their state governments, and more than half had been members of Congress under the Articles of Confederation.

Several delegates, such as Benjamin Franklin and Alexander Hamilton, had been active in the fight for independence. (Thomas Jefferson, author of the Declaration of Independence, could not attend the Constitutional Convention because he was overseas, serving as America's ambassador to France.) George Washington, who had led the American army to victory against Great Britain, was a delegate from Virginia. When the convention began, the delegates unanimously chose Washington to preside over the meeting.

KEY DECISIONS At the very start of the convention, the delegates made several important decisions. They agreed that each state would have one vote, no matter how many delegates were present from that state. They also agreed that a simple majority—in this case seven votes—would be enough to decide any issue.

The delegates also decided to keep everything that went on at the convention a secret. After all, the task they had taken on was quite controversial—they were supposed to revise the Articles of Confederation, not replace them. The delegates knew that public pressure could make it difficult for them to complete their work. A policy of secrecy would remove that pressure. It would allow the delegates to speak freely and to make deals with each other, without having to consider how people in their home states would react.

Because of this secrecy, there are virtually no written records of what went on at the convention. The only details we have came from a notebook kept by James Madison, of Virginia, who became a major force in shaping the new government.

TWO PLANS OF GOVERNMENT Shortly after the convention began, the Virginia delegates proposed a plan for how the new government should be set up. The Virginia Plan, as it came to be known, had been designed mostly by James Madison.

The Virginia Plan described a federal government very similar to the one we have today. It included a president, courts, and a congress with two houses. Representation in each house of the congress would be based on each state's population. Large states, in other words, would have more votes than smaller states.

Delegates from the smaller states were unhappy with the Virginia Plan. They feared that the large states would control the

The delegates to the Constitutional Convention had to make many compromises before they worked out a plan for the government of the United States.

Journalism

Journalists are people who gather information about important events and report it through newspapers, magazines, and radio and television newscasts. The television newscaster covering a war in the Middle East is a journalist, as is the sports reporter covering a local football game.

Journalism is hard work, with long hours and tremendous pressures. Some reporters go to the scenes of accidents or fires to gather information.

Others sit through hours of meetings so that they can report on them. And reporters are always under pressure to get the news to the public as quickly as possible.

Despite these drawbacks, journalism can be very rewarding. Through their work, journalists reach many people. Their names, or bylines, appear on articles they write; or they are seen or heard on TV or radio. Reporters may also influence events by exposing wrongdoing or airing important

issues. Some reporters travel all over the United States or the world.

Reporting and newscasting are only two of the positions available in journalism. There are also jobs for copy editors, film editors, columnists or editorial writers, and radio and TV producers. All of these jobs require a thorough knowledge of grammar and the ability to write

clearly. For most jobs, you need a bachelor's degree in liberal arts or journalism. Journalists start at low-level positions and work their way up.

Using Your Skills
1. What are some of the rewards and drawbacks of being a journalist?
2. How does the First Amendment protect journalists?

congress, leaving them with little or no power. After two weeks of angry discussion, delegates from the smaller states came up with their own plan of government. Because it was presented by William Paterson of New Jersey, it came to be called the New Jersey Plan.

The New Jersey Plan called for a government similar to the one set up by the Articles of Confederation. It included a one-house congress, in which states would have equal representation and therefore equal votes.

Naturally, the large states were unwilling to accept the New Jersey Plan. They considered it fair that larger states should have more power than smaller states. The delegates argued about the two plans for weeks, but neither side was willing to give in.

Constitutional Compromises

Finally, the delegates from Connecticut suggested a way in which both sides could be satisfied. They proposed that the new Congress should have two houses. In one house, each state would have equal representation. In the other house, representation would be based on each state's population.

Both sides agreed to this suggestion, which became known as the Connecticut Compromise, or the Great Compromise. (A **compromise** is an agreement in which each side agrees to give up something to get something more important.)

Two other compromises made at the convention involved slavery. The southern states wanted their slaves counted as part of their populations. In this way, they hoped to increase their voting power in Congress. Most of the northern states, which had few slaves, opposed the idea. Eventually, both sides reached a compromise. In the Three-Fifths Compromise, it was agreed that slaves would count as three-fifths of other persons. This number would be used to determine both representation and taxes.

Another compromise between the North and the South was the Commerce and Slave Trade Compromise. The northern states felt that Congress should have the power to regulate trade with other countries. The southern states, however, feared that Congress would use this power to tax **exports**, that is, goods sold to other countries. Since much of their income came from exporting tobacco, the southern states felt that such a tax would be an unreasonable burden. They also feared that Congress might interfere with the slave trade.

After some discussion, another compromise was reached. The South agreed to give Congress the power to regulate trade between the states, as well as with other countries. In exchange, the North agreed that Congress would not have the power to tax exports or to interfere with the slave trade for 20 years.

The Electoral College

Another important compromise dealt with how the President would be selected. Some delegates thought the President should be chosen by the members of Congress or by the state governments. They felt that ordinary citizens did not have enough knowledge or experience in government matters to elect a President.

Other delegates believed that the President should be elected by the people. Allowing Congress to choose the President, they thought, would give the legislature too much power.

The convention delegates settled on a system in which each state legislature would choose a number of electors. These electors, a group called the **Electoral College**, would select the President and Vice President. The Electoral College system is still used today, except that electors are now chosen directly by the voters.

After weeks of debate and compromise, the delegates were ready to put their ideas down on paper. A style committee, headed by a delegate named Gouverneur Morris, wrote the document that we call the Constitution. The Constitution was signed by the delegates on September 17, 1787.

Ratification

The delegates had decided that the Constitution would become law once it was ratified by 9 of the 13 states. They did not realize, however, how difficult that process would be. Groups of supporters and opponents soon emerged.

THE FEDERALIST PAPERS, NO. 51

The framers of the U.S. Constitution faced two formidable tasks in 1787. The first, of course, was to create a new national government. The second was to convince the people of the United States to accept it.

The second task may have been more difficult. Most Americans were very jealous of their liberties, and they feared the creation of a strong national government that might deprive them of their rights.

The supporters of the new constitution, the Federalists, wrote a series of newspaper articles and pamphlets explaining how the Constitution would work. These essays, written by James Madison, Alexander Hamilton, and John Jay, were later published as *The Federalist Papers*. The following passages are drawn from *The Federalist Papers*, No. 51, by James Madison. In this first exerpt, Madison discusses the nature of society and government:

If men were angels, no government would be necessary. If angels were to govern men, neither internal nor external controls on government would be necessary. In framing a government which is to be administered by men over men, the great difficulty lies in this: you must first enable the government to control the governed; and in the next place oblige it to control itself.

This second excerpt reveals Madison's thoughts about protecting individuals and groups against the will of the majority:

It is of great importance in a republic not only to guard the society against the oppression of its rulers, but to guard one part of the society against the injustice of the other part. Different interests necessarily exist in different classes of citizens. If a majority be united by a common interest, the rights of the minority will be insecure . . . In the federal republic of the United States . . . the society itself will be broken into so many parts, interests, and classes of citizens, that the rights of individuals, or of the minority, will be in little danger from interested combinations of the majority.

Scholars, judges, and political scientists still consult *The Federalist Papers* today whenever there is a disagreement over the meaning of a particular article or clause in the Constitution. They are the best guide we have for understanding the intentions of the nation's founders.

Using Your Skills
1. What was the purpose of *The Federalist Papers*?
2. What did Madison mean when he wrote that it was necessary "to guard one part of the society against the injustice of the other part"? How did he think that would happen?

One group, the **Anti-Federalists**, openly opposed the Constitution. They felt that it gave too much power to the national government and took too much away from the states. The Anti-Federalists also opposed the Constitution because it lacked a bill of rights. That is, it failed to provide for certain basic liberties, such as freedom of speech or religion.

The group that supported the new Constitution, the **Federalists**, included many of the delegates who had helped to write the document. They argued that the nation would not survive without a strong national government and pointed to the failure of the Articles of Confederation to support their view. In a series of essays known as *The Federalist Papers*, James Madison, Alexander Hamilton, and John Jay defended the Constitution to the American people. (See Great American Documents on page 75.) *The Federalist Papers* helped increase public support for ratification.

The Federalists agreed with the Anti-Federalists that a bill of rights was a good idea. They promised that if the Constitution was adopted, the first task of the new government would be to add a bill of rights.

That promise helped turn the tide for the Constitution. On June 21, 1788, New Hampshire became the ninth state to vote for ratification, and the Constitution became law. In time, the other four states voted for ratification of the Constitution. The last state, Rhode Island, ratified it in 1790. The 13 independent states were now one nation, the United States of America.

Alexander Hamilton was one of the authors of The Federalist Papers. *His words played an important part in convincing Americans that the Constitution was needed for the nation to survive.*

SECTION REVIEW

Define the Words

federal system	Electoral College
compromise	Anti-Federalist
export	Federalist

Check the Facts

1. Briefly identify the following: Constitutional Convention, Virginia Plan, New Jersey Plan, Connecticut Compromise, Three-Fifths Compromise, Federalist Papers.
2. What is the Electoral College, and why was it created?
3. For what reasons did the Anti-Federalists oppose the Constitution? On what point did the Anti-Federalists and Federalists agree?

Think About the Ideas

4. *Evaluate.* Was the Great Compromise fair to both sides? Why or why not?

SECTION 2

The Constitution

★ ★

VOCABULARY

Preamble	checks and
legislative	balances
executive	veto
judicial	override

The Constitution is the basic law of the United States. Although it is a relatively short document, it manages to accomplish much in very few words.

The Constitution's most obvious purpose was to provide a framework for the United States government. It did this by establishing three branches of government, listing the powers of each branch, explaining how the officials would be chosen, and defining the relationship between the national government and the states.

But the Constitution does more than outline the structure of our government. As the highest authority of the nation, it has legal and political force. The power of all the branches of government and of all elected officials, even the President, comes from the Constitution. No law or authority in the nation is above it.

Beyond everything else, the Constitution—like the American flag and the national anthem—is a symbol. It stands for our system of government and for our basic ideals and beliefs, such as liberty and freedom.

Every American President takes an oath to "preserve, protect, and defend the Constitution of the United States." In taking this oath, the President is not pledging loyalty to a piece of paper. He or she is promising to protect what the Constitution stands for—America's ideals and beliefs.

The Preamble

The Constitution begins with a **Preamble**, or introduction. The Preamble contains no laws, but it identifies certain ideas that the American government should stand for, and also states the purpose of the Constitution.

The Preamble is actually a single sentence. The beginning and end of this sentence says: "We the People of the United States . . . do ordain and establish this Constitution for the United States of America."

This statement expresses the most important idea behind our government: the people of the United States have the right and the power to govern themselves. They have chosen to place this power in the hands of a government set up by the Constitution. The government, in other words, depends on the people for its power and exists to serve them.

The middle of the Preamble lists six goals for the American government. These are:

1. "to form a more perfect Union"—to allow the states to operate as a single country, for the benefit of all;
2. "establish Justice"—to make certain that all citizens are treated fairly and equally;
3. "insure domestic tranquility"—to keep peace among the people;
4. "provide for the common defense"—to maintain armed forces to protect the country and its citizens;

The First Inaugural

George Washington became the first President of the United States on April 30, 1789. His inaugural, or swearing in, took place on the balcony of Federal Hall in New York City, which was then the nation's capital. A large crowd escorted the new President from his lodgings while bands played, cannons roared, and flags waved from nearly every house in the city.

As the large, joyful crowd looked on from the street below, Washington stood proud and tall on the second-floor balcony. Wearing knee breeches, an American-made coat, and a ceremonial sword, he placed his hand on a Bible and solemnly took the oath of office.

Today, each new President takes the same oath, and the ceremony and celebration of Inauguration Day are much the same as they were for Washington 200 years ago.

5. "promote the general Welfare"—to ensure, as much as possible, that citizens will be free from poverty, hunger, and disease;
6. "secure the Blessings of Liberty to ourselves and our Posterity"—to guarantee that no American's basic rights will be taken away, now or in the future. (*Posterity* means generations not yet born.)

Checks and Balances

To meet the goals listed in the Preamble, the writers of the Constitution divided the national government into three parts, or branches. The **legislative** branch—Congress—makes the laws. The **executive** branch—the President, the Vice President, and their assistants—makes sure those laws are carried out. The **judicial** branch—the court system, including the Supreme Court—decides how the laws should be applied in individual cases.

To keep any one of these three branches of government from becoming too powerful, the Constitution also set up a system of **checks and balances**. Under the system of checks and balances, each branch of government is able to check, or limit, the power of the others. This system helps maintain a balance between the three branches.

The President, for example, has an important check on the power of Congress. The President can **veto**, or reject, a bill proposed by Congress and keep it from becoming a law.

But Congress can also check the President's power. It has the power to **override**, or defeat, the President's veto. To do so, however, requires a vote by two-thirds of the members of both houses of Congress.

The judicial branch can check the power of both the legislative and executive branches.

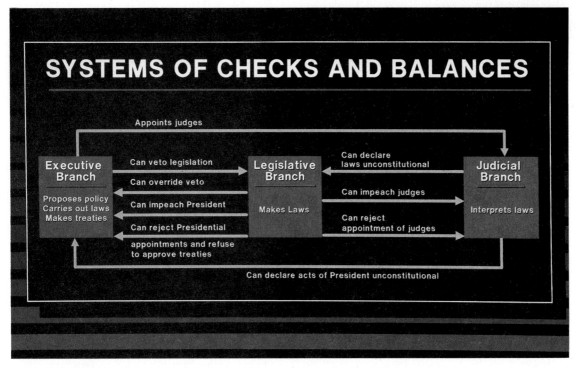

SYSTEMS OF CHECKS AND BALANCES

Appoints judges

Executive Branch

Proposes policy
Carries out laws
Makes treaties

Can veto legislation

Can override veto

Can impeach President

Can reject Presidential
appointments and refuse
to approve treaties

Legislative Branch

Makes Laws

Can declare
laws unconstitutional

Can impeach judges

Can reject
appointment of judges

Judicial Branch

Interprets laws

Can declare acts of President unconstitutional

This diagram shows how the three branches of government check and balance each other. In what way can the judicial branch overrule the executive branch?

The Supreme Court has the power to decide the meaning of laws and to declare that a law goes against the Constitution. In this way, it can overrule laws proposed by the President and Congress.

The Articles

Following the Preamble, the Constitution is broken into seven parts, or "articles." The first three articles describe the powers and responsibilities of the three branches of government.

Article I states that a Congress made up of two houses—the Senate and the House of Representatives—will carry out the legislative duties of government. The article then describes how each house must be organized and how its members will be chosen.

The article also lists the powers given to Congress, including the power to tax, to regulate trade, to coin money, and to declare war. Following this list is another that tells what powers are denied to Congress. This second list includes the power to tax exports, which was taken away from Congress by the Commerce and Slave Trade Compromise.

Article II deals with the executive branch and provides for a President and Vice President to carry out the duties of this branch. The article explains how these two leaders are to be chosen (by means of an Electoral College, described in Lessson 1). It then goes on to list the President's powers, including the power to command the armed forces, to make treaties with other nations, and to pardon criminals. The President is also given the power to appoint certain government officials, such as ambassadors and judges. Under the system of checks and balances, however, the Senate must approve the appointment of these officials.

Article III gives the judicial powers of government to a Supreme Court and other federal courts. The judges of these courts are appointed by the President, as described in Article II. Unless they commit crimes, these judges can never be removed from office.

Article III states that the courts will have the power to judge "all cases . . . arising under this Constitution." This statement allows the Supreme Court to prevent the President or Congress from doing things that go against the Constitution.

Article IV explains the relationship between the states and the national government; Article VI discusses general provisions about the government. Article V specifies how the Constitution can be changed. And Article VII states that the Constitution will go into effect after nine states ratify it.

The workings of all three branches of government (along with the system of checks and balances) will be examined much more closely in Unit 4, "The National Government." For now, you should become familiar with how the Constitution describes the structure of our government. You can read the entire Constitution on page 564.

SECTION REVIEW

Define the Words

Preamble	checks and balances
legislative	veto
executive	override
judicial	

Check the Facts

1. What are three purposes served by the Constitution?
2. What are the six goals of government listed in the Preamble?
3. What are some powers given to Congress and to the President in Articles I and II of the Constitution?

Think About the Ideas

4. *Analyze.* Why is it important for the United States government to have symbols?
5. *Explain.* How can the Constitution have more power than the Congress?

Although the President and Congress belong to separate branches of the government, they must work together to govern the nation.

****

SECTION 3

Underlying Principles

****

VOCABULARY
popular sovereignty   concurrent powers
enumerated powers   Supremacy Clause
reserved powers

As you discovered in Chapter 2, many of our ideas about government began in England. These ideas helped shape the Declaration of Independence and also the state constitutions that were written after independence.

By 1787, when the Constitution was written, Americans had already had experience in governing themselves. This practical experience added to, and sometimes changed, the ideas that had come from England. The Constitution reflected these changing ideas and expressed a uniquely American way of thinking about government.

The American view of government includes four basic principles: popular sovereignty, limited government, federalism, and separation of powers. These four ideas are the foundation on which our government was built.

Popular Sovereignty

Sovereignty means the right, or power, to rule. **Popular sovereignty** is the idea that people should have the right to rule themselves.

In England, the idea of popular sovereignty led to the growth of a democratic government. The legislature, Parliament, was made up of representatives elected by the people. By choosing representatives who shared their ideas and points of view, the people ruled themselves.

This idea remained important to the English colonists who came to America. The Declaration of Independence is really a statement about popular sovereignty. It says that Americans, like English citizens, must be given the right to govern themselves. The same idea is echoed in the "We the People" phrase with which the Constitution begins.

For the writers of the Constitution, however, popular sovereignty was more than just an abstract idea. They designed a government whose actions would always reflect the will of the people.

Under the Constitution, the will of the people is expressed most strongly through elections. Voters elect representatives to Congress; through the Electoral College, they elect a President and Vice President as well.

If elected officials fail to serve the people as they should, they can be removed from office. Under the Constitution, even the President can be dismissed if he or she commits a crime.

Limited Government

One danger of a democratic government is that the majority may try to limit or deny the rights of the minority. This is what happened to the American colonies before independence. Parliament, representing the majority of English citizens, passed laws to punish the small group of citizens who lived in America. As a result, some basic rights of citizens were denied to Americans.

The writers of the Constitution did not want to allow a similar situation to occur in the United States. They believed strongly that there are certain things a government must not be permitted to do, even if the majority of citizens feels that the government should do them. In other words, they felt that the power of government should be limited.

The limits of our government are expressed most clearly in Article I of the Constitution, which lists the powers denied to Congress. Among these are the powers to arrest people without charges or to punish people without a trial. The Bill of Rights, added to the Constitution in 1791, places many more limits on the government's power.

After the 1989 earthquake, residents of San Francisco received disaster relief from the federal government.

Federalism

Federalism is another name for the federal system of government, in which power is divided between the national government and the states. (In the United States, the national government is often called the federal government.)

Federalism is related to the idea of popular sovereignty—that people should govern themselves. Even in 1787, the United States was a large country, and people in different parts of the country had completely different ways of living. Many of the laws that made sense in a southern tobacco-growing state, for example, made little sense in a northern manufacturing state. By allowing each state to have its own government, the Constitution gave Americans the freedom to provide for their own local needs.

In setting up a federal system, the writers of the Constitution divided the powers of government into three types:

1. **Enumerated powers** are those powers that the Constitution specifically gives to the national government. These powers include the power to control immigration, to maintain an army, and to establish a postal system.

2. **Reserved powers** are those that the Constitution gives to the states. Among these are the power to regulate trade within the borders of a state, to set up and regulate schools, and to make rules for marriage and divorce.

3. **Concurrent powers** are those that are shared by the national and state governments. For example, both levels of government are allowed to collect taxes, to borrow money, and to set up courts and prisons.

In a federal system, the laws of a state and the laws of the national government may come into conflict. To deal with this possibility, the writers of the Constitution included a statement called the **Supremacy Clause**. Found in Article VI, the Supremacy Clause states that the Constitution and the laws of the national government are the "supreme law of the land." In other words, in any conflict between national law and state law, the national law has the higher authority.

Separation of Powers

English and European history is filled with stories of strong rulers who oppressed their people while gathering power and wealth for themselves. Having studied history, the framers of the Constitution understood that too much power in the hands of one person—or one group—could be dangerous. The framers were also influenced by the ideas of the French philosopher Baron de Montesquieu. Montesquieu believed that the best way to protect the liberty of the people was to separate the legislative, executive, and judicial functions of government and assign each to a separate governmental branch.

The writers of the Constitution combined these ideas to create a new form of government. To protect against the abuse of power, they divided the government into legislative, executive, and judicial branches. They then created a system of checks and balances, so that no one branch could gain too much power for itself.

Name three powers shared by the state and federal government.

FEDERAL AND STATE POWERS

Enumerated Powers (Powers given to the federal government)	Concurrent Powers (Powers shared by state and federal governments)	Reserved Powers (Powers given to the state governments)
★ Pass all laws necessary and proper to carry out its powers ★ Conduct foreign affairs ★ Raise and support an army ★ Regulate foreign trade with other countries and between the states ★ Coin and print money ★ Establish a postal system ★ Govern American territories, admit new states, and regulate immigration	★ Enforce the laws ★ Establish courts ★ Collect taxes ★ Borrow money ★ Provide for the general welfare	★ Regulate trade and commerce within the state ★ Establish local governments ★ Conduct elections, determine qualifications of voters ★ Establish a public school system ★ Provide for the public safety, health, and welfare within the state

Principles Versus Details

It is sometimes said that the U.S. Constitution is flawed, because so many compromises went into it. It is true that none of its signers was entirely satisfied with the document; each would have liked certain details to be different.

Even though they disagreed over details, however, the framers of the Constitution all believed strongly in the principles of popular sovereignty, limited government, federalism, and separation of powers. They disagreed only about how those principles should be reflected in a government.

Even if the Constitutional Convention had taken a different course, those four principles would still have played a major role. We can safely guess that any government based on these ideas would look very much like the government we have today.

SECTION REVIEW

Define the Words

popular sovereignty   concurrent powers
enumerated powers   Supremacy Clause
reserved powers

Check the Facts
1. What are the four basic principles on which the Constitution is based?
2. Name some enumerated powers, some reserved powers, and some concurrent powers.
3. Why did the framers of the Constitution divide the government into three branches?

Think About the Ideas
4. *Evaluate*. What are some advantages and disadvantages of our federal system of government?
5. *Put ideas together*. What problems might result if there were no Supremacy Clause?

A Living Constitution

VOCABULARY
amendment   implied powers

When the Constitution was signed in 1787, no one knew how well it would work. After all, the Articles of Confederation had been signed with high hopes, but they ended in near disaster. For all anyone knew, government under the Constitution might also turn out to be a failure. Yet the Constitution has lasted more than 200 years, and it still has as much strength and vigor as it did when it was first written.

One key to the Constitution's success is its flexibility—its ability to change with the times. The delegates to the Constitutional Convention could not have imagined a world in which automobiles, telephones, and computers were commonplace. And yet, they wrote a document that would be able to adapt to just such a world.

The Constitution's ability to adapt was built into the document from the very beginning. Its writers provided two ways for the Constitution to be changed—by amendment and by interpretation.

Amending the Constitution

Any change in, or addition to, the text of the Constitution is called an **amendment**. Article V of the Constitution explains exactly how amendments may be made.

The amendment process has two steps: an amendment must first be proposed, and then it must be ratified.

An amendment may be proposed in either of two ways: by a vote of two-thirds of the members of both houses of Congress or by a national convention. To call a national convention, two-thirds of the state legislatures must request one. (Such a convention has never been called.)

Once an amendment has been proposed, it must be ratified by three-fourths of the states. The states have two ways to ratify an amendment: either by a vote in each state legislature or by calling special state conventions. Only one amendment, the Twenty-First Amendment, was ratified by means of state conventions. All others were proposed by Congress and ratified by the state legislatures.

The writers of the Constitution deliberately made the amendment process difficult. After months of debate and compromise, they were aware of how delicate the structure of government can be. Making even one small change in the Constitution could have dramatic effects throughout the government. Therefore, the amendment process cannot, and should not, be carried out without the overwhelming support of the people.

At the same time, the ability to amend the Constitution is clearly necessary. Many freedoms that we take for granted today, such as the abolition of slavery and the right of women to vote, were accomplished by amendments to the Constitution.

The amendment process makes it possible for the Constitution to be changed to adapt to changing times. In what two ways can the Constitution be amended?

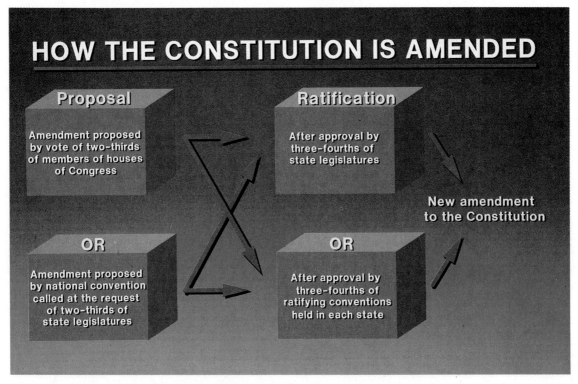

HOW THE CONSTITUTION IS AMENDED

Proposal

Amendment proposed by vote of two-thirds of members of houses of Congress

OR

Amendment proposed by national convention called at the request of two-thirds of state legislatures

Ratification

After approval by three-fourths of state legislatures

OR

After approval by three-fourths of ratifying conventions held in each state

New amendment to the Constitution

In the Declaration of Independence, Thomas Jefferson stated that people have the right to overthrow a government that does not protect their rights. If the Constitution could not have been amended to protect the rights of blacks, women, and other oppressed groups, it—and our government—surely would not have survived.

Interpreting the Constitution

The writers of the Constitution knew that the world would change in ways that they could not predict. For this reason, they tried to keep the document as general as possible. Although they went into great detail about some matters (such as the system of checks and balances), they left other matters open to interpretation.

One phrase in the Constitution has probably been interpreted more often than any other. It is called the Necessary and Proper Clause. In the section of Article I where it lists the powers of Congress, the Constitution gives Congress the power "to make all Laws which shall be necessary and proper" to carry out its duties.

Which branches of government were added to the government under the Constitution?

	ARTICLES OF CONFEDERATION	CONSTITUTION OF THE UNITED STATES
Organization	Strong, independent states with weak central government One house legislature with equal representation for each state	Strong central government with certain powers reserved to states Two house legislature: House of Representatives, representation based on state population; Senate, equal representation for each state
Powers	**Congress** ★ Declare war ★ Make treaties ★ Coin and borrow money ★ Make laws but not empowered to enforce them ★ No power to tax ★ No power to regulate trade	**Congress** ★ Declare war ★ Make treaties ★ Coin and borrow money ★ Make the nation's laws ★ Tax ★ Regulate trade
	No chief executive or separate executive branch	**President** ★ Commander in chief of armed forces ★ Carries out the nation's laws
	No federal court system	Supreme Court and lower federal courts interpret the laws
Procedure	No law could be passed unless 9 of 13 states voted for it No article could be amended unless all 13 states voted for it	Laws passed by majority vote in Congress Constitution can be amended by two-thirds vote in both houses of Congress and approval by three-fourths of state legislatures

John Marshall—Father of Constitutional Law

John Marshall was born on the Virginia frontier in 1755. As a young man, he served in the Revolutionary War, enduring the harsh winter of 1777 at Valley Forge. However, Marshall's contribution to the struggling new nation did not come on the battlefield but in the courtroom, where he helped shape the laws of the United States.

After the war, Marshall became a lawyer and a Federalist leader in Virginia. In 1801, President John Adams named him Chief Justice of the Supreme Court. Marshall remained on the Court for 34 years. During that time, he helped build the judicial branch into a powerful tool for protecting American democracy.

While Marshall was Chief Justice, the Court handed down several decisions that strengthened the power of the new national government and of its judicial branch. One ruling, for example, held that federal laws were superior to conflicting state laws. Marshall's most famous decision, in the case of *Marbury* v. *Madison*, established the power of judicial review (see page 280).

John Marshall saw the Constitution as a living document destined "to endure for ages to come, and consequently, to be adapted to the various crises of human affairs." Marshall played a major role in turning this vision into reality.

Using Your Skills
1. How did John Marshall help shape the role of the Supreme Court in the federal government?
2. How did the Court's ruling that federal laws were superior to state laws help strengthen the national government?

The Necessary and Proper Clause allows Congress to exercise powers that are not specifically listed in the Constitution. These powers are known as **implied powers**. Much of what the federal government does today—from regulating air pollution, to licensing television stations, to setting speed limits on interstate highways—is based on the implied powers of Congress.

Of course, not everyone agrees which laws are "necessary and proper" and which are not. Some people feel that Congress should be allowed to make any laws that are not specifically forbidden by the Constitution. These people believe in a loose interpretation of the Constitution.

Other people believe in a strict interpretation of the Constitution. They feel that Congress should only make the kinds of laws that the Constitution specifically mentions.

Another group of people say we should interpret the Constitution according to the intentions of its writers. These people feel that the writers of the Constitution, if they were alive today, would have approved of some implied powers but not others. Therefore, the proper way to interpret the Constitution is to try to discover the intentions of its signers, even if those intentions are not clearly stated in the Constitution itself.

The final responsibility for interpreting the Constitution rests with the Supreme Court. Over the years, the Court has interpreted the Constitution in different ways—sometimes strictly, sometimes loosely. Regardless of how it is interpreted, each new interpretation helps our government change and grow.

The Constitution of today is quite different from the document that was written in 1787. Two hundred years from now, it will no doubt have gone through many more changes. But the basic structure of our government—a finely tuned balance between the President, Congress, and the courts—will no doubt remain.

SECTION REVIEW

Define the Words

amendment   implied powers

Check the Facts
1. What are the two ways in which an amendment may be proposed?
2. What are the two ways in which an amendment may be ratified?
3. What are implied powers?

Think About the Ideas
4. *Analyze.* What might happen if amendments were easier to propose and ratify?

The nine justices of the U.S. Supreme Court bear the responsibility of interpreting the Constitution. They hear cases and hand down decisions in this building in Washinton, D.C.

CITIZENSHIP SKILLS

How to Interpret a Political Cartoon

Political cartoons are drawings that express a favorable or unfavorable opinion or point of view. They usually focus on public figures, political events, or economic or social conditions. Each cartoon contains useful clues to its meaning. These clues may come from labels or captions, the appearance and actions of figures, or the use of symbols—pictures that represent ideas or concepts.

The first step in interpreting a political cartoon is to try to identify the clues.

What is happening in the cartoon? What do the figures represent? What do the symbols refer to? Studying the clues helps you identify the subject and understand the cartoonist's point.

The cartoon on this page appeared on the cover of an almanac in 1788, soon after the ratification of the Constitution. Study the cartoon in terms of its historical context, and answer the questions that follow. Because visual clues can be interpreted in more than one way, some questions can have more than one correct answer.

Using Your Skills

1. How many figures are pulling the chariot? What do the figures pulling the chariot represent?
2. What do you think the chariot represents? To what political event does the cartoon refer?
3. The chariot has a folded umbrella, and the picture shows storm clouds overhead. How might this be interpreted?
4. What visual clues suggest the idea of government by law rather than by kings or queens?
5. Do you think the artist had a favorable or unfavorable opinion of the ratification of the Constitution? Explain.

CHAPTER 3 REVIEW

* *

MAIN POINTS

★ In 1787, a group of 55 delegates from 12 states met at a Constitutional Convention in Philadelphia to revise the Articles of Confederation. Instead, they wrote a new constitution, which established a new and stronger central government.

★ During the convention, numerous conflicts arose over how the new government would be set up. After much debate and many compromises, the delegates to the convention reached agreement and wrote the Constitution.

★ The ratification process pitted Federalists against Anti-Federalists. An agreement to add a bill of rights to the Constitution helped bring about ratification.

★ The Constitution serves three purposes: it is a plan of government, a legal and political force, and a symbol of American ideals and beliefs.

★ The Constitution set up a government in which power is divided among three branches: legislative, executive, and judicial. A balance of power is maintained among these branches by means of a system of checks and balances.

★ The Constitution is based on four underlying principles: popular sovereignty, limited government, federalism, and separation of powers.

★ The flexibility of the Constitution, and its ability to change to suit the times by means of amendment and interpretation, have been essential to the Constitution's survival.

WORDS IN REVIEW

Choose the word or phrase from the list below that best completes each sentence. Write the missing words on a separate sheet of paper.

federal system   Anti-Federalists
implied powers   checks and balances
legislative   judicial
enumerated powers   concurrent powers
amendment   popular sovereignty

1. Congress, in making laws, is carrying out the _____ function of government.

2. The division of power between the states and the federal government is part of our _____ of government.

3. In a democracy, the power of the people to rule themselves, reflects the idea of _____.

4. Changing the President's term of office to six years would require a(n) _____ to the Constitution.

5. The _____ were opposed to the power of the new central government.

6. The use of a presidential veto is an example of the system of _____.

7. _____ are specifically given to the federal government by the Constitution.

8. The Supreme Court and other federal courts are part of the _____ branch of government.

9. The Necessary and Proper Clause of the Constitution allows Congress to exercise its _____.

10. _____ are shared by both the federal government and the states.

CHAPTER 3 REVIEW

* *

FACTS IN REVIEW

1. What was the original purpose of the Constitutional Convention?

2. What key decisions did the delegates make at the very start of the Constitutional Convention?

3. Why were small states unwilling to accept the Virginia Plan?

4. Explain the importance of the system of checks and balances.

5. What is the purpose of the Preamble to the Constitution?

6. What is the purpose of Articles I, II, and III of the Constitution?

7. In what ways does the Constitution express the idea of popular sovereignty?

8. How is the idea of limited government expressed in the Constitution?

9. In what way did the writers of the Constitution allow for flexibility and change?

10. What is the difference between strict interpretation and loose interpretation of the Constitution?

THINKING ABOUT THE CONSTITUTION

1. *Analyze.* In what ways might the Constitution be viewed as not representative of the American people?

2. *Evaluate.* What, do you think, are the major strengths and weaknesses of the Constitution?

3. *Assess.* Do you think our Constitution has had an impact on other nations of the world? Explain how.

WRITING ABOUT THE CONSTITUTION

Your local American Legion is sponsoring a contest for the best one-page essay on "Democratic Principles in the Constitution." You decide to enter the contest. When you write your essay, remember to be concise and use specific examples. You have only one page, so avoid unnecessary information.

INTERPRETING A CHART

Look at the chart on page 86 comparing the features of government under the Articles of Confederation with government under the Constitution. How was the basic structure of government different? Which branches of government were added under the Constitution? What powers did Congress acquire under the Constitution? Under which system of government were laws easier to pass?

FOCUSING ON YOUR COMMUNITY

Investigate whether your community has a constitution or charter that defines the structure of the local government. How long is this document? What types of issues or information are included in it? In what ways is this document similar to or different from the U.S. Constitution? Prepare a short oral report for your class discussing the structure and purpose of your local constitution or charter.

CHAPTER 4

* *

The Bill of Rights

OBJECTIVES

After you have studied this chapter, you
will be able to:

★ Explain the purpose of the Bill of
  Rights.
★ Identify the rights guaranteed by the
  First Amendment.
★ Identify the rights guaranteed in the
  other nine amendments in the Bill of
  Rights.
★ Discuss the limits on First Amendment
  rights.
★ Explain how the Bill of Rights was
  extended by later amendments.

SECTIONS

1 The Bill of Rights
2 The First Amendment
3 The Bill of Rights Extended

When 39 weary delegates signed the Constitution in 1787, they knew that the work of establishing a new national government was not yet finished. The Constitution still had to be ratified by the states. Even before the ratification process began, controversy arose over the new document.

One of the strongest arguments of the Anti-Federalists against ratification was that the Constitution did not include a bill of rights. They warned that without a bill of rights, the strong national government might threaten individual liberties. So, to gain support for ratification, the Federalists promised to add a bill of rights to the constitution after the new government was established. That promise helped to win ratification.

In 1789, when James Madison took his seat in the new House of Representatives of the U.S. Congress, he introduced 12 amendments to the Constitution. These amendments had been modeled on the Bill of Rights of Virginia, his home state. Ten of those amendments were eventually passed by Congress and ratified by the states in 1791. They became the first 10 amendments to the Constitution—our Bill of Rights.

★ ★

SECTION 1

The Bill of Rights

★ ★

VOCABULARY

search warrant	due process of law
indict	eminent domain
double jeopardy	bail

The Constitution, as it was originally written, describes the powers and authority of the national government. The first 10 amendments to the Constitution, the Bill of Rights, describe the powers and rights of American citizens.

As you learned in Chapter 3, the writers of the Constitution believed strongly in the principle of limited government. The Bill of Rights reflects this principle by putting sharp limits on how the national government can use its power over the people.

First Amendment

The First Amendment to the Constitution is probably the best known and most cherished part of the Bill of Rights. It protects five basic freedoms that are essential to the American way of life: freedom of religion, freedom of speech, freedom of the press, freedom of assembly, and freedom to petition the government. Because this amendment is so important and so far-reaching, we will look at it more closely later in this chapter.

RIGHTS PROTECTED BY THE FIRST AMENDMENT

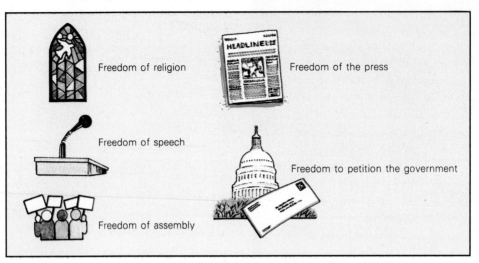

Freedom of religion

Freedom of the press

Freedom of speech

Freedom to petition the government

Freedom of assembly

Why is the First Amendment considered to be the most far-reaching of the amendments?

Second Amendment

The second Amendment guarantees Americans the right to serve in a state militia and to bear arms.

If you read the Second Amendment on page 574, you will see that it gives a specific reason for the right to bear arms: to maintain "a well-regulated militia." A militia, at the time this amendment was written, was a small, local army made up of volunteer soldiers. Such militias helped to fight against Great Britain in the American Revolution. After independence, they helped to defend the states and their communities. Because militias were not supported by government money, soldiers often had to supply their own weapons. The right of individuals to bear arms was necessary, therefore, for maintaining these militias.

Today, we no longer have local volunteer armies in the United States. For this reason, some Americans question whether the Second Amendment still gives individuals the right to have guns. Some federal court rulings reject the idea that this amendment gives

individuals the right to own firearms for private use. Leaders in Congress and in the state legislatures continue to discuss what the "right to bear arms" really means in today's society. This question is the subject of Issues of Our Time on page 300.

Third Amendment

The Third Amendment limits the power of the national government to force Americans to quarter, or house, soldiers. In peacetime, soldiers may not move into private homes except with the owner's consent. In times of war, the practice is also prohibited unless people are requested to do so by law.

During the colonial period, the law requiring American colonists to house and feed British soldiers was one of the leading causes of the independence movement. The Third Amendment has made it unlikely that Americans will ever be forced to open their homes to the military again. The amendment protects us, therefore, from an abuse of military authority.

EQUAL RIGHTS FOR WOMEN

As you have learned, changing the Constitution is not easy. The framers believed that any changes in our system of government should have the support of the overwhelming majority of the people. In the case of the proposed Equal Rights Amendment (ERA), the process worked just as the framers intended. The ERA amendment calling for equal rights for women won approval in Congress in 1972. At that time, the feminist, or women's rights, movement was at its height. The proposed amendment also gained broad support from labor organizations and civil rights groups.

Congress set a deadline of seven years for ratification by the states. By the end of 1972, the amendment seemed well on its way to passage. It had received the approval of 22 of the 38 states required for ratification. But in 1973, a strong opposition movement called STOP ERA emerged.

The goal of the ERA supporters was to ensure that women received the same rights under the law as men. They believed that the ERA would help end discrimination against women in such areas as hiring, pay, promotions, and credit ratings.

Opponents of ERA feared that it would force the government to impose equality, even when it might hurt women. They argued, for example, that women could be drafted and forced to fight in combat. They were also concerned that women would lose ground in legal areas, such as divorce and child custody.

By 1978, 35 states had ratified the ERA—but 5 states had changed their votes of approval. Although Congress extended the deadline by three years, ERA backers failed to win ratification.

While the ERA struggle was going on, however, women were gaining ground in other legislation. Congress passed law after law barring discrimination against women in education, school athletics, hiring, promotions, and financial matters. Many states added ERA's to their constitutions and passed similar antidiscrimination laws. The Supreme Court handed down dozens of decisions upholding these federal and state laws.

Women still earn only two-thirds as much as men for comparable jobs. In addition, salaries for jobs traditionally held by women (secretaries, teachers, and librarians, for example) remain low. But today women attend the nation's military academies, serve on ships, and pilot planes. Women have been hired as police and fire fighters, and they own banks and construction companies. One woman was nominated by the Democratic Party to be Vice President of the United States.

In 1988, the ERA was reintroduced in Congress. Again, it failed to win enough support, this time apparently because many people saw less need for it.

Using Your Skills

1. Why did the ERA gain broad support in 1972?
2. What legal gains have women made since 1972?
3. If you had the opportunity to vote on ERA today, how would you vote? Why?

Fourth Amendment

The Fourth Amendment, sometimes known as the Privacy Amendment, protects Americans against unreasonable searches and seizures. In other words, no soldier, government official, or law enforcement official can search a person's home or take a person's property without that person's permission.

There are, however, rules under which searches and seizures may be "reasonable." If law enforcement officers believe that an individual has committed a crime, they can ask a judge to issue a **search warrant**. A search warrant is a legal document that allows law enforcement officials to search a suspect's home and take specific items that they can use as evidence in court.

Judges do not give out search warrants easily, however. They must be convinced that good reasons, or probable cause, exist for believing that evidence will be found. Without this safeguard the Fourth Amendment would have little meaning. Warrants could be issued easily and our privacy invaded.

Without the Fourth Amendment we would have little feeling of security in our homes. At any time of the day or night, a knock on the door could bring the police into our homes to invade our privacy and confiscate our possessions.

The Fourth Amendment is one of the most important safeguards we have for protecting the rights of individuals from the abuse of government power.

Fifth Amendment

As you read in Chapter 2, the English philosopher John Locke wrote that every person has rights to life, liberty, and property. The Fifth Amendment protects these rights in several different ways.

The Fifth Amendment protects the life and liberty of citizens by protecting the rights of people accused of a crime. The first part of the amendment states that no one can be put on trial without first being **indicted**, or formally accused, by a group of citizens. A group

The police must have good reason for suspicion to obtain a search warrant. How does this protect a person's rights?

brought together for this purpose is called a grand jury. A person who is indicted is not necessarily guilty of a crime. An indictment simply indicates the grand jury's belief, based on evidence, that an individual *may* have committed a crime. This provision protects people from being brought to trial hastily, and perhaps needlessly.

The Fifth Amendment also protects an accused person from **double jeopardy**. This means that people who are judged not guilty of a crime may not be put on trial again for the same crime.

A third part of this amendment protects an accused person's right to remain silent. Many times throughout history, innocent people have been threatened, tortured, or bullied into confessing to crimes they did not commit. To prevent this from happening, the Fifth Amendment guarantees that persons cannot be forced to testify against themselves. This is called protection against self-incrimination.

Another part of the Fifth Amendment says that no one may be denied life, liberty, or property without **due process of law**. Due process means following procedures established by law and guaranteed by the Constitution. It also means that the laws themselves must be reasonable. Making it a crime to keep a diary would be unreasonable. Due process is therefore an important protection for everyone.

Finally, the Fifth Amendment protects a person's property rights. It limits the government's power of **eminent domain**. Eminent domain is the right of government to take private property—usually pieces of land—for public use. For example, if a home lies in the path of a proposed highway, the government may take the land and destroy the house. The Fifth Amendment limits this power and requires the government to pay a fair price for the property it takes.

The Fifth Amendment, is an important guarantee of the rights of innocent people against the abuses of government power.

Sixth Amendment

The Sixth Amendment guarantees additional rights to people who are accused of crimes. It requires that they be told exactly what crimes they are accused of committing. It also requires that the accused be given the opportunity to have a trial by jury. However, a person may ask to be tried only by a judge.

If an accused person asks for a trial, the trial must be speedy, public, and tried by an impartial jury. If possible, the trial should be held in the same area where the crime took place.

Accused individuals must have the right to hear and question all witnesses against them. They must also be permitted to call witnesses in their own defense. Finally, they are entitled to have a lawyer help them exercise these rights. Since the amendment was written, the Supreme Court has ruled that if an accused person cannot afford to hire a lawyer, the government must provide one. The fees of this court-appointed lawyer will be paid by the government.

Seventh Amendment

The Fifth and Sixth Amendments deal with people's rights in criminal cases—cases in which someone is accused of having committed a crime. Many court cases, however, result from disagreements between people or groups. For example, a person who is injured after falling off a ladder with a defective rung may take the ladder manufacturer to court. If the victim can prove that the rung broke because it was badly made, the court may

The Sixth Amendment to the Constitution provides that anyone accused of a crime has the right to a jury trial.

require the manufacturer to pay the victim's medical expenses. Cases like this one, in which no actual crime is involved, are called civil cases.

The Seventh Amendment guarantees the right to a jury trial in civil cases, providing that the amount of money involved is more than $20. It does not, however, require a trial. Both sides may decide to have their dispute settled by a judge instead.

Eighth Amendment

The Eighth Amendment is concerned with criminal cases. Although the Sixth Amendment guarantees a quick trial, sometimes several weeks or months may go by before a trial can be held. During that time, the accused person has two choices: to stay in jail or to pay a sum of money called **bail**. The purpose of bail is to make sure that the accused person will appear in court for the trial. If the person appears at the proper time, the bail is returned. If the person fails to appear, the bail is forfeited.

The judge decides how much bail a person must pay. The Eighth Amendment forbids the judge to set bail at an "excessive" amount—that is, an amount that is much too high. Excessive does not just refer to what a person can afford to pay. In determining bail, a judge considers various factors, including the type of crime committed, the record of the accused person, and the likelihood that the accused will appear in court. When a person is convicted of a crime, the Eighth Amendment protects him or her against having to pay excessive fines. Fines, however, may vary depending on the seriousness of the crime.

The Eighth Amendment also protects convicted persons against "cruel and unusual punishments." For many years, Americans have debated what this really means. It is generally agreed that it means that punishment should be in proportion to the crime committed. For example, branding someone for stealing a loaf of bread would be considered cruel and unusual. But people disagree strongly about whether punishment for some crimes—such as execution for murder— is cruel and unusual.

Ninth Amendment

The people who wrote the Bill of Rights realized that they could not list every right that citizens have under the Constitution. At the same time, they wanted to guarantee that Americans would have every right possible.

The Ninth Amendment makes clear that the rights spelled out in the Constitution are not the only rights of the American people. Other, unwritten rights are just as valuable, and they may not be taken away by the government. Therefore, although many basic freedoms we enjoy—such as the freedom to choose our friends, our spouses, and our careers—are not written down, they are still protected under the Constitution.

Tenth Amendment

The Tenth Amendment is also a reminder of what the Constitution does *not* say. But in this case, it concerns the principle of federalism. The Constitution talks about only certain powers of national and state government. But many other powers of government—such as the power to set up schools or to license lawyers—are not mentioned at all.

Under the Tenth Amendment, any powers not specifically given to the national government by the Constitution are reserved for the states or for the people. (This amendment is the source of many of the reserved powers you learned about in Chapter 3.)

In this way, the Tenth Amendment prevents Congress and the President from becoming too strong. The government of the United States can only have powers that are given to it by the people it governs.

Which amendments deal with people accused of crimes?

THE BILL OF RIGHTS

First Amendment	Protects five freedoms—of religion, speech, press, assembly, and petition
Second Amendment	Guarantees the right to serve in a state militia and to bear arms
Third Amendment	Limits the government's power to house soldiers in anyone's home
Fourth Amendment	Protects people from unreasonable searches and seizures
Fifth Amendment	Protects the rights of a person accused of a crime and guarantees that no one may be denied life, liberty, or property without due process of law
Sixth Amendment	Lists additional rights of a person accused of a crime, including the right to trial by jury and to be represented by a lawyer
Seventh Amendment	Guarantees the right to a jury trial in civil cases
Eighth Amendment	Prohibits excessive bail or fines; forbids cruel and unusual punishment
Ninth Amendment	Specifies that rights listed are not the only rights of the people
Tenth Amendment	Powers not specifically assigned to the national government belong to the states or to the people

SECTION REVIEW

Define the Words

search warrant   due process of law
indict   eminent domain
double jeopardy   bail

Check the Facts

1. Briefly explain the purpose of each of the first 10 amendments to the Constitution.
2. Why was the Bill of Rights added to the Constitution?
3. What is a civil case?

Think About the Ideas

4. *Analyze.* In what ways do the 10 amendments of the Bill of Rights reflect the principles of limited government and popular sovereignty?

A young man celebrates his Bar Mitzvah. People of all religions have the right to practice religion in their own way in this country.

★ ★

SECTION 2

The First Amendment

★ ★

VOCABULARY

slander   libel
treason   petition

For a democracy to work, its citizens must have access to information and ideas. They must be able to develop their own ideas and beliefs and to meet openly with others to discuss these ideas. They must also be able to express their ideas in public and to have their views on public matters heard by those who govern.

Such an open exchange of ideas is the hallmark of a free society. Access to new and different ideas allows a democracy to grow and change. It also ensures that the ideas of the people will be heard.

The First Amendment guarantees that Americans can do these things. The rights it discusses—freedom of religion, freedom of speech, freedom of the press, freedom of assembly, and freedom to petition—are the foundation on which American society rests. Without them, the rest of the Constitution would be meaningless.

Freedom of Religion

Americans have always placed a special value on religious freedom. Many early colonists came to America because they wanted to be free to practice their religion in their own way. Some had come from England, where they were treated badly because they did not follow the official religion, the Church of England. To prevent the same thing from happening here, the United States follows the principle of "separation of church and state." This principle is included in the First Amendment.

There are two parts to the section of the First Amendment dealing with religious freedom. The first part prohibits Congress from establishing an official religion in the United States. The second part guarantees the right to practice religion as we wish. The government may not favor one religion over another or treat people differently because of their religion. People may practice any religion they choose, or they may choose to practice no religion at all.

The principle of "separation of church and state" does not mean that religion is unimportant in America. It means only that the government may make no laws that interfere with the religious lives of its citizens.

Freedom of Speech

In some countries, people can be put in jail for criticizing the government or for expressing their ideas, even if this is done in private conversations.

Early Americans, however, realized the importance of an open exchange of ideas in a democracy. As a result, freedom of speech became an important part of the Bill of Rights. The First Amendment guarantees Americans the right to say what is on their minds, in public or in private, without fear of punishment.

There are, however, some limits to freedom of speech. This freedom does not permit us to harm other people. For example,

we are not permitted to tell lies about someone. Lying about another person, with the intent to harm that person's reputation, is a crime called **slander**. Yelling "Fire!" in a crowded theater is another example of speech that might cause harm to others. Such acts may be punished under the law.

Freedom of speech does not include the right to endanger our government either. Giving military secrets to enemies of the United States, for example, is a very serious crime called **treason**.

Over the years, freedom of speech has come to mean more than just spoken words. "Speech," as interpreted by the Supreme Court, can mean art, music, or even styles of clothing. The First Amendment thus allows us to decorate our houses as we like, to express our beliefs with posters and bumper stickers, or to wear unusual clothing or hairstyles. As a result, the phrase "freedom of speech" is often replaced by a much broader idea, freedom of expression. Almost all types of self-expression are protected by the First Amendment.

Freedom of the Press

The First Amendment allows Americans to express themselves in print as well as in speech. When the Bill of Rights was written, "the press" was a term that referred to printed publications such as books, newspapers, and magazines. Today, the press includes many other ways of communicating information, such as radio, television, and computer networks.

Freedom of the press is limited in many of the same ways as freedom of speech. For example, no one is permitted to publish information that will harm other people or endanger the government. The printing of lies about others is a serious crime called **libel**.

Although lies that are spoken may be easily corrected or forgotten, lies that are printed are permanent.

Freedom of the press not only protects our rights to publish information freely, but also allows us to read what other people have published. The United States government cannot ban books, magazines, newspapers, or other printed materials even if those materials contain ideas that people find alarming or offensive. As a result, the American people are exposed to a wide variety of points of view.

Governments may make rules about when and where such activities can be held, but they cannot ban them.

The right to form and join organizations such as social clubs, political parties, and labor unions is also protected by the First Amendment. Freedom of assembly does not refer only to a gathering of people at a particular time or place. It also guarantees your right to belong to any group or organization, even if you never attend a meeting.

Freedom of Assembly

Americans are free to assemble in groups for any reason, so long as the assemblies are peaceful. Activities such as meetings, parades, political rallies, and public celebrations are all protected by the First Amendment.

The First Amendment gives citizens the right to assemble, to meet in groups, and to join organizations. Groups often organize demonstrations to express their point of view.

Right to Petition

Finally, the First Amendment also guarantees all Americans the right to petition their government. A **petition** simply means a formal request. Often, we use the word *petition* to refer to a specific kind of document—a brief, written statement followed by the signatures of hundreds or thousands of people. But even a simple letter written by an individual can be a petition.

The right to petition means the right to express our ideas to the government. If we have a complaint, or would like to see a particular law passed, we can write to our elected representatives and express our views. Our representatives are not obligated to act on our ideas. Sometimes, though, if enough people express their feelings about an issue, our leaders change their minds.

Limits to These Freedoms

You have already seen that there are limits to freedom of speech and freedom of the press. In addition to those, there are other limits to our First Amendment rights. These freedoms do not allow us to do things that break the law. Freedom of religion, for example, does not permit practices, such as human sacrifice, that are against the law. Freedom of assembly does not permit groups to be so noisy or unruly that they break laws against disorderly conduct or disturbing the peace.

The First Amendment was never intended to allow Americans to do whatever they wanted. Unlimited freedom is not possible in a society of many people. The rights of one individual must be balanced against the rights of others and against the rights of the community. When the rights of the individual and the rights of the community conflict, the rights of the community must in most cases come first. Otherwise, the society will break apart.

SECTION REVIEW

Define the Words

slander	libel
treason	petition

Check the Facts
1. Name and describe the five freedoms covered by the First Amendment.
2. Describe two limits on freedom of speech and two limits on freedom of the press.
3. Explain the principle of separation of church and state.

Think About the Ideas
4. *Analyze.* Why do you think there are laws against libel and slander? What might happen if such laws did not exist?

A petition signed by a large number of citizens can have a great impact on government policies.

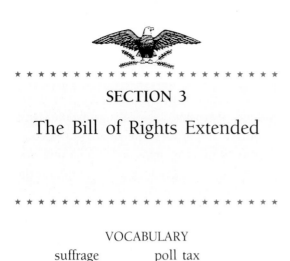

SECTION 3

The Bill of Rights Extended

* *

VOCABULARY

suffrage   poll tax

The Bill of Rights established rules for protecting the rights and liberties of citizens, but it did not apply to all Americans. In 1791, less than half of the American population enjoyed the full rights of United States citizens. Women, blacks, and adults under 21 were not granted the same rights as other Americans. None of these groups were permitted to vote, for instance. Most blacks, in fact, had no rights at all; as slaves, they were considered property rather than people.

Even those who had the most power in American society—white, adult males—did not always have the full protection of the Bill of Rights. Because the Constitution left a great deal of power to the states, individual states were able to pass laws that violated certain rights, and many did so.

Since 1791, the United States has experienced many changes. But the Constitution is flexible and has survived. It has been amended 26 times by the American people, as conditions and attitudes have changed over the years. Some of these amendments changed the way government works. Others extended the rights of Americans, offering basic freedoms to those groups of people who were previously ignored. We will look closely here at eight amendments that extended the Bill of Rights. All the Constitutional amendments are reprinted on pages 574–582.

Thirteenth Amendment (1865)

The Thirteenth Amendment was one of three important amendments passed after the Civil War. It officially ended all slavery in the United States and thus freed thousands of blacks throughout the country. It also outlawed any sort of forced labor, except as punishment for a crime.

Fourteenth Amendment (1868)

Although blacks gained their freedom in 1865, they did not receive full recognition as citizens until three years later. The Fourteenth Amendment defined a United States citizen as anyone "born or naturalized in the United States," a definition that included most black Americans.

To ensure the rights of black citizens, the Fourteenth Amendment went even further. It required every state to grant its citizens "equal protection of the laws." In other words, state governments must treat all citizens equally. This part of the Fourteenth Amendment has been extremely important. In recent years, it has been used to protect the rights of women, disabled people, and other groups whose rights have been abused.

Another part of the Fourteenth Amendment forbids state governments from interfering with the "privileges or immunities of citizens of the United States." In other words, state legislatures may not pass laws that interfere with rights granted by the national government. As a result of this provision, the protections in the Bill of Rights have been extended to state laws as well as national laws.

Over 200,000 people participated in this civil rights march on Washington in 1963. Many there heard Martin Luther King, Jr., give his famous "I have a dream" speech.

James Meredith, the first black to attend the University of Mississippi, was escorted to class in 1962.
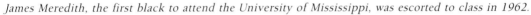

BROWN v. BOARD OF EDUCATION

In 1954, racial segregation (separation) was part of life in the United States. In many states, blacks went to separate schools, stayed at separate hotels, and even used separate restrooms and water fountains. Segregation was not only a social custom, but was also supported by hundreds of state laws. The U.S. Supreme Court had upheld these segregation laws in 1896 in the case of *Plessy* v. *Ferguson*. In that case, the Court ruled that states could maintain separate facilities—railroad cars—for whites and blacks as long as they were equal.

But separate often was not equal, particularly in the case of public schools. All-white schools usually got better teachers and better equipment than black schools. In 1950, Oliver Brown tried to enroll his daughter Linda in a white school in Topeka, Kansas. When she was refused, Brown filed suit against the Topeka Board of Education.

The U.S. Supreme Court heard Brown's case and four similar cases in 1953, but it did not hand down its decision until May 17, 1954. Chief Justice Earl Warren read the court's unanimous decision:

Does the segregation of children in public schools solely on the basis of race, even though physical facilities . . . may be equal, deprive the children of equal educational opportunities? We believe it does.

. . . We conclude that in the field of public education the doctrine of "separate but equal" has no place. Separate educational facilities are inherently unequal.

In other words, the Court decided that segregated schools violated the Fourteenth Amendment's guarantee of equal protection of the laws and was unconstitutional.

In 1955, the Court ordered states with segregated schools to pro-

ceed with desegregation "with all deliberate speed." The federal courts in each state were assigned to oversee the process.

The Court's ruling in *Brown* v. *Board of Education* met much resistance. In 1957, President Dwight D. Eisenhower had to send federal troops into Little Rock, Arkansas, to escort black students into an all-white school. Although school segregation is illegal today, many schools in this country are still segregated. This is because blacks and whites often live in different neighborhoods and belong to different school districts.

Using Your Skills
1. Why did the Supreme Court decide that segregated schools violated the Fourteenth Amendment's guarantee of equal protection of the laws?
2. Why do you think the Court's decision in the Brown case met with so much resistance?

Fifteenth Amendment (1870)

The Fifteenth Amendment extended the rights of black Americans even further by granting them **suffrage**, or the right to vote. This right was guaranteed only to men, however. Women, whether black or white, were not guaranteed suffrage until 1920.

The Fifteenth Amendment was largely unsuccessful in guaranteeing blacks the right to vote. Many states found legal ways to keep black citizens from voting. Some states, for example, required voters to pay a **poll tax**—a sum of money paid in exchange for the right to cast a ballot. Since many blacks were too poor to pay the poll tax, a large number remained unable to vote.

Seventeenth Amendment (1913)

According to Article I of the Constitution, members of the House of Representatives were to be elected directly by the people, but members of the Senate were to be chosen by the state legislatures. The Seventeenth Amendment changed that by allowing the voters to elect their senators directly. In doing so, it gave Americans a greater voice in their government.

Nineteenth Amendment (1920)

Although the Constitution did not grant suffrage to women, it did not explicitly deny women the right to vote. For this reason, the state legislatures, using the powers given to them under the Tenth Amendment, were able to make their own laws about women's suffrage. Wyoming granted women the right to vote in 1869, and several other states followed.

CIVICS SIDELIGHTS

Failed Amendments

For every amendment that is added to the U.S. Constitution, there are dozens, perhaps hundreds, that never make it. Although some of these are absurd ideas, others are reasonable attempts to deal with government or social problems. Among the recently proposed amendments that have failed to become part of the Constitution are amendments seeking to balance the federal budget and giving equal rights to women.

Here are a few other failed amendments:
★ The Senate shall be abolished (1876).
★ No U.S. citizen shall accept a foreign title of nobility (1810).
★ All acts of war shall be put to a national vote. All those affirming (voting yes) shall be registered as a volunteer for service in the United States Armed Forces (1916).
★ The nation shall hereafter be known as the United States of the Earth (1893).

Elizabeth Cady Stanton pictured here, and Susan B. Anthony began the National Women's Suffrage Association to fight for women's right to vote.

In the 1960's, Betty Friedan, a modern leader in the movement for women's rights, wrote about the role of women in a book called The Feminine Mystique.

Yet, national recognition of women's right to vote was slow in coming. Suffragists such as Susan B. Anthony and Elizabeth Cady Stanton struggled courageously to win the right to vote. They were opposed by many, however, who believed that women should not have the same rights as men. The fight continued for almost 50 years, but gradually the suffrage movement overcame this opposition. Finally, in 1920, the Nineteenth Amendment was added to the Constitution. It gave women the right to vote in all national and state elections. As a result of the Nineteenth Amendment, women were brought into the political system and were granted full citizenship alongside men.

Twenty-Third Amendment (1961)

Our nation's capital, the city of Washington, is not part of any state. It occupies an area called the District of Columbia.

Because the District of Columbia is not a state, its residents originally were not allowed to vote in national elections. The Twenty-Third Amendment granted the residents of the District of Columbia the right to vote for President and Vice President, just as other Americans do.

Twenty-Fourth Amendment (1964)

Nearly a century after the Fifteenth Amendment was adopted, many black Americans were still not able to vote. Many were among the poorer levels of society. As a result, they could not afford the poll taxes that several southern states required all voters to pay. These poll taxes affected not only blacks, but many poor whites as well.

In 1964, the Twenty-Fourth Amendment made poll taxes illegal in national elections. Two years later, the Supreme Court ruled that poll taxes were illegal in state elections as well. The elimination of the poll tax allowed many black citizens to enjoy their full rights as voters for the first time.

Twenty-Sixth Amendment (1971)

Throughout our nation's history, people under the age of 21 have been sent into battle to fight for their country. By law, however, they were not old enough to vote for the leaders who sent them there. Although the Constitution did not specify a minimum age for voters, most states set that age at 21.

That situation was finally changed in 1971, a year when many young Americans were fighting in Vietnam. The Twenty-Sixth Amendment lowered the minimum voting age to 18 for all national, state, and local elections. As a result, millions more Americans can now exercise their right to vote and enjoy the rights of full citizenship. (See Great American Documents feature on the Twenty-Sixth Amendment on page 160.)

The Twenty-Sixth Amendment was the last to be added to the Constitution. In the future, however, more amendments will certainly be proposed and ratified. One of the strengths of our Constitution has been its ability to respond to changes in society. The amendment process has contributed to that flexibility and will continue to do so in the future.

The voting age was lowered by a Constitutional amendment in 1971 when many young Americans were fighting in Vietnam.

CITIZENSHIP SKILLS

How to Run a Meeting

All organizations, clubs, and governing bodies hold meetings to take care of business and make important decisions. Whether you ever have to run a meeting or just participate in one, it is important to know how effective meetings are run.

The first thing to do is to prepare an agenda. An agenda is simply a list of matters to discuss and act on. On most agendas, the first items are usually to read and approve the minutes from the last meeting and the treasurer's report. The class secretary prepares the minutes, a record of each meeting. The treasurer's report should include income and expenses since the last meeting and the current balance in the treasury. Next, your agenda should list old (unfinished) business, items held over from previous meetings, and new business, items that have come up since the last meeting.

Since you are responsible for running the meeting, keep in mind that you are the one who should control it. Go through the agenda item by item until all the business is conducted. Give each person ample time to discuss each item before calling for a vote, but stop the discussion when it becomes repetitive or goes off the subject.

After an item has been discussed, call for a motion on the matter. A motion is a statement describing what action the group may want to take on the matter. For example, someone at the meeting may say, "I move that we approve the use of the school gym for our dance." Each motion requires a "second," or the backing of another person who says, "I second the motion." Then call for a vote, by either a show of hands, a secret ballot, or a voice vote (saying aye or nay). If a majority agrees with the motion, it is carried, or approved.

Sometimes a person at the meeting will make a motion to postpone or "table" the motion being considered. Perhaps the person wants to get more information, such as whether the gym is available the night of the dance. In that case, call for a vote on the motion to table the matter first.

These rules are quite formal and rigid, but they do not have to be followed precisely. Just keep in mind that a meeting should be conducted with common courtesy and common sense. Each member should respect the views and opinions of others.

Using Your Skills
1. Why is it important to prepare an agenda before each meeting?
2. How is being a class officer similar to being a member of a city council? How are the two jobs different?

AMENDMENTS TO THE CONSTITUTION (Nos. 11–26)

Eleventh Amendment	Places limits on suits against states
Twelfth Amendment	Revises procedure for electing the President and Vice President
Thirteenth Amendment	Abolishes slavery
Fourteenth Amendment	Defines U.S. citizenship; guarantees all citizens "equal protection of the law"
Fifteenth Amendment	Prohibits restrictions on the right to vote based on race and color
Sixteenth Amendment	Gives Congress the power to levy an income tax
Seventeenth Amendment	Enables voters to elect Senators directly
Eighteenth Amendment	Prohibits making, drinking, or selling of alcoholic beverages (Prohibition)
Nineteenth Amendment	Gives women the right to vote
Twentieth Amendment	Changes the date of Congressional and Presidential terms
Twenty-First Amendment	Repeals Prohibition (Eighteenth Amendment)
Twenty-Second Amendment	Limits Presidents to two terms in office
Twenty-Third Amendment	Gives residents of District of Columbia the right to vote
Twenty-Fourth Amendment	Abolishes poll taxes
Twenty-Fifth Amendment	Establishes procedures for succession to the Presidency
Twenty-Sixth Amendment	Sets voting age at 18 years

Which amendment deals specifically with the rights of women?

SECTION REVIEW

Define the Words

suffrage   poll tax

Check the Facts

1. Identify four amendments that affected the rights of black Americans, and briefly explain the purpose of each.
2. What was the significance of the Nineteenth, Twenty-Third, and Twenty-Sixth Amendments?
3. Why was the Fifteenth Amendment unsuccessful?
4. What do all the amendments discussed in this lesson have in common?

Think About the Ideas

5. *Explain.* Why do American minority groups consider the Fourteenth Amendment so important?

Civil rights legislation of the 1960's opened the way for many blacks in the South to participate in the election process.

111

CHAPTER 4 REVIEW

★ ★

MAIN POINTS

★ The Bill of Rights was added to the Constitution in 1791. Its purpose was to protect the rights of American citizens.

★ The First Amendment includes five rights that are essential to the American way of life. Those rights are freedom of religion, freedom of speech, freedom of the press, freedom of assembly, and freedom to petition the government.

★ The remaining amendments in the Bill of Rights also protect Americans against the power of government. These amendments concern protection against unreasonable search and seizure, various rights of persons accused of a crime, and the guarantee that Americans have other rights that are not listed in the Bill of Rights.

★ The rights listed in the First Amendment are not unlimited. They do not allow us to do things that would harm other people, nor do they allow us to do things that would break the law.

★ ~~Sixteen~~ Seventeen amendments have been added to the Constitution since the Bill of Rights. Some of these have changed the way government works. Eight of the amendments have extended rights to groups of people that were originally ignored.

WORDS IN REVIEW

Choose the word or phrase from the list below that best completes each sentence. Write the missing words on a separate sheet of paper.

suffrage
eminent domain
indicted
poll tax
slander

search warrant
due process of law
bail
double jeopardy
libel

1. Until 1964, in order to vote in several southern states, a person had to pay a(n) _____.

2. The government used its power of _____ to take several houses that were on the site of a proposed reservoir.

3. The person was charged with _____ as a result of damaging remarks made at a public meeting.

4. Before a person can be put on trial, he or she must be _____ by a grand jury.

5. Beginning in the 1800's, many women fought long and hard to win the right of _____.

6. The principle of _____ protects a person from being tried for the same crime more than once.

7. The right to a fair trial is an important part of the principle of _____.

8. The newspaper was being accused of _____ because of the lies and false accusations it had written about a person.

9. The police asked the judge to issue a(n) _____ so that they could look for evidence.

10. The lawyer for the accused claimed that the _____ set by the judge was excessive.

FACTS IN REVIEW

1. How does the Bill of Rights reflect the principle of limited government?

2. Why has the right to bear arms been questioned today?

CHAPTER 4 REVIEW

* *

3. Explain the rights of accused persons that are protected by the Fifth and Sixth Amendments.

4. What is the primary purpose of the Ninth Amendment?

5. Explain why the First Amendment is considered essential to a democratic society.

6. In what way is freedom of assembly limited?

7. What is treason?

8. Explain the significance of the Fourteenth Amendment.

9. How did the Seventeenth Amendment give Americans a greater say in their government?

10. In what way did the Twenty-Fourth Amendment extend the right to vote not only to blacks, but also to whites?

THINKING ABOUT THE BILL OF RIGHTS

1. *Analyze.* The Bill of Rights and other amendments provide a written guarantee of our rights. Do you think our rights would be as well protected if they were not written down? Why or why not?

2. *Evaluate.* Which of the first 10 amendments do you think is the most important guarantee of our rights? Explain why.

3. *Evaluate.* Should the U.S. government have the right to ban books that the majority of Americans find offensive? Why or why not?

WRITING ABOUT FREE SPEECH

Imagine that you have a cousin in Eastern Europe who has just returned home after a two- week visit with you and your family. She was very impressed by many things in the United States. She was very excited about the many political changes in Eastern Europe. She was especially excited about finally having the right to speak freely. She asked why free speech was so important to Americans.

You have been thinking about this since she left and have decided to write her a letter. In it, you will explain why the principle of free speech is so important to Americans.

INTERPRETING A CHART

Look at the chart on page 111 summarizing the amendments to the Constitution Nos. 11–26. Which of these amendments deal with how government works rather than with people's rights? Which of the amendments concern voting rights? What amendment reversed the ruling of an earlier amendment? Which amendments concern the office of President? How many amendments have been passed in the past 20 years?

FOCUSING ON YOUR COMMUNITY

Investigate your local community's rules about holding public assemblies (meetings, political rallies, parades, celebrations, and so on). Does the community require groups to get a permit to hold their activity? What restrictions does the community place on when and where activities can be held? Has the community ever prevented a group from holding an activity? Why? On what grounds did it prevent the activity from taking place? Present your findings to the class.

UNIT 2 REVIEW

* *

ESSAY QUESTIONS

The following questions are based on material in Unit 2. Answer each question with two or three written paragraphs. Be sure to give specific reasons to support your answers.

1. The framers of the Constitution believed that it was important to limit the power of government and protect individual rights. Explain what safeguards they devised to meet these goals.

2. The Constitution is not a rigid document. It was written in a way that makes it flexible and open to interpretation. Do you think this flexibility is a strength or a weakness? Explain your answer.

3. Do Americans enjoy more freedom and equality now than they did in 1789? Compare the situation today with that in 1789 and explain how any changes came about. Use examples to support your points.

CONNECTING CIVICS AND HISTORY

The Constitution was the product of a particular time in our nation's history. As such, it reflects the ideas, events, and situations existing at that time. For example, many parts of the Bill of Rights were written in response to experiences the colonists had had with Great Britain. In addition, ideas such as the separation of powers came from the writings of popular philosophers of the time. Be prepared to discuss the following in class: What specific parts of the Constitution were written in response to historical events? How have events influenced legislation in recent times (since 1960)? Give specific examples.

ANALYZING VISUALS

American painters and cartoonists in the late 1700's searched for symbols to represent the new nation. This early painting shows a number of symbols. Study the painting, and then answer the questions below.

1. The concept of liberty was often portrayed as a young woman, as in this painting. What is Miss Liberty stepping on? What is she holding in her right hand? What is the painter trying to show with these symbols?

2. The flag is the best-known symbol of the United States. Explain why this flag has one large star and 13 small ones. What other symbols do you see in the painting?

3. Why do you suppose an eagle was chosen to represent the United States?

4. Name some other symbols of the United States.

* * * * * * * * *

CLOSEUP ON THE NINETEENTH AMENDMENT

When the Constitution was adopted in 1789, it gave states the right to determine who could vote. Most states permitted only white male property owners to vote. Gradually, the states dropped property ownership requirements so that, by the 1830's, all white males could vote. Women, however, were expected to leave politics to men and devote their time to caring for their homes and children.

The women of the 1830's and 1840's were better educated than those who lived in earlier times. Many of them became involved in reform movements. Those working in the movement to abolish slavery realized that they were fighting for rights for black slaves that they themselves did not enjoy. At the time, women had virtually no legal rights.

In 1848, two abolitionist activists, Lucretia Mott and Elizabeth Cady Stanton, organized a Woman's Rights Convention in Seneca Falls, New York. The issues discussed at the meeting included property ownership, divorce, and voting rights for women. In the "Declaration of Sentiments" issued at the end of the convention, the delegates declared that "all men and women are created equal."

The Civil War interrupted the work of the feminist reformers. After the war, Congress adopted the Fifteenth Amendment to the Constitution, which extended suffrage or the right to vote, to former black male slaves. Women, however, still did not have this right, and the women's movement now focused on gaining suffrage.

Elizabeth Cady Stanton, Susan B. Anthony, Lucy Stone, and Henry Blackwell were among the leaders of the women's suffrage movement. At first, the movement was more successful in winning voting rights in individual states. In 1869, Wyoming became the first state to let women vote in all elections. By 1919, 27 states allowed women to vote.

In the early 1900's, a new generation of feminists, such as Carrie Chapman Catt, Lucy Burns, and Alice Paul, took over the leadership of the women's movement and brought new energy to it. These suffragists staged demonstrations, marches, and other forms of protest. Their actions helped increase support for the suffrage movement. The contributions of women during World War I also did much to win support for women's sufferage.

Starting in 1878, a women's suffrage amendment was introduced in Congress every two years. But it was always voted down. In 1918, however, the House of Representatives passed the amendment, and the Senate passed it the following year. By 1920, three-fourths of the states had ratified the amendment.

After struggling for more than 70 years, women had finally won the right to vote.

1. How did the movement to abolish slavery contribute to the women's rights movement?

2. What role did Elizabeth Cady Stanton play in the women's suffrage movement?

3. Why do you think that women's suffrage became the central issue of the women's rights movement?

The enumeration in the Constitution of certain rights shall not be construed to deny or disparage others retained by the people.

—NINTH AMENDMENT

The right of the citizens of the United States to vote shall not be denied or abridged by the United States or by any other state on account of race, color, or previous condition of servitude.

—FIFTEENTH AMENDMENT

The right of citizens of the United States to vote shall not be denied or abridged by the United States or by any state on account of sex.

—NINETEENTH AMENDMENT

* *

Citizenship: Rights and Responsibilities

By exercising the right to vote, Americans have the power to safeguard their rights and extend them beyond those listed in the Constitution. Voting is thus one of a citizen's most important responsibilities.

★ ★ ★ ★ ★

CHAPTER 5

★ ★

The Citizen and the Community

OBJECTIVES

After you have studied this chapter, you will be able to:

★ Identify the source of Americans' rights.
★ Explain and discuss the different categories of rights.
★ Explain how the government may limit certain rights.
★ Describe how the rights of American citizens have been broadened.
★ Identify some of the duties and responsibilities Americans have as citizens.
★ List some of the obligations people have to their communities.

SECTIONS

1 The Rights of Citizens
2 The Duties and Responsibilities of Citizens
3 The Citizen's Role in the Community

INTRODUCTION

It was 1967, and 500,000 American troops were fighting in Vietnam. In Washington, D.C., thousands of antiwar demonstrators marched past the White House chanting, "Hey, hey, LBJ, how many kids did you kill today?"

The protesters were calling President Lyndon Baines Johnson a murderer. In many other countries, the government would have responded to this by arresting the protestors or dispersing them with tear gas and gunfire. In Washington at this time, however, no one interfered with the marchers, and the demonstration ended peacefully, just as everyone expected.

The protesters had exercised their rights of free speech and assembly. While doing so, they also carried out certain responsibilities of citizenship. For example, it was their responsibility to make sure that the demonstration remained peaceful and that it did not deprive others of their rights. That meant that the protestors should not block streets and sidewalks or hinder bystanders.

It is the combination of rights with responsibilities that characterizes what it means to be a citizen in a free, democratic society. Citizens are free to exercise their rights, but they are also expected to fulfill certain duties and responsibilities of citizenship. Performing these duties is important if the government is to represent us and to protect our rights.

★ ★

SECTION 1

The Rights of Citizens

★ ★

VOCABULARY

civil rights	affirmative
discrimination	action
	segregation

The rights of Americans come from three basic sources—the Declaration of Independence and U.S. Constitution, the laws that are enacted by Congress and state legislatures, and the interpretation of those laws by the courts of the land.

In Chapter 2, you read Thomas Jefferson's beautiful words, contained in the Declaration of Independence:

> We hold these truths to be self-evident, that all men are created equal, that they are endowed by their Creator with certain unalienable rights, that among these are Life, Liberty, and the pursuit of Happiness.

The Declaration goes on to say that "to secure these Rights, Governments are instituted among Men, deriving their just powers from the Consent of the Governed."

Jefferson's words express the basic ideas of American democracy—that the government draws its power from the people and it exists to preserve their rights. But what exactly are those rights? As you learned in Chapter 4, the Bill of Rights guaranteed a number of very specific rights. In addition, in the 200 years since our government began, we have added more rights and safeguards through constitutional amendments and new laws. Most rights we now have as citizens can be grouped into three broad categories: security, equality, and liberty.

SECURITY Security, in this case, means protection from unfair and unreasonable actions by the government. The government, for example, cannot arrest, imprison, or punish people or search or seize their property without good reason and without following certain rules. As you learned in Chapter 4, protection from such government actions is guaranteed by certain amendments in the Bill of Rights. In addition, these rights are protected by the principle of "due process of law."

The due process clause, found in the Fifth and Fourteenth Amendments, states that no person shall be deprived of "life, liberty, or property, without due process of law."

Due process means that the laws must be fair and reasonable, must be in accordance with the Constitution, and must apply to everyone equally. Most often, due process is applied to criminal laws, the laws dealing with people accused of crimes. For example, a person who is arrested or charged with a crime must be advised of his or her right to remain silent and to have an attorney.

The due process also applies to property rights. For example, if a state takes private property to build a highway, it must pay the property owners a fair amount for their losses. Due process, as applied in this case, gives the property owners the right to appeal to a court of law if they think the payments are unfair.

EQUALITY The right of equality means that everyone is entitled to "the equal protection of the laws." That is, they have a right to be treated the same regardless of their race, religion, or political beliefs. This right, along with due process, is found in the Fourteenth Amendment. Equal protection means that the national, state, or local governments cannot enact any law that would deny you your rights or treat you differently from others because you are a woman, a black, a Hispanic, or a handicapped person. Every citizen has the right to enjoy the same freedoms and protections as every other citizen.

LIBERTY The rights with which we are most familiar—our fundamental freedoms—fall into this category. Most of these rights are spelled out expressly in the Bill of Rights. Our rights of freedom of expression—freedom of speech, press, religion, assembly, and petition—are found in the First Amendment.

All Americans who work must fill out an income tax return in which they report the amount of money earned during the year.

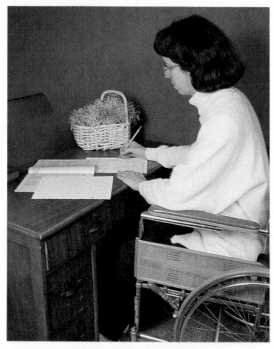

Our right to own private property and to a trial by jury are contained in other amendments of the Bill of Rights.

The Bill of Rights was expanded after the Civil War by the so-called Reconstruction or Civil Rights Amendments. These include the abolition of slavery and the extension of citizenship and voting rights to black males. In addition, the rights guaranteed by the Constitutional Bill of Rights were extended to the states. In this century, other amendments have extended the right to vote to women, to citizens of the District of Columbia, and to 18- to 20-year-olds.

Other rights of liberty, although not spelled out in the Constitution or in specific laws, also exist. These rights are derived from the Ninth Amendment, which states that the fact that certain rights are listed in the Constitution does not mean that the people have no other rights. For example, citizens have the right to travel and live anywhere they wish in the United States or to move to other countries. We are a free people, not confined to any local, state, or national borders. Another unwritten right is our right to engage in political activities and to support the political parties of our choice.

Limits on Rights

Our rights as Americans are not unlimited. The government can establish laws or rules to restrict certain rights to protect the health, safety, security, and moral stan-

At national party conventions, delegates often demonstrate to show their support for a candidate. It is part of the process of choosing the party's nominees for President and Vice President.

dards of a community. Moreover, rights may be limited to prevent one person's rights from interfering with the rights of others. The restrictions of rights, however, must be reasonable and must apply to everyone equally. Often, it is up to the courts to decide whether a law that restricts a Constitutional right is reasonable and fair.

Suppose you belonged to a group that wanted to hold a protest march down the main street of your city. Your right to do so is not completely unrestricted. Your organization may be required to obtain a permit from the city. The permit alerts the police department so it can reroute traffic and keep order. It also identifies the leaders of your group so that they can be held responsible for any problems that might arise during the march.

The purpose of such a permit or other similar limitations is to prevent people from interfering with the rights of others when they exercise their own rights. Consider another example. Suppose you made a speech in a public place in which you urged your listeners to loot nearby stores. You would be interfering both with the right of the shop owners to protect their property and with the right of other people in the area to enjoy peace and order. If you made such a speech, you would probably be arrested for inciting, or causing, a riot.

The government is also empowered to restrict rights when the exercise of those rights threatens the nation's security. A famous Supreme Court case in 1919, *Schenck v. the United States*, dealt with this issue. (The Schenck case is examined in Issues of Our Time on page 28.)

Sometimes it is not easy for the government to establish laws that protect individual rights on the one hand and the rights of the community on the other. In recent years, AIDS (Acquired Immune Deficiency Syn-

drome) has stricken many Americans. AIDS is a disease that destroys the body's immune system. This makes the body unable to fight back normally against infections and diseases. Since the AIDS epidemic began, public health officials and lawmakers have faced several dilemmas in trying to balance the rights of AIDS victims against the rights of the community. One such problem is concerned with the amount of funds and community resources that are to be used for AIDS research and to help AIDS victims. In a democratic society, such problems frequently arise. That is why we need the lawmakers and the courts to try to find fair and reasonable compromises.

Broadening Our Rights

In the 1950's and 1960's, many blacks in this country began an organized fight for their rights as citizens, or **civil rights**. The civil rights movement resulted in the enactment of several new laws that have increased the rights not only of blacks but also of all citizens.

Up to the 1960's, many state laws, particularly in the Southern states, denied blacks the same rights as other Americans. These laws allowed the states to practice **discrimination**, or unfair and less equal treatment toward a particular group. Some states, for example, forced black students to attend separate schools and colleges. Blacks were required to ride in the back of buses and sit in separate sections in theaters and restaurants. They also had to use separate public restrooms and water fountains and stay at separate hotels.

The civil rights struggle resulted in the Civil Rights Act of 1964 and the Voting Rights Act of 1965. These were designed to give blacks equal protection under the law, as

Martin Luther King, Jr., led many nonviolent protests against racial discrimination.

Uncle Sam

No one is really sure how Uncle Sam came to be a symbol of the United States. One story is that it came from the initials "U.S." stamped on government property during the War of 1812. A soldier supposedly asked what the "U.S." stood for, and another jokingly replied, "Uncle Sam." The nickname first appeared in print in 1813.

Cartoonists began to draw Uncle Sam with a goatee and striped trousers during the Civil War. He was used as a symbol of the United States during the Spanish-American War. But the most familiar portrait is the one on the "I Want You!" army recruiting posters of World Wars I and II.

guaranteed in the Constitution. The Civil Rights Act of 1964 banned discrimination against blacks in employment, voting, and public accommodations. This law, enacted to protect one group, also expanded the rights of everyone. It banned discrimination not only by race and color but also by sex, religion, or national origin.

The Voting Rights Act of 1965 gave the federal government the power to intervene in places where blacks were being discriminated against in voter registration. Although black males had been given the right to vote by the Fifteenth Amendment to the Constitution, that right was never very well enforced. By the 1960's, several states had found ways, such as the poll tax, to discourage blacks from registering and voting. Since the passage of the Voting Rights Act, black voter registration has risen sharply. The law has also helped Hispanics and other minorities register to vote.

AFFIRMATIVE ACTION New federal laws have also helped expand our rights through affirmative action. **Affirmative action** means taking special steps to help minorities and women gain access to jobs and opportunities that were denied them in the past because of discrimination. According to federal law, governments must apply affirmative action to give priority to hiring and promoting women and minorities in certain areas. This has affected fire departments, for example, where in the past jobs were available only to white males. Governments have also used affirmative action to award construction contracts to minority and female contractors because they were kept out of the building trades for many years.

Affirmative action was meant to be only a temporary, short-term means of helping minorities and women reach the same economic levels as white males. However, some affirmative action programs have existed for more than 20 years. In recent years, the Supreme Court has begun to interpret affirmative action cases more strictly. (Affirmative action is discussed in Issues of Our Time on page 446.)

EQUAL PROTECTION As you have already seen, the Fourteenth Amendment to the Constitution reaffirmed the principle of due process and established the idea of equal protection of the laws. It did much more than that, however. It made the Constitution and the Bill of Rights apply not only to federal laws, but to state laws as well. After the Fourteenth Amendment was adopted in 1868, no state could make a law that violated the Constitution or deprived anyone of the basic rights guaranteed in the Bill of Rights.

This meant that every citizen of the United States had the same rights as every other citizen. It also meant that if people felt their rights had been violated by a state or local law, they could take their complaint to a federal court, which could overturn the state or local law. This extension of federal laws to the state and local levels is called the nationalization of the Bill of Rights.

The most famous example of how the nationalization of the Bill of Rights helped expand American rights is the case of *Brown* v. *the Board of Education of Topeka, Kansas* in 1954 (see Legal Landmarks on page 106). In that case, the Supreme Court ruled that **segregation** in schools—separating students because of race—was unconstitutional because it violated the Fourteenth Amendment's principle of equal protection of the laws. The ruling overturned an 1896 Court decision, *Plessy* v. *Ferguson*, which had held that segregated schools were legal as long as each school provided "separate but equal" facilities.

In the Brown case, the Court decided that separate schools could never be truly equal and therefore were illegal. As a result of this interpretation of the Constitution, no state or public school district can maintain separate schools for children of different races.

SECTION REVIEW

Define the Words

civil rights	affirmative action
discrimination	segregation

Check the Facts
1. Identify and explain the three main categories of citizens' rights.
2. Explain how our rights may be limited.
3. Identify and describe two laws passed as a result of the civil rights movement.

Think About the Ideas
4. *Evaluate.* What is the importance of the due process clause found in the Fifth and Fourteenth Amendments?

★ ★

SECTION 2

The Duties and Responsibilities of Citizens

★ ★

VOCABULARY

duties	draft
responsibilities	toleration

Our democratic form of government is based on the principle of self-government. To function properly, it requires the active participation of informed citizens. Without citizen interest and involvement, government might become crooked and incompetent, bent on serving its own needs rather than the needs of its citizens.

As citizens of the United States, we are expected to carry out certain duties and responsibilities. **Duties** are things we are required to do; if we fail to perform them, we are subject to legal penalties, such as fines or imprisonment. **Responsibilities**, on the other hand, are things we should do; they are obligations that we fulfill voluntarily. Fulfilling both our duties and our responsibilities helps ensure that we have good government and that we continue to enjoy our rights.

Duties

Some countries require much from their citizens. In some countries, for example, citizens must serve in the armed forces for a period of time each year. In others, citizens are required to live in cities far away from their families and friends and to work at jobs assigned to them by the government.

The United States government asks much less of its citizens than many other countries. Nevertheless, the government does require its citizens to perform the following duties.

OBEY THE LAWS This is a citizen's most important duty. If citizens do not obey the

Why is it important for citizens to be informed about their community?

RIGHTS AND RESPONSIBILITIES OF CITIZENS

RIGHTS	DUTIES	RESPONSIBILITIES
Security—protection from government	Obey the laws	Be informed
Equality—equal treatment under the law	Pay taxes	Vote
Liberty—rights guaranteed under the Constitution	Defend the nation	Participate in your community and government
	Serve in court	Respect the rights and property of others
	Attend school	Respect different opinions and ways of life

law, the government cannot maintain order and protect the health, safety, and property of its citizens. The laws we must obey, including criminal laws, traffic laws, and local laws, all have a purpose. Criminal laws are designed to prevent citizens from harming one another; traffic laws prevent accidents; and local laws help people get along with one another. For example, most communities require their residents to have adequate sewage systems for their homes or to connect to a community sewage system. Without this law, sewage could pollute the environment or the water supply and endanger the health of people in the community.

PAY TAXES Taxes pay for the government's activities. Without them, the federal government could not pay its employees, maintain an army and navy to defend us, or help those in need. Your city could not hire police or fire fighters, and your state could not pave roads or maintain prisons.

Citizens pay taxes in several ways. The federal government and some states collect income taxes, a percentage of the money people make from their jobs. Most states collect sales taxes on the things people buy. Your school district collects taxes on the residential and commercial property within the district.

DEFEND THE NATION In the United States, all men age 18 and over are required to register with the government in case the country needs to **draft**, or call up, men for military service. Since the end of the Vietnam War, there has been no draft and all of America's military men and women have been volunteers. Nevertheless, the government has the authority to use the draft if the country should suddenly have to go to war.

SERVE IN COURT The Constitution guarantees every citizen the right to a trial by jury. To ensure this, every citizen must be prepared to serve on a jury. Jury duty usually requires only a few days of a person's time every few years or so. People can ask to be excused from jury duty if they have a good reason, but it is better to serve if possible. People on trial depend on their fellow citizens to render a fair and just verdict at their trials. Another duty of citizens is to serve as witnesses at a trial, if called to do so.

ATTEND SCHOOL In most states, people are required to attend school until age 16. This is important to both you and to the government because school is where you acquire much of the knowledge and skills you will need to be a good citizen. Thomas Jefferson once said, "If a nation expects to be ignorant and free, . . . it expects what never was and never will be."

In a free society, each person's opinion counts. You can voice your opinion in letters to the editor of a newspaper or to your Congressional representatives, at government meetings, and in the voting booth. But first, you need to learn how to arrive at an informed, well-reasoned opinion. This means examining all sides of an issue, separating facts from beliefs, and drawing your own conclusions. These are some of the skills you acquire in school.

Responsibilities

The responsibilities of citizenship are not as clear-cut as the duties. Since responsibilities are voluntary, people are not arrested or punished if they do not fulfill these obligations. However, the quality of our government and of our lives will diminish if our responsibilities are not carried out.

BE INFORMED Keep in mind that government exists to serve you. Therefore, one of your responsibilities as a citizen is to know what the government is doing and to voice your opinion when you feel strongly about something government has done or has failed to do. When the government learns that most people favor or oppose an action, it usually votes in accordance with their wishes.

Government leaders make decisions every day that have an important impact on your life. The state legislature, for example, may enact a new law that will raise or lower the rates your parents pay for auto insurance. Your town council may vote to ban skateboards from all streets or to allow your next-door neighbor to operate a day-care center at home. Keeping informed about these issues and expressing your feelings about them ensure that government will act in the interests of all of its people.

Being informed also means knowing your rights and exercising them when you feel it is necessary. For example, students who are expelled from school have a right to a hearing before the school board and, if necessary, to take their case to a court of law. If students were unaware of those rights, they might not try to defend themselves even if they felt the expulsion was unfair.

Knowing your rights is the best way of preserving them. You will learn about many of your rights in this course. You can learn more about other rights, and also keep informed about the government and its laws, by reading books, newspapers, and magazines, listening to the news on radio and television, and discussing issues and events with classmates, teachers, family, and friends.

VOTE Voting is one of American citizens' most important responsibilities. By voting, people exercise their right of self-government. Voters choose the people who run the government, and in doing so, they give their consent to that government. If people do not like the way an elected official is doing his or her job, it is their responsibility to choose someone else in the next election. Taking the responsibility to vote ensures that leadership is changed in a peaceful, orderly manner.

PARTICIPATE IN YOUR COMMUNITY AND GOVERNMENT Another responsibility of citizens is to participate in their community and in their government. People may do this in many ways: by voting, by attending public meetings and voicing opinions, by running for public office, and by doing volunteer work.

Participating in your government and community is extremely important. Think about what your community would be like if no one would serve as mayor, if no one would volunteer to fight fires or coach a baseball team, and if no one would ever speak out or do anything to help solve community problems. Communities and governments need people to participate. When people become involved in their communities, they are more likely to end up with honest and well-run governments.

RESPECT THE RIGHTS AND PROPERTY OF OTHERS To enjoy your rights to the fullest, you must be prepared to respect other people's rights as well. For example, if you live in an apartment building, you have an obligation to keep the volume on your radio or television down so that it does not disturb your neighbors. And you expect them to do the same for you. Many of our laws have been enacted to encourage people to respect each other's rights. A person who continues to play a radio or television too loudly can be arrested for disturbing the peace.

CAREERS

Social Work

If you get satisfaction from helping others, social work may be the career for you. Social workers help people deal with social and personal problems such as poverty, drug addiction, mental or physical illness, and criminal behavior.

The kind of problems social workers deal with depends on where they are employed. Social workers in schools help troubled students stay in school and overcome their family and academic problems. Those in child welfare agencies place children in foster or adoptive homes and help protect children from abusive parents.

Social workers employed by groups such as the Y.M.C.A. and some religious organizations run support groups for people with similar problems, such as single parents and alcoholics.

Hospitals hire social workers to help patients and their families adjust to physical disabilities, and psychiatric social workers specialize in helping people with mental or psychological problems.

Social workers also work for the courts, investigating charges of child neglect or abuse or running background checks on adolescents who are in trouble with the law. Some social workers are probation or parole officers.

To become a social worker, you usually need a master's degree in social work or psychiatric social work. Social work can be a very frustrating and challenging career, but it can also be extremely rewarding. To be a good social worker, you must really like people and you must possess excellent problem-solving skills.

Using Your Skills
1. Describe four kinds of jobs that social workers do. How are they alike?
2. What personal characteristics do you think social workers need to perform their jobs well?

Citizens have a responsibility to show the same respect for public property and for the property of others. Sometimes people who would not dream of breaking a neighbor's window will vandalize their school or a city bus because "no one owns it." Yet, such public property belongs to us all, and we all pay if it is stolen or damaged.

RESPECT DIFFERENT OPINIONS AND WAYS OF LIFE Citizens have a responsibility to respect the rights of people with whom they disagree. Respecting and accepting others, regardless of their beliefs, practices, or other differences, is called **toleration**. It means giving people whose ideas you dislike a chance to express their opinions. Without toleration

Students attending school can fulfill their responsibility to learn about their society and their government. Why is this important?

for the views of others, a real discussion or exchange of ideas is impossible. Under a democratic system of government, everyone should have a say. It is then up to the people to choose sensible ideas and discard offensive ones.

One of America's great strengths has always been the diversity of its people. Immigrants from all over the world have brought a variety of religions, traditions, and life-styles to this country, and they continue to do so. As citizens, we all have a responsibility to respect the practices and traditions of others when they are different from our own, just as we expect them to respect our differences. There are no degrees of citizenship in the United States. All citizens are equal and entitled to be treated the same.

SECTION REVIEW

Define the Words

duties   draft
responsibilities   toleration

Check the Facts

1. Explain the difference between duties and responsibilities.
2. Identify and explain four duties of American citizens.
3. Identify and explain five responsibilities of American citizens.

Think About the Ideas

4. *Evaluate.* Why are duties and responsibilities essential in a democratic system of government?

* *

SECTION 3

The Citizen's Role in the Community

* *

VOCABULARY

community	welfare
public	environment

A **community** is a group of people who share the same interests and concerns. People usually think of their neighborhood or town when they are asked to identify their community. Most people, however, belong to several different communities. Your family, your school, and your town are communities. For some purposes, your state is a community and so is the nation. You are even citizens of a global community that has common interests, such as peace and the health of our planet.

Each of the communities you belong to provides you with certain things. For example, your family and school teach you values, traditions, behavior, and cooperation. Your neighborhood may have a park, playground, library, theater, hospital, and stores. The government of your town or city provides laws, police and fire protection, schools, trash collection, and so on. These things are often called public services. **Public** means pertaining to the people in a community or for the use of all.

The services provided by a community vary according to the community's size and complexity. While a city provides police to protect its citizens from criminals, the federal government provides armed forces to protect the nation from attack by other nations. Similarly, while your town highway department plows the snow off the streets in your neighborhood, state workers plow the main roads and highways.

In return for the services our communities provide us, we have responsibilities toward our communities. For a community

The illustration shows the five factors that make each community a little different. Describe how these factors apply to your community.

WHAT MAKES A COMMUNITY SPECIAL

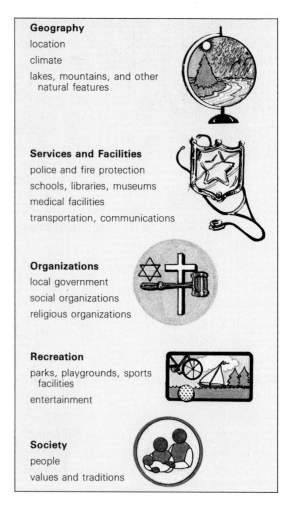

Geography
location
climate
lakes, mountains, and other natural features

Services and Facilities
police and fire protection
schools, libraries, museums
medical facilities
transportation, communications

Organizations
local government
social organizations
religious organizations

Recreation
parks, playgrounds, sports facilities
entertainment

Society
people
values and traditions

to be successful, its members must take an active role in it. One of the responsibilities of citizens is to help make their community a good place to work and live. Good citizens are concerned about the **welfare**—the health, prosperity, and happiness—of all members of the community. They are concerned about the poor, the elderly, the sick, and the dis-advantaged as well as the rich, the young, and the healthy.

Responsible citizens are also concerned about the welfare of the community as a whole. They may be concerned about the **environment**, or surroundings, of the community or about the overall safety or quality of life in the community. Safeguarding these

---

AMERICAN PROFILES

Rachel Carson

One person can make a great difference in our demo-cratic society. Rachel Carson is proof of that. Carson (1907–1964) was a marine biologist and a gifted author who wrote with great feeling about life in the seas. In 1958, she began writing a book about a differ-ent subject—the effects of using the powerful insecticide DDT to control plant pests.

In her book, Car-son examined how DDT and other toxic chemicals were passing up through the food chain. She found they were killing not only the insects they were intended for, but also birds, fish, plants, wildlife, and even farm animals. In addition, her research showed that these chemicals were causing cancer and other major dis-eases in humans who ate the poi-soned plants and animals.

Her book, *Silent Spring*, was pub-lished in 1962. Its title referred to the possibility that DDT might kill all birds and in time, all life on earth. Because of *Silent Spring*, the public became aware of the dangers of toxic chemicals for the first time and began to push for govern-ment regulation of them. In 1970, the federal government established the Environmental Protection Agency to regulate the use of toxic chemicals. And in 1972, the government finally banned all domestic uses of DDT.

Rachel Carson died in 1964. She never saw the results of her work, but she was awarded the Presidential Medal of Freedom in 1980.

Using Your Skills
1. Why was DDT so dangerous to ani-mals and humans?
2. What do you think America would be like today if Rachel Carson had not written *Silent Spring*?

things may require any number of government actions. It could mean cleaning up a toxic waste dump that is polluting the water supply, adding more police officers to combat drug trafficking, or building more parks and playgrounds for the community's residents.

When cities reserve land for parks and other recreational facilities, they are providing their citizens with a better environment in which to live.

Many communities depend on volunteer fire fighters for fire protection.

Concern for our communities is not enough, however. Our concern must be supported by action. No community or government has the money or resources to provide for the welfare of all its people or to solve all its problems. It counts on volunteers, or unpaid workers, to help by doing some of the things that the government cannot afford to pay people to do. People usually volunteer to do things they like. They may work in a hospital, fight fires, coach a team, lead a scout troop, or help out in a classroom. In the spring of 1989, after the Alaska oil spill, hundreds of people volunteered to help with the cleanup.

Some volunteers raise money to help a good cause, such as buying uniforms for the high school band or providing food and shelter for the homeless. People of all ages and backgrounds perform volunteer work. It is a very satisfying way of giving something back to the community for the help the community has given to them and their families.

SECTION REVIEW

Define the Words

community   welfare
public   environment

Check the Facts
1. Identify three types of communities to which you belong.
2. What types of services do communities provide their citizens?
3. Identify five types of volunteer activities that help communities.

Think About the Ideas
4. *Evaluate.* Why is it important for people to take an active role in their communities?
5. *Analyze.* How would our lives be different without the public services that communities provide?

CITIZENSHIP SKILLS

How to Get the Facts

How will you decide which candidate to vote for in an election? Responsible citizens find out about the candidates—their experience and their positions on issues.

Despite what you may have heard, there is no such thing as an "objective" source of information. No news report can include *all* the facts; someone has to decide which to include and which to leave out. Here are some common sources of information, along with warnings.

NEWSPAPERS Most newspapers, and many newsmagazines, such as *Time* and *Newsweek*, include both news and opinion. They usually indicate clearly which is news and which opinion. Do not assume, however, that the "news" section is accurate and complete. The people who write the news have their own political preferences, which are likely to influence their reporting.

NEWS BROADCASTS Commercial television and radio stations try to make stories dramatic, even if that means less accurate. They want to avoid being boring, because a bored viewer will not stay tuned. Therefore, they present news that is short and exciting.

Noncommercial news programs are a different matter. Some programs on public television and on National Public Radio provide in-depth discussions of news events and people.

POLITICAL ADVERTISEMENTS
Political advertising takes many forms: slick brochures, posters, newspaper ads, and TV commercials. Millions of dollars are spent each election year to get political messages into your hands. These political advertisements may be a good source of information, especially for finding out what a political party or candidate stands for or promises. But you should always question what one candidate's advertisements say about his or her opponents. Advertisements are designed to convince, not to inform.

LEAGUE OF WOMEN VOTERS
Founded in 1920, the League of Women Voters is a nonpartisan organization that includes both women and men. Its aim is to educate voters by presenting them with clear, accurate information. One of the ways it does this is by sponsoring political debates. Members of both parties respect the League for its thoroughness and fairness.

Using Your Skills
1. Identify three ways to get information about political candidates.
2. If political advertisements are so one-sided, why do you think people pay attention to them?

CHAPTER 5 REVIEW

★ ★

MAIN POINTS

★ The basic principle of American democracy is that the government draws its power from the people and exists to preserve their rights.

★ American rights come from three sources— the Declaration of Independence and the Constitution, the laws of the land, and the decisions of the courts.

★ American rights are grouped into three broad categories: security (protection from the government), equality (equal treatment under the law), and liberty (our guaranteed rights).

★ The government has the power to limit certain rights to protect the welfare of the nation.

★ American rights have been broadened by the reinterpretation of existing laws by the courts and by the enacting of new laws.

★ Citizens are required to fulfill certain duties, such as paying taxes, serving on juries, and obeying the laws.

★ Citizens also have responsibilities—voting, being informed—that help preserve our freedoms and our form of government.

★ Citizens have an obligation to participate in their communities.

WORDS IN REVIEW

Choose the word or phrase from the list below that best completes each sentence. Write the missing words on a separate sheet of paper.

segregation	draft
civil rights	community
responsibilities	welfare
discrimination	affirmative action
duties	toleration

1. By helping distribute food to the poor, the woman showed her concern for the _____ of the people in her community.

2. During the war, the thousands of men who fought in the armed services were fulfilling their _____ to their country.

3. The landlord was accused of _____ because he would not rent the apartment to the young black couple.

4. By hiring many blacks, women, and minorities, the company was responding to the policy of _____.

5. Before the 1960's, many schools in the South practiced _____ , separating white and black students.

6. Since the woman was not allowed to vote without paying a fee, her _____ were violated.

7. Although the two speakers disagreed completely, each showed a great deal of _____ by allowing the other to speak without interruption.

8. Most of the students who were 18 fulfilled their _____ as citizens by voting in the election.

9. When the war began, the government decided to _____ men to serve in the army.

10. The small religious group was a(n) _____ of similar beliefs and values.

FACTS IN REVIEW

1. What are the sources of our rights as citizens?

2. What two rights did the Fourteenth Amendment guarantee?

CHAPTER 5 REVIEW

* *

3. What rights were expanded by the Civil Rights Amendments?

4. Identify two examples of how government may restrict our rights.

5. Explain how affirmative action is used.

6. Identify three ways in which citizens pay taxes.

7. Identify three ways in which people can participate in their communities.

8. Explain why people have the responsibility to respect the rights of others.

9. Explain how the services a community provides may vary.

10. Identify three actions a government might take to safeguard the welfare of the community.

THINKING ABOUT CITIZENS AND THE COMMUNITY

1. *Evaluate.* Do you think that affirmative action laws are a fair way to change past discrimination? Why or why not?

2. *Analyze.* Which rights should have priority— the rights of individuals or the rights of the community? Explain.

WRITING ABOUT A COMMUNITY PROBLEM

Recently, you have been very disturbed by the increasing litter in the streets and parks throughout your community. You decide it is time to take action.

Write a letter to the editor, expressing your concern over the problem of litter. The tone of your letter should be forceful, yet not out of control. You want to make everyone see why it is a serious problem and perhaps suggest ways in which the community can solve the problem.

INTERPRETING A DIAGRAM

Every community is special—not quite like any other. Many factors play a role in making one community different from another. Some factors are the result of geography, but most are the work of people. Study the diagram on communities on page 130, and answer the following questions.

1. Which factors would be most important in making a community a suitable place for locating a business?

2. Which factors could citizens of a community change to make the community a better place to live?

3. Which factors would be most important to you in choosing a place to live?

FOCUSING ON YOUR COMMUNITY

The types of services communities provide vary according to various factors, such as the size of the community, the money available, and the community's needs. Find out what types of services your community offers. Research the different services that are available, who is eligible to receive these services, and how much money is available to provide these services. Find out also how interested citizens can become involved in helping to provide different community services. Present your findings to the class.

CHAPTER 6

* *

Parties and Politics

OBJECTIVES

After you have studied this chapter, you will be able to:

★ Discuss the advantages and disadvantages of a two-party system.

★ Describe multiparty and one-party systems.

★ Describe how political parties began in the United States.

★ Explain why third parties form in the United States.

★ Describe the organization of political parties and the responsibilities of political party members.

★ Identify five functions of political parties.

★ Discuss the power of political parties today.

SECTIONS

1 Kinds of Party Systems
2 U.S. Political Parties
3 The Organization of U.S. Political Parties
4 The Role of Political Parties in the United States Today

INTRODUCTION

Barbara Takagi is a Republican block captain. Before every election she distributes campaign literature to the neighbors on her block and urges eligible people to register to vote.

Mrs. Takagi is a volunteer and is not paid for this work. She does it because she agrees with the ideas of the Republican Party and its office seekers.

Michael Perry lives across the street from Mrs. Takagi. As a volunteer for the Democratic Party, he organizes other local party workers to stuff envelopes, make phone calls, and drive people to the polls on election day. Mr. Perry feels the same way about the Democrats as Mrs. Takagi does about the Republicans.

How did these two people come to work for different political parties, and what is a political party anyway? A political party is an organization made up of people who share similar ideas about the way the country should be governed. It offers people an opportunity to join forces with others in working for certain political goals. People like Mrs. Takagi and Mr. Perry work to have their political party's **candidates**, the people seeking elected office, chosen as the government's leaders. Once elected, these candidates organize and run the government. They also work to get laws passed to carry out their party's programs.

★ ★

SECTION 1

Kinds of Party Systems

★ ★

VOCABULARY

candidate	majority
plurality	coalition

Political parties are not unique to the United States. They exist in most countries. In America, we have a two-party system in which two major parties vie with each other to run the government. Some countries have a multiparty system in which several parties may compete. A third possibility is the one-party system in which only one party exists.

The Two-Party System

The United States has had a two-party system since its early days as a nation. Although the names of the parties have been different, one of two major parties has always been in power. Smaller political parties have also been formed, but these minor parties have had little or no impact on national elections.

For the most part, our two-party system has worked very well. If the voters are dissatisfied with the way one party is running the nation, they can elect candidates from the other party. The same process works on the state and local government levels as well.

The Donkey and the Elephant

Although the donkey and the elephant are now the proud symbols of the Democratic and Republican parties, they were originally created by a political cartoonist to poke fun at the two parties.

Thomas Nast was a cartoonist for a New York newspaper named *Harper's Weekly* from the 1860's to the 1880's. A Republican supporter, Nast often drew the Republican Party as an innocent lamb and the Democrats as a fierce tiger. Then, in the 1870's, he began to show the Republican Party as a long-suffering elephant, and the rival Democrats were pictured as a braying donkey or, occasionally, as a fox. Over time, people forgot that Nast's symbols had been invented to make fun of the two political parties, and gradually the parties adopted them as their emblems.

Sometimes it is difficult to tell the difference between the Republican and the Democratic Party. This is because the American people agree, to a large extent, about many political and social issues. Americans cherish their rights and freedoms. They believe that people should have an opportunity to get a good education and make a decent living. And they believe that the government has a duty to protect the nation, preserve the environment, and help its citizens.

The essential difference between the two major parties is that they disagree on how to achieve these ends. For example, the Democrats tend to believe that the federal government should be more directly involved in providing housing, income, education, and jobs for the poor. The Republicans tend to believe that if they help the nation's economy grow, poor people will have a better chance of finding work and meeting their needs on their own.

America's founders feared that political parties would divide the people and destroy the republic. But, on the whole, our two-party system has been a stabilizing force. Both parties tend to stay near the center of a wide range of political opinions. Most Americans do not support extreme political ideas, such as government ownership of factories, or desire a completely different system of government. Because each party wants to gain the support of the largest possible number of votes, party policies are designed to appeal to many different groups of people. This means that the parties usually avoid extreme positions that might cause voters to reject the party.

The two-party system has also provided continuity. Since each party is in power some of the time and out of power at other times, both have many members who are experienced not only in the art of politics, but also

1988 PARTY PLATFORMS

DEMOCRATIC PARTY	REPUBLICAN PARTY
Taxes	
★ Believes that the wealthy and corporations should pay their fair share	★ Opposes any increase in taxes
Defense	
★ Favors maintenance of nuclear deterrent ★ Supports the use of force when required	★ Favors reliance on nuclear weapons as the chief deterrent ★ Supports improvement of conventional deterrents
Equal Rights	
★ Pledges equal access to government services, employment, housing, business enterprise, education ★ Supports equal pay for women	★ Supports strict enforcement of laws to prevent discrimination ★ Supports equal pay for women
Child Care	
★ Seeks increase in federal funding and support ★ Favors aid to states for child care	★ Encourages families to choose type of child care that suits them ★ Favors reliance on traditional voluntary institutions
Education	
★ Promotes education as highest priority ★ Favors increase in federal funding	★ Encourages parents' participation in education ★ Supports federal funding of programs for disabled students
Crime	
★ Urges coordination of efforts to fight against drugs ★ Seeks increase in assistance to local law-enforcement agencies	★ Proposes goal of drug-free nation ★ Supports reestablishment of federal death penalty
Foreign Affairs	
★ Favors new initiatives to expand relations with the Soviet Union ★ Encourages negotiations leading to free elections in Central America	★ Favors working with Soviet leadership ★ Supports continuation of humanitarian and military aid to freedom fighters of Central America

Based on information from:
Kirk, Paul G.: *The 1988 Democratic National Platform*, Democratic Platform Committee, 1988.
Gribbin, William J. (editor): *An American Vision: Our Children and Our Future*, Republican Party Platform, 1988.

The platform of a political party describes the party's goals and its position on important public issues. Compare the Republican and Democratic positions on taxes.

in the business of government. Thus, when a Democratic President takes over from a Republican or vice versa, the transition is normally smooth and friendly.

Two-party systems are not without disadvantages, however. The most important is that a two-party system can stifle the views of minority groups. In the United States, the news media give a great deal of coverage to the Democratic and Republican candidates for President. Candidates from other, minor parties receive very little attention, even though they may have important ideas to contribute. For a minority viewpoint to be heard, it usually has to be accepted and championed by one of the major parties. For example, the civil rights and women's rights movements gained significant political power only when their ideas were taken up by the Democratic Party.

Multiparty Systems

In a multiparty system, three or more parties compete for control of the government. Multiparty systems are common in Europe and are also found in such countries as Israel and Japan.

An advantage of the multiparty system is that it provides voters with choices repre-

senting a broader range of political ideas. Its major weakness, however, is that with the vote divided among so many parties, it is sometimes difficult for one party to gain enough votes to form a government.

In countries where several major parties compete in each election, one party usually wins a **plurality**, which means that it wins more votes or seats in the legislature than any other party. It may not, however, win a **majority** of votes, or more than half the votes cast. In most multiparty systems, a party must hold a majority before it can form a government. In that case, the top vote-getting party must form a **coalition**, or an alliance with another party or parties, so that together they command a majority of the votes.

The major problem with coalition governments is that the parties in the coalition often have very different ideas about how to run the government. These differences can become so great that the government is unable to accomplish anything and collapses. When that happens, the parties are forced to hold another election and, very likely, form another coalition. In Italy, for example, the repeated failure of coalition governments has resulted in at least 48 governments since the end of World War II, an average of more than one a year.

One-Party Systems

A third type of party system is the one-party system. In a one-party system, the party and the government are very nearly the same thing. In the People's Republic of China, for

In Beijing, members of China's government vote on a resolution. Because China is a one-party state, the entire government is made up of members of the Communist Party.

example, only one party—the Communist Party—is allowed to exist. The party allows only candidates from its own party to run for office. As a result, positions in the government are filled only with Communist Party members. The role of government officials is simply to carry out the decisions made by the party. There is no opposition. In many one-party systems, the head of the government is the head of the party as well.

In a one-party system, the main job of party members is to recruit new members, maintain party discipline, and carry out the party's orders. In exchange for their work for the party and government, upper-level party members are sometimes rewarded with special privileges and favors such as vacation homes and the use of private stores and hospitals. Typically, only a small part of the population actually belongs to the party. In China, for example, only about 3 percent of the population belongs to the Chinese Communist Party.

SECTION REVIEW

Define the Words

candidate   majority
plurality   coalition

Check the Facts

1. What are some characteristics of America's two-party system?
2. What is a major disadvantage of a multiparty system?
3. Why do coalition governments frequently change?
4. What is the role of government officials in a one-party system?

Think About the Ideas

5. *Explain.* Why are the Democratic and Republican parties so alike? How are they different?

SECTION 2

U.S. Political Parties

VOCABULARY
third party

America's first political parties began to form during the debate over the Constitution. Those who desired a strong national government, the Federalists, supported the Constitution and campaigned for its acceptance. The Federalist Party became America's first political party. Those who favored strong state governments formed the Anti-Federalist or Democratic-Republican Party.

The two parties represented not only different ideas about the government but also different groups of the population. The Federalist Party drew much of its strength from New England merchants and bankers. The Democratic-Republicans relied on the support of the nation's small farmers, planters, shopkeepers, and laborers.

After winning only two Presidential elections, that of George Washington, who ran unopposed, in 1792 and John Adams in 1796, the Federalists gradually disappeared. For several years, the Democratic-Republicans were unopposed. By the mid-1820's, however, the party began to break up into several groups. One of these became the Democratic Party, which continued to represent small farmers and working people. Another party, the Whigs, arose to challenge the Democrats. The Whigs followed in the tradition of the Federalists and tended to represent northern bankers, merchants, manufacturers, and large plantation owners in the South.

In the 1850's, both parties split over the slavery issue. Proslavery voters stayed in the Democratic Party, and Whigs and antislavery Democrats formed a new party. This party was the Republican Party. In 1860, Abraham Lincoln was the first Republican to be elected President.

From the Civil War until today, the Democrats and the Republicans have remained the nation's two major parties. After the Civil War, the Republicans emerged as the stronger party. Between 1865 and 1931, the Democrats were able to elect only two Presidents—Grover Cleveland and Woodrow Wilson.

Then, in 1932, it was the Democrats' turn. Franklin Roosevelt was elected President four times and his successor, Harry S. Truman, served nearly eight years. Since then, the Presidency has gone back and forth between Democrats and Republicans, although the majority in Congress has been mainly Democratic.

Third Parties in the United States

From time to time a minor party has arisen to challenge the Democrats and the Republicans. In the United States, these minor parties are called **third parties**. That is because the minor parties are all challenging the two major parties rather than each other.

This time line shows which politcal parties won the Presidency between 1867 and 1992. Which party has held the office of President since 1980?

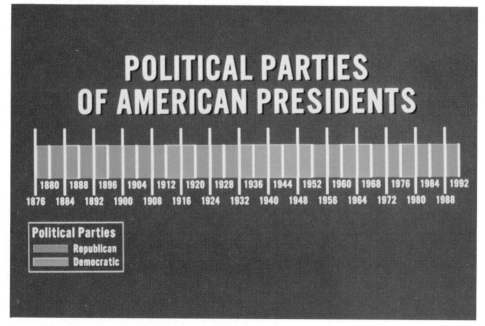

No third party has ever won a Presidential election. Third parties have, however, affected the outcome of some elections and influenced major changes in government and in social policy.

One of the most successful third parties was the Populist Party of the 1890's. A coalition of farmers and working people, the Populists called for the direct election of U.S. Senators and an eight-hour working day, as well as other reforms. Although the Populists never won a Presidential election, many of their reform ideas were eventually adopted by the two major parties and enacted into law.

Another important third party was the Progressive Party, which split off from the Republicans in 1912 and ran former President Theodore Roosevelt as its candidate. Roosevelt took so many votes from the Republican candidate, William Howard Taft, that the Democratic nominee, Woodrow Wilson, won the election. In this case, the Progressive Party is said to have played a "spoiler" role. It took votes away from the Republicans, the party closest to its own views, spoiling its chances of election.

There have been numerous third parties throughout the nation's history. In fact, there

Theodore Roosevelt, a former Republican President, ran as the Progressive Party's candidate in 1912.

are normally several third parties every election year, and their candidates usually receive a few hundred to several thousand votes. In general, there are three kinds of third parties. Some are tied to a single issue, some to a particular political belief, and some to a single candidate.

The Prohibition Party, which was formed in 1872 and still exists, is a single-issue party. It opposes alcohol and would like to see it banned as it once was in the 1920's. Parties such as the American Communist Party and the Libertarian Party are third parties based on political beliefs. They run candidates in elections year after year, even though their political beliefs are too extreme for the vast majority of Americans.

Third parties occasionally form around a single candidate when that person fails to receive support from one of the two major parties or does not fit in with those parties' political views. George Wallace failed to receive the support of the Democratic Party in 1968 and ran for President on the American Independent Party ticket. In 1980, John Anderson lost the Republican nomination and ran as the candidate of the Independent Party.

SECTION REVIEW

Define the Word
third party

Check the Facts
1. Why did America's first political parties form?
2. Identify three kinds of third parties, and give an example of each.
3. Explain how a third party can act as a "spoiler."

Thinking About the Ideas
4. *Evaluate.* Why are third parties important in our democratic system of government?

The Organization of U.S. Political Parties

★ ★

VOCABULARY

nominate	political
campaign	machine
patronage	platform
precinct	plank

In the United States, anyone can become a member of a political party. It is not necessary to pay a fee, or take a test, or even vote. In most states, it is only necessary to declare yourself a member of a party when you register to vote. Which party you choose to become a member of is entirely up to you.

In general, each of the two major parties has tended to attract certain kinds of people. Historically, the Democratic Party has tended to appeal more to working people, Catholics, minorities, union members, and people in favor of government involvement in social policies. The Republican Party has attracted more businesspeople, Protestants, and people against government involvement. These are only generalities, however. Each party includes members of all backgrounds, races, religions, and political beliefs. In Congress, for example, it is common to find Democrats whose political views are closer to those of some Republicans than to many of their fellow Democrats.

THE HIGH COST OF RUNNING FOR OFFICE

Running an election campaign has always cost money. But the amount of money required has increased dramatically in recent years. In 1976, the average cost of a U.S. Senate race was $610,000; by 1988, it was $4 million.

Although there are several reasons for this cost explosion, the most important is television. Candidates have discovered that the most effective way to win votes is to produce attractive television commercials and to show them during prime viewing hours. These commercials can cost tens of thousands of dollars per minute.

In 1971, Congress passed the Federal Election Campaign Act, which placed campaign financing under government control. Among other things, the law limited the amount that individuals could contribute to candidates to $1,000. This limit forced candidates to look for new sources of money. One source was the Political Action Committee (PAC).

PACs are usually formed by special-interest groups, such as members of labor unions, corporations, and educational and medical associations. PACs provide funds to candidates who favor their position on issues. Many people are concerned that when candidates accept large amounts of money from PACs, they are placing themselves under the control of these groups.

Some people believe that the government should pay for election campaigns. In the case of Presidential elections, a system is already in place. Presidential candidates who raise money from outside sources receive matching funds (an equal amount) from the federal treasury. Taxpayers are allowed to contribute $1 of their income taxes to this campaign fund.

Although this arrangement reduces the time a candidate must spend looking for money, it does not solve the problem of wasteful spending. One possibility is to limit the amount of money each candidate can spend. However, in a case called *Buckley* v. *Valeo*, the Supreme Court ruled that such a limit would be unconstitutional. The First Amendment guarantees everyone–including political candidates–the right to free speech. Restricting the amount of money a candidate can spend would be a violation of this right. Although some types of speech–such as TV commercials–are more expensive than others, all are equally protected by the First Amendment.

Using Your Skills
1. What is the possible effect of financing by a PAC?
2. Why has campaign fund-raising become more difficult and more controversial?

WHAT PARTY MEMBERS DO For most people, being a member of a political party involves little more than voting for the party's candidates on election day. Active party members do much more than just vote, however.

The major function of each party is to get its candidates elected to public office. To achieve that goal, party members must first **nominate**, or name, the candidates they want to run for each office. Once the candidates have been chosen, each party embarks on an election **campaign**, an effort to gather support for its candidates and inform the voters of the party's stand on issues. Campaigns are a lot of work, and many party workers and volunteers are needed to perform dozens of jobs. They may be asked to raise funds, poll voters, make telephone calls, stuff envelopes, arrange dinners and rallies, drive people to the polls, or register voters.

For some active party members, the work does not end when an election is over. Once a party's candidate is elected to office, the party helps the candidate organize and manage the government. For example, when a new President is elected, hundreds of job vacancies in the federal government must be filled. The President's party compiles lists of party members who contributed a great deal of time, energy, or money to the election campaign. The President consults these lists and often chooses people from them to fill positions in the government.

Giving jobs or special favors to party workers is called **patronage**. It is a way of rewarding people for their work and loyalty. Political patronage exists in both parties and at all levels of government and political organization. Many people work hard for their party in the hope of being rewarded with a patron-

This chart shows how political parties are organized at local, state, and national levels. What do you think a precinct captain does?

ORGANIZATION OF POLITICAL PARTIES

National Committee

Congressional Campaign Committee

National Convention

State Committee

Senatorial Campaign Committee

City, Town, or County Committee

Precinct Captain

Precinct Workers

age job for themselves or for other family members or friends.

PARTY ORGANIZATION The Democratic and Republican parties are organized at the local, state, and national levels, in very much the same way as the government. The local organization consists of a city, town, or county committee made up of people elected by their fellow party members. Each city or county is divided into election districts, or precincts. A **precinct** is a geographic area that contains a specific number of voters. A precinct can be an entire small town, or it can be made up of several adjoining neighborhoods in a large city.

For each precinct, the local party committee appoints a precinct captain whose job is to organize the party volunteers and get out the vote within the precinct. The precinct captain sends out volunteers to hand out literature, register voters, and try to convince voters to support the party's candidates.

The local party organization is very important because it works to elect candidates at every level of government, from President of the United States to town tax collector. In a well-organized local party committee, the precinct captain is expected to know about how many votes are likely to be cast for the party's candidate, and he or she is expected to deliver them.

Sometimes, a local party organization becomes so powerful that, year after year, only its candidates are elected to public office. Such a strong party organization is called a **political machine**. Political machines exist in some towns, cities, and counties throughout the United States.

Although political machines are not necessarily good or bad, most people think of them as harmful. If one party is in power for too long, it might become unresponsive to the needs of the community. Its politicians might

forget that the party's main function is to serve the public. At its worst, a political machine might elect corrupt leaders who seek to enrich themselves and their associates at the expense of the people they are supposed to serve. One of the most famous—or infamous—political machines was New York City's Tammany Hall. This organization, which ran New York in the late 1800's and early 1900's, was controlled by corrupt politicians.

Above the local party committees are the state party committees. State committee workers concentrate on electing candidates to state offices—the governor, the attorney general, representatives to the state legislature, and so on. They also work within their state to elect their party's candidates for national office, such as their U.S. Senators, Representatives, and the President.

Each political party also has a national committee made up of representatives from each state. The committee is headed by a national chairperson who directs the committee's staff and speaks for the party on national issues. The national committee helps raise funds for the presidential election and organizes the party's national convention.

The national convention is one of the most important responsibilities of the national committee. Held only once every four years, the national convention is where party members nominate their candidates for President and Vice President of the United States. During the national convention, party members also formulate the party's **platform**, the statement of its goals and positions on various public issues. Each item in the platform is called a **plank**. A plank on the party's platform might, for example, call for new programs to improve education.

In addition to the national, state, and local committees, each political party has two other party committees—a Congressional Cam-

At national party conventions—held every four years—Republicans and Democrats from across the country gather to nominate their candidates for President.

The Role of Political Parties in the United States Today

★ ★

VOCABULARY

grassroots   nonpartisan
accountable

paign Committee and a Senatorial Campaign Committee. These committees seek to elect and reelect party members to the United States Senate and House of Representatives. Made up of members of Congress, the committees help out when a party member is in danger of losing a seat or when a vacant seat is up for grabs.

SECTION REVIEW

Define the Words

nominate	political machine
campaign	platform
patronage	plank
precinct	

Check the Facts
1. List at least three jobs that party workers and volunteers perform during an election campaign.
2. What is the purpose of patronage?
3. What does a precinct captain do?

Thinking About the Ideas
4. *Put Ideas Together*. Explain why political machines do not usually result in good government. How do you think political machines could be controlled?

Although the primary purpose of American political parties is to elect their candidates to public office, they also play an important role in helping the people of the United States practice self-government. The parties enable people to communicate with their government leaders and help ensure that government remains responsive to the people. The parties fulfill this role in five ways:

★ They select and support candidates.
★ They inform the public.
★ They carry the message of the people to the government.
★ They act as a watchdog over government activities.
★ They serve as a link between different levels and branches of government.

SELECTING AND SUPPORTING CANDIDATES
Because candidates for public office have to compete in elections, each party tries to put up candidates who will win as many votes as possible. Each party wants to offer attractive, able candidates who have the experience needed to fill the offices they are seeking. This

competition between the parties means that the voters are usually offered a choice of two or more qualified candidates.

After the parties select their candidates, the election campaign begins. The parties support their candidates by helping to organize and raise money for election campaigns. They also help their candidates get their ideas and viewpoints across to as many voters as possible.

INFORMING THE PUBLIC In an election campaign, each party tries to tell the public what it has done and what it wants to do. It also points out what it believes the other party is doing wrong.

To get their views across, parties and their candidates for office make speeches, publish and distribute pamphlets, and place ads in newspapers and magazines and on television and radio. As the parties present their views, the voters have an opportunity to learn about, compare, and make judgments about these views. In this way, the political campaign informs and educates the voters.

CARRYING THE PEOPLE'S MESSAGE In addition to presenting their views to the people, the parties listen to what the people have to say. Voters have ideas and concerns of their own and issues they want their leaders to address.

For example, perhaps the voters in a particular area are concerned because the government is talking about closing several military bases there. Such an action would result in thousands of unemployed workers and a strain on the area's economy. The member of Congress representing the area responds

to the people's concern, promises to fight the closing of the bases, and vows to carry the people's message to the highest levels of government in Washington.

Sometimes a lot of people in different areas feel very strongly about an issue. They may be opposed to a government policy or want stronger laws to protect the environment. A political movement that begins with the people is known as a **grassroots** movement. When a grassroots movement becomes strong enough, its ideas will probably be taken over by a political party. This may happen first at the local level, but the local

Ron Brown became chairperson of the Democratic National Committee in 1988. It is his job to explain the party's position on many matters.

political party organizations are connected to the state and national party organizations. In this way, political parties provide a direct path by which individuals and groups can send their messages to the highest levels of government.

ACTING AS WATCHDOGS Between elections political parties act as "watchdogs" over government activities. Although it is not possible for an individual to keep a close watch on all government officials, political parties can do this very well.

Suppose, for example, that your town council has five Democrats and two Republicans. Although the Republicans lack enough votes to control the decision making on the council, they are still part of the government. They participate in all governmental meetings, inspect township records, talk to employees, and so on. For this reason, they are able to keep close track of the actions and behavior of public officials who belong to the Democratic Party. Although they are out of power, the Republicans are serving the public interest by bringing mistakes, wrongdoing, and problems to light. In this way,

During an election campaign, party volunteers go from door to door trying to persuade people to vote for their candidate.

the Republican minority is holding the Democratic majority **accountable** to the people. In other words, officials who want to keep their jobs must explain their actions to the voters.

Of course, the Republicans are acting as watchdogs out of self-interest. They would like to have more Republicans elected to the town council in the next election. The Democrats are also acting out of self-interest. If they know the public is watching, they will try to do a good job so they can be reelected.

Unfortunately, when a political machine has complete control of a government, the party out of power cannot be an effective watchdog. In Chicago, for example, all 50 City Council members are Democrats. There are no Republicans on the council to watch over the Democrats. The Democrats have been in control for so long that the city's Republican Party has grown weak and ineffective.

SERVING AS A LINK Just as political parties carry the people's message to the government, they also help different levels and branches of government communicate and cooperate with one another. For example, suppose both the mayor of Cincinnati, Ohio, and the governor of the state are Democrats. As public officials in the same state and members of the same party, they may share similar goals and ideas. They may know each other well and perhaps have worked together on election campaigns or party business in the past. These connections may make it easier for them to work together on mutual problems.

Political Parties Today

Many people believe that the two major political parties are no longer as powerful as they once were. Over the last 30 years, they appear to have lost considerable strength and may continue to decline in the future.

There are several reasons for this decline. The primary reason is a weakening of party loyalty. People move from place to place more often, and party leaders can no longer count on stable neighborhoods and election districts where they can deliver the same number of votes each election. In addition, fewer people vote in elections now than in the past. Although the reasons for this are unclear, it seems that many people believe their votes are no longer important.

Technological changes such as television have also weakened party loyalty. Years ago, many voters would have voted for a particular candidate simply because he or she was their party's choice. Now, many voters decide to vote for a candidate they have seen on television because they are attracted to the candidate, not the political party. In addition, because people are more sophisticated and better educated today than they were in the past, they are better able to make up their own minds about who to vote for. As a result, many voters prefer to register as independent voters rather than with the Democratic or Republican Party. More people today are likely to split their votes between candidates of different parties. For many voters, the qualifications and personal characteristics of a candidate are as important as the political party.

Special-interest groups also have an increasing impact on voters' decisions. Dedicated to advancing a specific cause, special-interest groups support candidates who have good records for backing their causes. Some voters decide to vote for a candidate because their labor union, women's rights group, environmental organization, or business association favors that candidate.

Another trend that is weakening the parties is the increase in **nonpartisan**, or nonparty, elections. Some states require that certain elections, such as municipal and school board elections, be nonpartisan. Political parties are prohibited from participating, and candidates run on the strength of their own qualifications and personal appeal. The candidates organize and run their campaigns without help from any political party.

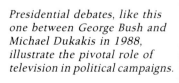

Presidential debates, like this one between George Bush and Michael Dukakis in 1988, illustrate the pivotal role of television in political campaigns.

WHO VOTES: PERCENT REPORTED VOTING, BY RACE, HISPANIC ORIGIN, SEX, AGE, AND LEVEL OF EDUCATION
NOVEMBER 1972–1988

RACE, HISPANIC ORIGIN, SEX, AND AGE	PRESIDENTIAL ELECTIONS					CONGRESSIONAL ELECTIONS			
	1988	1984	1980	1976	1972	1986	1982	1978	1974
Total, voting age	178,098	169,963	157,085	146,548	136,203	173,890	165,483	151,646	141,299
Percent voted	57.4	59.9	59.2	59.2	63.0	46.0	48.5	45.9	44.7
White	59.1	61.4	60.9	60.9	64.5	47.0	49.9	47.3	46.3
Black	51.5	55.8	50.5	48.7	52.1	43.2	43.0	37.2	33.8
Hispanic	28.8	32.6	29.9	31.8	37.5	24.2	25.3	23.5	22.9
Male	56.4	59.0	59.1	59.6	64.1	45.8	48.7	46.6	46.2
Female	58.3	60.8	59.4	58.8	62.0	46.1	48.4	45.3	43.4
18 to 24 years	36.2	40.8	39.9	42.2	49.6	21.9	24.8	23.5	23.8
25 to 44 years	54.0	58.4	58.7	58.7	62.7	41.4	45.4	43.1	42.2
45 to 64 years	67.9	69.8	69.3	68.7	70.8	58.7	62.2	58.5	56.9
65 years and over	68.8	67.7	65.1	62.2	63.5	60.9	59.9	55.9	51.4
Years of school completed									
Elementary: 0 to 8 years	36.7	42.9	42.6	44.1	47.4	32.7	35.7	34.6	34.4
High school: 1 to 3 years	41.3	44.4	45.6	47.2	52.0	33.8	37.7	35.1	35.9
4 years	54.7	58.7	58.9	59.4	65.4	44.1	47.1	45.3	44.7
College: 1 to 3 years	64.5	67.5	67.2	68.1	74.9	49.9	53.3	51.5	49.6
4 years or more	77.6	79.1	79.9	79.8	83.6	62.5	66.5	63.9	61.3

Source: U.S. Department of Commerce, Bureau of the Census

This table groups voters by race, sex, age, and education. Compare the voting records of men and women in Presidential elections since 1972.

Despite all of these factors, our two-party system is not about to disappear. Political parties are still the most effective means of raising the large sums of money necessary to campaign for national offices. In addition, state and federal election laws help preserve the two-party system by discouraging third parties and independent candidates. The two-party system is likely to remain an important part of our political system for many years to come.

SECTION REVIEW

Define the Words
grassroots   nonpartisan
accountable

Check the Facts
1. Identify five functions of political parties.
2. In what ways does a political party act as a watchdog over government activities?
3. What factors are causing political party loyalty to weaken?

Think About the Ideas
4. *Evaluate.* What are the advantages and disadvantages of nonpartisan elections?

CITIZENSHIP SKILLS

How to Register to Vote

When you become 18 years of age, you can begin to exercise one of your most important rights—the right to vote. But before you can walk into a polling place and vote for your candidates, you must first register to vote.

The procedure for registering varies from state to state. In some states, you can register by mail simply by filling out a special postcard obtained from any state or county office. The postcard will ask you to state your name, address, age, and party preference. You can register as a Democrat, a Republican, or a member of any other party you wish to join, or you can register as an independent voter.

If you register as a Republican or Democrat, you will be able to vote in primary elections. Primary elections are held to choose each party's candidates for the general election. If you choose to register as an independent voter, you cannot participate in primary elections, but you can vote for the candidates of your choice in the general elections.

Some states require you to register in person. This can be done at the county election bureau at any time. The bureau is usually located in the county courthouse or government office center and is listed in the telephone directory. Sometimes, the local Democratic or Republican Party or a citizens' group holds voter registration drives in which they go door to door or set up registration tables in local malls or firehouses. If you register to vote during a political party's voter registration drive, keep in mind that you are not required to register as a member of the party conducting the drive.

When registering, first-time voters are often required to show some proof of citizenship,

address, and age, such as a driver's license and birth certificate. Once you are registered to vote, you do not need to reregister except when you change your address, name, or party affiliation.

Although you can register to vote any time, some states have cutoff dates for registering to vote in a specific election. These deadlines vary from state to state.

After you register, you are assigned to an election district according to your address. On election day, the election bureau sets up voting machines at specified polling places, usually schools and government buildings, within each election district. When you register, be sure to find out where your polling place will be.

Using Your Skills
1. What advantage is there to registering as a Republican or a Democrat?
2. Why do you think that many eligible voters fail to register to vote?

CHAPTER 6 REVIEW

★ ★

MAIN POINTS

★ The United States has a two-party system in which two major parties compete with each other for control of the government.

★ Although our two-party system promotes stability and continuity, it also may stifle the views of minority groups.

★ Multiparty systems provide voters with a broad range of views but often lack stability and continuity.

★ In a one-party system, the government and the party are virtually the same.

★ The first American political parties developed out of debate over the U.S. Constitution.

★ In the United States, third parties usually form to promote particular issues, political beliefs, or individual candidates.

★ Active party members help nominate their party's candidates, work to have them elected, and occasionally serve in government positions.

★ Political parties are organized at the local, state, and national levels.

★ Political parties perform five functions—selecting candidates, informing the public, carrying the message of the people to government, acting as a watchdog, and serving as a link between levels and branches of government.

★ Although several factors have weakened the two major parties in recent years, they are still the dominant political organizations in the United States.

WORDS IN REVIEW

Choose the word from the list below that best completes each sentence. Write the missing word on a separate sheet of paper.

plurality   patronage
majority   precinct
coalition   platform
nominate   plank
grassroots   nonpartisan

1. An important _____ in the party's program was to reduce personal income taxes.

2. With 52 percent of the total vote, the candidate won by a _____.

3. During the convention, the party developed its _____ , its list of all the programs it wanted to accomplish.

4. The woman received her government job as a result of the system of political _____.

5. Although none of the candidates won more than 50 percent of the vote, one of them won by a _____.

6. With no political parties represented, the school board election was a _____ election.

7. The three largest parties formed a _____ government to govern the country.

8. The environmental movement was started as a _____ movement of people on the local level.

9. The party members met to _____ the candidate they wanted to represent their party.

10. The candidate was running as a representative from the city's fifteenth _____.

CHAPTER 6 REVIEW

* *

FACTS IN REVIEW

1. Explain how the two-party system works.

2. In what ways does the two-party system provide continuity?

3. What is the major disadvantage of a two-party system?

4. What are the disadvantages of a one-party system?

5. What role have third parties played in the American political system?

6. Identify different types of jobs that active party members are asked to perform.

7. What is the purpose of a party's national convention?

8. Identify three ways in which parties and their candidates inform the public.

9. Explain how political parties carry the message of the people to the government.

10. Identify two reasons why the two-party system is still strong.

THINKING ABOUT PARTIES AND POLITICS

1. *Analyze.* The United States has many different groups of people. Why has the two-party system worked so well in our nation, despite the differences among its people?

2. *Evaluate.* How do you think our political system would differ if all people were required to become members of a political party?

3. *Assess.* Are there cases in which a one-party system might be the best choice for a nation? Why or why not?

WRITING ABOUT A LOCAL ISSUE

You have become very concerned about an issue affecting your community. Perhaps it involves ways to save water or the lack of jobs for teenagers. You decide to attend a town board meeting and make a prepared statement about your feelings on the issue, including what you see the problem to be and how you would propose to solve it. Write the statement you will make before the board.

INTERPRETING A TIME LINE

Time lines can help you see the order in which events occurred and sometimes enable you to identify patterns and trends. The time line on page 142 shows the political parties of American Presidents since 1792. Study the time line, and answer the following questions.

1. Which party held the President's office for most of the period from 1876 to 1912?

2. What conclusion can you draw about the power of the Republican and Democratic parties since 1900?

FOCUSING ON YOUR COMMUNITY

Investigate the political preferences of your community. Are most voters registered as Democrats or Republicans? Over the last three Presidential elections, how did the majority of your community vote—Democratic or Republican? At the local level of government, which party does your community vote for most consistently? Report your findings to the class.

Voting and Elections

OBJECTIVES

After you have studied this chapter, you will be able to:

★ Summarize what voters need to do to prepare themselves for voting.
★ Discuss why people should vote and why people do not vote.
★ Explain the different methods of nominating candidates for office.
★ Describe the ways in which election campaigns "sell" their candidates.
★ Identify different sources of campaign funding.
★ Explain the electoral college system and how it works.

SECTIONS

1 Voting
2 Election Campaigns
3 Elections

It was election day, and Felicia Brown was walking to her polling place when she met her neighbor Sue. Felicia asked Sue if she had voted yet.

"No," replied Sue. "What's the point? I don't like either candidate very much, and I don't have time to wait in line. Besides, my vote won't make any difference."

Her statement bothered Felicia. "Just think what would happen if most people felt like that. Only a few people would vote, and those few would end up making all the decisions for the rest of us. I have a right to vote, and I'm going to use it!"

Felicia was correct when she said that voting is a right. It is also one of the major responsibilities of citizenship. Voting in elections is the only time that citizens can directly bring about change in their government. To take on this responsibility, voters must know about voting and about the election process.

★ ★

SECTION 1

Voting

★ ★

VOCABULARY

electorate   literacy test

apathy

Almost all Americans age 18 years or older have the right to vote. Like other rights, however, this right to vote is not absolute. It is subject to certain regulations and restrictions. The most significant regulation concerns who is actually eligible to vote on election day.

To be eligible to vote in most states, a person must be at least 18 years old, a resident of the state for a specified period of time, and a citizen of the United States. In most states, a person must be registered in order to vote. Registration usually takes place sometime before election day. (See How to Register to Vote on page 153.) The person's name is then added to a list of registered voters. On election day, election officials use this list to verify that the people who vote are eligible and to prevent people from voting more than once.

Preparing to Vote

Registering is only one part of getting ready to vote, however. It is equally important to learn about the candidates and the issues involved in the election. Voters can get this information from newspaper and magazine articles and from radio and television news programs. Political parties also provide information about their candidates and their party's programs. Responsible voters use these different sources of information to prepare themselves for voting on election day.

Most voters look for candidates whose opinions on particular issues are similar to their own. Voters who are concerned about protecting the environment, for example, would probably favor a candidate who advocates strong controls on pollution. Every election focuses on one or more issues.

Responsible voters learn about those issues and about the candidates' stands on them. That way, they know whether they agree or disagree with a particular candidate's positions.

In a Presidential election, there is usually a great deal of information about the Presidential candidates and the issues. On election day, however, voters will also be selecting candidates for local, state, and Congressional offices. They must choose town council members, judges, state legislators, tax collectors, governors, U.S. Senators, and so on. Although it is more difficult to learn about

Delegates to the 1988 Republican National Convention chose George Bush as their Presidential candidate. Dan Quayle was selected as his running mate.

local candidates and issues than Presidential ones, responsible voters try to get as much information as possible before going in to cast their ballots.

Who Votes?

Collectively, the people who are eligible to vote in an election are called the **electorate**. Not everyone in the electorate votes, however. In fact, in a typical Presidential election, only about 60 percent of the electorate actually votes. In the 1988 Presidential election, only about 57 percent of the 178 million people of voting age actually voted. It was one of the lowest voter turnouts in our history.

Why don't more people vote? Some are not allowed to, for one reason or another. For example, inmates of mental hospitals are not allowed to vote in any state. And in most cases, people who have been convicted of serious crimes are denied the right to vote. In addition, thousands of people cannot vote on election day because they moved recently and do not yet meet their state's residency requirements. Others fail to vote because they are ill or away from home on election day.

Voter registration appears to be a major obstacle to voting. Some people find the registration requirements too complicated. Others find it too difficult to get to a voter registration office during the working day. Some forget to reregister when they move. People without permanent addresses often cannot register because they do not meet state residency requirements.

In the past, racial discrimination often prevented blacks from registering to vote. Several Southern states discriminated against their black citizens by imposing poll taxes or by requiring people to pass a literacy test in order to register. The **literacy test** was a test to prove that the voter could read and write and understand public issues. In some cases, whites were not required to take the test. In others, whites and blacks were given different tests: whites only had to sign their names, while blacks had to explain complicated sections of the U.S. Constitution or the state constitution. Congress outlawed literacy tests in 1965. Since then, black voter registration has risen sharply, as has the number of elected black officials around the country.

Even among those people who are properly registered to vote, millions fail to do so. One reason for this is **apathy**, or lack of interest. Many people are not familiar with the candidates or the issues and do not care which candidate running in a particular election wins. Some people decide not to vote because they don't believe their vote will make any difference. That is not true, of course, but it is easy to see why some people feel that way, especially during Presidential elections. Why bother to vote, some people ask, when public opinion polls predict the probable winner weeks before election day?

REASONS FOR VOTING There are several reasons why people should exercise their right to vote. Voting gives citizens a chance to choose their government leaders. It also gives them an opportunity to voice their opinion on the past performance of public officials. If the voters are dissatisfied, they can elect new leaders. Voting also allows citizens to express their opinions on public issues. A vote for a candidate is also a vote for that candidate's party, ideas, and programs.

Some people find it difficult to take an active interest in politics. All concerned citizens should try to do so, however, because every level of government affects their lives. Perhaps the school board needs to raise money to build a new school. Or the local government wants to pass new regulations

THE TWENTY-SIXTH AMENDMENT

In the late 1960's and early 1970's, thousands of young men were sent to Vietnam to fight for their country. Many were only 18, 19, and 20 years old, old enough to die in a foreign war but not to vote for—or against—the leaders who sent them there.

The voting age had been 21 since colonial times. It was thought that people under 21 lacked the wisdom and experience needed to elect their leaders. Since young people often hold different ideas from their parents, it was also thought that lowering the voting age would threaten traditional American values.

But when the young soldiers in Vietnam took up the slogan "Old enough to fight; old enough to vote," the nation's leaders finally listened. On March 23, 1971, Congress passed the Twenty-Sixth Amendment to the Constitution, which said:

The right of citizens of the United States, who are eighteen years of age or older, to vote shall not be denied or abridged by the United States or by any State on account of age.

By June 30, the amendment had been ratified by the required two-thirds of the states. On July 1, 18-year-olds were officially given the right to vote. When the war in Vietnam ended, young Americans returned home to enjoy the full benefits of their newly won right.

Using Your Skills

1. Why did the young soldiers in Vietnam feel that they deserved the right to vote?

2. Why did Congress have to pass a constitutional amendment, rather than just a law, to lower the voting age?

3. The graph on this page shows the participation of 18- to 20-year-olds in Presidential elections. What conclusion can you draw from this graph?

4. Do you think the voting age should be lowered further, to 16? Why or why not?

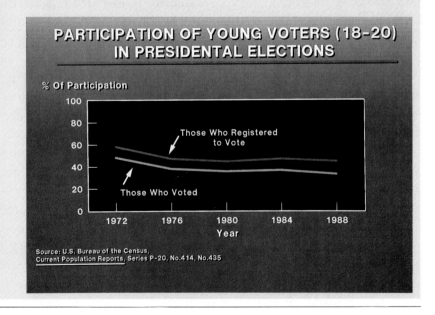

PARTICIPATION OF YOUNG VOTERS (18-20) IN PRESIDENTAL ELECTIONS

% Of Participation

Those Who Registered to Vote

Those Who Voted

Source: U.S. Bureau of the Census, Current Population Reports, Series P-20, No.414, No.435

to allow industrial development in the community. Or state and federal governments want to increase taxes. By participating in the political process and by using their right to vote, citizens determine who will make these decisions and influence how the decisions are made.

SECTION REVIEW

Define the Words

electorate   literacy test
apathy

Check the Facts
1. What are the eligibility requirements for registering to vote in most states?
2. List three reasons why some people do not vote.
3. Why is it important to exercise the right to vote?

Think About the Ideas
4. *Analyze.* Why is it important to weigh candidates' positions on all the issues, not just the one or two you feel most strongly about?

Reading and talking about current events is a good way to become an informed citizen.

★ ★

SECTION 2

Election Campaigns

★ ★

VOCABULARY

caucus   canvassing
primary election   PAC
propaganda

In the American political system, every election is a two-part process. First, each party nominates its candidates for public office, and then the candidates run against each other for election. The first part of this process, the nomination of candidates, varies widely from state to state.

Nominating Candidates

In state, local, and Congressional elections, a candidate can be nominated to run for a public office in three ways—in a caucus, a nominating convention, or a primary election. Each state decides which method it will use. In Presidential elections, the candidates are chosen by a combination of these methods.

CAUCUSES A **caucus** is a meeting of political party members to conduct party business. Originally, the caucus was a private meeting of important people in the community. Sometime in the 1720's it was used to nominate people for public office. Later, as political parties developed, party leaders took over the use of the caucus, including its role in nominating candidates. Today, the use of caucuses is limited pretty much to nominating candidates for local office, especially in New England. A few states hold caucuses for nominating Presidential candidates.

NOMINATING CONVENTIONS By the 1840's, caucuses were considered undemocratic and became very unpopular. People criticized the fact that only party leaders were involved in nominating candidates. Caucuses were replaced by nominating conventions, which were considered more democratic. The party members in a particular area elected delegates to attend the nominating convention. These delegates would then choose the candidates to run for various offices. Nominating conventions are used today in only a few places to choose candidates for state and local offices. The Presidential nominating conventions are discussed later in the chapter.

PRIMARY ELECTIONS A **primary election** is held among party members to nominate candidates to run for office. There are two kinds of primaries, the closed primary and the open primary. The closed primary is the more common. In a closed primary, only declared party members may vote. Voters can add their names to the list of one party or the other either when they register to vote or when they go to the polling place. Then, in the primary election, registered Democrats and Republicans are directed to voting machines or are given ballots that list only their party's candidates.

In an open primary, voters do not have to register with one of the parties. They choose the party to vote for after entering the voting booth. The major advantage of an open primary is that the privacy of voters is preserved. However, critics of open primaries say that they undermine party loyalty, because a voter can switch from party to party. They also point out that open primaries enable the voters of one party to cross over and vote in the opposing party's primary. In this way, party members can choose weak opponents to run against their own party's candidates.

GETTING ON THE PRIMARY BALLOT How do candidates get their names on a primary ballot to begin with? In most primary elections,

Ann Richards gave the keynote address at the 1988 Democratic National Convention. In 1990, she ran for governor of Texas.

party members meet and select one candidate for each office. This list of candidates, called a slate, is then placed on the party's ballot. Usually, each candidate also circulates a nominating petition that must be signed by a certain number of party members. If no one challenges these candidates, they run unopposed in the primary election. Party members who wish to challenge the party's nominees, however, may also circulate nominating petitions for other candidates. If these petitions receive enough signatures, these candidates are also placed on the primary ballot.

NOMINATING PRESIDENTIAL CANDIDATES
The Democratic and Republican parties each choose their Presidential and Vice Presidential nominees at a national nominating convention held during the summer of election year. Party delegates from all the states meet at this convention to vote for the candidate of their choice.

The nominating process actually begins in February of that year, when candidates seeking the parties' nomination run in the New Hampshire primary. From then until June, potential candidates run in other primaries or state caucuses throughout the country.

In some states with primary elections, voters vote directly for the candidates they prefer. In others, they vote for delegates to the national convention who support a particular candidate.

Although most states hold primaries, several, including Iowa, Minnesota, Maine, and Michigan, hold caucuses where party delegates meet and vote on Presidential candidates.

Each state sends a certain number of delegates to attend each party's national convention. The number of delegates is determined by the state's population. At the convention, the candidate who receives a majority of the delegates' votes wins the Presidential nomination. This candidate then chooses a Vice Presidential running mate. Together these two candidates are called "the ticket."

Running for Office

The nomination of candidates is only the first part of the election process. Once candidates are chosen, they spend several weeks or months in an election campaign, trying to convince the voters that they should be elected. Each candidate has a campaign organization to help run the campaign. In some races, such as for the city council or the school board, a candidate's campaign organization may have only a few workers. A Presidential campaign, on the other hand, can involve thousands of people.

A campaign organization is responsible for acquainting the voters with the candidate's name, face, and position on the issues. It must also make the voters like and trust the candidate. Each party uses several different techniques, or campaign tools, to accomplish this.

ENDORSEMENTS One common campaign tool is the endorsement. When a famous and popular person supports or campaigns for a candidate, it is an endorsement. The endorser may be a movie star, a famous athlete, a popular politician, or some other well-known individual. In 1988, for example, movie tough-guy Arnold Schwarzenegger often campaigned for the Republican candidate, George Bush. The idea behind endorsements is that if voters like the person making the endorsement, they may decide to vote for the candidate.

Endorsements are a kind of propaganda technique. **Propaganda** is an attempt to promote a particular person or idea. Propaganda

Candidates use symbols such as the American flag to suggest to voters that they represent the nation's best interests.

techniques are a means of trying to persuade or influence voters to choose one candidate over another.

Endorsements are only one type of propaganda technique used in political campaigns. You will read about others in Chapter 8.

ADVERTISING AND IMAGE MOLDING How the voters perceive a candidate is often more important than whether a candidate is qualified. Political campaigns therefore try to create an image of the candidate that will appeal to voters.

Political campaigns spend a lot of time and money to create the right image for a candidate. Much of that money goes for advertising. Political advertisements are a very effective campaign tool that allow a party to present only its candidate's position or point of view. They also enable a candidate to attack an opponent without offering an opportunity to respond.

For local campaigns, a party may do little more than buy newspaper advertisements and hang up posters. In state and national campaigns, however, a great deal of campaign advertising is done on television. Television ads can present quick and dramatic images of a candidate and his or her ideas. For example, the image of a candidate talking with unemployed steelworkers conveys a concern for industry and employment as well as a concern for people and their problems. Such television images tend to stay in the viewer's mind.

Television advertising has come under increasing criticism in recent years. Since most ads are only 30 seconds long, they do not allow candidates to discuss issues and ideas in detail. In addition, some candidates use TV ads to create negative images of their opponents instead of positive images of themselves. Although this "negative campaigning" is often viewed as unfair, it can also be very effective.

In addition to campaign advertisements, television is useful to candidates in other ways. In Presidential or statewide campaigns, candidates often appear in news broadcasts answering reporters' questions, making speeches, or talking to voters. Such appearances help them keep their names and faces in front of the voters.

CANVASSING Another important campaign tool is **canvassing**, or going through neighborhoods asking for votes or taking public opinion polls. At the local level, candidates and campaign workers often "knock on doors" to solicit votes and hand out campaign literature.

At the national level, campaign organizations conduct frequent polls to find out how their candidates are doing. News organizations and public opinion research companies also take polls to see which candidate is leading in a particular election.

Financing Election Campaigns

It takes money to buy the television ads, buttons, bumper stickers, posters, and literature that a candidate needs to run an effective campaign. How much is needed depends on the race.

A small-town mayoral race may require only a few hundred or a few thousand dollars. A state legislative or Congressional race can cost several hundred thousand dollars. And a Presidential race can cost hundreds of millions. The 1988 Presidential race, for example, is estimated to have cost $500 million.

PRIVATE FUNDING Where does all of this money come from? A small portion, probably less than 10 percent, comes from individual donors who feel strongly enough about a candidate to contribute money to his or her campaign. The political parties also work hard all year long to raise money for the party's campaign treasury. They hold $1,000-a-plate dinners or other fund-raising events such as concerts, rallies, and parties. Often, they also write to party members and ask them for donations.

In addition to money from individuals and fund-raising events, about one-fourth of each party's funds come from Political Action Committees, better known as PACs. (See the High Cost of Running for Office on page 145.) **PACs** are political fund-raising organizations established by corporations, labor unions, and other special-interest groups. PAC funds come from voluntary contributions of company employees, stockholders, and union members. A PAC uses its funds to support Presidential, Congressional, and state and local candidates who favor the PACs position on issues.

PUBLIC FUNDING The largest share of the money spent in Presidential campaigns comes from the public. Public funding of Presidential elections began in the 1970's. At that time, Congress created the Presidential Election Campaign Fund to prevent wealthy candidates from buying themselves into office by outspending their opponents. Taxpayers can contribute one dollar to the fund each

When taxpayers fill out their income tax form, they can check off a box to contribute one dollar to the Presidential Election Campaign Fund.

Presidential Election Campaign	Do you want $1 to go to this fund?	Yes	No	Note: Checking "Yes" will not change your tax or reduce your refund.
	If joint return, does your spouse want $1 to go to this fund? .	Yes	No	

year by checking off a box on their federal income tax form.

The Presidential Election Campaign Fund allots money for both the primary and general elections. In general, major party candidates can qualify for funds to campaign in the primary elections if they can raise $100,000 on their own. After the national convention, the two major party candidates receive equal shares of money from the fund, so long as they agree not to accept contributions from any other sources. In 1988, George Bush and Michael Dukakis each received $46.1 million. Minor party candidates also qualify for some federal funding if they receive 5 percent of the votes cast in the general election.

Congress also passed the Federal Election Campaign Act in 1971, which limits individual and PAC contributions to Presidential candidates to $1,000 and $5,000 respectively. This law was intended to prevent large contributors from buying special favors—such as appointment to public office or changes in the laws—from winning candidates.

SECTION REVIEW

Define the Words
caucus   canvassing
primary election   PAC
propaganda

Check the Facts
1. What is the difference between an open and a closed primary election?
2. Identify three important campaign tools.
3. What did the Federal Election Campaign Act do?

Thinking About the Ideas
4. *Analyze.* In what way could our present system of nominating Presidential candidates be considered undemocratic?

★ ★

SECTION 3

Elections

★ ★

VOCABULARY
polling place   electoral vote
straight ticket   initiative
split ticket   proposition
exit poll   referendum
popular vote   recall

Once the campaign hoopla is over and election day arrives, it is up to the voters to decide who will win or lose. These important decisions are made at the nation's **polling places**, or polls—the places where votes are cast. Polling places are usually set up in town halls, schools, firehouses, and other public buildings. Each voter must vote at an assigned polling place, determined by his or her place of residence.

At the Polls

Exact hours vary, but polling places are generally open from early morning until 7 or 8 P.M. to give people time to vote before or after work. Each polling place is staffed by election board workers who make sure that voters are properly registered and do not vote more than once. Typically, each party also stations a poll watcher at each polling place.

The poll watchers make sure that the election is conducted fairly and that only qualified voters are allowed to vote.

CASTING VOTES Upon entering the polling place, voters give their names to an election worker, who checks the names against a master list. The voters are then given a ballot and directed to a voting booth.

Voters cast their ballots in one of three ways—by computerized machine, by mechanical machine, or by paper ballot. In all three, the candidates are always listed according to their party and the office they are seeking. With a computerized voting machine, votes are cast by touching certain spots on the screen, by pushing certain buttons, or by marking a ballot. The machine then "reads" the ballot electronically and records the votes. With a mechanical voting machine, votes are cast by pulling small levers next to the names of the candidates chosen. With a paper ballot, a square is marked or a hole punched next to the names of the candidates chosen. All three systems also enable voters to vote a **straight ticket**, or for all the candidates of a

Ballots list all the candidates, their political parties, and the offices they are seeking. Here a voter marks her choices on a paper ballot.

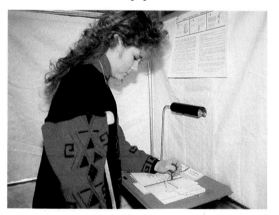

Gerrymandering is the practice of creating an oddly shaped election district that will favor a particular political party. The term dates back to 1812 when the Massachusetts legislature created a long, curving district north of Boston. A majority of voters in this "district" were loyal to the party of Governor Elbridge Gerry. As drawn by a political cartoonist, the district resembled a salamander. A political wit called it a "Gerrymander" after the governor.

Congress and the courts have ruled that an election district should be compact and made up of adjoining areas. In 1962, the U.S. Supreme Court also ruled that each election district should have nearly equal numbers of voters. These laws have reduced but not eliminated gerrymandering.

single party. Voting for candidates of different parties is called voting a **split ticket**. It is also possible to vote for someone not on the ballot. This is called a write-in vote.

Voters who cannot get to the polls on election day can vote by using an absentee ballot. Absentee ballots are commonly used by people who know they will be away from home on election day and by people who are too sick to get to the polls. A voter must request an absentee ballot from the local election board sometime before election day. On election day, these absentee ballots are opened and counted either at the polling place or at the election board.

COUNTING THE RESULTS In a major election, the news media and the party workers attempt to predict the winners as soon as possible. To do this, they often ask voters leaving polling places which candidate they voted for. This is known as an **exit poll**.

By taking a sample of voters at key polling places, specialists can predict who the winners will be.

When the polls close, the election workers count the votes at the polling place and bring the ballots and the results—called returns—to the election board. The election board then counts the returns for the entire city or county. Gathering all the returns and tallying the results can take several hours.

In national and state elections, the news media use the first returns that come in, as well as the results of their own exit polls, to make a projection of the winners. That is why a television network can project a winner at 8 P.M. in New York, while people are still voting in California.

General Elections

In a general election, the voters cast ballots for candidates for various national, state,

At election time, television networks receive frequent reports from key districts around the nation. These up-to-the-minute voting results and computer predictions are passed on to the viewers.

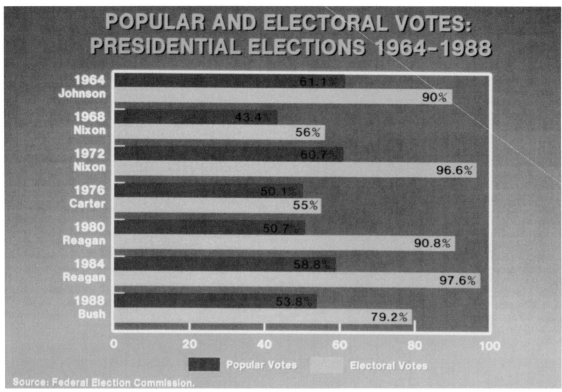

POPULAR AND ELECTORAL VOTES: PRESIDENTIAL ELECTIONS 1964-1988

1964 Johnson	61.1% / 90%
1968 Nixon	43.4% / 56%
1972 Nixon	60.7% / 96.6%
1976 Carter	50.1% / 55%
1980 Reagan	50.7% / 90.8%
1984 Reagan	58.8% / 97.6%
1988 Bush	53.8% / 79.2%

Popular Votes   Electoral Votes

Source: Federal Election Commission.

This graph shows the popular and electoral votes received by Presidents elected between 1964 and 1988. Who casts electoral votes?

and local offices. The general election is always held on the first Tuesday after the first Monday in November. The ballot may include the names of candidates for governor, the state legislature, the county government, and local offices. In certain years, the ballot will also list Presidential and Congressional candidates.

For all races except the Presidential race, the candidate who wins a majority of the **popular vote**—votes cast directly by the people—is elected to office. In a Presidential race, the voters are actually electing people called electors who hold **electoral votes** and are part of the Electoral College system. You read about the creation of the Electoral College in Chapter 3.

PRESIDENTIAL ELECTIONS IN THE ELECTORAL COLLEGE When a person votes for a Presidential candidate, he or she is really voting for a Democratic or Republican elector. About a month after the November general election, these electors assemble in each state to cast their votes for President. If the Republican Presidential candidate won the popular vote in the state, then the Republican electors get to cast all the state's electoral votes. The Democratic electors cast no votes. This is known as the "winner-take-all" system.

The number of electoral votes for each state is determined by its representation in Congress. For example, Michigan, which has 18 U.S. Representatives and 2 U.S. Senators, has 20 electors. There are a total of 538 electoral votes, and the candidate who receives 270 or more of these votes wins the electoral vote and the election.

Many people think that the Electoral College system should be changed or eliminated. They charge that large states—such as California and Texas, which have many more electoral votes than smaller states—have too much influence in deciding the election. One candidate might win five or six small states and yet not receive as many electoral votes as the candidate who wins just one large state. Critics also point out that with the Electoral College system a candidate can lose the popular vote but still win the election, as happened in 1888.

There have been several suggestions for reforming the Electoral College system. Under one plan, electoral votes would be based on the percentage of the popular vote. If a candidate won 55 percent of a state's popular vote, for example, he or she would also get 55 percent of the electoral votes. Any change in the system would take time, since it would require a constitutional amendment.

VOTING ON ISSUES In some elections at the state or local level, voters may be asked to vote on issues as well as on candidates. This allows voters to participate more directly in the lawmaking process. Twenty-three states provide for lawmaking through the **initiative**. The initiative is a method by which citizens propose laws or state constitutional amendments. They do this by circulating a petition asking for the proposed new law, or **proposition**. If the petition receives a certain number of signatures, the proposition is put on the ballot. In 1988, for example, California voters petitioned to put a proposition on the ballot that dealt with limiting auto insurance premiums.

A **referendum** is a method by which voters can approve or reject a measure passed by the state legislature or by the local government. All the states except Delaware use the referendum to vote on state constitutional amendments.

Special Elections

From time to time, state or local governments also hold certain kinds of special elections. Runoff elections may be held when none of the candidates for a particular office wins a majority of votes in the general election. The runoff is held to determine the winner.

Another kind of special election is the **recall** election. In a recall, voters can vote to remove a public official from office. Like the initiative, the recall begins with a petition. Voters may recall an official because of wrongdoing or because they do not like his or her position on issues. In many states, voters can recall only local officials, but in 14 states they can recall state officials as well.

DISPUTED ELECTIONS When an election is very close, the loser may sometimes contest, or challenge, the results. The loser then has the right to demand a recount of the votes. In very close races, a small mistake such as failing to include the votes from a single voting machine can change the results of the election.

Occasionally, a disputed election cannot be resolved by a recount and requires another election. In the case of a national election, a dispute may be referred to Congress for settlement. In Presidential elections, if neither candidate wins a majority of the electoral votes, the House of Representatives elects the President. This happened in the elections of 1800 and 1824.

In an election, voters use ballots to vote for candidates and to decide issues.

No campaigning is allowed beyond a certain point at a polling place. Voters who cannot get to the polls on election day can request an absentee ballot.

SECTION REVIEW

Define the Words

polling place
straight ticket
split ticket
exit poll
popular vote

electoral vote
initiative
proposition
referendum
recall

Check the Facts

1. Identify three methods of casting votes.
2. How does the election of Presidential candidates differ from the election of all other public officials?
3. What is the difference between an initiative and a referendum?

Think About the Ideas

4. *Analyze.* What are the advantages and disadvantages of the use of exit polls?
5. *Assess.* Is it a good idea to vote a straight ticket? Why or why not?

CITIZENSHIP SKILLS

How to Read an Election Map

Some special-purpose maps relate political information to geography. The information includes political boundaries and place names. Boundaries show the location and size of regions, populations, nations, alliances, states, districts, counties, or any other kind of political division. Place names identify the divisions and other political features, such as cities and ports.

The election map on the next page is an example of one type of special-purpose map. It shows the results of the Presidential election of 1988. The map identifies each state and the number of electoral votes it has. The map key explains the meaning of the colors. Blue, for example, identifies the states that cast their votes for George Bush. The key includes the totals of each candidate's electoral and popular votes. Use the map and key to answer the questions that follow.

Using Your Skills

1. Which state has the most electoral votes? Which candidate won this state?
2. In which geographic region did Dukakis get the most electoral votes?
3. Which vote was closer—the electoral or the popular vote?
4. A candidate needs a majority of electoral votes to win. If Dukakis had also won Texas, California, Illinois, Ohio, and Pennsylvania, would he have been elected President?
5. Summarize the information on this map in two or three sentences.

CITIZENSHIP SKILLS

How to Read an Election Map

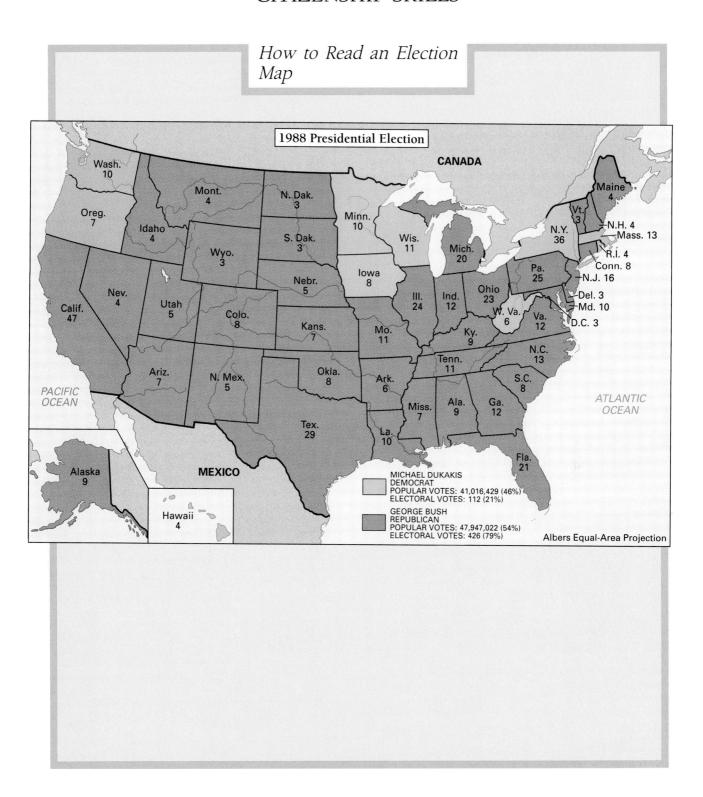

1988 Presidential Election

CANADA

Wash. 10
Mont. 4
N. Dak. 3
Minn. 10
Maine 4
Vt. 3
N.H. 4
N.Y. 36
Mass. 13
Oreg. 7
Idaho 4
S. Dak. 3
Wis. 11
Mich. 20
R.I. 4
Conn. 8
Wyo. 3
Pa. 25
N.J. 16
Nev. 4
Nebr. 5
Iowa 8
Ohio 23
Del. 3
Calif. 47
Utah 5
Colo. 8
Ill. 24
Ind. 12
W. Va. 6
Md. 10
Va. 12
D.C. 3
Kans. 7
Mo. 11
Ky. 9
N.C. 13
Ariz. 7
N. Mex. 5
Okla. 8
Ark. 6
Tenn. 11
S.C. 8
PACIFIC OCEAN
Tex. 29
Miss. 7
Ala. 9
Ga. 12
ATLANTIC OCEAN
La. 10
Fla. 21

Alaska 9
MEXICO
Hawaii 4

MICHAEL DUKAKIS
DEMOCRAT
POPULAR VOTES: 41,016,429 (46%)
ELECTORAL VOTES: 112 (21%)

GEORGE BUSH
REPUBLICAN
POPULAR VOTES: 47,947,022 (54%)
ELECTORAL VOTES: 426 (79%)

Albers Equal-Area Projection

CHAPTER 7 REVIEW

* *

MAIN POINTS

★ In most states, citizens must register before being allowed to vote.

★ Voters are responsible for finding out about the candidates and issues in an election.

★ Voting allows citizens to express their opinions and to directly affect their government. But many eligible voters do not vote.

★ Each party nominates its candidates for public office in primary elections or at caucuses or nominating conventions.

★ During the election campaigns each party tries to sell its candidates.

★ The money for election campaigns comes from both private contributions and government funding.

★ Voters may cast their ballots on computerized or mechanical voting machines or on paper ballots.

★ In the Presidential election, the voters choose members of the Electoral College who vote for the President.

★ Other kinds of elections include initiatives, referendums, runoffs, and recalls.

WORDS IN REVIEW

Choose the word or phrase from the list below that best completes each sentence. Write the missing words on a separate sheet of paper.

caucus	primary election
canvassing	straight ticket
split ticket	exit poll
electoral vote	initiative
referendum	recall

1. Many voters leaving the polling place were asked to answer questions for a(n) _____.

2. In most states, each party's candidate for governor is chosen in a(n) _____.

3. The new law proposed by the state legislature was submitted to the voters for their approval in a(n) _____.

4. The Republican Party _____ met to nominate its candidates for the town council.

5. The voters proposed a new tax law through a(n) _____.

6. In voting for only Democratic candidates, the man voted a(n) _____.

7. The _____ election was held to remove a corrupt official from public office.

8. The Republican Presidential candidate won the election by winning both the popular vote and the _____.

9. The party workers spent many hours _____ the neighborhood to get support for their candidate.

10. The woman voted a(n) _____, choosing a Republican President and a Democratic Senator and member of Congress.

FACTS IN REVIEW

1. What is the purpose of voter registration?

2. Name three groups of people who are not allowed to vote.

3. What methods did Southern states use in the past to prevent blacks from voting?

4. Identify three methods that have been used to nominate candidates for public office.

5. How do Presidential primaries work?

6. What is the purpose of endorsements?

CHAPTER 7 REVIEW

* *

7. What is the purpose of Political Action Committees, or PACs?

8. How can people vote if they are not able to go to the polls?

9. Why are television news programs able to predict the winners of elections before all the polls are closed?

10. What is the "winner-take-all" system?

THINKING ABOUT PARTIES AND POLITICS

1. *Analyze.* What do you think political parties could do about the problem of voter apathy?

2. *Evaluate.* Do you think it is better to have the government pay for election campaigns or to let each candidate raise funds privately? Why?

3. *Assess.* Do you think the Electoral College system should be abolished? Why or why not?

WRITING A CAMPAIGN BROCHURE

You have been working as a volunteer in the political campaign of one of the candidates for county legislator. One of your assignments is to help prepare a pamphlet on community issues.

Pick one of the major issues facing your community, and write a paragraph explaining the problem and your ideas on how it should be handled. Remember that what you write should help convince people to vote for your candidate.

INTERPRETING AN ELECTION MAP

Look at the map of the United States on page 173. It shows the number of electoral votes held by each state and the results of the 1988 election. Which three states have the largest number of electoral votes? What percentage of the total (538 electoral votes) is represented by these states? How do you think this affects the campaign plans of Presidential candidates?

FOCUSING ON YOUR COMMUNITY

Laws about registration vary from place to place. Contact the local election board to find out what the requirements are in your community. Then design a poster on voter registration. It should include the following information: local residency requirements, when and where people can register for an election, the procedure for registering, and the types of identification needed.

Public Opinion and Interest Groups

OBJECTIVES

After you have studied this chapter, you will be able to:

★ Identify the factors that influence public opinion.

★ Discuss the purpose of public opinion polls and how polls can affect public opinion.

★ Define interest group, identify different types of interest groups, and describe how they influence public opinion.

★ List three major contributions of interest groups.

★ Discuss the function and importance of lobbyists and lobbying activities.

★ Describe how the activities of lobbyists are regulated.

SECTIONS

1 Public Opinion
2 Interest Groups
3 Interest Groups and Public Policy

INTRODUCTION

Political discussions were common in the Miller household. Jason and his parents often spoke about the day's political news. One evening at dinner, the conversation focused on the proposed 51 percent pay raise that Congress was considering for itself and for other government employees.

"I think it's outrageous," Mr. Miller said. "How dare they take such a large increase at a time when they say government spending must be decreased and Americans must tighten their belts."

"I agree," said Mrs. Miller. "I don't think public opinion will stand for it. If those members of Congress want to be reelected, they'd better think twice about voting themselves such a large pay raise."

When Mrs. Miller spoke of public opinion, she was referring to the way most people felt about the proposed pay raise. **Public opinion** is the attitudes or opinions of a large group of people about a particular issue or person.

As our elected representatives, officials at all levels of government care about public opinion. It is the way in which these leaders learn what the people want. In this chapter you will learn more about public opinion and its effect.

* *

SECTION 1

Public Opinion

* *

VOCABULARY

public opinion	interest group
mass media	pollster

The term *public opinion* is misleading. It suggests a uniformity of opinion that does not exist. In fact, there are very few issues on which most Americans agree. On any given issue, different groups of the "public" may hold different viewpoints. For example, some may favor greatly increasing the nation's military forces; others may urge the government to do everything possible to halt the arms race. Between these two positions, however, are many shades of opinion on this issue. In other words, on almost any public issue, there are two or more public opinions.

Many factors affect a person's opinion on this or any other public issue. Age, sex, income, hobbies, race, religion, occupation, and so on, may play a role. The family of a government employee, for example, probably feels differently about the proposed government pay raise than Jason Miller's family. A black woman may favor affirmative action employment laws, while a white man may not.

Other factors affect public opinion as well. The economic situation usually has an enormous impact on public opinion. If America's steel mills are booming and the nation's steelworkers fully employed, most people would probably not object to allowing some foreign steel to be imported into the United States. But in hard times, when the steel mills were laying off workers, public opinion would probably oppose importing steel.

Public opinion is heavily influenced by the **mass media**, the sources of news information that include television, radio, newspapers, and magazines. Every day, newspapers sell about 60 million copies nationwide. They are read by more people than this, however, since more than one person in each household may read the same copy. Television news may reach another 60 million Americans each day, and some 10 million people subscribe to weekly newsmagazines.

These different media influence public opinion not only by the numbers of people they reach, but also by how they cover issues or events. The media can emphasize certain issues or events and downplay others in ways that can influence people's opinions. (See Citizenship Skills, page 133.)

Political leaders and public officials can also exert a strong influence on public opinion. When the voters elect people to office, they put their trust in those officials and rely on their opinions. Public officials get opportunities to state their views through speeches, press conferences, television interviews, and in newspaper and magazine articles. In doing so, they hope to persuade people to support their positions on issues.

People who share a similar point of view about an issue sometimes work together to promote that point of view. Such a group is called an **interest group** or a special-interest group. Interest groups try to influence public opinion by making people aware of issues and changing their attitudes. A recent example is the animal rights movement. Animal rights groups have worked to make people aware of the conditions of animals used for laboratory testing and for making fur coats. These interest groups hope to change people's attitudes about buying products that have been tested on animals. They also hope to persuade people not to buy fur coats.

Newspaper reports and magazine articles can have an important effect on how people view an issue.

Measuring Public Opinion

It is very difficult to determine just what the public's opinion is on any given issue. One way is to look at the results of elections. If a majority of voters elect a particular candidate, presumably they agree with that candidate's ideas and programs. Elections are not a very reliable guide to public opinion, however. People elect candidates for various reasons. Perhaps they liked a particular candidate's appearance or felt he or she was capable. Perhaps they voted a straight party ticket. Election results can provide only a broad idea of public opinion, not an accurate assessment of specific issues. The election of a Republican President, for example,

Interest groups, such as these animal rights activists, use various tactics to make the public aware of their concerns and to influence public policy.

may reflect a desire for less government spending. It does not, however, indicate which specific programs the public would like to see cut.

Public Opinion Polls

The most accurate way to measure public opinion is through a public opinion poll. In Chapter 7, you learned that people who take polls collect information by asking questions of certain groups of people. About a thousand companies are in the business of taking public opinion polls. Two of the best known are the Gallup Poll and the Harris Survey. Although most companies take polls about consumer products, some concentrate on public issues and political campaigns.

Polling companies have made a science out of taking polls. **Pollsters**, the people who take polls, follow careful methods to make sure their polls are accurate. By asking about 1,500 people their opinions on an issue, they can get an accurate idea of how most Americans feel about that issue.

Pollsters usually question a group of people selected at random all over the United States. They have found that such a random sample will probably include people of all races, incomes, sexes, ages, and viewpoints. Since the sample reflects the characteristics of the entire population, it presents a reasonably accurate picture of general public opinion.

To find out what people really think, pollsters must be careful how they word the questions in a poll. For example, the question, "Do

The Election Poll of 1936

In the last weeks before the 1936 Presidential election, a poll taken by the popular magazine *Literary Digest* showed Republican candidate Alf Landon winning by a landslide. Yet, when the election was over, President Franklin Roosevelt won reelection with over 60 percent of the vote.

Why was the poll so wrong? The *Literary Digest* had chosen its sample at random from automobile registration lists and telephone directories. The pollsters failed to realize that they were polling only those who could afford cars and telephones and who bothered to return the ballots.

The poll was thus not representative of the entire population. Today's pollsters are more careful about finding representative groups of voters to poll.

you favor cutting taxes?'' might get a different answer from the same person as the question, "Do you favor cutting taxes if it means letting poor people go hungry?'' The second question is called a loaded question because it is biased, or written in a way that will get a certain, in this case negative, response.

Political parties and news organizations frequently hire polling companies to take political polls. The results of the polls are then released to the public. Some critics feel that these polls not only measure public opinion, but also affect it. They argue that the polls may influence many voters to support a candidate who is leading in the polls.

Public opinion polls may also have the opposite effect of influencing people not to vote at all. For instance, in the last few weeks of the 1988 Presidential election, many polls predicted that George Bush would win the election. As a result, some voters did not bother to vote on election day because they thought the race had already been decided. This attitude probably contributed to the low voter turnout in that election.

What attitude does this cartoon show toward the election campaign?

Pollsters try to get a picture of public opinion by questioning a group of people selected at random.

SECTION REVIEW

Define the Words

public opinion	interest group
mass media	pollster

Check the Facts

1. How do the mass media affect public opinion?
2. How do public officials affect public opinion?
3. What are two ways to measure public opinion?
4. What is a random sample?

Think About the Ideas

5. *Put Ideas Together.* Why is a poll a more accurate measure of public opinion on an issue than an election?

★ ★

SECTION 2

Interest Groups

★ ★

VOCABULARY

bias	impartial

People form or join interest groups because there is strength in numbers. Although one person may not have much luck convincing the town board to start a waste recycling program, a homeowners' association of 300 members would be able to exert much more influence. The town board members would find it more difficult to oppose 300 voters than to oppose only one. Interest or special-interest groups are also called pressure groups because they try to influence or pressure the government into adopting certain policies or taking specific actions.

Interest groups are an important part of the American democratic process. Public officials are constantly bombarded by the opinions and demands of different interest groups. In fact, they are often pressured by groups that hold conflicting views on an issue. For example, while labor unions might demand an increase in the minimum wage, business groups might urge that it be kept at the current level. Because an interest group usually holds one particular viewpoint, we say it has a **bias**, or one-sided point of view. To be biased is the opposite of being **impartial**—or considering all viewpoints equally.

Interest groups can vary greatly in size and influence. Some may have only a handful of members and a few hundred dollars to spend a year. Others may have several million members and multimillion-dollar budgets. Some large interest groups have a national headquarters and hundreds of regional chapters, and others have a small local organization that meets in a member's living room.

An individual can belong to a number of different interest groups. Perhaps a person is a member of a labor union, the National Association for the Advancement of Colored People (NAACP), and the local Parent-Teacher Association and also contributes to the National Wildlife Federation. The right to belong to interest groups is protected by the First Amendment, which guarantees "the right of the people peaceably to assemble, and to petition the Government for a redress of grievances." Individuals are free to decide whether to belong to any interest groups and to choose which ones to join.

ECONOMIC INTEREST GROUPS Some of the largest and most powerful interest groups in America are those based on economic interests. These include business organizations, professional associations, labor unions, and industrial or trade associations.

The Chamber of Commerce, with more than 5 million members, and the National Association of Manufacturers (NAM), which represents more than 13,000 manufacturing companies, are two of the largest business organization interest groups. Many business organizations represent specific kinds of businesses. These are called industry or trade associations. One of the largest is the Tobacco Institute, which represents cigarette manufacturers. This association is frequently involved in fighting proposed laws to restrict or ban smoking around the country. Other trade associations include the National Association of Printing Ink Manufacturers and the California Redwood Association. There are trade associations for nearly every kind of business in the United States.

Business organizations are interested in shaping the government's policy on economic issues such as free enterprise, imports and tariffs, the minimum wage, new construction, and government contracts for construction and manufacturing. The Aerospace Industries Association of America, for instance, is interested in encouraging the federal government to build rocket ships, space stations, and satellites.

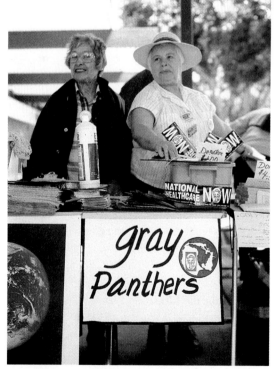

The Gray Panthers is an interest group that works for national health care and other legislation to protect the interests of older Americans.

Muller v. Oregon (1908)

The National Consumers' League was one of the first public interest groups to use the courts to bring about a major change in working conditions. The league was a reform group established in the 1800's to deal with the social problems and political corruption in American cities.

Throughout most of the 1800's, the working conditions of factory and mine workers were disgraceful. Around the turn of the century, reform groups like the league began to demand laws that would regulate working conditions for the women and children in the labor force.

Then, in 1906, Oregon passed a law that limited the hours women could work in factories and laundries to 10 hours a day. One laundry owner named Curt Muller ignored the law. He claimed that it interfered with his right of contract—his right to arrange working conditions with his employees.

Oregon prosecuted Muller, and he in turn took his case—*Muller* v. *Oregon*—to the U.S. Supreme Court. The National Consumers' League hired Louis Brandeis of Boston to defend the Oregon law before the Supreme Court. In his written brief, or argument, to the Court, Brandeis took an unusual tack. Instead of arguing about the law, he presented research showing that long hours of work affected the health and capabilities of working women. For example, he presented studies that showed people make more mistakes and become less productive when they are tired.

This kind of a brief, which uses sociological, historical, and scientific arguments to prove a case, came to be known as a Brandeis brief. Brandeis briefs have been used to argue many far-reaching Supreme Court cases successfully.

In unanimously upholding the Oregon law in *Muller* v. *Oregon*, the Supreme Court ruled that states could protect women workers if they could pro-vide a reasonable justification for doing so. In this case, the Court ruled that women's "unique physical structure and maternal functions" were sufficient justification for protecting them.

The Muller case opened the door for many similar social reforms. It was also the first time an interest group had convinced the Supreme Court to protect the interests of the general public instead of the interests of business tycoons and rich property owners.

Using Your Skills
1. Why did Muller believe the Oregon law was unconstitutional?
2. What role did the National Consumers' League play in *Muller* v. *Oregon*?
3. In what other cases have interest groups succeeded in championing their causes in court?

While business groups represent the owners and operators of businesses, labor unions represent the interests of the employees. The largest labor organization is the AFL-CIO (American Federation of Labor and Congress of Industrial Organizations), an association of over 100 unions whose members do all kinds of work. The International Airline Employees Association and the National Football League Players Association, for example, are both AFL-CIO unions. There are also many independent unions, such as the National Education Association for teachers, that represent workers in different industries.

Labor unions are concerned about wages, working conditions, and benefits such as pensions and medical care. Unions pressure the government to pass laws that will benefit and protect their workers.

Professional associations are made up of members of specific professions. Most doctors belong to the American Medical Association (AMA), and lawyers belong to the American Bar Association (ABA). Accountants, journalists, real estate agents, and many other kinds of professional people also have their own organizations.

OTHER TYPES OF INTEREST GROUPS Many people belong to interest groups that work to promote their particular ethnic group, age group, or sex. These organizations include the NAACP and Congress of Racial Equality (CORE) for blacks, the National Organization for Women (NOW) and National Women's Political Caucus for women, and the American Association of Retired Persons (AARP) and National Council of Senior Citizens for older Americans. Each of these kinds of groups is concerned with issues of particular interest to its members. The AARP, for example, seeks to influence legislation involving Social Security, insurance, and pensions.

Another category of interest groups covers those working for specific causes. For example, the Sierra Club, the National Wildlife Federation, and Greenpeace are all concerned with environmental issues. They might seek to protect an endangered species of plant or animal, work for legislation to set aside wilderness areas, or seek tougher laws to punish polluters.

Thousands of cause-oriented interest groups work on such issues as abortion, gun control, nuclear arms reduction, prayer in school, American Indian rights, and child and animal protection. The American Civil Liberties Union (ACLU) has been involved in several of these causes because its purpose is to defend the Bill of Rights. Sometimes, one or more of these organizations represent opposing sides of a cause or issue. For example, the National Rifle Association (NRA) opposes restrictions on the ownership of firearms, while Handgun Control, Inc., and the National Coalition to Ban Handguns seek a ban on handgun ownership.

All of the interest groups discussed so far are considered private groups, each pursuing issues of interest to its own members. Some groups, however, work to benefit all or most of society. These groups are called public interest groups. One example is Common Cause, an organization of 275,000 members that works to expose corruption and favoritism in government. The League of Women Voters is a nonpartisan group that seeks to promote voting and to educate voters about candidates and issues. The Consumer Federation of America seeks to protect consumers from fraudulent practices and from defective products.

Statisticians Make Things Count

Who will win the next election? How many consumers will buy a certain new product? The people who try to answer questions like these are statisticians. Their job is to collect and analyze numerical information.

Statisticians work for the government gathering and interpreting data about the economy, health trends, and so on. They also work for industries, such as banking and manufacturing. Public opinion research organizations use statisticians to prepare polls.

Statisticians often gather information by taking samples. They cannot question all the adults in this country about their leisure time activities. But statisticians can get a fairly accurate picture by asking a sample of only a few hundred people.

To become a statistician, you should have an aptitude and an interest in mathematics and computers. Although some jobs are available for people with a B.A. degree, many jobs require a graduate degree in mathematics or statistics. If you think you want a career in statistics, you should take business, mathematics, and science courses in high school.

Using Your Skills
1. How does taking a sample help a statistician gather information?
2. Why are statisticians important to government and business?

Techniques Used By Interest Groups

All interest groups want to influence public opinion both to increase their memberships and to convince people of the rightness of their causes. They attempt to do this in a number of ways. Many use direct-mail campaigns to recruit members. By using subscriber or membership mailing lists from magazines or groups with a similar viewpoint, these direct-mail campaigns are targeted to potential new members.

Interest groups also advertise on television or in newspapers and magazines. Perhaps you have seen ads urging you to drink milk or to buy clothing made of wool. These kinds of ads are sponsored by trade associations. Interest groups also seek free coverage in the news media by staging protests or organizing public events. For example, a peace group might stage a demonstration at a local defense plant or a business group might ask for coverage of its annual "Businessperson of the Year" dinner.

In Chapter 7, you learned that political parties use propaganda to promote a particular idea or viewpoint. Interest groups also use propaganda techniques to advance their causes. Here are some common propaganda

TYPES OF PROPAGANDA TECHNIQUES

NAME-CALLING

"Candidate A is the candidate of liberals and Communists."

ENDORSEMENTS

Big-shot movie star says, "I'm voting for Candidate A, and so should you."

GLITTERING GENERALITY

"Candidate A is the one who will bring us peace and prosperity."

THE BANDWAGON

"As the polls show, Candidate A is going to win the election. Vote for A and be a part of this great victory."

JUST PLAIN FOLKS

"My parents were immigrants. I understand the problems of ordinary Americans."

STACKED CARDS

"Candidate A has the best record on the environment."

SYMBOLS

"I pledge allegiance . . ."

This illustration shows various propaganda techniques used by political parties to promote their candidates. How is name-calling different from the other techniques?

techniques that political parties and their candidates and interest groups use:

★ **Endorsements**. Political candidates and interest groups often get famous people such as movie stars, rock stars, or sports figures to endorse, or support, them. In 1989, for example, movie actress Meryl Streep became a spokesperson for an interest group seeking to stop the spraying of apples with Alar, a possible cancer-causing chemical. The idea behind endorsements is that if people admire the person endorsing a product or idea, they will endorse it, too.

★ **Name-calling**. Name-calling is an attempt to turn people against an opponent or an idea by using an unpleasant label or description for that person or idea. In the 1970's, for example, supporters of women's liberation sometimes called men who did not support their ideas "male chauvinist pigs." Name-calling is meant to harm the image of a person, group, or idea. As such, the truth or falseness of the label must always be considered.

★ **Glittering Generality**. A glittering generality is a statement that sounds good but is essentially meaningless. For example, in the 1988 Presidential campaign, George Bush told the voters he wanted a "kinder, gentler America." His Democratic opponent, Michael Dukakis, said the election was about "competence." Both statements were glittering generalities.

★ **Just Plain Folks**. Political campaigns often use countless photographs of candidates wearing hard hats, talking to factory workers, eating pizza or tacos, or even milking cows. The idea of this plain-folks appeal is to make people think that the candidate is just like them, with the same desires and concerns.

★ **The Bandwagon**. Getting on the bandwagon means convincing people that everyone else agrees with the interest group's viewpoint or that everyone is going to vote for a certain candidate. This technique tries to appeal to the desire of many people to be on the winning team.

★ **Stacked Cards**. Card stacking is a technique that presents only one side of an issue by distorting the facts. For example, a group advocating nuclear power might present only facts that would make nuclear power seem safe, omitting any that might indicate safety problems.

★ **Symbols**. Political candidates and interest groups use and misuse symbols when appealing to the public. For example, one candidate for public office might salute the flag at every public event to appear more patriotic than his or her opponent.

SECTION REVIEW

Define the Words

bias   impartial

Check the Facts

1. Identify three kinds of economic interest groups.
2. What is a public interest group?
3. What methods do interest groups use to try to influence public opinion?

Think About the Ideas

4. *Analyze*. Why are some interest groups more influential than others?

SECTION 3

Interest Groups and Public Policy

★ ★

VOCABULARY

lobby   lobbyist

Many people think that special-interest groups are harmful to American democracy because they exert too much influence over political decisions. In reality, interest groups serve a number of useful functions.

The major contribution of interest groups is to bring issues and concerns to the attention of the public, lawmakers, and policymakers. They do this by presenting facts and opinions to support their positions and to counter the arguments of their opponents. For example, much of the current concern about air and water pollution can be traced to information and arguments presented by interest groups.

Another major contribution of interest groups is that they represent the interests and concerns of specific groups of Americans. For example, automobile assembly line workers are represented by a group, the United Auto Workers Union. Although politicians might not listen to the concerns of a single autoworker, they are very likely to listen to a group that represents hundreds of thousands of voters. As a member of an interest group, an individual can thus have a greater influence on the political system.

A third contribution of interest groups is their support of political candidates who favor their interests and goals. Many large groups, such as the American Association of Retired Persons (AARP), have PACs that contribute funds to selected candidates at election time. Some interest groups also rate lawmakers according to how they voted on issues of concern to the group. Such ratings help other voters decide which candidates to support.

Interest groups endorse political candidates who are sympathetic to their aims and are likely to support legislation beneficial to the group.

Lobbies

One of the primary goals of interest groups is to influence public policy. An anti-abortion group wants the government to pass laws outlawing abortion. Railway commuters want the government to operate more trains at lower fares. The NAACP wants the courts to enforce laws against discrimination. Interest groups bring about these kinds of changes and affect public policy by lobbying.

To **lobby** is the attempt to get government officials to support a group's goals. The word dates from the 1830's when it was used to describe how people would wait in the lobbies of statehouses and courthouses to ask politicians for favors. The people who lobby politicians are called **lobbyists**. They are either paid employees or volunteers who work for interest groups. Their job is to persuade government officials to change public policy so that it favors the group's goals or ideas.

Lobbying takes place at the local, state, and federal levels of government. It occurs in all branches of government, but most lobbying is focused on Congress and the state legislatures. Much of a lobbyist's time is spent trying to persuade these lawmakers to reject or enact laws that will affect their interest groups.

Lobbyists must have a good understanding of how the government functions. They must know where to go and whom to see. There are hundreds of departments, offices, and agencies in the federal government and in each state government, but a good lobbyist knows which department to contact about a particular concern. Lobbyists must also be skilled at making contacts with lawmakers, legislative aides, and other government officials. Some lobbyists are former legislators with many contacts in government. Others are lawyers or public relations consultants who specialize in lobbying.

Lobbyists often meet with politicians in an effort to persuade them to support certain policies. Here James Brady (seated) confers with Ohio Representative Chalmers Wylie (left) on gun control legislation.

WHAT LOBBYISTS DO How do lobbyists go about their jobs? Suppose Congress is considering a bill to allow oil exploration on national park lands in Alaska. Lobbyists for business and oil industry groups would promote the bill, and lobbyists for environmental groups would probably oppose it. Each side would research the issue and submit reports, news articles, and statistics favoring its views. The lobbyists might also testify at a House or Senate committee hearing on the bill.

These activities provide lawmakers with a tremendous amount of information. Since Congress deals with about 20,000 bills each year, lobbyists play an important role in making legislators aware of the merits and drawbacks of many bills. In some cases, lobbyists might even submit their own drafts of bills for consideration by lawmakers. Sometimes opposing lobbyists reach a compromise that enables both sides to accomplish their purpose.

Another way that lobbyists try to persuade lawmakers is by arousing public opinion. They often encourage their interest group's members to write or telephone key legislators. If these lawmakers receive enough mail supporting a proposed bill, they may be persuaded to vote for the bill. Yet lawmakers are usually aware of when they are being pressured by a small, but active, interest group rather than by a majority of the public.

The job of the lobbyists does not end once a law is enacted. Their interest groups are also concerned with making sure that laws are carried out, enforced, and stand up in court. For example, if an oil exploration bill is approved, environmental groups are likely to watch the whole operation carefully. They want to make sure that the oil companies observe any provisions aimed at protecting the environment. If not, lobbyists for the environmental groups will lobby various government departments or agencies to see that the law is enforced.

Sometimes lobbyists initiate court actions on behalf of their interest groups. The American Civil Liberties Union has gone to court to defend all kinds of interest groups, including students, police officers, and even Communists. Public Citizen, Inc., a consumer group led by Ralph Nader, has brought suits against various companies for violating consumer protection laws.

REGULATION OF LOBBIES In the past, lobbying was criticized severely because some lobbyists tried to win legislators' votes by providing them with fancy meals and free trips. Some lobbyists also provided large campaign contributions and even used bribery to win votes.

Today, most lobbyists are ethical and professional. Instead of trying to buy votes, they rely on their ability to present the facts and make persuasive arguments to influence public officials. Nevertheless, many people are still critical of lobbyists and their special-interest groups. They feel that some interest groups, because of their power and influence, have an unfair advantage over their opponents. These groups can afford to hire the best lobbyists and to spend a great deal of money trying to promote or defeat legislation. Groups such as the Chamber of Commerce, the National Rifle Association, and the Tobacco Institute can amass enormous PAC funds to spend on the campaigns of legislators who support their causes.

To prevent abuses among lobbyists, Congress passed the Federal Regulation of Lobbying Act in 1946. This law requires lobbyists at the federal level to register themselves and their interest groups and to report all lobby-

PACs: BIGGEST SPENDERS 1987-1988

	AMOUNT CONTRIBUTED
1. National Security Political Action Committee	$10,279,012
2. Democratic Republican Independent Voter Education Committee	8,475,552
3. Realtors Political Action Committee	5,930,618
4. American Medical Association Political Action Committee	5,385,951
5. National Rifle Association Political Victory Fund	4,672,291
6. National Congressional Club	4,140,237
7. Campaign America	4,025,876
8. National Committee to Preserve Social Security Political Action Committee	4,013,264
9. American Citizens for Political Action	3,870,927
10. Association of Trial Lawyers of America Political Action Committee	3,870,741

Source: Federal Election Commission

What are PACs trying to do when they make contributions to election campaigns?

The National Rifle Association, one of the most powerful lobbies in the country, explains its point of view in brochures and other publications.

ing expenditures. The law has not been very effective, however, because it applies only to people whose primary job is lobbying. People who claim that only a small portion of their time is spent lobbying are not required to register. As a result, only about one-fifth to one-quarter of all lobbyists are registered. The law does not provide for any means of enforcement. Most states have similar laws, some of which are more effective than the federal law.

Lobbying is also restricted by federal and state laws that require a waiting period before former officials can become lobbyists. The terms of these laws vary from state to state. A typical law might bar a former state legislator from lobbying the legislature or its committees for one or two years after leaving office. The purpose of these laws is to prevent ex–public officials from taking unfair advantage of their inside knowledge and close friendships with former associates on the behalf of special-interest groups. Unfortunately, these laws have proved inadequate, especially at the federal level. In recent years, for example, the Department of Defense has come under increasing criticism because many military officers retire and seek jobs with defense industries.

Public Opinion Poll

The following questions were asked during the 1988 presidential campaign.

---

1. If the presidential election were being held today, would you vote for the Republican ticket of George Bush and Dan Quayle or for the Democratic ticket of Michael Dukakis and Lloyd Bentsen?

Bush/Quayle	49%
Dukakis/Bentsen	43%
Undecided	8%

2. Do you support (preferred candidate) strongly or only moderately?

Bush	strongly	23%
	moderately	26%
Dukakis	strongly	19%
	moderately	24%
Undecided		8%

3. Is your overall opinion of (candidate) very favorable, mostly favorable, mostly unfavorable, or very unfavorable?

Bush	favorable	57%
	unfavorable	37%
	not sure	6%
Dukakis	favorable	49%
	unfavorable	44%
	not sure	7%

4. If you could vote separately for vice president, which candidate would you vote for—Dan Quayle, the Republican, or Lloyd Bentsen, the Democrat?

Bentsen	53%
Quayle	31%
Not sure	16%

Source: Based on a Gallup Poll, October 1988.

Why were the undecided voters so important when this poll was taken?

SECTION REVIEW

Define the Words
lobby   lobbyist

Check the Facts
1. Identify three functions of interest groups.
2. How do lobbyists try to persuade lawmakers?
3. How do interest groups bring issues and concerns to the attention of the public?

Think About the Ideas
4. *Evaluate.* In what ways do interest groups enjoy an unfair advantage over individual citizens?

CITIZENSHIP SKILLS

How to Distinguish Fact from Opinion

The first step in evaluating messages is to distinguish fact from opinion. Facts are statements that are known to be true or that can be verified. That is, you can prove or disprove a fact.

Opinions, on the other hand, are statements that express feelings, attitudes, or beliefs. You can agree or disagree with an opinion.

Although both facts and opinions are important in making decisions on political issues, it is important to consider them separately. Sometimes opinions are stated so persuasively that they are accepted as facts. However, opinions are not always based on the truth. For this reason, you might wish to check the accuracy of facts before deciding whether you agree or disagree with an opinion.

The language of a political message can help you distinguish facts from opinions. When writers or speakers state facts, they use neutral, impartial language that is free of bias. When they express opinions, they use emotional or subjective language that reveals a point of view.

The excerpt on this page is from President Theodore Roosevelt's message to Congress in 1907 calling for the conservation of America's natural resources. Read the excerpt and answer the questions that follow.

The conservation of our natural resources and their proper use constitute the fundamental problem which underlies almost every other problem of our national life . . .

. . . The land law system which was designed to meet the needs of fertile and well-watered regions of the Middle West has largely broken down when applied to the drier regions of the great plains, the mountains, and much of the Pacific slope, where a farm of 160 acres is inadequate for self support . . . . Three years ago a public-lands commission was appointed to scrutinize the law. . . . .

and recommend a remedy. Their examination specifically showed the existence of a great fraud upon the public domain . . .

The recommendations of the Public-Lands Commission are sound . . . . The Congress has not yet acted upon these recommendations, but they are so just and proper, so essential to our national welfare, that I feel confident, if the Congress will take time to consider them, that they will ultimately be adopted.

Using Your Skills
1. What facts did Roosevelt offer to support his claims about the land law system?
2. Why could you regard the information in the second paragraph as factual? How could you find out if the facts were true?
3. What words let you know that the third paragraph expresses an opinion?

CHAPTER 8 REVIEW

★ ★

MAIN POINTS

★ Public opinion is influenced by personal factors, economic and political conditions, the news media, public officials, and interest groups.

★ Interest groups attempt to influence public opinion by making people aware of issues and by trying to change people's attitudes.

★ Public opinion polls are used to measure public opinion.

★ There are many kinds of interest groups—economic groups, those based on particular personal characteristics, cause-oriented groups, and public interest groups.

★ Interest groups seek to influence public opinion by direct-mail campaigns, news media coverage, and propaganda techniques.

★ Interest groups bring issues and ideas to the public's attention, they represent the interests and concerns of specific groups of Americans, and they support political candidates.

★ Interest groups use lobbyists to advance their interests and goals at all levels and in all branches of government.

★ Lobbyists provide public officials with information and then argue for their interest groups' viewpoints.

★ Lobbying abuses have led to attempts to regulate and restrict lobbying activities.

WORDS IN REVIEW

Choose the word or phrase from the list below that best completes each sentence. Write the missing word(s) on a separate sheet of paper.

4 public opinion   2 interest group
6 mass media   8 pollster
1 bias   5 impartial
7 lobby   3 lobbyist

1. The interest group had a(n) _____ toward one particular candidate because his views were very similar to their own.

2. The homeowners' association could be considered a(n) _____ because members were all concerned with similar issues.

3. The _____ was employed by the oil industry to try to persuade lawmakers to pass laws in their favor.

4. _____ seemed to favor the Republican candidate over the Democratic one.

5. In considering all sides of the issue, the legislator tried to remain _____.

6. Most people look to the _____ as their source of news and information.

7. The group planned to _____ Congressional leaders to get them to change their views on the issue.

8. According to the _____, the results of the survey indicated that public opinion was divided on the issue.

FACTS IN REVIEW

1. What factors can influence public opinion?

2. Why do people form interest groups?

3. Why do some people criticize public opinion polls?

4. Why are interest groups an important part of our democratic system?

5. Identify three cause-oriented interest groups.

CHAPTER 8 REVIEW

* *

6. Identify and explain three propaganda techniques used by interest groups.

7. In what ways do interest groups support political candidates?

8. What skills must a lobbyist have to do his or her job well?

9 What are the main jobs of lobbyists?

10. What were the provisions of the Federal Regulation of Lobbying Act of 1946?

THINKING ABOUT PUBLIC OPINION AND INTEREST GROUPS

1. *Analyze*. What role do you think public opinion polls should play in the political process? Explain.

2. *Evaluate*. Do you think interest groups are a positive or a negative force in politics? Explain your answer.

3. *Assess*. How effective is lobbying as a means of influencing public officials to support a particular cause? Explain.

WRITING ABOUT PUBLIC OPINION

You are a member of an interest group concerned with expanding the amount of land included in the national park system. Your lobbyists will be going to Washington, D.C., in a few weeks to meet with a special Senate subcommittee that is discussing the issue. Your interest group has decided that it needs to gather some additional information about public opinion on this issue. You have been asked to prepare a public opinion questionnaire that will be sent out to gather this information. The poll should contain 20 questions dealing with people's attitudes about the national park system, their use of the park system, and their feelings about expanding the park system. Remember when you are writing the questions that they should not be biased in any way.

INTERPRETING A PUBLIC OPINION POLL

Look at the example of the public opinion poll on page 192. It includes some of the questions in the poll and the percentage of replies for each answer. What conclusions could be drawn from the answers on this poll? What types of questions are included on the poll? Why do you think these particular questions were included? How might some of the questions be rewritten so that they would be "loaded"?

FOCUSING ON YOUR COMMUNITY

Investigate some of the special-interest groups found in your community. How many of these interest groups have local offices with full-time staffs? How many are a local branch of a national organization? How many groups employ full-time lobbyists? Choose one of the interest groups to investigate further. Find out the major issues and concerns of this group. What methods does it use to try to inform the public and to influence public opinion? What activities is it involved in at the local, state, or national level? How effective has it been in changing policy or influencing the public? Share your findings with the class.

UNIT 3 REVIEW

★ ★

ESSAY QUESTIONS

The following questions are based on material in Unit 3. Answer each question with two or three written paragraphs. Be sure to give specific reasons to support your answers.

1. Our two-party system does not fully reflect the many views of the American people. Should we encourage the development of other political parties to represent the interests of particular groups? Why or why not?

2. Critics charge that the American political process discourages some of the brightest and most capable citizens from seeking political office. What factors make running for office so difficult? What might be done to encourage people to enter the political arena?

3. How does the use of television affect what the public knows and thinks about candidates and issues? Should the use of television in political campaigns be restricted in some way? Explain your answer.

CONNECTING CIVICS AND GEOGRAPHY

In choosing candidates, political parties try to have a "balanced ticket." One important way to balance a ticket is through geography. (See the chart below on the left.) Why is it an advantage to have Presidential and Vice Presidential candidates from different regions? Which regions or states have been represented most often in the last three elections? Why might it be important to select candidates from these states?

ANALYZING VISUALS

The line graph shows the percent of eligible voters of different age groups that voted in recent elections. Study the graph and answer the questions.

1. Which age group showed the greatest decline in voting participation?

2. Which age group showed an increase in participation? What factors might explain this increase?

3. Describe the general trend in voter participation since 1972.

CONNECTING CIVICS AND GEOGRAPHY

Presidential Elections, 1980 - 1988

Democratic

Year	President	Vice President
1988	Dukakis (Mass.)	Bentsen (Texas)
1984	Mondale (Minn.)	Ferraro (New York)
1980	Carter (Georgia)	Mondale (Minn.)

Republican

Year	President	Vice President
1988	Bush* (Texas)	Quayle (Indiana)
1984	Reagan* (Calif.)	Bush (Texas)
1980	Reagan* (Calif.)	Bush (Texas)

*Winning ticket

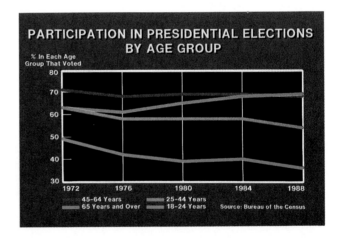

PARTICIPATION IN PRESIDENTIAL ELECTIONS BY AGE GROUP

% In Each Age Group That Voted

45–64 Years   25–44 Years
65 Years and Over   18–24 Years   Source: Bureau of the Census

****

CLOSEUP ON POLITICAL LABELS

What does it mean to be a liberal or a conservative, a moderate, a radical, or a reactionary? These are labels that people use about themselves and others to describe their position on various political issues and policies.

Political labels can be very confusing. It is helpful to think of these labels as describing a spectrum, or line, of political ideas. At one end of this spectrum are reactionaries, who favor a return to earlier, more traditional policies. At the other end are radicals, who favor extreme and sweeping changes in government policies. In between, and moving from reactionary to radical, are conservatives, moderates, and liberals.

Conservatives are generally people who want things to stay the way they are or who accept only slow, modest change. They favor political stability and also oppose government regulation of the economy. In recent years, conservatives have often opposed civil rights reforms and have sought to reinstate prayers in school, to ban abortions, and to curb affirmative action programs. Most conservatives tend to be Republicans.

Liberals are people who believe that government should do more to meet the needs of individual citizens and to protect and extend their rights. They generally support welfare programs, public housing, and affirmative action programs. Most liberals are Democrats or independent voters.

Moderates are people who follow a course between conservatism and liberalism. They may support government action in some areas and reject it in others.

In addition to these labels, the terms "the left" or "left wing" and "the right" or "right wing" are sometimes used in reference to liberals and conservatives, respectively. Moderates may also be referred to as "middle-of-the-road." These terms are based on the custom in the French National Assembly of seating liberals on the left, conservatives on the right, and moderates in the middle.

Each Presidential administration is usually identified with one of these political labels. Franklin D. Roosevelt, a Democrat whose government aid programs helped end the Great Depression, was considered a liberal. Dwight Eisenhower, a Republican, was thought of as a moderate or middle-of-the-roader. Ronald Reagan, a Republican who built up the military and favored a return to more traditional values, was considered a conservative.

1. What is the basic difference between conservatives and liberals?

2. Why are liberals sometimes referred to as left-wing?

3. If you had to put a political label on yourself, what would it be? Why?

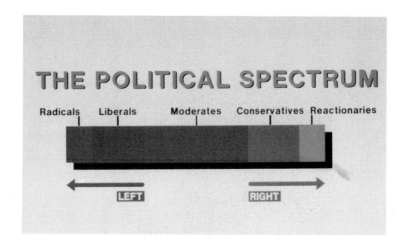

THE POLITICAL SPECTRUM

Radicals Liberals Moderates Conservatives Reactionaries

LEFT RIGHT

The right of the people to be secure in their persons, houses, papers, and effects, against unreasonable searches and seizures, shall not be violated.

—FOURTH AMENDMENT

198

The National Government

Americans do not fear their government.
We know that the Constitution and the Bill of
Rights contain important safeguards against
the abuse of government power. The Fourth
Amendment contributes to this sense of security
by stating that the government must not intrude
in our lives without following procedures
established by law.

* * * * *

Congress

OBJECTIVES

After you have studied this chapter, you will be able to:

★ Describe the qualifications for Senators and Representatives and the various benefits they receive.

★ Explain political party influence within Congress.

★ Identify several types of Congressional committees and explain the work of each.

★ Describe the different powers granted and denied to Congress.

★ Explain the process by which a bill becomes a law and how bills can be killed.

SECTIONS

1 How Congress Is Organized
2 How Congress Works
3 Congressional Powers
4 How a Bill Becomes a Law

INTRODUCTION

On March 4, 1789, the first Congress of the United States met in New York to begin the work of the new government formed by the Constitution. Two hundred years later, in March 1989, members of Congress met to celebrate their bicentennial and to continue the work of governing the nation. The ceremonies, which included poetry, music, and speeches, were a tribute to Congress's special place within our democratic system.

Congress is the most direct expression of American democracy. It is the means by which Americans govern themselves. When Americans express their views on public policy to members of Congress, they become part of the lawmaking process. Their ideas may eventually be incorporated into new laws.

Members of Congress serve as our voice in government. Through them, we have the power to change our nation and our lives.

* *

SECTION 1

How Congress Is Organized

* *

VOCABULARY

bicameral	immunity
gerrymandering	expulsion
constituent	censure
franking privilege	session

As you learned in Chapter 3, one of the major conflicts at the Constitutional Convention in 1787 concerned the way the states would be represented in the new Congress. Delegates from the smaller states wanted each state to have equal representation in Congress. Delegates from larger states wanted representation to be based on population, which would give them a greater voice in government.

The dispute was settled by the Great Compromise, which established a **bicameral**, or two-house, Congress. In the upper house, the Senate, each state would have an equal number of representatives—two. In the lower house, the House of Representatives, each state's representation would be determined by its population.

Although Article I of the Constitution makes some distinctions between the powers of the two houses, the houses are more alike than they are different. Each house is made up of elected members who carry out similar duties and enjoy similar privileges.

Profile of the 102nd Congress

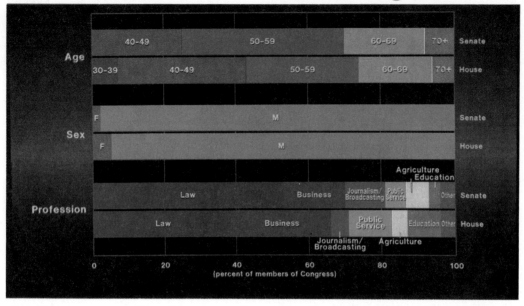

This chart presents a profile of the 102nd Congress according to the age, sex, and professions of its members. Which two professions are most highly represented in this Congress?

The House of Representatives

According to the Constitution, members of the House of Representatives, known as Representatives, must meet only three qualifications: they must be at least 25 years old, they must have been U.S. citizens for at least seven years, and they must live in the states they represent. In practice, however, Representatives usually meet several other qualifications as well. Most Representatives have had successful careers in law or business. Many have also had experience in state and local government or in other forms of public service.

Representatives are elected for two-year terms. Since these terms all begin and end at the same time, it is possible for the House to have an entirely new membership every two years. In reality, however, this never happens. In most elections, at least 90 percent of current House members are reelected. There is no limit to the number of terms a Representative may serve.

The number of Representatives is fixed at 435. The Constitution guarantees each state at least one Representative, but the number of additional Representatives depends on the state's population. Some small states, such as Wyoming and Vermont, have only one Representative. California, the state with the largest population, has 52.

When the Census Bureau takes a count of the population every 10 years, it studies population changes to see whether the number of Representatives for each state needs

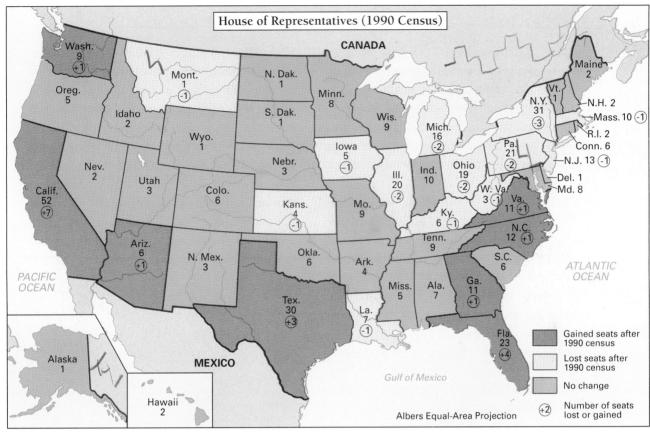

CANADA

Wash. 9 (+1)

Oreg. 5

Idaho 2

Mont. 1 (-1)

N. Dak. 1

Minn. 8

S. Dak. 1

Wis. 9

Mich. 16 (-2)

Maine 2

Vt. 1

N.Y. 31 (-3)

N.H. 2

Mass. 10 (-1)

R.I. 2

Conn. 6

N.J. 13 (-1)

Del. 1

Md. 8

Wyo. 1

Nev. 2

Utah 3

Colo. 6

Nebr. 3

Iowa 5 (-1)

Ill. 20 (-2)

Ind. 10

Ohio 19 (-2)

Pa. 21 (-2)

W. Va. 3 (-1)

Va. 11 (+1)

Calif. 52 (+7)

Ariz. 6 (+1)

N. Mex. 3

Kans. 4 (-1)

Mo. 9

Ky. 6 (-1)

Tenn. 9

N.C. 12 (+1)

S.C. 6

Okla. 6

Ark. 4

Miss. 5

Ala. 7

Ga. 11 (+1)

PACIFIC OCEAN

ATLANTIC OCEAN

Tex. 30 (+3)

La. 7 (-1)

Fla. 23 (+4)

Alaska 1

MEXICO

Gulf of Mexico

Hawaii 2

Albers Equal-Area Projection

Gained seats after 1990 census

Lost seats after 1990 census

No change

(+2) Number of seats lost or gained

This map shows how population changes of the 1990 census affected the number of representatives for each state. Which state lost the greatest number of representatives?

to be adjusted. After the 1990 census, for example, several western states such as Texas and Arizona gained Representatives, while some eastern states lost Representatives.

If a state has only one Representative in Congress, that person represents the entire state. States with more than one Representative are divided into sections, or districts; each of these Congressional districts elects one Representative to Congress.

Congressional districts are created by state legislators, who often try to draw the districts' lines in ways that will benefit them politically. For example, if most of a state's

legislators are Republican, they might draw the lines so that each district has more Republican voters than Democratic ones. Districts created in this way are often oddly shaped.

Dividing a state into odd-shaped districts for political reasons is called **gerrymandering**. Despite many attempts to stop this practice, gerrymandering remains legal under most circumstances. The major restriction is that all Congressional districts within a state must be approximately equal in population. This means that all of the state's Representatives should have about the same number of **constituents**, or people in their districts.

The Senate

The Constitution sets slightly stricter requirements for membership in the Senate. Senators must be at least 30 years old, U.S. citizens for at least nine years, and residents of the states they represent. Most Senators also have a great deal of government experience; many are former members of the House of Representatives.

Senators serve six-year terms, but not every Senator's term begins at the same time. Every two years, one-third of the Senators must run for reelection. As a result, at least two-thirds of the Senate always consists of experienced members. Like Representatives, there is no limit to the number of terms a Senator may serve.

Each state is represented by two Senators. There are, therefore, 100 members of the Senate. Unlike Representatives, Senators do not represent specific districts. Each of a state's Senators is elected by the entire state.

Salary and Benefits

Although members of Congress get to set their own salary, they rarely give themselves a raise. They are afraid of the public's response to such an action. Early in 1989, for example, Congress was considering a salary increase of 51 percent. Protests from angry voters caused the House and the Senate to vote down the raise, but a compromise was reached later that year. The yearly salary of Representatives was raised to $96,600 in 1990 and $120,700 in 1991. Senators now receive $98,400 a year.

In 1989, member of Congress proposed that they receive a large salary increase. In the view of the cartoonist, what happened when taxpayers learned about the plan?

In addition to their salary, members of Congress receive other benefits. They are given free office space, parking, and trips to their home states. They have budgets to pay for assistants, office staff, and supplies. They receive discounts on many services such as medical care, video production, and even haircuts. They are also given a **franking privilege**, the right to send job-related mail without paying postage.

The Constitution grants Senators and Representatives several kinds of **immunity**, or legal protection. For example, members of Congress may not be arrested while doing their jobs, or while traveling between home and work, unless they have committed a very serious crime. They also may not be sued for anything they say or write while carrying out their duties. This immunity allows members of Congress to say and do what they believe is right, without fear of interference from outsiders.

Of course, the guarantee of immunity does not mean that members of Congress are free to break the law. Senators and Representatives are expected to set an example of good, honest behavior for the rest of the country. A member of Congress who acts dishonestly or irresponsibly may face **expulsion**, and be forced to leave Congress. Expulsion requires a two-thirds vote of either house, and is reserved for only the most serious crimes. Less serious offenses may be punished by **censure**, or formal disapproval. Members who are censured must endure the embarrassment of having their misbehavior revealed to the public.

Now, thanks to cable television, Americans can sit at home and watch their representatives in Congress debate a bill, question appointees to public office, or probe the latest political scandal.

Television coverage of the House and Senate has only been available for a few years. "Gavel-to-gavel" (start-to-finish) coverage of daily proceedings began in 1979 for the House and in 1986 for the Senate.

Two cable networks are devoted primarily to broadcasting congressional sessions. The Cable-Satellite Public Affairs Network (C-SPAN) airs House sessions while C-SPAN-II covers the Senate. By tuning in these channels, you can see the government in action.

The Congressional Calendar

The entire House of Representatives is elected every other year, and each "new" Congress is given a number to identify its two-year term. For example, the first Congress met in 1789, and the 101st Congress began meeting in 1989.

Congress carries out its work in two regular time periods, or **sessions**. One session is held each year of the two-year term. In the early years of the Republic, each session of Congress lasted only a few months. Today, however, Congress meets regularly for most of the year. Sessions begin on January 3 and continue until November or December, although they are interrupted by recesses, or vacations.

In addition to regular sessions, Congress may also meet in special sessions. In times of crisis, the President has the power to call Congress into session to deal with pressing problems. Special sessions have been rare in recent times, since Congress is already in session during most of the year.

On some occasions, the House and the Senate may meet together in a joint session of Congress. Little real work can be accomplished at a joint session, so its value is mostly ceremonial. A joint session is held each year when Senators and Representatives gather to hear the President's State of the Union address.

SECTION REVIEW

Define the Words

bicameral	immunity
gerrymandering	expulsion
constituent	censure
franking privilege	session

Check the Facts

1. How many members are in the Senate and in the House of Representatives, and how is the number for each state determined?
2. In addition to their salary, what other benefits and privileges do members of Congress receive?
3. Identify the three types of Congressional sessions.

Think About the Ideas

4. *Analyze.* Why do you think the qualifications for Senators and Representatives differ?
5. *Evaluate.* Do you think the salary of members of Congress should be increased? Why or why not?

Newly elected members of Congress take their oath of office at the opening of a new session.

SECTION 2

How Congress Works

★ ★ ★ ★ ★ ★ ★ ★ ★ ★ ★ ★ ★ ★ ★ ★ ★ ★ ★ ★

VOCABULARY

majority leader	standing committee
minority leader	subcommittee
party whip	select committee
Speaker of the	joint committee
House	conference
president *pro*	committee
tempore	seniority system

Over the years, Congress has found it increasingly difficult to accomplish its work. This difficulty is due partly to the growing complexity of modern life and partly to the size of the two houses. The Senate, which began with 26 members in 1789, has 100 members today. The increase in the House has been even greater—from 65 to 435 members.

Such large groups are not always able to work together smoothly. As a result, the House has developed strict rules to help it conduct its business. These rules specify when bills can be introduced, how long they can be debated, and most other parts of the law-making process.

The Senate also has rules to help it work efficiently. Because it is much smaller, however, it can operate on a more informal basis. Few of the rules by which the House and Senate operate are written into the Constitution. But these regulations have become a permanent part of how our government works.

Congressional Leadership

Much of what happens in Congress is decided by the Democratic and Republican leaders of each house. Within the Senate and the House of Representatives, the party to which more than half the members belong is called the majority party. The other party is called the minority party.

At the beginning of each Congressional term, the members of each party meet to choose new leaders. Among the leaders chosen are floor leaders and party whips.

Floor leaders try to make sure that the laws passed by Congress are in the best interests of their own political party. Each house of Congress has two floor leaders—a Democrat and a Republican. The majority party's floor leader is called the **majority leader**; the minority party's floor leader is called the **minority leader**.

Each floor leader is assisted by a **party whip**. The whip's job is to keep track of how party members vote and to persuade all members of his or her party to vote together on issues.

In addition to these party leaders, each house also has one overall leader. In the House of Representatives, this leader is the **Speaker of the House**. A member of the majority party, the Speaker is usually an experienced, respected member of the House. The Speaker is in charge of nearly everything that occurs while the House is in session, including deciding who may speak, when a vote may take place, and how each proposed law will be handled.

According to the Constitution, the official leader and president of the Senate is the Vice President of the United States. The Vice President, however, takes no part in the legislative process of the Senate. Moreover, the Vice President may only vote when there is a tie.

Thomas S. Foley, a Democrat from the state of Washington, became Speaker of the House in 1989. The speaker controls most of the activities of the House of Representatives.

Because of other duties, the Vice President is rarely present while the Senate is in session. Day-to-day leadership of the Senate is handled by a **president *pro tempore***, or president "for the time being." Like the Speaker of the House, the president *pro tempore* is a respected and experienced member of the majority party.

Government by Committee

Each house of Congress must consider thousands of bills, or proposed laws, in the course of a session. These bills cover hundreds of complex topics, from nuclear energy to corporate finance. It would be impossible for each member of Congress to study the facts about every bill and decide whether or not it would make a good law.

As a result, each house of Congress has developed a system of committees to handle most of the legislative work. Every new bill goes to a committee, where it is researched, discussed, and often revised. The committee then decides whether the full House or Sen-

ate should vote on the bill. This committee system makes it possible for Congress to handle hundreds of bills at one time.

There are three types of committees in Congress: standing committees, select committees, and joint committees. A **standing committee** is a permanent committee that specializes in a particular topic. For example, both the Senate and the House have standing committees to deal with agriculture, commerce, the courts, and veterans' affairs. When a bill having to do with any of these topics is introduced, it is sent immediately to the appropriate committee.

Standing committees are divided into **subcommittees**, smaller groups that handle more specialized problems. In the House, for example, the Banking, Finance, and Urban Affairs Committee has subcommittees to deal with each of those three areas.

Both the Senate and the House sometimes form temporary committees to deal with issues that need special attention. These **select committees** meet for a few months or perhaps a few years, until they complete their assigned task.

Occasionally, the Senate and the House form **joint committees**, which include members of both houses. Like select committees, joint committees usually meet for a limited period of time to consider specific issues. A special type of joint committee is the **conference committee**, which helps the House and the Senate agree on the details of a proposed law. You will learn more about conference committees later in the chapter.

CONGRESSIONAL COMMITTEES

HOUSE OF REPRESENTATIVES	SENATE
Standing Committees	
Agriculture	Agriculture, Nutrition, and Forestry
Appropriations	Appropriations
Armed Services	Armed Services
Banking, Finance, and Urban Affairs	Banking, Housing, and Urban Affairs
Budget	Budget
District of Columbia	Commerce, Science, and Transportation
Education and Labor	Energy and Natural Resources
Energy and Commerce	Environment and Public Works
Foreign Affairs	Finance
Government Operations	Foreign Relations
House Administration	Governmental Affairs
Interior and Insular Affairs	Judiciary
Judiciary	Labor and Human Resources
Merchant Marine and Fisheries	Rules and Administration
Post Office and Civil Service	Small Business
Public Works and Transportation	Veterans' Affairs
Rules	
Science, Space, and Technology	
Small Business	
Standards of Official Conduct	
Veterans' Affairs	
Ways and Means	
Select Committees (as of April 1, 1988)	
Aging	Aging
Children, Youth, and Families	Ethics
Hunger	Indian Affairs
Intelligence	Intelligence
Narcotics Abuse and Control	Secret Military Assistance to Iran and the Nicaraguan Opposition
Joint Committees	
	Economic
	Library
	Printing
	Taxation

How are standing committees different from select and joint committees?

Committee Membership

Most members of Congress have strong preferences about which committees they would like to serve on. Sometimes, these preferences have to do with personal interests and experience. Sometimes members of Congress may want to join a particular committee because its work could benefit their home state. A Senator from an oil-producing state, for example, might be interested in joining the Energy and Natural Resources Committee.

In general, certain committees are considered more desirable than others. A Senator who belongs to the Foreign Relations Committee, for example, is likely to have an influence on international affairs. In contrast, a Senator who serves on the Human Resources Committee—which selects and oversees government employees—is not likely to accumulate much fame or power.

Committee membership is controlled entirely by the leaders of the political parties. By tradition, the chairperson of each committee is almost always a member of the majority party. Each chairperson is a powerful leader who controls the committee's activities.

The majority party is also allowed to select more than half of the committee members. For example, if 60 percent of House members are Democrats, 60 percent of each House committee will be Democratic as well. As a result, the majority party has a great deal of control over what takes place in each committee as well as in each house of Congress.

Party leaders nearly always make committee assignments according to the **seniority system**. In this system, the most desirable committee assignments are given to the Senators and Representatives who have served the longest in Congress. Moreover, within each committee, the member with the longest record of service is almost always made chairperson. Many people—especially younger members of Congress—feel that the seniority system is unfair. But the most influential Representatives and Senators, who earned their status through seniority, are unwilling to reduce their own authority by changing the system.

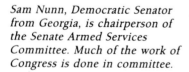

Sam Nunn, Democratic Senator from Georgia, is chairperson of the Senate Armed Services Committee. Much of the work of Congress is done in committee.

The President's budget proposal goes to the House and Senate Budget Committees for review. William Gray of Pennsylvania, right, chaired the House committee from 1984 to 1988.

★ ★

SECTION 3

Congressional Powers

★ ★

VOCABULARY

expressed powers   appropriations

impeach

SECTION REVIEW

Define the Words

majority leader
minority leader
party whip
Speaker of the House
president *pro
  tempore*

standing committee
subcommittee
select committee
joint committee
conference committee
seniority system

Check the Facts

1. How do political parties influence the legislative work of Congress?
2. Identify three types of Congressional committees.
3. What rules and traditions govern the assignment of members of Congress to committees?

Think About the Ideas

4. *Evaluate.* Do you think that government by committee makes the role of individual members of Congress less important? Why or why not?

The writers of the Constitution believed strongly in the principle of limited government. As a result, they placed clear limits on the powers of Congress. These restrictions determine what Congress and each of its houses may or may not do. You have already learned about Congressional powers and their limits in Chapter 3.

Expressed and Implied Powers

Expressed powers, also known as delegated powers, are one type of Congressional power. Expressed powers are those which are listed specifically in Article I of the Constitution. Among these are the power to collect taxes, to borrow money, to regulate foreign and interstate commerce, to set up a postal system, to maintain armed services, to declare war, and to regulate immigration and naturalization.

As you learned in Chapter 3, implied powers are those powers which are not stated explicitly in the Constitution. The implied powers of Congress come from the Necessary

Margaret Chase Smith Takes on McCarthy

The year was 1950. The United States and the Soviet Union were deeply involved in the "Cold War." At home, Americans were bombarded with newspaper headlines about Communist spies trying to infiltrate the government.

That same year, U.S. Senator Joseph R. McCarthy, a Wisconsin Republican, began making headlines for himself. He was accusing government workers, writers, actors, and other prominent Americans of being Communists and traitors. Although he had no proof, his accusations destroyed the careers and reputations of hundreds of people. But few people spoke out against McCarthy for fear of being called Communists and traitors themselves.

Margaret Chase Smith, a Republican from Maine, was elected to the Senate in 1948. As a newcomer and the only woman in the Senate, she had very little power. Although upset by McCarthy's accusations, Smith waited for her more senior colleagues to reprimand him. But when they remained silent, she decided to act. In her first important Senate speech, Smith criticized her fellow Senators for allowing the Senate to become "a forum for hate and character assassination." She reminded them that freedom of speech included the right to hold unpopular beliefs.

Smith's "declaration of conscience" speech cost her a great deal. Over the next four years, she and McCarthy clashed several times and McCarthy supporters made her life as a Senator difficult. Margaret Chase Smith weathered the storm of McCarthyism, however, and she went on to a long, distinguished career in the Senate.

Using Your Skills

1. Why was McCarthy so successful in his anti-Communist campaign?
2. Who had a better understanding of democratic principles, Smith or McCarthy? Why?

and Proper Clause, often called the elastic clause. That is because it allows Congress to stretch its power in order to carry out its expressed powers.

For example, one expressed power of Congress is to maintain an army and navy.

Using its implied powers, Congress has expanded this expressed power and has built a huge military network, including service academies and intelligence-gathering organizations in addition to the Army, Navy, Air Force, and Marines.

Additional Powers

The Constitution also grants Congress a number of nonlegislative powers. These enable the government to operate more effectively and help Congress serve as a check on the other branches of government. One such power, the power to propose amendments to the Constitution, was discussed in Chapter 4.

Congress also has the power to investigate. Most Congressional hearings and fact-finding commissions are part of the lawmaking process. Congress needs to gather information to use in drafting and evaluating legislation. But Congress can also use its investigative powers in another way. It can review the activities of the executive branch to find out whether the government is administering the laws efficiently and as intended by Congress.

One of Congress's most important nonlegislative powers is the power to **impeach**—to accuse government officials of wrongdoing, put them on trial and, if necessary, remove them from office. Any government official—including the President, the Vice President, or a federal judge—can be impeached if suspected of committing a serious crime.

The impeachment process begins in the House of Representatives, where a list of charges is drawn up against the accused official. If a majority of the House members vote to accept these charges, the Senate then has the power to act as a jury and decide the official's guilt or innocence. A two-thirds vote in the Senate is necessary to convict and to remove a person from office.

SPECIAL POWERS OF EACH HOUSE The Constitution has reserved special powers for each house of Congress. One of the House of Representatives' special powers, the power to begin impeachment proceedings, has just been discussed. The House also has the power to choose the President if no candidate wins a majority in the Electoral College. This has only happened twice—after the elections of 1800 and 1824.

One of the House's most important special powers is to introduce tax bills and **appropriations** bills, bills that involve the spending of money. The Senate votes on money bills, but all such bills must start in the House. For this reason, the political party that controls the House also has a great deal of control over the nation's purse strings.

The special powers of the Senate include acting as the jury in an impeachment trial and

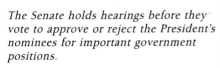

The Senate holds hearings before they vote to approve or reject the President's nominees for important government positions.

ratifying treaties with other nations. Although the President may sign a treaty, it is not binding unless it is ratified by a two-thirds vote in the Senate.

The Senate also has the power to approve or reject the President's appointments of certain high government officials. The Senate usually accepts the President's choice, but there have been several notable exceptions. In 1989, for example, the Senate refused to approve President Bush's appointment of John Tower as Secretary of Defense. The Senate expressed doubts about Tower's character and his ability to handle the job.

THE POWERS OF CONGRESS

Expressed Powers

Collect taxes and borrow money
Regulate foreign and interstate commerce
Coin money and regulate its value
Create federal courts
Regulate immigration and naturalization
Exercise authority over the District of Columbia
Set up a postal system
Declare war
Raise and support an army and navy
Organize the militia

Implied Powers

Make all laws "necessary and proper" for carrying out its expressed powers

Nonlegislative Powers

Ratify treaties (Senate)
Approve Presidential appointments (Senate)
Propose amendments to the Constitution
Bring impeachment charges against federal officials (House)
Try impeachment cases (Senate)
Investigate

Limits to Congressional Power

As you may remember, the Constitution includes some clear statements about what Congress may *not* do. According to Article I, Congress is not permitted to favor one state over another, to tax interstate commerce, or to tax exports.

Article I also forbids Congress from enacting laws that would interfere with the legal rights of individuals. Congress may not pass bills of attainder and *ex post facto* laws or suspend the writ of *habeas corpus*. These important legal rights will be discussed in Chapter 16.

The Constitution also reserves many powers for the states. These powers, such as the right to make marriage and divorce laws, cannot be interfered with by Congress. Certain powers are also denied to Congress by the Bill of Rights and by other amendments. These were discussed in Chapter 4.

Additional restrictions on Congressional power come from the Constitution's system of checks and balances. As you will see later in this chapter, the President has the power to veto a bill passed by Congress. The Supreme Court can also declare a law to be unconstitutional. This will be discussed in Chapter 12.

Which kind of Congressional power is the ratification of treaties?

A final restriction on the power of Congress is a result of economics. Nearly every law requires the government to spend a certain amount of money. Some government programs, such as Social Security, cost billions of dollars. While the government's budget is huge, it is still limited. Therefore, Congress cannot pass every law it might like to pass, simply because the money is not available. The power of Congress is limited by the need to set priorities and to consider what laws and programs the government can best afford.

SECTION REVIEW

Define the Words
expressed powers   appropriations
impeach

Check the Facts
1. Name three kinds of powers given to Congress by the Constitution.
2. Identify three powers reserved to the House and three reserved to the Senate.
3. Identify three powers denied to Congress by the Constitution.

Think About the Ideas
4. *Analyze.* Why do you think the power of impeachment was divided as it was between the House and the Senate?

SECTION 4

How a Bill Becomes a Law

* *

VOCABULARY
pigeonhole   standing vote
filibuster   roll-call vote
cloture   pocket veto
voice vote

Each year, Congress considers thousands of bills. Of these, only a few hundred become laws. The rest are killed by congressional committees, by negative votes in one or both houses of Congress, or by Presidential vetoes. The process by which a bill becomes a law is complicated and may require a great deal of effort.

Introducing a Bill

Every bill starts with an idea. Some of these ideas come from members of Congress. Some are suggested by citizens who write to their representatives. Many ideas come from lobbyists representing various interest groups. Others come from the President or from officials in the executive branch. To be considered by Congress, however, ideas for bills must be sponsored by a Senator or Representative.

Letters from constituents keep the members of Congress informed about the way people in their district feel about various issues.

A member of Congress who wants to sponsor a bill has to draft it, or put the idea in written form. The actual job of drafting a bill is usually done by the Representative's or Senator's staff.

A Senator introduces a bill by making a formal announcement in the Senate. In the House, a Representative introduces a bill by dropping it into the "hopper," a box used specifically for this purpose. The bill then receives a number. A House bill might be called HR 1266.

After a bill is introduced, it is sent to the standing committee that is concerned with the subject of the bill. For example, a bill dealing with airline safety would probably be sent to the Commerce, Science, and Transportation Committee in the Senate, or the Public Works and Transportation Committee in the House.

The Work of Committees

A committee has several options when it receives a bill. If the committee members dislike the bill, they can "kill," or reject it immediately, or they can **pigeonhole** it—set it aside without even considering it. This is what happens to most bills in committee.

Suppose, however, that most committee members like the bill. The committee might decide to keep the bill as it is, or it might decide to make some changes. It might even decide to throw out the bill and write a new one dealing with the same subject.

At this point, the bill would be passed to a subcommittee for further work and study. By law, the subcommittee must hold public hearings on the bill in which people affected by the bill can express their opinions about it. These people have an opportunity to present arguments in support of or against the bill.

Based on information from hearings and from other research, the subcommittee might make other changes in the bill. When the subcommittee has finished its work, the bill is returned to the full committee. The full committee may make additional changes before voting on the bill. If a majority of the committee votes to approve the bill, it is sent to the full Senate or House for consideration.

Debating a Bill

Because the House of Representatives has many members and a great deal of work to do, it can only devote a small amount of time to any one bill. The Rules Committee of the House helps to schedule the consideration of bills. This committee can decide when a bill will be debated and for how long. It can even kill a bill by refusing to give it time for debates.

The rules for debate in the House are fairly complicated. In some cases, the House speeds up the debate process by meeting as a "Committee of the Whole," a special gathering of all House members. The rules for debate within a committee are more informal, so debates can proceed more quickly and easily.

In the Senate, the debates are freer. For one thing, Senators are allowed to speak for an unlimited amount of time. This means that one or more Senators may kill a bill by talking indefinitely, refusing to stop until the bill is withdrawn by its sponsor. This tactic is known as a **filibuster**.

A filibuster can be ended by a vote for **cloture**, which requires a three-fifths vote of the Senate. Cloture limits a Senator to debate for no more than one hour. Cloture votes are rare, however, and a filibuster—or even the threat of one—is often an effective way to kill a bill.

Voting and Final Revisions

After a bill has been debated, it is brought to a vote. Voting is done in one of three ways. The simplest is a **voice vote**, in which everyone who supports a bill is asked to say "yea," and those opposed say "nay." A voice vote is usually used for bills that are clearly popular or unpopular.

A more exact method of voting is the **standing vote**. In this type of vote members who support a bill are asked to stand. Those standing are counted. Then members who oppose the bill are asked to stand and be counted.

A third method is the **roll-call vote**. In a roll-call vote, each member's name is called individually and he or she is asked to vote "yea," "nay," or "present." (A vote of "present" means "no opinion.") In a roll-call every person's vote is a matter of public record, so constituents can find out how their representatives in Congress have voted on an issue. The fact that a roll-call vote is a matter of public record may have an effect on the way a Senator or Representative votes.

Often, different versions of the same bill are passed by the House and the Senate. For example, the House version of a bill on airline safety might require aircraft to be replaced after 20 years. The Senate version, on the other hand, might specify 25 years. When two versions of the same bill are passed, the conflicting bills are sent to a conference committee made up of members from both houses. The conference committee works to reach a compromise and write a revised bill that will satisfy both houses. When its work is done, the conference committee sends the revised bill to the House and Senate for another vote. Unless both houses pass the same version of a bill, it cannot become a law.

When members of the House of Representatives cast their votes, the results are shown on a huge electronic display board behind the speaker's chair.

Signing the Bill

After a bill has been passed by both houses of Congress, it is sent to the President. If the President approves of the bill and signs it, the bill becomes a law. However, the President may also decide to veto the bill. Many bills survive months of work and debate in Congress, only to be killed by a Presidential veto.

A President may also choose to do nothing about a bill sent from Congress. If the President lets 10 days pass without signing a bill, and Congress is in session, the bill becomes a law without the President's signature. If Congress is not in session, the bill is considered dead after the 10 days. Killing a bill in this way is called a **pocket veto**.

Presidents sometimes use the pocket veto for political reasons. The President may want to veto a particular bill but know that the veto would be unpopular with the public. In that case, the President might prefer to let the bill die quietly.

If a bill is vetoed by the President, Congress has one last chance to save the bill. It can override the President's veto by a two-thirds vote in each house. Only the most popular bills can be rescued in this way, however. In order to keep a good relationship with the President, many members of Congress prefer not to challenge a veto—especially if the President is a member of their own party.

The President has the power to veto bills that have been passed by Congress. Here, President Reagan signs his veto of the National Defense Authorization Act.

SECTION REVIEW

Define the Words

pigeonhole   standing vote
filibuster   roll-call vote
cloture   pocket veto
voice vote

Check the Facts
1. Name three ways a standing committee can act when it receives a bill.
2. Identify three ways in which a bill can be killed in the House or the Senate.
3. Identify two ways in which a President can allow a bill to become law, and two ways in which a President can veto a bill.

Think About the Ideas
4. *Evaluate.* Do you think the process of passing a law should be made easier? Why or why not?

HOW A BILL BECOMES A LAW

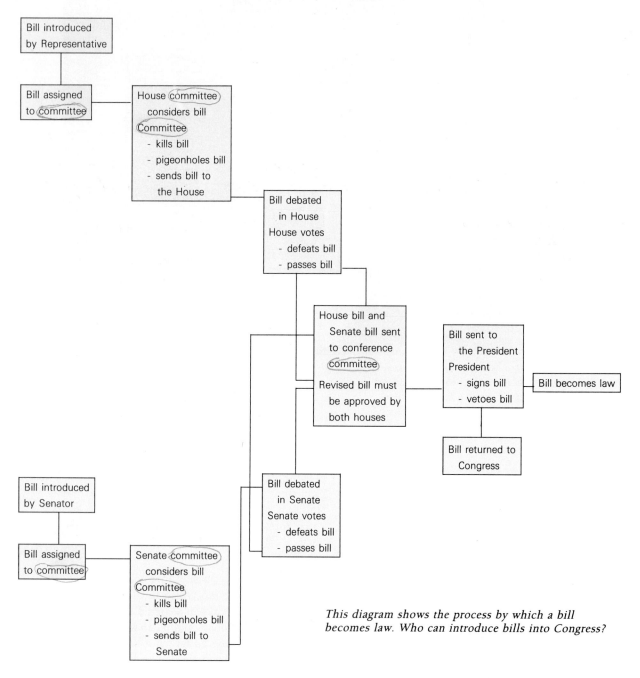

This diagram shows the process by which a bill becomes law. Who can introduce bills into Congress?

CITIZENSHIP SKILLS

How to Write to Your Representative

If you need help in dealing with a federal agency or getting information about the government, or if you want to voice your opinion about an issue, you can write to your U.S. Representative or your Senators. Our members of Congress depend heavily on their mail to find out how their constituents feel about specific issues.

If you do not know the name of your Senators or your Representative, just call your local library or county election bureau to get this information. You can also look up the names in the *Congressional Directory*, a book containing detailed information about Congress, its committees, and its members. This book is found in almost every library.

When you write your letter, here are some suggestions to follow:

★ Address the member of Congress as "The Honorable" (Name) on the envelope and inside and use the person's title (Representative or Senator) in the salutation.

★ A letter to your Representative should be addressed to the Longworth House Office Building, Washington, D.C., 20515. Letters to U.S. Senators should be addressed to the Dirksen Senate Office Building, Washington, D.C., 20510.

★ If you are writing to express an opinion about an issue, be courteous and stick to a single subject per letter.

★ If you are writing for help with a problem, explain the problem as clearly as possible and enclose photocopies of any documents that help prove your case.

★ Be sure to include your return address on the letter.

Using Your Skills
1. What two kinds of letters do members of Congress receive most frequently from their constituents?
2. Name an issue that you would like to write to your Congressional representatives about.

Here is a sample letter:

104 Michigan Avenue
Poplar Bluff, Mo.
February 15, 1989

The Honorable Mark Berger
Longworth House Office
 Building
Washington, D.C. 20515

Dear Representative Berger:

As you know, there is a bill pending in Congress to fund the building of a new veterans' hospital in our city. I am writing to urge you to support this bill.

The disabled veterans in our area have to travel a great distance to go to the nearest veterans' hospital. It is very inconvenient and time-consuming for the veterans and their families to have to travel so far to get medical care. In addition, a new hospital in our city would create many new jobs and help our economy.

Please let me know your position on this issue.

Sincerely,

Julia Imhoff

CHAPTER 9 REVIEW

★ ★

MAIN POINTS

★ Congress is a bicameral legislature. In the Senate, each state is represented by two Senators. In the House of Representatives, each state is represented in proportion to its population.

★ In addition to their salary, members of Congress receive other benefits such as the franking privilege and certain legal protections.

★ Power in Congress is tightly controlled by the two political parties. Party leaders influence the selection of Congressional leaders.

★ Most of the legislative process is accomplished by committees. Committees can kill, approve, pigeonhole, revise, or rewrite bills.

★ There are standing committees, select committees, joint committees, and conference committees in Congress.

★ Congress is given expressed powers and implied powers by the Constitution. A few special powers are reserved for each house.

★ The Constitution and its amendments also specifically deny certain powers to Congress, such as the power to suspend the writ of *habeas corpus*.

★ For a bill to become a law, it must be introduced in both houses of Congress, approved by committees, debated and voted on by each house, and signed by the President.

WORDS IN REVIEW

Choose the word or phrase from the list below that best completes each sentence. Write the missing words on a separate sheet of paper.

bicameral   censure
select committee   conference committee
seniority system   impeach
appropriations   pigeonhole
filibuster   pocket veto

1. The _____ met for only a few months to deal with the issue of Congressional ethics.

2. By not acting on the bill for 10 days, the President was using his _____.

3. The Congressional committee decided to _____ the bill when they set it aside without consideration.

4. The U.S. Congress is a _____ legislature consisting of two houses.

5. Only rarely have the House and Senate used their power to _____ government officials and remove them from office.

6. Without a three-fifths vote, the Senate was unable to stop the Senator's _____.

7. After the House and Senate passed their versions of the new bill, the bill was sent to a _____ for revision.

8. The Senators voted to _____ their colleague for conduct unbecoming a Senator.

9. All _____ bills, those involving the spending of money, must start in the House of Representatives.

10. Congressional committee posts are generally filled according to the _____.

CHAPTER 9 REVIEW

* *

FACTS IN REVIEW

1. What qualifications are required by the Constitution to be a Representative and a Senator?

2. What happens in the House of Representatives after the Census Bureau has counted the population?

3. Describe the responsibilities of floor leaders and party whips.

4. Why is most of the work in Congress done by committees?

5. Explain the difference between standing committees and select committees.

6. Describe three special powers granted to Congress by the Constitution.

7. Explain the difference between expressed and implied powers.

8. How are bills introduced in the Senate and in the House of Representatives?

9. How can the House of Representatives speed the process of debate?

10. Identify three methods of voting on bills in the House and Senate.

THINKING ABOUT CONGRESS

1. *Analyze.* Why do you think the Constitution did not include other qualifications for members of Congress?

2. *Evaluate.* Do you think Congress has enough power to assume its responsibilities and accomplish its work? Explain.

3. *Evaluate.* Do you think the people should play a greater role in making the laws that govern them? Why or why not?

WRITING ABOUT HOW A BILL BECOMES A LAW

Your neighbor is an immigrant from Central America who is preparing to become a naturalized American citizen. One of the things she wants to understand is how a bill becomes a law in Congress. She asks you to help her learn the different steps in the lawmaking process in both the House of Representatives and the Senate. You decide that the easiest way to explain the process is to prepare a simple outline showing the various steps taken in each house of Congress. Prepare this outline for your neighbor. Make the steps as clear and simple as possible.

INTERPRETING A FLOW CHART OF HOW A BILL BECOMES A LAW

Look at the chart of how a bill becomes a law on page 220. How does this flow chart differ from other types of charts and tables? How many steps are shown on this flow chart? At how many of the steps is more than one action possible? How often does the process flow in more than one direction? What is the advantage of using a flow chart?

FOCUSING ON YOUR COMMUNITY

One of the main responsibilities of members of Congress is to represent the interests of their constituents. Find out about an important issue in your community or state that has been the subject of Congressional debate in the last year. Find out what your Representatives' and Senators' stands were on this issue and how they voted on any related bills in Congress.

CHAPTER 10

★ ★

The Presidency

OBJECTIVES

After you have studied this chapter, you will be able to:

★ Explain the qualifications for the offices of President and Vice President.
★ Identify the President's primary duties.
★ Describe the President's roles and responsibilities and the limits on Presidential power.
★ Explain the purpose of the Executive Office of the President.
★ Identify and describe the functions of three offices within the Executive Office of the President.

SECTIONS

1 The President and Vice President
2 The President's Major Roles
3 The President's Other Roles
4 The Executive Office

The Constitution says very little about what a President is permitted or expected to do. As a result, the nation's first President, George Washington, established many traditions that have become part of the Presidency. Every President since Washington has followed and built upon these traditions, expanding and sharpening the President's role within the government.

One of the most important traditions established by Washington was the expansion of the Presidency into a team effort. Washington invited several of the most capable leaders of his time—among them, Thomas Jefferson and Alexander Hamilton—to help him govern the nation. This group, which became known as the President's Cabinet, advises and assists the President.

Over the years, Presidents have brought many additional individuals and agencies into the government. Today, some 3 million government employees carry out the duties of the executive branch. Although these positions are not called for in the Constitution, it would be difficult for the President to lead the nation without them.

★ ★

SECTION 1

The President and Vice President

★ ★

The Presidency is the most important office in America and one of the most important in the world. As head of the executive branch of government, the President must make decisions that will affect the lives of all Americans.

The President

The Constitution lists only three requirements to become President of the United States. The President must be a native-born (not naturalized) citizen of this country. He or she must be at least 35 years old and must have lived in the United States for at least 14 years. In theory, anyone who meets these qualifications can become President.

In practice, however, the requirements for becoming President are more complex. Almost all of our Presidents have shared similar characteristics. Every President in American history has been a white male. All but one have been Protestant, and many have been of British ancestry. Most, but not all, attended college, and many began their careers as lawyers.

It is only in the past few decades that the Presidency has become a possibility for a wider range of Americans. John F. Kennedy, a Catholic, was elected President in 1960.

The White House serves as both the residence and the office of the President. President Bush shows a group of visitors around the state floor of the White House.

In 1984, the Democratic Party nominated Geraldine Ferraro as its first female Vice Presidential candidate. Four years later, Jesse Jackson, a black man, ran a close second in the race to become the Democratic candidate for President.

SALARY AND BENEFITS The President receives a salary of $200,000 per year, plus another $50,000 per year for expenses and up to $100,000 per year for travel. The President's salary is fixed by Congress and cannot be changed during the President's term.

In addition, the President and his or her family receive free lodging in the White House. They have free use of Camp David, a mountain estate in Maryland. They receive the finest possible medical care and personal protection. They also have hundreds of assistants to help them with their public and per-

sonal activities. And, of course, the President enjoys the power, prestige, and respect that come with the office.

ELECTION AND TERMS OF OFFICE Presidential elections are held every four years. You have already learned much about the Presidential election process—how Presidential candidates are nominated and about the role of the Electoral College.

The Presidential election process—like the Presidency itself—depends heavily on tradition. The political parties are not required by law to nominate Presidential candidates. Nor are members of the Electoral College required by law to select either party's candidate. But these traditions have been with us for so long that they have almost taken on the force of law.

Sometimes long established traditions are turned into law. For example, the Constitution originally placed no limit on the number of terms a President could serve. George Washington, who felt that eight years was enough for any President, stepped down after two four-year terms. Following Washington's example, no President served more than two terms until 1940, when President Franklin D. Roosevelt was elected to a third term. In 1944, Roosevelt was elected to a fourth term.

After Roosevelt's death, Congress proposed a Constitutional amendment that would prevent any President from breaking the two-term tradition again. The Twenty-second Amendment, passed in 1951, limits each President to two terms in office.

The Vice President

The Vice President is the only other member of the executive branch mentioned in the Constitution. Article II says that if the President dies or leaves office, the Vice President automatically takes on all the powers of the President. For this reason, the qualifications for the Vice Presidency are the same as those for the Presidency.

As you may remember from Chapter 9, the Vice President serves as president of the Senate. Although the Constitution assigns the Vice President no other official duties, many Presidents have given their Vice Presidents major responsibilities. Most recent Vice Presidents have taken part in Cabinet meetings and have helped make important government decisions.

Vice President Lyndon Johnson became President when John F. Kennedy was assassinated in 1963. Here he is taking the oath of office aboard the Presidential plane, Air Force One.

SALARY AND BENEFITS The Vice President earns a salary of $125,000 per year, plus $10,000 per year for expenses. The Vice President also receives many of the same benefits as the President, including a free residence, a large staff, and a variety of personal services.

ELECTION AND TERMS OF OFFICE The procedure for electing the Vice President has changed since the Constitution was written. Originally, members of the Electoral College voted for two candidates for President. The candidate who received a majority of electoral votes became President, and the candidate who came in second became Vice President.

This procedure caused problems. With more than one person from each political party competing for the Presidency, it was difficult for any candidate to win a majority of the electors' votes. The problem was solved by the adoption of the Twelfth Amendment in 1804. This amendment allowed the Electoral College to vote separately for President and Vice President.

Although there is no limit to the number of four-year terms a Vice President can serve, no Vice President has ever served more than two terms.

Presidential Succession

In 1841, William Henry Harrison became the first President to die in office. His death raised many questions. While the Constitution says that the Vice President should assume the "powers and duties" of the Presidency, no one was sure what that meant. Should the Vice President remain Vice President while doing the President's job? Should the Vice President become President? Should a special election be called to elect a new President?

The matter was settled by Vice President John Tyler. He declared himself to be the new President and served out the remainder of Harrison's term. Since Tyler's time, eight other Vice Presidents have taken over the Presidency following the death or resignation of a President.

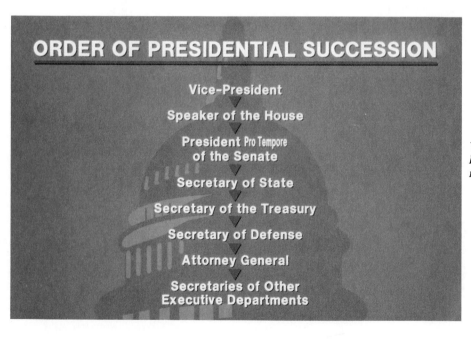

ORDER OF PRESIDENTIAL SUCCESSION

Vice-President

Speaker of the House

President Pro Tempore of the Senate

Secretary of State

Secretary of the Treasury

Secretary of Defense

Attorney General

Secretaries of Other Executive Departments

Why is an order of Presidential succession necessary?

Congress eventually decided that the selection of a President was too important to be left to tradition. In 1947, Congress passed the Presidential Succession Act, which indicates the line of succession after the Vice President. According to this law, if both the President and Vice President die or leave office, the Speaker of the House becomes President. Others in line include the president *pro tempore* of the Senate and the members of the Cabinet.

Twenty years later, Congress ended all remaining questions about Presidential succession by passing a Constitutional amendment. The Twenty-fifth Amendment, ratified in 1967, says that if the President dies or leaves office, the Vice President legally becomes President. The new President then chooses another Vice President, whose selection must be approved by both houses of Congress. The amendment also allows the Vice President to become "Acting President" if the President is temporarily unable to carry out the duties of office.

The Twenty-fifth Amendment has already been used three times. The first was in 1973, when Vice President Spiro Agnew resigned. President Richard Nixon replaced him with Gerald R. Ford, a Representative from Michigan. In 1974, when Nixon resigned from the Presidency, the amendment was used a second time. Gerald Ford became the new President and chose Nelson A. Rockefeller, former governor of New York, to be his Vice President.

In 1985, the Twenty-fifth Amendment was used again. President Ronald Reagan, who was about to undergo surgery, informed Congress that he would be unable to carry out his Presidential duties during the operation. As a result, Vice President George Bush served as Acting President for about eight hours, until Reagan awoke from his anesthesia.

Vice President Dan Quayle answers reporters' questions. The Vice President must be prepared to take over at any time if the President dies, leaves office, or is unable to carry out the duties of office.

SECTION REVIEW

Check the Facts

1. What are the written qualifications for both the Presidency and the Vice Presidency?
2. How has the procedure for electing the Vice President changed since the Constitution was written?
3. Describe the provisions of the Twenty-second and Twenty-fifth Amendments.

Think About the Ideas

4. *Evaluate.* Should a President be allowed to serve more than two terms? Why or why not?

★ ★

SECTION 2

The President's Major Roles

★ ★

VOCABULARY

bureaucracy   treaty
executive order   executive agreement
ambassador

The Constitution holds one person—the President—responsible for carrying out the duties of the executive branch of government. As the nation has grown, the duties and responsibilities of the executive branch have grown also. In carrying out these tasks, the President takes on several different roles. These include chief executive, chief diplomat, and commander in chief.

Chief Executive

The most important job of the President is to carry out the nation's laws. The responsibility to "take care that the laws be faithfully executed" is given to the President by Article II of the Constitution.

When Congress passes a law, a number of issues must be resolved before the law can take effect and be enforced. Suppose, for example, that Congress passes a law requiring all cosmetics to have labels listing their ingredients. Although the law seems relatively simple, there are many questions that must be answered. How big should the labels be? In what order should the ingredients be listed? Which products should be considered "cosmetics"? (For example, is hair spray a cosmetic or simply a grooming aid?) What should be done to punish manufacturers who break the law?

As chief executive, chief diplomat, and commander in chief of the United States, the President often makes statements on important events to the press and through it to the American public.

U.S. v. Nixon (1974)

For the most part, the doctrine of "separation of powers" works fairly well. Sometimes, however, one branch finds itself in conflict with another.

One of the most dramatic conflicts of recent years occurred in 1973–1974 between the executive and judicial branches. The trouble grew out of a burglary of the Democratic National Committee offices in Washington by people linked to President Richard Nixon's reelection committee. The offices were in a building called Watergate. (See Closeup on Watergate on page 293.) Part of the subsequent investigation concerned President Nixon's involvement in a cover-up of the break-in. President Nixon was asked to give Leon Jaworski, the special prosecutor assigned to investigate the case, 64 tapes of conversations he had had with his White House aides. Nixon refused on two grounds:

1. The tapes were protected by executive privilege, the right of the President to have confidential discussions with aides in order to conduct the nation's business.

2. The courts—the judicial branch—had no right to interfere in a dispute between the President and Jaworski who, as a member of the Justice Department, was an employee of the executive branch.

In 1974, in U.S. v. Nixon, the Supreme Court rejected President Nixon's arguments. The Court said that Presidents could claim executive privilege in cases where military and national security issues were involved but could not use it to conceal evidence of a crime.

The Court also ruled that, as a law enforcement officer, Special Prosecutor Jaworski represented the judicial branch. The fact that he was employed by the executive branch did not change this. Therefore, Jaworski had a right to seek evidence from the President in a criminal proceeding. Furthermore, the Court said, the President had a responsibility to uphold the law by cooperating with the prosecutor's request.

As a result of the Court's ruling in U.S v. Nixon, the President was forced to turn over the tapes. Conversations recorded on one of the tapes revealed Nixon's involvement in covering up the Watergate break-in and led to his resignation from office.

Using Your Skills

1. Why did President Nixon believe that he could withhold the 64 tapes from the special prosecutor?

2. What did the Supreme Court rule in U.S. v. Nixon?

3. What do you think would have happened if Nixon had destroyed the tapes or continued to withhold them after the Supreme Court handed down its ruling?

Congress cannot possibly deal with all these details when it writes a bill. Instead, the specific provisions of each new law are determined by the executive branch of the government. The President, of course, does not attend to such details personally. Overseeing the execution of national laws is the responsibility of the hundreds of agencies and millions of employees who make up the executive branch of the federal government. This large network of individuals and agencies is called the federal **bureaucracy**. The President heads this bureaucracy in his role as the chief executive.

ISSUING EXECUTIVE ORDERS One of the President's most important tools for executing laws is the power to issue **executive orders**. An executive order is a rule or command issued by the President that has the force of law. Executive orders are often, though not always, issued during times of crisis. During World War II, for example, President Franklin Roosevelt issued executive orders that put certain important industries under the direct control of the government.

According to the Constitution, only Congress has the power to make laws. But the issuing of executive orders is generally considered part of the President's duty to "take care that the laws be faithfully executed."

Decisions made by any agency of the executive branch are also considered executive orders, and have the force of law. For example, if the Federal Trade Commission— part of the executive branch—decides that cosmetics' labels must use lettering one-eighth of an inch high, cosmetics manufacturers must obey this rule as they would a law passed by Congress.

APPOINTING OFFICIALS Because the President shares power with others in the government, it is important that these people be reliable and competent. It is also important that these people share the President's values and ideas, so that they will support the President's policies and see that they are carried out.

The Constitution gives the President the power to appoint many government officials. Among these officials are ambassadors, judges, leaders of government agencies, and members of the Cabinet. Except for judges, the President can also remove most officials from office after they have been appointed. Almost all of the President's appointments must be approved by the Senate.

Chief Diplomat

Another role of the President is that of chief diplomat. The President and the executive branch have primary responsibility for dealing with other countries. The Constitution gives the President two important powers: the first is the power to appoint ambassadors; the second is the power to make treaties.

APPOINTING AMBASSADORS An **ambassador** is an official representative of a country's government. The President appoints about 150 ambassadors, each of whom is sent to a different country as a representative of the United States. As you may remember, the President needs the approval of the Senate in order to appoint ambassadors.

Ambassadors are sent only to those countries where the United States recognizes, or accepts, the legal existence of the government. If the government of a certain country is thought to hold power illegally, the President can refuse to recognize that government. In that case, no American ambassador will be

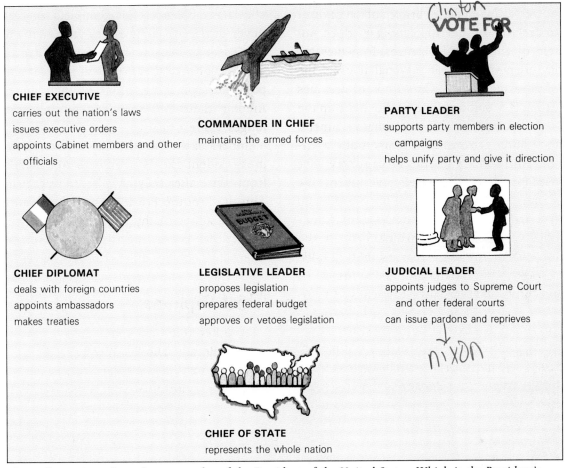

CHIEF EXECUTIVE
carries out the nation's laws
issues executive orders
appoints Cabinet members and other
  officials

COMMANDER IN CHIEF
maintains the armed forces

PARTY LEADER
supports party members in election
  campaigns
helps unify party and give it direction

CHIEF DIPLOMAT
deals with foreign countries
appoints ambassadors
makes treaties

LEGISLATIVE LEADER
proposes legislation
prepares federal budget
approves or vetoes legislation

JUDICIAL LEADER
appoints judges to Supreme Court
  and other federal courts
can issue pardons and reprieves

CHIEF OF STATE
represents the whole nation

These illustrations show the many roles of the President of the United States. Which is the President's most important role?

sent, and that country will not be allowed to send an ambassador to the United States.

MAKING TREATIES The second important power of the President as chief diplomat is the power to make treaties. A **treaty** is a formal agreement between two or more countries. The Constitution gives the President the power to make treaties with "the advice and consent of the Senate." The treaty must be approved by a two-thirds vote of the Senate. Only then can it be signed into law.

Sometimes, Presidents bypass the Senate by making executive agreements instead of treaties. An **executive agreement** is an agreement between the President and the leader of another country. It has the force of law but does not require Senate approval. Most executive agreements deal with fairly routine matters. In 1979, however, an executive agreement was made between the President of the United States and the leader of Iran. This agreement concerned the return of 52 Americans who had been held hostage in Iran.

Commander in Chief

The Constitution gives Congress the power to maintain an army and the power to declare war. But, in keeping with the system of checks and balances, it makes the President the commander in chief, or leader, of the armed forces. Only the President can order U.S. soldiers into battle.

Military power can sometimes be a threat to a nation's government. Many times in history, the military leaders of a country have used force to take over their government. The writers of the Constitution hoped to avoid this danger by making the President, a non-military person, the commander of the armed forces. For the same reason, they divided responsibility for the military between the executive and legislative branches.

Occasionally, however, the President has used the power as commander in chief in ways that have threatened this system of checks and balances. For example, Congress never declared war in Korea and Vietnam. Yet, America became involved in an armed conflict in Korea after President Truman sent troops to fight there, and in Vietnam under Presidents Eisenhower, Kennedy, Johnson, and Nixon.

In 1973, following the Vietnam War, Congress passed the War Powers Act, which limits the President's authority to wage war. This law requires the President to notify Congress immediately when troops are sent into battle. These troops must be brought home after 60 days unless Congress gives its approval for them to remain longer or unless it declares war.

The diplomatic efforts of President Jimmy Carter made it possible for Egypt's President Anwar Sadat and Israel's Premier Menachem Begin to sign the Camp David accord in 1979.

During an actual war—one declared by Congress—the President may be given special powers. For example, the President can order the U.S. Army to take over the government of another country.

During peacetime, the President can use the armed services for a variety of purposes. In April 1989, for example, President Bush asked the military to help clean up a large oil spill that occurred in Prince William Sound in Alaska. Presidents can also call out government troops to keep order within the United States. President Eisenhower did this in 1957, in Little Rock, Arkansas, when attempts to integrate public schools led to clashes between groups of angry citizens and the local police.

SECTION REVIEW

Define the Words

bureaucracy
executive order
ambassador
treaty
executive agreement

Check the Facts

1. Describe three important roles of the President.
2. What two powers does the President have as chief diplomat?
3. Which military responsibilities are given to Congress, and which to the President?

Think About the Ideas

4. *Analyze.* Why is the President given powers in times of war that would be unthinkable in peacetime?

★ ★

SECTION 3

The President's Other Roles

★ ★

VOCABULARY

pardon   amnesty
reprieve

In addition to acting as chief executive, chief diplomat, and commander in chief, the President plays several other important roles in the nation. These include legislative leader, party leader, judicial leader, and chief of state. Not all of these roles come directly from the Constitution, but all are vital parts of the President's job.

Legislative Leader

Every President comes into office with ideas about what kind of place the United States should be. Before George Bush was elected President, for example, he said frequently that he would like to make America a "kinder, gentler nation."

No President, however, can make major changes in American life without the cooperation of Congress. Any attempts to change the nation require new laws. And laws, as you know, can only be passed by Congress.

The President can, however, play a large part in the legislative process. By developing a close relationship with the members of Congress—especially those who belong to the

President John F. Kennedy used press conferences effectively to explain his administration's policies to the media and the American public.

President's party—the President can often get Congress to pass laws that will advance his program.

Suppose, for example, that the President wants a bill introduced in Congress. A member of the President's staff will first draft the bill according to the President's instructions. The President will then ask a Senator or Representative to introduce the bill in Congress. Once a bill has moved into Congressional committee, the President may speak individually to the committee members and encourage them to approve it.

When it is time for a bill that the President supports to be voted on by the full House or Senate, the President may use a variety of

tactics to encourage passage of the bill. Those tactics might include telephoning members of Congress, inviting them to the White House to discuss the bill, or even promising not to veto another bill that the member of Congress supports. Another tactic the President might use is to appeal to the American people by making a speech on television. If the speech is convincing enough, the voters may put pressure on their Senators or Representatives to pass the legislation. President Ronald Reagan, known as "the Great Communicator," used this technique successfully a number of times.

The President also has more formal ways to influence legislation. Once a year, as required by the Constitution, the President makes a State of the Union address to Congress. In this speech, the President presents the administration's goals for the coming year. Shortly afterward, the President submits a budget to Congress, which recommends how the government should raise and spend money in order to reach those goals. Congress is not required to accept the President's budget, but it often does.

The President may also call a special session of Congress to consider urgent matters. This is rarely necessary today, since Congress is now in session for most of the year.

President Reagan's meeting with Soviet President Mikhail Gorbachev, such as the Geneva Summit in 1985, helped improve relations between the United States and the Soviet Union.

Party Leader

When a political party's candidate is elected President, that person becomes the leader of the party. There are no special powers or privileges that come with this role. Like all political party members, however, the President does try to help out the party. One way a President can do this is by appointing party members to government jobs through the patronage, the system of rewarding party workers with jobs or special favors. Another way is by making speeches and personal appearances in support of party members who are running for election.

Although it is not always obvious, the President's role as party leader influences much of what happens in the national government. When making treaties, appointing officials, suggesting legislation, or executing laws, the President tries to consider the goals and interests of the party—as well as the country. In return, members of the President's party—in all levels and branches of government—try to act in ways that will help the President.

Judicial Leader

The Constitution gives the President the power to appoint judges to the Supreme Court and to other federal courts. This power is one of the most important that the President holds.

In 1974, President Gerald Ford pardoned former President Nixon for illegal acts he might have committed while President.

As you will discover in Chapter 12, the Supreme Court has a great deal of influence. It has final authority to determine whether or not a law is acceptable under the Constitution. Through this power to interpret the law and the Constitution, it can greatly affect life in America. Most Presidents try to appoint Supreme Court justices whose point of view is similar to their own. President Ronald Reagan, for example, appointed two Supreme Court justices—Antonin Scalia and Anthony Kennedy—who shared his views on civil rights, religion, and family values.

Once appointed, a Supreme Court justice usually holds that position for life. Therefore, by appointing new justices to the Supreme Court, Presidents can continue to influence the country long after they have left office.

The President also plays another, somewhat smaller, role in the judicial system. The Constitution gives the President the power to help an individual convicted of breaking federal laws. The President may grant a **pardon** to someone, that is, issue a declaration of forgiveness and freedom from punishment. Or the President may issue a **reprieve**, an order to delay a person's punishment until a higher court can rule on the case. If a large number of people have violated a federal law, the President has the power to grant **amnesty**. Amnesty is similar to a pardon, except that it applies to a group rather than to an individual.

Chief of State

Americans, like citizens all over the world, want their government to have a human face. Congress and the Supreme Court are groups with no distinct personality. The President, however, is an individual with familiar ways of speaking and acting. Unlike members of Congress, the President represents people from all the states. For most Americans, therefore, the President is a symbol of the U.S. government.

People want to admire the President and the First Family. They like to feel that the President is special. When the President greets a hero, or throws the first pitch at a baseball game, many Americans feel good about their country.

The President's role as chief of state is mostly symbolic. The President may demonstrate America's support of the arts by inviting musicians to perform at the White House. The President may express America's respect for another nation by attending the funeral of its leader.

The role of chief of state is often difficult to distinguish from the President's other roles. For example, when the President meets with leaders of other nations to discuss important matters, these meetings are accompanied by speeches and ceremonies in which the President acts as chief of state. But when the discussions turn to the business at hand, the President once again assumes the role of chief diplomat or chief executive.

SECTION REVIEW

Define the Words

pardon   amnesty

reprieve

Check the Facts

1. Identify five ways in which the President can influence Congressional legislation.
2. What can the President do as party leader to help the party and its members?
3. What two judicial powers are given to the President by the Constitution?

Think About the Ideas

4. *Analyze.* Is it possible for the President's role as party leader to interfere with other Presidential roles? How?

Presidential Pastimes

Each President brings a distinct personal style to the White House. Nothing illustrates this better than the many different ways that Presidents have chosen to spend their leisure time.

Harry Truman played the piano and went for walks. Dwight Eisenhower was a golfer. John Kennedy liked to sail, swim, and play touch football on the White House lawn.

Kennedy built a swimming pool in the White House, but Richard Nixon replaced the pool with a bowling alley. Nixon's successor, Gerald Ford, was an enthusiastic skier.

Jimmy Carter liked to jog in the early morning and Ronald Reagan rode horses and chopped wood at his California ranch. George Bush has brought a new sport to the White House. He installed a horseshoe court on the south lawn so he can pitch a few games of horseshoes to relax and help relieve stress.

VOCABULARY
administration   domestic

The executive branch of government is organized like a pyramid. The President, as chief executive, is at the very top of the pyramid. Directly below the President are a number of powerful officials, usually hand-picked by the President. Below these are many levels of lesser officials and managers. At the bottom of the pyramid are hundreds of thousands of people, from messengers to security guards to lawyers, who carry out the day-to-day work of the executive branch.

In general, the people at the top of the pyramid are the ones who set goals and make important decisions. Because they are appointed by the President, or by the President's closest advisers, they tend to be replaced every time a new President is elected. This group is usually referred to as the President's **administration**.

The Executive Office of the President

President Franklin D. Roosevelt created the Executive Office of the President (the EOP) in 1939. The people in the EOP are responsible for providing advice and help-ing Presidents do their job. Over the years, Presidents have changed the organization of the EOP according to their needs. The most important of the EOP offices are the White House Office, the Office of Management and Budget, and the National Security Council.

THE WHITE HOUSE OFFICE The core of the Executive Office of the President is the White House Office, which consists of the President's closest advisers and personal staff. Only the highest government officials get to meet with the President personally. Others must deal with the President's assistants in the White House Office.

The most powerful official in the White House Office is the Chief of Staff. The Chief of Staff decides who gets to see the President and which matters are important enough to be brought to the President's attention. It is often said that the Chief of Staff, rather than the President, really runs the White House.

Another member of the White House Office, the President's press secretary is often seen by the public. The press secretary provides reporters with news about, and statements from, the President. Most of the President's other assistants do their work behind the scenes. Among them are speechwriters, clerical staff, and experts in many fields who advise the President.

OFFICE OF MANAGEMENT AND BUDGET Earlier in this chapter, you learned that the President submits a proposed budget to Congress each year. Preparing this budget is the responsibility of the Office of Management and Budget, or OMB. In order to prepare a realistic budget, the OMB must gather many statistics about the country's economy.

The Budget Director, the head of the OMB, meets often with the President. Together, they decide how much money should be allotted to each government program and where that money should come from. They may decide to cut certain programs or to raise taxes to support others. The result of their work is presented in the proposed budget that is given to Congress. This budget is the clearest statement of the administration's plans and goals for the coming year.

THE NATIONAL SECURITY COUNCIL Matters affecting the safety and security of the United States are among the most urgent a President must deal with. Faced with a possible threat from a hostile country, the President must make life-and-death decisions in a matter of hours or even minutes. The National Security Council helps the President make such decisions. Its members include the Vice President, the Secretary of State, and the Secretary of Defense.

The National Security Council also supervises the Central Intelligence Agency, or CIA. The CIA is responsible for gathering information about other governments. To do so, it makes use of undercover agents, informants, spy satellites, and other techniques.

OTHER OFFICES WITHIN THE EOP The Office of Policy Development and the Council of Economic Advisors help the President make important decisions about domestic policy. **Domestic** refers to matters affecting only the United States. The Office of Policy Development advises the President about farm issues, urban affairs, energy policy, and interstate commerce. The Council of Economic Advisors advises the President about the nation's economy, and helps the President make decisions about taxes, inflation, and foreign trade.

The other offices within the EOP are the Council on Environmental Quality, the Office of Science and Technology Policy, the Office of Administration, and the Office of the United States Trade Representative. Together, the offices of the EOP allow the President to make careful and informed decisions about our country's future.

The chief of staff is a key figure in a President's administration. Here President Bush confers with Chief of Staff John Sununu in the Oval Office of the White House.

CITIZENSHIP SKILLS

How to Use Primary Sources

Much of what we know as history is really historians' interpretations of past events. How accurately these events are portrayed depends upon how much information historians have and on the quality of that information.

Accounts of events or descriptions of conditions made by participants and on-the-scene observers are called primary sources. Primary sources include people's diaries, journals, public records, and other personal and public documents.

Sources of information such as newspaper editorials and biographies are called secondary sources. Secondary sources are not the accounts of eye-witnesses, but they are based on those primary sources. Historians use both primary and secondary sources to reconstruct the past.

The following is a brief account of a historical event and a primary source related to that event.

In 1928, the National Convention of the Republi-can Party chose Herbert Hoover as its candidate for President. The chairman of the convention notified Hoover, saying that the United States was indebted to him for the great services he had performed for his country. Hoover had administered America's relief programs, which helped Europe recover from World War I, and had also served as Secretary of Commerce in the cabinets of Presidents Harding and Coolidge. Hoover won the election of 1928 and became the thirty-first President of the United States.

Following is an excerpt from Hoover's letter of reply. Read the excerpt and answer the questions that follow.

You convey too great a compliment when you say that I have earned the right to the presidential nomination. No man can establish such an obligation upon any part of the American people. My country owes me no debt. It gave me schooling, independence of action, opportunity for service and honor. In no other land could a boy from a country village, without inheritance or influential friends, look forward with unbounded hope.

My whole life has taught me what America means. I am indebted to my country beyond any human power to repay . . . . It has called me into the cabinets of two Presidents. By these experiences I have observed the burdens and responsibilities of the greatest office in the world. That office touches the happiness of every home. It deals with the peace of nations. No man could think of it except in terms of solemn consecration [dedication to a great cause].

Using Your Skills
1. What reasons does Hoover give for not accepting the chairman's compliment?
2. Why are primary sources so important to historians?

The Executive Departments and the Cabinet

The EOP is only a small part of the President's administration. Many more people work in the 14 executive departments. These executive departments can be distinguished from the EOP by the kind of work they do. The EOP exists to serve and advise the President. The executive departments, on the other hand, play a direct role in governing the country. The officials in these departments use the power given to them by the President to make and enforce regulations. The heads of the executive departments make up the President's Cabinet. The executive departments and the Cabinet will be discussed at length in the next chapter.

SECTION REVIEW

Define the Words

administration   domestic

Check the Facts
1. What is the general purpose of the EOP?
2. Identify the main responsibilities of the White House Office, the Office of Management and Budget, and the National Security Council.
3. How do the executive departments and the EOP differ?

Think About the Ideas
4. *Analyze.* Why do you think an EOP was not needed before 1939? How did previous Presidents manage without this office?

Why is the Executive Office of the President made up of so many different offices?

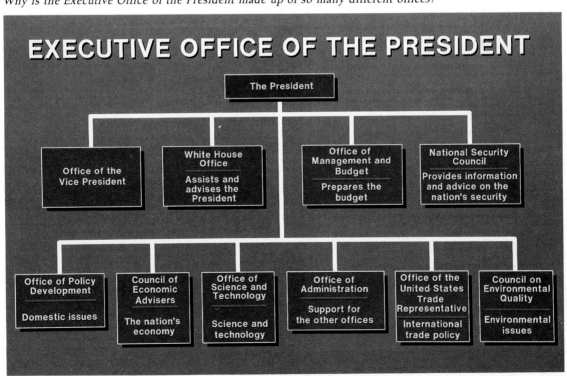

EXECUTIVE OFFICE OF THE PRESIDENT

The President

Office of the Vice President

White House Office — Assists and advises the President

Office of Management and Budget — Prepares the budget

National Security Council — Provides information and advice on the nation's security

Office of Policy Development — Domestic issues

Council of Economic Advisers — The nation's economy

Office of Science and Technology — Science and technology

Office of Administration — Support for the other offices

Office of the United States Trade Representative — International trade policy

Council on Environmental Quality — Environmental issues

CHAPTER 10 REVIEW

★ ★

MAIN POINTS

★ The President is the head of the executive branch. The President must be a native-born American citizen, at least 35 years old, and a resident of the United States for at least 14 years.

★ The Vice President must meet the same qualifications. The Vice President becomes President if the President dies or leaves office.

★ The President's primary duty is to carry out the nation's laws. The President may fulfill this duty personally or delegate authority to the federal bureaucracy.

★ The President's major roles include chief executive, chief diplomat, and commander in chief of the armed forces.

★ The President also acts as legislative leader, party leader, judicial leader, and chief of state. Often, the President performs more than one of these roles at the same time.

★ The Executive Office of the President exists to provide advice and assistance and to help the President govern effectively.

★ The EOP consists of several offices, including the White House Office, the Office of Management and Budget, and the National Security Council.

WORDS IN REVIEW

Choose the word or phrase from the list below that best completes each sentence. Write the missing words on a separate sheet of paper.

bureaucracy	executive order
ambassador	treaty
pardon	executive agreement
reprieve	amnesty
administration	domestic

1. The President granted the government official a _____, forgiving the official for his crime.

2. After her appointment, the new _____ to Italy was congratulated by the press.

3. The Council of Economic Advisers is concerned primarily with _____ issues, that is, with matters within the United States.

4. The executive branch of government includes a large _____ that deals with the day-to-day work of government.

5. The President's closest advisers are usually part of the _____.

6. During wartime, a President may need to issue an _____ to see that a policy is carried out quickly.

7. President Reagan granted the illegal aliens _____ so they would not be prosecuted for their illegal status.

8. The Senate voted to approve the _____ between the United States and Great Britain.

9. The convicted man's punishment was delayed when he was granted a _____.

10. Senate approval was not required for the _____ made between the President and the leader of the Soviet Union.

FACTS IN REVIEW

1. What characteristics have most U.S. Presidents shared?

CHAPTER 10 REVIEW

* *

2.Why were Presidents not elected for more than two terms before 1940?

3.What was the Presidential Succession Act of 1947?

4.What is the role of the federal bureaucracy?

5.Why did the Constitution place limits on the President's power to appoint officials?

6.Explain the purpose of the War Powers Act.

7.What is the purpose of the President's State of the Union address?

8.Why is the President's role as chief of state important?

9.Identify two important members of the White House Office and describe their responsibilities.

10.What is the responsibility of the CIA?

THINKING ABOUT THE PRESIDENCY

1. *Analyze*. Do you think that there should be more limits on the President's power? Why or why not?

2. *Evaluate*. Which of the President's roles do you think is the most important? Why?

3. *Put Ideas Together*. In Great Britain, the roles of chief executive and chief of state are played by two different people. Do you think this system would work in the United States? Why or why not?

COLLECTING INFORMATION ABOUT THE PRESIDENTS

Research the backgrounds of the Presidents elected since 1900. At what age did each President take office? What states were they from? What were their occupations? How many terms did each President serve? How many did not complete their terms of office? Put this information together in the form of a chart.

WRITING ABOUT THE PRESIDENT

Prepare a short biography of a President you admire. It should include information about the President's background, education, and political career. It should also discuss some of the President's major accomplishments. Conclude your biography by explaining why you admire this particular President.

INTERPRETING A CHART

Look at the chart on the Executive Office of the President on page 243. Which division do you think would be consulted in a foreign policy crisis? Which two offices are most directly concerned with taxes? What problems do you think might result from the way the EOP is organized?

FOCUSING ON YOUR COMMUNITY

How do the people in your community feel about the current President's performance in office? Interview various people in the community, including teachers, members of your family, neighbors, and friends. Limit your questions to one specific issue, such as the environment, foreign policy, or the drug problem. Based on your interviews, what do people think about the President's performance on this issue? Report your findings to the class.

CHAPTER 11

* *

The Executive Branch

OBJECTIVES

After you have studied this chapter, you will be able to:

★ Explain the role of the members of the President's Cabinet.

★ Explain why executive departments have been created as a part of the federal government.

★ Identify the 14 executive departments and describe their major responsibilities.

★ Identify three types of independent agencies.

★ Explain the role and workings of the federal bureaucracy.

SECTIONS

1 The Executive Departments
2 Other Executive Departments
3 Independent Agencies
4 The Federal Bureaucracy

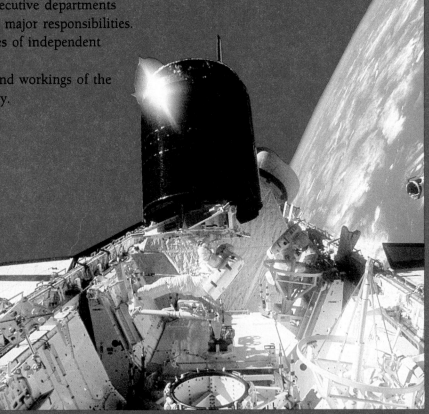

INTRODUCTION

Early in 1989, federal inspectors working for the Food and Drug Administration (FDA) found poison in some grapes imported from Chile. To protect American consumers, the FDA, part of the executive branch of government, halted the importation of all Chilean fruit until further notice. The order affected not only Americans, but also thousands of Chilean farmers and the economy of Chile.

This action by the Food and Drug Administration illustrates the far-reaching power of the executive branch. The executive branch affects almost every aspect of our lives. The quality of our food is controlled by the Department of Agriculture. The purity of our air and water is monitored by the Environmental Protection Agency. Our money is printed by the Bureau of Engraving and Printing, part of the Treasury Department. The television programs we watch are regulated by the Federal Communications Commission.

Not one of the hundreds of departments, agencies, commissions, bureaus, and corporations that make up the executive branch is mentioned in the Constitution. All of them, however, serve a single Constitutional purpose: to help the President "take care that the laws be faithfully executed."

★ ★

SECTION 1

The Executive Departments

★ ★

VOCABULARY

Cabinet	consul
foreign policy	passport
embassy	visa
consulate	

The executive departments are among the most important parts of the executive branch. With huge staffs and multi-billion dollar budgets, they carry out much of the work of the executive branch.

Each of these departments is responsible for a certain area of government. The head, or "Secretary," of each executive department is a member of the President's **Cabinet**. As Cabinet members, the Secretaries advise the President on issues related to their particular department. As department heads, the Secretaries often make policy decisions of far-reaching effect.

Development of the Cabinet

Although the Constitution mentions neither a Cabinet nor executive departments, it was clear from the start that the President would need assistance to carry out the Presidential duties. Right after he took office, President Washington asked Congress to provide funding for three executive departments.

EXECUTIVE DEPARTMENTS

DEPARTMENT OF STATE (1789)
Plans and carries out the nation's foreign policy

DEPARTMENT OF THE TREASURY (1789)
Collects, borrows, spends and prints money

DEPARTMENT OF DEFENSE (1947) WAR
Manages the armed forces

DEPARTMENT OF JUSTICE (1870)
Has responsibility for all aspects of law enforcement

DEPARTMENT OF THE INTERIOR (1849)
Manages and protects the nation's public lands and natural resources

DEPARTMENT OF AGRICULTURE (1889)
Assists farmers and consumers of farm products

DEPARTMENT OF COMMERCE (1903)
Supervises trade, promotes U.S. tourism and business

DEPARTMENT OF LABOR (1913)
Is concerned with the working conditions and wages of America's workers

DEPARTMENT OF HEALTH AND HUMAN SERVICES (1953)
Works for the health and well-being of all Americans

DEPARTMENT OF HOUSING AND URBAN DEVELOPMENT (1965)
Deals with the special needs and problems of cities

DEPARTMENT OF TRANSPORTATION (1966)
Manages the nation's highways, railroads, airlines, and sea traffic

DEPARTMENT OF ENERGY (1977)
Directs an overall energy plan for the nation

DEPARTMENT OF EDUCATION (1979)
Provides advice and funding for schools

DEPARTMENT OF VETERANS AFFAIRS (1989)
Directs services for veterans

What other role does the head of each executive department fill?

These were the Department of State, the Department of the Treasury, and the Department of War. Over the years, Presidents have continued to add departments to the executive branch. The most recent addition is the Department of Veterans Affairs, which was formed in 1989. Today there are 14 executive departments. (See the chart on page 248.)

As the number of departments has grown, the size of the President's Cabinet has increased as well. In addition to the department heads, most cabinets now include the Vice President and other important government officials. At the start of his term, President Bush invited two members of the Executive Office of the President—the Chief of Staff and the Budget Director—to participate in Cabinet meetings.

The only official members of the Cabinet, the heads of the 14 executive departments, are chosen by the President, but they must be approved by the Senate. Since the time of Washington, these Cabinet members have been called Secretaries. The head of the Labor Department, for example, is the Secretary of Labor. The only exception is the head of the Justice Department, who is the Attorney General.

Although the Secretaries have great power as leaders of their departments, they have virtually no power as members of the Cabinet. The President is not required to accept the Cabinet's advice on issues. Some Presidents, such as Franklin Roosevelt, relied heavily on advisers outside the Cabinet. But the Cabinet has played an influential role in the administration of many Presidents.

Three of the most important Cabinet departments are the original three executive departments: the departments of State, Treasury, and Defense. (The Department of War became part of the Department of Defense in 1947.)

Department of State

One of the responsibilities of the President is to create a **foreign policy**, a plan for dealing with other nations. The Department of State, or State Department, is the executive department that helps the President with this responsibility.

As a member of the Cabinet, the Secretary of State helps the President plan foreign policy. The Department of State is then responsible for carrying out this foreign policy and for managing America's relationships with other countries. To help in this task, the State Department employs many experts in foreign affairs. These experts gather information and help the President understand events and issues in different parts of the world.

The State Department also sets up American government offices, called **embassies**, in foreign nations. Each embassy is run by an ambassador, an official representative of the United States government. The details of foreign relations with a particular country are

As Secretary of State, James Baker meets with many foreign leaders. Here he confers with Fernando Salana.

Government Office Worker

The government is the largest employer in the United States. In 1986, nearly 17 million people worked for federal, state, or local governments. But most government employees work in offices and do the same kind of work—typing, word processing, and filing—as people in other businesses.

Employees who keep records up to date and in the right place are called file clerks. File clerks classify, store, update, and get information for other workers. They are also responsible for going through files from time to time and removing information that is no longer needed. File clerks handle several different kinds of files—paper files in folders, mechanized files that rotate, microfilm files, and computer disk files.

File clerks work for every agency and department at all levels of government, from the White House to a mayor's office. A file clerk is a job for people without work experience.

Because there is a lot of competition for government jobs, people sometimes become file clerks to get into government service. Then, they usually try to move up to more responsible, better-paying office jobs.

To become a government file clerk, you must graduate from high school and pass a civil service test. If you want to advance to other office jobs, however, you should take courses in typing, word processing, and other office skills.

Using Your Skills
1. What duties does a government file clerk perform?
2. What skills or abilities would a person need to be a good file clerk?

---

handled by these ambassadors and their staffs. From time to time, the Secretary of State also meets with foreign leaders to discuss matters of common interest.

Another function of the State Department is to protect the rights of Americans working or traveling abroad. In about 170 different locations around the world, the State Department has set up offices called **consulates** to help Americans in that country. These consulates are headed by an official called a **consul**. The consulates also work to improve American business opportunities and business interests in foreign countries.

The State Department is also responsible for issuing passports to American travelers. A **passport** is an official document that identifies a traveler as an American citizen. When a citizen of a foreign country visits the United States, the State Department issues a **visa**—a permit allowing the person to remain here for a certain amount of time.

Department of the Treasury

In 1990, the budget of the U.S. government was more than $1 trillion. The task of handling the nation's money belongs to the Department of the Treasury. It is responsible for collecting, borrowing, and spending the money that the nation requires. The head of the department, the Secretary of the Treasury, is an important adviser to the President on financial matters.

The Treasury Department has several divisions that carry out specific jobs. For example, the Internal Revenue Service (IRS) collects income taxes from individuals and businesses. The U.S. Customs service collects taxes on items that are brought into the United States from other countries. The Bureau of the Mint designs and produces U.S. coins, and the Bureau of Engraving and Printing prints paper money.

Some divisions of the Treasury Department perform tasks that are not directly related to money. The Secret Service, for example, was originally set up to find and punish counterfeiters—people who print imitation money and try to pass it off as real. Although the Secret Service still does this job, it now has a more important function—to protect the lives of the President and the Vice President and their families. Another division with little connection to money is the Bureau of Alcohol, Tobacco, and Firearms, which regulates the sale and use of those three items.

The highest positions in the Defense Department—the Secretary of Defense, and the secretaries of the Army, Navy, and Air Force—are held by civilians. Who is the commander in chief of the armed forces?

Department of Defense

Originally, the armed forces of the United States were managed by two executive departments: the Department of War and the Department of the Navy. In 1947, these were combined into the Department of Defense, which now oversees the Army, the Navy (including the Marine Corps), and the Air Force. The Department of Defense is the largest department in the executive branch, with more than a million employees and an annual budget of nearly 300 billion dollars.

Each of the three armed services has its own division within the Department of Defense. A Secretary of the Army, a Secretary of the Navy, and a Secretary of the Air Force head these subdepartments, but none of these leaders is a member of the Cabinet.

In Chapter 10, you learned that the writers of the Constitution were careful to place control of the military in the hands of a nonmilitary leader. They made the President, a civilian, commander in chief of the armed

forces. Today, most of the President's duties as commander in chief are carried out by the Department of Defense. In keeping with the intent of the Constitution, however, most of the Defense Department's power is held by civilians. By law, the Secretaries of the Army, Navy, and Air Force, as well as the Secretary of Defense, may not be military officers.

Military officers may, and do, serve as advisers to the President and to the Secretary of Defense. Among the most important of these advisers are the Joint Chiefs of Staff. The Joint Chiefs, made up of the highest-ranking officer from each of the armed services, are consulted whenever important defense decisions are made. Only the President, however, has the power to send American soldiers into battle.

SECTION REVIEW

Define the Words

Cabinet   consul
foreign policy   passport
embassy   visa
consulate

Check the Facts

1. What is the purpose of the President's Cabinet?
2. Identify the original three executive departments.
3. What are the responsibilities of the Department of State?

Think About the Ideas

4. *Analyze.* How do the responsibilities of the Departments of State and Defense overlap? How might the decisions made by one affect the other?

SECTION 2

Other Executive Departments

VOCABULARY
conservation

The original three executive departments were established in 1789. Over the next 200 years, as the nation grew, additional executive departments were added to help carry out the work of the government. In 1989, the creation of the Department of Veterans Affairs brought the number of these executive departments to 14. We will look briefly at each of these additional departments, in the order in which they were established.

Department of Justice

The Department of Justice was not established until 1870, after the Department of the Interior. Nevertheless, it is usually considered the fourth-oldest department because the Attorney General, who heads the department, was the fourth member of George Washington's original Cabinet.

The Attorney General was originally the nation's lawyer and represented the U.S. government in court. The Justice Department still fulfills this function, but the Attorney General almost never appears in court personally.

THE RIGHT TO PRIVACY

A 14-year-old student was seen smoking in the girl's lounge of a high school in New Jersey. One of the school's assistant principals searched her purse and found cigarettes—and also marijuana. The student was suspended from school and charged in juvenile court.

Did the assistant principal have a right to search the student's purse? Or was the student protected by the Fourth Amendment prohibition against unreasonable searches and seizures? In 1985, the U.S. Supreme Court ruled in favor of the school. It found that the assistant principal had reasonable grounds to suspect that the student was violating school rules or the law.

This case—*New Jersey* v. *T.L.O.*—is just one of the many cases involving the right to privacy that come before the courts each year. In 1965, in the case of *Griswald* v. *Connecticut*, the Supreme Court ruled that Americans do enjoy a right to privacy even though it is not mentioned in the Constitution. Some years before that, Supreme Court Justice Louis D. Brandeis wrote in a famous opinion that "the right to be left alone [by the government] is the most comprehensive of rights and the right most valued by civilized men."

Yet finding the balance between the right of privacy and the protection of society can be difficult. This is especially true today. Technological advances, such as computerized financial records, makes it easy to invade an individual's privacy. Moreover, some people believe that certain violations of privacy should be allowed if the health or safety of the community is at risk. Questions to consider:

★ Do co-workers have the right to know if they are working with a person who has AIDS?
★ Can job applicants be required to take lie detector tests?
★ Can a company sell the confidential information in its computerized personnel files to another company?
★ Can a company fire a person for dating an employee of a rival company?

These questions have all arisen in recent years, and most of them have not yet been resolved. However, Congress has already taken steps to protect people with AIDS from job discrimination and to limit the use of lie detector tests. Labor unions are also bringing suits and seeking contract clauses to protect workers from unjustified invasions of their privacy in the workplace. And more

juries are siding with people who take right-to-privacy cases to court.

Sometimes, however, public health and safety are judged more important than the right of privacy. In 1989, for example, the Supreme Court ruled that the crew members of a train involved in a serious accident could be tested for drug use.

Using Your Skills

1. What was the Court's ruling in *New Jersey* v. *T.L.O.*?
2. What did the Supreme Court rule in *Griswald* v. *Connecticut*?
3. Is it fair for the government to force train crews to submit to drug tests after an accident? Why or why not?

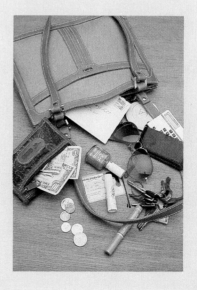

Over the years, the Justice Department's duties have grown to include a wide range of law enforcement activities. Whenever a federal law is broken, the Justice Department is responsible for investigating the crime, tracking down the lawbreakers, putting them on trial, and punishing them if they are found guilty.

Investigations and arrests are made by the Federal Bureau of Investigation, or the FBI, one of the best known bureaus in the Justice Department. Those convicted of breaking federal laws are usually sent to federal prisons, which are operated by the Bureau of Prisons.

Another part of the Justice Department is the Immigration and Naturalization Service, or INS. The INS is responsible for enforcing the nation's immigration laws.

The Department of the Interior

As pioneers moved westward in the mid-1800's, vast areas of land were added to the United States. The Department of the Interior was established in 1849 to manage that land. Today, the Interior Department is primarily responsible for the management and **conservation**, or protection, of the nation's public lands and natural resources.

The best known part of the Interior Department is the National Park Service, which oversees nearly 80 million acres of land in national parks across the country. The Interior Department also includes the Fish and Wildlife Service, which maintains wildlife refuges and protects endangered animals.

The Bureau of Indian Affairs, another division of the Interior Department, manages land set aside for the use of American Indians. These areas, called reservations, are home to more than 800,000 people.

Department of Agriculture

The Department of Agriculture, or USDA, became an executive department in 1889. Its job is to help both farmers and the consumers of farm products.

One agency within the USDA that benefits consumers is the Food Safety and Inspection Service, which helps maintain the quality and safety of meat and poultry. Another is the Food and Nutrition Service, which distributes food stamps to millions of needy families.

The Department of the Interior is responsible for managing the national forests. A forest ranger plants trees as part of a reforestation project.

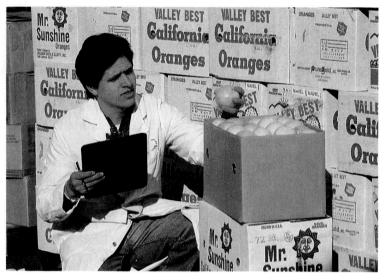

The Food Safety and Inspection Service of the Department of Agriculture oversees the safety and quality of food marketed in the United States.

Divisions of the USDA that benefit farmers include the Agricultural Research Service, which develops new crops and better ways to grow them, and the Farmers' Home Administration, which lends money to farmers who want to expand their farms.

Like the Interior Department, the Agriculture Department is also concerned with conservation. The USDA's Soil Conservation Service protects the rich soil of American farms, and its Forest Service maintains nearly 200 million acres of national forests.

Department of Commerce

The Department of Commerce was established in 1903 to encourage the growth of American business. It supervises international trade, promotes tourism and business, and collects information about the country's economic well-being.

The Commerce Department also offers a number of services that are less directly related to commerce. The Bureau of the Census, which you learned about in Chapter 1, is part of the Commerce Department.

So is the National Patent and Trademark office, which keeps official records of inventions and product names. The National Bureau of Standards, another part of the Commerce Department, sets standards for units of measurement such as inches, pounds, and quarts. These are the official measures against which all others are compared.

The Commerce Department also oversees the National Oceanic and Atmospheric Administration (NOAA), which conducts ocean research and keeps track of atmospheric conditions. Our daily weather forecasts usually come from the National Weather Service, part of the NOAA.

Department of Labor

In the late 1800's, labor unions put pressure on the federal government to pass laws against unfair labor practices. The Department of Labor was established in 1913 to enforce those laws.

One of the most important parts of the Department of Labor is the Occupational Safety and Health Administration (OSHA).

OSHA sets health and safety standards that employers must meet to protect their workers from physical harm. The Department of Labor also includes the Unemployment Insurance Service, which provides financial aid to workers who have been forced to leave their jobs.

The Bureau of Labor Statistics (BLS), another division of the Department of Labor, collects information about the job market and working conditions. This information is available to the public and is particularly useful to people planning their careers.

Department of Health and Human Services

In 1953, President Dwight D. Eisenhower established the Department of Health, Education, and Welfare to work for the health and well-being of Americans. It was renamed the Department of Health and Human Services in 1979, when the Department of Education was made a separate department.

The Department of Health and Human Services (HHS) still helps people in need. Several of its divisions, including the Social Security Administration and the Family Support Administration, provide financial support for people who might otherwise live in poverty. Most HHS programs, however, benefit all Americans.

The Public Health Service, for example, works to keep Americans free from illness. It includes the Center for Disease Control, which conducts research into prevention and cures for diseases, and the National Institutes of Health, which support other health-related research. The Food and Drug Administration (FDA), which oversees the safety of all foods, drugs, and cosmetics sold in the United States, is also part of HHS.

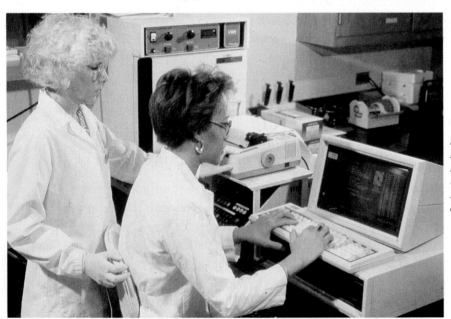

The Center for Disease Control is part of the Department of Health and Human Services. Research scientists at the center use technology in their search for ways to prevent and cure diseases.

Department of Housing and Urban Development

In 1965, President Lyndon Johnson established the Department of Housing and Urban Development, or HUD, to deal with the special problems of cities. HUD operates programs that distribute federal grants to state and local governments. These grants help pay for projects such as rebuilding slums, improving neighborhoods, and building low-income housing. HUD also works with cities and towns to plan for future growth.

Department of Transportation

The Department of Transportation (DOT) was formed in 1966 to manage the country's highways, railroads, airlines, and sea traffic. It also promotes transportation safety. Among its different agencies, the National Highway Traffic Safety Administration sets standards for the safety of automobiles, and the Federal Aviation Administration oversees the airline industry. One of the best-known parts of the DOT is the U.S. Coast Guard, which undertakes search and rescue operations at sea and also serves as an ocean-based police force.

Department of Energy

In 1973, America was hit by its first "energy crisis." The price of gasoline and home heating oil skyrocketed, and these widely used fuels were often in short supply. Americans wondered whether they would have to live with permanent shortages of energy. In 1977, President Jimmy Carter created the Department of Energy to work out and direct an overall energy policy for the nation. The department regulates the development and use of America's oil and gas resources. It also conducts research into ways to use these fuels more efficiently, and to develop other sources of energy such as nuclear energy and solar energy. The Department of Energy is also responsible for regulating the nation's nuclear power industry.

Department of Education

In the mid-1970's, critics charged that the United States was falling behind in education. Although America's goal was to provide free education for everyone, the number of people who could not read was increasing. Moreover, students in Europe and Asia were performing better than American students in science and mathematics.

The Department of Transportation and state governments work together to build and maintain highways and public transport systems across the nation.

Many people felt that the U.S. system of education had to be improved. To help meet this goal, President Carter set up the Department of Education in 1979. (Until that time, education had been part of the Department of Health, Education, and Welfare.)

Although responsibility for education lies primarily with the states and with local communities, the Department of Education offers advice and assistance whenever possible. It distributes federal money to states and school districts to help fund such programs as bilingual education, health and drug education, and vocational training. The department also helps schools meet the special needs of disadvantaged and disabled students.

Department of Veterans Affairs

More than 27 million living Americans have served in the armed forces. Many of these people receive special services from the government, such as inexpensive life insurance and financial aid for education. Some also have special needs, such as medical care for injuries or disabilities received during military service.

For many years, these needs were met by a government agency called the Veterans Administration. In 1989, however, the Veterans Administration became an executive department. It received a new name, the Department of Veterans Affairs, and the head of the department became a member of the Cabinet.

SECTION REVIEW

Define the Words
conservation

Check the Facts
1. Identify five executive departments discussed in this lesson and briefly describe their functions.
2. Identify the remaining nine executive departments discussed in this lesson.
3. Why was the Department of Education made a separate department?

Think About the Ideas
4. *Analyze.* Six of the 14 executive departments have been created since 1950. Why do you think this is so?

Classes held at a medical facility of the Department of Veterans Affairs keep the staff up-to-date on developments in health care.

★ ★

SECTION 3

Independent Agencies

★ ★

VOCABULARY
executive agency
regulatory commission
government corporation

Large as they are, the executive departments can handle only a small part of the executive branch's responsibilities. Other organizations within the executive branch, known as independent agencies, take care of the rest. Such agencies may be created by the President, and funded by Congress, whenever a need for a certain type of work arises.

As a result, today's government includes hundreds of independent federal agencies. Their responsibilities are not always clearly defined, and their work may sometimes overlap. In general, however, they can be divided into three types: executive agencies, regulatory commissions, and government corporations.

Executive Agencies

An **executive agency** is an independent agency responsible for dealing with certain specialized areas of government. The heads, or administrators, of the executive agencies are chosen by the President with the approval of the Senate.

The National Aeronautics and Space Administration (NASA) is an executive agency that we hear about every time a space shuttle is launched. Created in 1958, NASA is responsible for the nation's space flights and research program. About 23,000 people work for NASA, and its budget—more than $11 million in 1990—is larger than that of some executive departments. The chart on this page lists the names and functions of other executive agencies.

Who appoints the heads of the executive agencies?

EXECUTIVE AGENCIES

FARM CREDIT ADMINISTRATION (FCA)-1933
Supervises loans to farmers by federal banks

CENTRAL INTELLIGENCE AGENCY (CIA)-1947
Gathers political and military information on foreign nations

GENERAL SERVICES ADMINISTRATION (GSA)-1949
Maintains federal office buildings and property

NATIONAL SCIENCE FOUNDATION (NSF)-1950
Promotes scientific research

SMALL BUSINESS ADMINISTRATION (SBA)-1953
Protects the interests of small businesses

COMMISSION ON CIVIL RIGHTS-1957
Gathers and evaluates information on discrimination

NATIONAL AERONAUTICS AND SPACE ADMINISTRATION (NASA)-1958
Develops and administers the space program

NATIONAL FOUNDATION ON THE ARTS AND HUMANITIES-1965
Provides grants for the promotion of the arts

ACTION-1971
Administers programs of voluntary service including the Peace Corps

Regulatory Commissions

Regulatory commissions are independent agencies that protect the public by controlling certain types of businesses and industries. The federal government has 11 regulatory commissions. (See chart on this page.) In order to carry out their responsibilities, these commissions have been given special powers by Congress. Each commission has executive, legislative, and judicial powers.

For example, the Federal Communications Commission, or FCC, regulates the television, radio, and telephone industries. It exercises its executive power whenever Congress passes a law involving one of those industries. In 1970, for instance, when Congress banned cigarette commercials from television broadcasts, the FCC was responsible for enforcing the law.

More often, however, the FCC exercises its legislative power. Congress has given the FCC the power to regulate radio transmissions. Using this power, the FCC has set aside certain radio frequencies for special uses. One broadcast band, for example, may be used only for police communications. Another may be used only for cordless telephones. These FCC decisions have the force of law. Anyone who transmits music over the police band, for example, can be charged with a crime.

The FCC also has a judicial function. For example, anyone who wants to own a television station must obtain a license. In exchange for this license, the owner must demonstrate that the TV station will be run in a way that will benefit the general public. Often, when a TV station is put up for sale, two or more people apply to the FCC for a license to run the station. Just as they might do in court, the competing sides present evidence in support of their qualifications. The

---

REGULATORY COMMISSIONS

INTERSTATE COMMERCE COMMISSION (ICC)
Regulates interstate transportation

FEDERAL RESERVE SYSTEM
Establishes general monetary policies

FEDERAL TRADE COMMISSION (FTC)
Prevents monopolies and unfair business practices

SECURITIES AND EXCHANGE COMMISSION (SEC)
Regulates the stock market

FEDERAL COMMUNICATIONS COMMISSION (FCC)
Regulates radio and television

NATIONAL LABOR RELATIONS BOARD (NLRB)
Protects the rights of employees

EQUAL EMPLOYMENT OPPORTUNITY COMMISSION (EEOC)
Works to eliminate job discrimination

CONSUMER PRODUCT SAFETY COMMISSION (CPSC)
Develops standards of safety for consumer goods

NUCLEAR REGULATORY COMMISSION (NRC)
Regulates the building and operation of nuclear reactors

FEDERAL MARITIME COMMISSION (FMC)
Regulates shipping of commercial freight

COMMODITY FUTURES TRADING COMMISSION (CFTC)
Regulates trading

What ensures the impartiality of the regulatory commissions?

FCC then awards the license to one of the applicants. The FCC's decision in such cases is final.

To keep regulatory commissions impartial, Congress has been careful to protect them from political pressure. Each commission is run by a board rather than by an individual. Board members are selected by the

President with Senate approval. The terms of office of these board members are long, however—in some cases, as long as 14 years—and the starting dates of the terms are staggered. Furthermore, Democrats and Republicans must receive nearly equal representation on each commission's board. As a result, no President can fill a majority of seats on a commission, and a Republican President may be forced to appoint a Democrat to a vacant seat.

Because of these safeguards, regulatory commissions tend to be impartial. Their decisions are made to benefit the public rather than to please the members of political parties or interest groups. Nevertheless, many Americans feel that regulatory commissions are a bad idea. They feel that Congress has placed too much power in the hands of too few people. Some people also feel that regulatory commissions make unnecessary rules that interfere in people's lives.

Government Corporations

Many agencies, especially those that provide services to the public, are set up as **government corporations**. A government corporation is similar to a private corporation, except that it is owned and operated by the government rather than by individuals. The President, with Senate approval, chooses a board of directors and a general manager to run each government corporation.

Government corporations are expected to make a profit, so they are always working to cut costs. They are also much more likely to take risks and to find innovative ways of doing things than are other government agencies. Today, the executive branch includes more than 50 government corporations. Perhaps the best known of these is the U.S. Postal Service.

Originally an executive department called the Post Office Department, the Postal Service became a government corporation in 1970. As an executive department, the Post Office lost money. Since becoming a corporation, however, the U.S. Postal Service has begun to make money. In part, this is because, according to the Constitution, it is protected from competition. Only the federal government may deliver letters and bulk mail. In other areas, however, such as package delivery and air express, the Postal Service has had to compete with private businesses. It has met the challenge by cutting costs and making use of new technology such as computerized sorting machines.

SECTION REVIEW

Define the Words
executive agency
regulatory commission
government corporation

Check the Facts
1. Identify three types of independent agencies.
2. What is the purpose of regulatory commissions?
3. How do government corporations differ from private corporations?

Think About the Ideas
4. *Evaluate.* Government corporations, such as the U.S. Postal Service, are protected from certain types of competition. Do you think this is fair? Why or why not?

CIVICS SIDELIGHTS

Bureaucratic Doublespeak

Government officials sometimes seem to speak a different language from most other Americans. It's known as "bureaucratese" or "doublespeak" or "gobbledygook."

The first rule of bureaucratese is that the people who speak it never use one word when two or three or four will do. For example, the homeless might be referred to as "non-goal oriented members of society."

Here are some other examples of doublespeak. See if you can match them with the equivalent terms.

Energetic disassembly
Permanent prehostility
Revenue enhancement
Controlled flight into
  terrain
Frame-supported
  tension structure

Peace
A tent
Nuclear plant
  explosion
Tax increase
Airplane crash

---

* *

SECTION 4
The Federal Bureaucracy

* *

VOCABULARY

red tape	merit system
spoils system	civil servant

For 200 years, Americans have watched the executive branch grow and expand. Today, the President is assisted by over 3 million government employees.

The immense increase in the size of the government has occurred for several reasons. The most obvious is that the United States itself has grown. The U.S. population is now nearly 60 times larger than it was in George Washington's time. More important, however, the federal government has involved itself in the lives of Americans in ways that the writers of the Constitution never imagined. In 1787, there were no telephones, radios, cars, planes, or satellites. There were also no food safety inspections, no programs to provide low-cost housing, no unemployment insurance policies, and no social security benefits. These are things that we cannot imagine living without today. Each of these benefits requires regulation or administration by the federal government.

Structure of the Bureaucracy

The federal bureaucracy is well known for its **red tape**. Red tape is a term that refers to inefficiency caused by too many rules and regulations. For example, even a simple task—such as making a correction on an income tax return—can involve speaking with several different federal employees and filling out dozens of forms.

Some of this red tape results from poor planning or bad management. Most of it, however, is a necessary part of the way a bureaucracy works. Each person in a bureaucracy has a specialized function and operates within a strict chain of command. Only certain people have decision-making power; most people are responsible only for carrying out specific duties. A great deal of paperwork is required to get the proper authorization at different stages of any task. This system may be time-consuming and annoying to those who have to deal with it. It does, however, help ensure that cases are handled consistently. This way, everyone is treated equally by the bureaucracy.

Very specific procedures are also necessary to keep decision making to a minimum. If each person in the bureaucracy made individual decisions, the result would be chaos.

Bureaucracies function best when the people who work in them are well trained and well qualified. Managers should be good at giving clear instructions, and those who carry out the instructions should be skilled at their work.

Development of the Civil Service System

Originally, the executive branch was small enough for Presidents to be able to choose most of their employees personally. Early Presidents tried to appoint the most qualified people to federal jobs. They also, however, tended to appoint members of their own party, who shared similar views.

When Andrew Jackson became President in 1829, party loyalty became even more important. Jackson openly gave out federal jobs as rewards to people who had helped

Many of the agencies that make up the federal bureaucracy provide people with assistance. In some cases, applying for this assistance can require a great deal of paperwork.

his campaign or done him favors in the past. It didn't matter whether these people were qualified for the jobs they were given. This practice of giving jobs as a reward for party loyalty is called the **spoils system**, from the saying "to the victor belong the spoils."

The spoils system continued for more than 50 years. During that time, the executive branch grew larger, and the number of incompetent federal workers increased as well. In addition to being unqualified, many government employees were also dishonest and took advantage of their power. As a result, Americans began to demand that something be done about the spoils system.

After several unsuccessful attempts to end the spoils system, Congress passed the Pendleton Act (also called the Civil Service Act) in 1883. The Pendleton Act replaced the spoils system with a **merit system**, by which government jobs would be given to those who were most qualified.

The Pendleton Act divided government jobs into two categories, unclassified and classified. Jobs in the unclassified category could still be filled by appointment. Jobs in the classified category, however, would be given to those people who scored highest on tests relating to job skills. The Pendleton Act created an agency called the Civil Service Commission to give the tests and to award jobs to the highest scorers. The name of the agency reflected the idea that government workers are **civil servants**—workers whose primary duty is to serve the government and its citizens.

Workers who get jobs through the Civil Service system are supposed to be promoted based on their job performance. Many believed, however, that managers would tend to promote people who shared their political beliefs, rather than people who were good workers. They also feared that government employees would be asked to help one party or another in an election. To meet these concerns, Congress passed the Hatch Act in 1939. The act forbids any civil servant to work in a political campaign or to get involved in party politics.

As President, Andrew Jackson rewarded his most loyal supporters with government jobs—regardless of their qualification.

The Civil Service Today

In 1978, the Civil Service Commission was replaced by two federal agencies. The first, the Office of Personnel Management, administers Civil Service tests and hires workers for government jobs. It also trains new workers and decides on the salary and benefits for each job.

The second agency, the Merit System Protection Board, deals with promotions within the Civil Service system. It makes sure that promotions to higher positions are based entirely on merit. It also makes sure that no government worker is discriminated against for personal or political reasons.

The rise of the Civil Service system has not eliminated the red tape from the federal bureaucracy. It has, however, guaranteed that the executive branch, despite its large size, will work as efficiently as possible.

SECTION REVIEW

Define the Words

red tape   merit system
spoils system   civil servant

Check the Facts
1. Why is there red tape in the federal bureaucracy?
2. What were the provisions of the Pendleton Act?
3. What was the purpose of the Hatch Act?

Think About the Ideas
4. *Analyze.* Why is it important for the federal bureaucracy to be consistent in the way it does its job?
5. *Evaluate.* What are the advantages and disadvantages of the spoils system?

Most government workers had to pass Civil Service tests to qualify for their jobs.

CITIZENSHIP SKILLS

How to Read an Organizational Chart

An organizational chart is a diagram that shows the relationship of different offices or divisions within an organization. It shows the lines of command and the lines of communication. An organizational chart helps you understand the structure of the whole organization as well as the relationship of its various parts.

The organizational chart on page 267 shows the general structure of the Department of the Interior. At the head is the Secretary of the Interior, who is appointed by the President. The Secretary is assisted by the Under Secretary and six Assistant Secretaries, who are concerned with specific fields of interest.

Use the information on the chart to answer the questions that follow:

Using Your Skills

1. What role does the Under Secretary of the Interior play in the organization of the department?

2. Who is responsible for the National Park Service?

3. Suppose that an employee of the U.S. Geological Survey wanted to send a proposal to the Secretary of the Interior. What would be the normal route for this proposal to follow?

Yellowstone National Park

CITIZENSHIP SKILLS

DEPARTMENT OF THE INTERIOR

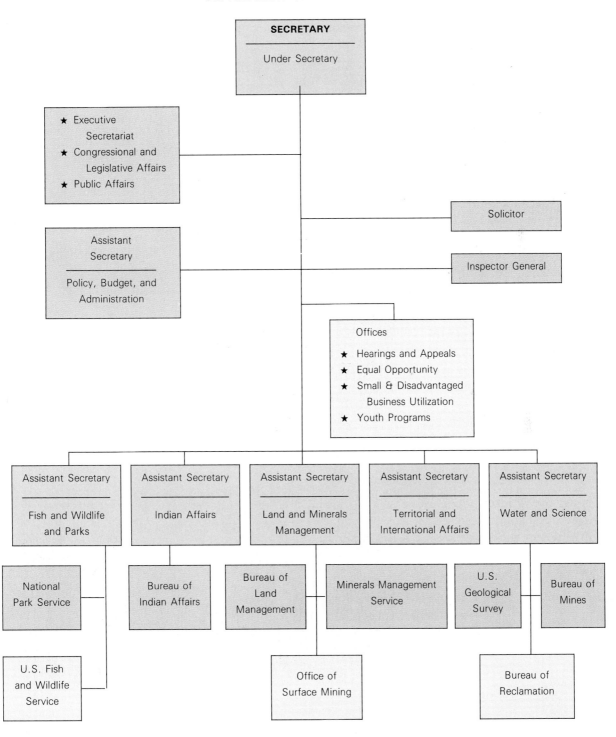

CHAPTER 11 REVIEW

★ ★

MAIN POINTS

★ The members of the Cabinet serve two important functions. They advise the President and they head executive departments.

★ Executive departments have been created over the years to meet certain needs and carry out the work of the government.

★ Fifteen executive departments share the President's executive power. These departments make broad policy decisions and enforce regulations.

★ Much of the work of the executive branch is also carried out by three types of independent agencies: executive agencies, regulatory commissions, and government corporations.

★ The federal bureaucracy has grown to meet the increased needs of the government and the executive branch in particular.

★ Today, government jobs are distributed on the basis of merit through the Civil Service system.

WORDS IN REVIEW

Choose the word or phrase from the list below that best completes each sentence. Write the missing words on a separate sheet of paper.

Cabinet	embassy
consulate	visa
conservation	regulatory commission
red tape	government corporation
spoils system	merit system

1. The foreign visitor applied for a _____, which would allow her to remain in the United States for three months.

2. Under the _____, people were given government jobs without regard to their qualifications.

3. The heads of the 14 executive departments are all members of the President's _____.

4. Government employees are promoted according to the _____.

5. The employees at the American _____ in Taipei, Taiwan, worked to improve U.S. business interests in that city.

6. The U.S. Postal Service is an example of a _____.

7. Many citizens have had frustrating experiences with bureaucratic _____.

8. The _____ was responsible for controlling use of radio frequencies throughout the nation.

9. The _____ was run by the newly appointed ambassador.

10. The _____ of the nation's resources is part of the job of the Interior Department.

FACTS IN REVIEW

1. Why did the Cabinet develop?

2. Name three important divisions of the Department of the Treasury.

3. What positions make up the Joint Chiefs of Staff?

4. What was the original role of the Attorney General?

5. Identify two important agencies within the Department of Health and Human services.

CHAPTER 11 REVIEW

* *

6. Why was the Department of Energy created in 1977?

7. What is an executive agency?

8. Why are regulatory commissions protected against political pressures?

9. Why is red tape a necessary part of a bureaucracy?

10. How did the spoils system change the federal bureaucracy?

THINKING ABOUT THE EXECUTIVE BRANCH

1. *Analyze*. Do you think the Department of Defense should be under civilian control? Why or why not?

2. *Evaluate*. Which of the executive departments do you think has the greatest effect on you and your family? Why?

3. *Analyze*. What effect does the Civil Service System have on the work of the federal bureaucracy?

WRITING ABOUT THE EXECUTIVE BRANCH

Prepare a written report on the work of the executive branch of the government. Your report should include a paragraph on each of the 14 executive departments. Each paragraph should include information on why the department was created, its main responsibilities, and the name of the current Secretary of the department.

COMPARING CHARTS

Look at the charts showing the executive departments and the executive agencies on pages 248 and 259. How many of the executive agencies have been created since 1970? Compare the responsibilities of the executive agencies with the responsibilities of the executive departments. Which ones seem to overlap? In what ways?

FOCUSING ON YOUR COMMUNITY

Jobs within the government bureaucracy are found at every level of government. For example, a secretary working in the mayor's office is a government employee. Research the different types of government jobs in your community. Find out how many people work for the local government. Find out how people apply for these jobs, what qualifications are necessary, and what the salaries are. Prepare a report to present to the class.

CHAPTER 12

★ ★

The Judicial Branch

OBJECTIVES

After you have studied this chapter, you will be able to:

★ Identify the different courts within the federal court system.
★ Describe the organization and jurisdiction of the federal court system.
★ Identify and describe the roles of various officials within the federal court system.
★ Discuss the importance of the Supreme Court and explain its jurisdiction and powers.
★ Discuss the roles and responsibilities of Supreme Court Justices and explain how the Supreme Court deals with cases.

SECTIONS

1 The Federal Court System
2 The Lower Federal Courts
3 The U.S. Supreme Court
4 The Court at Work

INTRODUCTION

Lisa Domenici was injured last year in an auto accident. Although the other driver was at fault, his insurance company refused to pay for Lisa's medical expenses and for the repairs to her car. Lisa therefore took the insurance company to court.

The writers of the Constitution knew that there would be disagreements and conflicts over the laws. The judicial system of judges and courts was set up to settle such disputes fairly and peacefully. While the legislative branch makes the laws and the executive branch carries them out, the role of the judicial branch is to interpret the laws and to preserve and protect the rights guaranteed by the Constitution. The judicial system is the nation's third branch of government.

The judicial branch can strike down a law passed by Congress if it conflicts with anything in the Constitution. The judicial branch can also overrule the actions of the President, or others in the executive branch, if those actions violate the laws or rights guaranteed in the Constitution. The judicial branch plays a vital role in the system of checks and balances that protects our democracy.

* *

SECTION 1

The Federal Court System

* *

VOCABULARY

inferior court	jurisdiction
criminal case	exclusive jurisdiction
civil case	concurrent jurisdiction
suit	

From 1781 to 1789, when the United States was governed by the Articles of Confederation, there was no national court system. Each state had its own laws and its own courts. There was no way to guarantee that people would receive equal justice in all states.

To deal with these problems the writers of the Constitution provided for a federal judiciary. Article III of the Constitution established a national Supreme Court. It also gave Congress the power to establish other **inferior courts**, or courts of lower authority. This power was given to Congress as a way of checking the power of the judicial branch.

Over the years, Congress has added two types of lower courts to the federal judiciary system. In 1789, it passed the Judiciary Act, which created the federal district courts. Much later, in 1891, Congress created the appeals courts. The federal court system now has three levels—the district courts on the bottom, the appeals courts in the middle, and the Supreme Court on the top. You will learn what each of these courts does later in this chapter.

Jurisdiction of the Federal Courts

There are really two separate court systems in the United States—the state courts and the federal courts. The state courts hear the vast majority of legal disputes in the United States. Most **criminal cases**—cases in which juries decide whether people have committed crimes—are tried in state courts. The state courts also hear most **civil cases**—cases in which two sides are in disagreement over some issue. Lisa's case, discussed at the beginning of this chapter, is a civil case. In a civil case, one party, or person, involved sues or takes legal action against another party. The complaint the first person makes to the court is called a **suit**, or lawsuit. A party in a lawsuit can be a person, a company or business, or a level of government. You will learn more about the state court system in Chapter 13.

Article III of the Constitution gives the federal courts **jurisdiction**—the authority to hear and decide a case—only in certain specific areas. These are cases that involve one of the following:

The words EQUAL JUSTICE UNDER LAW, *inscribed over the entrance to the Supreme Court building, describe the goal of the justice system.*

1. *The Constitution.* For example, if a person feels that a Constitutional right such as freedom of speech has been violated, that person has a right to be heard in a federal court.
2. *Laws enacted by the federal government.* The federal courts try people accused of federal crimes such as tax evasion, kidnapping, and bank robbery. Federal courts also hear civil cases that involve federal laws.
3. *Admiralty and maritime law.* These concern crimes and accidents that happen on the high seas, or are related to the seas. One recent case involved a dispute over rights to the riches recovered from a sunken ship 160 miles off the coast of South Carolina.
4. *Disputes in which the United States government is involved.* The government, for example, could take a company to court for failing to live up to a contract to deliver supplies to a government department. Individuals or companies can also take the government to court. For example, if your car was struck by a U.S. Army van or if the Department of the Interior failed to pay your company for equipment, you could sue the government.
5. *Controversies between states.* In any disagreements between states, the states can ask the federal courts to settle the matter.
6. *Controversies between citizens of different states.* For example, if a person in Massachusetts is cheated by a person in Nevada, the case can be brought before a federal court. Federal law limits the jurisdiction of federal courts in these cases to suits involving $10,000 or more.
7. *Disputes involving foreign governments.* In any dispute between a foreign country and the U.S. government, an American company, or an American citizen, the case will be heard in a federal court.
8. *U.S. ambassadors, ministers, and consuls serving in foreign countries.* For example, if a diplomat assigned to the U.S. Embassy in Moscow is accused of breaking an American law, the case may be heard in the federal courts.

In most of these areas, the federal courts have **exclusive jurisdiction**. This means that only the federal courts may hear and decide cases. By giving the federal courts jurisdiction in these instances, the writers of the Constitution left all other matters to the state courts. However, there are some circumstances in which a case can be heard in either the state or federal courts. In these instances, the state and federal courts are said to share the jurisdiction, or to have **concurrent jurisdiction**. For example, crimes that violate both state and federal laws may be tried in either the federal or state courts. Concurrent jurisdiction also occurs when a person appeals a conviction on Constitutional grounds. The conviction can be appealed through the state and federal courts up to the U.S. Supreme Court.

SECTION REVIEW

Define the Words

inferior court	jurisdiction
criminal case	exclusive jurisdiction
civil case	concurrent jurisdiction
suit	

Check the Facts
1. What was the Judiciary Act of 1789?
2. What is the difference between a criminal case and a civil case?
3. Give an example of concurrent jurisdiction.

Think About the Ideas
4. *Analyze.* Why do you think the federal courts were given exclusive jurisdiction over certain types of cases?

SECTION 2

The Lower Federal Courts

★ ★

VOCABULARY

district court	appellate
original jurisdiction	jurisdiction
magistrate	circuit
marshal	remand
subpoena	court-martial
court of appeals	

At the top of the federal court system is the Supreme Court. Then come the lower courts—the district courts and appeals courts.

District Courts

The United States District Courts make up the lowest level of the federal court system. **District courts** are the federal courts where trials are held and lawsuits are begun. Before a federal case can be filed and heard at an appeals court or the Supreme Court, it must be heard in a district court. For this reason, district courts are said to have **original jurisdiction**, or the authority to hear cases for the first time. They are also the only federal courts in which jury trials are held.

The district courts are so named because each has jurisdiction or authority over a specific geographical area or district. Each state has at least one district court, and more

populous states may have as many as three or four. There is one district court each in the District of Columbia and Puerto Rico. Also, there are district courts in some other United States' territories.

About 90 percent of the work of the federal courts is done in the district courts. They handle about 300,000 criminal and civil cases each year. Criminal cases can include such violations of federal laws as mail fraud, income tax evasion, bank robbery, and treason. Among the kinds of civil cases tried in district courts are disputes involving labor relations, public lands, copyright and patent laws, and civil rights.

The Constitution clearly states where federal cases shall be tried. Article III says that "such Trial shall be held in the State where the said Crimes shall have been committed." This provision helps ensure that people accused of federal crimes can get a fair trial. The accused will be tried by people familiar with the area where the crime was committed. In addition, witnesses for the defense will be available to testify without having to travel great distances.

DISTRICT COURT JUDGES Each district court has at least two judges who preside over the federal cases brought there. Some courts in more populous districts have many more judges because of a higher volume of work. It is the responsibility of each district court judge to decide on the procedures to be followed in court and to explain the law involved in a case to the jury. Judges also decide on the punishment or fine when the jury finds the defendant guilty. All district court judges are appointed by the President of the United States with the approval of the Senate. District court judges currently receive a salary of $96,000 per year.

The Constitution provides that federal judges be appointed "during good behavior."

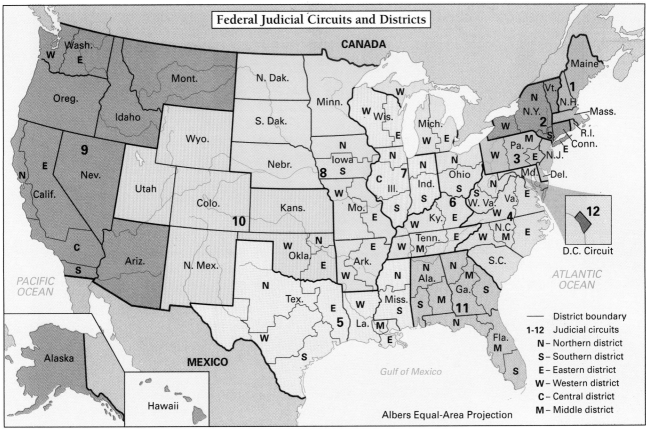

Federal Judicial Circuits and Districts

The map shows the geographical boundries of the federal judicial circuits and districts. Why do you think District 3 is so much smaller than District 10?

In effect, this means that they are appointed for life unless they are found guilty of some serious crime. The Constitution also provides that the government cannot reduce the salaries of federal judges during their term in office. The writers of the Constitution included these two provisions to help ensure an independent judiciary. Since judges cannot be removed from office without cause or punished with a reduction in salary, they can remain free from political influence and cannot be forced to make rulings favorable to anyone in power. They are free to decide each case strictly in terms of the legal issues, no matter how unpopular their decisions may be politically.

OTHER DISTRICT COURT OFFICIALS In addition to judges, district courts have several other officials who fulfill certain responsibilities. Each district court has a **magistrate**, who issues court orders and hears the preliminary evidence in a case to determine whether the case should be brought to trial. By doing this, the magistrate helps protect criminal suspects from being unfairly charged and tried. Magistrates may also hear minor cases.

Every district court also has a United States attorney. The United States attorney is the government's lawyer. It is his or her job to prove that a suspect has committed a crime. It is also the attorney's job to repre-

A courtroom's cast of characters includes the defendant, the prosecuting and defense attorneys, a clerk (next to judge), a stenographer (in front of the jurors), and a uniformed officer.

sent the government in civil cases in which the government is involved. Usually, a United States attorney runs a large office with dozens of assistant U.S. attorneys who perform most of the trial work.

Another district court official is the U.S. **marshal**. The marshal arrests suspects, delivers defendants to court, and serves subpoenas. A **subpoena** is a court order requiring people to appear in court. District court magistrates, attorneys, and marshals are all appointed by the President, with Senate approval.

In addition to these officials, each district court also has many clerks, deputy clerks, secretaries, and other workers who keep track of court cases, file legal papers, help the public, and perform other jobs that help the court operate efficiently.

U.S. Courts of Appeals

Above the district courts in the federal court system are the U.S. **courts of appeals**. These courts are also sometimes called federal appeals courts, circuit courts of appeals, or appellate courts.

When people who have been tried in district court feel that the verdict or penalty is unfair, they can take their case to a U.S. court of appeals.

The courts of appeals have only **appellate jurisdiction**. This means that they only hear cases that have come to them on appeal from the lower district courts or from federal regulatory agencies. For example, the lawyer for the losing side in a civil case may decide to appeal a district court's verdict. The lawyer may feel that the district court judge fol-

Court Reporter

Court reporters are stenographers, or shorthand reporters. They work in all levels of courts and are responsible for recording everything that is said in a legal proceeding. Speed and accuracy are very important, because the courts need a complete written record of their proceedings.

Court reporters use special stenotype machines with 21 keys to take notes. After the proceedings, they dictate their notes into a dictating machine for transcription by a typist or word processor. Every word said in the trial or hearing must be included in the official transcript.

Skilled court reporters are in high demand in state and federal court systems. In smaller areas, a court reporter may work in several courts within the municipal judicial system.

To become a court reporter, you must be able to take at least 160 words of dictation per minute. You

need at least a high school diploma, and preferably an associate degree or a certificate from a preprofessional training program.

In addition to being quick and accurate, court reporters must be able to concentrate on the task in a busy setting with many distractions. Most jobs involve repeti-

tive work with little independent decision-making. However, by keeping accurate records, court reporters play a vital role in the American system of justice.

Using Your Skills
1. What do court reporters do?
2. What are a court reporter's most important skills?

lowed the wrong procedure or did not apply the law correctly. Or some new evidence may have turned up that could change the outcome of the case.

Rulings by a federal regulatory agency may also be appealed if the people or groups involved feel the agency applied a rule or made a decision unfairly. Suppose, for example, that the Food and Drug Administration (FDA) refuses to approve the use of a new drug. The company that manufactures the drug can ask the appeals court to review the FDA's decision.

Congress created the appeals courts in 1891 to ease the burden of the U.S. Supreme Court, which was receiving more appeals each year than it could handle. There are 12 U.S. Courts of Appeals; each has jurisdiction over a **circuit**, or a particular geographical area. Each court receives cases from the district courts within its own circuit. If a person appeals a case that originated in the Federal District court in Denver, Colorado, for example, the case would go to the Court of Appeals for the 10th Circuit. (See the map on page 275.)

APPEALS COURT JUDGES Each appeals court has from 4 to 23 judges. Like other federal judges, they are appointed for life. Their salaries are currently $102,500 a year. Appeals court judges do not preside over trials. There are no juries in appeals courts. Instead, a panel of at least three judges hears arguments from the attorneys for each side and reviews trial records from the lower court.

The judges do not decide on the guilt or innocence of a defendant. They only rule on whether the defendant's rights have been protected and on whether he or she received a fair trial. The panel may make one of three rulings: to uphold the lower court's verdict, to overturn the lower court's decision, or to **remand** (return) the case to the lower court for a new trial. The decision of the appeals court is usually final. In some cases, however, the decision may be appealed to the U.S. Supreme Court, which can decide whether or not to hear the case.

Special Federal Courts

In addition to the district and appeals courts, Congress has also created several special courts to hear cases in certain instances. These include:

★ *The U.S. Tax Court.* This court hears appeals dealing with federal tax laws. Taxpayers who have a dispute with the Internal Revenue Service may take their case to this court.

★ *The U.S. Claims Court.* The Claims Court hears cases of citizens who bring suit against the government for money claims. If the court feels that the claim has merit, it will uphold the suit and award a sum of money. Congress must then appropriate the money to pay the claim.

★ *The Court of Military Appeals.* This is the appeals court for the armed forces. When people in the service are accused of breaking a federal or military law, they are tried

Most cases involving members of the armed services are handled in a Court of Military Review.

at a **court-martial**, a trial before a panel of military officers. Military personnel who have been court-martialed may appeal their verdicts to the Court of Military Appeals.

★ *The U.S. Court of International Trade.* This court hears disputes arising from tariff and trade laws. For example, if the government prevents an importer from bringing certain goods into the country, the importer may bring the case to the court of trade. This court is also called U.S. Customs Court.

SECTION REVIEW

Define the Words

district court	court of appeals
original jurisdiction	appellate jurisdiction
magistrate	circuit
marshal	remand
subpoena	court-martial

Check the Facts
1. What are the responsibilities of district judges?
2. What is the function of the U.S. Courts of Appeals?
3. Identify and describe the functions of three special federal courts.

Think About the Ideas
4. *Analyze.* Why is it important for federal judges to be protected from political pressures?
5. *Analyze.* Why do you think that military personnel are tried for crimes in court-martials instead of in district court?

SECTION 3

The U.S. Supreme Court

★ ★

VOCABULARY
judicial review   unconstitutional

The U.S. Supreme Court is the highest court in the land. It is the final court to which anyone can appeal a legal decision. According to the Constitution, the Supreme Court has original jurisdiction in only two instances. It can preside over trials in cases that involve diplomats from foreign countries and in cases in which a state is involved. For example, if one state sues another state, the Supreme Court can try the suit. In fact, the Court very rarely hears these two kinds of cases. They are usually tried in the federal district courts.

In all other instances, the Supreme Court has appellate jurisdiction. Its main responsibility is to hear appeals in cases originating in lower courts. Although about 5,000 cases are appealed to the Supreme Court each year, the Court selects only about 150 for a full hearing and review. In general, the Court hears appeals only in cases that pose significant legal or Constitutional questions or are of great public interest and concern. The Supreme Court decides not to hear many cases and remands others to the lower courts with a short opinion stating its reasons for ordering a retrial. Whether the Court hears a case or not, its decision cannot be appealed.

The justices of the Supreme Court pose for a group portrait. William J. Brennan, seated second from the left, resigned in 1990 after 33 years on the Supreme Court. He was replaced by David Souter.

The Supreme Court enjoys a great deal of power and prestige. The legislative and executive branches must follow the Supreme Court's rulings. The fact that the Court is removed from politics and from the influences of special interest groups makes it more likely that the parties involved in a case will get a fair hearing.

The Power of the Supreme Court

One of the most important powers of the Supreme Court is the power of judicial review. **Judicial review** means that the Court can review any federal or state law to see if it is in agreement with the Constitution. If the Court decides that a law or governmental action is **unconstitutional**—in conflict with the Constitution—it has the power to nullify, or cancel, that law or action. The power of judicial review thus makes the Supreme Court the final authority on the Constitution and laws of the United States.

MARBURY V. *MADISON* The power of judicial review is not mentioned in the Constitution. This power was established officially in 1803 in the case of *Marbury* v. *Madison*. On his last night in office, President John Adams signed an order making William Marbury a justice of the peace (a kind of judge) for the District of Columbia. When Thomas Jefferson took office the next day, he told Secretary of State James Madison not to carry out Adams' order.

DEMOCRACY IN AMERICA

*A*lexis de Tocqueville was a young judge from France who came to America in 1831 to study prison reform and American democracy. He spent two years traveling around the United States interviewing political leaders and ordinary citizens about how the American political system worked. At that time, American democracy with its system of checks and balances and separation of powers was still unfamiliar to most of the world.

Tocqueville returned to France and published the first part of his book *Democracy in America* in 1835. It was an instant success. The second part was published in 1840.

What Tocqueville tried to do was analyze how American society functioned and how its political system worked. He was particularly interested in learning how the American people were able to retain control of their government and prevent it from being taken over by dictators or kings

as had happened in France. In the following section of *Democracy in America*, Tocqueville discusses the role the Supreme Court plays in protecting democracy.

The peace, the prosperity, and the very existence of the Union are vested in [entrusted to] the hands of the seven Federal judges. * *Without them the Constitution would be a dead letter: the executive branch appeals to them for assistance against the encroachments [extension] of the legislative power; the legislature demands their protection against the assaults [attempts to gain power] of the executive; they defend the Union from disobedience of the states, the states from the exaggerated claims of the Union, the public against private*

---

* There were two vacancies on the high court during 1831 and 1832.

interests, and the conservative spirit of stability against the fickleness [changing nature] of the democracy. Their power is enormous, but it is the power of public opinion. They are all powerful as long as the people respect the law.

Democracy in America is considered an American classic, but it had an even greater impact abroad. This detailed blueprint of how to create a democratic government was widely read and debated in European countries as they struggled to establish democracies.

Using Your Skills

1. Why do you think Tocqueville was so interested in how American democracy worked?

2. What did he mean when he said that without the Supreme Court, the Constitution would be a "dead letter"?

3. Why was *Democracy in America* so important in Europe?

William Marbury took his case directly to the U.S. Supreme Court, which he claimed had jurisdiction as a result of a provision in the Judiciary Act of 1789. John Marshall, the Chief Justice of the Supreme Court, wrote an opinion turning down Marbury's claim. He noted that the Constitution did not give the Court jurisdiction to decide Marbury's case. (As you just learned, the Constitution says the Supreme Court can only preside over trials in cases that involve states or foreign diplomats.) In his opinion, Marshall set out three basic principles of judicial review:

★ The Constitution is the supreme law of the land.

★ When there is a conflict between the Constitution and any other law, the Constitution must be followed.

★ The judicial branch has a duty to uphold the Constitution. This means it must be able to determine when a law is in conflict with the Constitution and to nullify or cancel unconstitutional laws.

Which Supreme Court decision was overturned by Brown v. Board of Education?

LANDMARK DECISIONS OF THE SUPREME COURT

Marbury v. *Madison* (1803)
Established the Supreme Court's power of judicial review.

Dred Scott v. *Sandford* (1857)
Ruled that the federal government had the power to prohibit slavery in U.S. Territories, and that black slaves and their descendants could not be U.S. citizens.

Plessy v. *Ferguson* (1896)
Established the "separate but equal" doctrine which permitted segregation.

Muller v. *Oregon* (1908)
Ruled that states could protect women workers if the states had a reasonable justification.

Schenck v. *U.S.* (1919)
Held that free speech could be limited if there was a "clear and present danger" that illegal action might result from the speech.

Brown v. *Board of Education* (1954)
Established that the "separate but equal" doctrine was unconstitutional.

Gideon v. *Wainwright* (1963)
Declared that a person accused of a major crime has the right to legal counsel during a trial.

Reynolds v. *Sims* (1964)
Held that unequal representation violated the Fourteenth Amendment.
Established the principle of "one person, one vote."

Miranda v. *Arizona* (1966)
Ruled that policemen must inform suspects of their rights at the time of arrest.

New York Times v. *U.S.* (1971)
Held that prior restraint or censorship is unconstitutional unless the government can prove serious and immediate harm to the nation.

U.S. v. *Nixon* (1974)
Established that Presidents could claim executive privilege in cases where military and national security issues were involved but could not use it to conceal evidence of a crime.

Source: *Encyclopedia of American History*, 6th ed., Richard B. Morris Harper & Row, New York, 1982

The power of judicial review serves as an important check on the legislative and executive branches of government. It prevents them from straying too far from the Constitution when they make and carry out new laws.

CHECKING THE COURT'S POWER Judicial review gives the Court a position of great influence, but it does not make the Court all powerful. Congress can get around a Supreme Court ruling by changing a law in such a way that it is no longer in conflict with the Constitution. Congress can also adopt an amendment to the Constitution, which then changes the Constitution.

In addition, the Supreme Court must rely on the executive branch to carry out its decisions. The executive branch almost always enforces Supreme Court rulings, but in the case of *Worcester* v. *Georgia*, it did not. When Chief Justice John Marshall ordered the State of Georgia to stop violating federal land treaties with the Cherokee Indians in 1832, President Andrew Jackson refused to enforce the order. The President is reported to have said: "John Marshall has made his decision, now let him enforce it."

CONTROVERSY AND THE COURT Despite its power and prestige, the Supreme Court sometimes becomes involved in controversy. Some of its decisions anger certain groups of people. These people might put pressure on Congress to pass a new law or Constitutional amendment that will get around the Court's ruling. One of the Court's most controversial decisions was in the 1857 case of *Dred Scott* v. *Sandford*, in which the Court ruled that the Constitution did not prohibit slavery. That ruling was overturned by the passage of the Fourteenth Amendment in 1868.

Controversial decisions of recent years have included *Brown* v. *Board of Education* (1954), which outlawed school segregation, and *Wade* v. *Roe* (1973), which legalized abortion.

After the Supreme Court declared segregated schools unconstitutional, the President called in federal troops to enforce the decision.

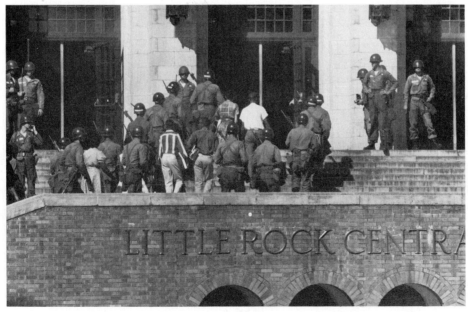

Supreme Court Justices

The Supreme Court is made up of eight Associate Justices and one Chief Justice. Until recently, all the justices who had served on the Supreme Court were men. But in 1981, President Ronald Reagan appointed Sandra Day O'Connor of Arizona to the Court. Thurgood Marshall, who was appointed in 1967, is the only black justice to ever serve on the Court. Supreme Court justices serve for life. Associate Justices currently receive a salary of $118,600 and the Chief Justice receives $124,000.

Although the Constitution does not set any qualifications for serving on the Supreme Court, all justices have been lawyers and most have been judges or law professors. Some have also been public officials. William

In the 1970's and 1980's, Supreme Court Justice Thurgood Marshall often found himself on the dissenting side of Court decisions. What is the purpose of a dissenting opinion?

In 1981, President Ronald Reagan appointed Sandra Day O'Connor (pictured here) to the Supreme Court. She was the first woman to serve as a Supreme Court justice.

Howard Taft was the only person to become Chief Justice of the Supreme Court after serving as President of the United States.

The Constitution gives the President the power to appoint Supreme Court justices, with the consent of the Senate. The Senate usually approves the President's choices. Occasionally, however, the Senate will turn down a President's nominee because of doubts about the qualifications or legal philosophy of that person. This happened most recently in 1987, when the Senate rejected Robert Bork because of his legal philosophy.

Presidents usually try to appoint justices who share their political beliefs or view of the law. Once appointed to the Court, however, a justice is under no obligation to follow the President's line of thinking. Nevertheless, if a President has the opportunity to name several justices to the Court, it is likely that the President's views will be reflected in many of the Court's decisions. In this way, a President may affect the way cases are decided far into the future.

SECTION REVIEW

Define the Words

judicial review   unconstitutional

Check the Facts

1. In what two instances does the Supreme Court have original jurisdiction?
2. Of the many cases appealed to the Supreme Court, which ones does the Court usually consider?
3. What was the significance of the case of *Marbury* v. *Madison?*

Think About the Ideas

4. *Analyze.* Why is it important that the Supreme Court not be influenced by politics?

★ ★ ★ ★ ★ ★ ★ ★ ★ ★ ★ ★ ★ ★ ★ ★ ★ ★ ★ ★

SECTION 4

The Court at Work

★ ★ ★ ★ ★ ★ ★ ★ ★ ★ ★ ★ ★ ★ ★ ★ ★ ★ ★ ★

VOCABULARY

brief	majority opinion
docket	concurring opinion
adversary	dissenting opinion
writ of certiorari	

The Supreme Court conducts its business each year from October until the following June or July. For the first two weeks of each of these months, the Court is said to be "sitting," or in session. This is the time when justices hear arguments—usually 30 minutes for each side in a case. The justices also announce what cases they have decided to hear, discuss and vote on current cases, and announce their decisions.

Each two-week session is followed by a two-week recess, during which the justices do most of their work. When the court is in recess, justices decide which cases to hear, research the cases that will come before them, and write their opinions on cases heard during the last session. They also use this time to read the written arguments, or **briefs**, that have been prepared by the attorneys for cases.

Deciding Which Cases to Hear

An important task of Supreme Court justices is to decide whether or not to hear a case. The justices review a list of possible cases and consider their merits. For a case to be heard, at least four justices must vote for it. After a case has been accepted, it is placed on the Court **docket**, or calendar. It is assigned a number as well as a date when it will be brought before the Court.

The justices of the Supreme Court decide to hear only certain kinds of cases. They usually decide to hear a case if it involves a Constitutional question. In most instances, these questions center on the Bill of Rights and other amendments, and deal with issues such as freedom of speech, equal protection of the laws, and fair trial.

The justices always choose cases that involve a real dispute between two **adversaries**, or opposing sides. In other words, the cases must deal with real people and events.

In 1986, William H. Rehnquist, center, became the fifteenth Chief Justice of the U.S. Supreme Court.

The justices also select cases that involve legal issues rather than political questions. By choosing these kinds of cases, the justices cannot be accused of interfering in matters that really should be decided by the legislative or executive branch.

Finally, the justices tend to select cases that are of importance to the entire country, rather than just to the individuals or groups involved. Such cases will have a broader application to the nation's laws.

How Cases Reach the Court

You have already learned that nearly all cases come to the Supreme Court because of an appeal from a lower court. Most of these appeals reach the Court by a request for a **writ of certiorari** (which is Latin for "to make more certain"). A writ of certiorari directs a lower court to send its records on a case to the Supreme Court for review. This happens if one of the parties involved in a case claims that the lower court made an error in conducting the case. Sometimes a lower court will ask the Supreme Court to make a ruling in a case because it is not sure how to apply the law to the case.

Court Decisions and Opinions

While the Court is in session, the justices meet privately on Wednesdays and Fridays to discuss and vote on each case. At these meetings, the Chief Justice asks each Associate Justice to give his or her opinion of the case. Opinions are given in order of the justices' time on the Court, with the longest-serving justice first and the newest justice last. Then a vote is taken in reverse order, starting with the newest justice and ending with the Chief Justice.

Facing the Music

Although the Supreme Court tries to choose cases that raise important legal or Constitutional questions, sometimes the circumstances of a case may take the Court into unusual areas.

In the case of *Ward* v. *Rock Against Racism*, which the Court heard in 1989, the issue was whether a New York City law violated the freedom of expression of rock and roll bands.

The law required musicians performing at a city-owned bandshell in Central Park to use a city-supplied sound system and a sound technician so that it could regulate the volume of the music. Rock Against Racism, a group of rock bands, argued that this interfered with artistic expression.

The Court upheld the New York Law. It ruled that the city could place certain restrictions on the "time, place and manner" of expression without violating the First Amendment. In other words, the city had the right to turn down the volume.

A majority vote of the Court determines the outcome of a case. If all nine justices are present, the vote must be at least 5 to 4. Sometimes, because of illness or other reasons, all nine justices do not vote. A minimum of six justices is required, however, to hear and decide a case. If only six justices vote, the vote must be at least 4 to 2. In the event of a tie vote, the lower court's decision is upheld.

Most Supreme Court decisions are accompanied by an opinion explaining why the justices made that decision. Usually the Chief Justice asks an Associate Justice who voted with the majority to write the **majority opinion**. A **concurring opinion** is written by a justice who agrees with the majority decision but has different reasons. **Dissenting opinions** are written by justices who oppose the majority decision.

Dissenting opinions sometimes become majority opinions in later cases. This happened when Justice Hugo Black argued in a dissenting opinion in 1942 that poor people suspected of crimes are entitled to an attorney. Black's dissenting opinion became the basis for a majority opinion he wrote 21 years later in *Gideon* v. *Wainwright*. (See Closeup on this case on page 407).

Justice Hugo Black, appointed by President Roosevelt in 1937, served on the Supreme Court for 34 years. Some of his dissenting opinions later became the basis of majority decisions.

SECTION REVIEW

Define the Words

brief
docket
adversary
writ of certiorari

majority opinion
concurring opinion
dissenting opinion

Check the Facts
1. How does the Supreme Court decide whether or not to hear a case?
2. What kinds of work do Supreme Court justices do during the Court's recess?
3. Explain the difference between a majority opinion and a concurring opinion.

Think About the Ideas
4. *Evaluate.* Which do you think is probably more important in Supreme Court cases, oral arguments or written briefs? Explain.

CITIZENSHIP SKILLS

How to Read a Flow Chart

A flow chart is a diagram that shows movement in a system or illustrates how a system works. The flow chart on this page shows how the various parts of the federal judicial system are related. The arrows indicate the flow of authority (appeals) from the lowest courts (shown at the bottom of the chart) up to the Supreme Court. You can trace the route of an appeal from any of the lower courts or agencies. The higher courts have the power to review the decisions of the lower courts under its jurisdiction.

Use the information on this flow chart to answer the following questions:

Using Your Skills

1. Which court has the power to review the decisions of the highest state courts?
2. To what court can decisions of district courts be appealed?
3. What courts review the decisions of federal regulatory agencies?
4. The Constitution established the Supreme Court and gave Congress the power to create lower courts. Why do you think the framers of the Constitution placed the Supreme Court above all courts?

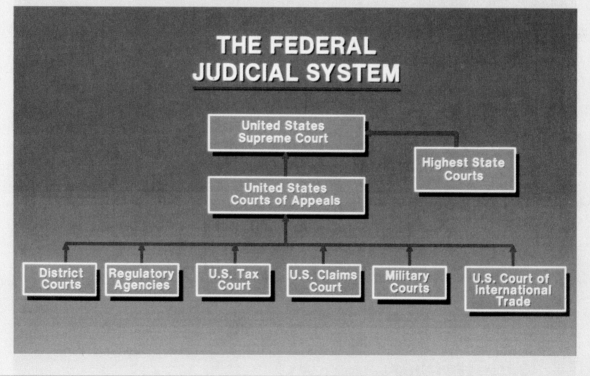

THE FEDERAL JUDICIAL SYSTEM

- United States Supreme Court
- United States Courts of Appeals
- Highest State Courts
- District Courts
- Regulatory Agencies
- U.S. Tax Court
- U.S. Claims Court
- Military Courts
- U.S. Court of International Trade

CHAPTER 12 REVIEW

★ ★

MAIN POINTS

★ The Constitution established the U.S. Supreme Court and gave Congress the power to create a federal court system.

★ The federal courts have jurisdiction in eight kinds of legal disputes. State courts have jurisdiction in all other kinds of cases.

★ In addition to the Supreme Court, the federal court system consists of district courts, appeals courts, and a number of special courts.

★ The main officials of the federal court system are judges, U.S. attorneys, magistrates, and marshals.

★ The U.S. Supreme Court is the highest court in the land. It is the final authority to which a case can be appealed.

★ One of the most important powers of the Supreme Court is judicial review, the right to decide whether a state or federal law is Constitutional.

★ The work of the Supreme Court is divided between periods when the Court is in session and when it is in recess. During the sessions, the justices hear arguments, announce which cases they will hear, and hand down opinions. During the recesses, the justices read briefs and write opinions on cases.

★ The Supreme Court hears cases that raise important legal or Constitutional questions, that involve real people or events, and that are of importance to the entire country.

WORDS IN REVIEW

Choose the word or phrase from the list below that best completes each sentence. Write the missing words on a separate sheet of paper.

criminal case   civil case
concurrent jurisdiction   appellate jurisdiction
district court   court of appeals
remand   judicial review
brief   writ of certiorari

1. In instances where either state or federal courts can hear a case, the courts are said to have _____.

2. The lower court received a _____ requesting that the records of a case be sent to the Supreme Court.

3. The burglary case was being tried in the _____.

4. The case against the man accused of robbing the store was a _____.

5. The appeals court judges decided to _____ the case to a lower court.

6. Convinced that the presiding judge had applied the law incorrectly, the defense lawyer decided to take the case to the _____.

7. After the case was accepted by the Supreme Court, the lawyer had to submit a _____ outlining the arguments of the case.

8. Courts that only hear cases sent to them from lower courts are said to have _____.

9. The Supreme Court used its power of _____ in deciding that the law was unconstitutional.

10. The case involving a boundary dispute between two neighbors was a _____.

CHAPTER 12 REVIEW

* *

FACTS IN REVIEW

1. Identify three types of cases in which the federal courts have exclusive jurisdiction.

2. In what instances do state and federal courts usually share concurrent jurisdiction?

3. What is the function of district courts?

4. What are the responsibilities of district court magistrates and marshals?

5. Describe the work of judges of the appeals court.

6. What was the basis for the decision in the *Marbury* v. *Madison* case?

7. What three principles of judicial review were established in the *Marbury* v. *Madison* case?

8. What are the two ways that Congress can get around a Supreme Court decision?

9. Identify three activities of Supreme Court justices while the Court is sitting, or in session.

10. What happens to a case before the Supreme Court in the event of a tie vote by the justices?

THINKING ABOUT THE JUDICIAL BRANCH

1. *Evaluate.* How important do you think appeals courts are in providing fair and equal treatment under the law? Explain.

2. *Analyze.* Why do you think the Supreme Court only deals with cases that involve real disputes between opposing sides?

3. *Evaluate.* What influence do you think the power of judicial review has on the legislative and executive branches of government? Explain.

WRITING ABOUT THE JUDICIAL SYSTEM

Judges and justices in the federal court system are appointed for life. What do you think would happen if judges had to run for election every four years like Presidents? Write a brief essay in which you discuss the advantages and disadvantages of appointing judges for life. Do you think elected judges could be relied upon to provide "equal protection of the laws" to all citizens?

INTERPRETING A MAP OF JUDICIAL DISTRICTS AND CIRCUITS

Look at the map showing U.S. judicial districts and circuits on page 275. How many judicial circuits are there in the United States? Which judicial circuits include the fewest states and territories? Which judicial circuit includes the most states? Which states have four judicial districts? Do you think that increasing the number of judicial districts and circuits would be a good idea? Why or why not?

FOCUSING ON YOUR COMMUNITY

Find out what courts are located in or near your community. Are these courts part of the state or federal court system? If there are no federal courts in your community, find out where the nearest federal district courts are located. Try to find out how many cases your district court handles each year. What types of cases does it handle? Where is the nearest appeals court? Present your findings in a written report.

UNIT 4 REVIEW

★ ★

ESSAY QUESTIONS

The following questions are based on material in Unit 4. Answer each question with two or three written paragraphs. Be sure to give specific reasons to support your answers.

1. Our nation's leaders come from many different backgrounds, and they have different goals. What qualifications and characteristics do you think are most important in a national leader? Name one political figure you admire and explain why you admire that person.

2. The framers of the Constitution sought to balance power among the legislative, executive, and judicial branches. In recent years, however, the executive branch has dominated the other branches. Why has this happened? Should measures be taken to correct the situation?

3. The Supreme Court makes decisions that affect all Americans. Yet, the American people do not elect Supreme Court justices to office. How are justices held accountable to the public for their decisions and behavior on the Court?

CONNECTING CIVICS AND LITERATURE

On retiring from office, many political leaders want to tell about their experiences in politics. In recent years, former Presidents Richard Nixon, Lyndon Johnson, Gerald Ford, and Jimmy Carter have written their memoirs, or recollections. Be prepared to discuss the following in class:

Memoirs are usually one-sided and very personal views of people and events. Why, then, do the memoirs of political leaders present a valuable contribution to the history of a period? What standards should be used to judge political memoirs? Should people close to political leaders also record their views of events, even though their accounts may be unflattering or contradictory?

ANALYZING VISUALS

The second half of the twentieth century has seen many changes in the federal government. The following pictograph shows the number of federal civilian employees from 1935 to 1985. Study the graph and then answer the questions.

1. How many people were employed by the federal government in 1935? In 1985?

2. Why do you think there were so many federal employees in 1945?

3. Explain the steady increase in the number of people employed by the federal government.

4. Do you think there has been a similar increase at the state and local level?

YEAR	Civilian Employees of the Federal Government, 1935–1985
1935	𝝅 𝝅
1945	𝝅 𝝅 𝝅 𝝅 𝝅 𝝅 𝝅 𝝅
1955	𝝅 𝝅 𝝅 𝝅 𝝅
1965	𝝅 𝝅 𝝅 𝝅 𝝅
1975	𝝅 𝝅 𝝅 𝝅 𝝅
1985	𝝅 𝝅 𝝅 𝝅 𝝅 𝝅

𝝅 = 500,000 people

Source: Bureau of the Census

* * * * * * *

CLOSEUP ON WATERGATE

On June 17, 1972, police arrested five men at the Watergate office complex in Washington, D.C. The men had broken into the Democratic National Party Headquarters located there. The burglary, which occurred during President Richard M. Nixon's campaign for re-election, marked the beginning of the so-called Watergate affair.

In the months that followed, *Washington Post* reporters Carl Bernstein and Bob Woodward investigated and wrote stories about the break-in. They found evidence linking the burglary and other illegal acts to the Committee to Re-elect the President (CREEP) and to members of the President's own staff. The White House denied any such connections.

The burglary suspects were tried and found guilty. One burglar agreed to testify before the Senate Committee investigating the Watergate case, and he named several White House and campaign officials. One of these officials, Presidential Counsel John Dean, declared that President Nixon himself had been involved in trying to cover up the break-in.

During its hearings, the Watergate Committee learned that President Nixon made tape recordings of conversa-

tions in his office. The committee believed it could discover the truth of the President's involvement by listening to these recordings. Nixon, however, claimed "executive privilege" and refused to turn over the tapes.

The situation came to a head in July 1974, when the Supreme Court ruled that Nixon must turn over all the tapes. On one of them, the President was heard discussing how to cover up White House involvement in the burglary only a few days after it took place. This tape was a "smoking gun"— concrete evidence of the President's personal involvement.

Meanwhile, the House Judiciary Committee held hearings on impeaching the President and voted to recommend impeachment. It charged Nixon with obstruction of justice, abuse of power, and contempt for Congress and the courts. The next step would have been a full House vote on the charges, and if approved, an impeachment trial in the Senate. The process never went that far. On August 9, 1974, Nixon announced his resignation—the first U.S. President ever to resign.

For more than two years, the nation had been in agony

over the Watergate affair. Americans were deeply divided over the affair and suspicious of their leaders. Yet, when Nixon relinquished the Presidency to Vice President Gerald R. Ford, it was done in a smooth, orderly manner without upheaval or violence. The U.S. Constitution had provided a process for dealing with official wrongdoing. The Watergate crisis showed that the Constitution and its system of checks and balances works to preserve democracy even in difficult times.

1. What role did Carl Bernstein and Bob Woodward play in the Watergate affair?
2. What was the "smoking gun"?
3. Why do you think that Nixon resigned from office rather than go through an impeachment trial?

The powers not delegated to the United States by the Constitution, nor prohibited by it to the states, are reserved to the states respectively, or to the people.

—TENTH AMENDMENT

State and Local Government

Our democracy is based on the ideas that power is both limited and to be shared. These principles are reflected in our Constitution. They are particularly evident in the Tenth Amendment, which guarantees that the power to govern will be shared among the federal government, the states, and the people.

★ ★ ★ ★ ★

CHAPTER 13

* *

State Government

OBJECTIVES

After you have studied this chapter, you will be able to:

★ Describe the federal system, including the powers of the state governments and the federal government.
★ Explain the similarities of the U.S. Constitution and the state constitutions.
★ Identify and describe the roles and responsibilities of the executive branch of state governments.
★ Discuss the responsibilities of the legislative branch of state governments.
★ Discuss the responsibilities of the judicial branch of state governments, including the organization of the state court system.

SECTIONS

1 The Federal System
2 The State Executive Branch
3 The State Legislative Branch
4 The State Judicial Branch

Few Americans know the names of their representatives in the state legislature. Fewer still have read their state's constitution. This lack of knowledge about state government is unfortunate. The daily lives of most Americans are affected much more by their state government than by the federal government.

Almost every time you make a purchase, you pay a state sales tax. Almost every time you ride in a car or bus, you travel on state roads. If you attend a public school, the courses you take were probably designed to fit state requirements. Your school lunch, your desk, and even this textbook may be paid for, at least in part, with state funds.

The government of each state is much smaller than the federal government. As a result, individual citizens have more influence over their state lawmakers than they have over their representatives in Congress. It pays, therefore, to become familiar with how the state government affects our lives. If the state government does something that we don't like, we may be able to help change it.

****

SECTION 1

The Federal System

****

VOCABULARY

extradition

As you learned in Chapter 2, the first American states behaved like 13 separate countries when the Articles of Confederation were in force. Each state wrote its own constitution, set up its own government, and made its own laws. When they banded together under the Constitution, the states gave up some of their independence. States could no longer print their own money, for example, or tax items imported from other states. Nevertheless, each state continued to govern itself much as it had in the past.

This system, in which the power to govern is shared between the national government and the states, is called the federal system, or federalism. Our federal system allows the people of each state to deal with their needs in their own way. At the same time, it lets the states act together to deal with matters that affect all Americans.

Constitutional Basis for Federalism

The Constitution does not list the powers of state governments, as it does for the national government. Instead, it specifies what the state governments may *not* do. Article I of the Constitution forbids the states to make treaties, coin money, tax imports or exports, keep an army in peacetime, or declare war. In addition, several amendments to the Constitution prevent state governments from taking away rights granted by the federal government. The most important of these amendments is the Fourteenth, which guarantees all Americans "equal protection of the laws."

While some powers are denied to the states, many others are given to both Congress *and* to the states. These concurrent powers include the powers to tax and to borrow money.

As you learned in Chapter 4, the Tenth Amendment to the Constitution gives the states additional authority. According to this amendment, state governments may exercise all powers not given to the federal government nor denied to the states. These powers, you may recall, are called reserved powers. Among them are the powers to make marriage and divorce laws, to regulate education, and to conduct elections.

In general, each state is responsible for the safety and welfare of its own citizens. State governments often use their reserved powers to meet this responsibility. They set up police forces and other law enforcement operations. They build roads and bridges. They regulate business and trade within their borders. They set educational requirements and provide funding for schools. They organize local governments for counties, cities, and towns. Almost every activity in Americans' lives is touched somehow by state government. (See the chart on Federal and State Powers in Chapter 3.)

The writers of the Constitution recognized that the powers of the states may sometimes come into conflict with those of the federal government. For this reason, they declared

in Article VI that the Constitution and the laws made by Congress shall be the "supreme law of the land." If there is a conflict between state and federal law, the federal law has the greatest authority and power. One famous use of this "supremacy clause" occurred after the Eighteenth Amendment was ratified in 1919. The amendment made it illegal to sell alcoholic beverages anywhere in the United States. Each state had had its own laws about the use of alcohol. But the Eighteenth Amendment became the supreme law of the land and the state laws lost their power.

State Constitutions

Every one of the 50 states has its own constitution. Like the U.S. Constitution, a state constitution is a plan of government. It is also the highest law in the state, just as the U.S. Constitution is the highest law in the nation.

Article IV of the U.S. Constitution requires each state to have a "republican form of government." (A *republic* is another term for a representative democracy.) Other than that, however, the Constitution does not say anything about how a state's government should be set up. It would be possible, therefore, for the 50 states to create 50 completely different systems of government.

Not surprisingly, however, nearly every state government closely resembles the federal government. The reason for this is simple: the early state constitutions served as models for the writers of the U.S. Constitution. Since then, most states have used the U.S. Constitution as a model for their own constitutions.

A typical state constitution begins with a preamble, which cites the goals and ideals of the state's citizens. All state constitutions provide for three branches of government—

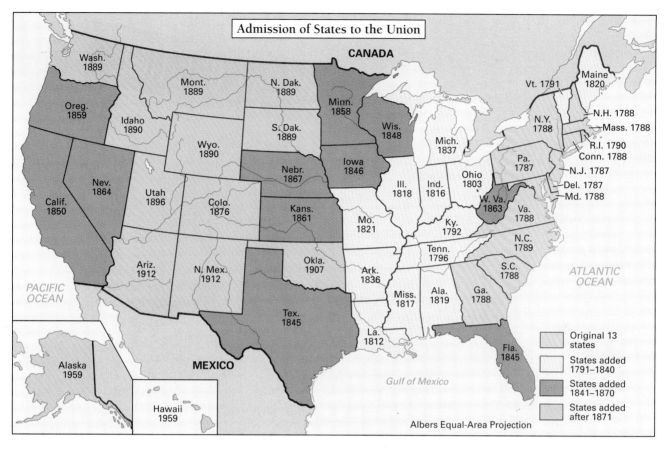

Admission of States to the Union

CANADA

Wash. 1889
Oreg. 1859
Idaho 1890
Mont. 1889
N. Dak. 1889
Minn. 1858
Wis. 1848
Mich. 1837
Vt. 1791
Maine 1820
N.H. 1788
Mass. 1788
N.Y. 1788
R.I. 1790
Conn. 1788
N.J. 1787
Nev. 1864
Utah 1896
Wyo. 1890
S. Dak. 1889
Nebr. 1867
Iowa 1846
Ill. 1818
Ind. 1816
Ohio 1803
Pa. 1787
Del. 1787
Md. 1788
W. Va. 1863
Va. 1788
Calif. 1850
Colo. 1876
Kans. 1861
Mo. 1821
Ky. 1792
N.C. 1789
Ariz. 1912
N. Mex. 1912
Okla. 1907
Ark. 1836
Tenn. 1796
S.C. 1788
Tex. 1845
Miss. 1817
Ala. 1819
Ga. 1788
La. 1812
Fla. 1845

PACIFIC OCEAN

ATLANTIC OCEAN

MEXICO

Gulf of Mexico

Alaska 1959

Hawaii 1959

Original 13 states
States added 1791–1840
States added 1841–1870
States added after 1871

Albers Equal-Area Projection

The map shows when each of the 50 states was admitted to the Union. Which states have been admitted since 1900?

legislative, executive, and judicial—and assign certain powers and duties to each branch. Every state constitution also includes a bill of rights which, in most cases, is similar to the U.S. Bill of Rights.

The amendment process is an important part of every state constitution. While the procedure for changing the constitution varies from state to state, it is usually a two-step process similar to amending the U.S. Constitution. An amendment must first be proposed, generally by the legislature; then it must be ratified by the voters. As the role of state governments has changed, some state constitutions have been amended hundreds of times.

Despite their basic similarities, there are important differences between the constitutions of different states. Every state has its own ideas about what makes a good government. Nebraska, for example, is the only state with a one-house legislature. (The other states have bicameral legislatures similar to the U.S. Congress.) In Delaware, constitutional amendments are ratified by the legislature rather than by the voters.

THE SECOND AMENDMENT AND GUN CONTROL LAWS

The Second Amendment of the Constitution deals with the right to bear arms. Of course, America has changed a great deal since 1791 when this amenument was adopted. At the time, most of the land beyond the 13 states was wilderness. Settlers needed guns to shoot animals for food and clothing and to defend themselves against Indians and outlaws.

Today there may be as many as 120 million guns in the United States—about one firearm for every two Americans. Most of these are rifles and handguns that law-abiding people keep for hunting or for protection. Still, every year many injuries and deaths are caused by guns, and Americans remain divided over the issue of gun control.

Groups, such as Handgun Control, Inc., that support gun control laws propose banning all handguns. They feel that these small, easily hidden guns make it too easy to kill people. In 1985, more than 9,000 Americans were murdered with handguns.

Opponents of gun control argue that gun ownership is as important a Constitutional right as freedom of speech. They say that gun control laws do not keep guns out of the hands of criminals. They argue that gun control laws would leave citizens no means of protecting themselves against armed criminals.

The National Rifle Association (NRA) has long opposed any kind of restraints on gun ownership. Over the years the NRA has built a powerful lobby of 2.8 million hunters, gun collectors, and police officers. It has been very successful at blocking gun control laws and defeating pro-gun control candidates at both the national and state level.

In recent years, attention has focused on semiautomatic assault rifles. These guns can hold 20 or more cartridges and fire a shot every time the trigger is squeezed.

There may be more than 1 million semiautomatic rifles in private hands.

Their spread has caused a change in public opinion about gun control. More than half of those polled in a recent survey favored a ban on semiautomatics, and many states have introduced or enacted laws to ban these weapons. But Americans remain deeply divided over the issue of gun control laws.

Using Your Skills

1. Why do you think the authors of the Bill of Rights wanted to make gun ownership a Constitutional right?

2. List the main arguments for and against gun control laws.

Federal-State Cooperation

The states and the federal government are not always in agreement. But they tend to work together most of the time.

A certain amount of federal-state cooperation is assured by the U.S. Constitution. Article IV, which requires every state to have a "republican form of government," includes the idea that the United States will defend that form of government if it is threatened. The Constitution says that the federal government will protect each state against invasion and domestic violence. When violent incidents within a state cannot be controlled by local or state police, the governor of the state may call for the assistance of federal troops.

In return, the states provide certain services to the federal government. For example, the states hold elections for federal offices—such as President and Vice President—as well as for state and local offices. This is considered to be part of the reserved powers of the states.

The states and the federal government also cooperate in ways not called for in the Constitution. For example, state and federal agencies often share information with each other. A state police force may help the FBI catch a criminal, or the Federal Bureau of Prisons may share prison management techniques with a state's justice department.

State governments also help carry out federal policies. In the late 1970's, for example, President Jimmy Carter required thermostats in government buildings to be turned down to conserve heating oil. Carter's order applied only to federal buildings, but many state governments followed his lead by lowering thermostats in state buildings as well.

Although not required to do so by the Constitution, the federal government provides funding for many state services. For example, federal agencies help pay for student lunches in public schools and for construction of state highways. By helping states pay for services that they could not otherwise afford, the federal government also helps the country as a whole.

When Hurricane Hugo struck Charleston, South Carolina, in 1989, the federal government sent funds and other assistance to state and local authorities.

Some of the money used to provide lunches for students in public schools comes from the federal government.

Cooperation Between States

The Constitution helps ensure that states cooperate with each other as well as with the federal government. According to Article IV, each state must give "full faith and credit" to the laws and court decisions of other states. This means that each state must accept and uphold these laws and decisions. For example, if a couple is married according to the laws of one state, every other state must accept that marriage as legal.

Article IV also ensures another type of cooperation. Often, someone who breaks the law in one state will flee to another state to avoid punishment. A state cannot legally punish a person for breaking the laws of another state. But if requested to do so, a governor usually orders that a person charged with a major crime be returned to the state where the crime was committed. Returning a suspected criminal in this way is called **extradition**.

States cooperate in other ways as well, especially when they share a border. The neighboring states of New York and New Jersey, for example, are partners in an agency called the Port Authority. The Port Authority controls an airport, a seaport, a bus terminal, and other transportation facilities that serve both states.

SECTION REVIEW

Define the Word
extradition

Check the Facts
1. Give an example of a concurrent power and an example of a reserved power.
2. Describe three ways in which the federal government helps state governments.
3. Describe three ways in which state governments cooperate with one another.

Think About the Ideas
4. *Analyze.* Each state has the power to tax its own citizens. Why then are federal funds sometimes used for state projects and programs?

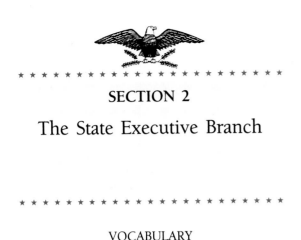

The State Executive Branch

VOCABULARY

commute   parole

The executive branch of a state government is similar to the executive branch of the federal government. The state executive branch is led by a chief executive, the governor. The governor plays a number of other roles in addition to chief executive, including those of party leader and chief of state. As in the federal government, the governor delegates powers to a number of executive departments and agencies.

The Office of Governor

Each state constitution includes a set of qualifications for the office of governor. In most states, a governor must be an American citizen, at least 30 years old, and a resident of the state for at least five years. As for most other elected offices, however, there are also unofficial qualifications for the governor's office. Most governors have held public office or been active in state politics. Many have had successful careers in law or business. In the past most governors have been men, and this has not changed very much. In 1990, only 3 of the nation's 50 governors were women.

Unlike the President, a governor is elected directly by the people—there is no Electoral College in state elections. Other than that, governors are nominated and elected in much the same way that a President is. Generally, each political party holds a primary election and nominates a candidate at a state party convention. The voters then choose their governor in a statewide election. The candidate who wins a majority of votes wins the election.

Because several states have more than two active parties, however, there are sometimes three or four candidates competing for the office of governor. When only two candidates are running for an office, one of them will almost always get a majority of the votes.

Before Madeleine Kunin was elected Vermont's governor in 1984, she was a teacher, a journalist, a state legislator, and lieutenant governor of the state.

When three or more candidates are running, however, a majority is rare. For this reason, many states allow their governor to be elected by a plurality rather than a majority vote. In other words, the candidate who gets the largest number of votes—even if it is less than a majority—wins.

Once elected, the governor in most states serves a four-year term. In nearly every state, a governor can be impeached if he or she commits a crime while in office. In 15 states, the voters themselves can take steps to remove a governor from office by demanding a special "recall" election.

Each state constitution sets up a line of succession in case the governor dies, resigns, or is removed from office. In most states, the first person in line is the lieutenant governor. The role of the lieutenant governor is similar to that of the Vice President in two respects. The lieutenant governor takes over the governorship if the governor dies or leaves office. The lieutenant governor usually presides over the state senate.

Powers and Duties of the Governor

Like the President, a governor plays several important roles. A governor's most important role is as the state's chief executive. As chief executive, the governor is responsible for executing laws passed by the state legislature. To help with this responsibility, the governor issues executive orders to a large state bureaucracy. The governor has the power to appoint some of the officials in this bureaucracy, usually with the approval of the state senate. The governor also has the power to veto bills passed by the legislature. And, in most states, it is the governor's

responsibility to prepare a budget for the state and submit it to the legislature. Many governors deliver a "state of the state" report at the same time that they submit their annual budget. In recent years, governors have been active in bringing foreign business to the state.

The governor is also the state's chief legislator. Although only the state legislature can pass laws, the governor can play a part in proposing laws. For example, the governor may suggest laws that he or she thinks should be passed. Governors also try to convince the legislature to pass certain bills. They may do this formally, by making speeches to the legislature, or informally, by speaking privately to lawmakers.

In addition to executive and legislative responsibilities, all governors have certain judicial responsibilities. Like the President, governors have the power to offer pardons and reprieves to convicted criminals. They may also **commute**, or reduce, a criminal's sentence. For example, if a criminal has been sentenced to death, a governor may decide to commute the sentence to life in prison. Governors also have the power to grant a prisoner a **parole**, an early release from prison, with certain restrictions. Usually, decisions regarding pardons, sentences, and paroles are not made by the governor personally, but by committees or boards under the governor's supervision.

Governors play a number of other roles as well. Every governor is commander-in-chief of the National Guard, a state militia that may be called up to protect the state and its citizens during emergencies. Every governor is a party leader who tries to help out his or her political party while governing the state. And finally, every governor is a chief of state, or ceremonial leader, who greets important visitors and represents the state on ceremonial occasions.

POWERS AND DUTIES OF THE GOVERNOR

CHIEF EXECUTIVE

★ carries out state laws
★ appoints officials
★ prepares a budget

CHIEF LEGISLATOR

★ proposes legislation
★ approves or vetoes legislation

JUDICIAL LEADER

★ offers pardons and reprieves
★ grants parole

COMMANDER IN CHIEF

★ in charge of the National Guard (state militia)

PARTY LEADER

★ leads political party in state

CEREMONIAL LEADER

★ greets important visitors
★ represents the state

This illustration shows the powers and duties of a state governor. Which of these is a governor's most important role?

Executive Officials and Agencies

Although not every governor has a cabinet, each state has a number of high officials who advise the governor on important issues. These officials are sometimes selected by the governor, but more often they are elected by the voters.

While the top government officials vary from state to state, most states have a few important officials in common. There is usually a secretary of state, who is responsible for keeping the state's records. An attorney general acts as the state's lawyer and legal adviser. A treasurer supervises the state's funds, pays money from the treasury, and sometimes acts as chief tax collector. The treasurer's work is supervised by an auditor or comptroller, who makes sure that no government money is spent without approval from the governor and the legislature. There is also a superintendent of public instruction (sometimes called a commissioner of education), who sets educational standards and oversees the state's public schools.

In addition, every state has a number of executive departments, agencies, boards, and commissions. Some of these, such as the Department of Justice, the Department of Agriculture, and the Department of Labor, are similar to departments in the federal government. Other departments exist only in state governments. For example, nearly all states have a Department (or Board) of Health, which administers programs in health education and disease prevention. Most states have a Department of Public Works and a Department of Highways to supervise construction of public buildings, dams, bridges, and roads. Most states also have a State Welfare Board, which helps people who are disadvantaged or unemployed.

SECTION REVIEW

Define the Words

commute   parole

Check the Facts

1. Identify two ways in which the election of a governor differs from the election of a President.
2. Describe three executive powers of state governors.
3. Name five top government officials found in many states and describe their roles.

Think About the Ideas

4. *Evaluate.* Which of the governor's roles do you think is most important? Why?
5. *Analyze.* High-level officials in many states are chosen by the voters rather than by the governor. How does this affect the governor's power?

★ ★

SECTION 3

The State Legislative Branch

★ ★

VOCABULARY

unicameral   item veto

apportionment

State legislatures vary in name and size. In some states, the legislature is called the general assembly; in others, it is called the legislative assembly. Most states, however, simply call it the legislature. New Hampshire has the largest legislature, with over 400 members, and Alaska has the smallest, with only 60 members.

The similarities, however, outweigh the differences. With one exception, every state legislature has two houses. The upper house is always called the senate, and the lower house is usually called the house of representatives. The one exception, as noted earlier in this chapter, is the state of Nebraska, which has a **unicameral**, or one-house, legislature. Its single house is called the senate.

Legislative Districts

Each state legislature divides its state into many election districts. The people in these districts elect their own representatives to the state legislature. Generally, there is one set of districts to elect state senators and another to elect state representatives. For many years,

Although 49 states have two-house legislatures. Nebraska's state legislature is unicameral. Why do you think all the other states have two-house legislatures?

senate districts were based on land area and house districts were based on population. This system resulted in unequal representation in many state senates. For example, a city district and a county district would each be represented by one senator, even though the city district might have 10 times more people.

This situation was ended in 1964 by the Supreme Court's "one person, one vote" decision (see the LEGAL LANDMARKS feature, "*Reynolds* v. *Sims*," in this chapter). The Court ruled that all election districts must be equal, or nearly equal, in population. As a result, many states had to change the **apportionment** of their legislatures. Apportion-

ment is the distribution of seats in a legislature according to a standard such as population.

Legislators

Each state constitution lists the qualifications for membership in its legislature. Generally, legislators must be American citizens and must live in the district they represent. They must also have reached a certain age—usually 25, 21, or 18. A legislator's term may be two or four years, depending on the state.

REYNOLDS V. SIMS

When the nation was young, each county or town had a representative in the state legislature. This system worked quite well as long as America remained a nation of farms and small towns.

By the early 1900's, however, more and more people were moving to cities and their suburbs. The old formula for assigning legislative seats was no longer fair. A county with 2,000 residents and a city with 100,000 people might each have one representative in the state legislature.

At the time, most states were largely rural with a few big cities. The legislators from rural areas controlled the state legislatures and paid little attention to the needs of city dwellers.

Many people realized that apportioning seats by area instead of population was very unfair. In 1964, the U.S. Supreme Court ruled in *Reynolds* v. *Sims* that voters in the most populous districts were underrepresented. According to the Court,

this unequal representation—even in a state body—violated the Fourteenth Amendment's guarantee of equal protection of the laws.

Reynolds v. *Sims* involved the apportioning of legislative seats in Alabama. At that time, the Alabama legislature had 43 rural state representatives for every urban one and 16 rural senators for every senator from a city or suburb.

The Court ruled that both houses of the state legislature had to be reapportioned according to population, not area. "Legislators represent people, not trees or acres," wrote Chief Justice Earl Warren. "Legislators are elected by voters, not farms or cities or economic interests."

The ruling required every state to draw up new voting districts. Each district had to have an approximately equal number of voters. For example, if a state had a population of 2 million and 100 seats

in the state senate, then each senator had to represent a district made up of about 20,000 voters.

This ruling has become known as the "one-person, one-vote" rule. It means that each vote counts equally no matter where the voter lives. The significance of *Reynolds* v. *Sims* stretched far beyond the state legislatures. Each state legislature also had to draw up new Congressional districts for the election of members of the U.S. House of Representatives. Today the "one-person, one-vote" rule applies to every election in the country from local school board races to the Presidency.

Using Your Skills
1. Why was apportioning legislative seats by area unfair to cities and suburbs?
2. How do you think the "one-person, one-vote" rule changed things for the people who lived in large cities and suburbs?

Originally, membership in the state legislature was not intended to be a full-time job. Many state legislatures met for only a few months every two years. Most legislators were members of the community who occasionally took time off from their jobs to serve in the state house or senate. For this reason, the pay for legislators is still fairly low—as little as $5 per day in Rhode Island.

As the duties of state governments have grown, however, the responsibilities of state legislators have increased. Many legislatures meet for at least six months a year, and some meet all year round. As a result, many state legislators have become full-time public servants, and their salaries and benefits have started to increase.

The Legislative Process

State legislatures operate much like the U.S. Congress. Ideas for bills come from many sources, including the executive branch, interest groups, individual citizens, and legislators themselves. After a state senator or representative introduces a bill in the legislature, the bill is sent to an appropriate committee. State legislatures, like Congress, have standing, select, and joint committees. These committees study bills, hold hearings, and revise the bills if necessary. They may recommend that a bill be passed or that it be killed. If different versions of a bill pass in different houses, the bill is sent to a conference committee to iron out the differences.

As in the U.S. Congress, each house of a state legislature has a leader. The state house of representatives usually is led by a speaker, and the state senate is usually led by a president (who, in many states, is the lieutenant governor). These leaders have a great deal of control over debate and voting on each bill.

After a bill is passed by the legislature, it is sent to the governor for approval. The governor may sign the bill, veto it, or pocket-veto it. In many states, the governor has another option as well—an **item veto**. This means that the governor can approve certain parts of the bill and veto other parts.

If the governor vetoes all or part of a bill, the legislature may vote to override the veto. As in Congress, however, few vetoes are successfully overcome.

Problems Facing State Legislatures

In recent years, Americans have begun to expect more and more from their state governments. They demand better public transportation, better schools, and better services for disabled, disadvantaged, and homeless people. They expect their state governments to protect the environment, regulate business, and reduce crime and drug abuse.

Unfortunately, most states have found it difficult or impossible to pay for the services that their citizens are demanding. Most legislators will not vote to raise taxes, because they know that such a decision may cost them the next election. So the states have come to depend a great deal on federal grants to help pay for programs that state taxes cannot support. Over the past decade, however, many of those grants have been eliminated as the federal government deals with its own shortage of funds.

As a result, many state governments have been faced with a difficult choice: to borrow increasing amounts of money or to cut essential services. Neither solution is satisfactory. Paying interest on borrowed money is expensive and adds to the drain on a state's treas-

The educational program of every state includes colleges and universities for the state's citizens. The extensive campus of the University of Illinois at Champaign-Urbana is shown here.

ury. On the other hand, cutting services—at a time when crime, homelessness, and pollution are rising rapidly—may be considered unwise and irresponsible.

Pressure on legislators was increased by the Supreme Court's "one-person, one-vote" ruling. As a result of that decision, city dwellers have greater representation in state legislatures than they did before. Since cities are the places where problems of crime, drug abuse, and unemployment are highest, legislators are under great pressure to deal with these issues. We'll look more closely at these and other problems in Chapter 15.

SECTION REVIEW

Define the Words

unicameral   item veto
apportionment

Check the Facts

1. How did the "one person, one vote" decision change the apportionment of state legislatures?
2. How has the job of state legislators changed in recent years?
3. What are some problems now being faced by the state legislatures?

Think About the Ideas

4. *Analyze.* What do you think might be the advantages and disadvantages of a unicameral legislature?

★ ★

SECTION 4

The State Judicial Branch

★ ★

VOCABULARY

misdemeanor	felony
justice of the peace	plea bargain
magistrate court	

The federal court system, which you read about in Chapter 12, handles only a small portion of the nation's judicial workload. Most of the legal matters that arise within a state—robberies, assaults, sale and use of illegal drugs, broken contracts, child custody battles, and so on—are the responsibility of the state court system.

Each year, millions of cases are decided by state and local courts. In order to handle the enormous number of cases as efficiently as possible, most states have set up several different kinds of courts. At the lowest level are justice courts, which handle minor matters in local communities.

Lower Courts

Less serious crimes, known as **misdemeanors**, are almost always handled by small, local courts. These courts do not have juries; instead, a single judge hears and decides each case. Judges in lower courts are usually elected by the voters of the community.

In many rural areas and small towns, the local court is called a justice court and the judge is called a **justice of the peace**. In larger towns and small cities, local courts may be called police courts or **magistrate courts**. These courts handle minor cases such as traffic violations or disturbing the peace. They may also handle civil cases involving small sums of money, usually less than $1,000. If someone is found guilty, the punishment may be a small fine or, occasionally, a short jail term.

Most larger cities have municipal courts that serve the same purpose. These are often divided into specialized courts—traffic courts, juvenile courts, and small claims courts. Small claims courts hear civil cases involving small amounts of money.

Higher Courts

More serious crimes, known as **felonies**, are handled by courts called general trial courts. These courts deal with criminal cases involving major crimes such as robbery, murder, and arson. They also hear civil cases involving large amounts of money.

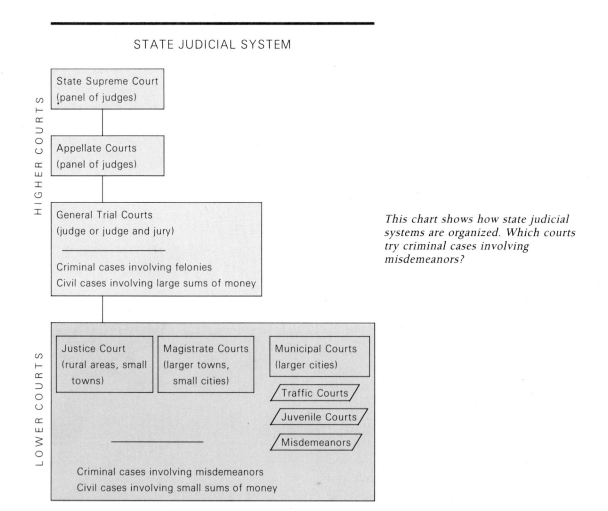

STATE JUDICIAL SYSTEM

This chart shows how state judicial systems are organized. Which courts try criminal cases involving misdemeanors?

Depending on the state and on the way the court system is organized, a general trial court may be called a district court, a county court, a common pleas court, a circuit court, or a superior court. No matter what they are called, however, general trial courts have the same responsibility: to determine whether someone is guilty or not guilty of a serious crime.

Unlike lower courts, general trial courts may use a jury to determine a defendant's guilt or innocence. The job of the judge in a general trial court is to guide the jury and, in some cases, to decide on a sentence.

APPELLATE COURTS Sometimes the decision of a general trial court may be appealed to an appellate court. The basis for appeal is usually that the general trial court violated one of the defendant's constitutional rights to a fair trial.

An appellate court has no jury. Instead, a panel of judges review the records of the lower court's proceedings. If they feel that the defendant did not have a fair trial, the panel can decide—by a majority vote—to overturn the lower court's decision.

The highest state court is the supreme court, in some states called the court of appeals. The supreme court consists of a panel of judges, usually elected by the voters. Like the U.S. Supreme Court, the state supreme court hears arguments from lawyers representing both sides of a case, reviews the evidence, and makes a decision by majority vote. Except for cases involving federal law or the U.S. Constitution, the decisions of the state supreme court are final.

Problems Facing the State Courts

Running a state court system is costly. It involves paying the salaries of court officials and clerical staff, and maintaining court buildings. Most state court systems face a severe shortage of funds. However, the U.S. Constitution guarantees a fair trial to every individual, no matter how much that trial costs. For this reason, state courts cannot cut their services.

Most state court systems have too few judges and too little space to handle the huge number of cases that come before them each year. Because of this, months may pass before a person who is accused of a crime finally receives a trial. A defendant who cannot afford bail may remain in jail during those months—even if he or she is innocent.

One way the courts have tried to speed the legal process and cut costs is by plea bargaining with defendants. In a **plea bargain**, a defendant agrees to plead guilty to a crime in exchange for a reduced sentence or some other form of leniency. A plea of guilty makes a court trial unnecessary. Few people believe that plea bargaining is a good solution to the problem of overcrowded courts. However, no one has yet found a better solution that does not involve spending money.

SECTION REVIEW

Define the Words

misdemeanor	felony
justice of the peace	plea bargain
magistrate court	

Check the Facts
1. Identify three types of lower state courts.
2. Identify three types of higher state courts.
3. What is plea bargaining and why is it used?

Think About the Ideas
4. *Evaluate.* Is it fair for people who commit misdemeanors to be convicted by a judge, without a jury? Why or why not?

CITIZENSHIP SKILLS

How to Read a Table

A table is a type of chart that presents information in columns under headings. It is a convenient way to analyze and compare facts, especially numerical data.

For example, look at the table of state finances on the following page. The table provides information on the revenue and expenditures of selected states. The column at the left lists the names of these states. Each of the five columns to the right of the states shows certain financial data about each state. By reading across the table, you can find out five different types of financial information for each state. By reading down a single column, you can compare all the states in terms of one type of financial data.

The first column is titled "Revenue." This is the income a state receives from taxes and other sources. The second column, "Expenditures," is the amount of money a state spends. The column titled "Debt" shows the amount of money a state owes. The fourth and fifth columns show per capita debt and per capita taxes. *Per capita* means "for each person." Per capita figures are averages. They are found by dividing the total amount of debt or taxes by the number of people in the state. It therefore shows the amount per person.

Using Your Skills

Use the table to answer the following questions.

1. What was Oregon's total revenue in 1986? Which two states had the highest revenues in 1986? Which two states had the lowest?
2. Which state spent about the same as it earned in 1986?
3. Which state had the largest debt in 1986? Which state had the smallest debt?
4. How much did people living in Alaska pay in state taxes, per capita, in 1986? How does this compare to per capita taxes in the other states shown?
5. Compare the financial information given for Oregon and Colorado. In what ways are the two states similar? In what ways do they differ?

CITIZENSHIP SKILLS

How to Read a Table

STATE FINANCES
(FISCAL YEAR 1986)

	REVENUE (THOUSANDS)	EXPENDITURES (THOUSANDS)	DEBT (THOUSANDS)	PER CAPITA DEBT	PER CAPITA TAXES
Alabama	$ 6,800,976	$ 6,347,706	$ 3,751,658	$ 926	$ 740
Alaska	6,115,297	4,220,878	6,961,334	13,085	3,490
Arizona	6,037,995	5,074,152	1,472,580	449	975
California	63,987,002	57,370,220	20,122,437	745	1,144
Colorado	5,994,542	4,952,058	1,998,327	612	718
Delaware	1,774,650	1,415,325	2,634,531	4,162	1,343
Florida	15,850,334	13,759,262	5,679,591	486	780
Hawaii	2,994,786	2,471,954	2,828,037	2,655	1,400
Idaho	1,743,619	1,516,579	658,164	657	743
Illinois	19,437,185	17,822,767	11,987,958	1,038	848
Indiana	8,485,339	7,548,547	2,180,275	396	810
Maine	2,388,932	2,156,438	1,558,447	1,330	940
Minnesota	9,540,193	8,581,248	3,759,541	892	1,163
Montana	1,753,593	1,642,736	1,240,239	1,518	755
Nevada	2,390,950	1,916,667	1,224,223	1,266	1,084
New Mexico	3,925,064	3,300,139	2,137,298	1,445	989
New York	50,908,739	43,138,967	36,371,158	2,044	1,278
Oregon	5,524,208	4,925,280	7,141,919	2,643	715
South Carolina	6,393,561	5,640,568	3,725,616	1,102	863
Texas	23,102,789	20,781,744	5,432,198	325	667
Utah	3,311,126	3,070,914	1,325,214	796	820
Washington	10,668,300	9,668,571	3,572,162	800	1,169
Wisconsin	10,885,758	9,124,918	4,659,656	974	1,148
Wyoming	2,003,511	1,632,973	825,059	1,627	1,569

Source: Census Bureau, U.S. Commerce Department

CHAPTER 13 REVIEW

MAIN POINTS

★ Under the federal system, the power to govern is shared by the national government and the states. The U.S. Constitution is the basis for the powers held by or denied to these two levels of government.

★ Each state has its own written constitution, similar to the U.S. Constitution, which sets up a government with executive, legislative, and judicial branches.

★ Each state's executive branch includes a governor, several other important government officials, and a number of departments and agencies.

★ Except for Nebraska, each state's legislative branch consists of a bicameral legislature. As the duties of state governments have grown, the responsibilities of the legislative branch have increased.

★ Each state's judicial branch includes lower courts to handle misdemeanors, higher courts to handle felonies, and appellate courts to review the decisions of the other courts. The highest court in each state is the supreme court.

WORDS IN REVIEW

Choose the word or phrase from the list below that best completes each sentence. Write the missing words on a separate sheet of paper.

extradition	unicameral
parole	item veto
apportionment	misdemeanor
felony	plea bargain
commute	justice of the peace

1. Some people in the state felt that the new _____ of election districts was unequal.

2. After reviewing the case, the governor decided to _____ the criminal's sentence to life imprisonment.

3. Though captured in Utah, the suspect was returned to Michigan where the crime was committed because of the _____ agreement between the two states.

4. The traffic violation was a _____ and was, therefore, handled by the local justice of the peace.

5. The defendant decided to plead guilty in a _____ in exchange for a reduced charge.

6. The governor used her _____ to reject one portion of the bill.

7. The murder case, a _____, was handled by the general trial court.

8. The convicted jewel thief was eligible for _____ after serving 10 years in prison.

9. Only one state, Nebraska, has a _____ legislature.

10. The marriage was performed by a _____ in a small rural town.

FACTS IN REVIEW

1. Identify three features of state constitutions that are similar to the U.S. Constitution.

2. What is the significance of the Supremacy Clause?

3. How does the U.S. Constitution help ensure cooperation among the states?

4. Why do some states allow governors to be elected by a plurality instead of by a majority vote?

CHAPTER 13 REVIEW

5. Identify three roles that a governor has in common with the President.

6. What judicial powers do governors have?

7. Identify three ways in which state legislatures are similar to Congress.

8. What are three problems facing state governments today?

9. What types of cases are usually handled by lower state courts?

10. Identify three ways lower state courts and higher state courts differ.

THINKING ABOUT STATE GOVERNMENT

1. *Analyze*. Why do you think the writers of the U.S. Constitution did not list the powers of the state governments?

2. *Evaluate*. What do you think is the best way for states to solve their money problems? Give reasons for your answer.

3. *Evaluate*. Do you think judges in state courts should be appointed or elected? Explain.

COLLECTING INFORMATION ABOUT STATE GOVERNMENT

Research and write a report about your own state government. Find information about the following questions: How many members are in each house of the legislature? What is the term of office for the members of each house and for the governor? What are the salaries of state legislators and the governor? How many election districts are there in your state?

WRITING ABOUT THE FEDERAL SYSTEM

The balance between state and federal authority is often a delicate matter. In recent years, the environment has been the source of numerous conflicts. For example, should the federal government be able to set up a toxic dump in a state? Should a state have control over mineral resources found in a national park within its borders? Write two or three paragraphs about the conflicts between federal and state governments. You can focus on one of the examples mentioned here or choose another one.

INTERPRETING A CHART

Study the chart on the Powers and Duties of the Governor on page 305. Then answer the following questions.

1. Which of the governor's roles do you think are most important? Why?

2. Compare the chart of the Powers and Duties of the Governor to the chart of the Powers and Duties of the President on page 233. Which powers are similar? What role does the President have that the governor does not have?

FOCUSING ON YOUR COMMUNITY

Find out about your local court system. What types of lower courts does your community have? Is there a general trial court or appeals court in your community? Prepare a short oral report of your findings.

* *

Local Governments: County, Town, and City

OBJECTIVES

After you have studied this chapter, you will be able to:

★ Describe the organization and responsibilities of county government, including the role of county officials.
★ Describe and compare the types of local government found in towns, townships, and villages.
★ Identify and explain the role of special districts.
★ Identify and describe four different types of city government.
★ Discuss some of the problems facing local governments today and ways to help solve these problems.

SECTIONS

1 County Government
2 Town, Township, and Village Governments
3 City Government

In March 1989, the U.S. Supreme Court ruled that New York City's government violated the "one person, one vote" rule. The court's decision referred specifically to the city's Board of Estimate, a powerful part of the government concerned with budgets. It found that people living in different boroughs, or divisions, of the city did not have equal representation on the Board of Estimate. The city was directed to come up with a new plan for government creating a government that would provide equal representation for people from different sections of the city.

Under our federal system, each city, town, and county has its own local government. These local governments deal with situations that are strikingly different. For example, each state has a number of different types of communities, such as seaports, resort areas, industrial centers, rural areas, and crowded cities. Our federal system allows each of these communities to govern itself and deal with its own special requirements.

There are thousands of local governments throughout the United States. Unlike the federal and state governments, which are all basically similar, local governments vary greatly in size and structure. All, however, allow ordinary citizens to play an important role in shaping their communities.

* *

SECTION 1

County Government

* *

VOCABULARY

charter ordinance

The U.S. Constitution grants no power to local governments; in fact, it doesn't even mention their existence. Instead, all local governments are established by the states. Usually, state constitutions describe the duties and powers of local governments. The only powers a local government has are those that are given to it by the state. Most often, a state grants these powers in a **charter**, or plan of government. This charter describes the local government and gives it authority over its affairs.

Because each state's history and geography is different, each has set up different kinds of local governments. One type—the county government—is found in every state except Connecticut and Rhode Island.

There are more than 3,000 counties in the United States. These counties vary greatly in size and in population. In some states, counties are known by other names. In Alaska, they are known as boroughs; in Louisiana, they are called parishes. No matter what their size is or what they are called, however, these counties have one thing in common—they provide services for their citizens.

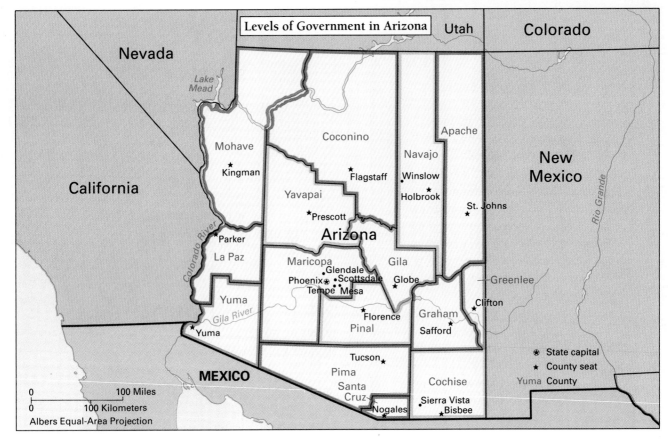

This map shows three levels of government in Arizona—state, county, and city or town government. What levels of government would you expect to find in the state capital of Phoenix?

Organization

Most counties are governed by a group of officials called a county board. In some places, this group may be called the board of supervisors, board of commissioners, or county court. The members of the county board, sometimes called supervisors, commissioners, or freeholders, are elected by the voters. Usually, each board member represents a particular district within the county. While board members' terms of office vary, the most common term is four years.

The county board has legislative powers and may pass laws for the county. A law passed by county boards or by other local governments is often known as an **ordinance**. These ordinances may deal with such matters as regulating business, improving regional transportation, and protecting the health and safety of county residents.

A county board may also raise money by imposing property taxes or sales taxes. This money is used to pay county employees, to maintain county roads and buildings, and to provide services such as law enforcement. Many counties also provide recreation facilities, hospitals, and public libraries for their residents.

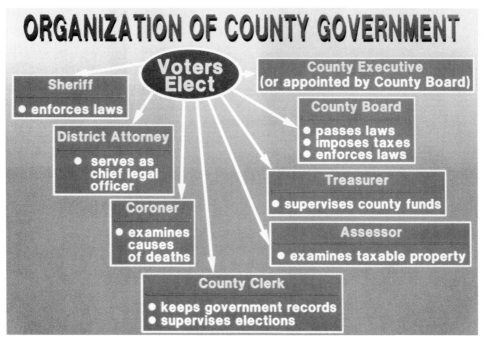

ORGANIZATION OF COUNTY GOVERNMENT

Voters Elect

Sheriff
• enforces laws

District Attorney
• serves as chief legal officer

Coroner
• examines causes of deaths

County Executive
(or appointed by County Board)

County Board
• passes laws
• imposes taxes
• enforces laws

Treasurer
• supervises county funds

Assessor
• examines taxable property

County Clerk
• keeps government records
• supervises elections

This chart shows how the government of a county might be organized. In what way do the county board and the treasurer work together?

Since it is also the county government's responsibility to administer and enforce laws, a county board may have executive powers as well as legislative powers. For example, many county boards employ inspectors to check buildings for safety violations. Many also set up special departments to enforce liquor and food service laws.

County Officials

The executive powers of a county board are often shared with a number of other elected officials. The roles of these officials are similar to those of executive officials in the state government.

The sheriff is the county's chief law enforcement officer. The sheriff's department, which usually includes deputies and uniformed officers, is responsible for enforc-

ing court orders and for managing the county jail. In some counties, the sheriff's department shares law enforcement duties with a separate police department.

The district attorney (DA) is the county's chief legal officer. The DA investigates crimes, brings charges against suspected lawbreakers, and prosecutes the cases in court.

The coroner is a medical doctor who tries to establish the cause of unusual or suspicious deaths. The coroner usually works closely with the sheriff's department or the police department.

The county clerk is similar to the state government's secretary of state. The clerk keeps official government records and often supervises county elections.

The assessor examines all taxable property within the county and estimates how much it is worth. The county's property tax is based on the assessor's estimate.

A major responsibility of local governments is to protect the health of its citizens. That is not always easy, and sometimes unusual action must be taken. Take the case of "Typhoid Mary." Mary Mallon was a carrier of typhoid fever, a contagious, sometimes fatal disease that is passed on through contaminated food or water. As a carrier, Mary did not suffer from the disease, but she passed it on to others. Worse, she worked as a cook and handled other people's food.

Mary was responsible for an outbreak of typhoid in New York City in 1907. A city health worker tracked her down and the city locked her up for three years. She was released in 1910 after promising never to work as a cook again.

However, a few years later Mary was found working as a cook and spreading typhoid. The city was forced to lock her up for the rest of her life. Mary Mallon infected at least 51 people with typhoid fever, and 3 people died. No one knows how many others she may have infected as well.

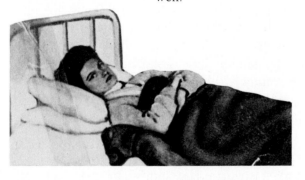

The county treasurer, like the state treasurer, supervises the county's funds and makes payments from the treasury. He or she may also be the chief tax collector. The treasurer's work is supervised by an auditor, who makes sure that none of the county's money is spent without approval from the county board.

Growth of County Government

County government began in rural areas of the South. People in these areas lived far apart and were largely self-sufficient. County governments were first set up to provide a few basic services that residents could not provide for themselves, such as law enforcement and road construction.

Over the past century, the role of county government has grown enormously throughout the United States. As large cities became increasingly crowded, many of their residents moved into the surrounding counties. Rural areas turned into densely packed suburbs, filled with shopping centers, highways, and housing developments.

Because of this growth, county governments have been forced to provide more and more services. Most counties provide water, sewer, and sanitation services. Many also operate large, modern police departments and hospitals. To manage these increased services, county governments have begun to maintain large bureaucracies similar to those of state governments. Among the government agencies found in many counties are the board of health, the welfare board, the hospital board, and the planning commission.

The increased demand for services has put a strain on many counties. The old form of county government, in which executive duties are divided equally among many officials, is often slow and inefficient. As a

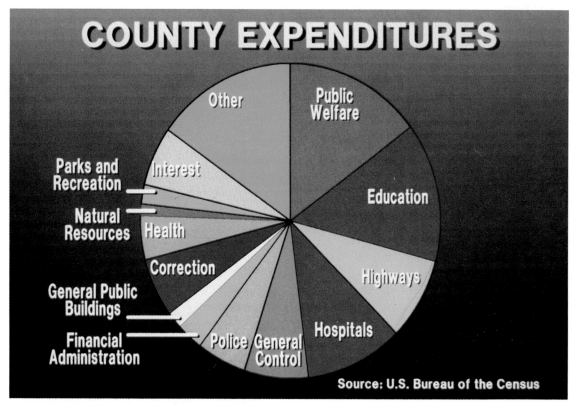

COUNTY EXPENDITURES

Other

Public Welfare

Parks and Recreation

Interest

Education

Natural Resources

Health

Correction

Highways

General Public Buildings

Hospitals

Financial Administration

Police

General Control

Source: U.S. Bureau of the Census

This pie graph shows how counties spend their money. Which are the two largest items (aside from "Other") in county budgets?

result, many county governments have been reorganized to operate more like state governments.

Under a new form of government adopted by many counties, the county board operates only as a legislature. All executive responsibilities are handled by a powerful official called a county executive, or county manager. The county executive is sometimes hired by the county board, but is more often elected by the voters. The county executive appoints top officials, manages the bureaucracy, and submits proposed bills to the legislature.

SECTION REVIEW

Define the Words

charter   ordinance

Check the Facts

1. What is a county board and what are its main responsibilities?
2. Identify three county officials and describe their duties.
3. List some of the services county governments often provide.

Think About the Ideas

4. *Analyze.* Why do you think the U.S. Constitution made no mention of local government?
5. *Evaluate.* What are the advantages and disadvantages of the county executive type of county government?

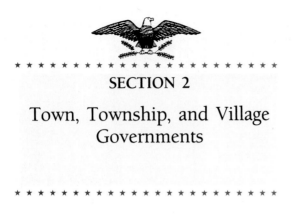

Town, Township, and Village Governments

★ ★

VOCABULARY

township   user fee
special district

Just as states are divided into counties, many counties are divided into smaller units. In New England, these units are called towns. In many other eastern and midwestern states, they are called **townships**. Each town or township also has its own government. Like county governments, local governments get their power directly from the state.

The relationship between county governments and local governments varies from state to state. In New England, the needs of most communities are met by their town governments, and counties are basically judicial districts. In some parts of the country, county and township governments share power, but in the South and West, counties tend to be more important than township governments. The two forms of government usually have a cooperative relationship, dividing responsibilities between them.

Officials of local government work closely with the people of the community.

Town Government

Town government is one of the oldest forms of government in the United States. It began in the New England colonies, where colonists generally settled in small villages and towns. In most cases, farmers living in outlying areas were also considered town members. From the very beginning, these New England colonists met regularly with their neighbors to discuss problems that involved everyone. Any disagreements were settled by a majority vote.

Eventually, "town meetings" became the colonists' form of local government. All important decisions were made by the citizens themselves, not by elected representatives. Since each citizen had a direct say in the government, the town meeting was a form of direct democracy. You learned about direct democracy in Chapter 1.

Fighting Fires for a Living

Why would anyone want to be a fire fighter? Putting out fires is hard, dangerous, dirty work. The hours are long and the working conditions are miserable. Nevertheless, many men and women do become fire fighters because they know that saving lives and property is a vital and rewarding job.

When a fire breaks out, seconds count in saving lives and keeping property damage to a minimum. Therefore, each fire fighter must perform a specific job as a member of a highly trained team. Some fire fighters drive the fire trucks, some connect and operate hoses, and others search burning buildings for fire victims.

Fire fighters are also concerned with preventing fires. Some become fire inspectors or fire science specialists. These specialists inspect buildings to spot fire hazards, and make sure the buildings have adequate fire-detection and fire-fighting equipment. Fire fighters also teach children and adults about fire safety measures.

Fire fighters usually work for towns and cities or for private companies. In many small towns, the fire fighters are unpaid volunteers who fight fires in their spare time. To become a professional fire fighter, you should be a high school graduate. You must pass a civil service test and a rigorous physical exam. If you pass the tests and are accepted by your local fire department, you will undergo several months of apprenticeship training.

Using Your Skills
1. What are some of the drawbacks and rewards of fire fighting?
2. Why do you think it is necessary for fire fighters to undergo so much testing and training?

A number of small New England towns still hold town meetings today. These meetings are usually held once a year. The time and place and the topics to be discussed are announced in advance. All town residents who are registered to vote are encouraged to attend the town meeting. One by one, the topics on the agenda are discussed and then voted upon.

Because town meetings are held so rarely, they are useful only for making broad policy decisions. They cannot handle the day-to-day details of government. For this reason, each New England town elects a number of officials, called selectmen, to run the local government between meetings. (Despite the name, selectmen may be women.) The town may also elect executive officers similar to those in a county government, such as a clerk, a treasurer, or an assessor.

Some New England towns have replaced the traditional town meetings with representative town meetings. In these towns, the citizens elect people to represent them at the town meeting. Other towns have eliminated town meetings entirely. These towns are run much like counties, with a board of selectmen or a town council doing the job of a county board. In some towns, the voters elect a town manager whose role is similar to that of a county executive.

Township Government

New York, New Jersey, and Pennsylvania were organized somewhat differently than New England. The counties in these states were divided into smaller units called townships, a term borrowed from Great Britian. These townships set up local governments similar to those of New England towns.

Midwestern townships have a different history. As the United States expanded westward, it acquired new land that was not yet settled. As this land was obtained, Congress divided it into square blocks, which were called townships. Townships were sections of land, not units of government. However, as settlers moved into these areas, they set up local governments similar to those in the eastern states. These governments, called civil townships, generally kept the same borders that Congress had established. For this reason, many midwestern townships appear perfectly square on a map.

Today, some township governments are like town governments, holding township meetings similar to town meetings in New England. Most townships, however, have governments similar to those of counties. There is often a small group of elected officials called a township committee, board of supervisors, or board of trustees, which has legislative responsibilities. This committee or board is usually headed by a township super-

visor. In addition, most townships have other elected officials, such as a treasurer, a tax collector, and an assessor.

Over the years, a number of responsibilities originally held by township governments have been taken over by county governments. In some cases, county and township governments work together to provide local services. Law enforcement duties, for example, may be divided between county and township police forces. Township officials may supervise county elections, and county officials may oversee the maintenance of township roads.

Village Government

A village is the smallest unit of local government. Villages almost always lie within the boundaries of other governments, such as townships or counties. In some areas, villages are known as boroughs. (These should not be confused with Alaskan boroughs, which are similar to counties rather than to villages.)

The population of some rural communities may be quite small—a few hundred people, or even fewer. Communities this small often have no need for their own government. Most of their needs are provided for by the county or township governments. Occasionally, however, community members find some reason to band together. They may be dissatisfied with the services provided by the county, or they may want to set up their own school system. In that case, they may organize the community as a village and request permission from the state to set up a village government.

As in a township, the government of a village usually consists of a small board of

Plowing the roads after a snowstorm can be a major expense for cities in cold climates.

trustees elected by the voters. Most villages also elect an executive, similar to a town manager. This official is usually known as the chief burgess, or president of the board, or sometimes as the mayor.

The village board has the power to collect taxes and to spend money on projects that benefit the community. Those projects may include building and maintaining roads, establishing schools and public libraries, or setting up recreation facilities. The board may hire officials to supervise these projects and to provide other services.

Becoming a village has both advantages and disadvantages. The main disadvantage is that residents must often pay higher taxes to support the village government. In return, however, they often get better services. Becoming a village also improves the community's status. As a result, visitors, new residents, and businesses may be attracted to the village, bringing money and other resources with them.

Special Districts

Local governments sometimes have special problems or needs. To deal with these matters, they may request permission from the state to create units of government called **special districts**. A special district is set up to deal with a single issue or provide a single service.

Special districts are sometimes set up for financial reasons. For example, one small village may not be able to afford a fully equipped fire department. By pooling their resources, however, several villages may be able to set up a fire department to serve the entire area.

In other instances, a special district may be established to deal with a regional issue. For example, the water in a reservoir may be used by several communities. Managing this water is beyond the authority of any of the individual communities.

Like a local government, a special district is run by a board or commission, which may be elected or appointed. The board sometimes has the power to collect taxes from district residents to pay for the service it provides. Some boards raise money by means of **user fees**. For example, a water district charges residents a fixed price for every gallon of water they use.

One of the most common types of special district is the school district. Small communities often band together to build schools and to hire faculty and staff. A school district is usually run by a school board or board of education whose members are elected by the voters. There are nearly 15,000 school districts in the United States today.

SECTION REVIEW

Define the Words
township   user fee
special district

Check the Facts
1. What are the differences between a town, a township, and a village?
2. Why is a New England town meeting not suitable for all communities?
3. Identify three kinds of special districts.

Think About the Ideas
4. *Compare.* In what ways are county, town, township, and village governments similar?

★ ★

SECTION 3

City Government

★ ★

VOCABULARY
home rule   member-at-large
mayor   metropolitan area
ward

City government is the most common form of local government. When people think of the word *city* they often think of skyscrapers, neon lights, and hundreds of thousands, or perhaps millions, of people. A city, however, can be as small as 2,500 people. Whether a community is called a city really depends on whether or not its residents consider it to be one.

Most of the features that characterize a city cannot be measured or counted. Cities are usually important centers of business, art, and education. Their residents often live more closely together than the residents of towns or suburbs. Cities frequently depend heavily on particular industries, such as manufacturing, high technology, or trade. They usually have special problems as well, such as high rates of crime or drug abuse.

For whatever reason, the people who live in a particular community sometimes begin to think of that community as a city. When that happens, they may apply to the state legislature for a city charter. As you know, a charter is a document in which a state legislature grants power to a local government.

A city charter is much like a constitution, describing the type of city government, its structure, and its powers. The state legislature still maintains control, however. It may change the powers granted to the city government at any time. In recent years, many state legislatures have begun to grant **home rule** to cities. Home rule allows cities to write their own charters, choose their own type of government, and manage their own affairs. While home rule limits the control of the state legislature, it does not eliminate it. Cities must still follow state law.

A city charter usually sets up one of four types of government: the mayor-council form, the council-manager form, the commission form, or the metropolitan form.

Governing the city of New York is a challenging and very complicated job.

Mayor-Council Government

The oldest and most widely used type of city government is the mayor-council form. Under this form of city government, responsibility for governing the city is divided between separate legislative and executive branches. The legislative branch consists of a group of officials called the city council. The executive branch is headed by a chief executive called the **mayor**. It also includes officials such as a clerk, a treasurer, a comptroller, and a city attorney. Separate departments handle police and fire protection, recreation, roads and buildings, health and welfare, and other matters.

Some cities are divided into voting districts called **wards**. Each ward elects a representative to the city council. In other cities, however, some or all of the members of a city council are known as **members-at-large**. A member-at-large is elected by the entire city.

The mayor is also elected by the voters, most often for a four-year term. The powers of the mayor vary from city to city. Some

The mayor-council system is the most common form of city government.

cities follow a strong-mayor plan which gives the mayor a great deal of power over city affairs. Under this plan, the mayor has many of the same powers as a governor or a President. He or she can veto bills passed by the city council, and also appoint and dismiss different city officials. A strong mayor also submits an annual budget to the city council and takes the lead in proposing legislation.

Many cities, however, still follow a weak-mayor plan. Under this plan, the mayor has only limited executive power. Most policy

This chart shows how a city government with a strong mayor plan is organized. To what division of government do the heads of city departments report?

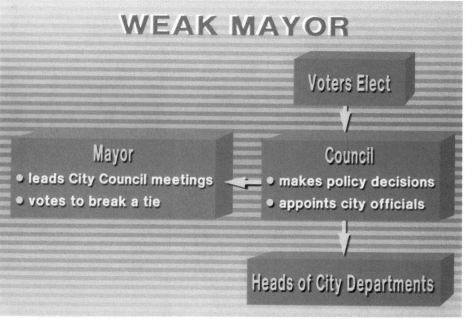

This chart shows how a city government with a weak mayor plan is organized. To what division of government do the head of city departments report?

decisions are made by the city council, and the mayor's veto power is restricted. In addition, the heads of most city departments are chosen by the city council rather than by the mayor. Under the weak-mayor plan, the mayor usually leads city council meetings and votes only to break a tie.

The weak-mayor plan dates from the early days of independence, when Americans still remembered how unfairly British officials had governed the colonies. Even today, many Americans want to prevent any one official from having too much power. The weak-mayor plan achieves that goal, but it also makes a city government much less efficient.

Council-Manager Government

Today, a growing number of cities use another type of city government—the council-manager form. In this type of city government, the voters also elect a city council. They may even elect a mayor, but he or she is given almost no power. Instead, most of the government's executive powers are given to an official called a city manager. This manager is responsible for carrying out the council's policies and running the city government.

Unlike a mayor, a city manager is hired by the city council rather than elected by the voters. Voters do not always elect a mayor who has the experience and the ability to run a city. City managers, however, are almost always professional executives who know how to get things done. In addition, since they are not elected, they are free from political pressures that might interfere with getting a job done.

A council-manager government operates like a large corporation. In the business world, an ineffective manager would probably be fired by the company's directors. In a city, the manager who doesn't run the city

efficiently is likely to be dismissed by the city council. Unlike a large corporation, however, the effectiveness of council-manager government may be limited by money. The top managers of successful corporations often receive millions of dollars in salaries and benefits. Most cities cannot afford to be this generous. As a result, they often have trouble attracting the best managers away from the business world.

Although the council-manager form of government is usually very efficient, many Americans do not approve of it. They feel that any official as powerful as a city manager should be elected, not appointed. Otherwise, the needs and wishes of voters—especially minority voters—may not be taken into account.

Commission Government

A third type of city government is the commission form. There is no separation of legislative and executive powers in a commission government. Instead, the city is governed by separate departments, each of which handles a different set of responsibilities. Some of the most common departments are police, fire, finance, health, and public works. The elected heads of these departments, called commissioners, perform executive duties for their particular department. They also meet together as a commission, with legislative power to pass city ordinances and make policy decisions.

In some cities, one commission is chosen to be mayor, either by the commission or by the voters. The mayor has no special powers, and usually has only a ceremonial role. However, he or she remains an equal member of the commission and continues to manage a government department.

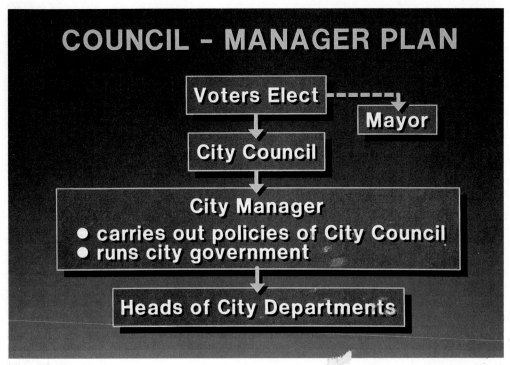

This chart shows the organization of a council-manager plan for city government. How is a city manager different from a mayor?

This chart shows the organization of a commission form of city government. What is the main feature of a commission government?

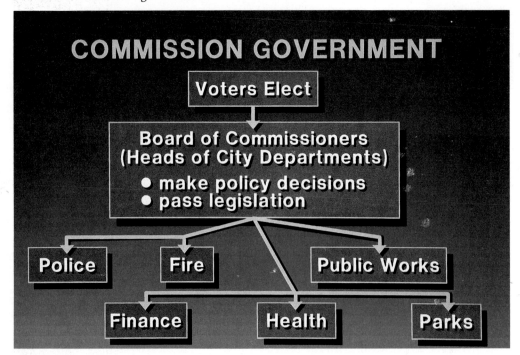

GREAT AMERICAN DOCUMENTS

THE SHAME OF THE CITIES

In the early years of this century, America had many problems. Penniless European immigrants poured into the cities and lived in cold, dark firetraps. Whole families worked six or seven days a week to scrape out a living. Business monopolies charged high prices for shoddy goods and drove honest merchants out of business. Meat packers sold rotten meat, and milk bottlers sold contaminated milk.

Into this unhappy world stepped the muckrakers, a group of magazine publishers, investigative reporters, novelists, and artists who set out to tell about the political corruption and social problems that plagued the country. President Theodore Roosevelt called these people muckrakers because he said they raked the "muck," or filth, to uncover wrongdoing.

One of the most famous muckrakers was Lincoln Steffens. Steffens chose political corruption in America's cities as his special area to investigate and expose. He traveled from city to city. In each place he described how local political leaders were stealing millions of dollars from the city's treasury while failing to provide services, such as water, sewers, and electricity.

Steffens' articles were printed in *McClure's* magazine, the most famous muckraking journal of the day. Some of the articles were collected in a book called *The Shame of the Cities* (1904). The following quotation is from Steffens' preface to that book.

The great truth I tried to make plain was that . . . bribery is no ordinary felony, but treason, that the "corruption which breaks out here and there and now and then" is not an occasional offense, but a common practice, and that the effect is literally to change the form of our government from one that is representative of the people to an oligarchy [government by an elite few], representative of special interests.

In every city that Steffens investigated, he found the same thing—a powerful political machine that continued in office year after year. During their time in power, the machine's leaders grew rich from taxpayers' dollars. And in each case, the voters who could have broken the power of the machine did nothing. Often this was because the machine had bribed them with jobs, money for drinks, or buckets of coal.

Steffens and other muckrakers tried to educate the public and set the American reform movement in motion. Soon people began demanding and winning changes.

Using Your Skills
1. Why was the work of the muckrakers so important to the American public?
2. What do you think Steffens meant when he said that bribery was treason?

The commission form of government was first developed in Galveston, Texas, in 1901. Nearly destroyed by a tidal wave, the city decided that a commission government seemed the best way to handle the emergency. Since that time, however, other cities have found that a commission government is not always efficient in running a city. Without clear leadership, a commission is often unable to set and meet goals. Each commissioner is likely to concentrate primarily on his or her own department, without considering the problems of the city as a whole.

Metropolitan Government

The influence of a city does not stop at the city borders. Nearly every major city is surrounded by—and closely tied to—a number of suburbs. Together, the city and its suburbs form a unit called a **metropolitan area**.

The different local governments within a metropolitan area often have many needs in common. For example, since many people live in the suburbs and work in the city, a good transportation system is essential to people in both places.

Because the rapid transit system of Washington, D.C., serves both the city and its suburbs, it requires the cooperation of a number of different local governments.

Some metropolitan areas have begun to deal with these regional issues by forming metropolitan governments. A metropolitan government is similar to a special district in that it involves several local governments. However, a metropolitan government usually has more than one area of responsibility. It may, for example, handle the transportation, water, and energy needs of people in the area. A metropolitan government is usually run by an elected board.

City and suburban residents may also form metropolitan councils to help them solve common problems. A metropolitan council is a regional organization made up of local elected officials, such as mayors and county supervisors. A metropolitan council does not have any special powers. It is simply an organization that discusses metropolitan issues, shares information, helps coordinate the policies of different local governments, and seeks solutions to regional problems.

Challenges Facing Local Government

The same financial problems that confront state governments also affect local governments. Community residents demand an increasing number of services, but are unwilling or unable to support those services through increased taxes.

This problem is especially serious in cities. Crime, homelessness, drug abuse, and pollution have been rising steadily in urban areas. At the same time, many of the industries and businesses that help provide cities with jobs and revenue have closed or moved elsewhere. In addition, as conditions in cities get worse, many people who can afford to leave move to the suburbs. Many of those who remain are poor and cannot afford higher taxes. As a result, cities are finding it increasingly difficult to raise enough money to solve their problems.

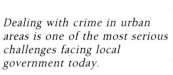

Dealing with crime in urban areas is one of the most serious challenges facing local government today.

Because of their financial difficulties, many local governments cannot afford to pay for services and the maintenance of buildings, parks, and roads. When a problem arises, they look to another unit of government to solve it. This happens because of the overlapping jurisdiction of different local governments. For example, most villages are located in townships, which, in turn, are located in counties. Most cities are located in townships or counties as well. Under these circumstances, it is often difficult to know which government is responsible for what. If a town bridge needs repair, for example, the town may ask the county to pay for the work. The county, in turn, may insist that the town should pay for the work. As the dispute goes back and forth, the bridge goes unrepaired.

Part of the solution to problems facing local governments lies in greater cooperation between the different levels of government. In some cases, this cooperation may be purely financial. Cooperation between governments may also take other forms. Increasingly, local governments are getting together to discuss their regional problems and to work out solutions. The idea of a metropolitan government, which was described earlier, is an important step in this direction.

SECTION REVIEW

Define the Words

home rule
mayor
ward

member-at-large
metropolitan area

Check the Facts
1. What are some characteristics of cities?
2. Identify and describe the four kinds of city government.
3. What is one way in which cities and suburban areas have worked together to solve common problems?

Think About the Ideas
4. *Evaluate.* What are the advantages and disadvantages of the council-manager form of government? Do you think it is a good form of city government? Explain your view.

Many American cities have experienced difficulty finding the money to keep their roads in repair.

CITIZENSHIP SKILLS

How to Deal with Government Bureaucracy

Dealing with government bureaucracy can be very frustrating and difficult. Sometimes you have to explain your problem over and over again before you reach the right department or official. In addition, you may have to stand in long lines for hours, or you may have to come back another day because you failed to bring the right form or document.

You can take a lot of the frustration out of dealing with the government by doing as much planning and information gathering as possible beforehand. Here are some ways you can prepare:

★ If you need to contact a federal, state, county, or municipal department, look up the number of the department in your local telephone directory. In some directories, government numbers are grouped together in a special section, and in others they are listed alphabetically in the white pages. If no num-ber is listed for a specific department or office, call the central switchboard number. Tell the operator which department you want or briefly explain your business. The operator should be able to connect you to the right office, but be patient if you are mis-routed. With some large government bureaucra-cies, you may be trans-ferred two or three times before you reach the right person.

★ Once you have reached the proper department, explain your problem and listen carefully for instructions. Have pencil and paper handy to take notes. Sometimes, you can take care of your business by mail. You may be instructed to write to a certain official, to send photocopies of specific documents, to send a processing or application fee, and so on. Be sure to get the correct names, addresses, and titles, and follow all instructions carefully.

★ In some cases, such as applying for a driver's license, you will have to appear in person. Get the address of the office and find out what hours it is open. Make a list of the documents you need to bring. Also, ask if you need to make an appoint-ment and how long you can expect to wait.

The key to dealing with a government bureaucracy is to expect delays and rerout-ing. If you are prepared for delays, you may be pleasantly surprised to find that gov-ernment workers will often help resolve your problems quickly and efficiently.

Using Your Skills
1. What steps can you take to make it easier to deal with a government bureaucracy over the telephone?
2. Why do you think it is difficult for a large government bureaucracy to serve the public efficiently?

CHAPTER 14 REVIEW

* *

MAIN POINTS

★ The U.S. Constitution does not grant any authority to local governments. The only powers held by a local government are those given to it by the state.

★ County government is one of the most wide-spread forms of local government. A county board, with both legislative and executive powers, and other elected officials are responsible for governing the county.

★ Towns, townships, and villages also have their own governments. The forms of these governments vary from state to state.

★ Some local governments share units of government called special districts, which are responsible for dealing with a single issue or providing a single service.

★ There are four different kinds of city government: mayor-council, council-manager, commission, and metropolitan. Each has advantages and disadvantages, but the mayor-council is the most common.

★ Today, local governments face greater responsibilities and greater problems. One way to help solve these problems is through increased cooperation, such as special districts and metropolitan councils.

WORDS IN REVIEW

Choose the word or phrase from the list below that best completes each sentence. Write the missing words on a separate sheet of paper.

charter
ordinance
special district

township
metropolitan area
user fee

home rule
mayor

ward
member-at-large

1. The city council included one _____, elected by the people of all the city's voting districts.

2. The three neighboring towns asked the state for permission to create a _____ to handle water use in the towns.

3. The state granted the village a _____, establishing its authority over local affairs.

4. The _____ led the executive branch of the government.

5. The city was granted _____, which allowed it to write its own charter.

6. In some areas, units of local government are called _____.

7. The influence of the city had spread to its surrounding suburbs, creating a _____.

8. Voters in the city's 23rd _____ voted for the Republican candidate in the last mayoral election.

9. To help pay for its operation and services, the district water commission required a _____ from the area's residents.

10. At the last meeting of the town board, the members passed an _____ requiring all new house lots to be at least one acre in size.

FACTS IN REVIEW

1. Give two examples of a county board's legislative power and two of its executive power.

2. Why has county government become more important in recent years?

3. What is the role of a county executive?

CHAPTER 14 REVIEW

* *

4. Describe the general organization of township government.

5. Why do small communities establish village governments?

6. What are some advantages and disadvantages of establishing a village government?

7. Identify two reasons for a special district.

8. What is one disadvantage of the city commission form of government?

9. Identify and describe the two types of mayor plan of city government.

10. Why are many cities having financial problems?

THINKING ABOUT LOCAL GOVERNMENT

1. *Evaluate*. Which do you think is more effective, state or local government? Why?

2. *Analyze*. What effect do you think increased suburbanization will have on town government?

3. *Apply*. What do you think could be done to encourage cooperation—instead of competition— among the local governments in a region?

COLLECTING INFORMATION ABOUT COUNTY GOVERNMENT

Find out about the county government in your area or, if there are no counties in your state, about the town government. What is the structure of your county (town) government? What are the main county (town) officials? What are some of the responsibilities of your county (town) government? Outline your findings and present them to the class.

WRITING ABOUT LOCAL GOVERNMENT

In recent days, your local government has run several articles dealing with a proposal for creating a special district in your area. You decide to write a letter to the editor expressing your feelings about this proposal. Decide what type of special district might be appropriate for your area. Then write your letter to the editor. In it, you should clearly give reasons why you feel this special district should be formed.

INTERPRETING A CHART OF CITY GOVERNMENT

Look at the chart on pages 330 and 332 that shows the different forms of city government. Answer the following questions for each type of government: Who do the voters elect? To whom are the different city departments responsible? Who holds legislative and executive power? Do you think this chart is helpful in showing the flow of power and authority in city government?

FOCUSING ON YOUR COMMUNITY

Find out about your local government and its leaders. If you live in a town, village, or city, find out who the chief executive is. Is the position a full- or part-time job? If you live in a city, who is the city council member for your district? What are some of the main issues and problems in your community? How are local officials trying to deal with these problems? Prepare a short oral report of your findings.

* *

Community Issues

OBJECTIVES

After you have studied this chapter, you will be able to:

★ Identify the sources of public policy.
★ Explain how public policy is made and how communities plan for the future.
★ Identify how communities finance public policy and explain the advantages and disadvantages of various types of funding.
★ Discuss some of the social issues facing communities today and how communities are dealing with these issues.
★ Discuss some of the environmental problems facing many communities today and what communities are doing to solve these problems.

SECTIONS

1 Dealing With Community Issues
2 Social Issues
3 Environmental Issues

In the early days of the nation, local governments provided only a few basic services, such as building roads, running schools, and keeping the peace. As communities grew larger, their governments gradually took on more responsibilities. In 1736, for example, Philadelphia set up America's first volunteer fire department. In 1833, the town of Peterborough, New Hampshire, established the nation's first free public library.

Over the past century, the responsibilities of governments have increased dramatically. Rapid change has produced many new issues and problems that have challenged government. For example, the increased use of electrical power and gasoline engines has led to pollution and energy shortages. The growing number of aged and disabled people has strained health care systems. Rising unemployment and overcrowded housing and schools have contributed to increases in crime and drug abuse.

While these are national issues, they are local issues as well. Every village, town, and city must find a way to deal with these and other problems. Solutions require both planning and cooperation. By preparing for change and working with other units of government, communities are better able to cope with their problems and reach their goals.

★ ★

SECTION 1

Dealing With Community Issues

★ ★

VOCABULARY

public policy	master plan
infrastructure	zoning board
priorities	bond
resources	

Schools, businesses, and other organizations usually have policies, or rules, that guide their actions. These policies allow decisions to be made consistently. Most businesses, for example, have policies about hiring, promoting, and firing employees.

Federal, state, and local governments also make policies. A policy made by a government is called a **public policy**, because it affects all members of the public. A public policy is not a law. In many cases, it is not even written down. Instead, a public policy is a general agreement among government leaders about how they intend to deal with certain issues or problems.

Making Public Policy

The ideas for policies, like those for laws, come from many different sources. They may originate with members of the legislative, executive, or judicial branches. They may be proposed by party leaders or by interest groups. They may even be suggested by members of the media, such as newspaper journalists or television commentators.

One other important source of policy ideas, especially at the local level, is private citizens. Often, just one person can have a great effect on the policies of local government. In Oakland, California, for example, a man named Robert Patten believed that the beauty of a scenic road near his home should be preserved. When a storage company began building a large, unattractive warehouse near the road, Patten acted immediately. He gathered his neighbors' signatures on a petition and complained to the city government. As a result, the city convinced the storage company to make some changes in the building's design. The city also changed its policy about what kinds of buildings would be allowed near the road.

Changing a public policy is not always easy however. It may take months or even years. During that time, there may be disagreements about what the public policy should be or how a policy should be changed.

By attending public hearings of local planning boards, citizens can often influence decisions about community development projects.

Like Congressional committees, local governments often do research and hold public hearings before making policy decisions. The policy that results is often a compromise that reflects many points of view.

Planning for the Future

Making policies to solve current problems is not always effective. The most useful public policies are usually those that try to prevent problems before they occur. This requires looking ahead at what is likely to happen in the future and planning for it now. A growing number of local governments are setting up planning commissions to do this kind of work. A planning commission is an advisory board whose members may include government leaders, business people, local residents, and architects.

Local governments and their planning commissions make both short-term and long-term plans. A short-term plan is a policy designed to be carried out over the next few years. For example, Oakland's decision to protect the scenic road near Robert Patten's home is a short-term plan. In the future, the Oakland planning commission may change its mind. It could decide that the rest of Oakland would benefit from having warehouses in that area, even if the structures marred the area's scenic beauty.

A long-term plan is a broader, less detailed policy than a short-term plan. It is designed to be followed over 10, 20, or even 50 years. In order to make long-term plans, a planning commission must make educated guesses about a community's future needs. For example, it might try to project the future population of the area by studying Census Bureau data. It might also try to determine future transportation, education, and recreation needs by looking at recent population and economic patterns.

In developing their plans, local governments and planning commissions often consult with the citizens or groups who will be most affected by particular policy decisions.

Facing Difficult Questions

Planning for a community always involves searching for answers to a number of difficult questions. Take, for example, a small town whose local computer software company suddenly becomes successful. As the company expands, it builds several new buildings. Attracted by the growing economy, other businesses move into the town. People flock to the town to work for these companies. Stores, theaters, and restaurants open to serve these new residents.

A situation like this raises a number of questions for a local government or planning commission. For example, where should offices and housing be built? Will increased traffic cause problems on local roads and highways? Should the town build new roads to accommodate more vehicles, or should it encourage the development of public transportation? What other demands will the growing population place on the town's **infrastructure**—its system of roads, bridges, water, and sewers? If the infrastructure needs to be expanded, how will the town pay for the work?

EVALUATING PRIORITIES AND RESOURCES
Hundreds of local governments and planning commissions around the country are faced with questions like these every year. The answers to these questions usually depend on two things—priorities and resources. **Priorities** are those goals a community considers most important or most urgent. In setting pri-

orities, a community must first decide what it values most. For example, is it more important to have commercial success or a peaceful place to live? Whose needs are more important—those of current residents or of future generations? While assessing its values, a community must also determine its more specific goals and must rank these goals in order of importance. For example, a community may decide that its most important goal is to attract business. Following that may

To prepare for the future needs of a growing population, a local government may have to plan, finance, and carry out major construction projects.

be goals of improving community services, preserving open spaces, upgrading the school system, and so on.

Once it has set its priorities, a community must look closely at its **resources**. These are the materials, people, and money available to carry out the community's goals. Suppose, for example, that a community has decided to improve its public transportation system. Is there enough money to build and maintain a new trolley system, or would an expanded bus system be more affordable? Which system will attract the most riders and earn the most revenue? To plan effectively, a community must consider how much money and other resources are available to it.

CREATING A MASTER PLAN After setting priorities and evaluating resources, a planning commission makes practical decisions about the community's future. It usually expresses these decisions in a document called a **master plan**, which states a set of goals and explains how the local government will respond to the changing needs of its citizens over time. It also describes the physical layout of the community in the present and what changes will be encouraged in the future.

A planning commission normally submits its master plan to the local government, which then decides whether to accept and enforce it. If the master plan is accepted, the local government is responsible for carrying

This diagram shows the layout of a city by its different land-use zones. Who determines how land can be used in most cities?

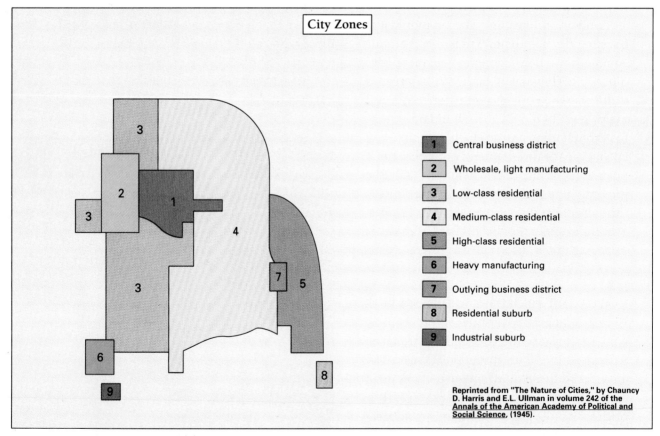

City Zones

1 Central business district
2 Wholesale, light manufacturing
3 Low-class residential
4 Medium-class residential
5 High-class residential
6 Heavy manufacturing
7 Outlying business district
8 Residential suburb
9 Industrial suburb

Reprinted from "The Nature of Cities," by Chauncy D. Harris and E.L. Ullman in volume 242 of the Annals of the American Academy of Political and Social Science, (1945).

it out. The legislative branch must approve funds for any projects outlined in the plan. The executive branch makes rules and regulations to enforce the plan. In many communities, a powerful commission called a **zoning board** decides where houses, stores, factories, and offices may be built. For example, the zoning board may set up a residential zone in which no businesses are allowed.

There is often a housing board as well, which makes sure that the community has safe, affordable housing. Often, a recreation department will set aside land for parks and athletic fields. If a public transportation system is part of the master plan, a special commission is usually set up to build or improve it.

Financing Public Policy

No local government can carry out any of its plans without first deciding how it is going to pay for them. Taxes are the most common source of revenue for local governments. There are several different kinds of taxes, each with its own advantages and disadvantages.

Nearly every local government imposes a tax on property—the land or buildings—within its borders. Some places also impose a property tax on things such as boats or cars. The advantage of a property tax is that it is a steady source of revenue. People within a community always own houses, land, or other types of property. The main disadvantage is that a property tax is difficult to apply fairly. There is no precise, scientific way to decide how much a piece of property is worth. Tax assessors must make estimates, and these estimates are not always accurate.

An increasingly popular source of local revenue is the sales tax. With a sales tax, you pay a fixed percentage of the purchase price—usually 5-8 percent—in addition to the purchase price. The advantage of a sales tax is that it is easy to collect; the seller collects taxes on every sale and gives this money to the government in a lump sum. The major disadvantage of a sales tax is that it puts an unfair burden on low-income families. People who can barely afford the purchase price of the goods they need find it difficult to pay sales taxes as well.

While an income tax is the chief source of revenue for the federal government and for many states, it is not common on the local level. Many large cities have income taxes, but most towns and villages do not. The primary advantage of an income tax is that the burden falls most heavily on those who can most afford to pay. The main disadvantage is that it is more difficult and costly to enforce. Many people find ways—legal and illegal—to avoid paying their fair share of income tax. It can also be expensive for a government to keep track of people's incomes and to investigate those who submit incorrect information on their tax forms.

Most of these kinds of taxes are paid by businesses as well as by individuals. In addition, local governments place a variety of taxes on businesses alone. For example, many communities require certain types of businesses to have a license to operate. In order to receive its license, a business must pay a certain fee to the government.

As you have discovered in previous chapters, local governments are finding it increasingly difficult to finance themselves and their projects. Taxes alone are not enough. In addition, grants from the federal government, another important source of income, have been cut back in recent years. As a result, towns and cities are turning to other means of raising funds.

One common source of revenue is the user fee. Examples of user fees are the tolls charged on a community's roads and bridges and the

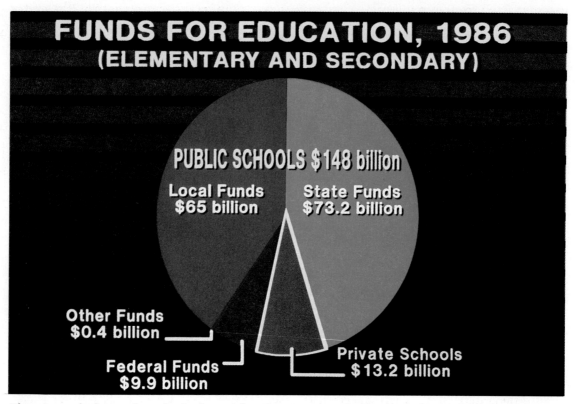

FUNDS FOR EDUCATION, 1986
(ELEMENTARY AND SECONDARY)

PUBLIC SCHOOLS $148 billion

Local Funds $65 billion

State Funds $73.2 billion

Other Funds $0.4 billion

Federal Funds $9.9 billion

Private Schools $13.2 billion

This pie graph shows where the funds used for education come from. What is still the largest source of funds?

fares charged on its public transportation system. User fees are often considered a fair way to raise money because they require only those who use government services to pay for them. Like sales taxes, however, user fees fall hardest on low-income people. The amount of money required just to travel to and from work can consume a significant fraction of a poor person's income.

As a last resort, many local governments find that they must borrow money to pay for the services they provide. They may borrow money from banks just as businesses do. More often, however, they borrow money from the public by issuing bonds. A **bond** is an I.O.U. or promissory note from the government. For example, if you pay $100 for a bond, the government promises to pay that $100 back to you—plus interest—by a certain date. Local governments most often sell bonds to pay for special projects, such as building schools or roads. Issuing bonds is an easy way for a local government to raise money quickly. The drawback, however, is that the government must eventually pay back not only the amount of the bond but also interest. Having to pay that interest may send the government further into debt.

CAREERS

City Manager

Running a city is a big job and many communities have decided they need a professional to do it. City managers are appointed by the city council or mayor to take charge of the daily operations of the city.

The city manager hires and supervises all of the people who run the different city departments such as public works, police and fire, streets and sanitation, and taxes. The manager is also expected to prepare the city's annual budget, negotiate contracts with the labor unions whose members work for the city, and keep the city's records in good order.

The job of a city manager can vary enormously depending on the size and complexity of the municipality where the manager is employed. In a rapidly growing area, the city manager may be required to determine the need for new parks, schools, streets, and utilities, and to propose ways to meet those needs. In an old, depressed city, it may be an important part of the city manager's job to propose ways to attract new businesses and population to the city.

Most municipalities require that their city managers have a college education and five years of experience. Many prefer to hire city managers who also have a master's degree in public administration, urban planning, or political science. City managers usually start out as interns or assistant city managers and work their way up.

Using Your Skills
1. What kinds of jobs do city managers do?
2. What high school courses do you think would help prepare you to be a city manager? Why?

SECTION REVIEW

Define the Words
public policy
infrastructure
priorities
resources
master plan
zoning board
bond

Check the Facts
1. What are some important sources of policy ideas?
2. What are some issues that a planning commission must consider when it develops its plans for the community?

3. Identify five ways a local government can raise money, and describe an advantage and a disadvantage of each.

Think About the Ideas
4. *Evaluate.* Do you think that governments should try to reduce taxes and raise more money through user fees? Why or why not?

SECTION 2

Social Issues

****

VOCABULARY
urban renewal   voluntarism

Cities are often portrayed as dirty, noisy, crowded, and dangerous places. The areas outside of cities, on the other hand, are portrayed as quiet, orderly, and clean. Such distinctions are becoming a thing of the past. As the populations of cities have spilled over into surrounding areas, urban troubles have followed. Changes in society and increased movement between different regions have also brought new problems to many areas in the nation. People everywhere must now deal with issues such as crime, inadequate housing, and declining standards of education. To meet these challenges, local governments are now calling on businesses and private citizens to help provide the funds and programs that are required.

Education

In 1986, more than $148 billion was spent on public education in U.S. elementary and secondary schools. About 40 percent was supplied by local governments; the rest came from federal and state funds. Of all the services provided by local governments, education is the most expensive.

Despite the money being spent, many Americans have become increasingly unhappy with the public education system. Students often feel that the subjects they study in school have little to do with their lives. Teachers, faced with students who seem uninterested in learning, are frustrated with their jobs, and work for a salary that is low compared to many other jobs. Parents complain that their children are not learning basic skills and are not being taught values and ideas from their own cultural traditions. In addition, many schools are plagued by problems such as high dropout rates, drug abuse, and crime.

Some problems have worsened as families move from the cities to the suburbs. Rapidly expanding suburban communities are unable to build schools or hire teachers fast enough to handle the growing number of students. Back in the cities, lower-income families cannot afford to maintain their school buildings or pay their teachers adequately.

Local governments have begun to tackle these problems in a variety of ways. To improve the quality of education, for example, some areas have begun experimenting with "magnet schools," which allow students to focus on learning particular skills, such as science or performing arts. Magnet schools bring together students from rich and poor communities, and they are supported by everyone in the area. By allowing students to concentrate on what they do best, they encourage students to work harder.

Competition from countries such as Japan has renewed Americans' awareness of the importance of education. With help from the U.S. Department of Education, many communities are making education a greater priority. They are now willing to pay more for public education, even if they must cut back on other government services.

Housing

A critical issue in many communities is providing adequate, affordable housing for the people who live there. In many communities and city neighborhoods, rising real estate values have forced out lower income families. Many move to less desirable areas, but some cannot find any affordable housing at all. These people join the growing number of homeless who roam America's streets. The homelessness problem has become increasingly serious in recent years.

Another aspect of the housing problem involves the decline of certain neighborhoods into slums. Many buildings in these areas are run-down and dangerous, and they often lack hot water and heat. Most people who live in slums are very poor and cannot afford to repair their homes. Life in slums is also dangerous because of high crime rates.

Cities have approached the housing problem in different ways. Some cities have tried to eliminate slums through **urban renewal** projects. Urban renewal means tearing down old buildings and replacing them with new ones. In recent years, the trend in urban renewal has been to convert old buildings into fashionable shops and living spaces. In many cities, young, well-to-do professional people are buying slum buildings and turning them into attractive residences. While urban renewal may improve the appearance of cities, it does not always solve the underlying problems. If poor neighborhoods become middle-class neighborhoods, poor families will have an even harder time finding affordable housing.

Many communities have tried to solve the housing problem by building low-income housing—blocks of houses and apartments set aside for low-income families. Unfortunately, most governments cannot afford to build enough housing units to satisfy the demand. Even after it has been built, low-income housing can be very expensive to

Special magnet schools are one way of giving talented students a chance to develop their skills.

A shortage of affordable housing has caused a dramatic increase in the number of homeless people in cities across the nation.

maintain. Many communities, faced with shortages of funds, have had to cut back on repairs and upkeep of their low-income housing. The result is often a government-owned slum.

As the housing problem grows more serious, many communities are opening temporary shelters for homeless people. Volunteer groups and religious organizations are also helping with donations of food and clothing. So far, however, communities have not found permanent solutions for the problems of housing and homelessness.

Crime

Crime is one of the most serious problems in many communities. The crime rates are usually highest in cities, where poverty and crime often go hand-in-hand. For people who have struggled in poverty with dead-end, minimum-wage jobs, robbery or drug dealing may seem like a practical way to make a better living. For others, employment may not even be an option. Many of the poorest inner-city residents—sometimes called the underclass—drop out of school early and spend much of their time on the streets. For these people, crime is the only way of life they know.

Many cities have set up programs to try to help poor people improve their lives.

By providing job-training programs, local governments help young people prepare for successful careers.

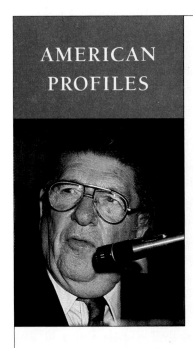

Howard Jarvis—Tax Rebel

They called him a crank and a nut, but Howard Jarvis proved them wrong. At the age of 76, he led the voters of California in the most successful tax revolt since the Boston Tea Party.

In the late 1970's, home prices in California were rising rapidly. The property tax rate, which paid for local government and schools, was linked to housing values so taxes were also skyrocketing. Many people complained that they would have to sell their homes because they could no longer afford to pay the taxes.

Jarvis, a retired businessman, started a campaign to hold an initiative on property taxes. On his first try, in 1976, he fell short of the 500,000 signatures he needed. Then in 1977, he joined forces with Paul Gann, leader of a state taxpayers group. Together they collected 1.2 million signatures for an initiative which came to be known as Proposition 13.

Nearly all of the state's political leaders and newspapers opposed the proposition. Cities and school districts believed that thousands of workers would be fired and many services would be cut if Proposition 13 was approved. But the voters did approve it, overwhelmingly, and California's property taxes were reduced by 57 percent. Proposition 13 also started a trend. Antitax propositions appeared on the ballot in several other states, and many people across the nation joined the revolt against high taxes.

Using Your Skills
1. Why did the state's political leaders oppose Proposition 13?
2. Why do you think California requires so many signatures to get a proposition on the election ballot?

These programs often include free job training and counseling. For young people, there are after-school tutoring services and government-funded summer jobs. Programs like these give people the skills they need to work their way out of poverty.

In recent years, with the increased use of illegal drugs, crime has become a major problem in suburbs and small towns as well as cities. Drug addicts often steal to get the money they need to buy drugs. Drug dealers often engage in violent crimes—including murder—as they fight over territory. These problems cannot be solved with job training and summer job programs.

Many communities are fighting drug-related crime through education. By teaching young people how to "say no" to drugs, they hope to put the drug dealers out of business. Communities are also teaching their residents to protect themselves against violent crime. Such simple techniques as walking in groups, or installing dead-bolt locks on doors, can protect life and property.

When possible, communities have tried to expand their police forces. Often, however, there are simply no funds available for more law enforcement officers. In that case, many communities have formed neighborhood watch programs in which ordinary citizens are trained to spot and report any suspicious activity in their neighborhoods.

Outlook for the Future

Given enough money, local governments could go a long way toward solving their social problems. They could raise teachers' salaries, build low-income housing for everyone who needs it, fix up decaying neighborhoods, hire additional police, and do much more. Unfortunately, as has been mentioned many times before, money is in short supply. The challenge facing communities, therefore, is to find solutions to their problems without relying on higher taxes or federal funds.

Many communities are beginning to meet that challenge by taking advantage of their greatest resource—their citizens. If given enough encouragement, citizens are often willing to devote time and energy to helping their communities. **Voluntarism**, the tradition of unpaid community service, has always been an important part of American life.

Community volunteers help their neighborhood schools by getting involved with parent-teacher organizations and by tutoring. They help homeless people by opening shelters, running soup kitchens, and organizing clothing drives. They help fight crime by participating in neighborhood watch programs. They help poor families by giving money, clothing, and food to community service organizations.

Recent court decisions extending the "one person, one vote" rule have given citizens a greater voice in their local governments. Many people—particularly minority groups such as blacks, Hispanics, and Asians—are able to participate more fully in the democratic process.

This increased participation has led to increased voluntarism as well. When people feel appreciated and valued as members of a community, they become more willing to devote themselves to that community.

SECTION REVIEW

Define the Words

urban renewal   voluntarism

Check the Facts
1. Identify two problems associated with the public education system.
2. What are two ways in which communities have tried to solve their housing problems?
3. Identify two ways in which communities are trying to solve the problem of crime.

Think About the Ideas
4. *Analyze.* What types of problems do you think can be solved most easily through voluntarism?

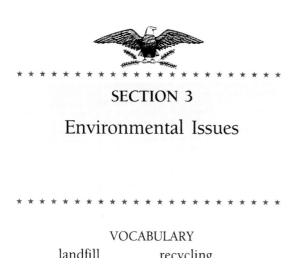

VOCABULARY

landfill   recycling

When the oil tanker *Exxon Valdez* ran aground off the coast of Alaska in March 1989, it spilled 10 million gallons of oil into Prince William Sound. Countless numbers of fish, birds, otters, and other wild creatures were killed by the oil, and hundreds of miles of coastline were blackened. The Alaskan fishing industry also suffered a severe blow from the accident.

The *Valdez* oil spill reminded Americans of the high price we pay for living in an industrialized society. Every time we turn on a light, drive a car, or throw away trash, we harm our environment. Often, that damage is small and easy to ignore. Sometimes, as in Prince William Sound, the damage is much greater.

Protecting the environment is a national, and worldwide, concern. Most often, however, the battles to protect the environment are fought on the local level. Nearly every town and city has its own environmental problems and is searching for ways to solve them.

Resource Shortages

As their populations grow, communities place greater demands on their energy and water resources. Many local areas are having trouble meeting this demand. Existing power plants often cannot produce enough electricity to meet people's needs, especially on hot summer days when air conditioners are running.

In many western states, where rainfall is limited, the demand for water is an even greater problem than the demand for electricity. As the population of these states grows, housing developments are built in

In 1989, extensive damage to the Alaska coastline caused by the Exxon Valdez *oil tanker helped focus public attention on environmental issues.*

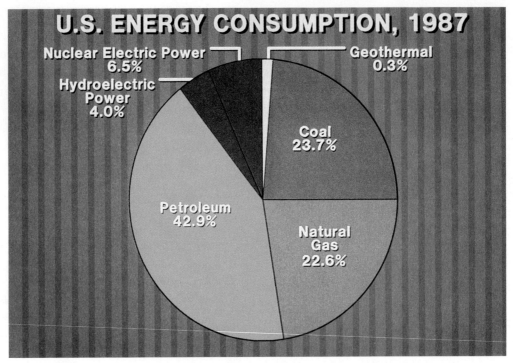

U.S. ENERGY CONSUMPTION, 1987

Nuclear Electric Power
6.5%

Geothermal
0.3%

Hydroelectric
Power
4.0%

Coal
23.7%

Petroleum
42.9%

Natural
Gas
22.6%

This pie graph shows the sources of energy used in the United States. Which three sources are likely to decline in consumption in the future?

desert areas and the demand for water is greatly increased. The growing populations of such states as California, Arizona, and New Mexico are pushing scarce water resources to the limit.

Americans disagree about solutions to these problems. Some believe that the best answer is new power plants and reservoirs. There are many drawbacks to this solution, however. Coal- and oil-burning power plants pollute the air. Nuclear power plants have been shown to be dangerous. Reservoirs alter the landscape and destroy the habitats of many wild creatures. Moreover, building power plants and digging reservoirs is very expensive.

Other people believe that the best answer is conservation. People can conserve electricity by buying energy-efficient appliances, adjusting thermostats, and turning off

unnecessary lights. They can conserve water by putting weights in toilet tanks, taking shorter showers, and reducing or eliminating the watering of lawns. This solution has drawbacks as well, however. Conservation is very difficult to enforce. Except in times of emergency, most Americans resent actions that interfere in their personal lives. They do not want to be told how much water or power to use. Legislatures are rarely successful in passing conservation laws. Conservation can only work if Americans do it willingly.

Scientists are working on a third solution—energy sources that do not harm the environment. In the future, we may get much of our electricity from sunlight, wind, water, or less harmful forms of nuclear energy. So far, however, none of these technologies is ready for large-scale use.

Air and Water Pollution

Pollution of our air and water is a nationwide problem. Cars and trucks pour fumes into the atmosphere. Factory smokestacks emit poisonous gases. Power plants and incinerators spew out ashes and smoke. Even cigarettes pollute the air. Air pollution can cause lung problems, heart disease, and cancer. It can also harm wildlife.

Water pollution comes primarily from factories, which produce all sorts of chemical waste. Some factories pour this waste directly into rivers and streams. Others bury it, allowing it to seep into underground water supplies. Water pollution kills fish and other sea life. Eating fish from polluted waters can also cause severe illness in people. Drinking polluted water can be dangerous or even deadly.

The federal government, through the Environmental Protection Agency, has done much to stop industrial pollution of air and water. Federal regulations strictly limit the amounts and kinds of waste that factories can discharge. Unfortunately, budget cutbacks in recent years have kept many of these regulations from being enforced. As a result, state

By how much did the amount of material recovered increase between 1960 and 1986?

CITY GARBAGE
(IN MILLIONS OF TONS)

	1960	1970	1980	1986
Total waste produced	87.5	120.5	142.6	157.7
Materials recovered	5.8	8.0	13.4	16.9
Processed for energy recovery	(NA)	0.4	2.7	9.6
Net waste disposed of	81.7	112.1	126.5	131.2
(NA—not available)				

Source: Statistical Abstract of the U.S. 1989

CIVICS SIDELIGHTS

Fluoridation

Today, about half the people in the United States drink water that contains fluoride. While this is taken for granted now, fluoridation was a controversial issue from the 1940's to 1960's.

Fluoride is a chemical that occurs naturally in some water supplies. Although harmful in large amounts, fluoride in very small amounts was found to reduce tooth decay. In 1945, the cities of Grand Rapids, Michigan, and Newburgh, New York, began to add fluoride to their water supplies to test the effect on tooth decay. The results of these tests led health officials to recommend fluoridation.

But not everyone supported the idea. People packed city council meetings and held long, heated debates over fluoridation. Supporters felt the prevention of tooth decay outweighed any risks. Opponents claimed fluoridation was forced medication and might have undesirable long-term effects.

In the end, many communities chose fluoridation. If your community has fluoridation, you probably have fewer cavities than your parents did at your age.

and local governments have had to take more responsibility for protecting the air and water.

Pollution produced by factories can be regulated much more easily than pollution produced by individuals. In many cities, cars and trucks are the primary source of air pollution. The only way to ease this problem is to persuade people to drive less. Local governments are trying to do this in two ways. First, they are building or improving public transportation systems. They hope that this will encourage people to take buses and subways instead of cars. Second, they are encouraging drivers to participate in car pools. Many highways now have carpool lanes in which cars with two or more passengers can travel more quickly—sometimes without paying the usual tolls.

Waste

Together, industries and private citizens produce millions of tons of garbage and trash each year. No satisfactory way has been found to dispose of this waste. Burning it in incinerators creates dangerous air pollution. Dumping it in the ocean doesn't work, as New Jersey residents discovered when hospital debris washed up on their beaches in 1988. Much waste in recent years has been buried at huge sites called **landfills**. Existing landfills are nearly full, however, and few Americans are willing to have new ones opened.

Recycling has become an increasingly popular way to dispose of some waste. In recycling, old materials are re-used to make new ones. For example, used paper and paper products can be shredded, bleached, and processed to make new paper. Many towns and cities now have voluntary recycling programs, and some have passed laws requiring recycling. Unfortunately, only a few kinds of waste are suitable for recycling. Glass, aluminum, paper, and certain kinds of plastic can be recycled successfully. Other common kinds of waste—such as plastic foam—cannot be recycled.

Once again, the best solution seems to be conservation. Many communities with active recycling programs are now encouraging *pre*cycling—using only products that can be recycled. Consumers are asked to buy milk in glass bottles instead of plastic ones, and to pack groceries in paper rather than plastic bags. Businesses are encouraged—and sometimes required by law—to eliminate unnecessary packaging. In Berkeley, California, for example, businesses are not allowed to sell products in plastic foam. In some communities, high school students have taken the initiative. They have led campaigns to ban the use of plastic foam in school cafeterias (see Closeup on page 497).

Land Use

Land is a scarce resource; we have only a fixed amount of it. Every time farmland is paved over for a shopping center, or a forest is replaced by a housing development, we lose a valuable part of the environment. Many communities have learned this lesson too late, after productive farmland and scenic areas have been destroyed.

Communities have begun to protect their land in several different ways. Many communities now set aside land for parks or wildlife refuges and put restrictions on the use of certain types of land. For example, a hotel built on beachfront property may be required to allow public access to the beach.

Many communities make an effort to hold on to their history as well as their land. To protect important historical sites, some communities set up historic districts in which no changes can be made without special approval. Individual buildings can be protected in a similar way by being declared landmarks.

The planning process described earlier in this chapter also helps preserve land and buildings. Planning commissions and zoning boards can help keep expansion under control. They can prevent developers from building houses or shopping centers in places where they would do more harm than good.

Not everyone agrees that limiting growth is a good idea, however. Many people object to restrictions that prevent businesses from bringing money into their community. There is always controversy when a piece of land is set aside as a park or a historic district. The controversy becomes especially strong when that land is known to contain an important resource, such as oil or minerals. In this time of energy shortages, many people feel that access to resources is more important than history or beauty.

Nevertheless, communities now tend to be more cautious in deciding land use issues. Too many farms, forests, marshes, and beaches have already been lost.

Boston's Faneuil Hall Marketplace is one of the most successful urban renewal projects of recent years. An old market and dockyards were turned into lively shops and restaurants.

Outlook for the Future

Solving environmental problems is difficult and expensive. Especially in these days of limited funds, state and local governments cannot do the job by themselves. Communities have had to find new ways to think about these issues and work on solutions.

One hopeful development is the increase in cooperation between governments. In Chapter 14, you read about special districts and metropolitan governments. Environmental issues have recently led to cooperation on an even larger scale. For example, the states of Connecticut, Maine, Massachusetts, New Hampshire, New Jersey, New York, Rhode Island, and Vermont recently announced a joint policy to reduce automobile emissions. Similarly, the states of Pennsylvania, Maryland, and Virginia have joined forces with the city of Washington, D.C., to fight water pollution in the Chesapeake Bay.

Communities are also beginning to depend more on the actions of private businesses and citizens. In many towns and cities, privately owned companies provide free recycling services to local residents. These companies make money by selling the bottles, cans, and stacks of paper to other companies that can recycle them.

Similarly, energy and water use in many communities is being reduced significantly through the efforts of individuals. As conservation becomes a way of life for more Americans, the nation may come closer to solving its environmental problems.

SECTION REVIEW

Define the Words

landfill   recycling

Check the Facts
1. Name two possible solutions to energy and water shortages and describe the disadvantages of each.
2. What are some of the sources of air and water pollution?
3. Describe ways in which communities try to protect their land.

Think About the Ideas
4. *Evaluate.* Do you think local governments should be allowed to make laws limiting how much a person can drive? Why or why not?

Because exhaust gases from cars and trucks are a major cause of air pollution, many states now use mobile emissions testing centers to check vehicles.

CITIZENSHIP SKILLS

How to Use a Library

Many times during your life you may need to find facts and information about a particular topic or issue. Where should you look for the information you need?

The best place to start is at your local library. There you can consult books, magazine and newspaper articles, reports of state and local governments, and other printed materials for information on your topic.

Libraries are set up to help you find the information you need. Most libraries still have card catalogs that organize references to books according to subject, title, and author. But many libraries are now replacing card catalogs with computers.

You can find references to magazine articles on your topic in the *Reader's Guide to Periodical Literature*, which is in the reference section of the library. The reference section also has encyclopedias, statistical almanacs, map atlases, dictionaries, and other research aids.

Most libraries also have a news index or news digest, such as *Facts on File*. This index will help you find references to newspaper articles on your topic. Most libraries keep back issues of various newspapers and magazines. If they don't have a copy of the newspaper or magazine itself, they may have it on microfilm or microfiche (a sheet of microfilm).

The librarian is there to help you locate the information you need. The librarian can help you use the library's resources and direct you to special collections of material that might be useful. Using the library is an important step in finding information on any topic.

Using Your Skills

Practice your library skills by researching a community issue in which you are interested. Complete the following tasks.

1. List the main topic and subtopics you will use to find information.
2. Write two facts about your topic that you find in an encyclopedia.
3. Write the author, title, and call number of a book about your topic.
4. Write the title of two magazine articles about your topic and the name and date of the magazine in which each article appears.
5. Write the headline of at least two newspaper articles or editorials about your topic and the name and date of the newspaper in which each appears.
6. Locate two of these articles and read them. Write short summaries of the main points made in these articles.
7. In researching your topic, what other sources of information could you use besides the library?

CHAPTER 15 REVIEW

MAIN POINTS

★ Ideas for public policy come from a variety of sources. Before setting policy, local governments must determine priorities and evaluate their resources.

★ Among the most effective public policies are those that prevent problems before they occur. Planning commissions are responsible for creating such policies.

★ Public policies are paid for primarily through taxes and user fees. Each source of revenue has advantages and disadvantages.

★ Local governments face social problems involving education, housing, crime, and poverty. Communities attempt to solve these problems in various ways. Some of the most promising solutions involve voluntarism on the part of individuals and groups.

★ State and local governments face environmental issues such as energy and water shortages, air and water pollution, waste disposal, and land preservation. While communities try various solutions to these problems, the most promising solutions involve cooperation among governments, businesses, and individuals.

WORDS IN REVIEW

Choose the word or phrase from the list below that best completes each sentence. Write the missing words on a separate sheet of paper.

public policy	bonds
priorities	infrastructure
master plan	zoning board
urban renewal	voluntarism
resources	recycling

1. The goal of the city's _____ project was to rebuild old neighborhoods.

2. The community residents were eager to start _____ their garbage.

3. In setting its _____, a community must balance its goals and its resources.

4. The town's _____ contained policies and goals for the next 25 years.

5. The ruling against selling the farm for development was part of the town's _____.

6. The people who devoted their time and energy to the community for free were showing a spirit of _____.

7. The planning board turned down a proposal to build a recreation center because the town lacked the _____ required.

8. The _____ ruled that only residential buildings could be built in that particular part of the town.

9. To pay for the new school, the community issued _____.

10. Much of the city's _____ was badly in need of repair.

FACTS IN REVIEW

1. What is the role of planning commissions?

2. Identify two groups found in many communities that help enforce the community's master plan.

3. Identify and explain two non-tax sources of local revenue.

4. What have local governments done to try to improve their systems of public education?

5. What effect does rising real estate values have on the housing problem?

CHAPTER 15 REVIEW

* *

6. Why has the problem of crime increased in suburban areas and small towns?

7. Identify three voluntary activities that can help solve a community's social problems.

8. Identify four environmental issues facing communities.

9. What are some ways in which communities have attempted to solve their waste problems?

10. Give an example of large-scale regional cooperation on environmental issues.

THINKING ABOUT COMMUNITY ISSUES

1. *Evaluate.* Which do you think is more important, long-term or short-term planning? Why?

2. *Analyze.* How do you think communities should try to deal with the problem of crime?

3. *Evaluate.* Which of the environmental issues discussed do you think is most critical today? Explain.

DEBATING THE USE OF RESOURCES

Some people claim that the country's need for resources is more important than a concern for the environment. Others believe that exploiting resources in this way is shortsighted. Without conservation and preservation, much of the environment will be destroyed and there will be nothing for future generations. Prepare arguments, pro or con, for debating the following statement: The country's need for resources is more important than environmental concerns.

WRITING ABOUT COMMUNITY ISSUES

Every community has its own special social problems. Choose one issue, such as housing, education, or crime, that you consider to be critical in your community. Research this issue and prepare a short report. Include tables, charts, graphs, and maps in your report to illustrate different aspects of the issue.

INTERPRETING A CITY ZONING MAP

Look at the zoning map on page 340. This shows how a typical city might be zoned—residential, commercial, industrial, and so on. Answer the following questions based on the map: Which type of zone is the largest? Which is the smallest? In what part of the city are the industrial zones located? Why do you think different types of zones are restricted to certain areas?

FOCUSING ON YOUR COMMUNITY

Find out about the most important environmental problems facing your community. What are the causes of these problems? What are the local government, businesses, and individuals doing to solve the problem? How successful have efforts to solve the problem been so far? What can you, as an individual, do to help solve environmental problems? Prepare a short oral report to present to the class.

UNIT 5 REVIEW

* *

ESSAY QUESTIONS

The following questions are based on material in Unit 5. Answer each question with two or three written paragraphs. Be sure to give specific reasons to support your answers.

1. Today most of us must pay taxes and obey the rules of three levels of government. Do you think that all these governmental units are necessary to deal with the problems of our complex society? Why or why not?

2. More and more American businesses are becoming involved in social issues, especially problems related to child care, drug abuse, and public education. What role do you think business should play in social issues? Discuss the advantages and disadvantages of relying on business for help in solving these problems.

CONNECTING CIVICS AND MUSIC

Almost every state in the Union has an official song. Be prepared to discuss the following in class: What type of music is played at government functions and official events? Is using music to influence people's feelings a proper activity of government?

ANALYZING VISUALS

The following diagram shows the organization of the executive branch of a typical state. Study the diagram and answer the questions.

1. Which state officials are usually chosen by the voters?

2. How can the voters show their approval or disapproval of the way the state attorney general and state treasurer perform their duties?

STATE GOVERNMENT
EXECUTIVE BRANCH

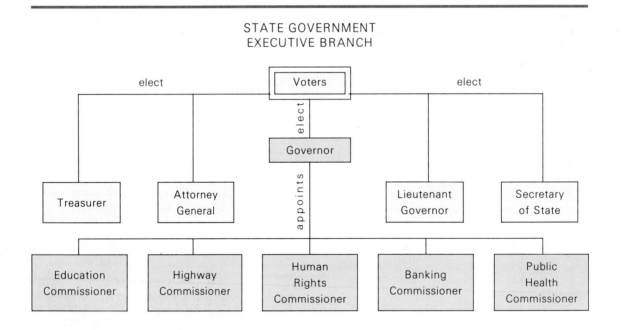

* * * * * * *

CLOSEUP ON THE *VALDEZ* OIL SPILL

On March 24, 1989, the oil tanker *Exxon Valdez* strayed off course and ran aground on a reef in Alaska's Prince William Sound. More than 10 million gallons of crude oil poured from the stricken tanker, causing the worst oil spill in American history. The oil fouled hundreds of miles of beautiful wilderness shoreline and killed untold numbers of coastal and marine wildlife. In addition, it threatened the livelihood of thousands of people in the Alaskan fishing industry.

The incident focused attention on the question of who is responsible for preventing such catastrophes, for punishing violators, and for making sure such spills are adequately cleaned up.

Some of the responsibility lies with the federal government. Under federal law, whoever causes an oil spill—in this case, the Exxon Oil Company—must clean it up. However, the U.S. Coast Guard is responsible for monitoring and coordinating any cleanup in ocean waters.

The state also shares responsibility in such matters. The Alaskan Environmental Conservation Department is in charge of regulating the safety and environmental aspects of the Alaskan oil industry, both to prevent spills and to draw up plans for any cleanup operations. The state, however, failed to carry out those duties. It had allowed the oil industry to reduce its emergency response measures because the industry claimed that such spills were highly unlikely. As a result, Exxon lacked the necessary manpower and equipment to begin immediate cleanup operations.

After the accident, both the state and federal governments asserted their authority. The state of Alaska charged the captain of the *Exxon Valdez* with several violations of state law, including operating a vessel while intoxicated and discharging oil. The state legislature repealed a long-standing tax break for two large oil fields on Alaska's North Slope. In addition to these actions, the state's fishing and tourist industries and injured property owners brought civil suits against Exxon in the state's courts.

At the federal level, Congressional committees held hearings to investigate the spill. One committee voted to impose a one-year moratorium on offshore oil drilling along most of the nation's coastline. Another voted to establish national minimum standards for cleaning up oil spills. Congress delayed a vote on a controversial bill to allow oil drilling in the Arctic National Wildlife Preserve in northern Alaska. It also passed a 1.3-cent-per-barrel oil tax to go toward a special fund for paying spill-related damage costs.

1. What action did the state of Alaska take against the captain of the *Exxon Valdez*?
2. Why do you think Congress postponed a vote on oil drilling in the Arctic National Wildlife Preserve?
3. What is the main difference between the role and responsibilities of the federal and state governments in protecting the environment?

In all criminal prosecutions, the accused shall enjoy the right to a speedy and public trial, by an impartial jury . . . and to be informed of the nature and cause of the accusation . . . and to have the assistance of counsel for his defense.

—SIXTH AMENDMENT

Law and the Individual

The provisions of the Sixth Amendment to the Constitution are fundamental to our legal system. They protect the right of any person accused of a crime to a fair hearing by the law. The provisions are based on the belief that a person should be considered innocent until proven guilty and they make the government provide proof of guilt.

* * * * *

CHAPTERS IN THIS UNIT

CHAPTER 16

★ ★

Legal Rights and Responsibilities

OBJECTIVES

After you have studied this chapter, you will be able to:

★ Explain the purpose of laws and identify the characteristics of good laws.
★ Identify and discuss the source of our nation's laws.
★ Identify and explain the legal rights of people accused of crimes.
★ Discuss the different responsibilities citizens have concerning the law.
★ Identify and describe five types of law.

SECTIONS

1 The Source of Our Laws
2 Legal Rights and Responsibilities
3 Types of Laws

Laws are rules that are binding on all the people living in a particular community, state, or nation. Imagine what life might be like if there were no laws. Without speed limits, red lights, or traffic signs, there would be many more car accidents. Without laws to deter or punish wrongdoers, there would be many more crimes such as robbery or murder. And without ways to settle disputes peacefully, many more disagreements would be settled with fistfights, rocks, or guns.

Laws help bring order into our lives. They help a community run smoothly by fulfilling several important functions. They discourage people from committing crimes by providing penalties. They enable people to settle disagreements peacefully by ensuring a fair means of justice. They protect our rights as citizens against abuses by other people, by organizations, and by government. And they promote the welfare of society as a whole by protecting it against certain dangers.

★ ★

SECTION 1

The Source of Our Laws

★ ★

VOCABULARY
jurisprudence   stare decisis

Although not all laws are good, good laws share certain characteristics. Good laws are fair. People in similar circumstances will be treated equally under the law. Good laws are also reasonable. In England in the 1700's, a person who stole a loaf of bread might have been hanged. Today, such harsh punishment for a similar crime would be considered unreasonable. Good laws must also be understandable. If laws are too complicated, people may sometimes break them without meaning to or realizing it. Finally, good laws are also enforceable. In a democracy, the government's ability to enforce a law often depends on the people's willingness to obey it. If most people ignore a law, the government will have difficulty enforcing it.

When the writers of the Constitution created a new government, they based the nation's system of laws on ideas, traditions, customs, and laws passed down from generation to generation. Some of these ideas date back thousands of years.

Early Systems of Law

The earliest laws were probably passed from one generation to the next by word of mouth. They were part of the traditions and customs of the people. Then, after people learned to write, they began to write their laws down.

About 4,000 years ago, King Hammurabi of ancient Babylon had a series of laws compiled into a list, or code of laws. This Code of Hammurabi is one of the earliest written codes of law. The Code of Hammurabi not only listed Babylon's laws, but also included the punishments for breaking them. Although some of the punishments were very harsh, the code was a great benefit to the people. It ensured that the law would be followed and everyone would be treated in the same way.

Another early set of written laws was the Ten Commandments found in the *Bible*. The Ten Commandments are a set of moral rules about how people should behave toward each other. Many of these rules still govern our behavior today. For example, the commandments "thou shalt not steal" and "thou shalt not kill" are reflected in our laws prohibiting theft and murder.

Religion was an important source for many of these early laws. Leaders believed that their authority and their laws came from God or from gods. One reason people obeyed the laws was because they feared the anger of their gods.

Roman Law

The ancient Romans developed an elaborate legal system which they took to all of the lands they conquered in Europe, Africa, and Asia. This legal system was the most highly organized in the ancient world. The Romans made a science of the law which they called **jurisprudence**, a word we still use to mean the study of the law.

Over the centuries, Roman law became very complex. In the 6th century, the Emperor Justinian I decided to simplify the Roman system of laws. His simplified system was called the Justinian Code.

Over a thousand years after it was written, the ideas of the Justinian Code were taken over by the French Emperor Napoleon. Napoleon updated the Justinian Code and called it the Napoleonic Code. Like the ancient Romans, Napoleon carried his laws to all the lands he controlled. One of those lands was Louisiana, which France sold to the United States in 1803. The laws in the state of Louisiana are still based on the Napoleonic Code.

English Law

The most important source of American laws is English law. Perhaps the greatest contribution has been the English system of common law, or law based on court decisions rather than on a legal code. Beginning in the 1100's, English monarchs sent judges all around the English countryside to hold trials and administer the law. The decisions of these judges set precedents that became part of the common law. A second significant contribution has been the idea of citizens' rights. As the power of English monarchs decreased, and the power of Parliament increased the English people began to acquire certain rights of citizenship (see Chapter 2).

When English settlers came to the American colonies in the 1600's and 1700's, they brought their traditions of common law and rights of citizenship with them. Today, these ideas are an important part of our legal system. This is true on the federal level and in all states except Louisiana.

Lawyers in the United States do not wear the wigs and robes of English barristers, but the influence of the English courts can be seen in our jury system.

THE EMANCIPATION PROCLAMATION

*W*hen the Civil War began in 1861, some Northerners argued that the only purpose of the war was to reunite the nation. By the summer of 1862, however, President Lincoln was under great pressure to take a stand against slavery.

In September, Lincoln acted. He issued a warning giving the Confederate states until January 1, 1863, to abandon their rebellion. On that day, he declared, the slaves would be set free in all those states still in rebellion. True to his word, Lincoln signed the Emancipation Proclamation on the first day of 1863.

The proclamation was an executive order stating that slaves would be freed only in the Confederate states. At the time, there was some question whether the President had the power under the Constitution to issue an order that would overrule state laws. Lincoln based his order on military necessity. As Commander-in-Chief of the armed forces, he believed he had authority to take any action against the rebels that would reunite the nation. And the freed slaves could help the cause by fighting in the ranks of the Union Army.

. . . All persons held as slaves within any State . . . in rebellion against the United States shall be then, thenceforward, and forever free; and the executive government of the United States, including the military and naval authority thereof, will recognize and maintain the freedom of such persons . . .

Now therefore, I, Abraham Lincoln, President of the United States, by virtue of the power in me vested as Commander-in-Chief of the Army and Navy of the United States in time of actual armed rebellion against the authority and government of the United States, and as a fit and necessary war measure for suppressing [putting down] said rebellion . . .

And upon this act, sincerely believed to be an act of justice, warranted [authorized] by the Constitution upon military necessity, I invoke [ask for] the considerate [thoughtful] judgement of mankind and the gracious favor of Almighty God.

The remaining slaves in the United States were officially freed after the war. On December 18, 1865, a majority of the Northern states ratified the Thirteenth Amendment to the Constitution abolishing slavery.

Using Your Skills
1. Why do you think Lincoln asked for "the considerate judgement of mankind . . ." in the proclamation?
2. The Emancipation Proclamation had very little effect on the lives of most slaves in 1863. Why, then, do you think that it is considered such an important document in American history?

The American Legal System

While our legal system has been influenced by ideas and traditions from the past, today's laws come from the authority of the Constitution. As you know, the Constitution is the basic law of the land. It is the most important source of our nation's laws. The Constitution gives each branch of government a role in making, enforcing, and interpreting the law.

Most laws are made by the legislative branches of government. These laws are created by Congress, state legislatures, and city and town councils.

While the main role of the executive branch is to carry out the laws, in doing so it sometimes makes laws as well. For example, you may remember from Chapter 10 that the President has the power to issue executive orders, which have the force of law. Executive departments and agencies also make rules and regulations to carry out the law. These, too, have the force of law.

Many laws come from the judicial branch as well. Although the courts do not pass laws or regulations, they do interpret them. They base their rulings on written laws and on the precedents of previous cases. These rulings are then used to guide decisions about similar cases in the future. This process is called **stare decisis** which is Latin for "let the decision stand." Such judicial rulings have the force of law unless they are overturned by a higher court. As you learned in Chapter 12, the Supreme Court has a special duty to make sure that local, state, and federal laws agree with the Constitution and to strike down any conflicting laws.

SECTION REVIEW

Define the Words

jurisprudence   stare decisis

Check the Facts
1. Identify four important functions of laws.
2. What was the Justinian Code?
3. How does the executive branch create laws?

Think About the Ideas
4. *Evaluate.* Do you think most of our laws are fair, reasonable, and understandable? Why or why not?

An increase in violent crimes in recent years has prompted Congress to hold hearings on gun control legislation.

★ ★

SECTION 2

Legal Rights and Responsibilities

★ ★

VOCABULARY

writ of habeas corpus	grand jury
	contempt of court
bill of attainder	petit jury
ex post facto law	bench trial

In some countries people can be arrested and put in jail for very little reason. They may be accused of things—such as demonstrating or criticizing the government—that would not even be considered crimes in the United States. These people may never be told the charges against them and are given no opportunity to defend themselves. Instead, they may be kept in prison for years or even executed without ever having a trial. Their families and friends may not be told where they are or even if they are alive.

In the United States, we have legal rights that protect us from these kinds of abuses. The Constitution outlines these rights, stating how we are to be treated if we are accused of a crime. These rights are an important safeguard of the freedom we cherish in our system of democracy.

What is the right of habeas corpus?

Basic Legal Rights

Our basic legal rights are guaranteed by the Constitution and its amendments. One of these rights concerns what is called a writ of habeas corpus. A **writ of habeas corpus** is a court order that guarantees an accused person the right to appear before a judge in a court of law. The officials holding the accused person must show good reasons why the prisoner should not be released. If they cannot give good reasons, the person must be set free. A writ of habeas corpus is an important legal right because it prevents people from being arrested and put in prison without cause. Article I, section 9 of the Constitution guarantees this right by stating that "The privilege of the writ of habeas corpus shall not be suspended, unless when in cases of rebellion or invasion the public safety may require it." Habeas corpus has been suspended only twice in the nation's history—during the Civil War and in Hawaii after the Japanese attack on Pearl Harbor

---

LEGAL RIGHTS OF PERSONS ACCUSED OF A CRIME

★ *Habeas corpus* (suspect cannot be held without a hearing)
★ to be told what the accusation is
★ to be represented by a lawyer
★ to refuse to answer any questions that may be incriminating
★ a grand jury hearing
★ a speedy and public trial
★ trial by an impartial jury
★ to hear and question opposing witnesses during trial
★ to subpoena their own witnesses
★ protection from double jeopardy
★ to appeal a verdict or sentence to a higher court
★ equal protection of the laws

Paralegal Aide

Paralegal aides assist lawyers by doing research in law books and public records. They perform much of the routine detail work involved in preparing lawsuits, contracts, wills, and other legal documents. They may interview clients, trace the ownership of properties, fill out income tax returns, write reports, and do a wide variety of other jobs.

Most paralegals work for private law firms. Some are employed by the government or by large corporations.

Paralegals who work for corporations are called corporate legal assistants. They are often involved in labor negotiations, contracts, and financial matters.

Paralegals need a high school diploma plus two to four years of instruction in a paralegal training program. Many private schools offer paralegal courses. Some colleges and law schools also offer paralegal training. The private schools usually provide help in placing their graduates in jobs.

Paralegals can become very knowledgeable about legal procedures and cases. They do most of their work in the law office or in public record offices. Sometimes they are asked to assist an attorney in court during a criminal or civil trial. Some paralegals go on to law school and become attorneys themselves. Paralegals must have a keen eye for detail and the ability to analyze complicated data. They must also be discreet and mature because they are

involved in handling many confidential matters.

Using Your Skills
1. Why do attorneys find it useful to employ paralegal aides?
2. Why is it necessary to complete two to four years of training to become a paralegal?

---

in 1941. In both instances, the Supreme Court later held that the suspensions were unconstitutional.

Article I of the Constitution states that "No bill of attainder or ex post facto law shall be passed." A **bill of attainder** is a law that punishes a person accused of a crime without a trial or a fair hearing in court. An **ex post facto law** is a law that would allow a person to be punished for an action that was not against the law when it was committed..For

example, an ex post facto law making it a crime to buy lottery tickets could be applied to someone who bought tickets *before* the law was passed. By banning ex post facto laws, the Constitution guarantees that people cannot be punished unfairly by changing the laws later.

Two other important legal rights guaranteed by the Constitution are the rights of due process and equal protection of the laws. In Chapter 4, you learned that due process

A judge may rule that a videotape of a suspect's confession cannot be allowed as evidence, if the suspect was not advised of his or her legal rights.

requires the government to follow certain procedures in enforcing the law. The right of due process helps guarantee that an accused person will receive a fair trial and will be granted all of his or her Constitutional rights before being convicted of a crime. Equal protection of the laws helps guarantee that a person accused of a crime will not be treated differently from others because of race, religion, sex, or other factors. For example, an Hispanic person accused of a crime has a right to a jury that includes other Hispanics, because non-Hispanics might be prejudiced against the accused.

One special legal safeguard included in the Constitution concerns the crime of treason. Treason is the only crime defined in the Constitution. Article III states that people can only be convicted of treason if they wage war against the United States, join their enemies, or give aid and comfort to the enemy. Moreover, no one can be convicted of treason

without positive proof. Treason is defined so that the government cannot misuse the law to punish people for political activities. In some countries, criticizing the government is considered treason. The Constitution prevents this from happening in the United States.

Rights of Persons Accused of a Crime

The Constitution includes several specific rights that protect citizens who are accused of crimes. These rights ensure that accused persons are treated fairly and receive every chance to defend themselves. Each of these rights is based on a time-honored principle of English and American law—a person is presumed innocent unless and until proven guilty in a court of law.

MIRANDA V. ARIZONA

Most people have probably seen policemen reading criminal suspects their rights on TV or in the movies. Under federal law, anyone who is arrested for a crime must be informed of these rights:

★ You have the right to remain silent.
★ Any statement you make can be used against you in court.
★ You have the right to have an attorney present during any questioning.
★ You have the right to have a court-appointed attorney if you cannot afford one.
★ You have the right to end this interview at any time.

Although informing a suspect of his or her rights is now routine, it wasn't until 1966, in the case of *Miranda* v. *Arizona*, that the Supreme Court ruled that this procedure must be followed. These rights are known as the "Miranda rules."

Ernesto Miranda was a poorly educated Arizonan who was tried and convicted of kidnapping and raping an 18-year old woman. After his arrest, Miranda was questioned by the police and made an oral and written confession. At his trial, the police testified that they had warned him that a written statement could be used against him. They had not warned him about making oral statements, however. Nor had they told him that he had the right to have an attorney present.

The Supreme Court voted 5 to 4 to overturn Miranda's conviction on the grounds that it violated his Fifth Amendment right to remain silent and his Sixth Amendment right to counsel.

The initial reaction to the Miranda ruling was highly unfavorable. Most police officers felt that it would make their jobs more difficult. Many people also felt that the ruling proved the Supreme Court was "soft on crime." Its defenders however, argued

that all the Miranda ruling did was make certain that suspects knew about their Constitutional rights.

Since 1966, the Supreme Court has continued to uphold the basic principles of the Miranda case. In 1984, for example, it ruled that the Miranda ruling applies to any case, no matter how minor, in which a person is taken into custody. One change, however, is that the Court has ruled that the right to have an attorney present only applies after a formal charge has been made, not from the time of arrest.

Using Your Skills
1. What are the four basic Miranda rights?
2. Why would it be important to a suspect to have his attorney present when he is being questioned by police?
3. Why do suspects have the right to stop answering the questions of police at any time?

Under the principle of "innocent until proven guilty," the police and the prosecutor, the government's lawyer, must prove that an accused person is guilty. The accused does not have to prove his or her own innocence. Furthermore, only a judge or jury can decide that a person is in fact guilty of a crime. Until convicted, or found guilty, of a crime, a person can only be considered a suspect.

The following are specific legal rights guaranteed by the Constitution. Each one protects people accused of committing a crime and ensures that they will be treated fairly.

GRAND JURY The Fifth Amendment provides that no person can be held for a serious crime unless the evidence is presented to a grand jury. A **grand jury** is a group of from 16 to 23 citizens that hears evidence presented by a prosecutor. It is the job of the grand jury to decide whether there is enough evidence to indicate that a crime has been committed. If there is sufficient evidence, the grand jury issues an indictment, or formal charge, that names the suspects and lists the charges against them. Grand juries protect citizens from being falsely accused of crimes.

SELF-INCRIMINATION The Fifth Amendment also states that "no person . . . shall be compelled in any criminal case to be a witness against himself." This means that a person does not have to answer questions that may incriminate, or show his or her involvement in a crime. Sometimes when being questioned by a prosecutor, a person may say, "I decline to answer on the grounds that it may tend to incriminate me." This is known as "taking the Fifth," or exercising the right to remain silent. If this right against self-incrimination is misused—to protect others, for example—the judge may hold the person in **contempt of court**. This means that the judge believes the person is obstructing or interfering with the judicial process. A person charged with contempt of court may be put in jail.

ADEQUATE DEFENSE Every person accused of a crime has the right to an adequate defense during a trial. The Sixth Amendment lists several specific rights to help ensure this. First of all, people accused of crimes have the right to be informed of the nature and cause of the accusations against them. They also have the right to hear and question the witnesses who testify against them. They have the right to subpoena witnesses who can testify and provide evidence on their behalf. (As you learned in Chapter 12, a subpoena is a court order requiring a person to appear in court.)

Every person accused of a crime has the right to be represented by an attorney. What are some of the services an attorney performs for a client?

Finally, they have the right to counsel, which means that they have a right to be represented by an attorney, or lawyer. This right to an attorney applies to every step in the legal process, from the moment a person is formally charged with a crime to the end of the appeals process.

Before 1963, people charged with crimes in state courts often had to face trial without an attorney if they were too poor to hire one. In that year, however, the U.S. Supreme Court in *Gideon* v. *Wainwright* ruled that states had to provide attorneys to people who were too poor to afford their own. (See Closeup on page 407.)

SPEEDY AND PUBLIC TRIAL The Sixth Amendment also guarantees accused persons the right to a speedy, public trial. This prevents accused persons from being forced to spend long periods in jail while awaiting trial. A federal criminal trial must begin within 100 days of a person's arrest, unless there are good reasons to delay it. Some states have also set specific time limits for the prosecution to bring a case to court. The suspect can ask for delays for certain reasons, but if the prosecutor causes the trial to be delayed for too long, the state must dismiss the charges against the defendant.

TRIAL BY JURY A person accused of a crime also has the right to a trial by an impartial jury. Impartial means that the jury members will be people who do not know anyone involved in the case and have not already made up their minds about the case. These jury members must also be drawn from the area where the crime was committed.

The juries that hear trials are called trial juries or **petit juries** to distinguish them from grand juries. A trial jury is usually composed of 12 citizens, although some states permit juries of as few as six people. The jury is usually required to reach a unanimous verdict.

An accused person can waive, or give up, the right to a jury trial and be tried by a judge instead. This kind of a trial is called a **bench trial**. A person might request a bench trial to avoid the long drawn-out process and greater expense of a jury trial.

The Sixth Amendment to the Constitution gives people accused of a crime the right to a public trial by an impartial jury.

DOUBLE JEOPARDY The Fifth Amendment protects an accused person from double jeopardy. You should remember from Chapter 4 that double jeopardy means a person cannot be tried twice for the same crime. Suppose, however, that a person breaks both federal and state law while committing a crime. In that case, the person could be tried for the federal crime in a federal court and for the state crime in a state court. A person can also be retried for the same crime if the first trial ends in a hung jury, a jury that cannot reach a verdict. In addition, people are tried again for the same crime when their case is appealed to a higher court.

APPEALS Anyone convicted of a crime always has the right to appeal an unfavorable verdict or sentence. The person may feel that the judge or prosecutor made errors in conducting the trial, that there was insufficient evidence for the jury to reach its verdict, or that new evidence would result in a different verdict.

Punishments and Fines

The Constitution also has provisions concerning the punishment of people accused and convicted of crimes. In Chapter 4, you learned that the Eighth Amendment bars the government from imposing excessive bail or fines or from using cruel and unusual punishment. These provisions ensure that courts must follow reasonable standards in setting bail and for determining fines or other punishments for people convicted of crimes.

When a person is arrested and brought before a judge, the judge determines the amount of bail. This amount must be reasonable in relation to the crime. A judge could not reasonably impose a $100,000 fine on a motorist for going through a red light, for example.

The main purpose of bail is to ensure that the accused person will appear in court for trial. After the trial, the person gets back the money. If a judge is convinced that a person will show up for trial and is unlikely to harm anyone, the judge may set a low bail or release the person without bail.

The prohibition against cruel and unusual punishment was originally meant to prevent such things as branding or burning at the stake. It has come to mean that the punishment should be in proportion to the crime. For example, it would be considered cruel and unusual punishment to sentence a person to life in prison as punishment for committing petty, nonviolent crimes such as writing a bad check.

As an alternative to prison, judges sometimes require people convicted of minor, nonviolent crimes to devote a certain amount of time to community service work.

In recent years, the Supreme Court has considered whether capital punishment (the death penalty) is cruel and unusual punishment. In 1972, the Court struck down all state capital punishment laws, although not because it found the death penalty cruel and unusual. Instead, it found that the death penalty was being applied unfairly, and was used primarily on poor or black people.

Since then, many states have passed new capital punishment laws, which have also been brought before the Supreme Court. State laws that made the death penalty mandatory for certain crimes, such as killing someone while committing another crime, were ruled unconstitutional. The Court ruled that these laws were too harsh because they did not allow judges to consider the individual circumstances of each case. Other state laws have established a two-stage process in capital punishment cases. First, a jury trial determines guilt or innocence. Then, a separate hearing determines the degree of punishment. The Court has upheld these laws. It has found that capital punishment is not cruel and unusual when applied in a fair manner.

Legal Responsibilities

American citizens have a number of responsibilities as well as legal rights. By fulfilling these responsibilities, citizens ensure that the legal system works as it should and that their legal rights are protected.

Serving on a jury is an important responsibility, as is testifying as a witness in court when required to do so. The legal right to a trial by jury can only be effective if people are willing to serve on juries and appear in court.

Other responsibilities include obeying the laws and cooperating with police and other law enforcement officials. Earlier, you learned

LEGAL RESPONSIBILITIES OF AMERICANS

To participate in our legal system by . . .
★ serving on a jury
★ testifying as a witness in court
★ obeying the laws
★ cooperating with police and law enforcement officials
★ calling attention to outdated or unfair laws

Which two legal responsibilities involve serving in court?

that the government's ability to enforce a law depends to a great extent on people's willingness to obey it. Similarly, the ability of law enforcement officials to arrest and prosecute criminals depends on people's willingness to become involved and tell what they know about a crime. When you help convict a mugger or drug pusher, you are not only protecting yourself and your family, you are helping to protect the entire community.

Another responsibility of citizens is to work peacefully to change unfair, outdated laws. This might include gathering voters' signatures on petitions to place issues on the ballot for a vote. It might include voting on state or local initiatives and referenda. Citizens might contact their state legislators or Congressional representatives and ask these officials to change the law. Sometimes, people might also hold public demonstrations to call attention to their concerns. For our legal system to be effective, people must care enough to participate in it.

SECTION REVIEW

Define the Words

writ of habeas corpus

bill of attainder

ex post facto law

grand jury

contempt of court

petit jury

bench trial

Check the Facts

1. Identify and explain three basic legal rights of all citizens.
2. What are three specific rights of persons accused of a crime?
3. Identify three things citizens can do to ensure that the legal system works effectively.

Think About the Ideas

4. *Analyze.* Do you think our legal rights adequately protect all citizens? Why or why not?
5. *Evaluate.* Which legal rights do you think are most important? Explain.

★ ★

SECTION 3

Types of Laws

★ ★

VOCABULARY

civil law

lawsuit

plaintiff

defendant

contract

Our legal rights and responsibilities are important because we are a nation of laws. The United States has many laws. There are laws against drunk driving, against robbing a store, against selling drugs, against harming another person, and so on. These laws can be divided into several categories—constitutional law, administrative law, international law, criminal law, and civil law.

CONSTITUTIONAL LAW The Eighth Amendment to the Constitution prohibits excessive fines and cruel and unusual punishment. This constitutional law serves as the guiding light for our courts and legislatures whenever they deal with punishments and fines. Constitutional laws are those laws found in the U.S. Constitution. As the highest laws in the land and the laws that dictate how the government works, constitutional laws have enormous influence on our lives.

Visitors to the nation's capital pay their respects to the Constitution of the United States, the source of our highest law.

ADMINISTRATIVE LAW If the Federal Aviation Agency issued an order requiring commercial airlines to install a new type of safety device, this would be an example of administrative law. Administrative law refers to all of the rules and regulations that the executive branch of government must make in order to carry out its job.

INTERNATIONAL LAW If Canada and the United States have a dispute over fishing in the territorial waters of either nation, that would be a matter of international law. International law refers to any laws that affect the United States and other nations. These laws might involve military and diplomatic treaties, trade regulations, international agreements concerning fishing rights, and so on.

CRIMINAL LAW Whenever people commit a crime, such as murder, they are not only harming their victims, they are also harming the victims' families, friends, co-workers, employees, and neighbors. Criminal laws are laws that seek to prevent people from deliberately harming one another or from harming each other's property. Law enforcement officers enforce criminal laws and the courts impose penalties such as fines and imprisonment for breaking these laws. The safety and well-being of the entire community is affected whenever someone breaks a criminal law.

CIVIL LAW Civil law is concerned with disputes between people (or groups of people) or between the government and its citizens. Suppose, for example, that you slip on ice on your neighbor's sidewalk and break a leg. According to your local law, property owners are responsible for keeping their sidewalks clear of ice. If your neighbor doesn't do this, and you are injured as a result, you have a

The Coast Guard patrols the territorial waters of the United States and stops foreign ships that are fishing within the two-mile limit.

right to sue your neighbor to recover the costs of your medical treatment and other damages.

When one person wrongs or injures another in any way, the injured person may decide to bring a lawsuit. A **lawsuit** is a legal action in which a person or group sues to collect damages for some harm that is done. The party (person, group, or organization) who files the lawsuit is the **plaintiff**. The party being sued, in this case the neighbor, is the **defendant**.

Many civil cases involve breach of **contract**. A contract is an agreement between two parties. It may be a written agreement or an

TYPES OF LAWS

Constitutional	Laws found in the U.S. Constitution
Administrative	Rules and regulations of executive branch of government
International	Laws that affect the U.S. and other nations
Criminal Law	Laws to protect people and property from deliberate harm
Civil Law	Law concerned with disputes between people or between government and its citizens

Which type of law describes the main duties of the United States Congress?

oral one. Breach of contract means the failure to fulfill the terms of a contract. The terms of any contract are enforceable by law. Suppose, for example, that you order something from a mail order catalogue and charge it to your credit card. The mail order company has, in effect, made a contract with you. If you do not receive the merchandise, the mail order company has broken the contract. If the company fails to return your money, you could take it to court.

Another type of civil law involves family issues and problems. Family law deals with such things as divorce, child custody, adoptions, alimony, child support, and spouse and child abuse.

SECTION REVIEW

Define the Words

civil law   defendant
lawsuit   contract
plaintiff

Check the Facts
1. Identify and give an example of administrative law.
2. What is breach of contract?
3. What kind of law is involved in a divorce?

Think About the Ideas
4. *Evaluate.* Which types of law do you think are most important to individuals? Explain.

Family law contains many provisions designed to safeguard the rights of children.

CITIZENSHIP SKILLS

How to Serve on a Jury

When you reach 18 years of age, you will be eligible to serve on a jury. Jury duty is one of the primary responsibilities, as well as privileges, of U.S. citizenship.

Procedures for jury selection vary from state to state, but in every case jurors are chosen at random. When your name is chosen, you will receive a notice to appear in court at a specific date and time. Failure to obey the jury notice is a punishable offense. In some cases, you might be able to postpone your jury duty.

The jury notice usually includes a form to be filled out and a confirmation card. Receiving a jury notice does not mean you will automatically be put on a jury. Many more jurors are called than are needed. Depending on the court's case load, you might be on standby or not needed at all. In some instances, you might be selected and then dismissed because the case to which you have been assigned is settled just before going to trial.

Jurors and alternate jurors are selected by the lawyers in a case. Possible jurors are questioned to determine whether they can be fair and impartial. Lawyers can reject any jurors they feel will not be favorable to their clients. After the jury selection is completed, the judge administers an oath to the jurors and gives them instructions on court procedures and rules of evidence.

Then the case goes to trial and each side presents its arguments and evidence. Then the judge instructs the jury on the rules of law that apply to the case. The jury is sent to a private room to discuss the evidence and decide on a verdict. In a criminal trial the verdict is "guilty" or "not guilty" and must be unanimous. In civil cases, the verdict is "for the plaintiff" or "for the defendant." After reaching its verdict, the jury returns to the courtroom, and announces its verdict.

A juror's responsibility is to determine the truth. It is important that jurors consider only the evidence presented in court. They must not be influenced by someone's personality or appearance, by speculation, information in the mass media, or public opinion. In determining the truth, they must set aside their emotions and personal prejudices. They must never discuss or investigate a case with anyone outside of the courtroom.

The role of a juror is an enormous responsibility. Justice is served only if each person serving on a jury upholds the right to a fair trial guaranteed by the Constitution.

Using Your Skills
1. Why is it that a jury summons does not guarantee that you will serve on a jury?
2. On what basis are jurors selected?
3. What are a juror's responsibilities?
4. Why is jury duty an important obligation of citizens?

CHAPTER 16 REVIEW

* *

MAIN POINTS

★ Laws bring order to society by regulating the way people and groups act toward one another. Laws protect people by discouraging criminals, enabling people to settle disagreements, and safeguarding our rights.

★ Good laws are fair, understandable, reasonable, and enforceable.

★ Our laws come from ideas and traditions established over generations. English common law is an important source of our law.

★ The Constitution outlines the legal rights of people accused of crimes. These rights include the principles of due process and equal protection of the laws.

★ The Constitution lists several specific legal rights including the rights of trial by jury, of counsel, and of appeal.

★ Citizens have the responsibility to obey the law, cooperate with law officers, serve on juries, testify in court, and work to change bad laws.

★ The United States has many laws. These laws fall into several categories; these include constitutional law, criminal law, and civil law.

WORDS IN REVIEW

Choose the words or phrase from the list below that best completes each sentence. Write the missing words on a separate sheet of paper.

stare decisis	writ of habeas corpus
ex post facto laws	grand jury
contempt of court	petit jury
bench trial	double jeopardy
plaintiff	contract

1. The case was being tried before a _____ of 12 citizens.

2. Although selling fireworks in the county became illegal in 1989, the provision against _____ meant that people who sold them in 1988 could not be accused of breaking the law.

3. The two partners signed a _____ specifying the terms of their agreement.

4. The _____ guaranteed the person's right to appear before a judge in a court of law.

5. The _____ had been injured in an accident and was bringing suit against the bus company.

6. By making its ruling based on the precedents of other cases, the Supreme Court was following the process of _____.

7. The constitutional provision against _____ protected the man from being tried for the crime a second time.

8. The accused waived his right to a jury trial in favor of a _____.

9. The _____ handed down the indictment after hearing the arguments of attorneys for both sides in the case.

10. The judge felt that the witness was obstructing the trial and held him in _____.

CHAPTER 16 REVIEW

* *

FACTS IN REVIEW

1. Identify four characteristics of good laws.

2. How did English law influence U.S. law?

3. Describe the role of the judicial branch in making laws.

4. What is meant by "taking the Fifth"?

5. Why is the crime of treason defined in the Constitution?

6. What is the role of the grand jury?

7. Identify three rights which guarantee that a person will have an adequate defense during a trial.

8. In what two situations can a person be retried for the same crime?

9. Name three types of law.

10. Give at least two reasons why a person might file a lawsuit.

THINKING ABOUT LEGAL RIGHTS AND RESPONSIBILITIES

1. *Evaluate*. Why do you think laws are important to our society?

2. *Analyze*. Are there any other legal rights you think people should have? Explain.

3. *Analyze*. Which types of law do you think might be most difficult to enforce? Why?

WRITING ABOUT LEGAL RIGHTS AND RESPONSIBILITIES

Legal rights and responsibilities are an important aspect of our democratic system. In many other nations, citizens have far fewer legal rights. Write a short essay about our legal rights and responsibilities. Why are they important? How would our society be different if we did not have them? What should we do as citizens to help protect our legal rights?

INTERPRETING A CHART OF LEGAL RIGHTS

Look at the chart showing Americans' legal rights on page 372. Which of these rights protect anyone suspected of a crime? Which rights apply specifically to a person who is charged with a crime? Which rights protect people who have been tried and convicted by a jury? Are there any legal rights not included on this chart?

FOCUSING ON YOUR COMMUNITY

Lawyers often specialize in a particular type of law. Find out about specialties of the lawyers in your community. How many lawyers deal with criminal law, with corporate law, with international law, and so on? What is the most common type of law practiced? With what types of law are most of the legal cases in the community involved? Prepare a short report for the class.

CHAPTER 17

★ ★

Civil and Criminal Law

OBJECTIVES

After you have studied this chapter, you
will be able to:

★ Identify and give an example of a lawsuit and a suit of equity.
★ Describe the court process in civil cases.
★ Identify several types of crimes against
persons and crimes against property.
★ Explain the function of criminal
penalties.
★ Describe the procedure for handling
criminal cases.
★ Discuss the role and operation of the
juvenile court system.

SECTIONS

1 Civil Cases
2 Criminal Cases
3 Court Proceedings in Criminal Cases
4 Juveniles and the Court System

Every year in the United States, millions of people file lawsuits and millions more are charged with committing crimes. Many of these crimes and lawsuits end up as cases that are tried in a court of law. Juries have to consider the cases and come to verdicts and judges have to hand down sentences. The people and agencies that carry out all of these activities make up the American legal system.

Most people think of the courts when they think about the legal system. It is the role of the courts to serve justice. That means that they should provide a fair hearing of each case that comes before them.

Our nation's courts hear both civil cases and criminal cases (see Chapter 12). But each type of case is handled somewhat differently, with its own rules and procedures. Legal cases involving juveniles are also handled differently from cases involving only adults.

★ ★

SECTION 1
Civil Cases

★ ★

VOCABULARY

suit of equity	complaint
injunction	pleadings

As you have learned, a civil case, or civil suit, is a legal action brought by one person or party against another. Civil cases usually involve disputes over rights, property, or agreements. For example, if an employer refuses to hire someone because the person is black or female, that person could bring a civil suit against the employer for discrimination. There are two basic kinds of civil cases—lawsuits and suits of equity.

Lawsuits

In a lawsuit, a person or group brings legal action to collect damages for some harm that has been done. Lawsuits involving damages of $5,000 or less are often handled in a small claims court, and the people involved can act as their own attorneys. Lawsuits involving more money, however, often require lawyers and juries in larger civil courts.

There are many different kinds of lawsuits. They may involve property disputes, or breach of contract, or family matters, such as divorce. Many lawsuits deal with negligence, or personal injury. A negligence suit

A person who causes an automobile accident may face a negligence suit brought by a person whose property has been damaged.

is filed when a person has been injured or killed or when property has been destroyed because someone else has been careless or negligent. Most cases involving auto accidents are negligence suits.

Suits of Equity

Suits of equity are a special kind of lawsuit that seeks fair treatment in a situation where there is no existing law to help decide the matter. Suits of equity are often brought to prevent a damaging action from taking place. For example, a group of citizens could file a suit of equity to try to prevent the state from building a highway through a local park.

While lawsuits may be decided by a jury, suits of equity are usually decided by a judge. In deciding a suit of equity case, a judge may issue an injunction. An **injunction** is a court order commanding a person or group to stop a certain action. In the case above, for example, the judge might issue an injunction to stop construction of the highway.

Court Procedure in Civil Cases

Each year, an enormous number of civil suits are filed in American courts. Some courts are faced with so many civil cases that it can take three or four years for a case to be scheduled for trial. Many civil suits, perhaps the majority, never make it to trial at all. They are usually settled out of court, when the parties involved agree on a settlement.

Let's look at how a lawsuit proceeds through the court system. Suppose John Maloney is riding in a city bus one day and suffers head injuries and a broken arm when the bus is in an accident. Mr. Maloney decides to file a lawsuit against the city to recover the costs of hospital and doctor bills, lost income from days missed at work, and other expenses. Mr. Maloney becomes the plaintiff, or person filing the lawsuit and making the complaint. The party he is suing, in this case the city, is the defendant.

Mr. Maloney hires an attorney who prepares and files a **complaint**, a formal notice that a lawsuit is being brought. It names the plaintiff and defendant and describes the nature of the complaint. The court then sends the defendant (the city) a summons, which announces that the defendant is being sued and sets a date and time for appearance in court.

After receiving the summons, the defendant's attorneys get a copy of the complaint and file a written answer with the court in which they deny or admit each of Mr. Maloney's claims. Next, the attorneys for each side exchange documents known as **pleadings**, which narrow down the issues and legal points raised by both sides in the case. For example, Mr. Maloney originally may have sued the bus manufacturer as well as the city. In the pleadings he may agree to drop that part of the suit because it is clear to both sides that the manufacturer was not at fault in the accident.

When the case finally goes to court, the attorneys for the plaintiff and defendant each present their side of the case, and then await a verdict.

SECTION REVIEW

Define the Words
suit of equity   complaint
injunction   pleadings

Check the Facts
1. What is the difference between a lawsuit and a suit of equity?
2. What is the purpose of an injunction?
3. Why do many civil cases fail to come to trial?

Think About the Ideas
4. *Analyze.* Do you think people in the United States file too many lawsuits? Why or why not?

Meetings between people involved in a lawsuit may result in an out-of-court settlement that saves both parties time and effort. How does the public benefit from an out-of-court settlement?

SECTION 2

Criminal Cases

When people break the laws, they are committing a crime and are subject to a certain punishment. In the United States, each state determines what actions are considered crimes within the state. These crimes are defined in the state's criminal laws, called the **penal code**. The federal government also has a penal code that defines federal crimes such as income tax evasion, kidnapping, airplane hijacking, and drug smuggling.

Crime is very costly to American society. Each year, thousands of people are killed, millions are injured, and billions of dollars in goods and services are lost as a result of crime. In addition, it costs the federal and state government billions of dollars annually to combat crime. Crime also takes a toll in the fear and anxiety it arouses in people throughout the nation.

Types of Crime

Crime can be divided into two general categories—crimes against persons and crimes against property. Most crimes against persons are violent crimes in which the victim is either injured or killed. These crimes include murder, manslaughter (the accidental killing of a person), rape, assault (physical injury or threat of injury), and kidnapping.

Crimes against property are the most common type of crime. Burglary, robbery, and theft are all forms of **larceny**, the taking of another's property unlawfully. Other common crimes against property are **vandalism** (the deliberate destruction of property) and fraud. **Fraud** means taking of property by dishonest means or misrepresentation. For example, if someone convinced another person to invest money in a nonexistent gold mine, that would be fraud.

Certain crimes, such as unauthorized gambling or the use of illegal drugs, are considered victimless crimes or crimes against morality. Laws against victimless crimes are very difficult to enforce because there is no victim to bring a complaint. Some people argue that these activities should not be crimes, since they do not hurt anyone except the person involved. Other people respond that victimless crimes do in fact harm others. People often steal to get money to purchase illegal drugs. Gamblers sometimes bet more than they can afford and borrow money from illegal money lenders called loan sharks. Moreover, victimless crimes are often under the control of criminal gangs that commit many violent crimes against society.

The penal code in most states establishes different degrees of seriousness to many of these crimes. For example, first degree murder is one in which a person plans and carries out a killing deliberately, or hires someone else to do it. A second-degree murder is one in which there is an intent to kill, but it is not planned beforehand. Instead, it is carried out on the spur of the moment, often in a fit of anger. Manslaughter is when one person kills another by accident without meaning to.

THE DEATH PENALTY

Should the United States execute people who commit murder or are involved in a crime in which someone is killed? Or does capital punishment (the death penalty) violate the Eighth Amendment which forbids "cruel and unusual punishment"? These questions have generated much debate over the last 20 years.

In 1972, the U.S. Supreme Court struck down the death penalty laws of all 50 states in the case of *Furman* v. *Georgia*. In that case, the Court did not base its decision on the Eighth Amendment but rather on the fact that capital punishment was applied disproportionately to convicted murderers who are poor and black.

In the next few years, 37 states enacted new death penalty laws. Some states required the death penalty for certain crimes, such as killing a police officer or hiring someone to kill a person. The Court struck down these death penalty laws in 1976. It ruled that the laws were too rigid and did not allow judges to consider individual circumstances.

Other states enacted two-stage death penalty laws. Under these laws, a jury must find the suspect guilty in one trial. A second jury trial then determines whether the suspect

should be executed or imprisoned. The Supreme Court has upheld these laws because they allow judges and juries to consider the circumstances of a case.

A recent Supreme Court case considered again the effect of race on sentencing. In the 1987 case, *McCleskey* v. *Kemp*, the defendant's attorney demonstrated to the Supreme Court that race still plays a large part in who is sentenced to execution. The Court, however, ruled that a defendant must prove that racial prejudice affected sentencing in his or her own particular case.

Social and moral issues play an important part in the debate over capital punishment. Opponents of the death penalty point out that the United States, South Africa, and Turkey are the only industrialized, Western nations that have the death penalty. They argue that it has never been shown that capital punishment prevents others from killing and that it is cruel and unusual punishment. They are especially concerned about teenaged murderers on death rows around the nation waiting to die. The Supreme Court ruled in 1988 that a state cannot execute a person who committed a murder at age 15 or under. Death penalty opponents would like this age limit raised to 18 or 21.

Those in favor of capital punishment argue that it is an appropriate punishment, that it prevents convicted murderers from killing again, and that it helps prevent others from killing. Supporters of the death penalty are especially bothered by indeterminate sentences, which sometimes allow convicted murderers to be released from prison after only 15 or 20 years. If a life sentence really meant life imprisonment without the possibility of parole, these people might not push as hard for the death penalty.

Using Your Skills

1. Why did the Court strike down mandatory capital punishment laws but not two-stage laws?
2. What arguments do opponents and proponents of the death penalty use to support their views?

The reason for establishing different classifications, or degrees of seriousness, for certain crimes is to set appropriate penalties. In general, the more serious the crime the harsher the punishment. The courts tend to treat crimes against persons more seriously than crimes against property because of the great harm these crimes can do to the victims and to society as a whole.

Penalties for Crimes

People convicted of crimes are usually punished by fines and/or imprisonment depending on the nature and severity of the crime. For many minor crimes and misdemeanors, punishment may be only a small fine or a few days or weeks in jail. Long-term imprisonment is the most common kind of punishment for felonies or serious crimes.

Criminal penalties serve several functions. First, they provide punishment in which a criminal is made to pay for an offense committed against a victim and against society. Criminal penalties also help protect society by keeping dangerous criminals "off the streets." Lawbreakers who are in prison cannot continue to commit crimes against others. Another function of criminal penalties is to keep others from committing the same crime.

This bar graph shows how the number of prisoners in state and federal institutions has increased since 1950. About how many more people were in prison in 1987 than in 1970?

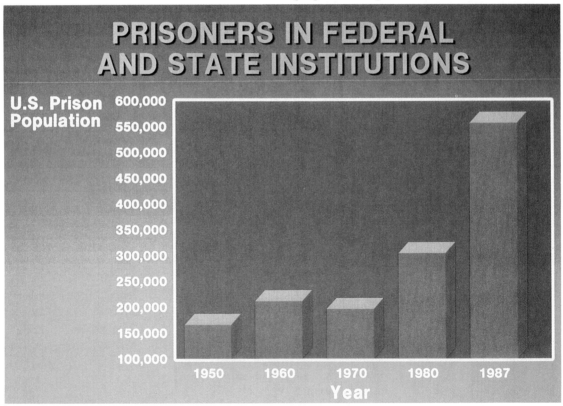

They serve as a warning or an example; others tempted to commit the same crime can see what their punishment would be if they were caught. Finally, criminal penalties can play a role in preparing lawbreakers to reenter society. Through counseling, education, and vocational training, some prisons help inmates learn skills that will help them lead productive lives after prison.

Determining the sentence, or punishment, of a person convicted of a crime is one of the most complicated and difficult aspects of the criminal justice system. Because the circumstances in each case are different, judges may hand down very different sentences for similar crimes.

Most states use a system of indeterminate sentences and parole in penalizing criminals. An indeterminate sentence is one in which a judge gives a minimum and maximum sentence instead of a specific length of time. A person may be released for good behavior after completing the minimum sentence.

A prisoner may also be eligible for parole, or early release, after serving a certain part of the sentence. A parole board will review each request for parole and decide whether or not to grant it. If parole is granted, the person is set free, but must report to a parole officer periodically until the maximum sentence has expired.

Some people are critical of indeterminate sentences and parole. They feel that many sentences turn out to be much shorter and less severe than originally intended. Some states have tried to deal with this issue by establishing mandatory sentences. With a **mandatory sentence**, a judge must impose whatever sentence the law directs. Mandatory sentences, however, present another problem. They sometimes force judges to impose much harsher sentences than are justified by the circumstances of the crime.

At the federal level, the courts are trying a third method in an effort to find a fairer system of sentencing criminals. Starting in 1987, the federal government abolished parole. Instead, it established a range of sentences that judges may apply to each of 43 "offense levels," or categories of crimes. Under this system, similar crimes receive similar punishments, although judges have some leeway in considering the individual circumstances in each case. If the new system proves to be workable and more just, individual states may model their sentencing procedures on the federal system.

SECTION REVIEW

Define the Words

penal code	fraud
larceny	sentence
vandalism	mandatory sentence

Check the Facts
1. What is victimless crime?
2. What is the purpose of classifying crimes by degree of seriousness?
3. Identify four functions of criminal penalties.

Think About the Ideas
4. *Evaluate.* Which system of determining punishment do you think is more fair, the use of indeterminate sentences or mandatory sentences? Explain.

SECTION 3

Court Proceedings in Criminal Cases

* *

VOCABULARY

summons   cross-examination
arraignment   acquittal
prosecution   hung jury
testimony

The justice system treats misdemeanor cases and felony cases quite differently. Misdemeanor cases are usually handled in a minor court such as traffic court or municipal court. Most felony cases are tried in district or circuit courts. The police do not usually arrest misdemeanor suspects. Instead, they issue a ticket, requiring payment of a fine, or a **summons**, directing someone to appear in court for a hearing on the charge. For felony cases, the procedure is much more formal and involved.

Arresting a Suspect

Suppose an undercover police officer observes Hannah Jones exchanging packets of white powder for money on a downtown street. The officer immediately arrests her, searches her, and finds a large amount of cash and 30 small packets of what seems to be cocaine. The officer also informs Ms. Jones of her rights as soon as she is arrested.

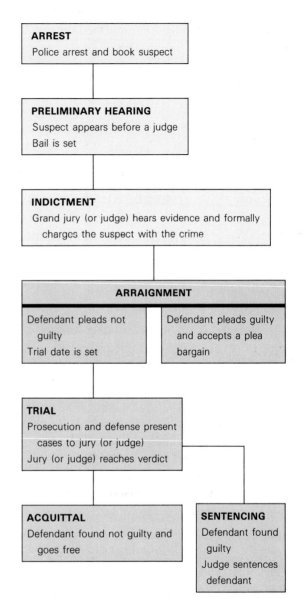

PROCEDURE IN A CRIMINAL CASE

ARREST
Police arrest and book suspect

PRELIMINARY HEARING
Suspect appears before a judge
Bail is set

INDICTMENT
Grand jury (or judge) hears evidence and formally charges the suspect with the crime

ARRAIGNMENT

| Defendant pleads not guilty. Trial date is set | Defendant pleads guilty and accepts a plea bargain |

TRIAL
Prosecution and defense present cases to jury (or judge)
Jury (or judge) reaches verdict

ACQUITTAL
Defendant found not guilty and goes free

SENTENCING
Defendant found guilty
Judge sentences defendant

This chart shows the procedure in a criminal case from the arrest of the suspect to acquittal or sentencing. What happens at an arraignment?

Whenever the police arrest anyone, they are required to read the suspect his or her rights. These include the right to remain silent and the right to have an attorney present when being questioned by police. (For a detailed discussion of the "Miranda rights," see Legal Landmarks: *Miranda* v. *Arizona* in Chapter 16.)

After her arrest, Ms. Jones is taken to the local police station where she is booked, or charged with a crime. As part of the booking procedure, Ms. Jones is photographed and fingerprinted. During this time, she is also allowed to call an attorney, or lawyer. If she doesn't have a lawyer, one will be provided by the state.

Hearing, Indictment, and Arraignment

A few hours later, Ms. Jones and her attorney appear before a municipal judge for a preliminary hearing. The judge hears the charges against the suspect and sets bail. For minor offenses, the judge has the option of releasing suspects on their own recognizance. This means they are released without having to pay bail. Instead, they promise to appear in court when they are called.

After the preliminary hearing, the judge sends Ms. Jones's case to a grand jury, which hears the evidence against the suspect. The grand jury decides whether to indict the suspect—to issue a formal charge—or to dismiss the case if it feels there is not enough evidence for a trial.

Some states do not have grand juries. Instead, the judge at the preliminary hearing will hear the evidence against the suspect and decide whether there is enough evidence to hold a trial.

After it is decided to charge a person with a crime, an arraignment is held. An **arraignment** is a hearing where the suspect pleads guilty or innocent to the charges. The judge at the arraignment will then set a court date for the trial.

Plea Bargaining

Sometimes, after reviewing the charges and evidence against a suspect, a lawyer may urge the defendant to accept a plea bargain. A plea bargain is an agreement in which the accused person agrees to plead guilty, but to a lesser charge. Plea bargaining helps avoid a lengthy and expensive trial. It also ensures that a person will receive some punishment for committing a crime.

Witnesses at at trial must swear to tell the truth about what they saw and heard. A witness who lies to the court can be prosecuted for the crime of perjury.

The majority of criminal cases never go to trial, but are handled through plea bargaining. While plea bargaining saves the government a great deal of time and money, many people object to it. They criticize the fact that it often results in serious crimes being punished with light sentences. Without plea bargaining, however, the criminal justice system would be even more backed up, and people accused of crimes would have very long waits before their cases came to trial.

Going to Trial

In preparing for her trial, Ms. Jones's lawyers interview witnesses, research the state's drug laws, and gather as much information about the case as possible.

When the trial begins, the first step is selecting the jurors. Following jury selection, the attorneys for each side make an opening statement in which they outline the case they will present. In criminal trials, the state's side of the proceedings is called the **prosecution**, and the lawyer for the state is called the prosecutor. The accused person's or defendant's side is the defense, and his or her lawyer is the defense attorney.

After the opening statements, the prosecution presents its case first, followed by the defense. Each side calls witnesses, who take an oath to tell the truth about what they know. The statements a witness makes under oath are called **testimony**.

After a witness testifies for one side, the other side is allowed to cross-examine, or question, the witness. The questions asked in **cross-examination** are often designed to cast doubt on the truth or reliability of the witness's testimony. Finally, each side makes a closing statement summarizing the testimony and evidence. The judge then "instructs" the jury, or explains the law that pertains to the case.

The Verdict

The last part of a trial is when the jury withdraws to deliberate, or think over and discuss the case and reach a verdict. After choosing a foreperson to lead the discussion, the jurors review the evidence and legal arguments they have heard. Finally, they take a vote. In most states, juries are required to reach a unanimous vote in finding a defendant guilty or not guilty.

If the jury feels that the prosecution has not proven its case, it can decide on **acquittal**—a vote of not guilty. To find a defendant guilty, a jury must believe that the evidence and testimony prove a suspect's guilt beyond a reasonable doubt. In the case of Hannah Jones, the jury finds her guilty of selling cocaine.

Sometimes, a jury cannot agree on a verdict. When that happens, the judge declares a **hung jury** and rules the trial a mistrial. With a mistrial, the prosecution must decide whether to drop the charges or ask for a retrial.

Sentencing

When a defendant is found guilty, the judge sets a court date for sentencing. In some cases, a jury recommends a sentence. Most often, however, the judge determines the sentence after considering the defendant's family situation, previous criminal record, employment status, and other relevant information.

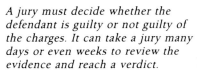
A jury must decide whether the defendant is guilty or not guilty of the charges. It can take a jury many days or even weeks to review the evidence and reach a verdict.

SECTION REVIEW

Define the Words

arraignment   cross-examination
prosecution   acquittal
testimony   hung jury

Check the Facts

1. What happens at an arraignment?
2. What is the purpose of cross-examining witnesses?
3. What happens when the jurors cannot agree on a verdict?

Think About the Ideas

4. *Evaluate.* Do you think plea-bargaining is an effective way to deal with persons convicted of crimes? Why or why not?
5. *Analyze.* How does the idea of "guilty beyond a reasonable doubt" protect the rights of defendants?

Although cases involving juvenile offenders are handled in separate courts, law enforcement officers take juvenile crime very seriously.

SECTION 4

Juveniles and the Court System

VOCABULARY

juvenile   offender
juvenile delinquent

Children and teenagers commit many crimes each year. Some of these crimes are misdemeanors such as speeding or driving without a license. Others, however, are serious crimes and felonies such as burglary, rape, and murder. Moreover, the number of serious crimes committed by children and teenagers seems to be increasing.

Each state establishes a certain age when people are considered adults for the purposes of applying criminal laws. In some states the age is 16, in others 18. Anyone under that age limit is considered a **juvenile**, a person not yet legally an adult. Our justice system treats juveniles who commit crimes somewhat differently than it treats adults.

Juvenile Delinquents

A child or teenager who commits a serious crime or repeatedly breaks the law, is often called a **juvenile delinquent**.

Some people have studied the problem of juvenile crime. Their aim is to find ways of preventing juvenile delinquency and also to prevent juvenile **offenders**, or lawbreakers,

Marion Wright Edelman
Lobbyist for Children

Although children can't vote or pay taxes, they have a powerful voice speaking for them—Marion Wright Edelman. She is the founder and president of the Children's Defense Fund (CDF), which works to get federal funds to help children get the medical care, nutrition, and education they need.

Edelman grew up in Bennettsville, South Carolina. She went to Spelman College in Atlanta and then to Yale Law School. She was the first black woman ever admitted to practice law in Mississippi, where she worked for the NAACP Legal Defense Fund during the Civil Rights years of the 1960's.

Edelman started the Children's Defense Fund (CDF) in 1973. Despite its name, the CDF has never had a lot of money to promote its causes. Instead, the CDF uses statistics to prove its points. Each year the fund produces many reports showing the effects of poverty, infant mortality, malnutrition, and poor education on the nation's children.

This strategy has helped convince Congress to increase funding for children's programs, even in years when other social programs were being cut. Edelman's work on behalf of children has been so effective that U.S. Senator Edward Kennedy calls her "the 101st Senator on children's issues."

Using Your Skills
1. How does the Children's Defense Fund seek to influence Congress to provide more money for children's programs?
2. If Congress reduced or eliminated funds for children's nutritional, medical, and educational programs, how do you think that would affect the children in the nation?

from becoming adult criminals. These studies have shown that children who are abused or neglected or who suffer from emotional or mental problems are more likely to get into trouble with the law. They have also shown that children who grow up in poverty, in overcrowded slums where drug and alcohol abuse are widespread, are also more likely to become delinquents. However, although these factors may contribute to juvenile delinquency, they do not explain why some children commit crimes. Many children who grow up in poverty or are abused do not become criminals. Moreover, children from all backgrounds and levels of society can and do become juvenile delinquents.

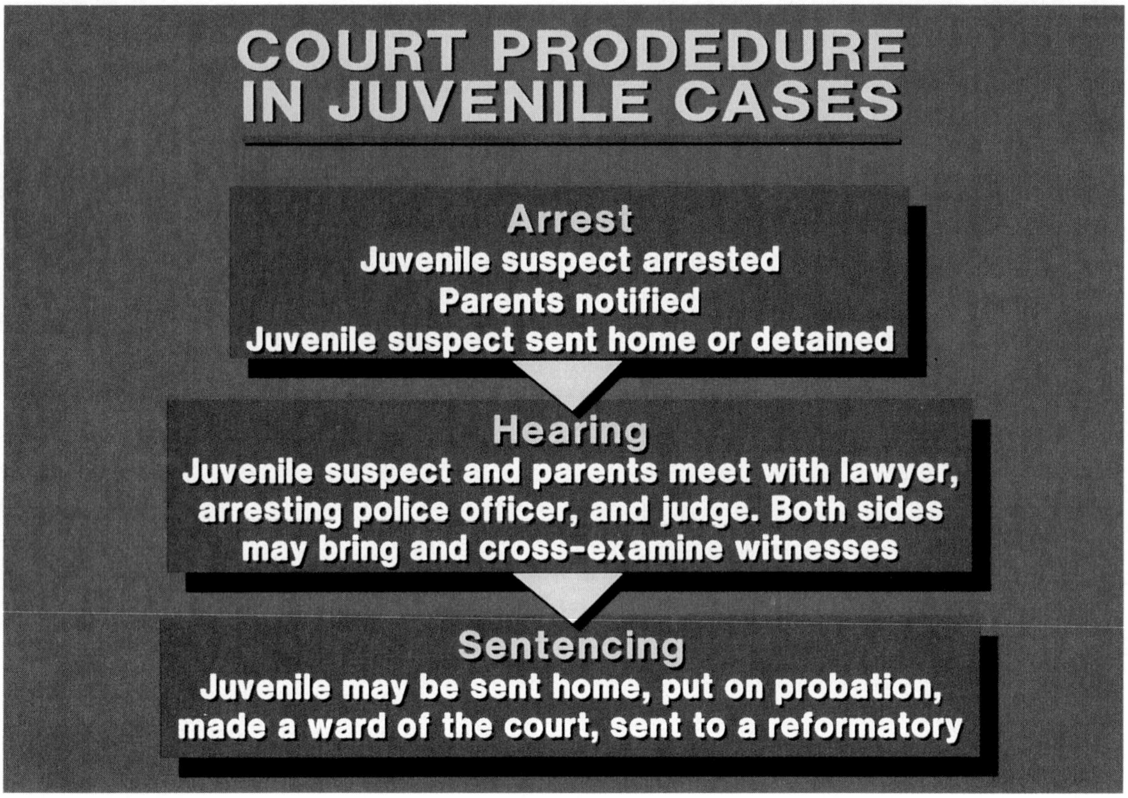

COURT PROCEDURE IN JUVENILE CASES

Arrest
Juvenile suspect arrested
Parents notified
Juvenile suspect sent home or detained

Hearing
Juvenile suspect and parents meet with lawyer,
arresting police officer, and judge. Both sides
may bring and cross-examine witnesses

Sentencing
Juvenile may be sent home, put on probation,
made a ward of the court, sent to a reformatory

This chart shows the court procedures followed in cases that involve juveniles. Who sets the age at which suspects are considered adults in the criminal justice system?

Juvenile Courts

When juveniles are charged with committing crimes, their cases are handled in separate courts called juvenile courts. The primary goal of juvenile courts is to try to rehabilitate juvenile offenders and correct their behavior, rather than to punish them.

The juvenile court system was set up in the late 1800's as a result of reforms in the judicial system. Before this time, juvenile offenders over age 14 were treated like adults. They received the same sentences for crimes and were sent to the same prisons as adult criminals. Some children were even executed for committing certain crimes.

Juvenile courts were set up to do whatever was in the best interest of the children, either to protect them from harm or to divert them from a life of crime. They handle two kinds of cases: neglect and delinquency. Cases of neglect involve children who are neglected or abused by their parents. A juvenile court has the power to place these children with other families in foster homes, where they will be protected and cared for. Delinquency cases involve children who commit crimes. Juvenile courts also handle offenses that are considered illegal for juveniles but not for adults. These offenses include such things as running away from home and playing hooky from school.

Dealing with Juvenile Offenders

What happens when a child is arrested for a crime? As soon as a child is arrested for a crime, the police notify his or her parents. Depending upon the seriousness of the crime, the child may be sent home or kept in a juvenile detention center until it is time to appear in court.

At the court appearance, the juvenile and his or her parents meet with their lawyer, the judge, the police officer who made the arrest, and the probation officer who investigated the case. This meeting, or hearing, is similar to a trial, but is less formal. Only the parties involved are allowed to attend the hearing. As in a trial, both sides are allowed to call and cross-examine witnesses. There is no jury, however. Juveniles do not have the right to a jury trial. Usually, the judge decides whether the juvenile is guilty or innocent.

The juvenile court system provides several special protections for juveniles. First of all, the juvenile's identity is kept secret. The criminal records of juveniles are also kept from the public, and in some cases they may be erased when the offender becomes an adult. In addition, when juveniles are arrested, they are not fingerprinted or photographed as adult suspects are.

In 1967, the Supreme Court established certain rules for juvenile cases:

★ The parents or guardians of the juveniles must be notified of their arrest as soon as possible.
★ Juveniles and their parents must be notified in writing of all the charges against them.
★ Juveniles have the right to remain silent and to be represented by an attorney.
★ Juveniles have the right to confront witnesses against them.

These rights were established as a result of the Supreme Court case, *In re Gault* (*in re* means in the matter of). In this case, 15-year old Gerald Gault of Phoenix, Arizona, was charged with making indecent telephone calls to a neighbor. His parents, who were not at home, were not informed of his arrest. When his case came up for a hearing, the neighbor was not called or questioned, and Gerald Gault was not represented by an attorney.

To protect the rights of juveniles, the Supreme Court has established certain guidelines for the way juvenile cases are handled.

After the hearing, the judge sent Gerald Gault to a reformatory until age 21. In effect, the judge sentenced Gault to six years imprisonment. If he had been an adult, the most he could have received was a $50 fine and two to three months in jail. In overturning the judge's decision, the Supreme Court ensured that juveniles would enjoy the same legal rights as adults.

Punishing Juvenile Offenders

Juvenile court judges can sentence juvenile offenders in several different ways. Very young children or first offenders may simply be returned to their families with a stern lecture. Offenders with a previous history of delinquency may be placed in a training school where they can learn a trade or in a reformatory, a prison that houses only juveniles.

Juveniles who have been neglected or have a poor home life may become wards of the court. This means that the court becomes their guardian and can supervise their life until adulthood. Judges may place juveniles with serious mental or emotional problems in a hospital or institution where they can receive proper medical treatment. Judges may also put juvenile offenders on probation, which means that they can continue to live at home and go to school as long as they obey the court's rules.

One criticism of the juvenile court system is that juveniles who commit major crimes sometimes receive very light sentences and are soon released to commit serious crimes again. In many states, juvenile court judges may now refer serious cases to the criminal courts, or prosecutors may ask the state courts to order the suspect to be tried as an adult.

Juvenile court judges have a variety of options available for dealing with young offenders.

SECTION REVIEW

Define the Words

juvenile   offender

juvenile delinquent

Check the Facts

1. What are two factors that contribute to juvenile delinquency?
2. What is the primary role of juvenile courts?
3. What special protections do the juvenile courts provide for juveniles?

Think About the Ideas

4. *Analyze.* Do you think juvenile offenders should be treated differently from adults? Why or why not?

CITIZENSHIP SKILLS

How to Evaluate Information

Throughout your life you will have to make decisions about different matters. You could make serious mistakes if you base your decisions on information that is faulty or not true. You may have already had the experience of making such a mistake.

There are ways, however, to help protect yourself from making mistakes because of bad information. You should always ask yourself the following questions when evaluating information:

★ *Is the information factual?* Information is often presented as fact when it is really a guess, a generalization, an assumption, or an opinion. Facts are statements or observations that can be verified or proven. They are supported by evidence. The better the evidence, the more reliable are the facts. When evaluating information start by deciding if the information seems believable. Then look for evidence that verifies the facts.

★ *Do I have ALL the facts?* People sometimes make mistakes when they draw conclusions from information that is incomplete, only partially true, or based on only one example. In evaluating information, try to learn all the facts that relate to an issue. The more facts and evidence you have the more confidence you can have in the reliability of the information.

★ *Where did this information come from?* People often make mistakes when they draw conclusions from information based on rumor or unreliable sources. Some of the best sources of information are personal observations, eyewitness accounts, and physical evidence. In many cases, information from an expert is better than information from a casual observer. Therefore, when evaluating information, always consider the source.

★ *How up-to-date is the information?* People can make mistakes when they draw conclusions from information that is no longer true. When evaluating information, always consider how current and timely it is.

★ *Is the information accurately stated?* An important step in deciding whether or not to trust information is to consider the way it is communicated. Information presented in a strongly emotional manner may be an expression of an opinion, bias, or point of view rather than of fact. When evaluating information, always consider the way the information is presented as a clue to its accuracy.

Using Your Skills
1. What questions should you ask about information before drawing conclusions?
2. What are some of the best sources of information?
3. What are some things that would lead you to believe information is not reliable?

CHAPTER 17 REVIEW

* *

MAIN POINTS

★ There are two basic kinds of civil suits—lawsuits and suits of equity.

★ Civil cases proceed through the courts in several steps, including filing a complaint, exchanging pleadings, and presenting the case in court.

★ Crime can be divided into two general categories—crimes against persons and crimes against property.

★ Criminal penalties serve several functions, including punishing the lawbreaker, preventing others from committing crimes, protecting society, and helping the lawbreaker reenter society.

★ The procedures in criminal cases include arrest, preliminary hearings, indictment and arraignment, trial, and sentencing.

★ A separate juvenile court system has been established to deal with youthful offenders.

WORDS IN REVIEW

Choose the word or phrase from the list below that best completes each sentence. Write the missing words on a separate sheet of paper.

fraud	injunction
complaint	sentence
prosecution	arraignment
plea bargain	testimony
acquittal	hung jury

1. The injured woman's lawyer filed a _____ against the city bus company.

2. After hours of deliberation, the jury felt the evidence was not convincing and voted for _____.

3. The _____ asked the jury to find the defendant guilty on all counts.

4. The defense attorney recommended that his client accept a _____ in exchange for a lighter sentence.

5. During the trial, the jury heard a great deal of _____ that seemed to support the prosecution's case.

6. At the _____, the defendant pleaded not guilty to the charge and a court date for the trial was set.

7. After the jury failed to reach agreement, the judge declared a _____ and ruled for a mistrial.

8. The two partners were accused of _____ for selling shares in a company that existed only on paper.

9. The judge issued an _____ to stop construction of a new highway after the community group filed a suit of equity.

10. The defendant was told that he would be eligible for parole after serving one year of his _____.

FACTS IN REVIEW

1. Identify and describe two types of lawsuits.

2. What is the purpose of a suit of equity?

3. In what ways are victimless crimes harmful to others?

4. Describe the parole system.

5. Describe the main steps in dealing with accused persons before a trial.

6. What is the purpose of plea bargaining?

7. What happens if a mistrial is declared?

8. What are some things a judge might consider in determining the sentences for convicted criminals?

9. Identify four important rules established by the Supreme Court for juvenile cases.

10. What are some of the options judges have in sentencing juvenile offenders?

THINKING ABOUT CIVIL AND CRIMINAL LAW

1. *Evaluate.* Do you think that civil cases should be tried before a jury? Why or why not?

2. *Evaluate.* Do you think that imposing longer prison sentences on people convicted of violent crimes would prevent others from committing similar crimes? Why or why not?

3. *Analyze.* What are some factors that contribute to juvenile delinquency? What do you think could be done to help prevent juveniles from committing crimes?

DEBATING THE MIRANDA RIGHTS

Some people argue that the Miranda rights interfere with the prosecution of guilty people. They claim that criminals are often allowed to go free because of technicalities. Others argue that the Miranda rights are an important protection for anyone accused of a crime. They claim that the Miranda rights only let people know the rights they already have under the Constitution. Prepare arguments, pro or con, for debating the following statement: The Miranda rights ruling should be suspended so that criminals can be prosecuted more easily.

WRITING ABOUT THE JUVENILE JUSTICE SYSTEM

The juvenile justice system is quite different than the justice system for adults. Write an essay comparing these two systems. In what ways are juveniles treated differently than adults? Why are they treated differently? What rights do juveniles have that adults do not? What rights do adults have that are not granted to juveniles. In what ways is the sentencing of offenders different?

INTERPRETING A CHART

Look at the chart on page 394 about the procedure in criminal cases. What is the first step after a crime is committed? What are police officers required to do when a suspect is arrested? At what point does a suspect plead guilty or not guilty? When does plea bargaining take place? Why do you think there are so many steps in the procedure?

FOCUSING ON YOUR COMMUNITY

The court systems of even the smallest communities must deal with many different types of cases, both civil and criminal, each year. Find out what types of civil cases are filed most frequently in your community? About what percentage of these cases are won by the plaintiff? What types of crimes are committed most often in your community? About what percentage of these cases result in a guilty verdict? How frequent is juvenile crime in the community? What types of crimes do the juveniles in the community commit most frequently? Prepare a short written report for the class.

UNIT 6 REVIEW

* *

ESSAY QUESTIONS

The following questions are based on material in Unit 6. Answer each question with two or three written paragraphs. Be sure to give specific reasons to support your answers.

1. The ever-increasing number of criminal cases has clogged the American court system. How does this congestion affect the legal rights of persons accused of crimes? What might be done to improve the situation?

2. The Constitution outlines the legal rights of people accused of crimes. Some people believe that the legal rights of victims of crime should also be recognized and protected by law. Discuss this idea and the rights that might be listed. Explain why you agree or disagree.

3. Lawyers and judges have criticized the American jury system because of its cost, inefficiency, and the quality of the jurors. Do you think the system needs reform? Why or why not?

CONNECTING CIVICS AND JOURNALISM

The First Amendment guarantees a free press. The Sixth Amendment promises a fair trial by an impartial jury. In recent years, these two rights have often collided in the courtroom. Be prepared to discuss the following in class: Why is it important for the news media to cover trials? Why do you think reporters and artists are allowed in courtrooms but photographic and recording equipment are usually barred? Will television coverage of trials endanger the rights of defendants? Should the news media be restrained in any way?

ANALYZING VISUALS

The criminal justice system has three parts—police work, judicial and legal proceedings, and corrections. (Corrections refers to prisons, jails, probation, and parole.) This bar graph shows what the federal, state, and local governments spent on the different areas of law enforcement in one year. Study the graph and answer the questions:

1. Which level of government spent the most money on police work?

2. Which level spent the largest portion of its criminal justice budget on corrections?

3. Why do you think the federal government spent less on all areas of the criminal justice system than state and local governments?

4. How can you explain the fact that local governments spent more on the judicial and legal process than states but less on corrections?

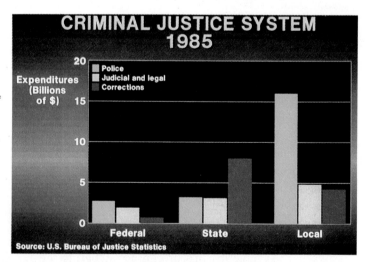

CRIMINAL JUSTICE SYSTEM 1985

Expenditures (Billions of $)

Police
Judicial and legal
Corrections

Federal   State   Local

Source: U.S. Bureau of Justice Statistics

CLOSEUP ON *GIDEON* V. *WAINWRIGHT*

The Sixth Amendment to the U.S. Constitution says that a person accused of a crime shall "have the assistance of counsel for his defense." Although this amendment was adopted in 1791, it was not applied to state courts until 1963. For all those years, people who could not afford to hire an attorney were forced to provide their own defense.

Most people did not see the unfairness of this situation. It was unfortunate if a defendant could not afford a lawyer. The government provided defendants with the right to a trial, to confront their accusers, to speak in their own defense, and to be tried by a jury. Many people questioned why the government should provide defense attorneys and thus pay to both prosecute and defend a suspect.

In 1942, the U.S. Supreme Court considered the issue in *Betts* v. *Brady*. Smith Betts had been accused of robbing a store in Maryland. Unable to afford an attorney to defend himself, he was convicted and sentenced to eight years in prison. In his appeal to the Supreme Court, Betts argued that his Sixth Amendment right to counsel and Fourteenth Amendment right to due process had been violated.

The Court, however, ruled against Betts. It stated that the Sixth Amendment applied only to the federal courts and to death penalty cases in the state courts.

The Supreme Court had another opportunity to consider the issue in 1963. Clarence Earl Gideon, an unemployed drifter, had been arrested and charged with breaking into a Florida pool hall and stealing some food and coins from a vending machine. The Florida courts refused to provide Gideon with an attorney for his defense. He was convicted and sentenced to five years in prison.

While in prison, Gideon studied law books and learned about the Constitution. He came to believe that his rights had been violated because he had been denied the Sixth Amendment right to counsel and the Fourteenth Amendment right to due process of law. In a neatly hand-written letter to the U.S. Supreme Court, Gideon asked the Court to hear his case. The Court agreed and assigned a very able lawyer, Abe Fortas, to represent him.

In 1963, the Court ruled unanimously in Gideon's favor, overturning the *Betts* v. *Brady* decision. Justice Hugo Black, who had dissented in the Betts case,

Clarence Earl Gideon

wrote the opinion for the Court. Black declared, ". . . any person . . . who is too poor to hire a lawyer, cannot be provided a fair trial unless counsel is provided . . . This seems to us to be an obvious truth."

As a result of the Court's decision, Gideon was given a new trial with a court-appointed lawyer and was acquitted. Now each state has a system for assigning attorneys to defendants who cannot afford one.

1. If the right to counsel is guaranteed in the Bill of Rights, why wasn't it recognized in state criminal cases before 1963?
2. What did Betts and Gideon mean when they argued that failing to provide them with attorneys violated due process of law?

*E*xcessive bail shall not be required, nor excessive fines imposed.

—EIGHTH AMENDMENT

*N*or shall private property be taken for public use without just compensation.

—FIFTH AMENDMENT

* *

The American Free Enterprise System

Americans work hard to achieve financial security. They accumulate savings, acquire property, start businesses, and make investments. They do so without fear that the government will come and take away their possessions. The Fifth and Eighth amendments, which protect our economic rights, have helped to make the United States a land of economic opportunity.

* * * * *

The American Economic System

OBJECTIVES

After you have studied this chapter, you will be able to:

★ Discuss the purpose of an economic system.

★ Explain the principles of supply and demand and how they affect production and price.

★ Identify and describe four elements that are required for the production of any good or service.

★ Identify and describe four basic types of economic systems and discuss the features of a capitalistic, free enterprise system.

★ Identify and describe three basic ways in which businesses are organized and managed.

SECTIONS

1 Making Economic Decisions
2 Economic Systems
3 Organization and Management

In a typical American shopping mall, you will probably see one store stocked with jeans, and another with records, tapes, and compact discs, and still others with shoes, jewelry, books, or toys. These stores offer a huge selection of different things to buy, many in various sizes, styles, colors, and prices.

Where do these products come from? Who makes them? How are they made? How do they get to the stores? Who buys them? Economics—the study of how things are made, bought, sold, and used—helps to answer these and other questions.

Every country has its own economic system, or way of producing the things its people want and need. A country's economic system helps determine how its basic economic decisions will be made.

* *

SECTION 1

Making Economic Decisions

* *

VOCABULARY

resources	division of labor
consumer	entrepreneur
supply	gross income
demand	profit
capital	marketing
capital goods	wholesaler

Goods and services are things that help satisfy people's needs and wants. Goods include food, clothing, cars, tools, jewelry, television sets, and anything else that can be grown or manufactured. Services are things that people do for others in exchange for money or something else of value. Barbers, doctors, waiters, and entertainers all provide services.

The goods and services that people can get depend upon their country's **resources**. Resources are the things used in making goods and providing services. They include money; natural resources such as wood, soil, and water; human resources—the people who provide the necessary labor, skills, and knowledge.

A country with many resources can satisfy its people's wants and needs better than a country with few resources. The United States is fortunate to be rich in resources such as minerals, fertile soil, trained workers, forests, and water. No country, however, has all of the

American consumers can choose from a wide range of goods available in stores and shopping malls across the country.

resources that it needs. Even the United States has a scarcity, or limited supply, of certain resources. Scarcity is a problem all countries must face.

A scarcity of resources affects the economic decisions a country and its people will make. For example, a country with a scarcity of good farmland might decide to buy most of its food from other countries rather than to grow its own. Scarcity affects individual decisions as well. A person with a limited amount of money must make decisions about how the money should be spent. Is there only enough to pay for rent and food, or is there also enough to buy a new television set?

Scarcity affects decisions concerning what and how much to produce, how goods and services will be produced, and who will get what is produced.

Deciding What and How Much to Produce

The people who buy and use things are called **consumers**. Much of a country's economy is geared to providing consumers with goods and services.

The amount of each kind of good or service available to consumers is the **supply**. The amount of a good or service that consumers are willing to buy is the **demand**. The demand for a product is influenced by its supply, its price, and the number of people who want to buy it.

Supply and demand are important factors in determining what kind of goods and services are made available and in what quantity. The following is an example of how these factors work:

With the invention of the compact disc (CD) player, there was a need for compact discs to play on the new machines. To fill this need, record companies began to produce compact discs. Their decisions about what music to put on disc were based on demand. If more people want to listen to rock than to classical music, recording companies will produce more rock CDs than classical ones. Decisions about how many CDs to produce are also based on demand.

The forces of supply and demand also affect the price of goods and services. When the supply of a product is low and the demand for it is high, the price will be high. When supply is high and demand low, however, the price will usually drop. For example, suppose there is a gasoline shortage during the summer when families are taking their vacations. This will probably cause the price of gasoline to increase because people will be willing to pay more to make sure they have gasoline. If the supply of gasoline increases, or the demand decreases, gasoline merchants will probably lower their prices.

Most often, there is a balance between supply and demand and price. This balance is based on what consumers are willing to pay for a product and on what producers are able to charge.

Under the system of supply and demand, the consumer plays the most important role in determining what goods and services will be offered and how much will be produced. The producer or manufacturer's role is to adjust production and price according to the decisions of the consumer.

Deciding How Goods and Services Will be Produced

What determines how goods and services are produced? Who makes them? How are they made? What resources are needed to produce them? The production of any good or service requires four elements—capital, land and natural resources, labor, and management. Let's look at how these four elements are involved in making a product.

CAPITAL The money needed to produce goods and services is called **capital**. Every business needs capital to get started and to continue operating. For example, several years ago, Robert and Marion Keller decided to start a business producing potato chips. The Kellers used some of their savings and also borrowed money from the bank to start their business. They used this capital to buy a small building and also to purchase several machines that would make the potato chips. The building and the machines are called **capital goods**—the tools, buildings, and machines used to make goods and provide services. Capital goods are different from consumer goods, which are the goods that are produced for people to buy. The potato chips are a consumer good.

LAND AND NATURAL RESOURCES Earlier, you read about resources. All businesses use land and natural resources—materials that come from the earth. A business might need some type of crop or a mineral such as iron or a supply of water to make its product. A business will also need a supply of energy, perhaps from electricity, coal, or gas.

Once their business was ready to go into operation, the Kellers needed several resources to produce their potato chips. First they needed potatoes, which they arranged to buy from several farmers in the area. They also needed vegetable oil in which to cook the chips and a good supply of water to clean the potatoes and machines. Finally, they needed electricity to provide light and to run the machines.

LABOR Workers are important in the production of all goods and services. Since the Kellers couldn't do all of the work themselves, they hired other people to help them. Some people move the potatoes from a storage area to the machines. Others operate the machines that wash and slice the potatoes and that cook and package the chips. Still others prepare boxes for shipment and deliver the potato chips to stores. Each person does just one kind of job. This is called **division of labor**. A division of labor helps manufacturers produce large quantities of goods more quickly and cheaply.

Labor is an important element of production not only because workers make goods, but also because they earn money that they use to buy other goods, thus providing jobs and money for other workers.

The flowchart shows how a product, such as potato chips, moves from the producer to consumers. What four elements are required to make any product?

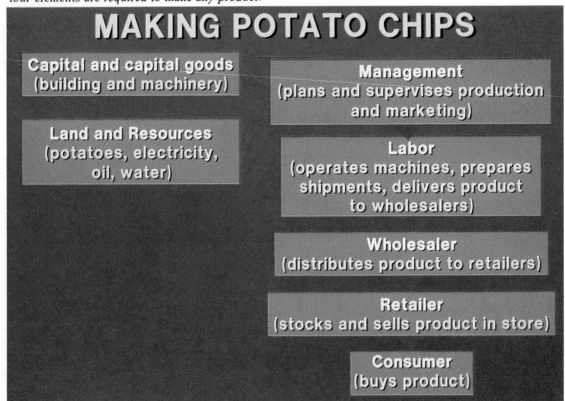

MAKING POTATO CHIPS

Capital and capital goods (building and machinery)

Land and Resources (potatoes, electricity, oil, water)

Management (plans and supervises production and marketing)

Labor (operates machines, prepares shipments, delivers product to wholesalers)

Wholesaler (distributes product to retailers)

Retailer (stocks and sells product in store)

Consumer (buys product)

MANAGEMENT Managers are the people who plan and supervise the production of goods and services. They make important decisions about what kind and how many goods will be produced, how and where they will be sold, and so on. The decisions managers make can have an important impact on a business and the people who work in it. For example, the managers of the Kellers' business may decide to make a new type of potato chip. If consumers don't like the new chip, it could result in decreased sales and a layoff of some workers.

Making management decisions involves taking risks. So does starting and owning a business. The people who start new businesses are called **entrepreneurs**. Entrepreneurs risk their money and devote their time and energy to building a successful business. If they are successful, one of their rewards will be making more money from their business than they put into it.

The total amount of money a business makes is its **gross income**. Much of this income is used to pay salaries, to pay bills for supplies and other expenses, and to pay off bank loans. After all of these payments are made, some money is put aside to pay taxes and some is saved to meet the future needs of the business. The money that remains is the **profit**. The business entrepreneurs and owners receive this profit as reward for taking the risk of starting the business.

One very successful entrepreneur of recent years was Steven Jobs. In 1975, when Jobs was only 20 years old, he started the Apple Computer Company with Stephen Wozniak in Jobs' garage. They had only $1,300 in capital. Jobs and Wozniak believed that they could produce an affordable, easy-to-use computer that people would want to use in their homes. Within five years the Apple Company was worth $1.2 billion and Jobs was a multimillionaire.

An airplane manufacturer can produce more airplanes at a lower cost by having each worker perform a specialized task, such as installing rivets in the fuselage.

Deciding Who Will Get What is Produced

Another important part of making economic decisions is deciding who will receive the goods and services that have been produced. The Kellers could make all the potato chips in the world, but they wouldn't make any money unless they got the chips to people who wanted them. Getting goods to consumers is called **marketing**.

Marketing involves several factors including advertising, shipping, storing, and selling. To encourage people to buy their product, the Kellers call their potato chips "Keller's Best." This name is put on the packages so people can recognize their brand of chips. The Kellers also advertise their chips on television to tell people about their product and to create a demand. When a company advertises its product, it tries to reach as many people in as wide an area as possible. The extent of the advertising depends, in large part, on how much money a company can afford to spend.

The Kellers have their own fleet of trucks to ship, or deliver, their potato chips. The trucks take the chips to **wholesalers**, businesses that buy large quantities of products and store them in warehouses. Wholesalers buy products from manufacturers at a wholesale price—a lower price than a consumer pays in a store. When the retail stores sell the product to consumers, they charge a higher price, called the retail price, to make a profit.

SECTION REVIEW

Define the Words

resources	division of labor
consumer	entrepreneur
supply	gross income
demand	profit
capital	marketing
capital goods	wholesaler

Check the Facts

1. How does a scarcity of resources affect economic decisions?
2. How does supply and demand affect prices?
3. What four elements are involved in the production of a good or service?

Think About the Ideas

4. *Evaluate.* Which element of production do you feel is most crucial to developing a successful business? Why?

Companies that are able to spend large amounts of money on advertising can reach and influence many people through television commercials.

SECTION 2

Economic Systems

* *

VOCABULARY

command economy   free enterprise
communism   socialist economy
market economy   socialism
capitalism   traditional economy

The way the United States makes its economic decisions is not the only way to make these decisions. Economists have identified four basic kinds of economic systems—the command economy, the market economy, the socialist economy, and the traditional economy. In each of these systems, economic decisions are made differently. In a command economy, economic decisions are made by the government; in a market economy, the consumers make these choices. Rarely, however, does a country have only one kind of system. Most nations have a combination of economic systems.

In which economic system is competition a fundamental element?

Command Economies

In a **command economy**, the government controls the means of production—the factories, farms, natural resources, transportation systems, and stores—and makes all economic decisions. It decides what products to make, how many to make, how they will be made, and who gets them. The leaders of the government "command" the economy as they see fit.

The economy of the Soviet Union has been primarily a command economy controlled by its Communist government. Under **communism**, the people, as a whole, are supposed to own the means of production, and the government is only supposed to represent the people when it makes economic decisions.

FOUR ECONOMIC SYSTEMS

MARKET ECONOMY (FREE ENTERPRISE):
- ★ means of production privately owned
- ★ supply and demand are the main factors in economic decisions
- ★ competition for business
- ★ individual profit is the motive

COMMAND ECONOMY:
- ★ government owns all means of production and distribution
- ★ government makes all economic decisions
- ★ no competition
- ★ businesses not run for profit

SOCIALIST ECONOMY:
- ★ major factories and resources noncompetitive, owned by government
- ★ smaller businesses and stores competitive, owned by individuals for profit

TRADITIONAL ECONOMY:
- ★ economic decisions made according to custom
- ★ people meet basic needs by hunting, gathering, farming
- ★ little technology

In practice, however, Communist governments have been run by a small group of self-chosen leaders who make all decisions. The people have had little or no say in economic or political matters.

For decades, the Soviet government planned what and how much to produce. The government told each farm and factory what to produce and provided them with the necessary money and raw materials. The government also determined how much to produce by setting weekly, monthly, and yearly production quotas, or goals, for each factory and farm. A shoe factory, for example, would be expected to produce a certain number of shoes each month.

One of the major characteristics of a command economy is that there is no competition. The government does not have its businesses compete against each other. As a result, consumers have little or no choice about what type of refrigerator or style of shoes to buy. In addition, consumer goods may be poorly made or be in short supply.

CAREERS

Bank Teller

When you go to a bank, perhaps to cash a check or put money into a savings account, your money is handled by a bank teller. The bank teller's job is to process a customer's transactions.

The work of a bank teller is very exacting. Tellers are responsible for every cent they handle during the workday. Their job includes helping customers who want to deposit or withdraw money or check on how much money is in their accounts.

Tellers also apply payments to Holiday Clubs and they sell travelers checks and money orders.

Tellers need an aptitude for mathematics, and they must be quick, accurate, and extremely honest. They should also have a pleasant personality and like to work with people since they deal with customers. Banks often hire high school graduates to be bank tellers. Applicants should have taken mathematics and business courses in high school.

A bank teller's job is considered an entry-level position in the banking industry. After a few years, a teller can be promoted to head teller, someone who trains and supervises the other tellers. Some tellers also move up to other important positions, such as the manager of a department or bank branch.

Using Your Skills
1. Why do tellers need to be quick, accurate, and honest?
2. What skills are necessary to be a bank teller?
3. Why might a person want to become a bank teller?

Businesses are more concerned with meeting quotas than in producing well-made goods. Farms and factories tend to be poorly run, which often results in shortages of goods.

On the other hand, since the government in a command economy owns the factories and farms, it is able to set the prices of goods produced. Factories and farms are in business to provide the goods that the government has decided to produce. Therefore, the government can set low prices for consumer goods, and can provide financial support for factories that lose money. Consumers can thus be assured of buying goods at a reasonable price when those goods are available.

In addition to setting low prices for goods, the Soviet system also had taken care of its citizens in other ways. It provided low-cost housing, free medical care, and free education. It also guaranteed everyone a job.

In the last few years, Soviet leader Mikhail Gorbachev has been trying to change the Soviet economy to make it more productive. His changes are aimed at making factories more self-sufficient, providing farmers with their own land to farm, and letting people own small businesses.

Market Economies

The word *market* refers to buying and selling. It can be a physical place, such as a supermarket or shopping mall. It can also mean a demand by consumers for certain goods.

In a **market economy**, the means of production are privately owned. Moreover, individual consumers, not the government, make economic decisions according to the principles of supply and demand. The United States can serve as an example of a market economy. A market economy is also called capitalism or free enterprise. In **capitalism**, individuals put their capital, or money, into businesses in hopes of making a profit. This profit motive is what influences people to take the risk of starting a business enterprise.

In a system of **free enterprise**, people enjoy economic freedoms. These include the freedom of individuals to own their own property, to go into business for themselves, and to buy and sell things to make a profit. Business owners are free to compete with others. Competition helps determine prices. Since consumers have freedom of choice, they are likely to choose the product that offers the best quality at the lowest price.

The price of food and other goods may be low in the Soviet Union, but people often have to spend hours in line to make their purchases.

How is the free enterprise system different than a command economy?

While the United States is primarily a market economy, it also combines features of other economic systems. For example, the federal, state, and local governments play a large role in regulating and promoting the American economy. Various government agencies regulate businesses to ensure that they sell safe products, that they do not pollute the environment, and that they do not cheat consumers. (You will learn more about the role of government in the American economy in Chapter 19.)

The U.S. government also promotes the economy by providing services to businesses and consumers. For example, the federal and state governments have built extensive highway systems that have helped promote travel and the transportation of goods. The government also owns and operates some businesses itself, such as the U.S. Postal Service and Amtrak, the federally owned passenger rail system.

The U.S. economy can be considered a mixed economy. A mixed economy is one in which most of the means of production are privately owned, but the government also plays an important role in guiding and regulating the economy. Mixed economies are the most common kinds of economies throughout the world. They are also the most efficient at providing consumers with goods and services. At the same time, government regulation prevents workers and consumers from being cheated and abused by business owners.

Socialist Economy

A **socialist economy** has features of both a market economy and a command economy. Like communism, **socialism** is an economic system in which the people, through their government, own the means of production. In a socialist economy, however, although the major factories and natural resources are owned by the government, smaller factories and stores are owned by individuals. Socialist economies are quite common in Europe. Great Britain, Sweden, and France all have socialist economies.

In addition to owning major industries, the governments of countries with socialist economies provide medical care for all their citizens.

PUNITIVE DAMAGES

When people bring civil suits, they can ask for two kinds of damages, compensatory damages and punitive damages. Compensatory damages is the amount that the plaintiff needs to pay for medical costs, lost income, damaged property, and other actual expenses. Punitive damages is an amount the jury may set to "punish" the defendant for negligence or wrongdoing.

Juries have been known to award punitive damages of as little as one dollar or as much as $20 million. In the case of *Browning-Ferris Industries* v. *Kelco Disposal*, the U.S. Supreme Court was asked to overturn a $6 million punitive damage award to Kelco Disposal as being "wildly excessive."

A Vermont jury had decided that Browning-Ferris had illegally tried to force its rival, Kelco Disposal, out of business. It awarded Kelco $51,000 in compensatory damages and $6 million—over a hundred times as much—in punitive damages.

Browning-Ferris argued that such a large punitive damage award was illegal under the Eighth Amendment to the Constitution which bars cruel and unusual punishment and "excessive fines." In 1989, the Court decided 7–2 not to overturn the punitive damage award. The Eighth Amendment, the Court said, was intended to prevent the government from imposing excessive punishments on citizens. It was not intended to restrict decisions in private lawsuits.

Punitive damages remains a concern for many businesses. Large punitive damage awards used to be very rare, but in recent years, many companies have been hit by multimillion dollar punitive damage awards. Insurance, investment, and news media companies have been among the hardest hit by these awards.

Plaintiffs, those bringing suits, also have reason to be wary of large punitive damage awards. In cases where one company is being sued by many different people, the first few plaintiffs whose suits are brought to trial may receive big awards. Those who file suit later, however, may find that little money remains. Some companies have been forced to go into bankruptcy by multiple claims.

Until and unless the Supreme Court reconsiders its refusal to limit punitive damages, some remedies do exist. At least six states limit the amount of punitive damages that may be awarded in civil suits. In other states, judges often reduce damage awards that they consider excessive.

Using Your Skills
1. What is the difference between compensatory and punitive damages?
2. Why did the Supreme Court rule against Browning-Ferris?
3. How can large punitive damage awards work against plaintiffs?

In a socialist economy, the government might own major businesses such as steel mills, coal mines, railways, and power companies. There is no competition among these government-owned industries. However, there can be a great deal of competition among smaller, privately owned businesses such as manufacturers of furniture and clothing and restaurants and retail stores.

As in a command economy, government-owned businesses in a socialist economy are operated not to make a profit, but to provide the goods and services the nation needs. The government, for example, might give financial support to an unprofitable steel mill to keep it producing. At the same time, privately owned businesses serve the consumer by responding to the principles of supply and demand, just as in a market economy.

Some countries have socialist economies but not democratic governments. Yugoslavia and China both have Communist governments and some form of socialist economy. In Yugoslavia, workers own and operate the factories where they work. In China, farmers and entrepreneurs in certain regions have been allowed to own their own small businesses, and foreign companies have been permitted to make and sell goods in China.

Traditional Economy

In a **traditional economy**, economic decisions are made according to traditions and customs handed down from one generation of people to another. In traditional economies, the people supply the goods they need by hunting, farming, gathering, and making things by hand. Traditional economies are largely untouched by technology. Farmers use the same methods their parents and grandparents did. The people make their clothing and tools and build their homes in the same way as their ancestors. Traditional economies are found among some rural groups in Africa, South America, and Asia.

SECTION REVIEW

Define the Words
command economy   free enterprise
communism   socialist economy
market economy   socialism
capitalism   traditional economy

Check the Facts
1. What are the main features of a command economy?
2. What economic freedoms are enjoyed in a free enterprise system?
3. In what ways is a socialist economy similar to a command economy? To a market economy?

Think About the Ideas
4. *Analyze.* What do you think are some of the advantages and disadvantages of a market economy?
5. *Evaluate.* In your opinion, which type of economic system is most favorable to an individual consumer? Explain.

★ ★

SECTION 3

Organization and Management

★ ★

VOCABULARY

single proprietorship	dividend
partnership	preferred stock
corporation	limited liability
incorporate	cooperative
stocks	nonprofit
stockholders	organization
common stock	

A new business must be organized and managed in a way that will help it produce goods or services as effectively and efficiently as possible. For example, as sole owners of a potato chip company, the Kellers make major decisions about the company. However, they also have managers who make decisions about specific aspects of the company, such as production, advertising, and shipping. The decisions these managers make have an important effect on the whole company. If a manager does not order enough potatoes, for example, the company will fall behind in production and lose sales and money as a result.

Businesses are organized and managed in three basic ways—single proprietorships, partnerships, and corporations. How a particular business is organized depends on its size, its purpose, and the number of owners.

Single Proprietorship

A **single proprietorship** is a business that is owned by a single individual. More than three-quarters of the businesses in the United States—over 11 million businesses—are single proprietorships. Single proprietorships are almost always small businesses, because very few individuals can afford to start a large business. Typical single proprietorships might include such businesses as gas stations, barbershops, restaurants, grocery stores, and newsstands.

Although owners of small businesses often need to work very long hours, they have the satisfaction of working for themselves.

Single proprietorships have both advantages and disadvantages. Single proprietors are their own bosses. They decide what to make or sell, how much to charge customers, and what hours to work. They also receive all of the profits when their businesses are successful. However, single proprietors must take all the risks of starting and operating a business. They provide all of the capital to start and run the business. They pay all the bills, hire all the employees, and usually must work long hours. If their business fails, they lose all of the money they put into it and must pay all of its debts. When the proprietor dies or retires, the business often comes to an end as well.

AMERICAN PROFILES

Wally Amos

Starting a new business is not easy. It takes a good idea, a good plan, and money to invest. One person who succeeded is Wally Amos—better known as Famous Amos, king of homestyle chocolate chip cookies.

Born in Tallahassee, Florida, Wally Amos went to live with his aunt in New York City when he was 12 years old. She was the first person to make him chocolate chip cookies. At age 17, he dropped out of school to join the Air Force. Four years later, Amos returned to New York City and eventually got a job in the mailroom of the William Morris Agency, a talent agency. After years of hard work, Amos rose from a mail clerk to become a talent agent for people in show business.

But Wally Amos wanted to start a business of his own—a cookie business. He used Ruth Wakefield's recipe for chocolate chip cookies and money from investors—the stars he had worked with as a talent agent. He also invested his own knowledge, skills, energy, and enthusiasm. In 1975, he opened a store in Los Angeles, and named his new business the Famous Amos Chocolate Chip Cookie Corporation.

Wally Amos's cookie business became a huge success. His story was featured in magazines and his business became nationally known. Amos wanted to share his success with others. One way he has done this is through the Literacy Volunteers of America, an organization devoted to helping people of all ages learn to read. Amos has been an active supporter and spokesperson for the organization. He has also made numerous visits to college campuses throughout the country, talking about the secrets of his success.

Using Your Skills
1. What is needed to start a business?
2. How did Wally Amos's experience at the William Morris Agency contribute to his success as an entrepreneur?

Partnerships

A **partnership** is a business owned by two or more people. Doctors and lawyers often form partnerships. Construction companies, auto dealerships, and advertising firms are also frequently partnerships. While partnerships tend to be larger than single proprietorships, they still are usually somewhat small businesses.

People set up partnerships for various reasons. Sometimes it is to pool their capital, because individually they don't have enough money to start a business. People may also form partnerships to combine different skills. For example, one partner in a clothing business may be a talented designer while the other is a good manager with a head for business. People often form partnerships to share the workload and the duties and decision-making required by a business.

In a partnership, the partners also share the profits and financial risks. If the business should fail, each partner is only responsible for his or her share of the losses and debts, not the whole amount. When people form a partnership, they usually sign a written partnership agreement that spells out the responsibilities and rights of each partner.

One of the greatest disadvantages of partnerships involves disagreements among partners. If partners have a serious falling out and want to end the partnership, it can be very complicated to do so. Disagreements over who will get what may have to be resolved in court. Another disadvantage is that if one partner dies, a new partnership must be legally formed.

Steven Jobs, right, and his partner, Stephen Wozniak, built the Apple Computer company from a small partnership into one of the most successful computer companies in the world.

Corporations

A **corporation** is a large business that has many owners. Starting and operating a large business requires more money than most individuals or even groups of partners can afford. However, a business of this sort can be set up and maintained by forming a corporation.

Suppose several entrepreneurs wanted to start a new computer company. The first thing they would do is **incorporate**. To do this, they apply for a charter from the state, which gives them permission to form a corporation. Incorporation gives a company some of the legal rights and obligations of individuals. For example, a corporation can enter into contracts and buy and sell property. But it must also pay taxes and it can be sued.

The entrepreneurs who formed the new corporation decide that they need $5 million to build a factory, purchase machinery, and hire workers. As a corporation, the company can raise this money by selling shares of ownership—shares in the business—to hundreds or thousands of people. The shares of ownership are called **stocks** and the people who buy them are called **stockholders**. When a person buys shares in a company, he or she is said to be investing money in the company. Like entrepreneurs, investors are gambling that the company will make a profit for them.

People who buy stock in a company receive stock certificates that indicate they are partial owners of the corporation.

An investor who buys stock in a corporation can share in its profits and its risks. Most people who invest in a corporation buy **common stock**. If the company makes a profit for the year, the owner of common stock receives a share of the profit called a **dividend** for each share of stock owned. The size of the dividend on common stock depends on how large a profit the company makes. Some people buy **preferred stock**. These people receive a dividend of a fixed amount each year the company makes a profit, and they are paid before common stockholders. Some investors buy corporate bonds. In effect, these people loan the company money. In return, the company pays them interest each year for the use of their money whether or not the company makes a profit.

Corporations offer several advantages. One advantage is that the risk is shared by a great many people. For example, if the company should fail, a stockholder who has invested $500 in the company can only lose that $500 and no more. This is called **limited liability**. Another advantage is that the death of an owner—a stockholder—does not interrupt the operation of the company. Even after an owner dies, his or her shares of stock continue to exist. This stock can be inherited by the stockholder's heirs or sold to other people.

A business with hundreds or thousands of owners must have a system for making important decisions. Corporations are run by a board of directors. This board makes important policy decisions and hires managers to oversee the day-to-day operations of the company. One way that stockholders can take part in a corporation is to attend its annual stockholders' meeting. Any stockholder can come to these meetings and question the company's directors. The stockholders can also elect the directors by voting their shares of stock. This means that a stockholder may cast one vote for each share of common stock owned. Thus stockholders can elect new directors if they do not like the way the company is being run.

People who buy the stock of a corporation own part of the company, and they can express their opinions about how the company is run at the annual stockholders meeting.

Cooperatives and Nonprofit Organizations

In addition to the three major types of business organization, there are two other ways in which people organize to conduct business.

A **cooperative** is an organization in which a number of people join together to share the costs of a business or to buy and sell goods at the lowest possible prices. Many farmers form cooperatives so they can share in the costs of storing and shipping their products.

Groups of consumers also form cooperatives. The most common kinds are food stores, preschools, and apartment buildings. A cooperative food store, for example, can sell food to members more cheaply than retail stores because it is not in business to make a profit. Cooperatives are often small enough so that all members can vote on business decisions. Sometimes, like a corporation, a cooperative may elect a board of directors to make decisions.

Nonprofit organizations are similar to cooperatives. They are in business to provide goods or services, not to make a profit. As a result, they can also charge lower fees for their goods or services. Many nonprofit organizations are charities, such as the American Red Cross or American Cancer Society, whose purposes are to collect money to help the victims of disasters, to pay for research, or to educate the public about their causes. Nonprofit corporations are usually run by boards of directors.

The American Red Cross, like other nonprofit organizations, uses the money it raises to provide important services to the public.

SECTION REVIEW

Define the Words

single proprietorship	dividend
partnership	preferred stock
corporation	limited liability
incorporate	cooperative
stocks	nonprofit
stockholders	organization
common stock	

Check the Facts
1. What are the three basic ways in which businesses are organized?
2. What are the advantages and disadvantages of a partnership?
3. How do corporations raise money?

Think About the Ideas
4. *Analyze.* Do you think buying stock in a corporation is a good way to invest money? Why or why not?

CITIZENSHIP SKILLS

How to Locate Government Figures

Statistics are facts expressed as numbers. You can find statistics on almost any topic. For example, you can find out the average life expectancy in the United States in 1920 (54 years of age), the amount of money the federal government spent on education in 1987 ($16.8 billion), or the average price of a gallon of gasoline in 1975 and 1985 ($.57 and $1.12).

One of the best sources of numerical facts about the United States is the *Statistical Abstracts of the United States*. It is published annually by the U.S. Department of Commerce and the Bureau of the Census. Locating facts in the *Statistical Abstracts of the United States* is easy. The table of contents shows the categories into which information is divided, and the index explains where to locate statistics on specific topics for each category. For example, in the table of contents you will find a section on Health and Nutrition, which contains a subsection on Food Con-

sumption. In the index under Food Consumption, you will find identification numbers and titles of all the tables of data on that topic. You use the identification numbers to locate the tables in the book. When you locate a table, you will discover that it further divides the topic and gives information that helps you interpret the figures.

The government also publishes the *Historical Statistics of the United States from Colonial Times to 1970*, and the *State and Metropolitan Area Data Book*. The *United States Government Manual* also has statistics, as well as descriptions of all current government agencies.

You can find statistics in other government documents as well. The U.S. Government Printing Office (GPO) in Washington, D.C., publishes thousands of books and pamphlets on American life, government, and the economy. You can locate these government reference materials by using a brochure called the *Sub-*

ject Bibliography Index. This index provides a list of about 270 separate subject bibliographies of GPO publications. Each of these subject bibliographies gives basic information about all GPO publications in a particular subject area, such as national parks or solar energy.

Many of these government reference materials can be found in the reference section of your library.

Your library will also have general almanacs that include both statistics and other information. The *World Almanac* and the *Information Please Almanac*, for example, include profiles on the world's nations, facts about U.S. states and cities, information on famous people, and data on many other topics.

Using Your Skills
1. What is one of the best sources of statistics about the United States?
2. Why is statistical information important?

CHAPTER 18 REVIEW

* *

MAIN POINTS

★ Economics is the study of how goods and services are made, bought, sold, and used.

★ In the American economic system, the principles of supply and demand determine what and how much will be produced and how much things will cost.

★ The production of any good or service requires four elements—capital, resources, labor, and management.

★ There are four basic types of economic systems—the command economy, market economy, socialist economy, and traditional economy. Economic decisions are made differently in each of these systems.

★ In a capitalist or free enterprise system, people can own property, make a profit, compete with others, and choose the goods they want to buy.

★ Businesses are organized and managed in three basic ways—single proprietorships, partnerships, and corporations.

★ Some businesses—cooperatives and nonprofit organizations—are formed to provide goods and services at low cost rather than to make a profit.

WORDS IN REVIEW

Choose the word or phrase from the list below that best completes each sentence. Write the missing words on a separate sheet of paper.

entrepreneur   profit
supply and demand   command economy
market economy   socialism
corporation   dividends
capital   limited liability

1. In a _____ the means of production are owned by individuals.

2. After forming a _____, the owners sold stock to raise capital.

3. In a capitalist system, most prices are determined by the forces of _____.

4. The owner's _____ was a result of sharing risk among many people.

5. The company had a very good year and was able to pay _____ to all the stockholders.

6. After investing her time and money to start the business, the _____ was happy to see the business prosper.

7. In a _____, the government owns all the means of production.

8. Although the man had a good idea, skills, and energy, he lacked the _____ needed to start a business.

9. After the partners paid their bills and taxes they found they had made a nice _____ for the year.

10. Under a system of _____, the government owns some major businesses and individuals own smaller businesses.

FACTS IN REVIEW

1. What factors affect decisions about what and how much to produce?

2. How do supply and demand affect each other?

3. How does a division of labor affect production?

4. What is the function of marketing and what does it involve?

CHAPTER 18 REVIEW

5. Identify and describe four different types of economic systems.

6. What are the main features of a command economy?

7. What is a "mixed economy"?

8. What are the disadvantages and advantages of a single proprietorship?

9. What are some of the reasons why people form partnerships?

10. What are some of the advantages of a corporation?

THINKING ABOUT THE AMERICAN ECONOMIC SYSTEM

1. *Analyze.* How can the supply of resources affect a country's economy?

2. *Evaluate.* Which type of economic system do you think provides the most stable economy? Explain.

3. *Analyze.* Do you think cooperatives and non-profit organizations serve a useful purpose? Explain.

COLLECTING INFORMATION ABOUT A CORPORATION

Choose a large corporation to research. When was it formed? Where is the corporate head-quarters? How large is the corporation today? How many employees does it have? What is its annual income? How many stockholders are there? Most corporations publish annual reports, which have much of this information. You can request a copy from the corporation.

WRITING ABOUT STARTING A BUSINESS

You want to start a business of your own and need capital to finance it. But in order to get capital, you need to prepare a business plan. Your plan should include a description of your product or service and an explanation of why you think the product or service is needed, how you plan to make or provide it, how your business will be run, what resources you need, and how you plan to use the capital you are requesting. Write a plan for your business.

INTERPRETING A FLOW CHART

Look at the flow chart on page 414. This chart follows the course of a potato chip business from the farm to the store. What roles does management play? Which people are involved in the distribution process? What different types of activities do they perform? What factors are likely to influence the sale of a particular brand of potato chip?

FOCUSING ON YOUR COMMUNITY

Find out about the different types of businesses in your community. What are the major businesses? What products or services do they provide? Which businesses employ the most people? Are there many single proprietorship businesses in your community? What types of goods or services do they provide? Which corporations have their main headquarters in the community? Prepare an oral report for the class.

CHAPTER 19

* *

Government and the Economy

OBJECTIVES

After you have studied this chapter, you will be able to:

★ Explain the business cycle and how it can be affected by government.

★ Identify ways in which the government measures the economy and explain the importance of these economic indicators.

★ Explain why and how the government regulates business.

★ Identify ways in which the government can assist businesses.

★ Describe the development of labor unions and explain their purpose and how they try to achieve their goals.

★ Explain the role of banks and how government regulates the banking industry.

SECTIONS

1 Measuring the Economy
2 Government and Business
3 Government and Labor
4 Government and Banking

INTRODUCTION

In 1981, the nation's air traffic controllers, the people who guide airplanes into and out of airports, went on strike. However, because they were federal employees, this action was illegal. President Ronald Reagan had the authority to fire the controllers, and that is exactly what he did. More than 10,000 controllers lost their jobs.

Reagan's action greatly affected the nation's economy. It created a shortage of trained air traffic controllers and disrupted airport operations for years afterward. On the other hand, the President upheld the nation's law. He also prevented a lengthy strike that would have paralyzed the airline industry and disrupted the economy. People still debate whether Reagan's action was right or wrong. Nevertheless, the point is that he had the authority to act as he did.

In the United States, the federal and state governments make many decisions that affect the nation's economy. These decisions are aimed at improving the economy and solving economic problems, as well as protecting the interests of the nation's citizens.

★ ★

SECTION 1

Measuring the Economy

★ ★

VOCABULARY

business cycle
recession
depression
fiscal policy
monetary policy

Gross National
   Product (GNP)
standard of living
inflation

The American economy continually changes as consumers, entrepreneurs, and the government make economic decisions. In order for the government to help the economy operate efficiently, it must know what the economy is doing. For this reason, the government regularly measures the economy and compares its performance to other years.

The Business Cycle

The ups and downs of the economy are known as the **business cycle**. This cycle has several phases, or parts. The first phase is when the economy is improving and business activity is increasing. During this period of expansion, businesses produce more goods and hire more employees, and people buy more goods and services. This phase is often called a period of prosperity.

The second phase takes place when economic activity has reached its peak. Businesses are working at full capacity and stores are selling in record amounts. Eventually, this boom period slows down and the economy enters its third phase. During this period of decline, people buy fewer goods and services than before. Companies do not sell as many goods, so they cut back on production and lay off workers. Some companies may be forced to go out of business.

During the fourth phase of the business cycle, production is at its lowest point and unemployment is very high. Most people have less money to spend on goods and services. Such a slowdown of economic activity is often called a **recession**. Eventually, however, the economy will enter a new expansion phase, and the business cycle will continue its ups and downs.

The model of the business cycle can help experts predict what will happen to the economy. Unfortunately, no one can predict how long a particular phase will last or how good or bad the economy will get. Sometimes, for example, a recession lasts for a long period of time and the economy becomes very bad. A severe recession is called a **depression**. The worst depression in the United States was the Great Depression, which began in 1929 and lasted until the start of World War II in 1941.

This illustration shows the four phases of a typical business cycle. When is a depression part of the business cycle?

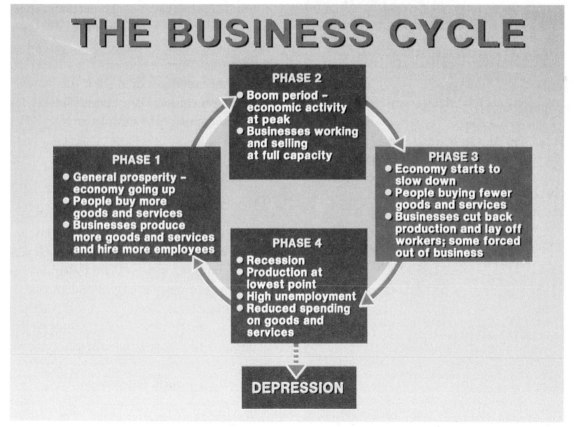

THE BUSINESS CYCLE

PHASE 1
- General prosperity – economy going up
- People buy more goods and services
- Businesses produce more goods and services and hire more employees

PHASE 2
- Boom period – economic activity at peak
- Businesses working and selling at full capacity

PHASE 3
- Economy starts to slow down
- People buying fewer goods and services
- Businesses cut back production and lay off workers; some forced out of business

PHASE 4
- Recession
- Production at lowest point
- High unemployment
- Reduced spending on goods and services

DEPRESSION

During the Great Depression of the 1930's, many people lost their jobs when businesses failed. People had to rely on food from the government and relief agencies.

THE GREAT DEPRESSION AND GOVERNMENT INVOLVEMENT During the Great Depression, thousands of businesses were forced to close and millions of people were unemployed. Families lost their homes and farms because they had no money to pay their mortgages. Banks failed and people lost their life savings. Millions of people were hungry and homeless.

Until the Great Depression, the government was not involved very much in the economy. Many people felt that the economy could take care of itself without government interference. However, in the early 1930's, the economy was so terrible that the government had to act.

When Franklin Delano Roosevelt took office as President in 1933, his administration took a number of steps to get the country back on its feet. Roosevelt's program, called the New Deal, put millions of people to work on government projects such as building dams, parks, hospitals, and schools. The government also provided low-cost loans so people could purchase homes, and it started the Social Security fund, which provided people with income during their retirement.

Many of the government agencies set up during the Depression still exist today. While these agencies cannot prevent economic slowdowns, they do help soften the effects of a long-term recession. The government also uses two other methods—fiscal policy and monetary policy—to help regulate the business cycle.

FISCAL AND MONETARY POLICIES Fiscal policy refers to the way in which the government taxes citizens and spends money. The government can use different fiscal policies to affect the business cycle. For example, in a recession, the government may spend more money. By spending money—to buy new fighter jets, for instance—the government helps keep companies in business and workers employed. People with jobs have money to spend on goods and services, which increases demand. With factories producing more goods to meet the demand of both government and consumers, the economy begins to expand and comes out of its recession. The government might accomplish the same thing by cutting taxes. A tax cut is a fiscal policy that also stimulates production, by giving people more money to spend on goods and services. The government can also use fiscal policy to control the peaks of the business cycle, by raising taxes or spending less.

Monetary policy refers to the way in which the government regulates the amount of money in circulation. The Federal Reserve System, which acts as a bank for banks, has an important role in the government's monetary policy. When individuals or businesses need money, they go to the Federal Reserve System, or the "Fed," as it is called.

One way the Fed can regulate the nation's monetary policy is by raising or lowering the interest rates on its loans to commercial banks. A higher rate, for example, will mean that commercial banks will borrow less money. They, in turn, will have less money to lend to individuals and businesses. As a result, spending will decrease and the economy will slow down.

By using its powers, the Fed can increase the money supply during a recession, and thus help the economy expand. It can also control the peaks of the business cycle by reducing the money supply.

Measuring Economic Performance

The government makes studies of different parts of the economy on a regular basis to find out how the economy is doing. In examining the economy, government economists seek answers to such questions as: How many people are working this month? How much did consumers spend last year? How much money did the steel industry make last year? The answers to these questions are called economic indicators because they indicate how the economy is performing.

One of the important indicators economists use is the **Gross National Product**, or **GNP**. The GNP is the total value, in dollars, of all the goods and services produced in the nation each year. That is, it is the total value

During a period of inflation, consumers can afford to buy fewer goods than before. What can the Federal Reserve do to reduce inflation?

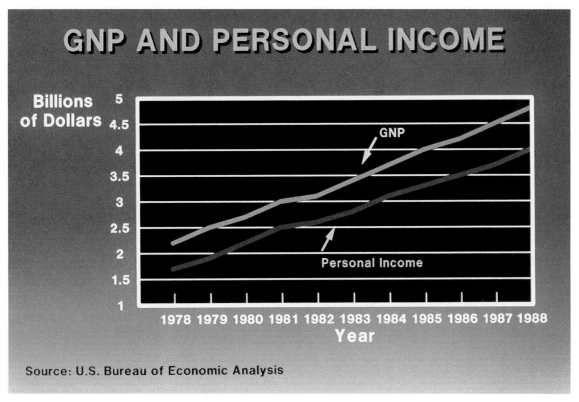

GNP AND PERSONAL INCOME

Billions of Dollars

Source: U.S. Bureau of Economic Analysis

This illustration shows the growth of the gross national product and personal income from 1978 to 1988. What happens to the GNP when the economy slows down?

of all the cars, planes, television sets, running shoes, toothbrushes, and so on produced. The GNP also includes all the money spent on doctors, restaurant meals, car repairs, and other services performed during the year.

The GNP tells economists how many goods and services are being produced, how much consumers are spending, and how these factors compare to other years. If the GNP is higher this year than last year, then the economy is expanding. If it is lower, the economy is slowing down. Economists study GNP figures over a period of years to analyze patterns in the business cycle. They also use the GNP to compare the economic performance of the United States with that of other countries.

Economists look at other economic indicators, such as personal income and disposable income, as well. Personal income is the total amount of money a person makes each year. Disposable income refers to the money people have to spend on goods and services after their taxes are paid. These indicators help tell economists about people's **standard of living**, their quality of life based on the amount of goods and services they can purchase and leisure time they have.

Inflation

During the business cycle, people's standard of living is sometimes threatened by inflation. **Inflation** is a general rise in the prices of most goods and services. Remember that when the economy is expanding, people have more money to purchase goods and services. As a result, the demand for those goods and services increases. As the demand increases, prices rise because people are competing to buy things. During a period of inflation, the prices of almost all goods and services will rise, and people have to keep paying more and more for the things they buy. Since their money buys less than it did before, their standard of living declines.

Sometimes, companies are able to pay their workers more to help them keep up with inflation. However, inflation is especially hard on retirees and other people with fixed incomes, because their incomes do not increase along with prices. Inflation also hurts people who save money. Their savings will probably buy less when they go to spend it.

The government tries to control inflation to prevent a decline in the standard of living. As you read earlier, government may try to slow the economy by raising the interest rate. This makes it more expensive to borrow money and puts a damper on economic activity (see page 436 on the Federal Reserve System). The government may also reduce the amount of money in circulation by raising taxes and cutting its own spending. Businesses, workers, and consumers can help control inflation as well. When businesses and workers increase their productivity (pro-

This map shows Federal Reserve Districts and the location of each district's Federal Reserve Bank. Who are the customers of Federal Reserve Banks?

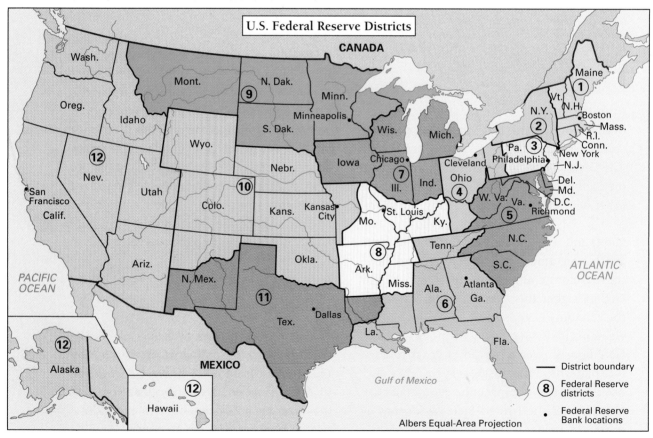

duce more goods) so that supply is greater than demand, prices drop. And when consumers save more money and spend less, this also reduces demand and causes a decrease in prices.

Controlling the economy is a complicated balancing act. Sometimes, an action the government takes to control one aspect of the economy has other, unavoidable consequences. For example, actions that help reduce inflation can also increase unemployment. The economy is very complex and changes constantly. Economic experts usually have different views on the course of action the government should take to keep the economy in good shape.

SECTION REVIEW

Define the Words

business cycle
recession
depression
fiscal policy
monetary policy

Gross National
    Product (GNP)
standard of living
inflation

Check the Facts

1. Describe the four phases of the business cycle.
2. In what ways can the government try to regulate the business cycle?
3. How does inflation affect people's standard of living?

Think About the Ideas

4. *Evaluate.* What is the importance of using economic indicators to measure economic performance?

★ ★

SECTION 2

Government and Business

★ ★

VOCABULARY

laissez-faire   trust
monopoly   conglomerate
merger   deregulation

At the beginning of the 1800's, most American businesses were small family-run concerns that made and sold a few goods. By the end of the 1800's, however, many businesses had become enormous, multimillion dollar enterprises. During this time, the government took a **laissez-faire** approach to businesses. (*Laissez-faire* is a French phrase that means to "allow to do.") In a laissez-faire economy, the government lets businesses do what they want and does not interfere. But in this century, the government has become more involved in regulating businesses.

The Growth and Regulation of Monopolies

As businesses grew larger, many became monopolies. A **monopoly** exists when one company or small group of people control the supply of all, or most of, a particular good or service. With a monopoly, there is little or no competition. Consumers, therefore, have no choice if they want to buy a product provided by a monopoly. For example, if a company has a monopoly of the sugar industry, anyone who wants sugar must buy it from that company. Because it has no competitors, a monopoly can produce goods of poorer quality or charge higher prices than it would if it had to compete with other companies.

Monopolies are formed in one of two ways—mergers or trusts. In a **merger**, two or more companies agree to join together and form one large company. A **trust** is when several companies remain separate, but have only one board of directors to make decisions for all the companies. Instead of competing, the companies cooperate in making decisions about their products. One of the best known trusts was the Standard Oil Trust, organized by John D. Rockefeller in the 1880's. Standard Oil controlled every aspect of the oil business—drilling, shipping, refining, and selling.

As monopolies grew stronger and competition decreased, the federal government began to take steps to regulate them. In 1890, Congress passed the Sherman Antitrust Act, which outlawed monopolies. Unfortunately, the law was very vague and therefore difficult to enforce. In 1914, Congress enacted a new law, the Clayton Antitrust Act, to correct the problems of the Sherman Act. The Clayton Act was easier to enforce because it listed specific business activities that were illegal. To help enforce the Clayton Act, Congress also created the Federal Trade Commission (FTC). The FTC could investigate businesses to determine whether they were monopolies and could order them to stop breaking the law. Today, the FTC still

The government passed legislation regulating trusts and monopolies. Why are the trusts represented as pigs in the cartoon?

"ISN'T IT JUST POSSIBLE THAT I'M OVERDOING THIS BUSINESS?"

enforces the Clayton Act and several other laws as well. It investigates charges of false advertising, makes sure companies label their products truthfully, and protects consumers against unfair business practices.

Monopolies and Regulation Today

Some monopolies still exist today. For example, the people of a community can only buy their electricity, water, or cable television service from one company. These companies are called public utilities because they provide services to everyone in a community. Public utilities are legal monopolies. They are allowed to exist because it is cheaper and more efficient to let only one company provide such services to a community. Public utilities, however, are closely regulated by the government. Almost each state has a commission or agency that monitors the utility companies in the state. If a company wants to raise its prices or change its services, it must first get permission from the state commission.

Sometimes, even legal monopolies are broken up. In 1982, the American Telephone and Telegraph Company (AT&T) was forced to break up its virtual monopoly on local telephone services throughout the United States. The government felt that competition would bring consumers lower prices and improved services.

The government also keeps a close eye on conglomerates. A **conglomerate** is formed by the merger of companies that supply a variety of different goods and services. For example, a communication conglomerate may own several newspapers, printing plants, paper mills, and television stations. Another conglomerate may own hotels, airlines, cereal companies, clothing stores, and so on. The danger with a conglomerate is that it might gain too large a share of a part of the economy and be able to control prices and competition. When that happens, the government can step in and break up the conglomerate.

For many years, the government closely regulated a number of important industries that were not monopolies or conglomerates. It did this to protect the interests of consumers. For example, trucking companies, airlines, and banks were regulated, and had to provide services and set prices according to rules established by the government. In the late 1970's and 1980's, some of the nation's leaders felt that the government was interfering too much in these industries. They felt that **deregulation**, removing government restrictions, would better serve the public by increasing competition. In the case of the airlines, the immediate effect of deregulation was to stimulate competition, which led to lower prices. However, deregulation also resulted in the merger of many airlines, the elimination of flights to many out-of-the-way destinations, and, after a while, in the raising of air fares again.

For many years, trucking companies were regulated and prices were set according to rules established by the government.

Government Assistance to Business

The government's relationship with business is not limited to regulating and restricting. Various government departments and agencies also provide services to businesses. For example, farmers can learn about soil conditions from the Soil Conservation Service, fishermen can find out about ocean weather conditions from the National Weather Service, and a business owner can get help selling goods to Italy from the Department of Commerce.

The Department of Commerce also includes the Bureau of the Census, which compiles records on the nation's population.

This data is very useful to businesses. Census records tell a great deal about consumers, such as where people live, how much they earn, and how many children they have. Business can use this information to help decide where to locate a factory, shopping mall, or movie theater.

Another federal agency, the Small Business Administration, helps people start new businesses. It advises them on how to go about setting up and operating a business, and also makes low-cost loans to help them get their businesses underway.

SECTION REVIEW

Define the Words

laissez-faire   trust
monopoly   conglomerate
merger   deregulation

Check the Facts
1. Why are monopolies a threat to consumers?
2. What did the federal government do to help regulate monopolies and trusts?
3. What types of assistance does the government provide to business?

Think About the Ideas
4. *Evaluate.* What are the advantages of monopolies?

In the past, most agricultural land was owned and farmed by families. Today, most farmland is controlled by large corporations.

* *

SECTION 3

Government and Labor

* *

VOCABULARY

labor union   open shop
collective bargaining   mediation
strike   arbitration
closed shop

The nation's work force is an important part of the economy. Workers not only produce goods and services, but also use their wages to buy the goods and services that are available. Because of their importance, government takes a special interest in workers and in their relation to businesses.

The Growth of Unions

For much of the 1800's, the nation's workers were treated very badly. Wages were low, and working conditions were poor and often dangerous. Workers who complained were fired and quickly replaced with others. Many workers began to band together to try to get better working conditions, shorter hours, and higher pay. They formed organizations of workers called **labor unions** to achieve their goals.

The first groups of workers to form unions were crafts workers—skilled workers such as plumbers, shoemakers, and carpenters who worked at specific trades. In 1886, many different craft, or trade, unions joined together to form a large association of unions called the American Federation of Labor (AFL). Within 15 years, the AFL had grown to nearly half a million members.

In the meantime, factory and mine workers began to form unions called industrial unions. These unions were organized not by craft, but by factory or industry. For example, people who worked in a textile factory could join that factory's union regardless of what type of work they did. These industrial unions also formed an association of unions, which was called the Congress of Industrial Organizations (CIO). In 1955, the AFL and CIO joined together to become the AFL-CIO, which represents more than 100 unions and 16 million workers. There are also many other unions that are independent of the AFL-CIO.

Labor-Management Relations

Once workers had formed unions, they had to find ways to convince employers to raise wages and improve working conditions. Business owners often resisted the unions' demands, however, because paying higher wages or buying safer equipment would force them to raise the prices of their products or reduce their own profits. In addition, business owners could no longer arrange hours and wages with individual workers. Instead, they had to negotiate conditions and terms of employment with representatives of the union. This kind of negotiation is called **collective bargaining**.

If a business owner rejected a union's demands, union members might **strike**, or refuse to work. Striking workers usually formed a picket line, or a kind of human fence, at the entrance to the business. The purpose of this picketing was to prevent non-union workers from entering and taking the strikers' jobs. Striking and picketing are still the major methods unions use to force companies to negotiate with them. In addition, unions might call for a work slowdown, in which workers perform their jobs so slowly that production decreases.

Business owners quickly developed ways of getting back at striking workers. In some cases, they went to court and obtained injunctions. With these court orders, they could use the police, and sometimes even federal troops, to break up a strike. Companies would also keep blacklists of the names of union leaders and strikers. These blacklists would be sent to other companies. When union workers went looking for new jobs, these other companies would often refuse to hire them. Sometimes, a company might simply lock its doors and wait until the workers ran out of money and had to return to work.

Today, companies and unions still use collective bargaining to settle their disputes. In addition to higher wages, unions often seek other benefits such as medical, dental, and life insurance, longer paid vacations, more sick days, and safer working conditions. Unions are also very concerned about job security. They want to ensure that members can only be fired or laid off under certain conditions.

Government Actions in Labor-Management Relations

During the early years of the labor movement, many strikes and lockouts were very violent. By the 1930's, the government had moved into the role of referee between labor and management. In 1935, Congress enacted the National Labor Relations Act. This law guaranteed the right of all workers to join a union. It also created a government agency, the National Labor Relations Board (NLRB),

When union leaders are not able to secure better wages and benefits for their members, they may call a strike to force a company to negotiate with the union.

which would judge the fairness of actions by employers and unions.

In 1947, Congress passed the Taft-Hartley Act, which imposed some limits on unions. The Taft-Hartley Act banned closed shops and featherbedding. A **closed shop** is a factory or business in which workers cannot be hired unless they are union members. Featherbedding refers to a union practice that forces a company to employ more workers than are needed. However, the law did allow union shops. In a union shop, workers do not have to be union members to be hired, but they must join the union within 30 days to keep their jobs.

Many states now have right-to-work laws, which guarantee that no one may be forced to join a union. These states only allow **open shops**, in which workers are free to choose whether or not to join a union. Unions do not like open shops because non-union workers receive the benefits that the unions have negotiated for their own members, without having to pay union dues or support the union.

Labor Unions Today

Labor unions are not as strong as they once were. In some cases, unions have lost power because industries in which unions were prominent—such as steel and automaking—have become less important to the American economy. In other cases, businesses have moved to areas of the country where there are no unions or unions are weak.

Nonetheless, labor unions are still a significant factor in the economy. In the 1960's, Cesar Chavez formed the United Farm Workers union and organized the migrant farm workers who harvest the nation's food crops.

AFFIRMATIVE ACTION

One of the most important results of the Civil Rights movement of the 1960's was the development of affirmative action programs. The purpose of these programs was to give an advantage to minority groups and women, who had long been denied the educational and employment opportunities of white males.

Affirmative action programs took many forms. All-white, all-male fire departments were required to hire a certain number of women and blacks. Contractors working on public projects had to use a certain percentage of minority subcontractors and workers. For some jobs, blacks, Hispanics, and women had to be hired and promoted before white men, even if they scored lower on

qualifying examinations. State-supported colleges and graduate schools were required to actively recruit minority students.

Supporters of affirmative action argue that women and minorities need special consideration to help them catch up in school and on the job. Before affirmative action, there were very few blacks and virtually no women in high-paying blue-collar jobs such as construction, or in police and fire departments. Today, blacks and women routinely fill many of those jobs.

Opponents of affirmative action argue that it results in reverse discrimination against white males. Many affirmative action programs establish quotas specifying numbers or percentages of minorities and women who must be hired. Quotas, the critics contend, violate the Constitutional principle of equal protection of the laws.

The Supreme Court has repeatedly upheld the constitutionality of affirmative action. Over the years, however, it has gradually limited the ways in which affirmative action can be used.

One important Court decision was in the case of *Regents of the University of California* v. *Bakke* in 1978. The university had reserved 16 out of 100 slots in each class of its

medical school for minorities. Allan Bakke, a white male, sued the school, claiming that he had been denied admission to medical school because of reverse discrimination. In a 5-4 decision, the court ruled that the university's quota system had denied Bakke equal protection of the laws.

The Court's recent rulings on affirmative action have set new limits on how such programs may be applied. For example, in the case of *City of Richmond* v. *Croson* (1989), the Court ruled that the city could not set aside a fixed percentage of public works money for minority contractors unless it could prove that there had been discrimination against minority contractors in the past. This ruling does not overturn affirmative action as a remedy for past discrimination. It will, however, make it more difficult for government agencies to carry out affirmative action programs in the future.

Using Your Skills
1. What is reverse discrimination?
2. Do you think it is fair to choose a female candidate over a male candidate who has scored higher on a job aptitude test? Why or why not?

LABOR UNIONS, 1955-1988

Percent of Union Workers in U.S.

30 29 28 27 26 25 24 23 22 21 20 19 18 17 16 15

1955 1960 1965 1970 1975 1980 1985 1988
Year

Source: U.S. Department of Labor

This chart shows the decline in union membership among American workers from 1955 to 1988. What factors contributed to this decline?

In recent years, unions have successfully organized many public and service employees such as hospital workers, restaurant workers, teachers, police, and fire fighters.

Strikes are far less common today than they were 10 or 15 years ago. In most cases, employers and unions prefer to settle disputes peacefully, through mediation and arbitration. In **mediation**, a third party listens to both sides and then suggests a solution, which is not binding on either side. If both sides accept the mediator's recommendation, the dispute is settled. **Arbitration** is similar to mediation except that both sides agree beforehand to accept the arbitrator's decision no matter what it may be.

SECTION REVIEW

Define the Words
labor union
collective bargaining
strike
closed shop
open shop
mediation
arbitration

Check the Facts
1. Why were labor unions formed?
2. What methods did employers use to get back at striking workers?
3. What actions did the government take in labor-management relations?

Think About the Ideas
4. *Analyze.* Do you think labor unions will continue to be an important force in America? Why or why not?

SECTION 4

Government and Banking

VOCABULARY

interest   cash reserve

collateral

Banking is a business that deals in money. It is a very large and important part of the American economy. Like business and labor, the banking industry is regulated by the federal government.

Banks Provide Services

Most people keep their money in a bank, either in a checking or savings account, or both. When depositors put money into a bank, they are, in effect, lending it to the bank. The bank can use this money to make loans and investments. In return, the bank pays its depositors **interest**, a fee for the use of their money. This interest is based on a percentage rate that varies depending upon the type of account and the state of the economy.

Of course, banks also lend people money to make purchases, such as a house or a car, that they could not usually pay for from their own savings. When people borrow money from a bank, they usually have to pledge something they own of equal value as **collateral**. For example, someone who wants to borrow $5,000 to buy a car might put up

$5,000 worth of stock shares as collateral. This collateral is used as a guarantee that the loan will be repaid. If the borrower fails to pay back the loan, the bank can recover its money by taking the collateral and selling it.

Borrowers must also pay interest on the money they borrow. In other words, they pay a fee to the bank for using its money just as the bank pays a fee to depositors for using their money.

Types of Banks

The most common types of banks in the United States are commercial banks. Commercial banks are banks that have charters, or licenses, from the federal government or state governments, which allows them to receive deposits and make loans. Banks chartered by the federal government are called national banks. Those chartered by state governments are called state banks. Commercial banks are usually large businesses with large cash reserves. A **cash reserve** is the amount of money that the government requires each bank to keep on hand in order to pay depositors who want to withdraw their money.

Another type of bank is a savings and loan association. Savings and loan associations, sometimes known as S&L's, are owned and operated by people who have shares in the S&L. Until recently, S&L's only offered savings accounts and loans. Most of their loans were long-term loans—usually 20 years or more—for the purpose of buying or building homes. Their activity was limited by government regulations. However, in 1980, the banking industry went through deregulation, and most government restrictions were removed. Today, savings and loans can offer all the services that commercial banks offer, such as checking accounts and safe deposit boxes.

During the savings and loan crisis, the House Banking Subcommittee held hearings to determine how much money would be needed to protect depositors' savings.

In the late 1980's, however, savings and loans in some parts of the country began to have financial problems. They had made bad loans with little or no collateral to guarantee them. The federal government was forced to provide funds to rescue the failing S&L's so that the banks' customers would not lose their savings. This S&L "bail out" cost the taxpayers billions of dollars.

Credit unions are a special kind of private bank that offer savings accounts and loans for their members. Credit unions are usually started by labor unions or businesses, and can be used only by members or employees.

Government and the Banking Industry

During the 1800's, many American banks lent out too much money and did not keep enough cash reserve. As a result, depositors sometimes lost faith in a bank and demanded their money back. This was called "a run on the bank." If the bank did not have enough money in reserve to pay its depositors, it might fail, and depositors who did not withdraw their money in time would lose their savings.

In 1913, Congress created the Federal Reserve System to put a stop to these bank failures. (You learned about the Federal Reserve System's role in monetary policy in the first section of this chapter.)

The Federal Reserve System set up one Federal Reserve Bank in each of 12 districts around the nation. All national banks were required to keep part of their cash reserves on deposit at a Federal Reserve Bank. Then, in the event of a run on the bank, the bank could use this cash reserve to meet its depositors' demands. Today, all banks are required to be part of the Federal Reserve system.

The Federal Reserve is, in effect, the government's bank. It is where the government deposits money and borrows money.

The Federal Reserve is also the bank for other banks. Individuals and companies cannot do business with Federal Reserve Banks. Commercial banks, however, may borrow money from the Federal Reserve to lend to their customers. Just like any other borrower, the bank must then pay interest to the Federal Reserve.

Despite the establishment of the Federal Reserve System, many banks failed in the 1930's during the Great Depression. In addition, many savings and loans failed during the 1980's.

To protect individual depositors from losing their life savings in cases like these, the federal government created the Federal Deposit Insurance Corporation (FDIC) for bank depositors and the Federal Saving and Loan Insurance Corporation (FSLIC) for savings and loan depositors. These two programs insure that depositors in member banks will be repaid up to $100,000 in the event that the bank fails.

SECTION REVIEW

Define the Words
interest   cash reserve
collateral

Check the Facts
1. What are some of the services banks provide?
2. Originally, how were savings and loan associations different from commercial banks?
3. Why did the government create the Federal Reserve System?

Think About the Ideas
4. *Analyze.* What do you think might be the advantages and disadvantages of deregulation of the banking industry?

Commercial banks keep cash reserves on deposit in the huge vaults of the Federal Reserve System.

CITIZENSHIP SKILLS

How to Read a Pie Graph

A pie graph, or a circle graph, shows the relationship of parts to each other and to a whole. In a pie graph, the circle represents the whole, or 100 percent. Sections of the pie—the wedges—represent parts or fractions of the whole. For example, half of the pie is 50 percent; a quarter of the pie is 25 percent.

In reading a pie graph, first look at the graph's title to determine what the whole circle represents. Then look at the different wedges, each of which is labeled on the graph or in the key. You can interpret the information on a pie graph by comparing the size of the wedges. Pie graphs are helpful because you can make comparisons easily by looking at the division of a whole into its parts, the size of each part, and the relationship of the parts to the whole.

The pie graph on this page shows the U.S. government's budget receipts for fiscal, or financial, year 1988, which runs from October 1, 1987, through September 30, 1988. The whole circle represents the total amount (100 percent) of money received by the government that year—more than $900 billion. The wedges of the circle represent the different sources of that money. "Other" is a category that lumps together sources of money that are too small to include as separate wedges. In this graph, "other" includes excise taxes and customs duties.

Using Your Skills

Look at the pie graph, then answer the following questions.

1. According to the graph, what were the sources of budget receipts for 1988?
2. What percent of the budget receipts came from corporate taxes?
3. What percent of the budget receipts came from social insurance taxes?
4. Which two budget categories made up about three quarters of the government's budget receipts?
5. From what category did the government receive the largest amount of money?

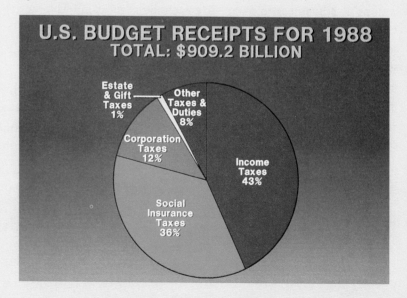

U.S. BUDGET RECEIPTS FOR 1988
TOTAL: $909.2 BILLION

Estate & Gift Taxes 1%
Other Taxes & Duties 8%
Corporation Taxes 12%
Income Taxes 43%
Social Insurance Taxes 36%

CHAPTER 19 REVIEW

★ ★

MAIN POINTS

★ The American economy can be described in terms of a business cycle, which consists of high and low phases of economic activity. The government can affect this business cycle through fiscal and monetary policy.

★ The government regularly measures certain economic indicators, such as the Gross National Product (GNP) and personal income, to determine the state of the economy.

★ The government regulates business in different ways in order to prevent unfair business practices, such as monopolies. The government also assists businesses by providing information and loans.

★ Labor unions developed as workers banded together to seek higher wages and better working conditions. These unions use methods such as collective bargaining and strikes to achieve their goals.

★ The government acts as a referee between unions and business to make sure each side is treated fairly.

★ Banks are businesses that provide people with services such as checking and savings accounts, and loans.

★ The Federal Reserve System was created to regulate banks and prevent them from losing depositors' money.

WORDS IN REVIEW

Choose the word or phrase from the list below that best completes each sentence. Write the missing words on a separate sheet of paper.

recession	merger
inflation	monopoly
deregulation	collective bargaining
strike	open shop
mediation	collateral

1. Since it had no competition, the _____ could charge whatever price it wanted for its product.

2. To get the loan from the bank, the couple had to use their car as _____.

3. With business very slow and unemployment increasing, the country seemed headed for a _____.

4. Because of _____, the company had to negotiate with union representatives and treat all union members the same.

5. The newspapers reported the _____ of the two publishing firms to form a new company.

6. As an _____, the company could choose to hire either union or non-union employees.

7. Prices kept going up and up because of the high rate of _____.

8. _____ removed many government controls from the industry.

9. After _____, the third party recommended that the company meet the union's demands.

10. Unable to reach agreement with the company, the union called for a _____.

CHAPTER 19 REVIEW

* *

FACTS IN REVIEW

1. How does the business cycle affect the economy?
2. What is the difference between fiscal policy and monetary policy?
3. What is the Federal Reserve System and how can it regulate the economy?
4. Why was the Sherman Antitrust Act difficult to enforce?
5. Why does the government allow public utility companies to operate as monopolies?
6. What methods can unions use to try to improve wages and working conditions?
7. What government actions have reduced the power of the unions?
8. In what ways can employers and unions try to settle disputes peacefully?
9. What is featherbedding?
10. How does the government protect depositors' savings in banks?

THINKING ABOUT GOVERNMENT AND THE ECONOMY

1. *Analyze.* What are the advantages and disadvantages in using fiscal and monetary policies to regulate the nation's economy?
2. *Analyze.* Do you think a laissez-faire approach to business is good for individuals and small companies? Explain.
3. *Analyze.* What factors do you think have helped lead to the decline of labor unions in the United States?

COLLECTING INFORMATION ABOUT ECONOMIC PERFORMANCE

Find out the latest figures for economic indicators such as the Gross National Product (GNP), per capita income, inflation rate, and economic growth rate. Compare these figures to those of 1960, 1970, and 1980.

WRITING ABOUT LABOR UNIONS

Labor unions have played an important part in improving the lives of workers. Write a short essay discussing the role of labor unions today and how their significance has changed because of changes in the nation's economy.

INTERPRETING A LINE GRAPH

Look at the line graph on page 437. Between which years did the GNP increase the most? How would you describe the growth of the GNP since 1978? How does it compare to the growth of personal income?

FOCUSING ON YOUR COMMUNITY

Some local governments initiate policies that will stimulate business activity in the community. This might include such things as tax breaks and development of better roads. Find out what types of assistance your local government provides businesses in the community. Also, investigate local policies that would either encourage or discourage businesses to locate in your community.

Financing Our Governments

OBJECTIVES

After you have studied this chapter, you will be able to:

★ Explain the basis for taxation in the United States and how taxation is limited.
★ List the basic characteristics of a "good" tax.
★ Identify the various sources of government revenue.
★ Describe the budget process and explain why budgets are necessary.
★ Explain the problems associated with a budget deficit and how governments attempt to deal with deficits.

SECTIONS

1 The Power to Tax
2 Types of Revenue
3 How Governments Spend their Money

Every government has expenses. It must pay the salaries of elected and appointed officials and public employees. Most important, it must pay for the services it provides—services such as enforcing laws, building roads, and protecting the health and welfare of its citizens.

Even a small local government is likely to spend at least $1 million each year on expenses. Large cities, such as Los Angeles, Chicago, or New York, may spend more than $1 billion a year. State governments spend from $1 to $60 billion annually.

Large as these amounts are, they seem small when compared to the expenses of the federal government. In 1987, the federal government spent over $1 trillion in a single year. Since then, it has continued to spend more than $1 trillion every year.

One trillion dollars is an unimaginably large number. If you were to spend $1 million every day, you would need nearly 3,000 years to spend $1 trillion. Raising, managing, and spending that much money in one year is an enormous task. It is also one of the most controversial aspects of government. Some people feel that governments should spend less. Others feel that governments should spend more. Moreover, almost everyone has different ideas about what this money should pay for. People's feelings about public spending generally reflect their deepest beliefs about the purpose of government.

* *

SECTION 1

The Power to Tax

* *

VOCABULARY

revenue   regressive tax

progressive tax

Governments, like individuals, must receive money before they can spend it. Money received by governments is generally called **revenue**. While governments get revenue from a variety of sources, the most important source is taxes. A tax is a sum of money that individuals or businesses are required to pay to the government. State and local governments usually get 60 to 80 percent of their revenue through taxes. The federal government gets nearly all of its revenue from taxes.

The Basis for Taxation

The power to tax is an important source of a government's strength. Laws and regulations are worthless unless a government can raise the money necessary to carry them out. For this reason, governments have almost always required their citizens to pay some form of taxes. For example, ancient Mesopotamian farmers had to give a portion of their crops to the government. Ancient Romans paid sales taxes, just as we do today.

Sometimes, governments abuse their power to tax. Many times throughout history, citizens have turned against their government because they believed their tax burden was unfair. One such revolt led to the American colonists' decision to declare independence from Great Britain in 1776.

When the American Revolution was over, citizens denied their new government the power to tax in order to avoid similar revolts. Under the Articles of Confederation, the government could request—but not demand—contributions from the states. The lack of ability to raise money was a major weakness of the Confederation government.

The U.S. Constitution, on the other hand, included provisions on the power of taxation. The writers of the Constitution realized that the federal government needed a reliable source of revenue in order to operate effectively. At the same time, they wanted to prevent Congress from abusing its power to tax, as the British Parliament had done. For this reason, they gave Congress a *limited* power to tax.

THE BIPARTISAN APPROACH

© 1989, Herblock, The Washington Post

The title "Bipartisan Approach" suggests that the President and Congress must work together to plan how the federal government will spend its money. Why is the list of where to save money blank?

Limits on Taxation

The writers of the Constitution gave Congress "the power to lay and collect taxes." However, they placed certain restrictions on this power to prevent abuses. They wanted to make sure that the people being taxed would have a voice in the tax law. For this reason, all tax bills must be introduced in the House of Representatives, where representation is based on population. They also wanted to be sure that the taxes would fall fairly on all citizens. For this reason, the Constitution requires that any tax imposed by the federal government must apply uniformly throughout the country, not just to one region.

In addition, the Constitution restricts the power of state governments to collect taxes. Unlike Congress, states are not permitted to tax interstate or foreign commerce. Also, as the result of an 1819 Supreme Court decision, states are not allowed to tax the federal government.

One of the most important limits on the taxation power of state governments is the Fourteenth Amendment. The amendment's guarantee of "equal protection of the laws" to all citizens prevents states from taxing one group of citizens more heavily than another—without good reason. For example, a state government may not require Republicans to pay heavier taxes than Democrats. It may, however, require wealthy people to pay more taxes than poor people.

Many state constitutions place further limits on taxation. These may include the kinds of taxes the state legislature can pass and how high those taxes can be. As you discovered in Chapter 14, local governments get their powers directly from state governments. Therefore, all restrictions on state taxation—whether found in the U.S. Constitution or in state constitutions—apply to local governments as well.

Principles of Taxation

No one enjoys paying taxes. Taxpayers complain less, however, when they feel that their government is collecting taxes fairly and using the money wisely. In 1776, the English economist Adam Smith developed four guidelines for taxation. According to modern economists, any tax system that follows these guidelines can be considered a "good" tax.

Adam Smith, an eighteenth-century English political economist and philosopher, included guidelines for fair taxation in his book The Wealth of Nations.

The first guideline is that taxes should be *based on a person's ability to pay*. In other words, wealthy people should be taxed at a higher rate than poor people. Such a tax, in which people who earn more money pay more taxes, is known as a **progressive tax**. A **regressive tax**, on the other hand, is one in which people pay the same amount no matter how wealthy or poor they are. A regressive tax places a heavier burden on the poor.

Smith's second guideline is that a tax should be *clear and straightforward*. Each person should be able to figure out exactly how much he or she must pay in taxes. When this guideline is followed, people can plan their finances wisely. They can determine how much money they will be able to spend, to save, and to invest.

The third guideline is that a tax should be *collected in the most convenient way possible*. A sales tax, for example, should be paid when the sale is made.

Smith's final guideline is that each tax should be *collected efficiently*. Whenever a government collects a tax, a small portion of the revenue goes to pay for the cost of tax collection. According to this guideline, collection costs should be kept as low as possible, so that more tax money can be spent for the public good.

Give an example of a tax that is collected in the most convenient way possible.

GUIDELINES FOR TAXATION

Taxes should be:
★ based on a person's ability to pay
★ clear and straightforward
★ collected in the most convenient way possible
★ collected efficiently
★ reasonable

Most economists add a fifth guideline that Adam Smith did not include. This guideline is that taxes should be *reasonable*. When taxes are high, people and businesses have less money to save and invest. Moreover, people may not work as hard, because they know they will have to pay the government a large portion of the money they earn. As a result, high taxes can sometimes damage an economy, and actually raise less money for the government than low taxes.

SECTION REVIEW

Define the Words

revenue   regressive tax

progressive tax

Check the Facts

1. Why did the writers of the Constitution limit the federal government's power to tax?
2. Describe three restrictions on the taxation powers of state governments.
3. Identify and explain five guidelines for good taxation.

Think About the Ideas

4. *Analyze.* What guidelines do you think should be used to determine whether a tax is "reasonable"? Explain.

* *

SECTION 2

Types of Revenue

* *

VOCABULARY

income tax	property tax
tax return	sales tax
exemption	excise tax
deduction	tariff
taxable income	

There is no such thing as a perfect tax. No single form of taxation can satisfy all of the guidelines you read about in the preceding lesson. For this reason, most governments use several different kinds of taxes to raise revenue. The advantages of one tax can help to make up for the disadvantages of another.

Income Taxes

An **income tax** is a tax on income—the money earned by an individual or business. The Sixteenth Amendment, passed in 1913, gave the government the power to levy, or collect, such a tax. Today, the federal government gets more than half its total revenue from income taxes. Most states have income taxes as well, and rely on these as an important source of revenue.

There are two types of income taxes—personal and corporate. Personal income

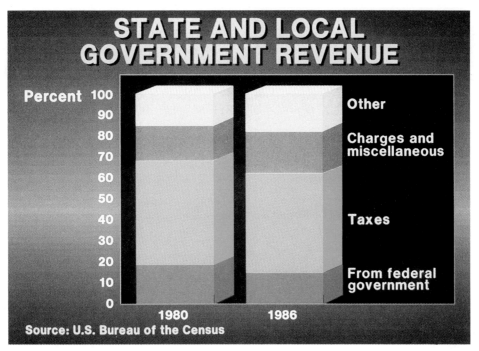

STATE AND LOCAL GOVERNMENT REVENUE

Percent

100
90
80
70
60
50
40
30
20
10
0

Other

Charges and miscellaneous

Taxes

From federal government

1980   1986

Source: U.S. Bureau of the Census

This graph shows the sources of state and local government revenue in 1980 and 1986. How does the federal government raise the money it gives to the states?

taxes are paid by individuals, based on the money they earn each year. Corporate income taxes are paid by corporations, based on their annual profits.

The deadline for paying personal income tax is generally April 15 of each year. By that date, each taxpayer must submit a form called a **tax return** to the Internal Revenue Service, the government's tax collector. To fill out the tax return, taxpayers must first figure out exactly how much income they received during the past year. Each taxpayer then subtracts a certain amount of money called an **exemption**. In 1989, the legal exemption allowed by the government was $2,000, plus an extra $2,000 for each dependent, or person supported by the taxpayer. For example, a taxpayer with an unemployed spouse would claim an exemption of $4,000.

A taxpayer may sometimes subtract additional amounts of money as well. These additional amounts are called **deductions**, and often include such things as medical expenses and charitable contributions. The amount that remains after the taxpayer has subtracted all possible exemptions and deductions is called **taxable income**. The taxpayer must pay the government an income tax based on a certain portion of this taxable income.

In order to make the payment and collection of personal income taxes more convenient, the federal and state governments have set up a system of tax withholding. Under this system, employers regularly subtract a certain portion of money from each employee's paycheck. This money is sent directly to the federal and state governments. As a result, most taxpayers owe only a small amount of income tax when they submit their tax returns. Some taxpayers may have too much money withheld from their paychecks.

Simplifying Taxes?

Whenever Congress overhauls the federal income tax system, the Internal Revenue Service (IRS) has to publish new tax forms to reflect the changes. After the Tax Reform Act of 1986, for example, the IRS promised new "simplified" tax forms for the 1987 tax year.

Instead, people found themselves buried in a blizzard of paper and stumped by dozens of complicated mathematical formulas. They had to fill out schedules A, B, C, D, and E. They had to read page after page of confusing instructions and practice on worksheets before tackling the tax form itself.

The new forms caused a lot of people to give up doing their own taxes. According to one economist, the new forms did not represent tax simplification but rather "tax complexification."

These taxpayers are entitled to a tax refund after submitting their tax returns.

The federal income tax and most state income taxes are progressive. That is, people with higher incomes must pay a greater percentage in taxes. For example, in 1989, an unmarried taxpayer whose taxable income was less than $18,550 had to pay 15 percent (or no more than $2,782.50) to the federal government. An unmarried taxpayer whose taxable income was between $18,550 and $44,900 had to pay 15 percent on the first $18,550 and 28 percent on the rest. The reason for this system is that people with lower incomes must spend a larger percentage of their earnings on necessities such as food and housing. People with higher incomes, on the other hand, generally have more money to spend on non-necessities. As a result, they can afford to take on a bigger share of the tax burden.

Property Taxes

A **property tax** is a tax based on the value of property. Governments usually define "property" to mean real estate, but personal items such as cars and jewelry may also be taxable. Property taxes are the primary source of revenue for local governments. Some state governments impose property taxes as well, as do many of the nation's school districts.

Before it can collect property tax, a government must send an assessor to examine a taxpayer's property. Using written reference material and past experience, the assessor decides what each piece of property is worth. Property tax is usually worked out as a certain percentage of the assessed value. This tax rate is set by the local government according to the needs of the community. In one community, it might be 4 percent

Taxes paid by owners of houses and other properties help pay for schools, local roads, and other services provided by local governments.

($2,000 on a house assessed at $50,000). In another, it might be only 2 percent ($1,000 on a house assessed at $50,000).

As the costs of government have increased, property owners have had to pay higher and higher property taxes. In recent years, many property owners have objected to paying these high taxes. In 1978, for example, California taxpayers voted to lower property taxes throughout the state. Voters in other states followed with similar "taxpayer revolts." As a result of this pressure to lower property taxes, many state and local governments have been forced to cut their spending drastically.

Sales Taxes

A **sales tax** is a tax placed on the sale of various products. It is paid by the purchaser at the time of purchase. The seller collects the sales tax and sends the money to the government. Sales taxes are a popular way to raise revenue because they are so easy to collect. Almost every state government has some form of sales tax, as do many county and city governments.

There are two kinds of sales taxes, general and selective. A general sales tax is one collected on the sale of nearly any product. A selective sales tax, also called an **excise tax**, is one collected only on specific products. Every state, for example, places excise taxes on gasoline, cigarettes, and alcoholic beverages.

A sales tax is set as a percentage of the purchase price. This percentage rate varies from place to place. Among the states, the rate varies from 3 to 7.5 percent. When local governments charge sales taxes, those taxes are added on to the state tax. For example, residents of Berkeley, California, pay a 7 percent general sales tax. That rate includes 4.75 percent for the state, 1.25 percent for the county, and 1 percent for the city.

A sales tax is a regressive tax, meaning that the tax rate is the same for everyone. Lower-income people are hit hardest by sales tax, because they must spend nearly all of their earnings on necessities. Higher-income people, on the other hand, rarely spend everything they earn; they usually have money left over to save or invest. Therefore, wealthy people pay sales tax on a smaller portion of their earnings.

In order to make sales taxes less regressive, many governments exclude certain basic, necessary items. In most states, for example, sales of groceries and medical supplies are not taxable. As a result, poor people, who spend much of their incomes on these necessities, are able to pay a smaller share of taxes.

Other Taxes

The federal government and most state governments impose several other kinds of taxes in addition to income taxes and sales taxes. For example, when a person dies, the property and money left behind are known as that person's estate. If the estate is worth more than $600,000, the federal government may claim a portion of its value as an estate tax. Most states also collect an estate tax, or a similar tax called an inheritance tax.

In order to avoid paying an estate tax, some people try to give away their property before they die. This property, however, is subject to a gift tax. Under this tax, anyone who gives gifts of more than $10,000 per year must pay the federal government a percentage of the total amount as a gift tax. State governments may also collect gift taxes.

Several other kinds of taxes are collected only by the federal government. The best known of these is the Social Security tax. In 1935, the Social Security Act set up a federal fund to provide financial support for elderly people. This fund is supported by a 15.02 percent tax on wages and salaries, half of which is paid by employers, the other half by employees.

A **tariff** is a special kind of import tax. Its primary purpose is not to raise revenue, but to protect American industries. Many products, such as clothing and automobiles, can be produced more cheaply in countries other than in the United States. When those products are imported and sold in this country, people are more likely to buy them than to buy more expensive American products. American businesses may suffer as a result.

Tariffs may help protect American businesses by making it more expensive to buy foreign goods.

To help make American-made products more competitive, importers may be required to pay a tariff to the federal government. The importers must raise the selling price of their products to cover the cost of the tariff.

The use of tariffs is quite controversial. Some people feel that tariffs are necessary to protect American businesses from unfair competition. Others feel that tariffs hurt U.S. consumers by forcing importers to raise the prices of products. One problem is clear to everyone: when the federal government places tariffs on foreign products, foreign governments respond by placing tariffs on American products. For this reason, the federal government usually imposes tariffs only as a last resort.

Non-Tax Revenue

Taxes are not the only way for the federal, state, and local governments to raise revenue. Governments may collect money from their citizens in a variety of other ways.

Many governments own land that they no longer need or cannot use. Occasionally, a government will sell unneeded property to private buyers. More often, however, the government will rent or lease the land. For example, the federal government often leases the rights to dig mines or drill for oil on federal land. Renting or leasing is preferable to selling because it provides a steady source of income.

Tolls are another regular source of income. State and local governments often charge tolls for the use of highways and bridges. The federal government charges tolls for the use of U.S.-owned canals.

All governments also collect fees and fines. State governments, for example, require licenses for driving, getting married, hunting, and fishing. People who want to obtain such licenses must pay a fee to the government. The federal government charges fees for such services as registering copyrights, preparing passports, and providing copies of documents. In addition, governments collect fines from individuals and organizations. The fines might be for violations of traffic regulations or for failing to meet clean air and water standards.

In recent years, an increasing number of states have begun to raise revenue through government-run lotteries. These games of chance, in which people buy numbered tickets, offer large amounts of cash as prizes for those whose numbers are drawn. Lotteries have proven to be very successful at raising revenue, and more than half the states now have them. Many people disapprove of lotteries, however, because they feel that states should not be encouraging gambling.

Many state and local governments get 10 to 25 percent of their revenue from non-tax sources such as rents, tolls, and fees. The federal government, however, gets less than 2 percent of its revenue from non-tax sources.

In more than half of the states, people can help increase the revenue of their state government by purchasing lottery tickets.

SECTION REVIEW

Define the Words

income tax	property tax
tax return	sales tax
exemption	excise tax
deduction	tariff
taxable income	

Check the Facts

1. Why is the income tax considered a progressive tax?
2. What are the two kinds of sales taxes, and what is the difference between them?
3. Identify three sources of non-tax revenue.

Think About the Ideas

4. *Evaluate.* Do you think state-run lotteries are a good idea? Why or why not?

April 15 is generally the deadline date each year for taxpayers to submit their tax return to the Internal Revenue Service.

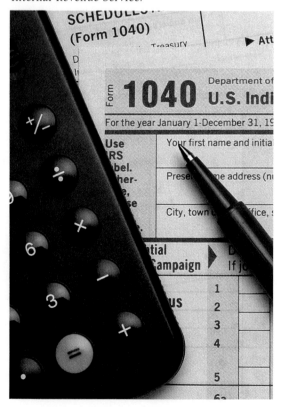

* *

SECTION 3

How Governments Spend Their Money

* *

VOCABULARY

budget	national debt
expenditures	balanced budget
deficit	grant-in-aid

Since governments have limited revenues, they must make choices. If more money is spent on one item, less money must be spent on another. Spending an extra $1 million on AIDS research, for example, may mean spending $1 million less on education. Spending an extra $1 billion on space exploration may result in less money for programs to feed the hungry. Making decisions like these is one of the most difficult duties of government.

In order to decide how best to spend its money, a government must set priorities. In other words, it must determine the importance of its various goals and spend its money accordingly. The greatest amount of money will be spent on the most important items. Lesser amounts of money will be spent on less important items. For some less important items, there may be no money available.

The Budget Process

A government's spending priorities are presented in the form of a **budget**, a plan for managing and spending money. A budget always has two parts. The first part lists the government's revenues, or receipts, and indicates how much money is expected from each source. The second part lists the government's outlays, or **expenditures**—the items that the government plans to spend money on and the amount it plans to spend on each.

Budgets are almost always annual; that is, they list revenues and expenditures for a one-year period. This one-year period is usually a fiscal year rather than a calendar year. While a calendar year always runs from January 1 to December 31, a fiscal year can begin at any time. For example, the federal government's fiscal year runs from October 1 of one calendar year to September 30 of the next. Most state and local governments also use those dates for their fiscal years.

Because the federal government spends such an immense amount of money—over $1 trillion, as you may recall—the federal budget is a huge document. Preparing the budget requires the work of hundreds of people over several months.

The budget process begins each year in the Office of Management and Budget (OMB), a division of the Executive Office of the President. The head of the OMB, the Budget Director, asks every federal department and agency to estimate the amount of money it will need for the coming fiscal year. At the same time, members of the OMB staff estimate the amount of money the government can expect to take in during the same period.

With this information, the Budget Director meets with the President to discuss priorities. Based on recommendations of the

This chart shows how state and local governments spend their money. What document outlines a government's spending plans?

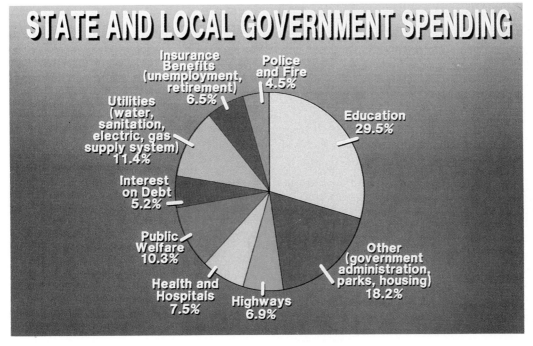

STATE AND LOCAL GOVERNMENT SPENDING

Insurance Benefits (unemployment, retirement) 6.5%

Police and Fire 4.5%

Utilities (water, sanitation, electric, gas supply system) 11.4%

Education 29.5%

Interest on Debt 5.2%

Public Welfare 10.3%

Health and Hospitals 7.5%

Highways 6.9%

Other (government administration, parks, housing) 18.2%

As budget director, Richard Darman is responsible for explaining the Bush administration's spending priorities to Congress.

President and the President's advisers, the Budget Director works out the first draft of the budget with the help of the OMB staff, who fill in the details. The completed budget is often more than 1,000 pages long.

Once the President has approved the OMB's work, the budget is sent to Congress for approval. The President usually marks the occasion with a nationally televised speech, explaining and defending the spending priorities that have been established. Congress, however, almost never accepts the President's budget as it is. Many members of Congress have different priorities from those of the President. As a result, after weeks or months of debate by Congressional committees, the budget usually emerges with a number of major changes.

By the time the budget is passed by both houses of Congress, it includes a great many compromises. Many federal agencies must accept less funding than they requested. The President may have to abandon some goals that were considered important. Members of

Congress may have to give up programs that would benefit their constituents. As a result of these compromises, however, the federal budget is better able to meet the needs of the country as a whole.

Most state and local governments follow a similar process in preparing their own budgets. The leader of the executive branch, with the advice of experts and political leaders, submits a budget to the legislature. The legislature then makes some changes and passes the revised version. Of course, no state or local budget requires as much work as the federal budget. In a small town, the budget process may take days rather than months, and the finished document may be only a few pages long. Nevertheless, the task of making choices and compromises is a difficult and often painful process at all levels of government.

Expenditures

Each year's budget tends to be somewhat different from the one before. Some budgetary changes are due to outside events, such as world crises or natural disasters. More often, however, the changes are due to political developments such as the election of new leaders who have new ideas and priorities.

During the 1980's, there had been some shifts in priorities but there have been no radical changes in the pattern of spending of the federal government. Each year, the greatest amount of money spent by the government has been on Social Security and Medicare (28 percent in 1988). A slightly smaller amount has been spent on national defense (27 percent in 1988). Surprisingly, the next largest amount of money spent by the government has gone toward interest payments on loans (nearly 14 percent in 1988).

The expenses in state and local budgets are much different than those of the federal budget. State governments do not have to pay for national defense or Social Security. They also borrow much less money than the federal government does, so interest payments are not a major expenditure. Therefore, the federal government's three most expensive budget items are missing from state and local budgets.

The largest expense for nearly every state and local community is education. Educational spending accounts for nearly one-third of the average state budget. Among the major expenses are social services (aid to needy people), transportation, and public safety. You can see how state and local governments spend their money by looking at the graphs on page 465.

Debt

Governments often choose to spend more money than they can take in. An excess of government expenses over government revenues is called a **deficit**. The federal government has had a deficit every year since 1964. In 1986, this deficit was at its peak—221 billion dollars. Since then, the amount of the deficit has gone down slightly.

In order to make up for a deficit, governments must borrow money to meet their expenses. Although some of the money is borrowed from banks, most of it comes from issuing bonds. A bond is a way for a government to borrow money from individuals. If you have ever bought a U.S. Savings Bond, you have lent money to the federal government. The government has promised to pay back what you paid for the bond, plus interest.

This graph shows how the federal deficit has increased sharply in the 1980's. In which year was there not a deficit?

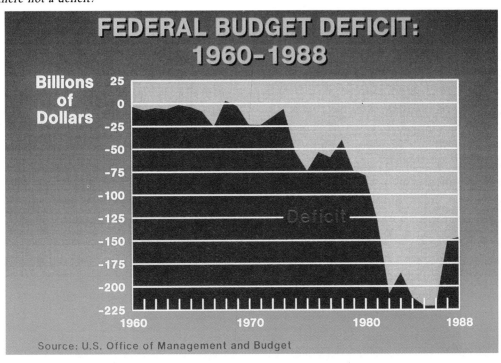

FEDERAL BUDGET DEFICIT: 1960–1988

Billions of Dollars

25
0
-25
-50
-75
-100
-125
-150
-175
-200
-225

1960   1970   1980   1988

Deficit

Source: U.S. Office of Management and Budget

The reasons for government deficits have been discussed in a number of previous chapters. As you may recall, American citizens have demanded much more of their governments in recent years. At the same time, many Americans are unwilling to pay higher taxes. Candidates who pledge to raise taxes almost always lose elections. As a result, government leaders have been left with a difficult choice. They can either cut back on government programs or borrow more money. They have almost always decided to borrow more money.

The huge federal deficit has caused a number of problems for the country. The most severe problem is the effect it has on the national debt. The **national debt** is the total amount the government owes on money it has borrowed. Each year's deficit adds to this debt and increases the interest that must be paid on it. In 1989, that interest payment was nearly $152 billion. In order to pay this interest without cutting other expenses, the federal government has to continue borrowing money, which adds to the national debt.

Another problem is the deficit's effect on the economy. Only a limited amount of money in the country is available for borrowing. If much of that money is borrowed by the federal government, very little is left for individuals and businesses to borrow. As a result, interest rates—the "price" for borrowing money—tend to rise because of a reduced supply and increased demand. Higher interest rates discourage investment and slow the growth of the economy.

To overcome these problems, the federal government has been making great efforts to cut the federal deficit and "balance the budget." A **balanced budget** is a budget in which expenditures do not exceed revenues—in other words, a budget with no deficit. So far, the government has been unsuccessful. However, an important step toward reducing the deficit came in 1985, when Congress passed the Gramm-Rudman Act. This law requires federal spending to be reduced by a certain amount each year.

Many state and local governments are required by their constitutions to have balanced budgets. When these governments cannot raise enough revenue to meet their expenses, they are not allowed, by law, to borrow money. Instead, they must cut services. In many communities, library hours have been cut and school activities have been limited in order to meet the restrictions of a balanced budget.

Intergovernmental Revenue

When state and local governments are short of funds, they often turn to the federal government for help. Financial aid from the federal government may take several different forms.

By far the most common form of federal assistance is the **grant-in-aid**. A grant-in-aid is given for a specific purpose only, such as building highways or low-income housing. In order to receive a grant-in-aid, a state or local government must meet certain conditions set by the U.S. government. For example, it might have to agree to let minority-owned companies do a certain part of the work on the project that is funded. A block grant is a combination of specific grants-in-aid. The federal government usually gives block grants for general categories, such as transportation or drug enforcement. The grant may be used for any purpose within that category only.

States also provide grants to local governments. For an expensive item such as education, a city or town may depend on assistance from both the state government and the federal government. In many schools, for example, state grants help to pay for text-

Large-scale projects, such as the construction of Nevada's Hoover Dam, are too expensive for state and local governments to undertake without assistance from the federal government.

books and hot lunch programs. The same schools may also receive federal grants to set up new programs, such as education for learning-disabled students.

Many Americans are critical of federal grants. They feel that the huge bureaucracy needed to manage these grants is too expensive. They also argue that state and local governments often waste money by requesting grants for projects they do not really need. These critics feel that states should find a way to raise necessary revenue. Then, the federal bureaucracy could be reduced and federal taxes could be cut.

Other people disagree. They argue that federal grants enable communities to provide services they could not afford otherwise, especially services for people who need help. They feel that the tax money of Americans who are better off should be shared with those who have less. In their view, while the federal government may not be completely efficient, it is the best way we have of providing help to people who need it.

The debate over federal aid has quieted in recent years, simply because federal grants are no longer easily available. In its efforts to reduce the budget deficit, the federal government has had to make fewer and smaller grants than in the past. As a result, many states and cities are searching for ways to reduce their own growing deficits.

SECTION REVIEW

Define the Words

budget
expenditures
deficit

national debt
balanced budget
grant-in-aid

Check the Facts
1. What is a fiscal year?
2. Describe the steps involved in the federal budget process.
3. What problems has the federal deficit caused?

Think About the Ideas
4. *Analyze.* What do you think the federal government should do to solve its deficit problem?
5. *Evaluate.* Do you think there should be a Constitutional amendment requiring the federal government to have a balanced budget? Why or why not?

CITIZENSHIP SKILLS

How to Compare Line Graphs and Bar Graphs

Although most statistics can be expressed in various forms, some graphs are more useful than others in certain situations. A line graph, for example, is a good way to illustrate trends, or changes in something from year to year. Bar graphs are very useful for showing comparisons between things. To trace the changes in the federal deficit over a number of years, a line graph would be most appropriate. To compare the gross national product of a number of different countries in a given year, a bar graph would be best.

The graphs below illustrate how line and bar graphs can be used most effectively. The line graph shows how much of the federal budget went to defense spending between 1970 and 1988. The bar graphs show how U.S. military spending compares to that of other nations.

Using Your Skills
Study the graphs and answer the following questions.

1. What do the points on the line graph represent?

2. What does the line graph show about defense spending in the 1970's? In the 1980's?

3. Which two countries shown on the bar graph spent about the same percent of their GNP on the military in 1985?

4. Could the information shown on the line graph be shown on a bar graph? Why or why not?

5. Could the information shown on the bar graph be shown on a line graph? Why or why not?

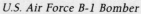

U.S. Air Force B-1 Bomber

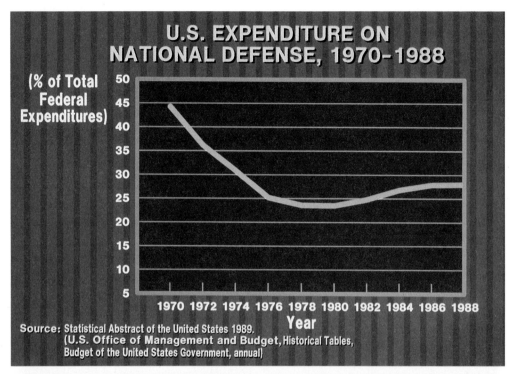

U.S. EXPENDITURE ON NATIONAL DEFENSE, 1970–1988

(% of Total Federal Expenditures)

Year

Source: Statistical Abstract of the United States 1989.
(U.S. Office of Management and Budget, Historical Tables,
Budget of the United States Government, annual)

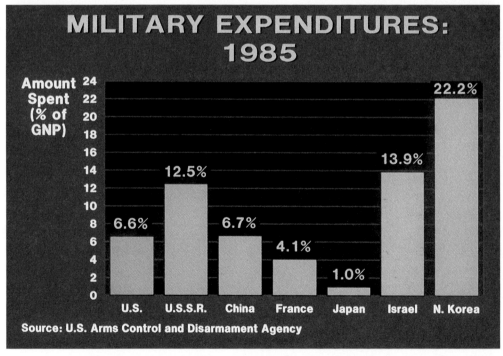

MILITARY EXPENDITURES: 1985

Amount Spent (% of GNP)

U.S.	U.S.S.R.	China	France	Japan	Israel	N. Korea
6.6%	12.5%	6.7%	4.1%	1.0%	13.9%	22.2%

Source: U.S. Arms Control and Disarmament Agency

CHAPTER 20 REVIEW

* *

MAIN POINTS

★ The writers of the Constitution set limits on the taxation power of the federal and state governments to prevent abuses of this power.

★ Most economists agree that taxes should be based on ability to pay, and be straightforward, convenient, efficient, and reasonable.

★ The most common sources of government revenue are income taxes, property taxes, and sales taxes. Among non-tax sources are tolls, fees, and government-run lotteries.

★ Governments set priorities in spending their money. These priorities are reflected in government budgets, which are prepared in a process that requires difficult choices and compromises.

★ When the federal government fails to raise enough revenue to meet its expenses, it must borrow money to make up its deficit. This deficit has caused a number of problems for the country.

★ State and local governments often seek federal aid when they are short of funds.

WORDS IN REVIEW

Choose the word or phrase from the list below that best completes each sentence. Write the missing words on a separate sheet of paper.

revenue
progressive tax
deductions
tariff
deficit

regressive tax
property tax
sales tax
expenditure
grant-in-aid

1. For the last several years, the government had a _____, as its expenses exceeded its receipts.

2. The town hired an assessor to help determine residents' _____.

3. Over half of the federal government's _____ comes from income taxes.

4. The federal government gave the town a _____ to build low-income housing.

5. The government placed a high _____ on all foreign-made televisions.

6. The tax was a _____ because the wealthy paid more.

7. The state placed a 4 percent _____ on all products except food.

8. An important _____ in the federal budget is for defense.

9. The _____ placed a heavier tax burden on the poor.

10. The family was able to claim several _____ on their income tax return.

FACTS IN REVIEW

1. Why is taxation such an important government power?

2. How does the Constitution limit the federal government's power to tax?

3. What is the difference between progressive and regressive taxes?

4. Explain how a taxpayer determines his or her taxable income.

5. What is tax withholding and what is its purpose?

CHAPTER 20 REVIEW

* *

6. How are property taxes determined?

7. What is the role of the Office of Management and Budget in the federal budget process?

8. In what ways is the federal budget a compromise document?

9. What choices do government leaders have when faced with a deficit?

10. What factors may contribute to annual changes in the federal budget?

THINKING ABOUT FINANCING OUR GOVERNMENTS

1. *Analyze.* Do you think Americans would be willing to pay higher taxes in return for more services? Why or why not?

2. *Evaluate.* What type of government revenue do you think is the most fair? Explain.

3. *Evaluate.* What do you think the government's spending priorities should be? Explain.

COLLECTING INFORMATION ABOUT THE FEDERAL BUDGET

Research the current federal budget. Find out what the major categories of revenue and expenditures are. What amounts of money does the government plan to raise and spend in each category? Which categories are the largest? Which are the smallest? How much of the budget is spent for interest on the national debt? What is the projected budget deficit for the current year?

WRITING ABOUT THE FEDERAL DEFICIT

For some time now, people have been concerned about the federal deficit and the problems it has caused for the nation's economy. Write a short essay discussing the federal deficit. In your essay, include the cause of the deficit, recent trends in the deficit, what problems the deficit has caused, and how government is attempting to deal with the deficit problem.

INTERPRETING A GRAPH

Look at the graph on page 467. This graph shows the growth of the federal deficit from 1960 to 1988. Between which years did the deficit increase the most? Between which years did it increase the least? In which year was there a budget surplus? What is the total increase in the deficit over the years shown on this chart? How would you describe the trend of the deficit?

FOCUSING ON YOUR COMMUNITY

The revenues and expenditures of every community are somewhat different depending on the community's needs and resources. What are your community's major expenditures, and what is the amount of each? What are your community's major sources of revenue, and how much does the community receive from each? What are the community's property tax rates and sales tax rates? What grants, if any, does the community receive from the federal government? Has the community had to cut services in recent years because of budget problems? If so, what services have been cut? Prepare a brief oral report for the class.

CHAPTER 21

The Economy and the Individual

OBJECTIVES

After you have studied this chapter, you will be able to:

★ Explain how to be a responsible consumer.
★ Discuss the decisions individuals must make concerning their income and expenses, including the different ways to save, invest, and borrow money.
★ Explain the importance of savings and investments to individuals and to the nation's economy.
★ Identify different types of credit, and discuss the advantages and disadvantages of buying on credit.
★ Explain the purpose of insurance, and identify and discuss different types of insurance.
★ Explain how the federal and state governments and private organizations help protect the rights of consumers.

SECTIONS

1 Buying Goods and Services
2 Saving, Borrowing, Buying on Credit
3 Insuring Against Risk
4 Protecting Consumer Rights

INTRODUCTION

Suppose that a neighbor gives you $10 for helping her clean out her garage. You can do a number of things with that money. You may decide, for example, to spend it on movie tickets. In that case, your money will be helping to pay the expenses of a local movie theater, including the salaries of the people who work there.

Or you may decide to put the $10 into a savings account at your bank. If you do that, your money might end up as part of the money the bank lends to a new business, or to someone who wants to buy a home.

There are many other choices you might make. You might decide to give the money to charity or to lend it to a friend. Now, imagine hundreds of millions of Americans making similar decisions while you make yours. These decisions affect not only the individuals who make them, but many other people as well. Thus, your economic choices often have far-reaching effects.

★ ★

SECTION 1

Buying Goods and Services

★ ★

VOCABULARY

fixed expenses   unit price
flexible expenses

Every time you buy a product, you expect to receive good quality merchandise and to be treated with respect in exchange for your money. If stores and businesses fail to satisfy you, you can look for others that will work harder to please you. This is one of your rights as a consumer.

In earlier chapters, you discovered that with every right, there are certain responsibilities. With the right to vote, for example, comes the responsibility of staying informed about issues and candidates. In the same way, our rights as consumers require some responsibility on our part. We should find out as much as we can about the products we buy so that we can recognize good quality. We should also find out where we can get the best value for our money. We cannot rely on stores and businesses to protect us; we must protect ourselves.

Planning A Budget

In the last chapter, you read about how governments use budgets to manage their finances. Individuals and families also use budgets to plan their spending. Although governments usually plan budgets for an entire year, most individuals plan their budgets month by month.

As you learned, a budget has two parts: income and expenditures. The first step in planning a monthly budget is to determine monthly income. Common sources of income include a job, an allowance, or interest from money in the bank.

Once income has been determined, an individual or family must decide how that money will be spent. A large portion of the money in most people's budgets goes toward **fixed expenses**—expenses that are the same from month to month. Common fixed expenses include rent, loan payments, or insurance premiums. Other expenses vary from month to month. Some of these **flexible expenses**, such as heating bills and clothing purchases, vary according to the time of year. Others, such as entertainment expenses,

depend on the changing needs and wants of the spender.

Not all money in a budget goes toward expenses. Most people try to set some money aside for saving or investing. We will look more closely at saving later in the chapter.

Very few people have enough income to cover all their needs and wants. As a result, people must set priorities and make decisions that will allow them to balance their budgets—that is, to make sure that expenditures do not exceed income. There are several possibilities. One is to increase income by getting a better-paying job or by working more hours each week. Another is to decrease fixed expenses, by moving to a less expensive apartment, for example. Most people, however, find that the most practical decision is to decrease their flexible expenses. They may try to spend less on food or clothing, or to avoid buying things they do not really need, such as jewelry or candy.

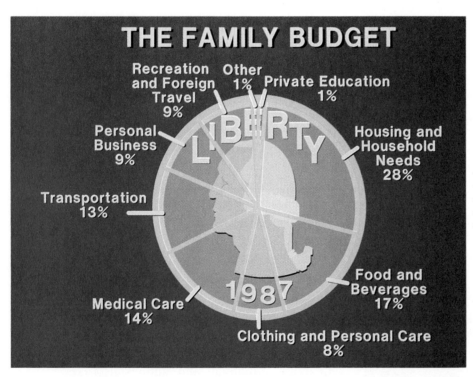

THE FAMILY BUDGET

Recreation and Foreign Travel 9%
Other 1%
Private Education 1%
Personal Business 9%
Housing and Household Needs 28%
Transportation 13%
Medical Care 14%
Food and Beverages 17%
Clothing and Personal Care 8%

If a family has an income of $30,000, about how much money should be set aside for housing and household needs?

Food Store Manager

A food store manager is a person in charge of running a supermarket or grocery store. He or she is responsible for ordering merchandise, hiring and supervising employees, and making all decisions concerning the store's operation and maintenance.

Some food store managers run large supermarkets. Others manage small independently owned grocery stores. At a large store, the manager usually supervises several assistant managers, who each run a separate department of the store.

Being a food store manager is a challenging job. Managers work long hours and must be at the store when it opens and closes. They are responsible for all the money the store makes, and they must keep very accurate records of the store's operations. They also oversee the advertising and promotion of the store and its products.

Food store managers must make hundreds of decisions each day about what products to order. They also must work well with people and be good at solving problems.

Most food store managers are high school graduates. They usually work their way up to the position of manager, perhaps starting as a checkout clerk and then becoming a department head, an assistant manager, and finally a manager.

Using Your Skills
1. What are the major responsibilities of a food store manager?
2. What high school courses do you think would best prepare you for a job as a food store manager?

Shopping for Quality

Since income is limited, it makes sense to try to "get the most for your money." This does not necessarily mean buying a large number of products; it means buying good-quality items that will last longer than poorly made goods.

There are several ways to find out about the quality of a product before buying it. One way is to talk to trusted people, such as parents and friends, who may be familiar with the product. Another is to visit the library and check recent issues of magazines such as *Consumer Reports* and *Consumers' Research*. These and similar magazines test thousands of products each year for safety, effectiveness, convenience, and reliability. They then publish the results for the benefit of consumers, those who buy products or services. Evaluations of certain kinds of products, such as computers, stereos, or cars, can also be found in specialized magazines such as *PC Magazine*, *High Fidelity*, or *Car and Driver*.

CONSUMER RATINGS: COMPACT-DISC PLAYERS

BRAND AND TYPE	PRICE	BASIC RATING	ABILITY TO WITHSTAND DAMAGE	DYNAMIC RANGE	CONVENIENCE	REMOTE CONTROL	PAUSE FEATURE	HEADPHONE JACK
Corvac ZX-600	$350	4	4	3	3	✔	—	✔
Vonex CD-NL80	400	2	4	2	2	—	✔	✔
Vonex Mini CD-2B	230	3	2	1	4	—	—	—
Top-Tech CDP-R2L	410	5	5	4	5	✔	✔	—
Tku DL-9990	320	4	4	4	2	✔	✔	—
Automain C16-3000	515	4	3	4	2	—	✔	✔
Centura 8PLX	225	2	1	1	1	—	—	✔

Scale: 1 ——— 5
Poor   Excellent

Source: *Consumer Reports*, May, 1987, p. 286.

Which compact-disc player received the highest overall rating in this consumer evaluation?

Another important way to determine the quality of a product is to look at it carefully and, if possible, to try it. It is always a good idea to try on clothing, test out electronic equipment, or examine furniture before buying it. The more that is known about a product, the easier it is to judge its quality.

Much of what consumers need to know about a product can often be found on its label. A number of federal and state labeling laws require manufacturers to attach certain information to the product itself or to the package the product comes in. Packaged foods, for example, must have all their ingredients listed on the outside of the package. Many foods and medicines must be stamped with a date that indicates how long they will be safe to use. Tags on clothing must describe what the clothing is made from and how it can be cleaned. Labels on many kinds of products must identify any safety or health risks associated with using the product. Even if two products seem to be alike, the labels may reveal that one is better than the other. For example, one brand of lemonade may contain real juice while another contains only lemon flavoring.

Shopping For Value

Once a consumer decides that a product is worth buying, the next step is finding out where to buy it for the best possible price.

Many grocery stores now display labels with the unit price of the item.

To do this, it is useful to check advertisements in newspapers, call stores and ask about prices, or visit stores in person.

In some areas, grocery stores help shoppers compare prices by displaying **unit prices** for many of the products. A unit price is the price for a standard unit of measurement. For example, a four-ounce bar of soap for 52 cents may seem like a better buy than a six-ounce bar for 72 cents. A unit price, however, would show that the four-ounce bar costs 13 cents per ounce, while the six-ounce bar costs only 12 cents per ounce. An increasing number of local governments are requiring their stores to use unit pricing.

Another good place to check prices is in a mail-order catalog. Many products available from mail-order companies are cheaper than items sold in stores because mail-order companies do not have to rent and decorate stores or pay salaries to salespeople. A disadvantage of buying by mail, however, is that the consumer does not see a product before buying it. But some mail-order companies will allow people to return items if they are not satisfied with them.

A good way to get products at lower prices is to wait for a sale. Many stores sell items at a discount, or lower price, at particular times of the year. For example, outdoor barbecue grills may go on sale in September as the summer is ending.

Avoiding Impulse Buying

While buying wisely requires a good deal of work and thought, many businesses try to get consumers to buy without thinking. For example, supermarkets may place certain items near checkout lines, hoping that shoppers will toss them into their carts while waiting to pay for purchases. Many stores hold special "one-day sales" as a way to encourage people to buy products without taking time to compare prices at other stores. Salespeople may try to put pressure on shoppers to buy products they do not need.

These sales techniques can be very effective. Many people do not realize their mistake until after they have spent their money. Wise shoppers often make it a rule never to buy anything without planning in advance. Even if a salesperson offers a deal that seems too good to resist, a wise shopper will insist on thinking about it, and will then do some research and comparison shopping. If the salesperson persists and says that the deal is "now or never," it is best to hold off. Consumers should never be pressured into making a purchase they may regret later.

The best protection is to buy from businesses that allow customers to change their minds after they have made a purchase. Before handing over money, first find out a store's return policy. This policy may be posted on a wall, or printed in small type on a store's "sales contract." An acceptable policy will allow merchandise to be returned within a few days, in exchange for a full refund. It is always important to save sales receipts as proof of the price and date of purchase. These receipts are usually required to be able to return merchandise.

SECTION REVIEW

Define the Words
fixed expenses   unit price
flexible expenses

Check the Facts
1. What is the difference between fixed and flexible expenses?
2. Identify three ways in which people might balance their budget.
3. List several ways that consumers can evaluate the quality of a product.

Think About the Ideas
4. *Evaluate.* Would you be willing to pay more for a product if the people who sold it to you were particularly friendly and helpful? Why or why not?

★ ★

SECTION 2

Saving, Borrowing, Buying on Credit

★ ★ ★ ★ ★ ★ ★ ★ ★ ★ ★ ★ ★ ★ ★ ★ ★ ★ ★ ★

VOCABULARY

certificate of   principal
deposit   bankruptcy
investment   repossess

People's income and expenses vary widely. Some people take in much more money than they need to cover their basic expenses. These people usually save or invest the money they have left over. Other people take in much less money than they need. These people must make up the difference by borrowing money or by buying on credit.

Saving

Saving money can be a difficult habit to establish. Some people feel that they should enjoy every penny they earn. As a result, they spend their money as quickly as it comes in, often buying things they may not really need.

There are, however, many good reasons for saving money. Certain major purchases, such as a car or a house, usually cannot be made without putting aside money to help pay for them. Savings also come in handy in emergencies. And, of course, savings can be used for luxuries—such as a new stereo system or a trip to Hawaii.

To make it easier for people to save, some employers offer to withhold a fixed amount from their employees' paychecks. This money is automatically deposited into participating employees' savings accounts. Many people, however, handle the responsibility themselves. Each week or month, they budget a small amount of money to be put aside for savings.

At one time, people saved money by stuffing it into a mattress or hiding it under the floor. Today, however, most people put their savings in a bank, a savings and loan association, or a credit union. Depositing money in any one of these is a way of increasing your savings, because the money in a savings account earns interest.

Banks and credit unions offer several kinds of savings accounts. A regular savings account pays a relatively small amount of interest. A savings certificate, or **certificate of deposit** (CD), pays higher interest, but requires that a certain amount of money be kept in the account for a specific length of time. Although keeping money in a bank generally does not earn depositors the highest interest rates, it is a relatively risk-free way of saving. As you learned in Chapter 19, the federal government insures each depositor's account up to $100,000.

Another way to save money is to buy government bonds. After a certain number of years, a savings bond can be sold for a higher price than was paid for it.

A third way of saving money is to invest it. **Investment** means buying something that is expected to increase in value. Investment carries a risk, but it can also pay off hand-

A major purchase such as a new car often requires working out a savings plan that involves putting aside a certain amount of income each month.

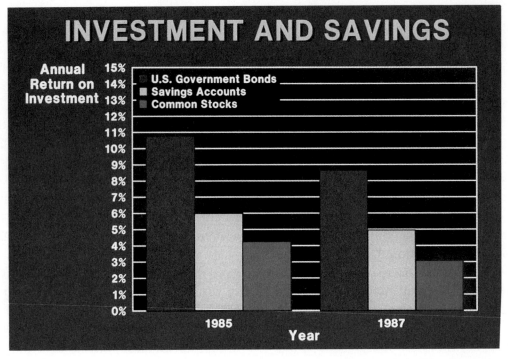

INVESTMENT AND SAVINGS

Annual Return on Investment

- U.S. Government Bonds
- Savings Accounts
- Common Stocks

15%
14%
13%
12%
11%
10%
9%
8%
7%
6%
5%
4%
3%
2%
1%
0%

1985   1987

Year

This graph compares the average return on savings accounts and on stocks and bonds. What do banks do with the money people deposit in savings accounts?

somely. Imagine, for example, that you and several friends buy shares in a small record company. If the company is successful, your investment might earn you a good deal of money. If it is unsuccessful, however, you might lose all the money you invested. You can also invest in a business by buying stock in it. This, too, can be risky. A share of stock may increase—or it may decrease—in value.

People who are looking for a safer investment may put money in mutual funds or money market funds. The experts who manage these funds use the money to buy stocks and bonds in many different areas. Because the investments are varied and carefully selected, these funds usually make money for their investors.

Investment benefits not only individuals, but also the economy. It helps individuals increase their savings. It also helps businesses by giving them the money they need to grow

and expand. Banks invest their depositors' money in stocks, in bonds, and in loans to people and businesses, which keeps the economy running and expanding. If people went back to keeping their savings in mattresses, the nation's economy would grind to a halt.

Borrowing

Often, people have to spend more money than they have in their savings accounts. Very few people, for example, can save the thousands of dollars needed to pay for a college education, to start a business, or to buy a home. In situations like these, it is necessary to borrow money.

The usual places to borrow money are banks, savings and loan associations, and credit unions. In order to borrow money, a person must prove that he or she is a good risk. It is necessary to show that the loan can be repaid, with interest, in a reasonable amount of time.

Some people who cannot get loans from banks borrow money from finance companies instead. Finance companies are private businesses that lend money. They often lend to high-risk borrowers, but they charge very high rates of interest in return.

If a bank or finance company feels there is some chance that a person will not be able to repay a loan, it will ask for collateral. (You learned about collateral in Chapter 19.) If you borrow money to buy a car, for example, the bank may require that you offer the car as collateral. In this case, although you have full use of the car, the bank remains the car's legal owner until you have repaid the loan.

Most loans must be paid back in installments, usually a certain amount of money each month. At first, these monthly payments cover only interest payments on the loan. Little by little, however, they also begin to pay back some of the **principal**—the amount of money that was originally borrowed. After a certain number of installments, the entire loan is paid off.

Borrowing money can be dangerous. If a borrower is unable to keep up with loan payments, the bank may seize the collateral. For example, even if 80 percent of a car loan has been repaid, the bank may take the car along with the money already paid on the loan.

Sometimes, people borrow money from a finance company in order to pay back other loans. Eventually, they may have borrowed more money than they can possibly repay. People in this situation may be forced to declare **bankruptcy**, a legal statement that one cannot pay one's debts. When people declare bankruptcy, their financial assets are taken over by the courts and distributed to the people to whom they owe money.

Buying on Credit

Buying on credit is another way to borrow money. In this case, the money is borrowed from a store or business rather than from a bank.

The simplest way to buy on credit is to use a charge account. A charge account is a line of credit that a particular store extends to its regular customers. For example, a customer may make several purchases during a month without paying for them. At the end of the month, the store sends the customer a bill for that month's purchases.

Another way to buy on credit is with a credit card. Credit cards are issued by banks and some businesses. A person may use a credit card to buy items from any store that accepts the card for payment. The store collects the purchase price from the bank or business, which then sends a monthly bill to the cardholder. A credit card bill may be paid all at once, or in installments. Although fees

Paying for a purchase with a credit card is convenient. However, credit cards also make it easy for people to spend more money than they can afford.

CONTRACTS

A contract is any legally binding agreement between two or more people. The parts or terms of a contract spell out the rights and obligations of each of the parties under the terms of the agreement. Contracts can be oral. For instance, if you say that you will cut your neighbor's grass for $5 an hour, you have made an oral contract. Most contracts, however, are in writing. A written contract helps settle or prevent disputes between the parties since the terms are spelled out in considerable detail. If one party fails to comply with a contract, the other party may sue in court.

A contract has three elements: an offer, an acceptance, and a "consideration"—an exchange of something of value. Your neighbor *offered* you a job cutting the grass, which you *accepted*. In exchange, your neighbor agreed to pay you a *consideration* of $5 an hour.

The language in contracts may seem difficult to understand. When writing a contract, lawyers use terms that have very specific legal meanings. In an apartment lease, for example, the contract will refer to the Landlord, the Tenant, and the Premises. The *Landlord* is the person who owns the apartment (the *Premises*) and the *Tenant* is the person who rents it.

Here are a few of the terms and conditions that might be included in an apartment lease:

1. Tenant shall pay Landlord as rent for the Premises the sum of $500 monthly in advance, until termination of this lease.
2. Tenant shall not permit anything to be thrown out of the windows; nothing shall be hung from the outside of the windows or placed on the outside window sills; no parrot, dog, or any other animals shall be kept within or about the Premises.
3. Landlord will supply hot and cold water to the Premises for the use of the Tenant at all faucets and fixtures. Landlord will also supply heat, by means of the heating system and fixtures provided by the landlord.

Each paragraph or clause of a lease contract spells out one or more specific rights or obligations of each party. A typical lease may have 10 to 20 such paragraphs.

The main purpose of any contract is to protect all of the parties involved. The contract provides a clear understanding of what is expected of each party and thus reduces the chances of a disagreement.

Using Your Skills
1. What is the purpose of a written contract?
2. What are the three elements of a contract?
3. What obligations did the tenant have in paragraph 2 above? What were the obligations of the landlord in paragraph 3?

are not usually added to the unpaid portion of the bill, the interest rates are often very high. Late charges may be added to bills that are not paid on time.

Buying on credit can be an easy and convenient way to make purchases. Unfortunately, the availability of easy credit encourages people to spend money they do not have. When customers are unable to pay their bills, a store has the right to **repossess**, or take back, the items that were bought on credit, as well as keep any money that has already been paid. In addition, the high interest rates on credit cards cause people's debts to mount rapidly. The use, and abuse, of credit has led people into bankruptcy.

In the past, the federal government encouraged the use of credit cards by allowing taxpayers to deduct interest payments on their federal income taxes. In recent years, however, this policy has changed, and interest payments are no longer fully deductible. The government now hopes to encourage saving rather than buying on credit.

SECTION REVIEW

Define the Words

certificate of deposit bankruptcy
investment repossess
principal

Check the Facts
1. Why are savings important?
2. Describe four ways to save money.
3. What are the dangers of borrowing money or buying on credit?

Think About the Ideas
4. *Evaluate.* What are the advantages and disadvantages of saving for major purchases?

★ ★

SECTION 3
Insuring Against Risk

★ ★

VOCABULARY

insurance   Social Security
premium   Medicare
liability insurance Medicaid
beneficiary

Life is full of dangers and surprises. A breadwinner may die suddenly, leaving his or her family with no source of income. A farmer's crop may be washed away by a flood. An apartment building may be destroyed by fire, leaving dozens of residents injured and hundreds of others homeless. Few people are prepared to deal with events like these. Even if they have money in the bank, it is rarely enough to meet the challenge of rebuilding their lives.

For these reasons, many Americans rely on **insurance** to help them through a crisis. Insurance is a type of investment that protects the investor against unpredictable events. It can help pay for hospital bills and for repairs to homes or cars. It can also supply financial support to people who have lost their primary source of income.

Insurance can be classified into two basic categories, depending upon who provides it. One kind of insurance is provided by private companies, the other by the federal government.

Although homeowners hope never to file a claim, most of them buy property insurance so that they will be able to rebuild if disaster strikes.

Private Insurance

Most Americans have some type of insurance on their car, their home, their health, and perhaps even their life. This insurance is provided by private insurance companies, and is paid for by individual consumers and businesses. Insurance companies sell insurance policies, which protect policyholders against certain risks. A car insurance policy, for example, will protect against the risks of car accident or theft.

To get an insurance policy, people must make payments, called **premiums**, to the insurance company. These premiums must be paid regularly—usually, a certain amount each month or every few months. If the premiums are not paid, the insurance policy is cancelled. An insurance company keeps some of the money it receives from premiums in a reserve fund that is used to pay the claims of policyholders.

An insurance policy guarantees that a policyholder will collect money for any expenses covered by the policy. For exam-

ple, if the holder of a car insurance policy has an accident while driving, the insurance company will pay the driver's medical expenses. It will also pay the medical expenses of other people hurt in the crash, and it may pay to repair the damage to the car. An insurance company might end up paying many thousands of dollars for a single accident. Insurance companies are able to make these large payments because many other policyholders never have accidents. Their premiums become part of the reserve fund and are used to pay the expenses of the unfortunate policyholders who do have an accident.

Automobile insurance is only one of many kinds of insurance. Other common types of insurance include health insurance, liability insurance, property insurance, and life insurance. Health insurance is often paid for by a person's employer. It is one of the benefits an employee may receive in addition to salary.

Most property owners have **liability insurance**. If someone is injured while on another person's property, the property owner may be legally liable, or responsible, for paying the injured person's medical expenses. Liability insurance pays these expenses for the property owner and helps protect against such a financial liability.

Property insurance helps to repair or replace property that is damaged, lost, stolen, or destroyed. It is possible to get insurance policies that cover specific events such as fire or flood. More often, however, people get "umbrella policies" that protect against any number of dangers.

Life insurance provides money to help support a policyholder's family after the policyholder dies. With a life insurance policy, the policyholder must provide the name of a **beneficiary**—the person who will receive the money from the insurance company.

Social Insurance

Much of the social insurance program run by the federal government began during the Great Depression in the 1930's, when millions of Americans lost their jobs and their savings. To help them, President Franklin D. Roosevelt proposed an assortment of government programs that he called the New Deal. Within a very short time, Congress passed most of these programs into law.

The cornerstone of the New Deal was the Social Security Act, passed in 1935. The **Social Security** program now covers two different kinds of insurance: old age and survivors insurance and unemployment insurance. This federal insurance system is funded by required contributions from businesses and from all taxpayers.

As you read in Chapter 20, every employer and employee must pay a Social Security tax on wages and salaries. This tax, which is similar to an insurance premium,

goes into a special federal fund. When a person reaches age 62, he or she can begin to receive payments from that fund. These old-age benefits continue for the rest of the person's life. If a worker is forced to retire early due to illness or disability, benefits may begin before age 62.

Some people die before they are old enough to collect old-age benefits. In this case, surviving family members—the spouse and children under 18—receive Social Security payments instead. In this way, Social Security is similar to a life insurance policy.

Unemployment insurance is not paid for by Social Security taxes. Instead, every employer must pay a payroll tax—a small percentage of what the company pays its employees—to the federal government. This money is used to help support people who are out of work. Although it is a federal program, unemployment insurance is managed by the states. Workers who have lost their

The Social Security tax employees pay is an investment that they will be able to enjoy when they retire.

jobs must register with a state employment office and report there regularly. If they can prove they are looking for work, unemployed people can receive small, weekly payments for a certain number of months.

The Social Security Act has been amended many times since 1935, and other insurance programs have been added. Two of the most important—Medicare and Medicaid—went into effect in 1965. **Medicare** provides health and hospitalization insurance to people aged 65 and older. **Medicaid** helps pay the health care costs of low-income people, no matter what their age. Medicaid is a federal program that is administered by the states.

Because health care costs have been rising rapidly, the cost of the Medicare and Medicaid programs has been rising as well. Together, Social Security, Medicare, and Medicaid account for more than $300 billion of federal spending each year.

SECTION REVIEW

Define the Words

insurance   Social Security
premium   Medicare
liability insurance   Medicaid
beneficiary

Check the Facts
1. Identify and describe five kinds of private insurance.
2. What types of insurance are covered by Social Security?
3. How are insurance companies able to pay policyholders amounts greater than the premiums paid?

Think About the Ideas
4. *Evaluate.* Most states require drivers to have car insurance. Do you think people should be required to have other kinds of insurance as well? Why or why not?

★ ★

SECTION 4

Protecting Consumer Rights

★ ★

Throughout much of history, the rights of consumers could be summed up in one Latin phrase: *caveat emptor*, or "let the buyer beware." Sellers routinely lied and cheated, and any buyers who fell for the sellers' tricks were thought to deserve what they got.

Today, numerous government regulations protect consumers and help ensure that they will be treated fairly and honestly. In addition, there are a number of private organizations that consumers can turn to if they feel they have been treated unfairly.

The Role of Government

Over the years, Congress has passed a number of laws that protect the rights of consumers. Many of these laws involve labeling. For example, the Fair Packaging and Labeling Act requires that every package have a label identifying its contents and how much it weighs. In addition, the Food, Drug, and Cosmetic Act requires packages to list their ingredients according to the amounts of each. Other laws are intended to protect the health and safety of consumers. An early example is the Pure Food and Drug Act, passed in 1906. It requires manufacturers of foods, cos-

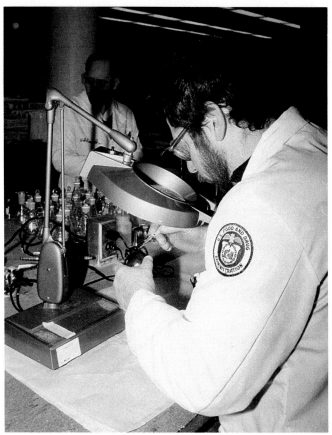

Inspectors for the Food and Drug Administration check food imported from other countries to make sure it meets the safety standards set by the government.

metics, and drugs to prove that their products are not dangerous.

Much of the work of enforcing the laws that protect consumer rights is handled by executive agencies of the federal government. As you learned in Chapter 11, there are hundreds of such agencies, with responsibilities that often overlap. One important federal agency is the Food and Drug Administration, or FDA, which oversees the safety of food, drugs, and cosmetics. Other agencies include the Federal Trade Commission, which guards against false advertising; the Consumer Product Safety Commission, which prevents manufacturers from selling hazardous products; and the U.S. Postal Service, which cracks down on individuals and companies that sell fraudulent products through the mail.

State and local governments also play a role in protecting consumers. Many states, for example, have laws regulating car repair services or used car sales. Some states also have their own restrictions on advertising or labeling. One such state is California, where any product that is suspected of causing cancer—even gasoline—must be labeled with a health warning.

On the local level, nearly every city or county has commissions to deal with consumers' complaints about public utilities, such as electricity, water, and cable television. Most cities also have health inspectors who check restaurants and food processing plants for unsanitary conditions.

The Role of Private Organizations

The federal and state governments have been quite successful in regulating manufacturing, advertising, and sales practices. However, government bureaucracies do not usually have the time or money to deal with the problems of individuals.

As a result, the task of protecting individual consumers has largely been taken on by private groups and organizations. Sometimes, these organizations are able to resolve consumers' problems by themselves. At other times, they pressure the appropriate government agencies to come up with solutions.

Mail Fraud

Your mailbox can be a dangerous place. It brings all kinds of irresistible offers and heart-tugging appeals for funds. Not all of them are legitimate. Here are some of the most common mail frauds:

★ Vacation condos. These are usually official-looking letters telling you that you may have won a car or a television. To claim your prize, you must go to the vacation site and hear a sales pitch. No one ever wins the big prizes, but many people are pressured into buying an overpriced vacation package.

★ Mail-order rip-offs. Most mail order companies are legitimate, but a few specialize in selling cheap, worthless goods. Diet aids, tanning pills, and imitation perfumes are among the products sold this way.

★ Charities. Some so-called charities solicit funds for cancer research, crippled children, and so on. The "charity" keeps 95 percent of the donations.

One of the oldest consumer groups in the United States is the Better Business Bureau, founded in 1912. There are more than 100 local Better Business Bureaus in communities around the country, in addition to a national bureau that sets standards for the local groups. Surprisingly, Better Business Bureaus are run by business owners rather than by consumers. These businesspeople recognize that the key to success lies in earning the trust of their customers. Better Business Bureaus provide information about local businesses and warn consumers about dishonest business practices. They also investigate consumer complaints and try to resolve them in a way that will satisfy everyone concerned.

Many communities also have local consumer leagues. These groups serve much the same purpose as Better Business Bureaus, but they are run by consumers rather than by businesspeople. In addition to handling customer complaints, they may help to educate consumers about their rights. They may also issue "seals of approval" to businesses or products they recommend.

Over the past 30 years, another type of group—the consumer interest group—has become quite common. The primary purpose of consumer interest groups is to bring consumer problems to the attention of government. These groups put pressure on the government to pass new laws and regulations that will protect consumers. Through education, publicity, and organizing efforts on the national and local levels, consumer interest groups have attracted broad public support for their causes.

The growth of these groups is due largely to the leadership of Ralph Nader, who has worked tirelessly on behalf of consumers' rights. Early in his career, Nader worked for the passage of stricter automobile safety laws. He also helped convince Congress to ban dangerous chemicals from foods. In 1971, he

People who are not satisfied with the products or services provided by a local business can have their complaints investigated by the Better Business Bureau.

Many of the laws passed by Congress to protect American consumers were proposed by consumer advocates such as Ralph Nader.

founded a consumer interest group called Public Citizen, Inc. Nader's group has since been joined by other national groups such as the National Consumer League. Many states and communities now have consumer interest groups as well.

SECTION REVIEW

Check the Facts
1. What role has the government played in protecting the rights of consumers?
2. Identify two federal agencies that help protect the rights of consumers.
3. Describe three kinds of private organizations that help protect the consumers' rights.

Think About the Ideas
4. *Analyze.* What role do you think people should play in protecting their rights as consumers?

CITIZENSHIP SKILLS

How to Protect Your Rights as a Consumer

While many federal and state laws protect consumers, you can help protect yourself by reading and understanding the labels and warranties that accompany a product.

A warranty is a guarantee of a product's performance. An "implied" warranty comes with all products, in that you have a right to expect a product to do what it is supposed to do. Some products come with a written warranty, which specifies the purchaser's rights and responsibilities. Before buying a product, you should check its warranty. Here's what you should look for:

★ *What kind of warranty is it?*
A "full" warranty is one in which the manufacturer agrees to repair or replace the entire product. A "limited" warranty covers only certain parts.

★ *How long is the warranty good for?*
Warranties are valid for a specified time after the date of purchase, for example, 1 year.

★ *Who is protected by the warranty?*
Most warranties protect only the original purchaser.

★ *What is covered in the warranty, and what will the manufacturer pay for?*
Most warranties cover defective parts and defective workmanship, and specify what the manufacturer will pay for.

★ *What is NOT covered?*
Most warranties do not cover products purchased outside the United States or from unauthorized dealers, nor products damaged by accident, misuse, neglect, fire, water, unauthorized repairs, or improper installation. In addition, warranties usually contain an "exclusion" clause stating that the manufacturer will not pay for "incidental and consequential" damages. This means the manufacturer will not pay for damages you have caused or for personal damages you might claim, such as your inconvenience.

★ *What are your obligations under the warranty?*
You must sometimes register a warranty by mailing an enclosed card to the manufacturer. When returning defective goods, you must usually supply the sales receipt as proof of purchase and effective date of coverage.

Using Your Skills
Study the sample warranty on the next page and answer the questions that follow.

1. What kind of warranty is this? What expense would you have if the product had to be repaired after 90 days?
2. Is the product covered by warranty if you bought it from your neighbor? If the movers dropped it?
3. Do you think warranties provide adequate protection for consumers? Why or why not?

CITIZENSHIP SKILLS

How to Protect Your Rights as a Consumer

LIMITED WARRANTY
CENTURY CASSETTE RECORDERS

Century warrants this product to be free from defects in materials and workmanship for 1 year from the date of purchase. This warranty may be enforced only by the first purchaser.

This warranty covers all defects in material or workmanship except for any product that is purchased or used outside the U.S.; purchased from an unauthorized dealer; damaged in transit; damaged by accident, misuse, abuse, unauthorized repair, or improper installation.

Century will pay all labor and materials expenses for covered items except shipping, removal, and installation.

Century's liability for any defective product is limited to the repair or replacement of the product at our option.

CHAPTER 21 REVIEW

* *

MAIN POINTS

★ Becoming a responsible consumer requires time and thought. In addition to planning a budget, a responsible consumer determines which products are of the best quality, and finds out where those products are available for the lowest price.

★ Individuals, like governments, must make decisions concerning their income and expenses. Among these are decisions about how to save and invest and whether to borrow money or use credit.

★ Savings and investments help individuals reach their goals, and also help the nation's economy grow.

★ Most people who need money can borrow it from a variety of sources. Buying on credit is a type of borrowing.

★ People can protect themselves against some of life's risks by buying insurance. The federal government also provides protection under the social security system.

★ The federal and state governments work actively to protect the health, safety, and rights of consumers. In addition, various private organizations deal with consumer complaints and work to bring consumers' concerns to the attention of government leaders.

WORDS IN REVIEW

Choose the word or phrase from the list below that best completes each sentence. Write the missing words on a separate sheet of paper.

fixed expenses	unit price
investments	Social Security
bankruptcy	principal
insurance	premium
repossess	beneficiary

1. The woman had _____ to protect her against accidents and other risks.

2. Peter was worried that the company might _____ his car, because he had fallen behind in his payments.

3. The man felt that his stocks and bonds were good _____.

4. The shopper checked the _____ to see which product was really cheaper.

5. The family's mortgage payments were finally paying off the _____ rather than interest.

6. The policyholder always paid the _____ on her policy on time.

7. The student was looking for a cheaper apartment because his _____ were much too high.

8. The store owner was so far in debt that he had to declare _____.

9. The woman named her son as _____ of her life insurance policy.

10. After his retirement, the man began receiving monthly _____ benefits from the federal government.

CHAPTER 21 REVIEW

* *

FACTS IN REVIEW

1. What are some of our responsibilities as consumers?
2. What are the advantages and disadvantages of buying from mail-order catalogs?
3. What are some methods stores use to encourage impulse buying?
4. Why is it important to invest money?
5. Describe two ways to buy on credit.
6. What are the general requirements for getting a loan?
7. What is the purpose of insurance?
8. Why did the federal government set up the Social Security system?
9. Why is the task of protecting individual consumers primarily the concern of private groups and organizations?
10. What actions do Better Business Bureaus take in protecting consumers?

THINKING ABOUT THE ECONOMY AND THE INDIVIDUAL

1. *Evaluate.* What do you think are the most important factors to consider when shopping for a product? Explain.
2. *Analyze.* Compared to many industrialized nations, the savings rate of Americans is very low. Why do you think this is so?
3. *Evaluate.* Do you think there are sufficient government regulations to protect consumers? Why or why not?

COLLECTING INFORMATION ABOUT INVESTMENT POSSIBILITIES

Find out the interest rates for different types of savings accounts at several local banks. Also find out the current interest rates for 6-month, 1-year, 2-year, and 5-year Certificates of Deposit (CDs) at those banks. Report your findings to the class.

WRITING ABOUT CREDIT

Some people feel that charge accounts and credit cards are a dangerous way to spend money because people tend to spend more than they have and, as a result, they go into debt. Others feel that buying on credit is a convenience that allows people more freedom as consumers and, if used wisely, presents no danger. Write a short essay on the use of credit. Discuss both points of view and then explain how you feel about buying on credit.

INTERPRETING A BAR GRAPH

Look at the bar graph on page 482. Of the investments shown, which have shown a decrease in value over the period shown? Which have shown an increase? In which would you invest your money? Why?

FOCUSING ON YOUR COMMUNITY

Investigate ways in which your local community or groups in the community protect the rights of consumers. What ordinances protect consumers? How are complaints handled? Are there any private organizations that help consumers? Prepare a report for the class.

UNIT 7 REVIEW

★ ★

ESSAY QUESTIONS

The following questions are based on material in Unit 7. Answer each question with two or three written paragraphs. Be sure to give specific reasons to support your answers.

1. Foreign-made goods frequently outsell American-made goods. Discuss steps that could be taken—by the government or by industry—to make American products more competitive.

2. Many Americans are unable to obtain affordable private health insurance. Should the government do more to ensure that all Americans have access to needed health services? Why or why not?

3. Americans rely heavily on credit for everyday expenses. What problems are caused by this "way of life"? What might be done to change the situation?

CONNECTING CIVICS AND SCIENCE

The Constitution empowers Congress "to promote the progress of science . . . by securing, for limited times, to . . . inventors, the exclusive right to their . . . discoveries." Under this power, Congress created the U.S. Patent Office in 1836. The government also promotes science by funding research. Be prepared to discuss the following in class: What role should the government play in promoting scientific research? What are some of the advantages and disadvantages of government involvement and support? Which areas should receive priority—research related to military technology, space programs, medicine, or the environment? In what other ways could the government promote and support science?

ANALYZING VISUALS

Consumers are often asked to give their opinions about products and services. This information helps other consumers make choices. It also helps businesses improve their performance. The following chart shows consumers' ratings of fast-food chains. Study the chart and then answer the questions.

RATINGS OF FAST-FOOD CHAINS

CHAIN	FRESHNESS OF FOOD	VARIETY OF FOOD	SPEED OF SERVICE	EMPLOYEE COURTESY	CLEANLINESS OF DINING AREA	CONVENIENT LOCATION	GOOD PLACE FOR KIDS
Mickey O's	3	2	2	2	2	1	1
Happy Days	3	2	3	3	4	3	3
Barby's Best	2	3	2	3	3	5	5
Burgers n' BBQ	3	2	2	5	3	2	1
Chicken Licken	5	5	4	4	5	5	5

1 Top rating —— 5 Lowest rating

1. Which fast-food chain did consumers like the most?

2. Which fast-food chain received the worst overall rating?

3. What did consumers think was the best feature of the chains?

4. What were consumers' two biggest complaints about the chains?

★ ★ ★ ★ ★ ★ ★

CLOSEUP ON RECYCLING

In 1989, a 15-year-old high school student became concerned about the environment and helped launch a campaign to ban the use of polystyrene trays in her school cafeteria. Polystyrene is a plastic foam that does not decompose and, as a result, takes up a great deal of space in the nation's landfills. It also releases harmful air pollutants when it is burned. The student-led campaign was so successful that the local school board eliminated polystyrene products from all township schools.

Today, many states, counties, and municipalities are wrestling with similar problems concerning what to do with the millions of tons of trash and solid wastes that Americans generate each year. Some are banning the use of certain products so that they do not become disposal problems later on. Minneapolis, Minnesota, for example, has banned the use of most throwaway plastic food packaging in grocery stores and fast-food outlets. Although the ban was opposed by supermarkets and plastics manufacturers, who claimed it would increase grocery prices, Minneapolis residents strongly supported it.

Plastic products are not the only materials contributing to the nation's waste disposal problems. Newspapers, aluminum cans, old tires, glass, and even leaves and grass clippings are rapidly piling up in landfills throughout the country. As these landfills reach capacity, communities are searching for other, more acceptable solutions to the waste problem. One alternative has been to burn waste products in incinerators. This method, however, can also be harmful to the environment. Even the most modern incinerators release some toxic fumes that can pollute the air and endanger the environment.

More and more local governments are turning to recycling as a solution to the waste problem. In a number of communities across the country, residents are required to sort out their cans, glass, plastics, and

newspapers and place them in special receptacles.

An increasing number of private companies have discovered that there are profits to be made in recycling. For example, one plant in California burns old tires to produce electricity. The process, which creates very little air pollution, also recovers the minerals zinc and gypsum for resale.

Sometimes recycling efforts can be too successful. In 1989, local municipalities throughout the nation had collected more newspapers for recycling than could be processed by the paper mills. The resulting glut of newspapers has caused storage problems for some recycling programs. Several states have passed laws to encourage the papermaking industry to catch up with the supply of newspaper awaiting recycling.

1. Why did the high school student want her school to ban polystyrene products?

2. Why has solid waste become such an enormous problem for most American cities?

3. What measures does your community take to recycle waste?

*C*ongress shall make no law
. . . abridging the freedom of
speech, or of the press . . .

—FIRST AMENDMENT

498

The United States and the World

It sometimes seems that the press serves as a fourth branch of government in our American system of checks and balances. On many occasions in our history, members of the press have spoken out against corruption, negligence, deceit, and the policies of the government at home and abroad. A free press is an essential element in a democratic society.

* * * * *

CHAPTER 22

* *

Comparative Government

OBJECTIVES

After you have studied this chapter, you will be able to:

★ Describe the system of government in Great Britain, and explain how the British system of government differs from American government.

★ Describe the system of government in the Soviet Union, and discuss the role of the Communist Party.

★ Describe the system of government in Japan, and discuss the effect of Japan's economic success on its relationship with the United States.

SECTIONS

1 Great Britain
2 The Soviet Union
3 Japan

In a ceremony that dates back hundreds of years, Britain's Queen Elizabeth II presides over the official opening of Parliament. Seated on a magnificent throne and wearing the crown of her country, she reads a speech outlining the legislative program for the coming session. Her speech, however, does not express her own political opinions. It expresses the opinions of the ruling government; for the queen is only a symbolic ruler with little real authority.

In contrast, the President of the United States, in the State of the Union address, outlines plans for the coming year. These plans are backed by real political power.

The United States and Great Britain, although both democracies, have forms of government that differ in many respects. This is because each nation has a different history, different cultural values, different political interests, and different economic needs. All of these factors influence how each nation governs itself. The same is true of other nations.

The kind of government a nation has affects not only its own people, but also its relations with other countries. For example, the Soviet Union, which has a Communist system of government, was in conflict with the United States for decades. During the period of the cold war both countries had sought to expand their influence to other parts of the world.

★ ★

SECTION 1

Great Britain

★ ★

VOCABULARY

constitutional monarchy	constituency
	by-election
parliamentary government	shadow cabinet

The United Kingdom of Great Britain and Northern Ireland is made up of England, Scotland, Wales, and Northern Ireland. Many of the early European settlers in the United States came from the British Isles. They brought with them a tradition of representative government and the idea that citizens have certain basic rights, such as freedom of speech.

Nevertheless, this country's democratic form of government is quite different from that of Great Britain. The United States is a republic, while Great Britain is a **constitutional monarchy**. It has a monarch, a king or a queen, who serves as the symbolic head of state but does not run the government. In the presidential system of the United States, the executive, legislative, and judicial branches of government are separated. In the **parliamentary government** of Great Britain, the executive, legislative, and judicial functions overlap. There is no separation of powers.

Furthermore, the United States has a written Constitution that guides our government.

Former Prime Minister Margaret Thatcher attends the annual state opening of Parliament.

Great Britain, as you learned in Chapter 2, has what is called an unwritten constitution. Instead of one single document, it has a collection of documents, Parliamentary acts, and court decisions that serve as a guide to government.

The Parliament

For centuries, England was governed by powerful monarchs who ruled the land as they saw fit. Many early rulers did, however, consult with the nation's nobles and religious leaders. Late in the 1200's, the monarchs began to include representatives of towns and counties in their meetings. They needed the help of prominent citizens in winning approval for various tax laws. Gradually, these meetings, or parliaments, began to take on more and more of the duties and powers of government, while the kings and queens became less and less powerful.

HOUSE OF COMMONS Today, the British Parliament makes and executes all of the nation's laws. The Parliament is made up of two houses—the House of Commons and the House of Lords. The lower house, the House of Commons, is the main legislative body. It is made up of 650 elected representatives called MPs (Members of Parliament). The head of the government, the prime minister, is the leader of the party that holds a majority in the House of Commons.

Each member of the House of Commons represents a **constituency**, or the people in an election district. Each member is elected in a general election. There are no set dates for these general elections as there are in the United States. However, the government must hold an election at least once every five years. The prime minister can call an election any time he or she feels that members of the ruling party have a good chance of being re-elected. In addition, if an MP dies or resigns between general elections, a special **by-**

election will be held in his or her district to choose a new MP.

HOUSE OF LORDS The upper house of Parliament, the House of Lords, is not an elected body. It is made up of about 800 nobles, such as dukes and earls, who have inherited their titles. It also includes 26 archbishops and bishops of the Church of England, 15 judges or "law lords," and 230 life peers. Life peers are people who have been rewarded with a title because of some service or achievement.

The House of Lords has no real legislative power. Any bill it defeats can simply be passed again by the House of Commons, after which it becomes law. The House of Lords does, however, act as a moderating force by watching closely and criticizing the work of the House of Commons.

The Government

Great Britain's government (or administration as it would be called in the United States) is formed by the prime minister. The prime minister chooses ministers, or officials, to run various executive departments. Most of these ministers are members of the House of Commons and the majority party. The 17 to 23 ministers who head the most important departments make up the Cabinet, with the prime minister at its head.

Once a government is formed, it serves until the next general election. If the government's party fails to recapture a majority of seats in Parliament, the government falls and a new prime minister is chosen to form a new government. A government may also fall if it loses the support of Parliament. This hap-

This chart shows how the British parliamentary system is set up. What position in the United States is comparable to that of the British Prime Minister?

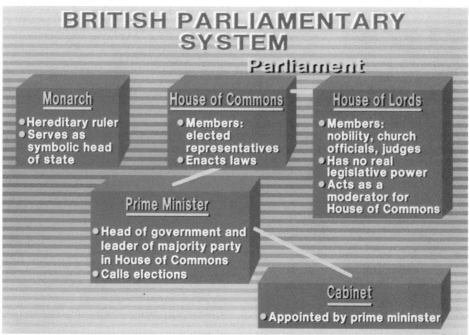

BRITISH PARLIAMENTARY SYSTEM

Parliament

Monarch
- Hereditary ruler
- Serves as symbolic head of state

House of Commons
- Members: elected representatives
- Enacts laws

House of Lords
- Members: nobility, church officials, judges
- Has no real legislative power
- Acts as a moderator for House of Commons

Prime Minister
- Head of government and leader of majority party in House of Commons
- Calls elections

Cabinet
- Appointed by prime mininster

pens when the House of Commons defeats an important bill proposed by the government. In that case, the government resigns and a new election is held.

A major difference between the American and British systems of government is that, in the United States, the President can belong to one party and the majority of Congress may belong to the other. In Britain, the prime minister and his or her government are always chosen from the majority party in Parliament. As a result, there are fewer checks and balances between the executive and legislative branches. On the other hand, there are

Queen Elizabeth II, shown with her husband Prince Philip, has little real political power. However, she plays an important role as the symbolic head of state in Great Britain.

also fewer disagreements between the government and Parliament, and they work together very efficiently.

The Monarchy

The British monarchy is hereditary. This means that the title of king or queen is passed from a monarch to his or her son or daughter. The present monarch of Great Britain is Queen Elizabeth II. Her role in the government is largely ceremonial. She symbolizes the nation and its people at home and around the world. Although the government is called "her majesty's government," the queen cannot make any important decisions. She does give her assent to new laws and she appoints the prime minister, but these are only formalities. In both cases, the monarch always follows the wishes of Parliament.

Political Parties

Like the United States, Great Britain's political system is dominated by two major parties. Since 1979, the Conservative Party, headed by Prime Minister Margaret Thatcher, has been in power. The Conservative Party is similar to the Republican Party in the United States. It believes in free enterprise and less government regulation, and attracts its main support from business and from middle- and upper-class voters.

The major opposition party is the Labor Party, which resembles the Democratic Party in the United States. The Labor Party favors socialism and more government aid to the poor, and attracts working-class voters. The primary role of the opposition party in Parliament is to question and criticize the government. The opposition also forms a **shadow cabinet** made up of members of its own party.

THE UNITED NATIONS CHARTER

On January 1, 1942, 26 nations signed the "United Nations Declaration," which set up a wartime alliance. Roosevelt, however, was concerned with maintaining such an alliance after the war. He ordered the U.S. State Department to begin working on a plan for a permanent international organization.

In 1945, representatives of four nations met in Washington, D.C., to discuss a new United Nations. Over a period of four months, the United States, Great Britain, the Soviet Union, and China hammered out a constitution, or charter, for the new world organization. Later, delegates from 50 nations met in San Francisco to adopt the proposed charter of the United Nations. The United Nations officially came into being on October 24, 1945.

The following is the preamble to the United Nations Charter:

We the peoples of the United Nations determined to save succeeding generations from the scourge of war which twice in our lifetime has brought untold sorrow to mankind, and

to reaffirm faith in fundamental human rights, in the dignity and worth of the human person, in the equal rights of men and women and of nations large and small, and

to establish conditions under which justice and a respect for the obligations arising from treaties and other sources of international law can be maintained, and

to promote social progress and better standards of life in larger freedom,

and for these ends

to practice tolerance and live together in peace with one another as good neighbors, and

to unite our strength to maintain international peace and security, and

to ensure, by the acceptance of principles and the institution of methods, that armed force shall not be used, save in the common interest, and

to employ international machinery for the promotion of the economic and social advancement of all peoples,

have resolved to combine our efforts to accomplish these aims.

Accordingly, our respective Governments, through representatives assembled in the city of San Francisco, who have exhibited their full powers found to be in good and due form, have agreed to the present Charter of the United Nations and do hereby establish an international organization to be known as the United Nations.

Using Your Skills

1. What was the purpose of the original United Nations Declaration?
2. What role did the United States play in creating the United Nations?
3. How does the preamble of the United Nations Charter compare to the preamble of the United States Constitution?

Each shadow cabinet member follows the activities of one of the government's cabinet members and is ready to take over should the government fall. A third party, the Social Democrats, and several small political parties hold a few dozen seats in Parliament.

Great Britain and the World

In the 1800's, people used to say that "the sun never sets on the British Empire." Britain possessed numerous colonies throughout the world. Today, those colonies are independent nations. Most of them, however, remain members of the Commonwealth of Nations, a loose association of former British colonies, that includes Canada, Australia, India, Kenya, and 43 other countries. The prime ministers of these countries meet periodically to discuss common military, economic, and political matters. While Great Britain often plays a leadership role, it has no real authority over Commonwealth members.

Great Britain also belongs to two powerful European organizations: the North Atlantic Treaty Organization (NATO) and the European Economic Community (EEC), often called the Common Market. NATO is a 15-nation military alliance in which the United States is also a leading member.

This map shows which countries in Europe are members of the European Economic Community. How many nations belong to the European Economic Community?

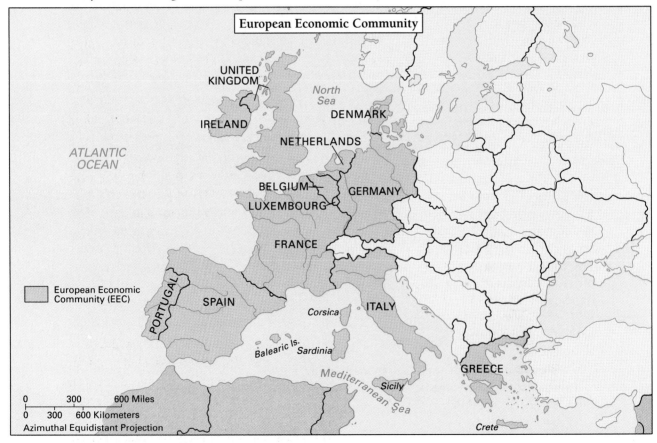

The EEC was formed in the 1950's to enable European nations to work together for economic improvement. The EEC has worked so well that, in 1992, Western Europe will become one nation for economic purposes. Although national borders will remain, the EEC will act as a single nation when doing business with the rest of the world. This will generally strengthen the economies of Great Britain and the other EEC nations.

Through the years, Great Britain has had an especially close relationship with the United States. Millions of British immigrants have settled in America, and the two countries share the same democratic ideals. Moreover, the United States and Britain were military allies in both World War I and World War II. During the 1980's, the conservative governments of Margaret Thatcher and Ronald Reagan had similar goals and views of world affairs.

SECTION REVIEW

Define the Words

constitutional monarchy

constituency

parliamentary system

by-election

shadow cabinet

Check the Facts

1. Describe several ways in which Great Britain's democratic government is different from that of the United States.
2. What is the role of each of the following: House of Commons, House of Lords, prime minister, Queen Elizabeth II?
3. What is the role of the opposition party in the House of Commons?

Think About the Ideas

4. *Evaluate*. What are some of the advantages and disadvantages of the parliamentary system? Explain.

★ ★

SECTION 2

The Soviet Union

★ ★

VOCABULARY

perestroika   Politburo

glasnost

The Soviet Union is the largest country in land area in the world. It spans the European and Asian continents and has a population made up of hundreds of different groups and nationalities. Starting in the late 1940's, the United States was engaged in a so-called "cold war" with the Soviet Union. A bitter competition has been waged to influence other nations to support the ideas of either the United States or the Soviet Union.

Now, relations between the United States and the Soviet Union have grown warmer, signaling an end to the cold war. The two countries share many technological and scientific developments, and their leaders meet frequently to discuss world issues.

Soviet Communism

Until the beginning of this century, the Soviet Union was known as Russia, and was ruled by powerful monarchs called czars. In 1917, a revolution in Russia overthrew the monarchy of Czar Nicholas II. In its place, a group of Communist revolutionaries, called Bolsheviks, set up a new government. Led by

Vladimir Lenin, this new government was a dictatorship in which a handful of Communist Party leaders made all the decisions for the nation.

After Lenin died in 1924, Joseph Stalin became leader of the Soviet Union and ruled the nation ruthlessly for nearly 30 years. Stalin forced farmers to give up their land and go to work on state-owned farms. He murdered and imprisoned millions of Soviet citizens who tried to oppose him. In 1953, Stalin died and was replaced by a succession of Communist Party leaders who continued many of the harsh policies established by Lenin and Stalin.

In 1917, Lenin led the Bolshevik party in a revolt that established a Communist government in Russia.

A Nation in Transition

The Soviet Union is made up of 15 republics or self-governing regions. Each republic is the homeland of a major national group, such as the Ukrainians, and has its own government. The largest and most populous republic is the Russian Soviet Federal Socialist Republic or "Russia." That is why the Soviet Union is often referred to as Russia.

Until recently, the Soviet Union was a totalitarian nation. Although it had a constitution, its provisions were ignored and the civil rights of citizens were not protected. The government also held elections, but the voters were not offered a choice of candidates. Only one person, selected by the Communist Party, could run for a particular office.

In 1985, Mikhail Gorbachev became the new premier, or head of state, of the Soviet Union. Younger and more open to new ideas than any of the previous premiers, Gorbachev set out to make radical changes in the government and economy of the Soviet Union.

GLASNOST AND PERESTROIKA Gorbachev introduced several reforms aimed at making Soviet society more democratic. These changes are called *glasnost*, which means openness. The Soviet people are now permitted to criticize the government openly and even to hold public demonstrations. Gorbachev also freed thousands of political prisoners, and he relaxed censorship rules on books and films. Today, people are allowed to go to church, and many Jews have been allowed to emigrate from the Soviet Union.

Glasnost is part of a broader policy called *perestroika*, which means "restructuring." It has come to symbolize Gorbachev's efforts to revive the failing agriculture and economy of the Soviet Union. Under the old Communist system, the government owned all the

Burgers from America

The opening of the first McDonald's restaurant in Moscow represents one aspect of President Mikhail Gorbachev's policy of restructuring the economy of the Soviet Union.

It was January 31, 1990. The citizens of Moscow were lining up around the block in the bitter cold. Each of them was waiting to buy a burger, a milkshake, and some fries. Fast food had finally arrived in the Soviet Union.

President Gorbachev had invited foreign companies to invest in businesses in the Soviet Union. McDonald's of hamburger fame decided to accept. Its 700-seat restaurant in Moscow can serve 15,000 customers a day. But first, McDonald's had to teach Soviet farmers how to grow potatoes for its french fries and lettuce for its salads. In a country where salespeople are notoriously surly, it also spent time training its Soviet workers to smile and say, "Have a nice day."

The Soviets claim to have invented the hamburger. They say it was an old Russian dish of raw meat and hot spices. Russian sailors exported it to Hamburg, Germany, where it got its name. Today, a cheeseburger, french fries, and soft drink cost the average Moscovite about half a day's pay.

nation's factories, stores, farmlands, and homes. Gorbachev's reforms include giving people the right to own private property and to start small businesses, such as restaurants and shops. New legislation would allow farmers to hold lifetime leases on land and permit individuals and companies to lease government-owned factories. Gorbachev also plans to set up a stock exchange so that people can buy stock in Soviet industries.

The Soviet Government

The Soviet Union is a nation in transition. Many of Gorbachev's proposals have been adopted, and the nation is moving rapidly toward a more democratic government.

CONGRESS OF PEOPLE'S DEPUTIES In 1989, the Soviet Union held free and open elections for the first time since 1917. Soviet citizens elected representatives to the Congress of People's Deputies, a 2,250-member legislature that meets once a year to vote on major national issues. Many of the new deputies were not members of the Communist Party. In the past, the Soviet legislature had always approved government decisions without debate or opposition. Now, members were criticizing the Soviet leadership and openly debating government policies.

The Congress also elected Gorbachev to the new position of president. As president, Gorbachev is the nation's chief executive. In 1990, the Congress agreed to increase the power of the Soviet president. Gorbachev can now make economic changes by decree and declare civil and military emergencies.

Starting in 1995, the Soviet president will be chosen by the people in direct elections. The president will serve a five-year term. This marks a historic departure from the days

when the Soviet ruler was chosen by a small group of Communist Party leaders and then remained in power indefinitely.

THE SUPREME SOVIET The Congress of People's Deputies elects the members of the Supreme Soviet from its own ranks. The Supreme Soviet, the government's main legislative body, consists of two houses, each with 271 members. The Council of Union, elected on the basis of population, is similar to the U.S. House of Representatives. Members of the Council of Nationalities, the equivalent of the U.S. Senate, represent the different republics or regions of the Soviet Union.

In 1989, free and open elections were held for the first time in the Soviet Union. A voter in Moscow casts his ballet in the 1990 parliamentary elections, under the watchful gaze of Lenin.

Mikhail Gorbachev, the President of the Soviet Union, has tried to reform his country's economy. Shortages of food and consumer goods have made this a difficult task.

The Supreme Soviet makes all the nation's laws, approves the budget, and has the power to declare war. It can override a presidential veto by a vote of two-thirds of its members. The Supreme Soviet has two executive bodies that carry out the laws and policies of the government. The Council of Ministers is the equivalent of the American or British cabinet. It is made up of the ministers or heads of government departments and state committees. The second executive body, the Presidium, operates like a steering committee that coordinates the activities of the Supreme Soviet. It is chaired by the president and includes a vice president from each of the 15 republics.

THE SOVIET JUDICIARY The Soviet judiciary belongs to the executive branch. It does not have the power to declare laws unconstitutional. Government reformers are developing plans for a stronger and more independent judiciary.

The Communist Party

One of the most important actions of Congress of Deputies in 1990 was to repeal Article 6 of the Soviet Constitution. Article 6 allowed only one political party in the Soviet Union, the Communist Party. Before Gorbachev took office, the party and the government were virtually the same. The party made the decisions and the government carried them out. The party ran all areas of the nation. Only party members could win promotion to high positions in government and industry, but less than 7 percent of the population belonged to the party.

At the local level, the Communist Party is divided into units or cells. The cells send delegates to local and regional committees, which in turn choose delegates to the National Party Congress. The Party Congress meets every few years to elect the Central Committee, which runs the party and appoints the Politburo. The **Politburo**, made up of top party officials, makes party policy. Before Gorbachev's reforms, the Politburo actually ran the country. Little by little, Gorbachev has been transferring power from the party to the government.

Since the repeal of Article 6, voters have elected many nonparty candidates to municipal and regional positions around the country. The Communist Party remains the major political party in the Soviet Union, but many people expect that the party will split and that other political parties will develop in the next few years.

The Soviet Union at Home and Abroad

As the Soviet Union moves toward a more democratic form of government, it faces three

The events in Europe in 1989 inspired this cartoon in which Eastern European countries and Soviet republics are shown as children being released from school. What does the little red schoolhouse stand for?

critical problems. Most of the people working in government offices are loyal Communist Party members. They form a bureaucracy that is stubbornly resisting the changes that Gorbachev is trying to make. Second, Gorbachev's economic reforms have not yet led to improvement in the stagnant Soviet economy. Finally, the Soviet Union itself is in danger of coming apart. A number of the republics are trying to secede and form independent nations.

Since Gorbachev came to power, he has worked hard to improve the Soviet Union's image abroad. He has tried to convince the world that his country is no longer interested in dominating the world but in cooperating to solve world problems. Gorbachev withdrew Soviet troops from Afghanistan after eight years of fighting, and he signed a major arms reduction treaty with the United States. In 1989, Soviet support for democratic movements in Eastern European countries led to the fall of five Communist governments and the toppling of the Berlin Wall. This wall dividing the two Germanys had been a symbol of the cold war for almost 30 years.

SECTION REVIEW

Define the Words
glasnost   Politburo
perestroika

Check the Facts
1. How did the 1989 Soviet elections differ from previous elections?
2. What is the role of the Central Committee of the Communist Party?
3. How are the policies of *glasnost* and *perestroika* changing the Soviet Union?

Think About the Ideas
4. *Evaluate.* Which of Mikhail Gorbachev's policies do you think will have the greatest effect on the Soviet Union? Explain why.

* *

SECTION 3

Japan

* *

VOCABULARY
oligarchy   consensus
sovereignty   faction

Great Britain's government developed slowly over hundreds of years, and the Soviet Union's government has been taking shape since 1917. The government of Japan, on the other hand, changed almost overnight following its defeat in World War II.

Japan is a small, island nation like Great Britain. Before the war, its leader was Emperor Hirohito, a hereditary monarch who many Japanese believed to be divine, or descended from the gods. At that time, Japan was an **oligarchy**, a system of government in which power is held by a small group of people. It was ruled by the emperor and a small group of nobles and warlords. After the war, the United States occupied Japan for seven years and helped restructure its government and rebuild its economy.

The Japanese Constitution

The Japanese constitution was enacted in 1947, during the American occupation. It established a parliamentary system of government that recognizes the **sovereignty**, or supreme power, of the people. It also guarantees many of the same civil rights as those in the U.S. Constitution. Under the constitution, the emperor and his descendants continue to reign, but have no power. Like the British monarchs, they serve only as symbols and representatives of their country. The Japanese constitution also includes a unique statement in which the Japanese people forever reject war as a part of national policy and declare that offensive military forces will never be maintained.

Japanese Government

Japan has a bicameral national legislature called the Diet. Its upper house, the House of Councilors, has 252 members who each serve six-year terms. The House of Councilors is elected by the people, but it has very little power. Its main role is to advise the government.

The lower house, the House of Representatives, has 511 members elected from 123 election districts. Each of these districts elects three or four representatives to serve four-year terms. However, they may stand for election sooner if, as happens in a parliamentary system, the government is dissolved and new elections are required. Like the British House of Commons, the Japanese House of Representatives is the most powerful legislative body in Japan. Its duties are to make laws and treaties, approve budgets, determine taxes, and spend public funds.

Like the United States, Japan has a national legislature made up of two houses. In what way is the House of Councilors, Japan's upper house, different from the U.S. Senate?

The Japanese people have a long tradition of group cooperation, political unity, and social harmony. They like to conduct business in a low-key, quiet manner that avoids confrontation. Members of the Diet thus try to reach decisions through compromise and **consensus**—by broad, general agreement—and avoid argument and dissent.

Japan's head of state, the prime minister, is elected by the Diet. As in Great Britain, the head of state is usually the leader of the majority party in the House of Representatives. The prime minister selects the members of the cabinet and the ministers of government departments. Together, the prime minister and these leaders form the executive branch of the government. The prime minister and at least one-half of the cabinet ministers must be members of the Diet. As a result, the executive and legislative functions are combined rather than separated.

Political Parties

Japan is a multiparty democracy. Although there are four major parties, one party, the Liberal Democratic Party, has been in power since 1955. Despite its name, the Liberal Democratic Party (LDP) is a conservative party that represents Japan's powerful business interests and middle class. The LDP is really a coalition of parties made up of several smaller **factions**, or groups. While these factions differ from one another in certain respects, all favor free enterprise and close ties with the United States.

The major opposition party is the Japanese Socialist Party (JSP). Much of its support comes from union members and various groups that want greater change in the nation. Generally, the JSP favors placing more controls on capitalism and a break with the United States.

The two other large parties are the Japanese Communist Party and the Komeito (Clean Government) Party. The Communist Party has gained supporters in many of Japan's large cities by focusing on social problems. The Komeito Party is closely associated with a religious organization, and seeks a return to a simpler, more spiritual way of life.

Japanese Bureaucracy

Japan has a large bureaucracy, or civil service, that carries out many of the administrative and technical duties of the government. Japanese civil servants work hard to help solve the enormous problems caused by Japan's rapidly growing population, such as waste disposal and traffic congestion. Civil servants enjoy a great deal of power and esteem because of their dedication to the people and the nation.

Japan and the World

Since its devastation in World War II, Japan has rebuilt its economy so successfully that it has become one of the world's richest nations. Its spectacular economic success has been a model for many other Asian regions, such as South Korea, Singapore, Taiwan, and Hong Kong. In fact, some experts predict that the next century will be the "Pacific Century." They foresee that the Asian countries on the Pacific Ocean will be very important in world affairs, both politically and economically.

Japan's economic development has already made it a major world power. Yet, the nation has been reluctant to take on a role of political leadership. Slowly, however, its reluctance is disappearing, and it has begun to provide foreign aid and technical assistance to other nations.

GETTING IN

Who may come to the United States and who may not? That question has long been a subject of controversy. So many foreigners want to come here to visit or to stay, that the United States has had to impose limits.

One way in which the United States controls immigration and visitors is through the issuing of visas, permission to enter the country for a certain period of time. In 1952, during the height of the anti-Communist hysteria, Congress enacted the McCarran-Walter Act. This law denied visas to certain classes of foreigners—criminals, terrorists, ex-Nazis, the mentally ill, people with contagious diseases, homosexuals, Communists, and people "who engage in activities prejudicial to the public interest."

The law has enabled the government to prevent visits by a wide variety of prominent people whose ideas were not in line with those of the administration then in power. The Carter administration, for example, used McCarran-Walter to prevent visits by right-wing extremists from Rhodesia (now Zimbabwe) and El Salvador.

The Reagan administration used the law to prevent visits and speeches by such prominent figures as Canadian environmentalist Farley Mowat and Colombian writer Gabriel García Márquez because of their politics. The law has even been used to keep foreigners with AIDS from attending AIDS conferences in the United States.

The McCarran-Walter Act has long been under attack and will probably soon be repealed. Critics say it is unconstitutional because it is so vague and is applied unfairly. Furthermore, they charge that it violates the principle of freedom of speech in two ways. It prevents American citizens from hearing speeches by foreigners supporting unpopular political ideas. It also excludes foreigners because of what they have said, not what they have done.

The question of who the government admits as refugees is equally controversial. The U.S. government claims its refugee policy is "nation-neutral." It says that it accepts refugees from any country as long as they can prove "a well-established fear of persecution" in their own countries. However, refugees from nations that are not on good terms with the United States gain asylum fairly easily. Those from nations with which the United States has friendly relations have a much harder time. (The table on the next page shows the number of refugees to the United States from several regions of the world between 1979 and 1989.)

American refugee policy also changes with world events. In 1989, the Chinese government killed thousands in an effort to crush the democracy movement among Chinese students. America immediately offered long-term visa extensions to an estimated 40,000 to 50,000 Chinese students studying in the United States who were afraid to go home.

GETTING IN

REFUGEES TO THE UNITED STATES

	AFRICA	ASIA	EASTERN EUROPE	SOVIET UNION	LATIN AMERICA	MIDDLE EAST/ SOUTH ASIA	TOTAL
1979	0	76,521	3,393	24,449	7,000	0	111,363
1980	955	163,799	5,025	28,444	6,662	2,231	207,116
1981	2,119	131,139	6,704	13,444	2,017	3,829	159,252
1982	3,326	73,522	10,780	2,756	602	6,369	97,355
1983	2,648	39,408	12,083	1,409	668	5,465	61,681
1984	2,747	51,960	10,285	715	160	5,246	71,113
1985	1,953	49,970	9,350	640	138	5,994	68,045
1986	1,315	45,454	8,713	787	173	5,998	62,440
1987	1,994	40,105	8,606	3,694	315	10,107	64,821
1988	1,588	35,347	7,818	20,421	2,497	8,415	76,086
1989	1,922	45,684	8,948	39,553	2,605	6,908	105,620
TOTAL	20,567	752,909	91,705	136,312	22,837	60,562	1,084,892

Source: U.S. Department of State Bureau of Refugee Programs: Summary of Refugee Admissions, August 31,1989.

Using Your Skills

1. How does the McCarran-Walter Act violate the principle of free speech?
2. What provisions of the McCarran-Walter Act would you keep? Which would you repeal? Why?
3. According to the table, in what year did the United States receive the largest number of refugees?
4. According to the table, from which region did the largest number of refugees come to the United States between 1979 and 1989?
5. Why do you think the government makes it harder for refugees from friendly nations to gain asylum than for refugees from hostile and Communist nations?

Japan's relationship to the United States is also changing. In recent years, Japan's economic strength has led to increased tensions with the United States. For example, Japan now exports many more goods to the United States than it imports. The Japanese are also investing heavily in American real estate and businesses. These situations alarm many American political leaders and citizens. They feel that Japan's economic success is hurting the economy of the United States. In response, many Americans are demanding that Japan adopt fairer trade policies with the United States. And, despite Japan's constitutional ban on maintaining offensive military forces, the United States is pressuring the country to take on more of its own defense burden. This defense has been provided and paid for by the United States since World War II.

SECTION REVIEW

Define the Words

oligarchy   consensus

sovereignty   faction

Check the Facts

1. What is unique about the Japanese constitution?
2. How have Japan's traditions affected political activities and decision-making?
3. How has Japan's relationship with the United States been changing in recent years?

Think About the Ideas

4. *Analyze.* Do you think that Japan will be able to continue and build upon its great economic success? Why or why not?

Under the leadership of Takoko Doi, the Japanese Socialist Party has gained ground in recent elections.

CITIZENSHIP SKILLS

How to Use an Atlas

Atlases are reference books that contain maps. They usually have various types of maps that present different kinds of geographic and social information.

Atlases often contain general-purpose maps. *Physical maps*, for example, show natural features such as mountains and deserts and river systems. *Political maps* show the boundaries between countries and often smaller divisions such as states or counties.

Atlases may also contain special-purpose maps. For example, *geologic maps* might show the location and distribution of the earth's volcanoes and earthquake zones. *Oceanographic maps* focus on the structure of the ocean floors, and perhaps the location of ocean currents or the distribution of marine life. *Climate maps* present information about rainfall, air temperature, humidity, and winds. Various other types of maps might show the location of different kinds of soils or plants, or the distribution of natural resources.

Maps can also present information about people. For example, maps can show the distribution and movement of people in a region or where different religions are practiced and different languages are spoken. Information about human activities and relationships among the world's peoples can also be shown. For example, *economic activity maps* might show how land is used, what crops are grown, and what products are manufactured. *Transportation maps* might show roads, railroads, air routes, shipping lanes, and systems of communication. Other special-purpose maps can show forms of government, how people voted in elections, and political alliances.

Changes in political, economic, social, and cultural conditions are the special concern of *historical atlases*. A historical atlas presents maps on specific places, events, and conditions in the past.

When presenting information, maps can focus on areas of any size— nations, regions, cities, voting districts, historic sites, or the entire world.

Although atlases are made up mainly of maps, they usually contain useful information in other forms as well. Some atlases contain a great deal of written information such as chronologies, glossaries, geographical dictionaries, and statistics. Many also include captioned pictures, tables, diagrams, charts, and graphs. As you can see, an atlas is a valuable resource to use when looking for information about places in the world.

Using Your Skills
1. What types of information can be shown in maps?
2. What other kinds of information, besides maps, are often found in atlases?
3. Why do you think it is important, in most instances, to use the most recent atlas available?

CHAPTER 22 REVIEW

★ ★

MAIN POINTS

★ Great Britain is a constitutional monarchy with a parliamentary system of government. Its Parliament is made up of two houses, the House of Lords and the House of Commons. The real legislative power is held by the House of Commons.

★ Great Britain's prime minister is the head of government.

★ The Soviet Union was a Communist dictatorship. Under the leadership of Mikhail Gorbachev, it is moving toward democracy and a free market economy.

★ The new Soviet government has a strong president and a legislature called the Supreme Soviet.

★ After World War II, Japan adopted a parliamentary system of government. The government is headed by a prime minister.

★ Japan has achieved great economic success, but it has been reluctant to take on a role of political leadership in the world.

WORDS IN REVIEW

Choose the word or phrase from the list below that best completes each sentence. Write the missing words on a separate sheet of paper.

parliamentary	by-election
government	Politburo
constitutional monarchy	*perestroika*
shadow cabinet	consensus
glasnost	sovereignty
oligarchy	

1. Under the policy of _____, the Soviet people are experiencing more freedom than ever before.

2. The members of Japan's parliament, or Diet, try to make decisions based on _____ rather than confrontation.

3. In Great Britain's _____, executive, legislative, and judicial functions overlap.

4. The _____ of the people is the basic principle of democratic government.

5. Members of Britain's opposition party maintain a _____ that is ready to rule should the majority party lose power.

6. In a _____, power is controlled by a small group of people.

7. A special _____ was held to choose a new Member of Parliament.

8. The goal of _____ is to reform both the political and economic systems of the Soviet Union.

9. The real power in the Soviet Union is held by members of the _____.

10. In a _____, the power of the king or queen is largely ceremonial.

FACTS IN REVIEW

1. Describe the main features of the British Parliament.

2. Compare the political parties of Great Britain with those of the United States.

3. Describe the relationship between Great Britain and the United States.

4. How did the Soviet Union become a Communist country?

5. In what ways is the Soviet government similar to the U.S. government?

6. How does Gorbachev plan to change the Soviet economy?

CHAPTER 22 REVIEW

* *

7. Discuss the role of the Communist Party in the Soviet Union.

8. How did Japan's government change after World War II?

9. What is the role of the emperor in Japan today?

10. How has Japan's economic success affected its role in the world?

THINKING ABOUT COMPARATIVE GOVERNMENT

1. *Analyze.* Why do you think Great Britain continues to have a monarchy, even though the monarch has no real power to rule the country?

2. *Analyze.* Do you think the Soviet Union has really changed? Does it allow a free and open society with a democratic government? Explain your answer.

3. *Analyze.* What do you think might be the advantages and disadvantages of Japan's consensus-type decision-making?

WRITING ABOUT POLITICAL SYSTEMS

Write an essay comparing the political system of the United States to that of either Great Britain, the Soviet Union, or Japan. You may need to do some additional reading about one of these for-eign governments. After a brief comparison of the structures of the two governments, your essay should analyze the advantages and dis-advantages of different features of the political systems. Focus also on how each type of govern-ment affects the citizens of each country. You might consider using a chart to help compare the structures of the two governments.

INTERPRETING A POLITICAL CARTOON

Look at the political cartoon on page 512. What is the significance of the symbol on the steeple of the schoolhouse? Who do the children in the cartoon represent? Who is the teacher inside the schoolhouse? Why do you think the cartoonist used a schoolhouse? What is the main point of the cartoon?

FOCUSING ON YOUR COMMUNITY

Find out if any people in your community have come from Great Britain, the Soviet Union, Japan, or other countries. Try to interview these people and ask them questions about the politi-cal system of the country they came from. Find out what it was like to live under that system of government, and what role citizens had in government. Find out also how local government in that country compares to the local govern-ment of your community. Prepare an oral report for the class.

International Relations

OBJECTIVES

After you have studied this chapter, you will be able to:

★ Discuss basic American foreign policies, including isolationism, containment, and collective security.

★ Explain how U.S. foreign policy toward the Soviet Union has changed.

★ Describe the role of the President, Congress, the Departments of State and Defense, the National Security Council, and the American people in making foreign policy.

★ Discuss different aspects of foreign policy, such as diplomacy, foreign aid, and alliances.

★ Describe the purpose of the United Nations and the roles of its various divisions and agencies.

★ Identify and discuss foreign policy challenges facing the United States today.

SECTIONS

1 Elements of U.S. Foreign Policy
2 The United Nations
3 Foreign Policy Challenges Today

During much of its history, the United States remained isolated from the political upheavals and struggles of other nations. Bordered on two sides by enormous oceans, the nation was distant from conflicts in Europe, Africa, and Asia.

This isolation enabled the United States to grow and develop on its own. The invention of modern transportation and communications changed everything, however. The telegraph, the telephone, and then the airplane brought the rest of the world much closer to America's shores.

In 1917, America became immersed in world affairs when it entered World War I. Since that time, the United States has had a great deal of experience in international relations. It has had to develop a **foreign policy**—plans outlining U.S. positions on world issues and relations with other countries. As the United States has moved into a position of world leadership, foreign policy has assumed a central place in American government.

* *

SECTION 1

Elements of U.S. Foreign Policy

* *

VOCABULARY

foreign policy	disarmament
isolationism	diplomacy
containment	alliance
détente	

Before World War I, America's foreign policy was characterized by **isolationism**. This meant that the nation did not form alliances or military pacts with other countries. It remained neutral in other nations' disputes or wars. An exception to this policy was in Latin America, where the United States sometimes stepped in to protect U.S. interests.

World War I ended American isolationism. After the war, however, the nation moved back toward isolationism. It avoided many international involvements, and refused to join the League of Nations, the new world organization. This isolationism was shattered once again when Japan bombed the U.S. naval base at Pearl Harbor, Hawaii, on December 7, 1941, and the nation entered World War II.

Postwar Foreign Policy

Two events at the end of World War II changed American foreign policy forever. The first was the use of the atomic bomb, the most fearsome weapon the world had ever seen.

THE PENTAGON PAPERS:
THE BILL OF RIGHTS V. NATIONAL SECURITY

One of the basic principles of freedom of the press is the idea of "no prior restraint." This means that the government cannot decide beforehand what members of the press cannot discuss or write about. To do so would amount to censorship and would violate freedom of the press. In 1971, the federal government tried to prevent the *New York Times* from publishing a series of articles. The articles were based on secret documents taken from the Pentagon, the headquarters of the Defense Department, by a former employee.

The documents, which became known as the "Pentagon Papers," detailed the history of America's involvement in the Vietnam War. They showed that the government had misled the public about its early involvement in Vietnam.

The *New York Times* printed its first articles on June 13 and June 14, 1971. The Nixon administration sought, and won, an injunction from a federal court halting publication of any further articles. The *Times* immediately appealed to the U.S. Supreme Court. In the meantime, the *Washington Post* also began printing articles based on the Pentagon Papers. It soon became apparent that other newspapers would do the same, forcing the government to seek injunctions against each one.

The Supreme Court took the case. The *Times* argued that the injunction was unconstitutional and amounted to censorship. The government charged that the articles were damaging to national security because the war was still going on.

The Supreme Court handed down its decision in the Pentagon Papers case (*New York Times Co. v. U.S.*) on June 30. It ruled 6–3 against the injunction, finding that the government had not shown sufficient "justification for the imposition of such a restraint." The

Court upheld the principle that prior restraint or censorship is a violation of the First Amendment.

In a very few cases, the federal courts have allowed prior restraint for the sake of national security. In 1979, for example, in the case of *United States v. Progressive, Inc.*, a magazine was barred from publishing an article on how to build an atom bomb. The government had argued that the article would have made it easier for terrorist groups and small, hostile nations to build such weapons and use them against the United States.

Using Your Skills

1. Why would allowing the government to decide beforehand what can be printed or broadcast destroy freedom of the press?
2. Do you agree with the decisions in the Pentagon Papers and the *United States v. Progressive, Inc.*, cases? Why or why not?

The other was the Soviet occupation of Eastern Europe, which turned Eastern Europe nations into Soviet dependencies with Communist governments. This Soviet action convinced the United States and its allies that the goal of communism was to take over the world. These events led to fierce competition between the forces of democracy and communism. Called the "cold war," this competition involved the clash of ideas more often than the clash of armies.

To prevent the spread of communism in Europe and Asia, President Harry Truman developed the policy of **containment**. Under this policy, the United States would use both money and military power to "contain" the Soviet Union and prevent it from expanding its territory. To promote containment, nations signed defense treaties in which they agreed to protect each other in the event of Communist attack.

The policy of containment prevented Communist advances in Greece and Turkey. It also defeated Soviet attempts to take over the western half of the divided city of Berlin. In the 1960's, the policy of containment led the United States into the unpopular and unsuccessful Vietnam War.

Another postwar foreign policy was the idea of collective security, or joining together to protect each other. In 1949, the United States, Canada, and several Western European nations formed NATO, the North Atlantic Treaty Organization. Collective security is the basis of NATO. Its main purpose has been to protect member nations from Soviet aggression and maintain a balance of power in Europe.

DÉTENTE In the 1970's, the United States and the Soviet Union began a policy of peaceful coexistence. During this period of **détente**,

In the years since World War II, the nations of the world have met regularly to work together toward common goals.

or easing of tensions, relations between the two superpowers improved, but the cold war continued. Thousands of Soviet and NATO troops were still stationed in central Europe. In addition, the governments of the Soviet Union and other Communist countries continued to deny basic civil rights to their citizens.

One of the signs of the improved relations was some progress in arms control and **disarmament**, or arms reduction. After World War II, the United States and the Soviet Union were engaged in an escalating arms race. In an effort to gain the upper hand, each side increased the numbers and kinds of weapons, both nuclear and conventional (nonnuclear). Since the 1970's, however, the two nations have signed several arms control treaties that limit the growth of nuclear arms.

In 1989, events in the Soviet Union brought the cold war to an end. Gorbachev allowed free elections and began to move his country toward democracy. He also presented no opposition when one after another of the countries of Eastern Europe ousted their Communist governments. Relations between the Soviet Union and the United States improved dramatically.

Who Conducts Foreign Policy?

One of the U.S. President's most important roles is formulating the nation's foreign policy. Among the President's powers are the power to negotiate treaties and to appoint ambassadors and other diplomats.

Several government officials and agencies help the President plan and carry out foreign policy. The Department of State has the primary responsibility for carrying out American foreign policy around the world. It supervises U.S. diplomats and gathers information to help the President make decisions on foreign policy issues.

The Department of Defense carries out the President's military decisions. It maintains about 2 million troops at hundreds of military bases around the world. It ensures that the United States will be ready to react quickly to any military crisis that arises.

The National Security Council (NSC) also informs and advises the President on foreign policy issues. It analyzes information, and coordinates the nation's military and foreign

The United States maintains troops at hundreds of military bases around the world. The troops shown here are on maneuver in Germany.

policy goals. In addition, the NSC supervises the Central Intelligence Agency (CIA). Known as America's spy agency, the CIA gathers information about governments and political movements around the world.

Congress and the American people also play important roles in making foreign policy. Only Congress has the power to declare war or appropriate money needed to carry out foreign policy goals. In addition, the U.S. Senate must ratify all treaties negotiated by the President. It must also approve the President's nominees for ambassadors.

The American people affect foreign policy through the leaders that they elect. They can also participate in special interest groups, such as environmental, peace, and human rights organizations and lobbies.

How the United States Conducts Foreign Policy

Foreign policy is carried out in three basic ways—diplomacy, foreign aid, and alliances. **Diplomacy** is the process of conducting business between foreign governments. As the nation's chief diplomat, the President frequently meets with the leaders of other nations to discuss foreign policy issues or to negotiate treaties and agreements. The Secretary of State, ambassadors, and other officials are engaged in most of the nation's day-to-day diplomacy.

Another way of carrying out foreign policy is through foreign aid. Foreign aid might be given in the form of money, military assistance, food, or other supplies. The United States often provides large amounts of foreign aid to nations in an effort to limit Communist influence.

One of America's greatest foreign aid triumphs was the Marshall Plan. In 1947, Secretary of State George Marshall proposed that the United States give Western Europe $12.5 billion to help rebuild factories and businesses destroyed during World War II. The Marshall Plan was so successful that, within a decade, Western Europe had fully recovered from the war.

A third way of carrying out foreign policy is through **alliances**—formal agreements or unions among nations. NATO, as you have already learned, is a defense alliance. The United States belongs to several alliances in other regions as well.

Not all alliances are formed for defense. Some are formed for economic or other reasons. For example, the European Economic Community, or Common Market, works to improve the economy of Western Europe. The Organization of Petroleum Exporting Countries (OPEC) is an alliance of several oil-rich nations that works to control the quantities and price of oil around the world. The Antarctic Treaty Alliance, formed by the United States and 12 other nations, conducts peaceful scientific research in Antarctica.

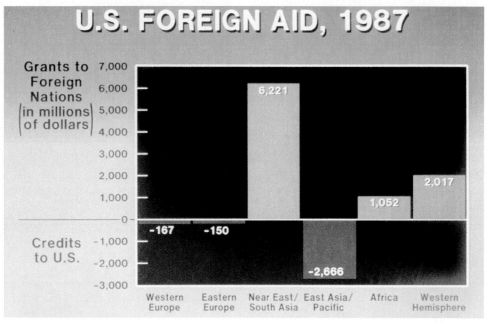

This graph shows the distribution of U.S. foreign aid in 1987. Which area received the most aid from the United States?

Decisions made at meetings of the Organization of Petroleum Exporting Countries (OPEC) often affect oil prices around the world.

SECTION REVIEW

Define the Words

foreign policy
isolationism
containment
détente

disarmament
diplomacy
alliance

Check the Facts

1. How did U.S. foreign policy change after World War II?
2. What role does Congress play in America's foreign policy?
3. Describe three ways in which foreign policy is carried out.

Think About the Ideas

4. *Analyze.* What are the advantages and disadvantages of a foreign policy of isolationism?

★ ★

SECTION 2

The United Nations

★ ★

VOCABULARY
developing nations   developed nations

Without the participation of the United States, the League of Nations was a weak, ineffectual organization that was unable to prevent World War II. As that war ended, America realized it could not make the same mistake again. The United States therefore became a leader in forming a new international organization—the United Nations. (See Great American Documents: The United Nations Charter on page 505.)

The United Nations Today

Today, the United Nations has 159 member nations and is headquartered in New York City. According to the UN charter, the organization's main purposes are to maintain international peace, develop friendly relations among nations, promote justice and cooperation, and seek peaceful solutions to international problems.

THE GENERAL ASSEMBLY The General Assembly is the legislative body of the United Nations. Each member nation is represented in the General Assembly and has one vote.

UNITED NATIONS

International Court of Justice

Security Council
Peacekeeping arm of UN

General Assembly
★ Discusses international issues
★ Elects Secretary General

Secretariat
Handles administrative work of the UN

Trusteeship Council
Concerned with non-self-governing territories

Economic and Social Council
Concerned with social, educational, and health conditions

Specialized Agencies
World Health Organization (WHO)
Studies diseases and maintains worldwide health clinics

United Nations Children's Fund (UNICEF)
Provides food and medicine to children around the world

International Monetary Fund (IMF)
Promotes world trade

World Bank
Provides loans and technical assistance to developing countries

The chart shows the main divisions of the United Nations and some of its specialized agencies. What is the function of the Secretariat?

AMERICAN PROFILES

Eleanor Roosevelt: First Lady of the World

As First Lady of the United States, Eleanor Roosevelt was a tireless worker on behalf of America's poor, minorities, women, and children. In 1945, her husband President Franklin Roosevelt died. His successor, Harry Truman, appointed her one of the first American delegates to the new United Nations. Although some people thought she was a terrible choice for the position, she soon won everyone's respect. She forced the Soviet delegates to back down on an important issue concerning refugee rights.

In 1947, Eleanor Roosevelt was named chairperson of the UN Commission on Human Rights. After a year and a half of her determined and patient leadership, the commission produced the Universal Declaration of Human Rights. This document spelled out the basic rights and freedoms that should be enjoyed by all the people of the world. Now more than 40 years old, the document still serves as a model for democratic governments all over the world.

Mrs. Roosevelt resigned from her UN post in 1952. For the next decade, she traveled the world as an unofficial ambassador of goodwill, visiting world leaders and welcoming them to her home. In 1961, she was reappointed to the United Nations. On her return, the General Assembly gave her a standing ovation—the first ever given. She truly was, in President Truman's words, "First Lady of the world."

Using Your Skills
1. What role did Mrs. Roosevelt play in the United Nations?
2. Why is the Declaration of Human Rights an important document?

The General Assembly meets in regular and special sessions to debate international issues and make recommendations to member nations. The General Assembly also elects a Secretary General to serve as chief executive of the United Nations.

THE SECURITY COUNCIL The Security Council is the peacekeeping arm of the United Nations. Its 15 members include 5 permanent members—the United States, Great Britain, the Soviet Union, France, and China—and 10 nonpermanent members elected for two-year terms by the General Assembly. Although each country is given one vote, a veto by any of the permanent members can defeat any motion. This gives the five permanent members a great deal of power. The Soviet Union, for example, has vetoed over 150 actions and the United States has vetoed about 50.

The Security Council meets throughout the year. It often asks quarreling nations to try to settle their differences peacefully. It can also send UN troops, drawn from various nations, to try to keep war from breaking out between nations. In 1988, the United Nations peacekeeping forces won the Nobel Peace Prize for their efforts to maintain peace around the world.

INTERNATIONAL COURT OF JUSTICE The International Court of Justice, also known as the World Court, hears disputes between nations and issues decisions based on international law. The 15 judges are appointed by the General Assembly. Decisions are not binding, but if a nation does not comply, the case may be brought before the Security Council.

UN AGENCIES Much of the most important and least recognized work of the United Nations is done by its 27 specialized, semi-independent agencies. These agencies work for world peace by helping the developing nations of the world cope with hunger, dis-

UNESCO, the UN agency concerned with education, sponsors literacy programs in developing nations.

ease, poverty, and ignorance. **Developing nations** are the poorer nations of the world, which are struggling to build an industrial economy and meet the basic needs of their people. These countries are primarily agricultural, and many of the people are farmers or miners. Most of the developing nations are located in Africa, Asia, and Latin America. The **developed nations**—such as the United States, Canada, Japan, Australia, and most of Europe—have already developed their resources and built their industries. As a result, the people in these countries generally enjoy a higher standard of living than those in developing countries. Some of the United Nation's specialized agencies include The World Health Organization (WHO), The United Nations Children's Fund (UNICEF), The International Monetary Fund (IMF), and The World Bank (International Bank for Reconstruction and Development).

The UN's Effectiveness

The United Nations has not been as effective in settling disputes and preventing wars as many had hoped. Some critics feel that it is now dominated by many small nations, which contribute little to the organization.

They point out that the United States pays one-fourth of the cost of the United Nations. Yet it has no more say in UN operations than a country that pays much less and has only a fraction of the population of the United States. That is because each country gets one vote in the General Assembly.

Nevertheless, the UN's peacekeeping forces and specialized agencies have been extremely important in dealing with global problems and fostering international cooperation. The United Nations gives the nations of the world a place to discuss their grievances and seek justice. For these reasons, it offers one of the best opportunities for achieving world peace.

SECTION REVIEW

Define the Words

developing nations   developed nations

Check the Facts

1. What are the purposes of the United Nations according to its charter?
2. How can the five permanent members of the Security Council hinder its work?
3. Explain the difference between a *developing* and a *developed* nation.

Think About the Ideas

4. *Evaluate.* Do you think it is fair for each member nation to have one vote in the UN General Assembly? Why or why not?

In Lebanon and other trouble spots around the world, United Nations peacekeeping forces try to enforce cease-fire agreements and prevent the outbreak of hostilities.

VOCABULARY

guerrilla   apartheid

As the 1990's began, the global situation seemed hopeful. Fighting was ended in several countries, and many dictatorships in Latin America and the Communist world turned toward democracy. Still, major challenges remain.

Regional Conflicts

During the 1980's, several regional conflicts occurred between neighboring nations or among different factions within a nation. In 1979, the Soviet Union invaded its neighbor, Afghanistan. Soviet troops remained there through most of the 1980's. Iran and Iraq waged a long, bloody war with each other for most of the 1980's. And Vietnam occupied its neighbor Kampuchea (Cambodia) for several years. All of these conflicts have now come to an end.

The Middle East, however, remains a regional hot spot. The state of Israel, created in 1948, is surrounded by Arab nations that have tried over the years to destroy it. Although Israel has repelled several Arab attacks, the Arab-Israeli conflict continues to dominate the region. The United States, a strong ally of Israel, is working with both Israel and the Arab nations to try to find a peaceful solution to this conflict.

Iraq invaded Kuwait in August 1990. Responding to the invasion, the nations of the world, through the UN, banned together against Iraq.

Latin America is also a trouble spot. In 1962, Cuba became the first nation in the Americas to turn Communist. Since that time, the United States has been dedicated to preventing the spread of communism in this hemisphere. To this end, the United States has supported almost every anti-Communist government in Latin America, even those ruled by harsh dictators. In Central America, the United States supported the government of El Salvador in its civil war with bands of Communist **guerrillas**, or rebel soldiers. In Nicaragua, on the other hand, the United States armed and supplied a guerrilla group called the Contras, who were fighting the

Border disputes have been a source of continuing conflict between Israel and its neighbors.

The Name Game

At least one or two countries a year change their names, making even the most recently published maps and atlases out of date. In 1989, for example, Burma chose to adopt the name of Mayanmar.

Here are some other countries that have changed their names since 1960. The new names are first, then the old names and the year of the change:

★ Malaysia—Malaya, Sabah (North Borneo), and Sarawak (1963)
★ Zambia—Northern Rhodesia (1964)
★ Tanzania—Tanganyika and Zanzibar (1964)
★ Guyana—British Guiana (1966)
★ Namibia—South-West Africa (1968)
★ Zaire—Belgian Congo (1971)
★ Bangladesh—East Pakistan (1971)
★ Sri Lanka—Ceylon (1972)
★ Benin—Dahomey (1975)
★ Zimbabwe—Rhodesia (1980)
★ Vanuatu—New Hebrides (1980)
★ Belize—British Honduras (1981)
★ Burkina Faso—Upper Volta (1984)

Communist government. In 1990, free elections were held in Nicaragua and the government was defeated by an anti-Communist coalition. Also in Central America, the United States invaded Panama in 1989 to depose its dictator, Manuel Noriega, and install the elected government. The invasion angered many in Latin America who believe that the United States is too eager to intervene in the affairs of Latin American nations.

Movements Toward Democracy

The cold war ended suddenly in 1989 when the Soviet Union held free elections and the countries of Eastern Europe forced out the ruling Communist governments. In rapid succession, Poland, Hungary, East Germany, Bulgaria, Czechoslovakia, and Romania all deposed their Communist leaders and scheduled elections. The governments of East and West Germany, separated since 1945, became a reunited Germany in October 1990.

Some of the new Eastern European governments have asked the Soviet Union to reduce or remove troops and weapons from their countries. All are drawing up trade agreements with the West. They look forward to participating more fully in the European Economic Community after 1992.

In the western part of the Soviet Union, voters in the republics of Latvia, Estonia, Lithuania, and Georgia elected nationalist majorities to their legislatures. In March 1990, Lithuania declared itself an independent nation and other Soviet republics moved in the same direction. The United States was concerned that these demands for independence might cause a Soviet crackdown and a return to more repressive policies.

Such a crackdown occurred in China in 1989, when hundreds of thousands of students

This political protest in a region of the Soviet Union would not have been permitted before the reforms of 1989.

This map shows the per capita income of people around the world. Which two continents have the lowest average per capita income?

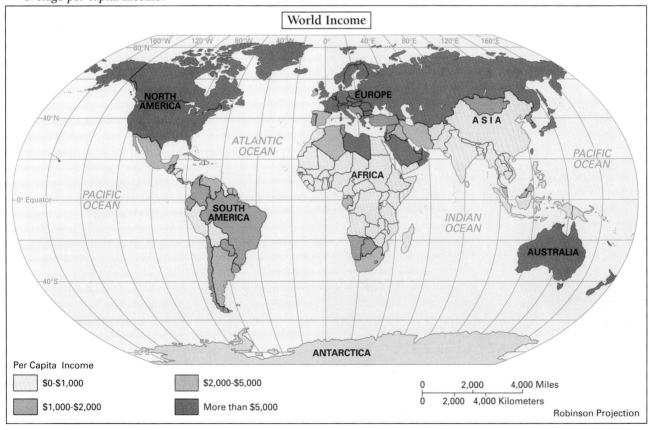

World Income

NORTH AMERICA

EUROPE

ASIA

ATLANTIC OCEAN

PACIFIC OCEAN

AFRICA

PACIFIC OCEAN

0° Equator

SOUTH AMERICA

INDIAN OCEAN

AUSTRALIA

40°S

80°S

ANTARCTICA

Per Capita Income

$0-$1,000

$2,000-$5,000

$1,000-$2,000

More than $5,000

0   2,000   4,000 Miles
0   2,000   4,000 Kilometers

Robinson Projection

and workers demonstrated in the capital city of Beijing, demanding democratic reforms. Hundreds, perhaps thousands, were killed when army troops fired on the demonstrators.

Changes are also taking place in Africa. The former South African colony of Namibia became an independent nation in 1990. It is expected to become the 160th member of the United Nations. South Africa also took some steps toward solving its racial problems. The government released black leader Nelson Mandela after 28 years in prison. This was seen as a sign that the country may change its policy of **apartheid**, keeping black citizens powerless and separate from whites. The United States and other nations have long maintained a trade embargo against South Africa because of its apartheid policy.

The Debt Crisis

Another foreign policy challenge is the issue of foreign debt. Many of the world's developing nations have borrowed large sums of money to build their economies. As a result, many debtor nations must spend a large part of their annual budgets to repay the loans and pay the interest on them. For some nations, this debt has become a tremendous burden. To make their payments, they have had to deprive their people of basic services such as schools, hospitals, and roads.

Many loans to developing nations come from American banks. If these nations cannot repay the money, the banks could lose millions of dollars, and perhaps even fail.

The United States is working closely with the International Monetary Fund and the World Bank to find solutions to this problem. In some cases, countries have been allowed to make smaller payments over a longer period of time. In others, countries have been told they only have to repay part of the loans.

Black South African leader Nelson Mandela addressed the Congress of the United States on a recent trip to this country.

Because it needs money to make payments on its foreign debt, the government of Brazil cannot afford to provide adequate housing for some of the nation's citizens.

Human Rights Issues

Human rights is a continuing concern of the United States. It became an important part of foreign policy during President Carter's administration. In 1975, the United States, Canada, the Soviet Union, and 32 European nations signed the Helsinki Accords, in Helsinki, Finland. This agreement dealt with basic human rights and freedoms in Europe. Until Mikhail Gorbachev came to power, however, the Soviet Union made no effort to adhere to the human rights provisions.

One important aspect of the human rights issue is the refugee problem. These people, who have been forced to flee their homelands

Refugees face a stark existence in refugee camps. Food shortages are among the most serious problems.

Years of war and brutality have forced thousands of Cambodians to leave their homeland and live in crowded refugee camps.

because of war, persecution, famine, or natural disaster, often end up in countries that are unable or unwilling to provide for their needs. Many refugees are forced to live in temporary camps and are at the mercy of the host nation. Life is often quite harsh.

The United Nations and several countries, including the United States, are concerned with solving the refugee problem. The hope is that refugees will be able to build new lives in their adopted countries, or else return safely to their homelands.

SECTION REVIEW

Define the Words

guerrilla   apartheid

Check the Facts

1. Name two regions that are currently world trouble spots and explain the trouble that exists.
2. Why is the United States concerned about changing conditions within the Soviet Union?
3. What are the Helsinki Accords?

Think About the Ideas

4. *Evaluate.* Which foreign policy challenge do you think is potentially the most threatening to the United States? Explain.

CITIZENSHIP SKILLS

How to Read a Newspaper

Newspapers are an important source of information about current events. A good newspaper has the facts you need to make informed decisions as an American citizen.

Newspapers are organized into sections by topic. Section headings on political topics might refer to world, national, regional, state, metropolitan, or local news. The editorial page includes articles, letters, and cartoons that express political opinions or points of view. Other section headings include, for example, "Business," "Classified Ads" or "Help Wanted," and "Sports." Such sections are listed in the paper's *Index*, which usually appears on page 2.

Headlines serve as brief summaries of the news. They help you locate the articles you want to read. The size of the headline and the placement of an article indicate the relative importance of a story—in the judgment of the paper's editors. Articles on the front page cover the stories the editors have decided are the most important.

News articles are supposed to present facts, not the opinions of the writer. (Personal opinions can be expressed on the editorial page of the paper.) An article's byline and dateline appear below the headline. The byline identifies the article's source—the reporter or agency that supplied the article. News agencies, or wire services carry stories from reporters all around the world. Today the largest and best known wire services are United Press International (UPI), Associated Press (AP), and Reuters. The dateline often names the place where the event took place, as well as the date.

Each news article is organized to give you maxi-

mum information in as few words as possible. The first sentence or paragraph, called the lead, should give you the main facts of the story. The body of a news article gives additional details, including the quoted statements of the people who were involved or who were asked for their comments.

If a newspaper is well written, you do not have to read everything to be reasonably well informed. You can scan the headlines to select the articles you are interested in and read the lead paragraph. Then you can decide whether to skim or read the rest of the article or to move on to another headline.

Using Your Skills
1. What information do headlines give? What information can be found in the byline and the dateline?
2. What is the difference between a news article and an article on the editorial page?

CHAPTER 23 REVIEW

* *

MAIN POINTS

★ America followed a policy of isolationism until World War I and again after the war. After World War II, however, U.S. policy changed to containment and collective security.

★ In recent years, U.S.-Soviet relations have improved greatly, leading to major arms control treaties and cooperation on common problems.

★ The U.S. President develops foreign policy with the help of the Departments of State and Defense and the National Security Council.

★ The United States conducts foreign policy through diplomacy, foreign aid, and alliances.

★ The United Nations was formed in 1945 to maintain international peace and promote justice and cooperation throughout the world.

★ The UN's legislative body is the General Assembly; the Security Council is its peace-keeping arm; and specialized agencies help developing nations cope with their problems.

★ Regional conflicts, U.S.-Soviet relations, the world debt crisis, and human rights issues are the major foreign policy challenges facing the United States today.

WORDS IN REVIEW

Choose the word or phrase from the list below that best completes each sentence. Write the missing words on a separate sheet of paper.

foreign policy	containment
isolationism	diplomacy
disarmament	developing nations
alliance	guerrilla
developed nations	apartheid

1. The _____ were struggling to build industrial economies.

2. The President hoped to arrive at a solution through _____, by talking and negotiating with the other nation's leader.

3. The nation was torn apart by civil war as _____ forces fought to overturn the government.

4. By trying to avoid any entanglements with other countries, the nation was following a policy of _____.

5. Many nations have refused to do business with South Africa because of its policy of _____.

6. After World War II, the United States followed a policy of _____ to prevent Communist expansion throughout the world.

7. The _____ are among the world's wealthiest nations, and are able to meet most of their citizens' needs.

8. The United States and several European nations formed an _____ for mutual cooperation and protection.

9. Negotiations were underway to reduce the number of nuclear weapons and to bring about complete _____.

10. In a speech on _____, the President announced plans for a new trade agreement with Japan and aid to debtor nations.

FACTS IN REVIEW

1. What events after World War II caused a change in American foreign policy?

2. What is the main purpose of NATO?

3. How has the arms control issue changed since the 1970's?

CHAPTER 23 REVIEW

4. How do American citizens play a role in foreign policy?

5. Why was the United States a leader in forming the United Nations?

6. What is the role of the UN General Assembly?

7. What actions can the UN Security Council take to try to keep peace?

8. Identify two regional conflicts that have ended within the last few years.

9. What major changes took place in Eastern Europe in 1989?

10. Why is the world refugee situation a problem?

THINKING ABOUT INTERNATIONAL RELATIONS

1. *Evaluate*. How do you think the United States should deal with the Soviet Union today?

2. *Analyze*. Do you think the United States should continue to support the United Nations as much as it does? Why or why not?

3. *Analyze*. How do you think the United States should deal with regional conflicts in other parts of the world?

DEBATING UN MEMBERSHIP

At times, some people have criticized the United Nations because they feel that small nations, which contribute little financial support, have too much power in the organization. Others argue that power in the United Nations should not be related to the amount a nation can

contribute. Prepare arguments, pro or con, for debating the following statement: The United States should reduce its support to the UN.

WRITING ABOUT FOREIGN POLICY

Write an essay explaining your views about U.S. foreign policy today. Discuss what policy you think the United States should follow toward any two of the following places: the Soviet Union, China, Japan, Western Europe, Eastern Europe, Latin America, the Middle East. Give reasons why you feel a particular policy should be followed. Also indicate how you would try to carry out these policies.

INTERPRETING A MAP

Look at the map on page 535 showing per capita income in the nations of the world. On which continents are the poorest countries found? What is the income level of the developed countries of North America, Western Europe, and Australia? In what other area are the richest nations found? Why do you think this is so?

FOCUSING ON YOUR COMMUNITY

Interview several members of your community, including relatives and neighbors, to find out their views on U.S. foreign policy. Find out how they feel about U.S. policy toward one particular nation, such as the Soviet Union, China, Japan, or Nicaragua. Prepare an oral report to present to the class.

Citizens of the World

OBJECTIVES

After you have studied this chapter, you will be able to:

★ Explain how the nations of the world are economically interdependent.
★ Discuss the problem of world hunger and what is being done about it.
★ Identify and discuss the advantages and disadvantages of protectionist and free trade policies.
★ Discuss the problems of environmental pollution and identify ways in which countries are trying to deal with these problems.
★ Discuss how individuals, including yourself, can work to solve environmental problems and to influence world affairs.

SECTIONS

1 The Global Economy
2 The Global Environment
3 Citizens of the World

INTRODUCTION

In the spring of 1989, thousands of Chinese students assembled in the main square of Beijing, demanding democratic reforms in their country. The Chinese leaders responded by sending in troops and tanks, killing perhaps thousands of people.

People all over the world watched these events on television or read about them in newspapers. The Chinese government tried to stop the flow of information by forbidding the use of cameras or tape recorders. But the news got through. Foreign reporters and Chinese citizens described the events over long-distance telephone lines. Pictures and reports were transmitted around the world by fax machines. Space satellites picked up China's own television broadcasts and relayed them to viewers in other countries.

In today's world, it is difficult for any country to sever connections with the rest of the world. The world is tied together by telephones, by satellites, and by jet planes. It is connected by a vast international trade network, which allows Europeans to drive Japanese cars and Africans to use American computers. In many ways, the world has become a single, small community. As a result, problems that occur in one part of the world often affect people living thousands of miles away.

$\bigstar$ $\bigstar$

SECTION 1

The Global Economy

$\bigstar$ $\bigstar$

VOCABULARY

interdependence	free trade
trade deficit	multinational
protectionism	corporation

Today, no nation is truly independent. Every country depends on other countries for some of the things it needs to survive. The United States, for example, depends on oil-rich countries such as Saudi Arabia for much of its energy supply. The Soviet Union depends on the United States for agricultural products such as wheat. This relationship among the countries of the world is called **interdependence**. Interdependence means that countries must depend on each other for products, services, and raw materials.

Economic Inequality

As you read in the last chapter, the countries of the world are often divided into developed and developing nations. Despite their differences, developed and developing nations are interdependent. Developing nations depend on developed nations for manufactured goods such as cars, telephones, and farm equipment. Developed nations depend on developing nations for raw

In 1989, the world watched as Chinese students defied the government in the main square in Beijing.

materials such as iron ore and coal, and for crops such as sugar cane and rice.

Developed countries are much wealthier than the developing countries. Their wealth comes from the high prices they are able to charge for their goods and services. They also have a great variety of goods and services to offer. Developing nations, on the other hand, usually sell only what they grow or take from the ground. These types of products are generally less costly than manufactured goods. In addition, developing nations generally have only a few products to offer.

Most developing nations would like to improve their economies and become industrialized. With so little income from the world market, however, they are unable to build factories or train and hire skilled workers. Many

developing nations have barely enough money to survive, and their citizens must endure poverty, illness, and hunger.

Many of the world's wealthier countries have made efforts to help their poorer neighbors improve their economies. Many American businesses, for example, have built factories in developing nations. These factories provide jobs for unskilled workers and help teach them useful skills. This arrangement also benefits American companies. Since wages are lower in developing nations, American businesses can manufacture products more cheaply than in the United States.

The U.S. government often helps developing nations by providing them with foreign aid. In 1987, for example, the United States gave over $6 billion in nonmilitary aid to for-

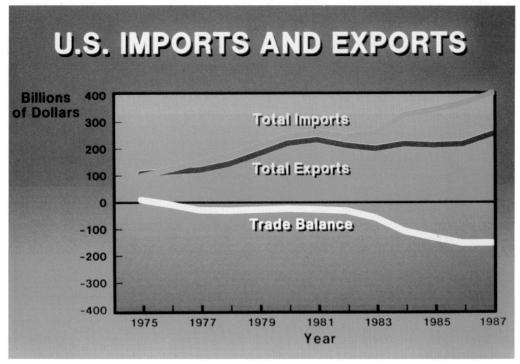

U.S. IMPORTS AND EXPORTS

This graph shows the value of the goods imported and exported by the United States. When is a country's trade balance a positive number?

eign governments. Although this aid is given partly out of a sincere wish to help, there are also other reasons. U.S. leaders realize that, by helping poorer countries, they are building friendly relations and developing markets for American products.

American citizens also help developing nations. For example, many young people join volunteer groups such as the Peace Corps. Peace Corps volunteers are sent to developing nations to teach important skills, such as how to grow better crops or prevent disease.

World Hunger

Hunger is probably the most pressing problem of developing nations. More than one and a half billion of the world's people,

most of them in developing nations, do not receive enough food. Moreover, as the world's population continues to grow, hunger becomes a greater concern for all nations.

The developed nations have worked hard over the past 40 years to end world hunger. During that time, for example, the United States has contributed more than $30 billion worth of food to developing countries. By itself, and through the United Nations, the U.S. government has also contributed billions of dollars more in cash and technical assistance. Private organizations, such as Oxfam America, have also raised millions of dollars each year for hunger relief.

Much of this money is spent not on food, but on research. In the 1960's and 1970's, research scientists were able to develop disease-resistant seeds and new chemical fertilizers. These products, together with mod-

Peace Corps volunteers help citizens of developing countries improve their health and standard of living.

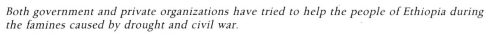

Both government and private organizations have tried to help the people of Ethiopia during the famines caused by drought and civil war.

ern farming techniques, began a "Green Revolution." Farmers in many developing nations were able to grow more and better crops. Even so, the Green Revolution has made only a small dent in world hunger. Many developing countries cannot afford the expensive supplies and equipment needed to grow new kinds of crops. Others lack more basic necessities, such as an adequate supply of water. Nevertheless, scientists continue to look for ways to make better use of the world's farmland.

Unfortunately, the supply of food is only part of the hunger problem. Even when countries have food on hand, it is often difficult to get that food to the people who need it. Some countries lack adequate transportation to move food from farms to markets. In others, political problems may prevent food from being distributed fairly. Wars, droughts, and floods can wipe out food supplies. The world hunger problem is really a number of different problems, some of which will take a very long time to solve.

International Trade

The nations of the world are trading with one another more than ever before. U.S. supermarkets are stocked with beef from Argentina, lamb from New Zealand, coffee from Brazil, grapes from Chile, and oranges from Israel. An "American-made" car may contain a Japanese engine, Italian upholstery, French tires, and a Korean radio. Shoppers in other countries often encounter a similar international mix.

Increased international trade has many advantages for those involved. Businesses can make greater profits selling to a world market instead of to a single country. International trade usually leads to increased competition among businesses worldwide,

and this may result in lower prices for the consumer. Consumers also enjoy a greater variety of products to choose from.

However, international trade also has its drawbacks. For example, many products can be produced less expensively in other countries than in the United States. Those products can then be sold in the United States at lower prices than similar American-made products. Since World War II, Americans have tended to buy more and more foreign products. As a result, U.S. businesses have lost money and American workers have lost jobs. Furthermore, since the late 1970's, the United States has had a **trade deficit**. That is, it has spent more money each year on imports, goods brought in from other countries, than it has earned from exports, goods sold to other countries.

As you read in Chapter 20, many Americans want to try to reduce the trade deficit by placing tariffs on foreign goods. The policy of placing barriers such as tariffs in the way of trade is called **protectionism**. Tariffs increase the price of imported goods, making them less desirable to American consumers.

The tariff paid by the importer of this Italian handbag will increase the price paid by the American consumer. Who is this tariff supposed to protect?

Customs Inspector

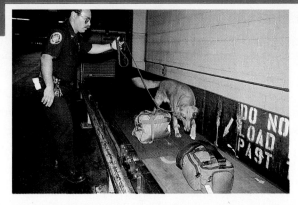

When you travel to other countries, you have to pass through "customs." Customs inspectors are responsible for enforcing laws that regulate the flow of goods into a country. Much of the work that customs workers perform is done behind the scenes. They process applications for goods entering the country and inspect shipments as they arrive.

The U.S. Customs Service employs thousands of inspectors to examine the belongings of travelers entering the United States. The inspectors look for illegal items, such as narcotics, certain furs, animals, and plants. Customs inspectors also check to see whether tourists have purchased expensive items such as jewelry and cameras abroad. If the value of the goods exceeds a certain amount, the traveler must pay a duty, or tax, on the goods.

Customs inspectors must be high school graduates and have some further education or law enforcement experience. It is useful for customs workers to know a foreign language and to take courses in business and law. To become a customs inspector, an applicant must pass a civil service test. Customs workers may be stationed at any port or point of entry along the United States border or at any international airport within the United States.

Using Your Skills
1. Why would knowledge of a foreign language be helpful to a customs inspector?
2. Why would experience in law enforcement be useful?

Experience has shown, however, that protectionist policies often backfire. Other countries respond by placing tariffs on American goods, making them too expensive for consumers abroad. As a result, all prices increase, the trade deficit continues, and consumers pay more for the products they buy. Many Americans feel that countries should follow a policy of **free trade**, in which tariffs and other economic barriers are eliminated.

In one way, the idea of imports and exports is becoming increasingly obsolete. Many products today are made by **multinational corporations**—businesses based in one country but with branches in several other parts of the world. For example, a multinational corporation may have its headquarters in Europe, make parts in Asian factories, and assemble its finished products in the United States. In these cases, it is often difficult to decide whether a product is foreign or domestic. The rise of multinational corporations is making the world's economy more and more interdependent. The future of the global economy will be shaped in large part by these multinational corporations.

SECTION REVIEW

Define the Words

interdependence   free trade
trade deficit   multinational
protectionism   corporation

Check the Facts

1. What are some of the differences between developed and developing nations?
2. What are some of the causes of world hunger?
3. How have multinational corporations affected international trade?

Think About the Ideas

4. *Evaluate.* Do you think the United States should give so much money to other countries without first eliminating hunger and poverty at home? Why or why not?

★ ★

SECTION 2

The Global Environment

★ ★

VOCABULARY

acid rain   greenhouse effect
ozone layer

The world is not only economically interdependent, it is also interdependent environmentally. When one country harms its environment, the damage can affect other countries as well. In 1986, for example, a Soviet nuclear reactor at Chernobyl exploded and caught fire. Radioactive particles were swept up by the wind and spread to other countries. Within days, scientists in Scandinavia and Eastern Europe detected higher-than-normal levels of radiation in the air. Later, scientists in Western Europe also reported increased radiation. While no one is yet sure of the long-term damage, it is clear that the effects of the Chernobyl accident were not stopped by national borders. A more severe accident might have affected the whole world.

Pollution

In Chapter 15, you read about the growing pollution problem in much of the United States. Air and water pollution are not, however, confined to this country. All industrialized countries have similar problems, as

The accident at the Chernobyl nuclear reactor released radioactive particles that spread far beyond the Soviet Union. Vehicles that pass through the affected region must be checked for radiation.

they pour toxic gases into the air and industrial wastes into the water. This pollution poses a danger not just to the country involved, but to the entire planet.

Pollution of the world's oceans, lakes, and rivers affects all the creatures that live there. Many fish die, causing food shortages in places where fish is an important part of the food supply. Other fish absorb toxic chemicals into their bodies and do not die. If caught and eaten, however, they can cause serious illness. In this era of international trade, fish from one polluted area may be shipped all over the world, endangering people thousands of miles from the source of pollution.

In the same way, the effects of air pollution can be felt far from its source. For example, many factories in Indiana, Ohio, and western Pennsylvania get power by burning coal. Burning this coal releases a chemical called sulfur dioxide into the air. This chemical is carried by the winds for hundreds of miles. While in the air, it combines with water vapor to form sulfuric acid, which later falls to earth as **acid rain**.

Much of this acid rain falls in Canada, where it is killing large areas of forests. In addition, it is raising the acid level in

Acid rain, an unwelcome product of coal-powered factories, threatens the health of forests in Canada and the eastern United States.

hundreds of Canadian lakes, killing many fish. The Canadian government, which cannot control the wind or the rain, is helpless to stop the destruction.

Ending the spread of pollution will require two kinds of action. First, individuals, businesses, and governments must work to end pollution in their own countries. Second, national governments must work together to solve pollution problems that extend beyond national borders. The United States and Canada, for example, have formed a joint commission to explore solutions to the acid rain problem.

Simply talking about these issues will not make them go away. In order to eliminate acid rain, American coal-burning factories may have to install expensive anti-pollution devices and switch to higher-priced, low-sulfur coal. The hope is that businesses and countries will be willing to spend large amounts of money to reduce their own pollution and thus the pollution of their neighbors.

Ozone Destruction and the Greenhouse Effect

Much of our environmental pollution can be reversed by eliminating the sources of pollution. In two cases, however, irreversible damage may already have been done to the environment. This damage is potentially very serious, because it affects everyone on earth.

The first case involves the **ozone layer**—a thin layer of gas in the earth's atmosphere that acts as a natural shield against the sun's ultraviolet radiation. In recent years, scientists have discovered that the ozone layer is being destroyed by human-made gases called chlorofluorocarbons (CFCs), which are used in such things as refrigerators and air conditioners. These gases escape into the air and

rise as much as 30 miles into the atmosphere, where they damage the ozone layer.

The gradual destruction and thinning of the ozone layer allows greater amounts of ultraviolet radiation to reach the earth. This radiation can cause skin cancer or other illnesses in people. It can also harm or destroy animals, forests, and food crops. Most scientists believe that the damage to the ozone layer is not yet great enough to produce these results. Any further damage, however, may have serious consequences.

The other case of irreversible damage to the environment concerns the **greenhouse effect**. When oil and coal are burned to produce energy, they release a gas called carbon dioxide into the atmosphere. In small quantities, carbon dioxide is not especially harmful. After decades of energy use, however, huge amounts of carbon dioxide and other gases build up in the atmosphere. These gases act like a greenhouse, allowing the sun's heat to enter the atmosphere, but preventing it from escaping. As a result, the temperatures on earth grow steadily warmer.

The destruction of the world's forests contributes to the greenhouse effect. Trees are the earth's natural protection against carbon dioxide buildup. Their leaves absorb carbon dioxide and emit oxygen, which humans and animals need to survive. As millions of acres of forest—particularly in South America—are cut down each year, this natural protection is lost.

If global warming continues, the earth will change dramatically. Polar ice caps may melt, raising the level of the world's oceans and submerging vast coastal areas, including many cities and towns. Climates throughout the world may change, and fertile farming regions may become deserts. Up to now, the greenhouse effect has caused only minor problems, and global warming is barely detectable.

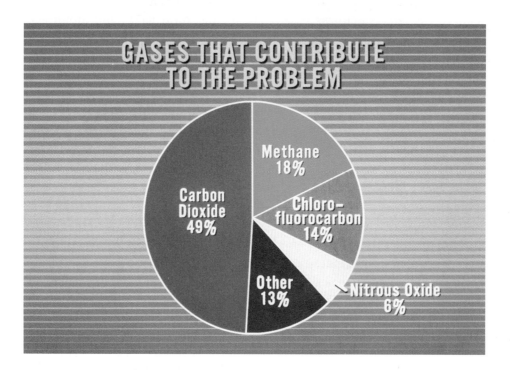

These pie graphs show which gases contribute to the greenhouse effect and where the gases come from. How might conserving energy reduce the greenhouse effect?

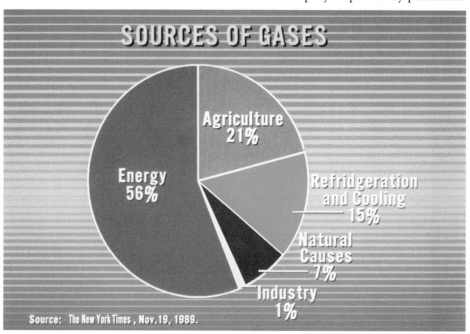

Many countries have started to treat the greenhouse effect and the destruction of the ozone layer as genuine emergencies. Although the damage already done may be permanent, further damage can be prevented if nations are willing to cooperate. So far, more than 80 countries have agreed to ban the use of chlorofluorocarbons by the year 2000. Scientists all over the world are investigating the causes of global warming and searching for practical solutions. In the meantime, the U.S. government has passed strict new regulations to limit energy use and reduce emissions of carbon dioxide. Many other countries expect to pass similar regulations.

SECTION REVIEW

Define the Words

acid rain   greenhouse effect
ozone layer

Check the Facts

1. What is the probable cause of acid rain, and what are its effects?
2. How does the destruction of forests contribute to the problem of global warming?
3. What actions are being taken to deal with global environmental problems?

Think About the Ideas

4. *Analyze*. Do you think all countries should be forced to follow the same anti-pollution standards? Why or why not?

* *

SECTION 3

Citizens of the World

* *

Although the world is led by governments, it is made up of individuals. If every person on earth decided to live peacefully, there would be no more war. If every individual decided to respect the environment, there would be no environmental problems.

Such notions, of course, are unrealistic. People are complicated creatures, with conflicting needs, emotions, and ideas. Many people tend to act selfishly, even though they realize that acting unselfishly would make the world a better place to live.

You have probably wrestled with conflicting ideas in your own life. You may feel compassion for people who are poor or starving. You may feel afraid of the poisons that pollute the environment. At the same time, however, you may find it difficult to give up time or money to work for a better world. In addition, you may feel that, as an individual, you cannot solve the world's problems. At one time or another, most people have asked, "I'm just one person. What could *I* possibly do?"

Working To Solve Environmental Problems

The environment is one area in which the actions of individuals, no matter how small,

"Think Globally. Act Locally" is a rallying cry for some of the many activists who join together to work for a cleaner environment and world peace.

can make a difference. As an individual, you can help preserve the environment by using resources wisely. Avoid using a car when you can walk, bicycle, or take public transportation instead. Turn off lights and appliances when you are not using them. Open windows instead of using an air conditioner. Be careful not to waste water. Buy products in reusable containers instead of disposable ones whenever possible. Recycle paper, cardboard, glass, aluminum, and, if possible, plastic.

You can also help by staying informed about environmental issues and expressing your opinions to local, state, or national leaders, as well as to those responsible for pollution or environmental destruction. Finally, you can volunteer your time to help improve the environment. If there is an organization in your community devoted to the environment, you can join it. Volunteer

groups can help clean up dump sites, set up recycling centers, and educate the public about environmental issues.

Participating In World Affairs

Before you can do anything to change the world, you must become familiar with the world as it is. The best way to find out about world events is to make a daily habit of reading a newspaper. In addition, you may want to watch television news reports and read weekly newsmagazines.

If you really want to understand world affairs, you must also try to learn how people in other countries think and feel. There are various ways to do this. You can read translated articles and books by foreign authors. You can study a foreign language so that you can read foreign newspapers and magazines. You can make an effort to meet and talk with people from different racial, ethnic, and religious backgrounds. You can travel to other countries, or talk to people who have done so.

As an individual, you can help relieve poverty and oppression throughout the world by contributing time or money to charitable organizations. The money you give to groups such as the International Red Cross or UNICEF may pay for medicine or food that will save human lives. The time you devote to a human rights group such as Amnesty International may help free political prisoners.

Looking at the world through the eyes of people whose experiences are different from your own will broaden your knowledge and understanding of the world.

CIVICS SIDELIGHTS

Fighting River Blindness

River blindness, or onchocerciasis, is a disease that strikes millions of people in Central and West Africa. It is caused by worms carried by black flies. The disease causes severe skin problems, and as many as 10 percent of adult victims eventually go blind.

In the 1970's, an American pharmaceutical company developed a drug called ivermectin. It was intended to kill worm parasites in cows and horses. However, in the early 1980's the company discovered that a human formulation of ivermectin would be a safe and effective treatment of river blindness in humans.

Since then, the company has committed itself to giving African health organizations all of the ivermectin necessary to treat river blindness victims. It is hoped that river blindness will eventually be controlled. By sharing their resources and skills with others, corporations can also be good citizens of the world.

Your greatest power to change the world, however, lies in your rights as an American citizen. Your voice, through the President and other elected representatives, can have an effect on world affairs. You can campaign and vote for candidates whose views you support. You can write to your representatives and express your ideas and opinions. You can join a political party or other political organization and work together with citizens who share your point of view. One day, you may even decide to run for office yourself.

The United States is a powerful and respected nation. The decisions of its leaders affect the lives of people throughout the world. As a citizen of the United States, your decisions also affect the lives of all people. In many ways, we are truly citizens of the world.

SECTION REVIEW

Check the Facts
1. Describe three ways that you, as an individual, can help solve environmental problems.
2. Why is it important to try to learn how people in other countries think and feel?
3. Describe three ways that you, as an individual, can influence world events.

Think About the Ideas
4. *Evaluate.* What issues do you feel strongly about and would like to get involved in?

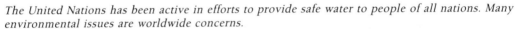

The United Nations has been active in efforts to provide safe water to people of all nations. Many environmental issues are worldwide concerns.

CITIZENSHIP SKILLS

How to Get a Passport

The United States and other countries regulate the foreign travel of their citizens by issuing passports. Most countries require that foreign visitors present an up-to-date passport before entering the country.

Some countries require foreign visitors to have visas as well. A visa is a permit issued by a government and stamped or attached to a passport. A transit visa allows a foreigner to pass through a country; a tourist visa to visit it; a student visa to attend school.

In planning a trip to a foreign country, you must apply well in advance for your passport and for visas or any other documents you need. To receive a U.S. passport in your own name for the first time, you must apply in person at a passport agency, a state or federal court building, or an authorized post office. Here is what you need to bring:
★ a completed application form.
★ your official birth certificate, certificate of naturalization, or previous passport as proof of your citizenship.
★ a document, such as your driver's license, with your signature and physical description as proof of your identity.
★ two identical recent passport photos.
★ the fee (currently $35 for adults 18 years and older, $20 for persons under 18, plus a $7 handling charge).

If you were born in a foreign country of a native-born or naturalized American parent, you must present a certificate of citizenship issued by the Immigration and Naturalization Service, or a Consular Report of Birth issued by the Department of State. You will also need your parents' marriage certificate and record of the places and periods of their residence in the United States and abroad. If you claim citizenship through a naturalized parent, you must present proof of your parent's admission to the United States as a permanent resident.

It may take as long as six weeks to process a passport application. Your passport is then valid for five years if you are under 18 and for ten years if you are 18 or older. If you have an out-of-date passport in your own name, you can apply for renewal by mail. You send in your old passport along with an application form, new photos, and the fee.

Your passport is a valuable, personal document that gives you legal status in a foreign country. It is illegal for anyone else to use your passport. If you lose it when you are abroad, you should report immediately to the nearest United States embassy or consulate.

Using Your Skills
1. Why do you need a passport? What other documents might you need for traveling?
2. What documents must you present when you apply for a passport?
3. What is the significance of a passport to you when you are away from your own country?

CHAPTER 24 REVIEW

* *

MAIN POINTS

★ The nations of the world are economically interdependent. Developed nations depend on developing nations for raw materials and inexpensive labor. Developing nations depend on developed nations for manufactured goods.

★ Some Americans favor free trade because increased imports give consumers more variety and lower prices. Others believe tariffs are necessary to protect American jobs and businesses.

★ The problems of hunger and environmental damage present a challenge to everyone on the planet. In order to deal with these issues, national governments will have to learn to work together.

★ Individual action can have real, measurable effects on the United States and the world. Every person must assume the responsibility of working for change.

WORDS IN REVIEW

Choose the word or phrase from the list below that best completes each sentence. Write the missing words on a separate sheet of paper.

interdependence   free trade
trade deficit   ozone layer
tariff   acid rain
protectionism   greenhouse effect

1. The President's belief in _____ caused him to oppose tariffs or other economic restrictions.

2. Many eastern forests seem to be dying because of the effects of _____.

3. Some scientists are concerned about global warming brought on by the _____.

4. Modern technology has increased the _____ of nations.

5. The country had a policy of _____, with high trade tariffs and other economic barriers.

6. With its imports exceeding exports, the United States has had a _____ for the last several years.

7. Chlorofluorocarbons have been blamed for the destruction of the earth's _____.

8. The union wanted the government to place a _____ on all imported shoes.

FACTS IN REVIEW

1. Why are no nations truly independent?

2. In what ways are developed and developing nations interdependent?

3. What efforts have wealthy countries made to help poorer nations?

4. Summarize the arguments for and against a protectionist trade policy.

5. Why is an adequate supply of food only part of the world hunger problem?

6. How can water pollution at one source affect people thousands of miles away?

7. Why is the destruction of the ozone layer a problem?

8. What are the possible consequences of the greenhouse effect?

9. What can individuals do to help preserve the environment?

10. How can being informed help you become a better citizen?

CHAPTER 24 REVIEW

* *

THINKING ABOUT CITIZENS OF THE WORLD

1. *Analyze.* How would the United States be affected if we stopped trading with other countries? How would the rest of the world be affected?
2. *Evaluate.* What do you think are the best approaches to solving environmental problems and preventing further destruction of the earth's environment?
3. *Analyze.* Why is it important for individual citizens to become involved in world issues?

COLLECTING INFORMATION ABOUT ENVIRONMENTAL PROBLEMS

People concerned about the environment often use statistics and other facts to support their views. Choose an environmental problem such as water pollution or forest destruction. Collect as many facts and figures as you can about this problem. Identify important sources of information and groups that are working to solve this particular problem. Present your findings to the class.

WRITING ABOUT INDIVIDUAL RESPONSIBILITY

Write an essay discussing why individuals should become involved in local, state, national, and world issues. In addition to explaining why personal involvement is important, describe what individuals can do to participate. Conclude by discussing how you plan to become more involved in world affairs.

INTERPRETING PIE GRAPHS

In 1989, experts from 68 nations met in the Netherlands to discuss the problem of global warming. They focused on ways to reduce the gases that are causing the greenhouse effect. The two pie graphs on page 552 show which gases contribute to the problem and where these gases come from. Study the graphs and answer the questions.

1. Which gas is the major contributor to the greenhouse effect? Name one way that it is produced.
2. What is the greatest source of gases that cause the greenhouse effect? What do you think contributes to this source?

FOCUSING ON YOUR COMMUNITY

Find out what opportunities exist in your community for individual involvement on issues. For example, does your community have a recycling program? Are there any community groups monitoring and working to reduce or prevent environmental pollution? Are there any groups working to reduce world hunger or to protect human rights around the world? Find out what you or your classmates might do to assist in these efforts. Report your findings to the class.

UNIT 8 REVIEW

* *

ESSAY QUESTIONS

The following questions are based on material in Unit 8. Answer each question with two or three written paragraphs. Be sure to give specific reasons to support your answers.

1. After World War II, the United States helped Western Europe get back on its feet by providing economic assistance through the Marshall Plan. Should the United States develop a similar program to help the countries of Eastern Europe in the 1990's? Explain your answer.

2. The United States has been a world leader for most of the twentieth century. Do you think this country will have the same role in world affairs in the future? Why or why not?

3. What is the major challenge facing the United States today in the area of foreign policy?

CONNECTING CIVICS AND THE ENVIRONMENT

When the twentieth anniversary of Earth Day was celebrated on April 22, 1990, people around the world heralded the coming decade as the Green Nineties. Be prepared to discuss the following in class: What role will environmental concerns play in American politics in the coming years? What problems should receive attention first? Why is international cooperation so important in this area?

ANALYZING VISUALS

As the cold war seemed to be ending, many American political leaders proposed major cuts in the defense budget. The money to be saved was termed the "peace dividend." Study the political cartoon and answer the questions.

1. How does the cartoon portray various social and foreign-policy programs? Why are they lined up outside the office of Defense Spending?

2. What does the cartoon suggest about the relation of defense spending to spending for social and foreign-policy programs?

3. Which program would you put at the head of the line? Why?

* * * * * * *

CLOSEUP ON SAVING THE FORESTS

When astronauts went into space in the 1960's, they saw only one sign of the human race on earth—the Great Wall of China. Today's astronauts can see other, startling, evidence of human life—the smoke of gigantic fires consuming the world's largest forest, the Amazon rain forest.

The fate of the entire world may depend in part on saving what remains of this forest and other forests around the world. The use of fossil fuels, such as oil and coal, is greatly increasing the amount of carbon dioxide in the atmosphere. This carbon dioxide is a major contributor to the "greenhouse effect," a gradual warming of the earth's temperatures. Forests help to reduce the greenhouse effect by absorbing carbon dioxide from the air.

There are other reasons to save the world's forests as well. When forests and their habitats are destroyed, many species of plants and animals become extinct. Destroying forests can also cause or worsen natural disasters such as floods and droughts. In 1988, for example, annual flooding killed 1,200 people in the nation of Bangladesh. The destruction of forest watersheds in the Himalaya Mountains, the source of Bangladesh's rivers, has increased the severity of these floods. In large areas of Africa, the destruction of woodlands has contributed to increased "desertification," or growth of the Sahara Desert. Each year as the desert expands into once-valuable farmland, millions of Africans face starvation.

Efforts to save the world's forests sometimes pit nation against nation. Developed nations, which destroyed most of their forests long ago, are pressuring developing nations to preserve virgin forests. These developing nations, however, feel that they must use their forests to meet the needs of their people. Brazil, for example, has built dams in the Amazon region to provide electricity for its mushrooming population. This has submerged vast areas of the Amazon forest. Brazilians also burn millions of acres of forest each year to open the land for farming,

cattle grazing, and new settlements. Tensions also exist between neighboring nations. For example, Canada is angry at the United States because of acid rain. This acid rain, caused by American industries in the Midwest, is destroying Canadian forests.

World leaders are looking for ways to ease tensions and also preserve the environment. The World Bank and International Monetary Fund have instituted programs to reward developing nations that conserve their forests and to penalize those that do not. The United States and Canada have been negotiating agreements to reduce acid rain. Increasingly, environmental issues, such as saving the world's forests, are moving to the top of the agenda of economic or political summit meetings among nations. World leaders now recognize that these problems cross international borders and affect all of the world's people.

1. Why is the Amazon rain forest so valuable to the whole world?

2. How does forest destruction increase the severity of flooding and drought?

3. What are some ways that governments can save forests?

THE DECLARATION OF INDEPENDENCE
July 4, 1776

* * * * * * * *

When in the Course of human events, it becomes necessary for one people to dissolve the political bands which have connected them with another, and to assume among the powers of the earth, the separate and equal station to which the Laws of Nature and of Nature's God entitle them, a decent respect to the opinions of mankind requires that they should declare the causes which impel them to the separation.

We hold these truths to be self-evident, that all men are created equal, that they are endowed by their Creator with certain unalienable Rights, that among these are Life, Liberty and the pursuit of Happiness. That to secure these rights, Governments are instituted among Men, deriving their just powers from the consent of the governed; That whenever any Form of Government becomes destructive of these ends it is the Right of the People to alter or to abolish it, and to institute new Government, laying its foundation on such principles and organizing its powers in such form, as to them shall seem most likely to effect their Safety and Happiness. Prudence, indeed, will dictate that Governments long established should not be changed for light and transient causes; and accordingly all experience hath shown, that mankind are more disposed to suffer, while evils are sufferable, than to right themselves by abolishing the forms to which they are accustomed. But when a long train of abuses and usurpations, pursuing invariably the same Objects evinces a design to reduce them under absolute Despotism, it is their right, it is their duty, to throw off such Government, and to provide new Guards for their future security.—Such has been the patient sufferance of these Colonies; and such is now the necessity which constrains them to alter their former Systems of Government. The history of the present King of Great Britain is a history of repeated injuries and usurpations, all having in direct object the establishment of an absolute Tyranny over these States.

To prove this, let Facts be submitted to a candid world.

He has refused his Assent to Laws, the most wholesome and necessary for the public good.

He has forbidden his Governors to pass Laws of immediate and pressing importance, unless suspended in their operation till his Assent should be obtained; and when so suspended, he has utterly neglected to attend to them.

He has refused to pass other Laws for the accommodation of large districts of people, unless those people would relinquish the right of Representation in the Legislature, a right inestimable to them and formidable to tyrants only.

He has called together legislative bodies at places unusual, uncomfortable, and distant from the depository of their public records, for the sole purpose of fatiguing them into compliance with his measures.

He has dissolved Representative Houses repeatedly, for opposing with manly firmness his invasions on the rights of the people.

He has refused for a long time, after such dissolutions, to cause others to be elected; whereby the Legislative powers, incapable of Annihilation, have returned to the People at large for their exercise; the State remaining in the mean time exposed to all the dangers of invasions from without, and convulsions within.

He has endeavored to prevent the population of these States; for that purpose obstructing the Laws of Naturalization of Foreigners; refusing to pass others to encourage their migration hither, and raising the conditions of new Appropriations of Lands.

He has obstructed the Administration of Justice, by refusing his Assent to Laws for establishing Judiciary powers.

He has made Judges dependent on his Will alone for the tenure of their offices, and the amount and payment of their salaries.

He has erected a multitude of New Offices, and sent hither swarms of Officers to harass our people and eat out their substance.

He has kept among us in times of peace, Standing Armies, without the Consent of our legislatures.

He has affected to render the Military independent of, and superior to, the Civil power.

He has combined with others to subject us to a jurisdiction foreign to our constitutions, and unacknowledged by our laws; giving his Assent to their Acts of pretended Legislation:

For quartering large bodies of armed troops among us;

For protecting them, by a mock Trial, from punishment for any Murders which they should commit on the Inhabitants of these States;

For cutting off our Trade with all parts of the world;

For imposing Taxes on us without our Consent;

For depriving us, in many cases, of the benefits of Trial by Jury;

For transporting us beyond Seas, to be tried for pretended offenses;

For abolishing the free System of English Laws in a neighboring Province, establishing therein an Arbitrary government, and enlarging its Boundaries, so as to render it at once an example and fit instrument for introducing the same absolute rule into these Colonies;

For taking away our Charters, abolishing our most valuable Laws, and altering, fundamentally, the Forms of our Governments;

For suspending our own Legislatures, and declaring themselves invested with Power to legislate for us in all cases whatsoever.

He has abdicated Government here, by declaring us out of his Protection, and waging War against us.

He has plundered our seas, ravaged our Coasts, burned our towns, and destroyed the lives of our people.

He is at this time transporting large Armies of foreign Mercenaries to complete the works of death, desolation and tyranny, already begun with circumstances of Cruelty and perfidy scarcely paralleled in the most barbarous ages, and totally unworthy the Head of a civilized nation.

He has constrained our fellow Citizens taken Captive on the high Seas to bear Arms against their Country, to become the executioners of their friends and Brethren, or to fall themselves by their Hands.

He has excited domestic insurrections amongst us, and has endeavored to bring on the inhabitants of our frontiers the merciless Indian Savages whose known rule of warfare is an undistinguished destruction of all ages, sexes, and conditions.

In every stage of these Oppressions We have Petitioned for Redress in the most humble terms. Our repeated Petitions have been answered only by repeated injury. A Prince whose character is thus marked by every act which may define a Tyrant, is unfit to be the ruler of a free people.

Nor have We been wanting in attentions to our British brethren. We have warned them from time to time of attempts by their legislature to extend an unwarrantable jurisdiction over us. We have reminded them of the circumstances of our emigration and settlement here. We have appealed to their native justice and magnanimity, and we have conjured them by the ties of our common kindred to disavow these usurpations, which, would inevitably interrupt our connections and correspondence. They too have been deaf to the voice of justice and of consanguinity. We must, therefore, acquiesce in the necessity, which denounces our Separation, and hold them, as we hold the rest of mankind, Enemies in War, in Peace Friends.—

We, therefore, the Representatives of the United States of America, in General Congress, Assembled, appealing to the Supreme Judge of the world for the rectitude of our intentions, do, in the Name, and by the Authority of the good People of these Colonies, solemnly publish and declare, That these United Colonies are, and of right ought to be Free and Independent States; that they are Absolved from all Allegiance to the British Crown, and that all political connection between them and the State of Great Britain, is and ought to be totally dissolved, and that as Free and Independent States, they have full Power to levy War, conclude Peace, contract Alliances, establish Commerce, and to do all other Acts and Things which Independent States may of right do. And for the support of this Declaration, with a firm reliance on the protection of Divine Providence, we mutually pledge to each other our Lives, our Fortunes and our sacred Honor.

THE CONSTITUTION OF THE UNITED STATES

Sections of the Constitution that are no longer in effect are crossed out in blue. Explanations and comments appear in the side column.

Preamble

We the people of the United States, in Order to form a more perfect Union, establish Justice, insure domestic Tranquility, provide for the common defence, promote the general Welfare, and secure the Blessings of Liberty to ourselves and our Posterity, do ordain and establish this Constitution for the United States of America.

Article I

Section 1

All legislative Powers herein granted shall be vested in a Congress of the United States, which shall consist of a Senate and House of Representatives.

Section 2

1. The House of Representatives shall be composed of Members chosen every second Year by the People of the several States, and the Electors in each State shall have the Qualifications requisite for Electors of the most numerous Branch of the State Legislature.

2. No Person shall be a Representative who shall not have attained to the Age of twenty-five Years, and been seven Years a Citizen of the United States, and who shall not, when elected, be an Inhabitant of that State in which he shall be chosen.

3. Representatives and direct Taxes shall be apportioned among the several States which may be included within this Union, according to their respective Numbers, which shall be determined by adding to the whole Number of free Persons, including those bound to Service for a Term of Years, and excluding Indians not taxed, three-fifths of all other Persons. The actual Enumeration shall be made within three Years after the first Meeting of the Congress of the United States, and within every subsequent Term of ten Years, in such Manner as they shall by Law direct. The Number of Representatives shall not exceed one for every thirty Thousand, but each state shall have at Least one Representative; and until such enumeration shall be made, the State of New Hampshire shall be entitled to chuse three, Massachusetts eight, Rhode Island and Providence Plantations one, Connecticut five, New-York six, New Jersey four, Pennsylvania eight, Delaware one, Maryland six, Virginia ten, North Carolina five, South Carolina five, and Georgia three.

Side Column

Preamble

The Preamble, or introduction, to the Constitution lists six goals: 1) to join the states in a single nation, 2) to ensure fair and equal treatment for all Americans, 3) to keep the peace, 4) to maintain armed forces to protect the country, 5) to promote the well-being of the people, and 6) to guarantee their basic rights.

ARTICLE I: The Legislative Branch

Section 1: Congress

The power to make laws is given to the two houses of Congress, the Senate and the House of Representatives.

Section 2: House of Representatives

1. Members of the House of Representatives are elected by qualified voters for two-year terms.

2. Representatives must be at least 25 years old. They must also be U.S. citizens for at least seven years and residents of the state they represent.

3. The number of Representatives in a state is based on state population. A census must be taken every 10 years to determine the population. The number of Representatives will be adjusted after each census.

4. When vacancies happen in the Representation from any State, the Executive Authority thereof shall issue Writs of Election to fill such Vacancies.

5. The House of Representatives shall chuse their Speaker and other Officers; and shall have the sole Power of Impeachment.

4. State governors can call special elections to fill vacancies in the House of Representatives.

5. Members of the House of Representatives choose their own officers, including a Speaker of the House.

Only the House of Representatives has the power to impeach government officials.

Section 3

1. The Senate of the United States shall be composed of two Senators from each State, chosen ~~by the Legislature thereof~~, for six Years; and each Senator shall have one Vote.

2. Immediately after they shall be assembled in Consequence of the first Election, they shall be divided as equally as may be into three Classes. The Seats of the Senators of the first Class shall be vacated at the Expiration of the second Year, of the second Class at the Expiration of the fourth Year, and of the third Class at the Expiration of the sixth Year, so that one-third may be chosen every second Year; and if Vacancies happen by Resignation, or otherwise, ~~during the Recess of the Legislature of any State~~, the Executive thereof may make temporary Appointments ~~until the next Meeting of the Legislature, which shall then fill such Vacancies~~.

3. No person shall be a Senator who shall not have attained to the Age of thirty Years, and been nine Years a Citizen of the United States, and who shall not, when elected, be an Inhabitant of that State in which he shall be chosen.

4. The Vice President of the United States shall be President of the Senate, but shall have no vote, unless they be equally divided.

5. The Senate shall chuse their other Officers, and also a President pro tempore, in the absence of the Vice President, or when he shall exercise the Office of the President of the United States.

6. The Senate shall have the sole Power to try all Impeachments. When sitting for that purpose, they shall be on Oath or Affirmation. When the President of the United States is tried, the Chief Justice shall preside: And no person shall be convicted without the Concurrence of two thirds of the Members present.

7. Judgment in Cases of Impeachment shall not extend further than to removal from Office, and disqualification to hold and enjoy any Office of Honor, Trust, or Profit under the United States: but the Party convicted shall nevertheless be liable and subject to Indictment, Trial, Judgment, and Punishment, according to Law.

Section 3: Senate

1. Each state has two Senators, who serve six-year terms. Originally, Senators were chosen by state legislatures. (The Seventeenth Amendment provided for the direct election of Senators by the people.)

2. One-third of the Senators must run for election every two years. State governors can make temporary appointments to fill Senate vacancies.

3. Senators must be at least 30 years old. They must also be U.S. citizens for at least nine years and residents of the state they represent.

4. The Vice President is the leader of the Senate. The Vice President may vote only to break a tie.

5. Members of the Senate choose their own officers, including a president *pro tempore*, the Senate leader when the Vice President is absent.

6. Only the Senate has the power to try impeachment cases. Conviction requires a two-thirds vote.

7. Persons convicted in impeachment cases are removed from office. An impeached official cannot hold office in the future. Convicted persons can also be tried in courts of law and punished if found guilty.

Section 4

1. The Times, Places and Manner of holding Elections for Senators and Representatives, shall be prescribed in each state by the Legislature thereof: but the Congress may at any time by Law make or alter such Regulations, except as to the Places of Chusing Senators.

Section 4: Congressional Elections and Sessions

1. Each state legislature determines its own rules for Congressional elections. Congress, however, can overrule state election laws.

2. The Congress shall assemble at least once in every Year, ~~and such Meeting shall be on the first Monday in December, unless they shall by Law appoint a different Day~~.

2. Congress must meet at least once every year beginning on the first Monday in December. (This day was changed to January 3 by the Twentieth Amendment.)

Section 5

1. Each House shall be the Judge of the Elections, Returns and Qualifications of its own Members, and a Majority of each shall constitute a Quorum to do Business; but a smaller Number may adjourn from day to day, and may be authorized to compel the Attendance of absent Members, in such Manner, and under such Penalties, as each House may provide.

2. Each House may determine the Rules of its Proceedings, punish its Members for disorderly Behavior, and with the Concurrence of two thirds, expel a Member.

3. Each House shall keep a Journal of its Proceedings, and from time to time publish the same, excepting such Parts as may in their Judgment require Secrecy; and the Yeas and Nays of the Members of either House on any question shall, at the Desire of one fifth of those Present, be entered on the Journal.

4. Neither House, during the Session of Congress, shall, without the Consent of the other, adjourn for more than three days, nor to any other Place than that in which the two Houses shall be sitting.

Section 5: Congressional Organization and Rules

1. Each house of Congress decides whether its members are qualified to serve. Each house also decides if members have been elected fairly.

A quorum, or more than half of the members, must be present to conduct business. Each house may require the attendance of members.

2. Each house of Congress sets its own rules, punishes its own members for misconduct, and can expel a member by a two-thirds vote.

3. Each house must keep an official record of its business and publish it regularly (*The Congressional Record*). Members' votes must be included in this record if one-fifth of the members request it.

4. Neither house of Congress may stop meeting for more than three days, or move to another place, without the approval of the other house.

Section 6

1. The Senators and Representatives shall receive a Compensation for their Services, to be ascertained by Law, and paid out of the Treasury of the United States. They shall in all Cases, except Treason, Felony, and Breach of the Peace, be privileged from Arrest during their attendance at the Session of their respective Houses, and in going to and returning from the same; and for any Speech or Debate in either House, they shall not be questioned in any other Place.

2. No Senator or Representative shall, during the Time for which he was elected, be appointed to any civil Office under the Authority of the United States, which shall have been created, or the Emoluments whereof shall have been increased, during such time; and no Person holding any Office under the United States shall be a Member of either House during his continuance in Office.

Section 6: Congressional Privileges and Restrictions

1. Members of Congress are paid salaries by the U.S. government. They cannot be arrested while Congress is in session, except for treason or felonies. They cannot be sued or prosecuted for anything they say while in Congress.

2. Senators and Representatives may not hold other government jobs while serving in Congress.

Section 7

1. All Bills for raising Revenue shall originate in the House of Representatives; but the Senate may propose or concur with Amendments as on other bills.

2. Every Bill which shall have passed the House of Representatives and the Senate, shall, before it become a Law, be presented to

Section 7: Passing Laws in Congress

1. All bills to raise money must begin in the House of Representatives. The Senate can amend these bills.

2. All bills passed by Congress must be signed by the President

the President of the United States; If he approve he shall sign it, but if not he shall return it, with his Objections, to that House in which it shall have originated, who shall enter the Objections at large on their Journal, and proceed to reconsider it. If after such Reconsideration two thirds of that House shall agree to pass the bill, it shall be sent, together with the objections, to the other House, by which it shall likewise be reconsidered, and if approved by two thirds of that House, it shall become a Law. But in all such Cases the Votes of both Houses shall be determined by Yeas and Nays, and the Names of the Persons voting for and against the Bill shall be entered on the Journal of each House respectively. If any Bill shall not be returned by the President within ten Days (Sunday excepted) after it shall have been presented to him, the Same shall be a Law, in like Manner as if he had signed it, unless the Congress by their Adjournment prevent its Return, in which Case it shall not be a Law.

3. Every Order, Resolution, or Vote to which the Concurrence of the Senate and House of Representatives may be necessary (except on a question of Adjournment) shall be presented to the President of the United States; and before the Same shall take Effect, shall be approved by him, or being disapproved by him, shall be repassed by two thirds of the Senate and House of Representatives, according to the Rules and Limitations prescribed in the Case of a Bill.

before becoming law. If the President vetoes a bill, it is returned to Congress. Congress can pass a bill over the President's veto by a two-thirds vote in each house. If the President does not sign or veto a bill within 10 days (excluding Sundays), the bill becomes law. If Congress adjourns during this 10-day period, however, the bill is dead. (This is a "pocket veto.")

3. Every action that requires approval by both houses (except for adjournment) must be approved or vetoed by the President.

Section 8

The Congress shall have Power

1. To lay and collect Taxes, Duties, Imposts and Excises, to pay the Debts and provide for the common Defence and general Welfare of the United States; but all Duties, Imposts and Excises shall be uniform throughout the United States.

2. To borrow money on the credit of the United States;

3. To regulate Commerce with foreign Nations, and among the several States, and with the Indian Tribes;

4. To establish an uniform Rule of Naturalization, and uniform Laws on the subject of Bankruptcies throughout the United States;

5. To coin Money, regulate the Value thereof, and of foreign Coin, and fix the Standard of Weights and Measures;

6. To provide for the Punishment of counterfeiting the Securities and current Coin of the United States;

7. To establish Post Offices and post Roads;

8. To promote the Progress of Science and useful Arts, by securing for limited Times to Authors and Inventors the exclusive Right to their respective Writings and Discoveries;

9. To constitute Tribunals inferior to the Supreme Court;

10. To define and punish Piracies and Felonies committed on the high Seas, and Offenses against the Law of Nations;

11. To declare War, grant Letters of Marque and Reprisal, and make Rules concerning Captures on Land and Water;

12. To raise and support Armies, but no Appropriation of Money to that Use shall be for a longer Term than two Years;

13. To provide and maintain a Navy;

Section 8: Powers Given to Congress

The following are things the federal government CAN do:

1. Collect taxes. Spend money to pay debts and provide for the defense and welfare of the nation and its people. Taxes must be the same for all states.

2. Borrow money.

3. Regulate all foreign domestic commerce.

4. Pass laws on the naturalization of foreigners and on bankruptcies.

5. Coin money and determine its value; establish a system of standard weights and measures.

6. Punish people who print or coin money illegally.

7. Set up post offices and a highway system.

8. Regulate copyrights and patents.

9. Establish a system of federal courts under the Supreme Court.

10. Make laws concerning piracy and other crimes committed at sea.

11. Declare war.

12. Create and support an army.

13. Create and support a navy.

14. To make Rules for the Government and Regulation of the land and naval forces;

15. To provide for calling forth the Militia to execute the Laws of the Union, suppress Insurrections and repel Invasions;

16. To provide for organizing, arming, and disciplining the Militia, and for governing such Part of them as may be employed in the Service of the United States, reserving to the States respectively, the Appointment of the Officers, and the Authority of training the Militia according to the discipline prescribed by Congress;

17. To exercise exclusive Legislation in all Cases whatsoever, over such District (not exceeding ten Miles square) as may, by Cession of particular States, and the acceptance of Congress, become the Seat of Government of the United States, and to exercise like Authority over all Places purchased by the Consent of the Legislature of the State in which the Same shall be, for the Erection of Forts, Magazines, Arsenals, dock-Yards, and other needful Buildings;—And

18. To make all Laws which shall be necessary and proper for carrying into Execution the foregoing Powers, and all other Powers vested by this Constitution in the Government of the United States, or in any Department or Officer thereof.

Section 9

1. The Migration or Importation of such Persons as any of the States now existing shall think proper to admit, shall not be prohibited by the Congress prior to the Year one thousand eight hundred and eight, but a tax or duty may be imposed on such Importation, not exceeding ten dollars for each Person.

2. The privilege of the Writ of Habeas Corpus shall not be suspended, unless when in Cases of Rebellion or Invasion the public Safety may require it.

3. No Bill of Attainder or ex post facto Law shall be passed.

4. No capitation, or other direct, Tax shall be laid unless in Proportion to the Census or Enumeration herein before directed to be taken.

5. No Tax or Duty shall be laid on Articles exported from any State.

6. No Preference shall be given by any Regulation of Commerce or Revenue to the Ports of one State over those of another: nor shall Vessels bound to, or from, one State, be obliged to enter, clear, or pay Duties in another.

7. No Money shall be drawn from the Treasury, but in Consequence of Appropriations made by Law; and a regular Statement and Account of the Receipts and Expenditures of all public Money shall be published from time to time.

8. No Title of Nobility shall be granted by the United States: And no Person holding any Office of Profit or Trust under them, shall, without the Consent of the Congress, accept of any present, Emolument, Office, or Title, of any kind whatever, from any King, Prince, or foreign State.

14. Regulate the army and navy.

15. Call up state militias (national guards) when needed to enforce laws or deal with uprisings or invasions.

16. Regulate state militias.

17. Set up a federal capital district.

18. Make laws needed for carrying out all its powers. (This is the "necessary and proper," or "elastic clause.")

Section 9: Powers Denied to the Federal Government

The following are things the federal government CANNOT do:

1. Ban the slave trade until after 1808.

2. Suspend the writ of habeas corpus, except during invasions or rebellions. (A writ of habeas corpus is the right of an accused person to be brought before a court of law to determine whether he or she is being held legally.)

3. Pass bills of attainder (laws that punish a person accused of a crime without a court trial).

Pass ex post facto laws (laws that make an action illegal after the action has taken place).

4. Levy direct taxes, except in proportion to the population. (This was changed by the Sixteenth Amendment.)

5. Tax exports.

6. Pass laws that favor the commerce of one state over another. Tax ships that cross state lines.

7. Spend any money that has not been appropriated by Congress. An official record of federal spending must be kept.

8. Grant titles of nobility. No public official can accept any gift, office, or title from any foreign country without Congressional approval.

Section 10

1. No State shall enter into any Treaty, Alliance, or Confederation; grant Letters of Marque and Reprisal; coin Money; emit Bills of Credit; make any Thing but gold and silver Coin a Tender in Payment of Debts; pass any Bill of Attainder, ex post facto Law, or Law impairing the Obligation of Contracts, or grant any Title of Nobility.

2. No State shall, without the Consent of the Congress, lay any Imposts or Duties on Imports or Exports, except what may be absolutely necessary for executing its inspection Laws: and the net Produce of all Duties and Imposts, laid by any State on Imports or Exports, shall be for the Use of the Treasury of the United States; and all such Laws shall be subject to the Revision and Control of the Congress.

3. No State shall, without the Consent of Congress, lay any duty of Tonnage, keep Troops, or Ships of War in time of Peace, enter into any Agreement or Compact with another State, or with a foreign Power, or engage in War, unless actually invaded, or in such imminent Danger as will not admit of delay.

Article II

Section 1

1. The executive Power shall be vested in a President of the United States of America. He shall hold his Office during the Term of four years, and, together with the Vice President chosen for the same Term, be elected, as follows:

2. Each State shall appoint in such Manner as the Legislature thereof may direct, a Number of Electors, equal to the whole Number of Senators and Representatives to which the State may be entitled in the Congress: but no Senator or Representative, or Person holding an Office of Trust or Profit under the United States, shall be appointed an Elector.

3. ~~The Electors shall meet in their respective States, and vote by Ballot for two Persons, of whom one at least shall not be an Inhabitant of the same State with themselves. And they shall make a List of all the Persons voted for, and of the Number of Votes for each; which List they shall sign and certify, and transmit sealed to the Seat of the Government of the United States, directed to the President of the Senate. The President of the Senate shall, in the Presence of the Senate and House of Representatives, open all the Certificates, and the Votes shall then be counted. The Person having the greatest Number of Votes shall be the President, if such Number be a Majority of the whole Number of Electors appointed; and if there be more than one who have such Majority, and have an equal Number of Votes, then the House of Representatives shall immediately chuse by Ballot one of them for President; and if no Person have a Majority, then from the five highest on the List the said House shall in like Manner chuse the President. But in chusing the President, the Votes shall be taken by States, the Representation from each State having one Vote; a quorum for this Purpose shall consist of a Member or Members from two-thirds of the States, and a Majority of all the States shall~~

Section 10: Powers Denied to the States

The following are things the states CANNOT do:

1. Make treaties or alliances; coin money or use anything but gold or silver as money; pass bills of attainder, ex post facto laws, or laws that interfere with contracts; grant titles of nobility.

2. Tax imports or exports without Congressional approval.

3. Tax shipping, raise armies or navies in peacetime, make agreements with other states or countries, or make war (unless invaded or in danger of being invaded) without Congressional approval.

ARTICLE II: The Executive Branch

Section 1: The President and Vice President

1. The President has the power to execute laws. The President and Vice President are elected for four-year terms.

2. The President and Vice President are elected by electors from each state. Each state has the same number of electors as its total number of Senators and Representatives.

3. The procedure described here for electing the President and Vice President was changed by the Twelfth Amendment.

4. Congress decides when Presidential elections will be held. The date set is the first Tuesday after the first Monday in November. Electors vote on the Monday after the second Wednesday in December.

5. The President must be at least 35 years old and a U.S. citizen by birth. The President must also have lived in the United States for at least 14 years.

6. If the President dies, resigns, or is unable to carry out his or her duties, the Vice President takes over. If neither official is able to serve, the order of Presidential succession established by Congress is followed. (Also see the Twenty-Fifth Amendment.)

7. The President receives a salary that cannot be changed during

~~be necessary to a Choice. In every Case, after the Choice of the President, the Person having the greatest Number of Votes of the Electors shall be the Vice President. But if there should remain two or more who have equal votes, the Senate shall chuse from them by Ballot the Vice President.~~

4. The Congress may determine the Time of chusing the Electors, and the Day on which they shall give their Votes; which Day shall be the same throughout the United States.

5. No person except a natural-born Citizen, or a Citizen of the United States, at the time of the Adoption of this Constitution, shall be eligible to the Office of President; neither shall any Person be eligible to that Office who shall not have attained to the Age of thirty-five years, and been fourteen Years a Resident within the United States.

6. In Case of the Removal of the President from Office, or of his Death, Resignation, or Inability to discharge the Powers and Duties of the said Office, the same shall devolve on the Vice President, and the Congress may by Law provide for the Case of Removal, Death, Resignation, or Inability, both of the President and Vice President, declaring what Officer shall then act as President, and such Officer shall act accordingly, until the disability be removed, or a President shall be elected.

7. The President shall, at stated times, receive for his Services a Compensation, which shall neither be increased nor diminished during the Period for which he shall have been elected, and he shall not receive within that Period any other Emolument from the United States, or any of them.

8. Before he enter on the execution of his Office, he shall take the following Oath or Affirmation:—"I do solemnly swear (or affirm) that I will faithfully execute the Office of President of the United States, and will, to the best of my Ability, preserve, protect, and defend the Constitution of the United States."

Section 2

1. The President shall be Commander in Chief of the Army and Navy of the United States, and of the Militia of the several States, when called into the actual Service of the United States; he may require the Opinion, in writing, of the principal Officer in each of the executive Departments, upon any subject relating to the Duties of their respective Offices, and he shall have Power to Grant Reprieves and Pardons for Offenses against the United States, except in Cases of Impeachment.

2. He shall have Power, by and with the Advice and Consent of the Senate, to make Treaties, provided two-thirds of the Senators present concur; and he shall nominate, and by and with the Advice and Consent of the Senate, shall appoint Ambassadors, other public Ministers and Consuls, Judges of the supreme Court, and all other Officers of the United States, whose Appointments are not herein otherwise provided for, and which shall be established by Law: but the Congress may by Law vest the Appointment of such inferior Officers, as they think proper, in the President alone, in the Courts of Law, or in the Heads of Departments.

his or her term of office. The President cannot receive any other salary from the federal or state governments.

8. The President must swear to uphold the Constitution before taking office.

Section 2: Powers of the President

1. The President is commander in chief of the military. The President may seek advice from executive department heads (the Cabinet).

The President may grant pardons and reprieves for all federal crimes except impeachment.

2. The President may make treaties with foreign countries; these must be approved by two-thirds of the Senate.

The President may appoint ambassadors, federal judges, and other high officials with Senate approval.

3. If the Senate is not in session, the President may appoint officials to fill vacancies temporarily.

3. The President shall have Power to fill up all Vacancies that may happen during the Recess of the Senate, by granting Commissions which shall expire at the End of their next Session.

Section 3

He shall from time to time give to the Congress Information of the State of the Union, and recommend to their Consideration such Measures as he shall judge necessary and expedient; he may, on extraordinary occasions, convene both Houses, or either of them, and in Case of Disagreement between them, with respect to the Time of Adjournment, he may adjourn them to such Time as he shall think proper; he shall receive Ambassadors and other public Ministers; he shall take Care that the Laws be faithfully executed, and shall Commission all the Officers of the United States.

Section 4

The President, Vice President and all civil Officers of the United States, shall be removed from Office on Impeachment for, and Conviction of, Treason, Bribery, or other high Crimes and Misdemeanors.

Article III

Section 1

The judicial Power of the United States, shall be vested in one supreme Court, and in such inferior Courts as the Congress may from time to time ordain and establish. The judges, both of the supreme and inferior Courts, shall hold their Offices during good Behaviour, and shall, at stated Times, receive for their Services, a Compensation, which shall not be diminished during their Continuance in Office.

Section 2

1. The judicial Power shall extend to all Cases, in Law and Equity, arising under this Constitution, the Laws of the United States, and treaties made, or which shall be made, under their Authority;—to all Cases affecting ambassadors, other public ministers and consuls;—to all cases of admiralty and maritime Jurisdiction;—to Controversies to which the United States shall be a party;—to Controversies between two or more States;—between a State and Citizens of another State;—between Citizens of different States;—between Citizens of the same State claiming Lands under Grants of different States, and between a State, or the Citizens thereof, and foreign States, Citizens or Subjects.

2. In all Cases affecting Ambassadors, other public Ministers and Consuls, and those in which a State shall be Party, the supreme Court shall have original Jurisdiction. In all the other Cases before mentioned, the supreme Court shall have appellate Jurisdiction, both as to Law and Fact, with such Exceptions, and under such Regulations as the Congress shall make.

Section 3: Duties of the President

The President must report the condition of the nation to Congress (the State of the Union address), and recommend policies or actions. The President may call special sessions of Congress.

The President receives representatives from foreign countries.

The President must see that the nation's laws are carried out.

Section 4: Impeachment

The President, Vice President, and other government officials can be impeached for treason, bribery, or other serious crimes.

ARTICLE III: The Judicial Branch

Section 1: The Federal Courts

Judicial power is given to the Supreme Court and to any lower courts established by Congress. All federal judges hold office for life (unless impeached).

Section 2: Jurisdiction of the Federal Courts

1. The federal courts hear cases involving the Constitution, federal laws, or treaties. They also hear cases involving foreign diplomats, ships or shipping, the federal government, and conflicts between states. Federal courts can also hear cases involving disputes between citizens of different states, disputes over land claims, and disputes between a state or citizen and a foreign country or its citizens.

2. Certain cases—those involving foreign diplomats and states—can be heard directly by the Supreme Court. In all other instances, the Supreme Court hears cases on appeal from lower courts.

3. The trial of all Crimes, except in Cases of Impeachment, shall be by Jury; and such Trial shall be held in the State where the said Crimes shall have been committed; but when not committed within any State, the Trial shall be at such Place or Places as the Congress may by Law have directed.

Section 3

1. Treason against the United States, shall consist only in levying War against them, or in adhering to their Enemies, giving them Aid and Comfort. No Person shall be convicted of Treason unless on the Testimony of two Witnesses to the same overt Act, or on Confession in open Court.

2. The Congress shall have power to declare the Punishment of Treason, but no Attainder of Treason shall work Corruption of Blood, or Forfeiture except during the Life of the Person attained.

Article IV

Section 1

Full Faith and Credit shall be given in each State to the public Acts, Records, and judicial Proceedings of every other State. And the Congress may by general Laws prescribe the Manner in which such Acts, Records, and Proceedings shall be proved, and the Effect thereof.

Section 2

1. The Citizens of each State shall be entitled to all Privileges and Immunities of Citizens in the several States.

2. A Person charged in any State with Treason, Felony, or other Crime, who shall flee from Justice, and be found in another State, shall on demand of the executive Authority of the State from which he fled, be delivered up, to be removed to the State having Jurisdiction of the crime.

3. ~~No Person held to Service or Labour in one State, under the Laws thereof, escaping into another, shall, in Consequence of any Law or Regulation therein, be discharged from such Service or Labour, but shall be delivered up on Claim of the Party to whom such Service or Labour may be due.~~

Section 3

1. New States may be admitted by the Congress into this Union; but no new State shall be formed or erected within the Jurisdiction of any other State; nor any State be formed by the Junction of two or more States, or parts of States, without the Consent of the Legislatures of the States concerned as well as of the Congress.

2. The Congress shall have Power to dispose of and make all needful Rules and Regulations respecting the Territory or other Property belonging to the United States; and nothing in this Constitution shall be so construed as to Prejudice any Claims of the United States, or of any particular State.

3. Any person accused of a crime has a right to a trial by jury (except for impeachment cases). Trials must be held in the state where the crime was committed.

Section 3: Treason

1. Treason is defined as carrying on war against the United States or helping the enemies of the United States. No one may be convicted of treason without the testimony of two witnesses or a confession of the accused in court.

2. Congress may decide the punishment for treason. The families or descendants of those found guilty may not be punished.

ARTICLE IV: Relations Among the States

Section 1: Official Acts

Each state must accept the laws, records, and court decisions of other states.

Section 2: Mutual Duties of States

1. Each state must treat the citizens of other states the same as its own citizens.

2. If a person accused of a crime in one state is captured in another, the person must be returned to the state where the crime was committed.

3. This provision that escaped slaves be returned to their owners was canceled in 1865, when the Thirteenth Amendment outlawed slavery.

Section 3: New States and Territories

1. Congress may add new states to the nation. No new states may be formed by changing existing states, unless approved by the states involved.

2. Congress may make rules concerning U.S. territory and property.

Section 4

The United States shall guarantee to every State in this Union a Republican Form of Government, and shall protect each of them against Invasion; and on Application of the Legislature, or of the Executive (when the Legislature cannot be convened) against domestic Violence.

Article V

The Congress, whenever two-thirds of both Houses shall deem it necessary, shall propose Amendments to this Constitution, or, on the Application of the Legislatures of two-thirds of the several States, shall call a Convention for proposing Amendments, which, in either Case, shall be valid to all Intents and Purposes, as part of this Constitution, when ratified by the Legislatures of three-fourths of the several States, or by Conventions in three-fourths thereof, as the one or the other Mode of Ratification may be proposed by the Congress; Provided that no Amendment which may be made prior to the Year One thousand eight hundred and eight shall in any Manner affect the first and fourth Clauses in the Ninth Section of the first Article; and that no State, without its Consent, shall be deprived of its equal Suffrage in the Senate.

Article VI

1. All Debts contracted and Engagements entered into, before the Adoption of this Constitution, shall be as valid against the United States under this Constitution, as under the Confederation.

2. This Constitution, and the Laws of the United States which shall be made in Pursuance thereof; and all Treaties made, or which shall be made, under the Authority of the United States, shall be the supreme Law of the Land; and the Judges in every State shall be bound thereby, any Thing in the Constitution or Laws of any State to the Contrary notwithstanding.

3. The Senators and Representatives before mentioned, and the Members of the several State Legislatures, and all executive and judicial Officers, both of the United States and of the several States, shall be bound by Oath or Affirmation to support this Constitution; but no religious Test shall ever be required as a qualification to any Office or public Trust under the United States.

Article VII

The Ratification of the Conventions of nine States shall be sufficient for the Establishment of this Constitution between the States so ratifying the same.

Done in Convention by the Unanimous Consent of the States present the Seventeenth Day of September in the Year of our Lord one thousand seven hundred and Eighty seven, and of the Independence of the United States of America the Twelfth. In Witness whereof We have hereunto subscribed our Names.

Section 4: Federal Protection for the States

Each state is guaranteed a government of elected representatives of the people. The federal government will protect states against invasion and, upon request of the state legislature or governor, against internal riots or rebellion.

ARTICLE V: The Amendment Process

Amendments to the Constitution may be proposed by a two-thirds vote of both houses of Congress or by request of two-thirds of the state legislatures. Proposed amendments take effect when approved by three-fourths of the state legislatures or by conventions in three-fourths of the states.

No amendment may take away a state's right to have two U.S. Senators.

ARTICLE VI: Debts, National Supremacy, Oaths of Office

1. The United States will pay back any debts owed before the Constitution was adopted.

2. The Constitution, federal laws, and treaties are the supreme law of the land. State laws may not conflict with federal laws.

3. All federal and state officials must promise to uphold the Constitution.

There can be no religious requirement for holding federal office.

ARTICLE VII: Ratification of the Constitution

The Constitution was to go into effect after approval by nine states.

The Constitution was signed by the delegates to the Constitutional Convention on September 17, 1787.

Amendment I

Congress shall make no law respecting an establishment of religion, or prohibiting the free exercise thereof; or abridging the freedom of speech, or of the press; or the right of the people peaceably to assemble, and to petition the Government for a redress of grievances.

Amendment II

A well regulated Militia, being necessary to the security of a free State, the right of the people to keep and bear Arms shall not be infringed.

Amendment III

No soldier shall, in time of peace, be quartered in any house, without the consent of the Owner, nor in time of war, but in a manner to be prescribed by law.

Amendment IV

The right of the people to be secure in their persons, houses, papers, and effects, against unreasonable searches and seizures, shall not be violated, and no Warrants shall issue, but upon probable cause, supported by Oath or affirmation, and particularly describing the place to be searched, and the persons or things to be seized.

Amendment V

No person shall be held to answer for a capital or otherwise infamous crime, unless on a presentment or indictment of a Grand Jury, except in cases arising in the land or naval forces, or in the Militia, when in actual service in time of War or public danger; nor shall any person be subject for the same offence to be twice put in jeopardy of life or limb; nor shall be compelled in any criminal case to be a witness against himself, nor be deprived of life, liberty, or property, without due process of law; nor shall private property be taken for public use, without just compensation.

AMENDMENTS TO THE CONSTITUTION

Amendment 1: Freedom of Religion, Speech, Press, and Assembly (1791)

Congress may not pass any law that establishes an official religion for the country or prevents people from worshiping as they choose.

Congress may not limit the right of people to speak or write freely, to gather together peacefully, or to take their complaints to the government.

Amendment 2: The Right to Bear Arms (1791)

Citizens have a right to serve in their state militia.

Amendment 3: The Quartering of Troups (1791)

People may not be forced to keep soldiers in their homes during peacetime, and in wartime only as prescribed by law.

Amendment 4: Searches and Seizures (1791)

People may not be arrested or have their houses and property searched or taken without a warrant issued by a judge. Warrants should only be given for good reason and must describe the place to be searched and the person or items to be taken.

Amendment 5: Rights of Accused Persons (1791)

A person may not be tried for a serious crime unless a grand jury finds enough evidence to make a formal charge. (Military cases in wartime are an exception.)

A person found innocent of a crime may not be tried again for the same crime (double jeopardy).

A person may not be forced to testify against himself or herself (self-incrimination).

A person may not be denied life, liberty, or property without the proper legal procedures (due process of law).

The government may not take private property without paying a fair price (eminent domain).

Amendment VI

In all criminal prosecutions, the accused shall enjoy the right to a speedy and public trial, by an impartial jury of the State and district wherein the crime shall have been committed, which district shall have been previously ascertained by law, and to be informed of the nature and cause of the accusation; to be confronted with the witnesses against him; to have compulsory process for obtaining witnesses in his favor, and to have the Assistance of Counsel for his defence.

Amendment 6: Right to a Speedy and Fair Trial (1791)

Accused persons have the right to a speedy public trial by an impartial jury. The trial must take place in the state or district where the crime was committed.

Accused persons have the right to be told of the charges against them, to question witnesses against them, to call in witnesses to testify on their behalf, and to be represented by a lawyer.

Amendment VII

In suits at common law, where the value in controversy shall exceed twenty dollars, the right of trial by jury shall be preserved, and no fact tried by a jury, shall be otherwise re-examined in any Court of the United States, than according to the rules of the common law.

Amendment 7: Civil Suits (1791)

In civil lawsuits involving more than $20, people have the right to a trial by jury.

Amendment VIII

Excessive bail shall not be required, nor excessive fines imposed, nor cruel and unusual punishments inflicted.

Amendment 8: Bail and Punishment (1791)

Bail, fines, and punishments must be fair and reasonable.

Amendment IX

The enumeration in the Constitution, of certain rights, shall not be construed to deny or disparage others retained by the people.

Amendment 9: Powers Reserved to the People (1791)

People have other rights not listed in the Constitution. The government may not take away those rights even though they are not listed.

Amendment X

The powers not delegated to the United States by the Constitution, nor prohibited by it to the States, are reserved to the States respectively, or to the people.

Amendment 10: Powers Reserved to the States (1791)

All powers not given to the federal government or denied to the states belong to the states or to the people.

Amendment XI

The Judicial power of the United States shall not be construed to extend to any suit in law or equity, commenced or prosecuted against one of the United States by Citizens of another State, or by Citizens or Subjects of any Foreign State.

Amendment 11: Suits Against States (1795)

Lawsuits brought against states by citizens of other states or by foreign citizens must be tried in state courts.

Amendment XII

The Electors shall meet in their respective States and vote by ballot for President and Vice President, one of whom, at least, shall not be an inhabitant of the same State with themselves; they shall name in their ballots the person voted for as President, and in distinct bal-

Amendment 12: Election of the President and Vice President (1804)

This amendment changed the electoral procedure by providing that electors in each state vote separately for the President and

lots the person voted for as Vice President, and they shall make distinct lists of all persons voted for as President, and of all persons voted for as Vice President, and of the number of votes for each, which lists they shall sign and certify, and transmit sealed to the seat of the government of the United States, directed to the President of the Senate;—The President of the Senate shall, in the presence of the Senate and House of Representatives, open all the certificates and the votes shall then be counted;—The person having the greatest number of votes for President,. shall be the President, if such number be a majority of the whole number of Electors appointed; and if no person have such majority. then from the persons having the highest numbers not exceeding three on the list of those voted for as President, the House of Representatives shall choose immediately, by ballot, the President. But in choosing the President, the votes shall be taken by states, the representation from each state having one vote; a quorum for this purpose shall consist of a member or members from two-thirds of the states, and a majority of all the states shall be necessary to a choice. And if the House of Representatives shall not choose a President whenever the right of choice shall devolve upon them, before the fourth day of March next following, then the Vice President shall act as President, as in the case of the death or other constitutional disability of the President.—The person having the greatest number of votes as Vice President, shall be the Vice President, if such number be a majority of the whole number of Electors appointed, and if no person have a majority, then from the two highest numbers on the list, the Senate shall choose the Vice President; a quorum for the purpose shall consist of two-thirds of the whole number of Senators, and a majority of the whole number shall be necessary to a choice. But no person constitutionally ineligible to the office of President shall be eligible to that of Vice President of the United States.

Vice President. The candidate who receives the most electoral votes (provided it is a majority) is elected President. If no candidate receives a majority, the House of Representatives chooses the President from the three leading candidates.

If no candidate for Vice President receives a majority of the electoral votes, the Senate chooses from the two leading candidates.

Amendment XIII

Section 1

Neither slavery nor involuntary servitude, except as a punishment for crime whereof the party shall have been duly convicted, shall exist within the United States, or any place subject to their jurisdiction.

Section 2

Congress shall have power to enforce this article by appropriate legislation.

Amendment XIV

Section 1

All persons born or naturalized in the United States, and subject to the jurisdiction thereof, are citizens of the United States and of the State wherein they reside. No State shall make or enforce any law which shall abridge the privileges or immunities of citizens of the United States; nor shall any State deprive any person of life, lib-

Amendment 13: Abolition of Slavery (1865)
Slavery is banned in the United States and all U.S. territories. Involuntary servitude is permitted only as punishment for a crime.

Amendment 14: Rights of Citizens (1868)
This amendment gave U.S. citizenship to former slaves.
1. Anyone born or naturalized in the United States is a citizen.
States may not make or enforce laws that limit the rights of U.S. citizens.

erty, or property, without due process of law; nor deny to any person within its jurisdiction the equal protection of the laws.

Section 2

Representatives shall be apportioned among the several States according to their respective numbers, counting the whole number of persons in each State, excluding Indians not taxed. But when the right to vote at any election for the choice of electors for President and Vice President of the United States, Representatives in Congress, the Executive and Judicial officers of a State, or the members of the Legislature thereof, is denied to any of the male inhabitants of such State, being twenty-one years of age, and citizens of the United States, or in any way abridged, except for participation in rebellion, or other crime, the basis of representation therein shall be reduced in the proportion which the number of such male citizens shall bear to the whole number of male citizens twenty-one years of age in such State.

Section 3

No person shall be a Senator or Representative in Congress, or elector of President and Vice President, or hold any office, civil or military, under the United States, or under any State, who, having previously taken an oath, as a member of Congress, or as an officer of the United States, or as a member of any State legislature, or as an executive or judicial officer of any State, to support the Constitution of the United States, shall have engaged in insurrection or rebellion against the same, or given aid or comfort to the enemies thereof. But Congress may by a vote of two-thirds of each House, remove such disability.

Section 4

The validity of the public debt of the United States, authorized by law, including debts incurred for payment of pensions and bounties for services in suppressing insurrection or rebellion, shall not be questioned. But neither the United States nor any State shall assume or pay any debt or obligation incurred in aid of insurrection or rebellion against the United States, or any claim for the loss or emancipation of any slave; but all such debts, obligations, and claims shall be held illegal and void.

Section 5

The Congress shall have the power to enforce, by appropriate legislation, the provisions of this article.

Amendment XV

Section 1

The right of citizens of the United States to vote shall not be denied or abridged by the United States or by any State on account of race, color, or previous condition of servitude.

States may not execute a person or take away a person's freedom or property without due process of law. States may not deny to any individual equal treatment under the law.

2. If a state denies citizens the right to vote, the state's representation in Congress will be reduced.

3. Government officials who once swore to support the Constitution and later rebelled against the United States or helped its enemies may not hold any federal or state office (unless approved by a two-thirds vote of Congress).

4. The federal government shall pay all its debts including debts contracted in putting down rebellion. Neither the federal government nor a state government may pay debts contracted by aiding a rebellion against the United States. No payments will be made for lost or freed slaves.

Amendment 15: Right to Vote (1870)

No U.S. citizen can be denied the right to vote because of race, color, or having been a slave.

Section 2

The Congress shall have power to enforce this article by appropriate legislation.

Amendment XVI

The Congress shall have power to lay and collect taxes on incomes, from whatever source derived, without apportionment among the several States, and without regard to any census or enumeration.

Amendment 16: Income Tax (1913)

Congress may levy an income tax.

Amendment XVII

The Senate of the United States shall be composed of two Senators from each State, elected by the people thereof, for six years; and each Senator shall have one vote. The electors in each State shall have the qualifications requisite for electors of the most numerous branch of the State legislatures.

When vacancies happen in the representation of any State in the Senate, the executive authority of such State shall issue writs of election to fill such vacancies: *Provided*, That the legislature of any State may empower the executive thereof to make temporary appointments until the people fill the vacancies by election as the legislature may direct.

This amendment shall not be so construed as to affect the election or term of any Senator chosen before it becomes valid as part of the Constitution.

Amendment 17: Direct Election of Senators (1913)

Senators are to be directly elected by the voters of each state.

A Senate vacancy will be filled by a special election called by the state governor. State legislatures may give governors the power to make temporary Senate appointments until elections are held.

Amendment XVIII

Section 1

After one year from the ratification of this article the manufacture, sale, or transportation of intoxicating liquors within, the importation thereof into, or the exportation thereof from the United States and all territory subject to the jurisdiction thereof for beverage purposes is hereby prohibited.

Section 2

The Congress and the several States shall have concurrent power to enforce this article by appropriate legislation.

Section 3

This article shall be inoperative unless it shall have been ratified as an amendment to the Constitution by the legislatures of the several States, as provided in the Constitution, within seven years from the date of the submission hereof to the States by the Congress.

Amendment 18: Prohibition of Alcohol (1919)

The manufacture, sale, or transportation of alcoholic beverages is forbidden. (This was repealed by the Twenty-First Amendment.)

Amendment XIX

The right of citizens of the United States to vote shall not be denied or abridged by the United States or by any State on account of sex.

Congress shall have power to enforce this article by appropriate legislation.

Amendment 19: Women's Suffrage (1920)

This amendment gave women the right to vote.

Amendment XX

Section 1

The terms of the President and Vice President shall end at noon on the 20th day of January, and the terms of Senators and Representatives at noon on the 3d day of January, of the years in which such terms would have ended if this article had not been ratified; and the terms of their successors shall then begin.

Section 2

The Congress shall assemble at least once in every year, and such meeting shall begin at noon on the 3d day of January, unless they shall by law appoint a different day.

Section 3

If, at the time fixed for the beginning of the term of the President, the President elect shall have died, the Vice President elect shall become President. If a President shall not have been chosen before the time fixed for the beginning of his term, or if the President elect shall have failed to qualify, then the Vice President elect shall act as President until a President shall have qualified; and the Congress may by law provide for the case wherein neither a President elect nor a Vice President elect shall have qualified, declaring who shall then act as President, or the manner in which one who is to act shall be selected, and such person shall act accordingly until a President or Vice President shall have qualified.

Section 4

The Congress may by law provide for the case of the death of any of the persons from whom the House of Representatives may choose a President whenever the right of choice shall have devolved upon them, and for the case of the death of any of the persons from whom the Senate may choose a Vice President whenever the right of choice shall have developed upon them.

Section 5

Sections 1 and 2 shall take effect on the 15th day of October following the ratification of this article.

Section 6

This article shall be inoperative unless it shall have been ratified as an amendment to the Constitution by the legislatures of three-fourths of the several States within seven years from the date of its submission.

Amendment XXI

Section 1

The eighteenth article of amendment to the Constitution of the United States is hereby repealed.

Amendment 20: Terms of Office (1933)

1. The President and Vice President shall take office at noon on January 20th. Senators and Representatives shall take office at noon on January 3rd.

2. Congress must meet at least once a year beginning at noon on January 3, unless it passes a law to change this date.

3. If a President-elect dies before taking office, the Vice President becomes President. If a President is not elected by January 20, or if the President-elect is not qualified, the Vice President becomes President until a qualified candidate is elected. If both President-elect and Vice President–elect die or fail to qualify, Congress may appoint a temporary President or Vice President until qualified candidates are elected.

Amendment 21: Repeal of Prohibition (1933)

1. The Eighteenth Amendment is repealed.

2. States may ban the sale of alcoholic beverages.

Section 2

The transportation or importation into any State, Territory, or possession of the United States for delivery or use therein of intoxicating liquors, in violation of the laws thereof, is hereby prohibited.

Section 3

This article shall be inoperative unless it shall have been ratified as an amendment to the Constitution by conventions in the several States, as provided in the Constitution, within seven years from the date of the submission hereof to the States by the Congress.

Amendment XXII

Section 1

No person shall be elected to the office of the President more than twice, and no person who has held the office of President, or acted as President, for more than two years of a term to which some other person was elected President shall be elected to the office of the President more than once.

But this Article shall not apply to any person holding the office of President when this Article was proposed by the Congress, and shall not prevent any person who may be holding the office of President, or acting as President, during the term within which this Article becomes operative from holding the office of President or acting as President during the remainder of such term.

Section 2

This article shall be inoperative unless it shall have been ratified as an amendment to the Constitution by the legislatures of three-fourths of the several States within seven years from the date of its submission to the States by the Congress.

Amendment XXIII

Section 1

The District constituting the seat of Government of the United States shall appoint in such manner as the Congress may direct:

A number of electors of President and Vice President equal to the whole number of Senators and Representatives in Congress to which the District would be entitled if it were a State, but in no event more than the least populous State; they shall be in addition to those appointed by the States, but they shall be considered, for the purposes of the election of President and Vice President, to be electors appointed by a State; and they shall meet in the District and perform such duties as provided by the twelfth article of amendment.

Section 2

The Congress shall have power to enforce this article by appropriate legislation.

Amendment 22: Limit on Presidential Terms (1951)

A President may be elected to only two terms of office. A Vice President who serves more than two years as President may be elected for only one term.

Amendment 23: Voting Rights for the District of Columbia (1961)

This amendment gave residents of the District of Columbia the right to vote in Presidential elections.

Amendment XXIV

Section 1

The right of citizens of the United States to vote in any primary or other election for President or Vice President, for electors for President or Vice President, or for Senator or Representative in Congress, shall not be denied or abridged by the United States or any State by reason of failure to pay any poll tax or other tax.

Section 2

The Congress shall have the power to enforce this article by appropriate legislation.

Amendment XXV

Section 1

In case of the removal of the President from office or his death or resignation, the Vice President shall become President.

Section 2

Whenever there is a vacancy in the office of the Vice President, the President shall nominate a Vice President who shall take the office upon confirmation by a majority vote of both houses of Congress.

Section 3

Whenever the President transmits to the President pro tempore of the Senate and the Speaker of the House of Representatives his written declaration that he is unable to discharge the powers and duties of his office, and until he transmits to them a written declaration to the contrary, such powers and duties shall be discharged by the Vice President as Acting President.

Section 4

Whenever the Vice President and a majority of either the principal officers of the executive departments, or of such other body as Congress may by law provide, transmit to the President pro tempore of the Senate and the Speaker of the House of Representatives their written declaration that the President is unable to discharge the powers and duties of his office, the Vice President shall immediately assume the powers and duties of the office as Acting President.

Thereafter, when the President transmits to the President pro tempore of the Senate and the Speaker of the House of Representatives his written declaration that no inability exists, he shall resume the powers and duties of his office unless the Vice President and a majority of either the principal officers of the executive departments, or of such other body as Congress may by law provide, transmit within four days to the President pro tempore of the Senate and the Speaker of the House of Representatives their written declaration that the President is unable to discharge the powers and duties of his office. Thereupon Congress shall decide the issue, assembling within 48 hours for that purpose if not in session. If the Congress within

Amendment 24: Abolition of the Poll Tax (1964)
Poll taxes are prohibited in federal elections.

Amendment 25: Presidential Disability and Succession (1967)
1. If the President dies or resigns, the Vice President becomes President.
2. When the office of Vice President is vacant, the President may appoint a Vice President with the approval of a majority of both houses of Congress.
3. If the President is unable to fulfill the duties of office, the Vice President serves as Acting President.
4. If the Vice President and a majority of Cabinet members decide that the President is unable to fulfill the duties of office, the Vice President becomes Acting President.
The President may resume the duties of office by notifying Congress. However, if the Vice President and a majority of the Cabinet feel that the President is still unable to resume duties, Congress must decide the issue by a two-thirds vote of both houses.

21 days after receipt of the latter written declaration, or, if Congress is not in session, within 21 days after Congress is required to assemble, determines by two-thirds vote of both houses that the President is unable to discharge the powers and duties of his office, the Vice President shall continue to discharge the same as Acting President; otherwise, the President shall resume the power and duties of his office.

Amendment XXVI

Section 1

The right of citizens of the United States, who are eighteen years of age or older, to vote shall not be denied or abridged by the United States or any State on account of age.

Section 2

The Congress shall have power to enforce this article by appropriate legislation.

Amendment 26: Lowered Voting Age (1971)

This amendment gave citizens 18 and older the right to vote in all elections.

THE AMERICAN FLAG

★ ★ ★ ★ ★

Honoring the Flag

A great many rules and customs have grown up about how to use and display the American flag. These rules and customs were incorporated in a flag code passed by Congress in 1942 and amended in 1976. No one is expected to know all of the regulations. The important thing is to treat the flag with respect. Here are some of the rules of the flag code.

★ The flag should be displayed from sunrise to sunset. It should not be flown at night except on special occasions or in certain places.
★ The flag should not be flown in bad weather.
★ No other flag should be flown above the American flag or to the right of it at the same height.
★ The flag should not be used to cover a statue or painting at an unveiling.
★ On Memorial Day, the flag should be flown at half-mast in the morning and at full-mast in the afternoon.
★ The flag may be flown at half-mast to mourn the death of public officials. When it is flown at half-mast, it should first be hoisted all the way up and then lowered.
★ When the flag is used to drape a coffin, it should be placed so that the union (the stars) is at the head and over the left shoulder of the casket.
★ The flag should never touch the ground or floor beneath it.

★ The flag may be flown upside down only to signal distress.
★ If the flag is suspended over a street, the union should face north or east.
★ The flag should never be used as a drapery or displayed in festoons or folds. It should always fall free.
★ The flag should never be used for advertising purposes.
★ The flag should never be dipped to any person or thing.

The Pledge of Allegiance

"I pledge allegiance to the Flag of the United States of America and to the Republic for which it stands, one Nation under God indivisible, with liberty and justice for all."

Francis Bellamy, a magazine editor, wrote the Pledge of Allegiance in 1892 to celebrate the 400th anniversary of Columbus's discovery of America. In 1954, Congress amended the Pledge by adding the words "under God." Over the years, it has become an American tradition to recite the Pledge of Allegiance in school and at many public gatherings.

When you recite the Pledge of Allegiance, you should stand facing the flag and place your right hand over your heart. People in military uniform should give a military salute with their right hand.

THE MAYFLOWER COMPACT
November 11, 1620

In late 1620, a group of Pilgrims left England for Virginia. Somehow their ship, the *Mayflower*, went off course and landed in Massachusetts. The Pilgrims decided to settle where they were, but they had no charter to form a colony. Before they left the ship, the settlers drew up a compact, or agreement, establishing a government ("civil Body Politick") for the new colony. The government would enact laws necessary for the common good, and the 41 men who signed the compact agreed to obey those laws.

In the name of God, Amen. We, whose names are underwritten, the Loyal Subjects of our dread Sovereign Lord, King James, by the Grace of God, of Great Britain, France and Ireland, King, Defender of the Faith, &. [etc.]

Having undertaken for the Glory of God, and Advancement of the Christian Faith, and the Honour of our King and Country, a voyage to plant the first colony in the northern Parts of Virginia; do by these Presents, solemnly and mutually in the Presence of God and one of another, covenant and combine ourselves together into a civil Body Politick, for our better Ordering and Preservation, and Furtherance of the Ends aforesaid; And by Virtue hereof to enact, constitute, and frame, such just and equal Laws, Ordinances, Acts, Constitutions and Offices, from time to time, as shall be thought most meet and convenient for the General good of the Colony; unto which we promise all due Submission and Obedience. In Witness whereof we have hereunto subscribed our names at Cape Cod the eleventh of November, in the Reign of our Sovereign, Lord, King James of England, France and Ireland, the eighteenth, and of Scotland the fifty-fourth. Anno Domini 1620

GETTYSBURG ADDRESS
November 19, 1863

Four months after the terrible battle of Gettysburg in the midst of the Civil War, President Lincoln paused to honor those who had died on the battlefield. In his speech, Lincoln pledged that the nation the soldiers had died for, a nation based on the ideas of freedom and equality, would survive.

Fourscore and seven years ago our fathers brought forth on this continent a new nation, conceived in liberty and dedicated to the proposition that all men are created equal.

Now we are engaged in a great civil war, testing whether that nation or any nation so conceived and so dedicated can long endure. We are met on a great battle field of that war. We have come to dedicate a portion of that field, as a final resting place for those who here gave their lives that that nation might live. It is altogether fitting and proper that we should do this.

But, in a larger sense, we can not dedicate—we can not consecrate—we can not hallow—this ground. The brave men, living and dead, who struggled here, have consecrated it, far above our poor power to add or detract. The world will little note, nor long remember, what we say here, but it can never forget what they did here. It is for us the living, rather, to be here dedicated to the great task remaining before us—that from these honored dead we take increased devotion to that cause for which they gave the last full measure of devotion—that we here highly resolve that these dead men shall not have died in vain—that this nation, under God, shall have a new birth of freedom—and that government of the people, by the people, for the people, shall not perish from the earth.

THE PRESIDENTS OF THE UNITED STATES

1. George Washington
   1732–1799
   Party: Federalist
   Elected from: Virginia
   In office: 1789–1797

2. John Adams
   1735–1826
   Party: Federalist
   Elected from: Massachusetts
   In office: 1797–1801

3. Thomas Jefferson
   1743–1826
   Party: Democratic-Republican
   Elected from: Virginia
   In office: 1801–1809

4. James Madison
   1751–1836
   Party: Democratic-Republican
   Elected from: Virginia
   In office: 1809–1817

5. James Monroe
   1758–1831
   Party: Democratic-Republican
   Elected from: Virginia
   In office: 1817–1825

6. John Quincy Adams
   1767–1848
   Party: Democratic-Republican
   Elected from: Massachusetts
   In office: 1825–1829

7. Andrew Jackson
   1767–1845
   Party: Democratic
   Elected from: Tennessee
   In office: 1829–1837

8. Martin Van Buren
   1782–1862
   Party: Democratic
   Elected from: New York
   In office: 1837–1841

9. William H. Harrison
   1773–1841
   Party: Whig
   Elected from: Ohio
   In office: 1841

10. John Tyler
    1790–1862
    Party: Whig
    Elected from: Virginia
    In office: 1841–1845

11. James K. Polk
    1795–1849
    Party: Democratic
    Elected from: Tennessee
    In office: 1845–1849

12. Zachary Taylor
    1784–1850
    Party: Whig
    Elected from: Louisiana
    In office: 1849–1850

13. Millard Fillmore
    1800–1874
    Party: Whig
    Elected from: New York
    In office: 1850–1853

14. Franklin Pierce
    1804–1869
    Party: Democratic
    Elected from: New Hampshire
    In office: 1853–1857

15. James Buchanan
    1791–1868
    Party: Democratic
    Elected from: Pennsylvania
    In office: 1857–1861

16. Abraham Lincoln
    1809–1865
    Party: Republican
    Elected from: Illinois
    In office: 1861–1865

17. Andrew Johnson
    1808–1875
    Party: Democratic
    Elected from: Tennessee
    In office: 1865–1869

18. Ulysses S. Grant
    1822–1885
    Party: Republican
    Elected from: Illinois
    In office: 1869–1877

19. Rutherford B. Hayes
    1822–1893
    Party: Republican
    Elected from: Ohio
    In office: 1877–1881

20. James A. Garfield
    1831–1881
    Party: Republican
    Elected from: Ohio
    In office: 1881

21. Chester A. Arthur
    1829–1886
    Party: Republican
    Elected from: New York
    In office: 1881–1885

22, 24. Grover Cleveland
    1837–1908
    Party: Democratic
    Elected from: New York
    In office: 1885–1889,
              1893–1897

23. Benjamin Harrison
    1833–1901
    Party: Republican
    Elected from: Indiana
    In office: 1889–1893

25. William McKinley
    1843–1901
    Party: Republican
    Elected from: Ohio
    In office: 1897–1901

26. Theodore Roosevelt
1858–1919
Party: Republican
Elected from: New York
In office: 1901–1909

27. William H. Taft
1857–1930
Party: Republican
Elected from: Ohio
In office: 1909–1913

28. Woodrow Wilson
1856–1924
Party: Democratic
Elected from: New Jersey
In office: 1913–1921

29. Warren G. Harding
1865–1923
Party: Republican
Elected from: Ohio
In office: 1921–1923

30. Calvin Coolidge
1872–1933
Party: Republican
Elected from: Massachusetts
In office: 1923–1929

31. Herbert C. Hoover
1874–1964
Party: Republican
Elected from: California
In office: 1929–1933

32. Franklin D. Roosevelt
1882–1945
Party: Democratic
Elected from: New York
In office: 1933–1945

33. Harry S. Truman
1884–1972
Party: Democratic
Elected from: Missouri
In office: 1945–1953

34. Dwight D. Eisenhower
1890–1969
Party: Republican
Elected from: New York
In office: 1953–1961

35. John F. Kennedy
1917–1963
Party: Democratic
Elected from: Massachusetts
In office: 1961–1963

36. Lyndon B. Johnson
1908–1973
Party: Democratic
Elected from: Texas
In office: 1963–1969

37. Richard M. Nixon
1913–
Party: Republican
Elected from: California
In office: 1969–1974

38. Gerald R. Ford
1913–
Party: Republican
Elected from: Michigan
In office: 1974–1977

39. Jimmy Carter
1924–
Party: Democratic
Elected from: Georgia
In office: 1977–1981

40. Ronald W. Reagan
1911–
Party: Republican
Elected from: California
In office: 1981–1989

41. George Bush
1924–
Party: Republican
Elected from: Texas
In office: 1989–Present

Hillary an Bill Clinton

THE STATES OF THE UNITED STATES

* * * * *

State	Year Entered Union	Capital	Population (1990 Census)	Number of Representatives in Congress
Alabama	1819	Montgomery	4,062,608	9
Alaska	1959	Juneau	551,947	3
Arizona	1912	Phoenix	3,677,985	8
Arkansas	1836	Little Rock	2,362,239	6
California	1850	Sacramento	29,839,250	54
Colorado	1876	Denver	3,307,912	8
Connecticut	1788	Hartford	3,295,669	8
Delaware	1787	Dover	668,696	3
Florida	1845	Tallahassee	13,003,362	25
Georgia	1788	Atlanta	6,508,419	13
Hawaii	1959	Honolulu	1,115,274	4
Idaho	1890	Boise	1,011,986	4
Illinois	1818	Springfield	11,466,682	22
Indiana	1816	Indianapolis	5,564,228	12
Iowa	1846	Des Moines	2,787,424	7
Kansas	1861	Topeka	2,485,600	6
Kentucky	1792	Frankfort	3,698,969	8
Louisiana	1812	Baton Rouge	4,238,216	9
Maine	1820	Augusta	1,233,223	4
Maryland	1788	Annapolis	4,798,622	10
Massachusetts	1788	Boston	6,029,051	12
Michigan	1837	Lansing	9,328,784	18
Minnesota	1858	St. Paul	4,387,029	10
Mississippi	1817	Jackson	2,586,443	7
Missouri	1821	Jefferson City	5,137,804	11
Montana	1889	Helena	803,655	3
Nebraska	1867	Lincoln	1,584,617	5
Nevada	1864	Carson City	1,206,152	4
New Hampshire	1788	Concord	1,113,915	4
New Jersey	1787	Trenton	7,748,634	15
New Mexico	1912	Santa Fe	1,521,779	5
New York	1788	Albany	18,044,505	33
North Carolina	1789	Raleigh	6,657,630	14
North Dakota	1889	Bismarck	641,364	3
Ohio	1803	Columbus	10,887,325	21
Oklahoma	1907	Oklahoma City	3,157,604	8
Oregon	1859	Salem	2,853,733	7
Pennsylvania	1787	Harrisburg	11,924,710	23
Rhode Island	1790	Providence	1,005,984	4
South Carolina	1788	Columbia	3,505,707	8
South Dakota	1889	Pierre	699,999	3
Tennessee	1796	Nashville	4,896,641	11

THE STATES OF THE UNITED STATES
(Continued)

State	Year Entered Union	Capital	Population (1990 Census)	Number of Representatives in Congress
Texas	1845	Austin	17,059,805	32
Utah	1896	Salt Lake City	1,727,784	5
Vermont	1791	Montpelier	564,964	3
Virginia	1788	Richmond	6,216,568	13
Washington	1889	Olympia	4,887,941	11
West Virginia	1863	Charleston	1,801,625	5
Wisconsin	1848	Madison	4,906,745	11
Wyoming	1890	Cheyenne	455,975	3
District of Columbia	— —	— —	609,909	0
Total			249,632,692	535

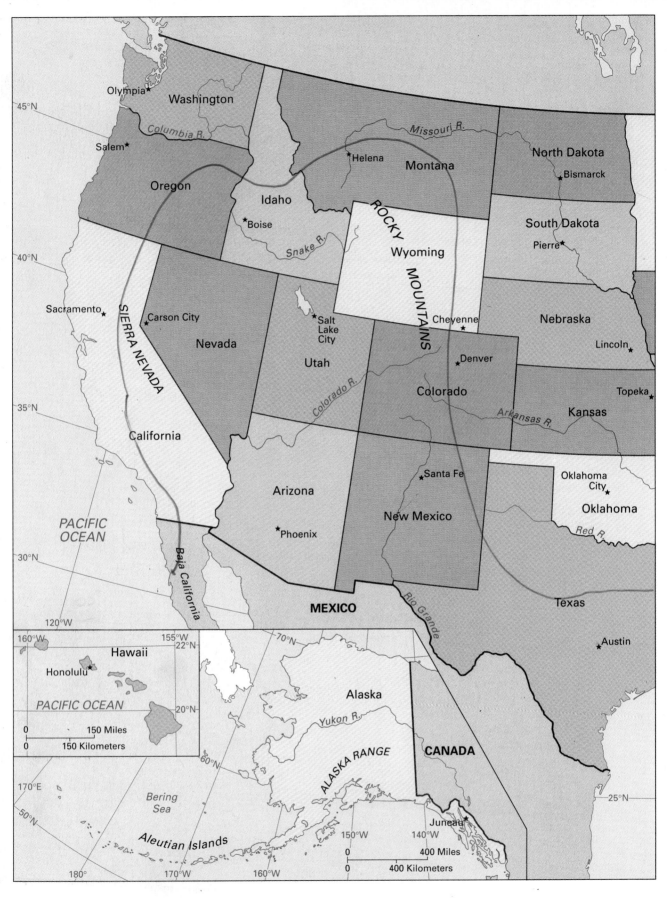

Olympia ★

Washington

Columbia R.

Salem ★

Oregon

Idaho

Boise ★

Snake R.

SIERRA NEVADA

Sacramento ★

Carson City ★

Nevada

Salt Lake City ★

Utah

California

PACIFIC OCEAN

Baja California

Helena ★

Montana

ROCKY MOUNTAINS

Missouri R.

Wyoming

Cheyenne ★

Denver ★

Colorado

Colorado R.

Arkansas R.

Arizona

Phoenix ★

New Mexico

Santa Fe ★

North Dakota

Bismarck ★

South Dakota

Pierre ★

Nebraska

Lincoln ★

Kansas

Topeka ★

Oklahoma City ★

Oklahoma

Red R.

Texas

Austin ★

MEXICO

Rio Grande

45°N

40°N

35°N

30°N

120°W

Hawaii

Honolulu ★

PACIFIC OCEAN

0   150 Miles

0   150 Kilometers

160°W

155°W

22°N

20°N

170°E

70°N

Alaska

Yukon R.

ALASKA RANGE

CANADA

Juneau ★

Bering Sea

Aleutian Islands

180°

170°W

160°W

150°W

140°W

60°N

50°N

25°N

0   400 Miles

0   400 Kilometers

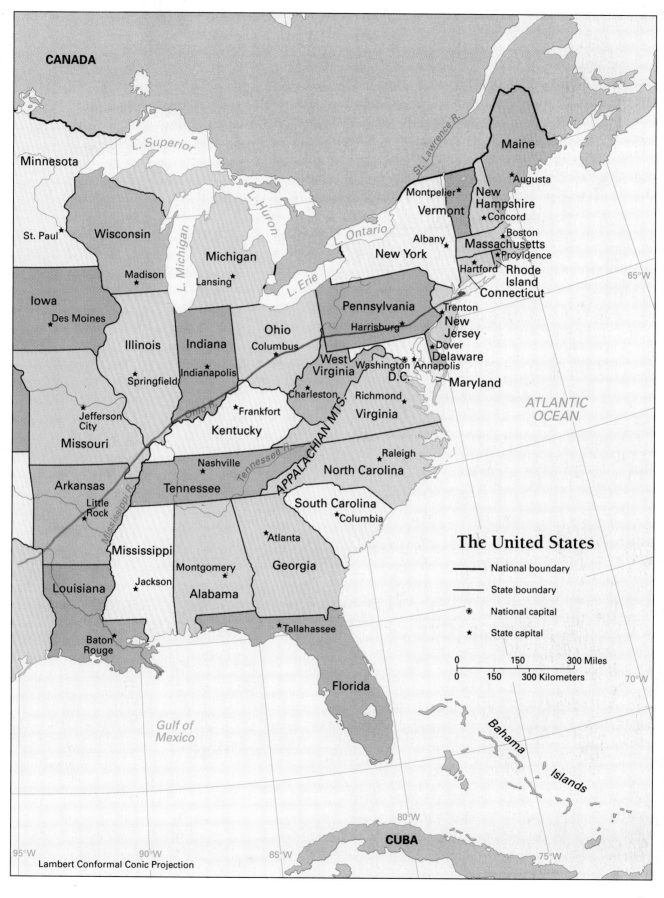

CANADA

Minnesota

L. Superior

Wisconsin

St. Paul ★

Madison ★

Iowa

Des Moines ★

Illinois

Springfield ★

Jefferson City ★

Missouri

Arkansas

Little Rock ★

Louisiana

Baton Rouge ★

Michigan

L. Huron

L. Michigan

Lansing ★

Indiana

Indianapolis ★

Ohio R.

Mississippi R.

Kentucky

Frankfort ★

Nashville ★

Tennessee

Tennessee R.

Mississippi

Jackson ★

Alabama

Montgomery ★

Gulf of Mexico

L. Erie

L. Ontario

New York

Albany ★

Ohio

Columbus ★

West Virginia

Charleston ★

APPALACHIAN MTS.

Pennsylvania

Harrisburg ★

Richmond ★

Virginia

Raleigh ★

North Carolina

South Carolina

Columbia ★

Atlanta ★

Georgia

Tallahassee ★

Florida

St. Lawrence R.

Maine

Augusta ★

Montpelier ★

New Hampshire

Vermont

Concord ★

Boston ★

Massachusetts

Providence ★

Hartford ★

Rhode Island

Connecticut

Trenton ★

New Jersey

Dover ★

Delaware

Washington ✷

D.C.

Annapolis ★

Maryland

ATLANTIC OCEAN

65°W

70°W

Bahama Islands

80°W

75°W

CUBA

85°W

90°W

95°W

Lambert Conformal Conic Projection

The United States

———— National boundary

——— State boundary

✷ National capital

★ State capital

0   150   300 Miles

0   150   300 Kilometers

591

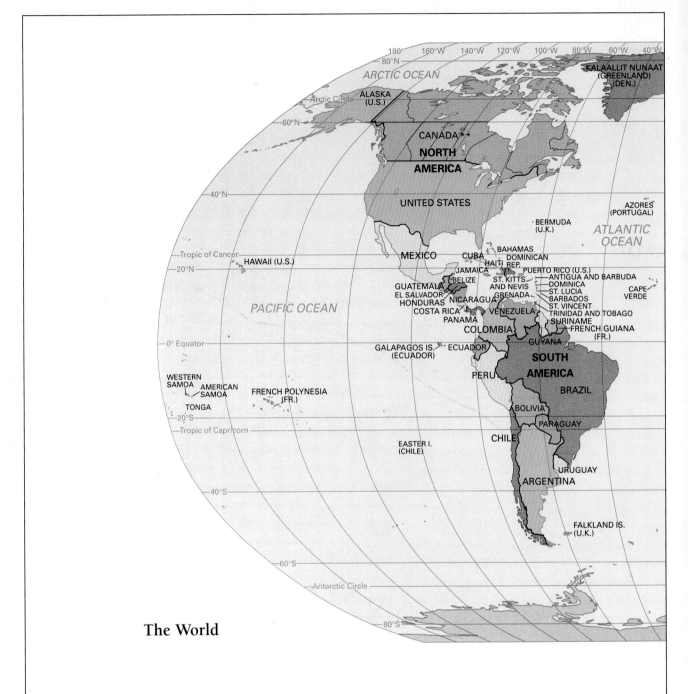

ARCTIC OCEAN

KALAALLIT NUNAAT
(GREENLAND)
(DEN.)

180° 160°W 140°W 120°W 100°W 80°W 60°W 40°W

80°N

Arctic Circle

ALASKA
(U.S.)

60°N

CANADA

NORTH
AMERICA

40°N

UNITED STATES

AZORES
(PORTUGAL)

BERMUDA
(U.K.)

ATLANTIC
OCEAN

Tropic of Cancer

HAWAII (U.S.)

20°N

MEXICO

CUBA

BAHAMAS

DOMINICAN
REP.

HAITI

JAMAICA

BELIZE

PUERTO RICO (U.S.)

ANTIGUA AND BARBUDA

ST. KITTS
AND NEVIS

DOMINICA

GUATEMALA
EL SALVADOR
HONDURAS

NICARAGUA

ST. LUCIA

BARBADOS

ST. VINCENT

GRENADA

CAPE
VERDE

PACIFIC OCEAN

COSTA RICA

PANAMA

VENEZUELA

TRINIDAD AND TOBAGO

SURINAME

COLOMBIA

GUYANA

FRENCH GUIANA
(FR.)

0° Equator

GALAPAGOS IS.
(ECUADOR)

ECUADOR

PERU

SOUTH
AMERICA

WESTERN
SAMOA

AMERICAN
SAMOA

FRENCH POLYNESIA
(FR.)

BRAZIL

TONGA

BOLIVIA

20°S

Tropic of Capricorn

PARAGUAY

CHILE

EASTER I.
(CHILE)

URUGUAY

40°S

ARGENTINA

FALKLAND IS.
(U.K.)

60°S

Antarctic Circle

80°S

The World

0   1,000   2,000 Miles

0   1,000 2,000 Kilometers

Robinson Projection

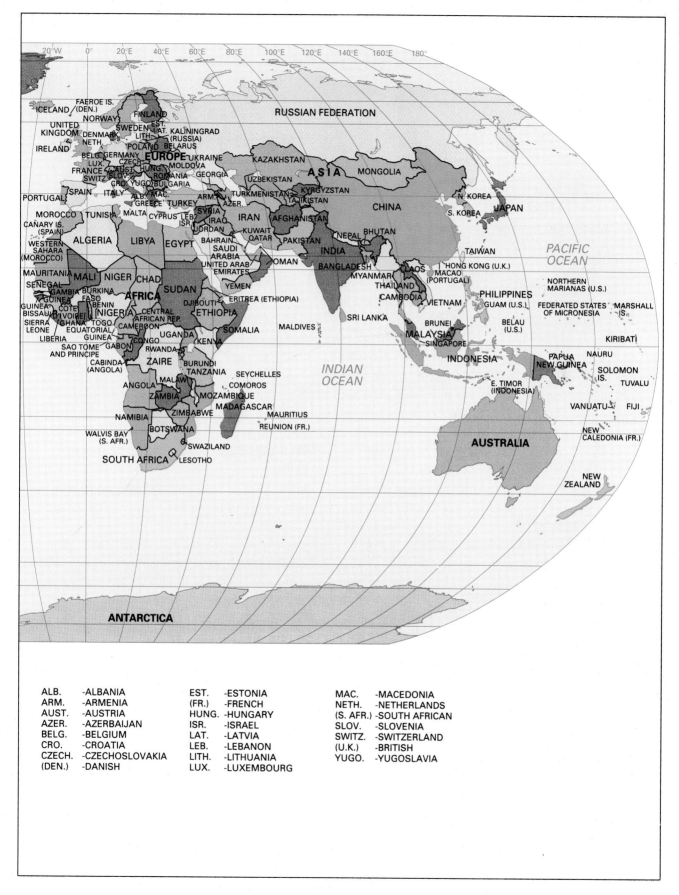

ALB.	-ALBANIA	EST.	-ESTONIA	MAC.	-MACEDONIA
ARM.	-ARMENIA	(FR.)	-FRENCH	NETH.	-NETHERLANDS
AUST.	-AUSTRIA	HUNG.	-HUNGARY	(S. AFR.)	-SOUTH AFRICAN
AZER.	-AZERBAIJAN	ISR.	-ISRAEL	SLOV.	-SLOVENIA
BELG.	-BELGIUM	LAT.	-LATVIA	SWITZ.	-SWITZERLAND
CRO.	-CROATIA	LEB.	-LEBANON	(U.K.)	-BRITISH
CZECH.	-CZECHOSLOVAKIA	LITH.	-LITHUANIA	YUGO.	-YUGOSLAVIA
(DEN.)	-DANISH	LUX.	-LUXEMBOURG		

GLOSSARY

The number that appears in parentheses after each definition indicates the chapter and section in which the definition appears.

accountable having to explain one's actions to the voters (6-4)

acid rain rain containing sulfur dioxide, which destroys forests and pollutes water (24-2)

acquittal a vote of not guilty (17-3)

administration the officials and agencies of the executive branch that help the President plan and carry out policy (10-4)

adversary the opposing side in a dispute (12-4)

affirmative action a program designed to help minorities and women gain access to jobs and opportunities (5-1)

alien a person who lives in a country but is not a citizen of that country (1-2)

alliance a formal agreement among nations (23-1)

ambassador an official who represents his or her nation in a foreign country (10-2)

amend to change (2-4)

amendment a change in the text of the Constitution (3-4)

amnesty a pardon granted to the members of a group for breaking a law (10-3)

Anti-Federalist a person who opposed the Constitution before 1789 (3-1)

apartheid in South Africa, the policy of keeping black people powerless and separate from whites (23-3)

apathy lack of interest (7-1)

appellate court a court that hears cases appealed from lower courts (12-2)

appellate jurisdiction authority to review cases from lower courts or federal agencies (12-2)

apportionment the distribution of seats in a legislature according to population (13-3)

appropriations funds set aside for a particular purpose (9-3)

arbitration the settlement of a dispute by acceptance of the decision of a third party (19-3)

arraignment a hearing in which a suspect is charged and pleads guilty or innocent (17-3)

bail money paid to the court by an accused person as guarantee that he or she will appear for trial (4-1)

balanced budget a budget in which expenditures do not exceed revenues (20-3)

bankruptcy a legal statement that a person or corporation is unable to pay its debts (21-2)

bench trial a trial by a judge (16-2)

beneficiary a person named to receive money in an insurance policy (21-3)

bias a one-sided or slanted point of view (8-2)

bicameral having a legislature with two houses (9-1)

bill of attainder a law that punishes a person accused of a crime without a fair hearing in court (16-2)

bond a certificate from the government or a corporation pledging to repay a certain amount of money at a fixed rate of interest at a certain time (15-1)

borough a county (in Alaska) (14-1)

boycott to refuse to buy or use a product or service (2-3)

brief a written argument prepared by an attorney (12-4)

budget a plan for managing and spending money (20-3)

bureaucracy a large, complex organization with many departments and different levels of responsibility (10-2)

business cycle a pattern of economic expansion and decline (19-1)

by-election a special election to replace a member of Parliament in Britain (22-1)

Cabinet a group of Presidential advisers made up of the heads of the executive departments, the Vice President, and other important government officials (11-1)

campaign an organized effort to gather support for a candidate (6-3)

candidate a person seeking an elected office (6-1)

canvassing going through a district asking for votes and taking polls (7-2)

capital money and property used to produce goods and services (18-1)

capital goods the tools, buildings, and machines used by businesses to make goods and provide services (18-1)

capitalism an economic system in which people put their capital into businesses in hopes of making a profit (18-2)

cash reserve the amount of money a bank must keep on hand (19-4)

caucus a meeting of members of a political party to select candidates (7-2)

censure in government, a legislature's formal disapproval of the conduct of one of its members (9-1)

census a process for counting the nation's population (1-3)

certificate of deposit a savings account in which money deposited for a certain amount of time earns a fixed rate of interest (21-2)

charter government document that gives individuals or organizations authority to carry on certain activities (14-1)

checks and balances a system in which each branch of government can check (restrain) the actions of the other branches (3-2)

circuit one of the twelve divisions of the United States Courts of Appeals (12-2)

citizen a member of a community with a government and laws (1-1)

civics the study of citizenship and government (1-1)

civil cases legal disputes that do not involve criminal charges (4-1)

civil law the laws concerned with disputes between individuals or groups or between the government and its citizens (16-3)

civil rights the rights guaranteed to American citizens (5-1)

civil servant an employee of the government (11-4)

closed shop a factory or business that cannot hire nonunion members (19-3)

cloture a vote to end debate on a bill in the Senate (9-4)

coalition a political alliance with another party or parties (6-1)

collateral property used as a guarantee that a loan will be repaid (19-4)

collective bargaining negotiations between representatives of a union and business owners about wages and hours (19-3)

colonists the members of a colony; those who settle a new place (2-2)

colony a group of people in one place who are ruled by the government of another place (2-2)

command economy an economy in which the government controls the means of production and makes all economic decisions (18-2)

common law unwritten law based on precedent (2-1)

common stock a share of a corporation that pays a dividend if the corporation makes a profit (18-3)

communism an economic and political system of government in which all property and means of production belong to and are controlled by the state (18-2)

community a group of people who share the same interests and concerns (5-3)

commute to reduce a criminal's sentence (13-2)

compact an agreement or contract (2-2)

complaint a formal notice that a lawsuit is being brought (17-1)

compromise an agreement between two groups in which each side agrees to give up something in order to get something more important (3-1)

concurrent jurisdiction cases in which both federal and state courts have the right to sit in judgment (12-1)

concurrent powers powers that are shared by the national government and the state governments (3-3)

concurring opinion an opinion written by a justice who supports the majority decision but for different reasons (12-4)

confederation a group of individuals or individual states who band together for a common purpose (2-4)

conference committee a joint committee of Congress that tries to work out differences between the House and Senate versions of a bill (9-2)

conglomerate a company formed by the merger of other smaller companies (19-2)

congress a formal meeting at which delegates discuss matters of common concern (2-3)

consensus broad, general agreement (22-3)

conservation the protection of natural resources (11-2)

constituency the people in an election district (22-1)

constituent a person from a legislator's district or state (9-1)

constitutional monarchy a government that has a monarch who serves as the symbolic head of state (22-1)

consul the official who runs the consulate (11-1)

consulate a government office in a foreign country that works to protect and promote the interests of its citizens (11-1)

consumer a person who buys products and services (18-1)

containment U.S. foreign policy after World War II that was designed to prevent the Soviet Union from expanding (23-1)

contempt of court a charge of obstructing or interfering with the judicial process (16-2)

contract an agreement between two parties (16-3)

cooperative an organization formed to share the costs of a business or to buy and sell goods at the lowest possible price (18-3)

corporation a large business that has many owners (18-3)

court-martial a trial before a panel of military officers (12-2)

court of appeals the federal court that hears only cases appealed from the lower district courts or from federal regulatory agencies (12-2)

criminal case a case in which juries decide whether people have committed crimes (12-1)

cross-examination the process of questioning a witness (17-3)

deduction money subtracted from income before taxes for items such as medical expenses and charitable contributions (20-2)

defendant the person accused of a crime or the party sued in a lawsuit (16-3)

deficit an excess of government expenses over government revenues (20-3)

delegate a representative (2-3)

demand the amount of a product or service that people are willing to buy (18-1)

democracy a government in which the citizens hold the power to rule and to decide what laws will be made (1-1)

deport to expel from the country (1-2)

depression a severe recession, or slowing down of economic activity (19-1)

deregulation the removal of government regulations (19-2)

détente the easing of tensions between nations (23-1)

developed nations the countries that have developed their resources and established industries (23-2)

developing nations the poor nations that are working to meet the basic needs of their people (23-2)

dictatorship a government that is controlled by one person or by a small group of people (1-1)

diplomacy the process of conducting relations with foreign governments (23-1)

disarmament the reduction of arms (23-1)

discrimination unfair or less equal treatment of a particular group (5-1)

dissenting opinion the written statement of a judge who disagrees with the majority decision (12-4)

district court the lowest level of the federal court system (12-2)

dividend a share of the profit paid to stockholders (18-3)

division of labor a system of production in which each worker does only one part of the job (18-1)

docket the list of cases to be heard by the Supreme court (12-4)

domestic referring to matters that affect only the United States (10-4)

double jeopardy the retrial of a person who was judged not guilty of the crime in a previous trial (4-1)

draft to call up men for military service (5-2)

due process of law judicial procedures established by law and guaranteed by the Constitution (4-1)

duties the things we are required to do (5-2)

Electoral College the group of people who elect the President and the Vice President (3-1)

electoral vote a ballot cast by an elector in the Electoral College system (7-3)

electorate the group of people who are eligible to vote in an election (7-1)

embassy a government office in a foreign nation, which is run by an ambassador (11-1)

eminent domain the right of the government to take private property for public use (4-1)

entrepreneur a person who starts and runs a new business (18-1)

enumerated powers powers of the federal government that are specifically mentioned in the Constitution (3-3)

environment the surroundings of a person or a community (5-3)

excise tax a tax on the manufacture or sale of certain items (20-2)

exclusive jurisdiction the right of only one court to hear a case (12-1)

executive having the power to carry out laws (3-2)

executive agency an independent agency responsible for dealing with specialized areas of government (11-3)

executive agreement an agreement between the President and the leader of another country (10-2)

executive order a rule issued by the President that has the force of law (10-2)

exemption the amount of money that can be subtracted from income before taxes for each person in a family (20-2)

exit poll a survey taken at polling places to find out how people voted (7-3)

expenditures money spent by a government (20-3)

export a product sold to another country (3-1)

ex post facto law a law that would allow a person to be punished for an action that was not against the law when the action took place (16-2)

expressed powers see *enumerated powers* (9-3)

expulsion forcing a member of Congress accused of a serious crime to resign (9-1)

extradition the return of a person accused of a crime to the state in which the crime was committed (13-1)

faction a party or group within a larger group (22-3)

featherbedding a union practice of forcing a company to employ more workers than are needed (19-3)

Federalist someone who supported the Constitution and a strong national government (3-1)

federal system a form of government in which power is shared between a national government and the states (3-1)

felony a serious crime such as robbery, murder, or arson (13-4)

filibuster in the Senate, the practice of talking for hours to delay the vote on a bill (9-4)

fiscal policy the way in which the government taxes citizens and spends money (19-1)

fixed expenses expenses that are the same from month to month (21-1)

flexible expenses expenses that vary from month to month (21-1)

foreign policy the government's positions on world issues and relations with other countries (11-1)

franking privilege the right of members of Congress to send work-related mail without paying postage (9-1)

fraud taking property by dishonest means or misrepresentation (17-2)

free enterprise a system in which people have certain economic freedoms and in which competition determines price (18-2)

free trade a policy in which economic barriers such as tariffs are eliminated (24-1)

gerrymandering dividing a state into odd-shaped election districts to gain political advantage (9-1)

glasnost in the Soviet Union, Gorbachev's policy of "openness," which has removed many restrictions on personal freedoms (22-2)

government the power or authority that rules a country (1-1)

government corporation a business owned and operated by the government that provides services to the public (11-3)

grand jury a group of citizens that hears evidence and decides whether a person should be formally accused of a crime (16-2)

grant-in-aid federal assistance to a state or local government for a specific purpose (20-3)

grassroots beginning with the people (6-4)

greenhouse effect the gradual warming of the earth caused by the high level of carbon dioxide in the atmosphere (24-2)

gross income the total amount of money a business or individual makes (18-1)

Gross National Product (GNP) the total value of all the goods and services produced in the nation each year (19-1)

guerrilla a rebel soldier (23-3)

home rule the power granted by state legislatures to cities to manage their own affairs (14-3)

hung jury a jury that cannot agree on a verdict (17-3)

immigrant a person who moves to a new country with the intention of becoming a permanent resident (1-2)

immunity legal protection from prosecution (9-1)

impartial not favoring any particular side (8-2)

impeach to formally accuse a government official of wrongdoing (9-3)

implied powers Congressional powers not specifically listed in the Constitution but suggested by the Constitution's "necessary and proper" clause (3-4)

income tax a tax on the money earned by an individual or business (20-2)

incorporate to receive a charter from the state to form a corporation (18-3)

independence self-reliance and freedom from outside control (2-3)

indicted to be formally accused by a grand jury (4-1)

inferior courts courts of lower authority (12-1)

inflation a general rise in the prices of most goods and services (19-1)

infrastructure a community's system of roads, bridges, water, and sewers (15-1)

initiative a procedure by which citizens can propose laws through the use of petition (7-3)

injunction a court order to a person or group to stop a certain action (17-1)

insurance an arrangement in which an individual or group makes regular payments in return for protection against loss or major expenses (21-3)

interdependence the reliance of countries on each other for products, services, and raw materials (24-1)

interest money paid for the use of money (19-4)

interest group a group of people who share a similar point of view and who join together to promote that point of view (8-1)

interpret to decide the meaning of (2-4)

investment buying something that is expected to increase in value (21-2)

isolationism the policy of avoiding alliances or military pacts with other countries (23-1)

item veto the power to approve certain parts of a bill and veto other parts (13-3)

joint committee a committee that includes members from both the House and the Senate (9-2)

judicial having the power to interpret laws (3-2)

judicial review the power of the courts to decide whether actions of the executive and legislative branches of government are in agreement with the Constitution (12-3)

jurisdiction the authority of a court to hear and decide a case (12-1)

jurisprudence the study of the law (16-1)

justice of the peace a judge of a local court who hears misdemeanors and minor cases (13-4)

juvenile a person not yet legally an adult (17-4)

juvenile delinquent a child or teenager who commits a serious crime or repeatedly breaks the law (17-4)

labor union an organization of workers that tries to improve the wages and working conditions of its members (19-3)

laissez-faire "to allow to do," a government policy of letting businesses do what they want without interference (19-2)

landfill a site for burying waste (15-3)

larceny taking the property of another unlawfully (17-2)

legislative having the power to make laws (3-2)

legislature a group of people that makes laws for a state or country (2-1)

liability insurance insurance that protects property owners against damages or injuries that occur on their property (21-3)

libel the crime of printing lies about other people (4-2)

limited liability the sharing of the responsibility and risk of a business venture among many people (18-3)

literacy test a test to prove that a voter can read, write, and understand public issues (7-1)

lobby to try to persuade government officials to support the cause of a special-interest group (8-3)

lobbyist a person who tries to persuade politicians to support a particular group or position (8-3)

magistrate the official in a district court who issues court orders and determines whether cases should be brought to trial (12-2)

magistrate court a local court that handles minor cases such as traffic violations and civil cases involving small sums of money (13-4)

majority more than half (6-1)

majority leader the leader of the majority party in each house of Congress (9-2)

majority opinion a statement explaining the majority view in a case in which the justices are divided (12-4)

mandatory sentence the punishment that is required by law for a certain crime (17-2)

market economy an economy in which the means of production are privately owned (18-2)

marketing selling a product or service, a process involving advertising and distribution (18-1)

marshal the district court official who serves subpoenas and arrests and delivers defendants to court (12-2)

mass media the sources of information that are widely distributed, including television, radio, newspapers, and magazines (8-1)

master plan a document that states a community's goals and outlines plans for dealing with its changing needs over time (15-1)

mayor the chief executive of a city or town government (14-3)

mediation a way of settling disputes in which a third party listens to both sides and suggests a solution (19-3)

Medicaid federal insurance that pays for the health care of low-income people (21-3)

Medicare health and hospitalization insurance for people 65 and older (21-3)

member-at-large a member of city council who is elected by the entire city (14-3)

mercantilism the theory that a country should sell more goods to other countries than it buys (2-3)

merger the joining of two or more companies to form one large company (19-2)

merit system a system in which government jobs are given to those who are the most qualified (11-4)

metropolitan area a city and its suburbs (14-3)

migration a movement of people from one area or country to another (1-3)

minority leader the leader of the minority party in each house of Congress (9-2)

misdemeanor a relatively minor or less serious crime (13-4)

monetary policy the way in which the government regulates the amount of money in circulation (19-1)

monopoly the control of the supply of a particular product or service by a company or small group of people (19-2)

multinational corporation a business that is based in one country but has branches in several other countries (24-1)

municipal court the lower court of a large city (13-4)

national debt the total amount the government owes on money it has borrowed (20-3)

naturalization the process by which resident aliens become citizens (1-2)

nominate to choose a candidate to run for office (6-3)

nonpartisan not involving political parties (6-4)

nonprofit organization an organization that exists to provide certain goods or services, not to make a profit (18-3)

offender a person who breaks the law (17-4)

oligarchy a system of government in which power is held by a small group of people (22-3)

open shop a factory or business in which workers can choose whether or not to join a union (19-3)

ordinance a law, usually of a city or county (14-1)

original jurisdiction the authority of a court to be the first to hear a case (12-2)

override to defeat a veto on a bill (3-2)

ozone layer a thin layer of gas in the earth's atmosphere that shields us against the sun's ultraviolet radiation (24-2)

PAC Political Action Committee; an organization established to raise money for a political candidate (7-2)

pardon a declaration of forgiveness and freedom from punishment (10-3)

Parliament the British legislature (2-1)

parliamentary government a system in which the power to make and execute laws is controlled by the legislative body (22-1)

parole an early release from prison with certain conditions (13-2)

partnership a business owned by two or more people (18-3)

party whip a party official in Congress who keeps track of how party members vote and persuades party members to vote together on issues (9-2)

passport an official document that identifies a traveler as a citizen of a particular country (11-1)

patronage giving jobs or special favors to loyal party workers (6-3)

penal code the criminal laws of a state (17-2)

perestroika Gorbachev's plan to change the political and economic structure of the Soviet Union (22-2)

petition a formal request for government action (4-2)

petit jury a jury that hears trials (16-2)

pigeonhole to set a bill aside in legislative committee without considering it (9-4)

plaintiff the party filing a lawsuit (16-3)

plank a section of a political party's platform (6-3)

platform the statement of a political party's goals and positions on various public issues (6-3)

plea bargain an arrangement in which a defendant in a criminal case agrees to plead guilty in exchange for some form of leniency (13-4)

pleadings legal documents detailing the issues and points of law raised by both sides in a case (17-1)

plurality in an election, winning more votes than any other party or candidate but not necessarily a majority (6-1)

pocket veto a way the President can kill a bill, when Congress is not in session, by refusing to sign it (9-4)

Politburo an executive body of the Communist Party (22-2)

political machine a strong party organization that can control political appointments and deliver votes (6-3)

polling place the place where votes are cast (7-3)

pollster someone who takes polls, or samples, of public opinion (8-1)

poll tax a sum of money paid in exchange for the right to cast a ballot (4-3)

popular sovereignty the idea that people should have the right to rule themselves (3-3)

popular vote votes cast directly by the people (7-3)

Preamble the introduction to the U.S. Constitution (3-2)

precedent a ruling in an earlier case that is used as the basis for a judicial decision (2-1)

precinct a geographical area that contains a specific number of voters (6-3)

preferred stock stock that earns a fixed amount each year the corporation makes a profit (18-3)

premiums regular payments made on an insurance policy (21-3)

president *pro tempore* the official who presides over the Senate when the Vice President is away (9-2)

primary election an election in which party members choose candidates to run for office (7-2)

principal the original amount of money that was deposited or borrowed and on which interest is paid (21-2)

priorities the goals a community considers most important (15-1)

profit the money that remains after a business has paid its expenses and taxes (18-1)

progressive tax a form of tax in which people who earn more money pay more (20-1)

propaganda techniques used to promote a particular person or idea (7-2)

property tax a tax based on the value of property (20-2)

proposition a petition asking for a new law (7-3)

prosecution the state's side of the proceedings in a criminal trial (17-3)

protectionism the use of tariffs or other barriers to protect a nation's industry (24-1)

public pertaining to the people in a community (5-3)

public opinion the attitudes or opinions of a large group of people on a particular issue or person (8-1)

public policy a policy made by a government (15-1)

quota a fixed number of people allowed or required for a particular function or activity (1-3)

ratify to vote approval of (2-4)

recall an election in which the voters can remove a public official from office (7-3)

recession a slowdown of economic activity (19-1)

recycling reusing old materials to make new ones (15-3)

red tape inefficiency caused by too many rules and regulations (11-4)

referendum an election by which voters can approve or reject a law (7-3)

refugee a person who has left his or her home because of war, famine, or political oppression (1-3)

regressive tax a tax that requires everyone to pay the same amount (20-1)

regulatory commission an independent agency that protects the public by controlling certain types of businesses and industries (11-3)

remand to return a case to a lower court for a new trial (12-2)

repeal to cancel (2-3)

repossess to take back property bought on credit because of nonpayment (21-2)

representative a person who represents other citizens in a government (1-1)

reprieve a delay in carrying out a court order or sentence (10-3)

reserved powers the powers that the Constitution gives to the states (3-3)

resources the materials, people, and money available to a community (15-1)

responsibilities obligations that are fulfilled voluntarily (5-2)

revenue money collected by the government to pay for its activities (20-1)

roll-call vote a procedure in which each person is called upon to announce his or her vote (9-4)

sales tax a tax on the sale of goods (20-2)

search warrant a legal document that allows law enforcement officials to search a suspect's home for evidence (4-1)

segregation the separation of people because of race or ethnic origin (5-1)

select committee a temporary committee formed to deal with a particular issue (9-2)

seniority system a system that gives the most desirable committee assignment to members of Congress who have served the longest (9-2)

sentence the punishment for a crime (17-2)

session the period of time when Congress meets (9-1)

shadow cabinet In Britain, the leaders of the opposition party who follow the activities of the government's cabinet members and who are ready to take over should the government fail (22-1)

single proprietorship a business that is owned by one person (18-3)

slander telling lies about another person with the intent to harm that person (4-2)

socialism an economic system in which the people, through their government, own the means of production (18-2)

socialist economy an economy with features of both a market economy and a command economy (18-2)

Social Security federal insurance, financed by a special tax, that provides benefits to retired and unemployed workers (21-3)

sovereignty the supreme power to govern (22-3)

Speaker of the House the leader of the House of Representatives, who is chosen from the majority party (9-2)

special district a special unit of government set up to deal with a single issue or to provide a single service (14-2)

split ticket the practice of voting for candidates of different parties in an election (7-3)

spoils system the practice of giving jobs as a reward for party loyalty (11-4)

standard of living the quality of life of people as determined by their goods and services and leisure time (19-1)

standing committee a permanent committee in Congress that specializes in a particular area (9-2)

standing vote a way of voting that requires those in favor and then those opposed to a measure to stand and be counted (9-4)

stare decisis the practice of using earlier judicial decisions as the basis for deciding cases (16-1)

stockholders people who purchase shares of ownership in a corporation (18-3)

stocks shares of ownership in corporations (18-3)

straight ticket the practice of voting for all the candidates of one political party (7-3)

strike to refuse to work until an employer meets certain conditions (19-3)

subcommittee a group within a standing committee that handles special problems (9-2)

subpoena a court order requiring a person to appear and testify in court (12-2)

suffrage the right to vote (4-3)

suit a complaint that is made to the court (12-1)

suit of equity a special kind of lawsuit that seeks fair treatment in a situation where there is no law to decide the matter (17-1)

summons a notice directing someone to appear in court to answer a complaint or a charge (17-3)

supply the amount of goods and services available (18-1)

Supremacy Clause the statement in the Constitution that national law has authority over state law (3-3)

tariff a tax on imports that is designed to protect American industries from foreign competition (20-2)

taxable income the amount of money that remains after a taxpayer's exemptions and deductions have been subtracted (20-2)

tax return the form for reporting income, deductions, and so on that each taxpayer must fill out and submit to the government (20-2)

testimony the statements a witness makes under oath (17-3)

third party a minor political party in the United States that challenges the two major parties (6-2)

toleration respect for and acceptance of people of a different race, religion, or life-style (5-2)

town meeting a gathering of the town's citizens to discuss and vote on important issues (2-2)

township a division of a county that has its own government (14-2)

trade deficit the amount by which a country's spending on imports exceeds the amount received from exports (24-1)

traditional economy an economy in which decisions are made according to age-old customs (18-2)

treason an act that endangers one's country or gives assistance to its enemies (4-2)

treaty a formal agreement involving two or more countries (10-2)

trust several separate companies that are run by one board of directors (19-2)

unconstitutional in conflict with the Constitution (12-3)

unicameral having a legislature with one house (13-3)

unit price the price per ounce, pound, or other standard unit of measure (21-1)

urban renewal a project to rebuild a run-down area in a city (15-2)

user fee a tax for the use of a service or product (14-2)

vandalism deliberate destruction of property (17-2)

veto to reject (3-2)

visa a permit that allows a foreign citizen to remain in a country for a certain amount of time (11-1)

voice vote a method of voting in which those favoring a proposal say "yea" and those who are opposed say "nay" (9-4)

voluntarism the tradition of unpaid community service (15-2)

ward a voting district in a city (14-3)

welfare the health, prosperity, and happiness of a community; also public assistance programs for people unable to provide for their own welfare (5-3)

wholesaler a person who buys goods directly from the manufacturer (18-1)

writ of certiorari a request that a lower court send its records on a case to the Supreme Court for review (12-4)

writ of habeas corpus a court order that guarantees an accused person the right to appear before a judge in a court of law (16-2)

zoning board a commission that decides where houses, stores, factories, and offices may be built (15-1)

INDEX

Lenin, Vladimir, 508
Libel, 101-102
Libertarian Party, 144
Limited government, 81, 84, 93
Lincoln, Abraham, 29, 142, 370
Literacy test, 159
Lobbies, 189-190
  regulation of, 190-191
Locke, John, 56, 96

M

McCarthy, Joseph R., 212
McCarthyism, 212
Madison, James, 72, 76, 93, 280
Magazines, consumer, 477
Magna Carta, 45, 48, 59
Marbury v. *Madison*, 280, 282
Marshall, George, 527
Marshall, John, 87, 282, 283, *ill.* 87
Marshall, Thurgood, 284, *ill.* 284
Marshall Plan, 527
Massachusetts, 50, 60
Mayflower Compact, 50, 584
Medicaid, 488
Medicare, 466, 488
"Melting pot," 38
Mercantilism, 52
Merit System Protection Board, 265
Metropolitan area, 334
Middle East, 533
Military service, 126
Minorities, 120, 123, 124, 352. *See also*
  Black Americans; Hispanics; Women.
"Miranda rights," 373, 395
Miranda v. *Arizona*, 375, 395
Money and monetary policies, 297, 436,
  448-450
Monopoly, 439, 441
Morris, Gouverneur, 74
Muller v. *Oregon*, 183
Multiparty system, 140

N

Nader, Ralph, 490, 491, *ill.* 491
Napoleonic Code, 369

National Aeronautics and Space Administration
  (NASA), 259
National Bureau of Standards, 255
National Consumer League, 491
National Highway Traffic Safety Administra-
  tion, 257
National Institutes of Health, 256
National Labor Relations Act, 444
National Labor Relations Board (NLRB),
  444-445
National Oceanic and Atmospheric
  Administration (NOAA), 255
National Park Service, 254
National Patent and Trademark Office, 255
National Security Council (NSC), 241, 526-527
National Weather Service, 255, 442
Naturalization, 33-34
Necessary and Proper Clause, 86, 87
New Jersey Plan, 73
News broadcasts, 133, 158
Newspapers, 133, 149, 178
Nineteenth Amendment, 107
Ninth Amendment, 99, 121
Nixon, Richard, 229, 231, 293
North Atlantic Treaty Organization (NATO),
  506, 525, 526

O

Oath of Allegiance to the United States, 34
Occupational Safety and Health Administration
  (OSHA), 255-256
O'Connor, Sandra Day, 284, *ill.* 284
Office of Administration, 241
Office of Management and Budget, 240-241,
  465-466
Office of Personnel Management, 265
Office of Policy Development, 241
Office of Science and Technology Policy, 241
Office of the United States Trade
  Representative, 241
Oil, 353, 363
One-party system, 140-141
Opinions, respecting, 128-129
Organization of Petroleum Exporting Countries
  (OPEC), 527
Ostracism, 23

* *

ACKNOWLEDGMENTS

Alcoa, 497

Apple Computer, Inc., 425

American Antiquarian Society, 37, 89, 167(right)

Arnold & Brown, 95, 150, 191, 340, 418

James L. Ballard, 401

Roger B. Bean, 120, 128, 132(top), 250, 337, 349, 350(bottom), 378, 388, 477, 487, 539

The Bettmann Archive, 31, 44, 52, 65, 92, 108(left), 115, 123(bottom right), 138, 369, 435, 508, 530

Black Star
 Dennis Brack, 123(top left), 148, 189, 210, 224, 229, 280, 284, 286, 371, 380, 466, 536
 Dannemiller, 249
 Jim Domke, 542
 Rick Friedman, 162, 164
 Andrew Holbrooke, 118, 350
 Shelly Katz, 32
 James Kamp, 149
 Lockwood, 236
 Mike Mauney, 293
 Doug Mazzapica, 16
 Clause Meyer, 561
 Pedro Meyer, 546
 Christopher Morris, 510, 532, 533
 Robin Moyer, 537
 Rob Nelson, 486
 D. B. Owen, 234, 237
 H. K. Owen, 526
 Vladimir Pcholkin, 419
 Ted Spiegel, 550(bottom, inset)
 Ken Rogers, 351
 Pat Tehan, 554
 Peter Turnley, 15, 500, 522, 525, 535, 538
 E. Walter, 528(bottom)
 Fred Ward, 105(top)
Chip Bok, Akron Beacon Journal, 204

Bradley University Library, Peoria, Roger B. Bean, 53, 185

Burlington Coat Factory, Roger B. Bean, 483, 547

C-SPAN, 205

CS&A, 38, 79, 85, 142, 146, 160, 169, 196, 197, 202, 228, 243, 289, 292, 321, 323, 330, 332, 346, 354, 392, 400, 406, 414, 434, 437, 447, 451, 459, 465, 467, 471, 476, 482, 503, 528(top), 545, 552

Centers for Disease Control, Atlanta, 256

City of Chicago Dept. of Streets & Sanitation, 327

Children's Defense Fund, Rick Feinhard, 399

Comstock, 1, 20, 66, 98, 116, 198, 270, 272, 377, 396, 402, 410, 432, 464, 498
 Michael Geissinger, 8
 Russ Kinne, 397
 Stuckey, 13

Consolidated News Pictures, 251, 514, 518
 Peter Girugeon, 504
 Keith Jewell, 218
 Arnie Sachs, 449
 Ron Sachs, 230

David Cornwell, Honolulu, 424

Council for Better Business Bureaus, Roger B. Bean, 491(top right)

Coventry Creative Graphics, 479

Culver Pictures, Inc., 440

Dallas Democratic Party Headquarters, Ann Garvin, 136, 145

Faneuil Hall Marketplace, Inc., 357

Folio, Everett C. Johnson, 364

David R. Frazier Photolibrary, Inc., 12, 14, 24, 25, 132(bottom), 156, 254, 255, 266, 296, 318, 324, 358, 366, 454, 462, 470, 548

David R. Frazier Photolibrary, Inc./David Falconer, 381

WORLD UPDATE

Consultant: Alexey A. Pankin, Directorate of Foreign Relations
Academy of Pedagogical Sciences, Moscow, Russia

A Changing World

AS 1992 DAWNED, the Soviet Union no longer existed; the cold war was at an end; and a new world order was emerging. Only a year earlier, the Soviet Union, although a troubled nation facing economic and ethnic problems, had been a superpower.

In an extremely short period of time during 1991, the 74-year-old Soviet experiment was swept away by an unforeseen series of events. First, an inept group of Communist party hardliners ousted Soviet President Mikhail Gorbachev and proclaimed a new government in the old Communist tradition.

They failed, however, to take into account Russian President Boris Yeltsin, who rallied the Russian people against the new leaders. When the coup collapsed and Gorbachev returned to Moscow, everything had changed: Yeltsin not Gorbachev—was the person in charge.

Gorbachev resigned as head of the Communist party three days later and urged that it be abolished, but nothing could stem the tide of change. First, the

Examining Photographs
Citizens of Moscow, riding a tank and carrying the white, blue, and red flag of pre-Communist Russia, celebrate the collapse of the coup staged by Communist hardliners in August 1991. One factor in the coup's failure was the refusal of the military to carry out the orders of coup leaders to suppress demonstrations.

Baltic republics won their freedom, and then the remaining 12 republics. By year's end, 11 of them had joined in a Commonwealth of Independent States. Russia and Yeltsin were dominant—Gorbachev was forced out of office.

While the Soviet Union entered history, profound changes heralded an uncertain future in eastern Europe. Yugoslavia, once held together by a loyalty to its own brand of communism, began to unravel as communist ideology throughout the region waned. As a result, the country plunged into Europe's first large-scale civil war since 1945.

Meanwhile, the opposite was occurring in western Europe, where the 12 members of the European Community took the first crucial steps toward complete economic and political union. With the forging of a large European market, the European Community hoped to emerge as a global trading power equal to the United States and Japan.

The Soviet Collapse

IN EARLY 1991, many of the Soviet republics were demanding independence from Moscow. To halt the breakup of the Soviet Union, Soviet President Mikhail Gorbachev proposed a new Union Treaty. The treaty was to establish a new constitutional basis for the relationship between the Soviet central government and the republics that made up the Soviet Union. Under the treaty, the republics would gain more control over their industrial and natural resources, while the Kremlin would have a say in economic and political reforms.

Hardliners Oust Gorbachev Fearing the loss of central government authority over the republics, Communist hardliners in August tried to force Gorbachev to declare a state of emergency. When Gorbachev refused, the hardliners ousted the Soviet President from power and formed a ruling committee.

The new leaders immediately clamped down on the press, banned demonstrations, and introduced curfews. After imposing a national state of emergency, the committee tried to use force to consolidate its power. Tanks, armored personnel carriers, and trucks loaded with soldiers swarmed through Moscow. The crackdown, however, was heaviest in the independence-minded Baltic republics. Soviet military officials took control of Lithuania, Latvia, and Estonia, and Soviet troops forced their way into TV and radio stations. Soviet warships blocked the main harbor in Estonia.

People Against the Coup As the coup leaders sought to consolidate their power, Soviet citizens began to respond. Small bands of Moscow residents built barricades of concrete blocks, iron bars, benches, and parked buses to prevent tanks from passing through the streets. In an afternoon of heated exchanges with civilians who climbed aboard their

Examining Photographs Russian President Boris Yeltsin addresses a cheering crowd of pro-democracy supporters outside the Russian parliament building in Moscow, where he had led public resistance against the coup. As a result of the coup's collapse, Yeltsin emerged as the most powerful figure in the Soviet Union.

Examining Photographs *During the days of the coup, supporters of Boris Yeltsin built barricades around the Russian parliament building to protect the Russian President and his staff inside. Many young citizens of Moscow were involved in the resistance to coup leaders.*

tanks, Russian soldiers stationed in Moscow said they did not want to shed Russian blood.

Russian President Boris Yeltsin rallied public support against the coup and for democracy. Appearing before a throng gathered in front of the Russian parliament building, he called for nonviolent resistance and urged military officials to refuse to carry out committee orders.

In response to Yeltsin's appeal, Moscow citizens set up barricades outside the parliament building and in neighboring streets. Tens of thousands of them defied the curfew to stand guard in the rain to protect Yeltsin and his aides, who remained holed up in the parliament building. Aside from a barricade of eight tanks that defected to the side of anti-coup forces, the protesters were unarmed.

Even though a column of tanks maneuvered nearby, no attack occurred. Inside the parliament building, Yeltsin supporters operated fax machines and photocopiers to print makeshift newspapers for distribution throughout the country. The resistance inspired by Yeltsin soon spread beyond Moscow, despite the ban on demonstrations. In Leningrad, 200,000 people jammed the city's main square and cheered for their liberal mayor, Anatoli Sobchak. About 400,000 demonstrators in Kishinev, the capital of Moldova, demanded the resignation of coup leaders and the return of Gorbachev. Coal miners in Siberia and the north carried out strikes, although in other parts of the country, industries were operating normally. In the Baltic republics, the parliaments of Estonia, Latvia, and Lithuania declared full independence from the Soviet Union.

In a startling development, many KGB (secret police) and military units throughout the nation refused to carry out orders from coup leaders.

Collapse of Coup In the face of public resistance, international condemnation, and growing splits within its ranks, the coup crumbled two days after it was announced. As troops and tanks withdrew from Moscow, the Soviet Parliament announced that it had formally reinstated Gorbachev as President. Meanwhile, Soviet police jailed many of the committee members and other conspirators.

Although Gorbachev was back in power, the coup and its failure had made him lose face. It was now

Examining Photographs After the coup's collapse, a wave of anti-Communist feeling swept the Soviet republics. In response to the public mood, Soviet President Mikhail Gorbachev resigned as Communist party leader and ended the party's 74-year rule of the Soviet Union. In Moscow and other Soviet cities, crowds cheered as statues of Lenin and other Communist leaders were removed from public squares and parks.

widely recognized that the coup stemmed from Gorbachev's inability to solve the Soviet Union's many problems and his unwillingness to break with the Communist old guard. The failed coup, on the other hand, had boosted the standing of Boris Yeltsin. Having rallied his people to resistance, Yeltsin was acclaimed as a world-respected leader.

End of Communist Rule Within a few days of the coup's collapse, Gorbachev and Yeltsin began forging a new relationship, one in which Yeltsin had the upper hand. Gorbachev removed from government posts the men who had tried to oust him and promised a renewed push for democratic reforms. He also announced the appointment of committed reformers to government positions. These people were chosen with the consent of Yeltsin and other leaders.

Meanwhile, anti-Communist demonstrations swept the Soviet Union. In Moscow, crowds cheered wildly as giant cranes toppled a large statue of the founder of the KGB. In other areas of the Soviet Union, statues of Communist leaders were removed from public squares. In the weeks that followed, many cities throughout the country began adopting their pre-1917 names. For example, Leningrad, the city that gave birth to the 1917 Bolshevik Revolution, reverted to its historic name: St. Petersburg.

Responding to the rising wave of anti-communism, Gorbachev on August 24 resigned as Communist party leader while remaining Soviet president. He urged the Central Committee—the Communist party's decision-making body—to disband, thus signaling the political collapse of the institution that had ruled the Soviet Union with an iron hand for nearly seven decades.

Gorbachev saw the further erosion of his authority as a number of Soviet republics declared their independence from the central government. Armenia, Georgia, Moldova, and the Baltic republics acted on earlier declarations and declared their full separation from the Soviet Union. The republics of Ukraine and Belarus took the first steps toward independence. The Baltic republics and eventually many of the other republics received recognition from the Soviet Union, the United States, and the European Community.

The Commonwealth

DURING LATE 1991, the Soviet republics faced a deepening economic and political crisis, and growing social tensions were erupting into ethnic conflicts. Declaring that the Soviet Union had ceased to exist, the leaders of the three Slavic republics of Russia, Ukraine, and Belarus announced the formation of a new Commonwealth of Independent States. They named themselves the first three members of the new union, and opened membership to all republics of the former Soviet Union.

The three cofounders of the Commonwealth—President Boris Yeltsin of Russia, President Leonid Kravchuk of Ukraine, and Stanislav Shushkevich, Chairman of the Belarus Parliament—stated that their authority to dissolve the Soviet Union rested on

Examining Photographs *Former Soviet President Mikhail Gorbachev gives a news conference following his resignation speech on December 25, 1991. Although Gorbachev's reforms had failed to halt Soviet economic decline, the Soviet leader won worldwide acclaim for his efforts to make the Soviet Union a freer society.*

the fact their countries were three of the four original cosigners of the 1922 treaty that had created the Union of Soviet Socialist Republics.

The new declaration—signed in Mensk, the capital of Belarus—nullified the Union Treaty proposed by Gorbachev. It stated that the Commonwealth assumed all international responsibilities of the former Soviet Union, including control over the Soviet nuclear arsenal.

In late December at Alma Ata in the republic of Kazakhstan, eight other former Soviet republics joined Russia, Ukraine, and Belarus in signing an accord that made them members of the Commonwealth of Independent States. Only the republic of Georgia did not join the new union.

New Beginning The loosely structured Commonwealth was intended to replace the highly centralized Soviet Union. Under the new arrangement, each member republic was sovereign and independent. A central administration, however, was established in Mensk to coordinate economic and monetary policies. In matters of defense, Commonwealth leaders agreed to a permanent unified command over the nuclear weapons held by Russia, Ukraine, and Kazakhstan, but each republic asserted the right to organize and maintain its own conventional military forces.

Resignation of Gorbachev On December 25, Mikhail Gorbachev resigned the Soviet presidency. "We are now living in a new world," he declared

COMMONWEALTH OF INDEPENDENT STATES

Examining Maps *The Commonwealth of Independent States is a loose alliance of republics, shown above with their capitals. Formed in December 1991, the Commonwealth replaced the Soviet Union, which Mikhail Gorbachev had tried unsuccessfully to reform during the late 1980s and early 1990s.*

THE EMERGING COMMONWEALTH

Republic (Date Independence Declared)	Capital	Population Estimates	Ethnic Groups	Major Products	Before Union Breakup
Armenia (9/23/91)	Erivan	3,305,000	90% Armenian 5% Azeri 5% Russian,	chemicals, machinery, textiles, grapes	0.2% land 1.2% pop. .9% GNP
Azerbaijan (8/30/91)	Baku	7,145,600	80% Azeri 8% Russian 8% Armenian 4% Daghestani	oil, copper, chemicals, cotton, rice, grapes, tobacco, silk	0.3% land 2.4% pop. 1.7% GNP
Kyrgyzstan (8/31/91)	Bishkek	4,372,000	52% Kirghiz 22% Russian 13% Uzbek 4% Ukrainian 2% Tatars	wool, livestock, machine and instrument production	0.9% land 1.5% pop. 0.8% GNP
Belarus (8/25/91)	Mensk	10,200,000	79% Byelorussian 12% Russian 4% Polish 2% Ukrainian 1% Jewish	chemicals, agri-cultural machinery, paper, building materials, potatoes, livestock	1.0% land 3.5% pop. 4.2% GNP
Georgia* (8/23/91)	Tbilisi	5,538,000	69% Georgian 9% Armenian 9% Russian	tea, citrus fruits, grapes, silk, tobacco, manganese, coal	0.3% land 1.9% pop. 1.6% GNP
Kazakhstan (10/26/90)	Alma Ata	16,538,000	36% Kazakh 41% Russian 6% Ukrainian	cotton, millet, coal, oil, lead, zinc, copper	12.1% land 5.7% pop. 4.3% GNP
Moldova (8/27/91)	Kishinev	4,321,000	64% Moldovan 14% Ukrainian 13% Russian	wines, tobacco, grain, vegetables	0.2% land 1.5% pop. 1.2% GNP
Russia (6/12/90)	Moscow	147,386,000	83% Russian more than 100 ethnic groups	chemicals, building materials, machine steel, cars, trucks, wheat, barley, rye, potatoes, sugar beets	76.6% land 51.4% pop. 61.1% GNP
Tajikistan (9/9/91)	Dushanbe	5,112,000	59% Tajik 23% Uzbek 10% Russian	cattle, sheep, fruit, hydroelectric power	0.7% land 1.8% pop. 0.8% GNP
Turkmenistan (8/22/90)	Ashkhabad	3,621,000	68% Turkmeni 13% Russian 9% Uzbek	oil, sulphur, cotton, dates, olives, figs	2.2% land 1.3% pop. 0.7% GNP
Ukraine (8/24/91)	Kiev	51,704,000	74% Ukrainian 21% Russian 1% Jewish	wheat, sugar beets, iron, oil, chemicals, machinery	2.7% land 18.0% pop. 16.2% GNP
Uzbekistan (8/31/91)	Tashkent	19,906,000	69% Uzbek 11% Russian 4% Tatar	cotton	2.0% land 6.9% pop. 3.3% GNP

*has not yet decided to join Commonwealth

Examining Photographs *In late December 1991, leaders of the new Commonwealth of Independent States met in Mensk, the capital of Belarus, to discuss military policies. They agreed to have a permanent unified command over nuclear weapons, but allowed each republic the right to maintain its own conventional forces.*

on state-run television. The former leader expressed concern for the new Commonwealth of Independent States: "I'm worried by the fact the people have lost the citizenship of a great country. The consequences can be unpredictable."

Following Gorbachev's speech, the red hammer and sickle Soviet flag that had flown over the Kremlin for 74 years was lowered and replaced with the white, blue, and red flag of Russia.

Yeltsin and Russia While signaling the end of Gorbachev's presidency, the formation of the Commonwealth confirmed Yeltsin's rise to power. Although the leaders of the 11 republics in the Commonwealth considered themselves equal, Yeltsin was the first among equals. His Russian Federation was the most powerful nation in the Commonwealth. By far the largest nation in land area and population, Russia produces about 90 percent of the oil and natural gas in the Commonwealth.

Just as his country far outstripped the other 10 in the Commonwealth, so did Boris Yeltsin's powers outstrip those of the other leaders—in fact, if not on paper. During the final months of the Soviet Union, Yeltsin assumed complete control over production and export of Russia's resources. He began monetary reforms designed to force the other republics to follow Russia's pace of change, and persuaded the Russian Parliament to vote him any powers necessary to implement reforms.

Yeltsin further expanded his leadership when he engineered the Commonwealth. As the new arrangement became more and more of a reality, Yeltsin took control of the Kremlin and all Soviet central government agencies. He assumed command of former Soviet President Mikhail Gorbachev's staff and office, and placed the Soviet Foreign Ministry and embassies under Russian control. With Gorbachev's resignation and Yeltsin's responsibility for the former Soviet Union's nuclear arsenal, Yeltsin, along with United States President Bush, became one of the world's most powerful leaders.

Although Yeltsin was the most influential Commonwealth leader, he had to assume responsibility for Russia's problems: a shattered economy, deteriorating public services, and ethnic strife. The Russian government had to carry the brunt of the Soviet Union's budget and debt load. As Russia's leader, Yeltsin also had to lead the Commonwealth into the international free market system, make good on his promise to revive a shattered economy, improve public services, and settle ethnic unrest. Finally, he had to demonstrate to the other republics and to the global community that Russia would not use its power to turn the Commonwealth into a new authoritarian Russian empire.

Economic Crisis Although the Commonwealth broke decisively with the Soviet past, its member republics faced a host of economic problems. These included rising prices, stagnant overseas trade, a decaying transportation system, and a declining standard of living. Continuing political instability also hindered the former Soviet republics from introducing workable economic reforms.

The economic crisis was particularly severe in the area of agriculture. Unresolved problems of food production and distribution, inherited from the previous centralized and subsidized system, had been heightened by months of political turmoil and governmental neglect.

Small farms and state-run complexes had long blamed the Soviet government for failing to deliver promised farm machinery and other equipment. In retaliation, farmers routinely "hid" thousands of tons of grain to use as barter on the black market. The results were seen in the fact that state stores had continual shortages of produce.

Examining Charts
In January 1992, Yeltsin and other Commonwealth leaders lifted long-standing price controls in an effort to bring more food to store shelves in their individual republics. As the figures here indicate, prices of goods in government-run stores immediately rose to high levels, while prices continued even higher in free-enterprise markets. Although ordinary citizens grumbled, Commonwealth leaders saw the ending of price controls as a necessary, though painful, step in the process of moving their economies toward capitalism.

Price Increases in Russia, January 1992						
	Old subsidized state price	Hours of work*	New price at state stores	Hours of work*	Price at private market stores	Hours of work*
Smoked sausage rubles per pound	35.5	17.8	49.1	24.5	68.2	34.1
Chicken rubles per pound	15.5	7.8	21.6	10.8	40.9	20.5
Butter rubles per pound	4.5	2.3	20.5	10.3	50	25
White bread rubles per loaf	.6	18 minutes	49.1	54 minutes	n/a	n/a
Milk rubles per quart	.69	21 minutes	2.1	1.1	37.1	18.6
Gasoline (93 octane) rubles per quart	.42	13 minutes	1.3	39 minutes	3.2	1.6

*Number of hours an average worker must work to earn that amount, based on about 175 hours of work per month.

Source: AP

Manufacturers of farm machinery also had complained of the same neglect and government disinterest as the farmers. During 1991, plants reported production drops of as much as 90 percent because of a lack of parts and supplies.

Another problem inherited from the past was the antiquated method of harvesting and getting crops to market. On many farms, harvesting was still done by hand; students and soldiers were drafted to pick, load, and unload crops. The poor transportation system also contributed its share to agricultural shortcomings. The system was not capable of delivering the goods.

Plagued by long-standing problems of machine shortages, outdated farming practices, and inadequate transportation, the agricultural sector was further afflicted by new problems arising from the political unrest of 1991. Many farmers, now free to sell crops to the highest bidder, refused to sell any to the crumbling state system at rock-bottom prices. As a result, government grain houses were empty during the months of the autumn harvest.

The collapse of Gorbachev's government meant that no central agency was in control of the flow of food and supplies between the republics. In the absence of central leadership, the republics began taking matters into their own hands. Early in October, Ukraine—the traditional "breadbasket" of the Soviet Union—banned grain exports to other republics. The other republics followed suit as winter approached. By December, a lack of food exports was causing serious food shortages in many of Russia's cities, most notably Moscow and St. Petersburg, and other nonagricultural areas. Some locations officially reserved all meat and milk supplies for schools and hospitals. Adding to food shortages was 1991's lowered grain production.

The economy's disintegration was seen in other areas. Inflation skyrocketed as government presses printed more currency to cover growing government expenditures. Fuel shortages led to cold living facilities, the shutdown of many airports, and the cancellation of most domestic flights. Consumers stood in long lines at stores, people foraged in fields, and older citizens and the poor combed garbage dumps for food and clothing.

In a rapid shift to free enterprise, the governments of Russia and the other republics lifted price controls

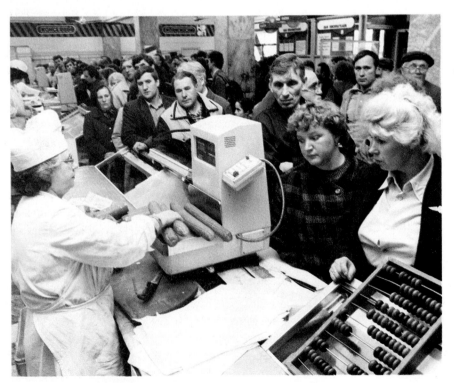

Examining Photographs
Russian shoppers form lines to purchase scarce food items in a government-run produce store. By early 1992, declining production, inadequate distribution, and widespread hoarding had led to food shortages in many towns and cities throughout Russia and the other republics.

Examining Photographs *A woman in the Georgian capital of Tbilisi stands in front of her house that was burned to the ground as a result of street violence between troops loyal to President Zviad Gamsakhurdia and opposition forces. Gamsakhurdia was later ousted from power, but he continued to resist the new military government that succeeded him.*

in early January 1992. Although prices rose significantly as a result, officials hoped that the move would in the long run spur production, stimulate competition, and lower prices. By late February, however, prices still had not declined, although more food had appeared in produce stores and emergency supplies were arriving from the United States and other foreign nations.

As the economic crisis continued, public opinion became divided. Many older Russians expressed a longing to return to the Communist system, while younger Russians preferred to support Yeltsin and to give his reforms more time to work. Meanwhile, critics of Yeltsin's reform plans emerged within the government. Vice-President Alexander Rutskoi led the attack, calling for an end to economic "shock therapy" and a return to government controls.

Future Prospects At the beginning of 1992, predictions about the future of the Commonwealth varied. Pessimists concluded that continuing economic distress could deepen into famine. Such a situation, they said, might lead to riots, civil war, and the return of dictatorship.

Optimists, while acknowledging the critical economic situation, did not expect widespread famine. They predicted continued shortages, long lines of dissatisfied shoppers, and perhaps "pockets of poverty" at the mercy of the decaying transportation system. They did not necessarily believe that the Commonwealth was headed for dictatorship.

Whether pessimists or optimists, experts agreed that the Commonwealth's job of converting to a free market economy would be long-term and would not bring prosperity for many years. During the transition, they stated, unemployment in the republics would rise as inefficient industries closed. Inflation would continue as the lifting of price controls took effect. Very few citizens anywhere in the Commonwealth would adjust easily to these changes.

Georgia Beset by internal conflict, Georgia was the only former Soviet republic that did not immediately join the Commonwealth of Independent States. In December 1991, heavy fighting flared between troops loyal to President Zviad Gamsakhur (zvee·AHD gahm·sah·KOOR·dee·ah) and rebel forces. Gamsakhurdia had become increasingly unpopular since his election in May. In recent months, the president had closed opposition newspapers, fired government officials who questioned his policies, and persecuted non-Georgian groups. Gamsakhurdia's opponents accused him of being a dictator and resorted to force to remove him from power.

Vowing not to resign, Gamsakhurdia sought refuge in the parliament building, while his troops battled rebels in the streets of Tbilisi, the capital. Finally, in early January 1992, Gamsakhurdia's forces were defeated by the rebels, and the president fled to neighboring Armenia. A military junta came to power, promising new elections in the spring for a civilian government that would establish a democratic system.

Support for the deposed president, however, re-mained strong, as daily pro-Gamsakhurdia rallies took place in Tbilisi. During the first week in January, gunmen loyal to the military junta fired on the demonstrators, killing at least two civilians and wounding as many as 30 others. The junta, which had declared a state of emergency, regretted the shootings but defended the need for law and order. Meanwhile, Georgia's political leaders contin-ued to debate the country's future.

Changes in Europe

DURING THE PERIOD of the Soviet collapse, Europe underwent a number of significant changes. In eastern Europe, nations newly freed from Commu-nist rule experienced difficulties adjusting to democracy and free enterprise economies. In western Europe, the nations of the European Community pushed for closer political and eco-nomic union.

Yugoslav Civil War In June 1991, the Yugoslav republics of Croatia and Slovenia declared their independence from Yu-goslavia. Both had long-standing differences with the neighboring Yugoslav republic of Serbia. For months, both Croatia and Slo-venia had demanded that they would leave the Yugoslav federation if Serbia did not meet their demands to trans-form the nation into a community of equal and sovereign republics. Serbia favored the present federal system, while Croatia and Slo-venia wanted a looser

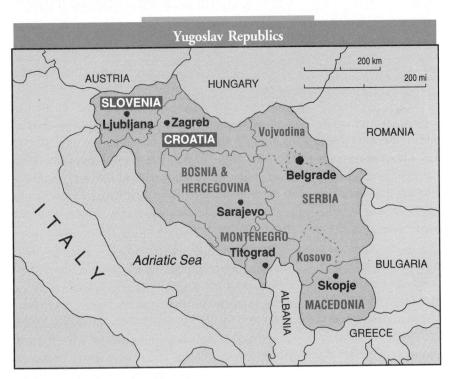

Yugoslav Republics

Examining Maps *Formed as a Communist republic in 1945, Yugoslavia until recently was a federation of six republics (Serbia, Croatia, Slovenia, Macedonia, Montenegro, and Bosnia and Hercegovina) and two provinces (Kosovo and Vojvodina). During the 1980s, Communist authority declined, the federal government weakened, and traditional ethnic rivalries surfaced once again. In 1991, civil war fragmented Yugoslavia following declarations of independence by Slovenia and Croatia. By early 1992, many foreign governments had recognized the independence of the individual Yugoslav republics.*

Examining Photographs
A young Croatian soldier fires on federal Yugoslav forces attacking a Croatian town. In early 1992, United Nations peacekeeping forces prepared to end the Yugoslav civil war, Europe's first full-scale conflict since 1945.

arrangement that would end what they regarded as Serb domination of their affairs.

The declarations of independence led to an outbreak of hostilities. Following Slovenia's announcement, Slovene citizens blocked many roads in their republic to prevent Yugoslav federal army units from reaching federal customs posts on the Italian, Austrian, and Hungarian borders. The federal troops, composed mainly of Serbs, battled Slovene militia units for control of the posts.

In early July, Slovenia freed captured federal troops, and the federal government stated that its army would not strike at Slovenia again. Federal and Slovene officials agreed to a cease-fire, accepting mediation from the European Community. Negotiators, who included the foreign ministers of Portugal, Luxembourg, and the Netherlands, agreed to start talks on aspects of Yugoslavia's future.

Meanwhile, Croatia's declaration of independence heightened already strained relations between the republic's Croatian majority and its Serb minority. The Serbs, who live in the northwestern part of Croatia, had declared their independence from Croatia in March, affirming their desire to unite with Serbia. Serb guerrillas then barricaded the roads, destroyed rail lines leading into their communities, and seized Croatian government buildings in the region.

In May, the Yugoslav federal government sent troops to Croatia in an effort to maintain order. The presence of the federal army, however, only fueled tensions between Serbs and Croatians. Because Yugoslavia's military was dominated by Serbs, Croatians accused the army of backing the guerrillas.

Fighting between the Croatians and ethnic Serbs continued into the early summer and intensified Croatian desires for independence. During July, the Serbs battled Croatian militia forces over a wide area of Croatia, thwarting the peace efforts of the European Community.

By late 1991, the conflict had become the first full-scale war in Europe since 1945. In November, Croatia appealed to the United Nations for help. By that time, Serb-dominated forces controlled more than a third of the republic. In January 1992, a cease-fire agreement finally was reached, and the United Nations prepared to send a peacekeeping force.

While peace efforts continued, various European nations became increasingly involved in the crisis. In January 1992, Germany announced that it was recognizing the independence of Slovenia and Croatia as well as any other Yugoslav republic that also requested such recognition. Other foreign ministers of the European Community followed Germany's lead, agreeing to diplomatic ties if the Yugoslav republics met a series of criteria, including respect for the rights of minorities within each republic's borders. Serbia warned that these moves would only deepen and expand the civil war.

European Unity While eastern Europe was torn by ethnic strife, western Europe took steps toward greater unity. During a December 1991 summit meeting at Maastricht in the Netherlands, leaders of the 12-nation European Community approved two treaties designed to move their countries closer to political and economic union. One treaty provided for the eventual creation of a common European currency and monetary system; the other paved the way for common defense, foreign, and economic policies. The heads of government also pledged Community economic assistance to the poorest members—Greece, Ireland, and Portugal.

Britain, which was very reluctant to cede any national sovereignty, succeeded in having removed from the second treaty a provision establishing common social welfare and labor policies. British Prime Minister John Major had insisted that each nation should set its own standards in each of these areas.

THE EUROPEAN COMMUNITY 1992

Examining Maps As it moves toward full economic and political unity, the 12-nation European Community is playing a larger role in European and world affairs. In late 1991, it intervened as a mediator in the Yugoslav civil war. In early 1992, the Community provided emergency aid to eastern Europe and the Commonwealth republics.

At Britain's request, members also removed from the treaties any references to the creation of a federal system for Europe, the expansion of the European Parliament's powers, and the requirement that all members must accept the change to a single currency.

"We have different traditions and different points of view," said Ruud Lubbers, Prime Minister of the Netherlands. "But if you take that into account, it is quite a miracle that we agreed." Although progress had been made on specific issues, European Community leaders still disagreed over how close a European union would be, what powers a central European government would have, and the steps to take toward union.

The European drive for economic and political union was powered by the desire to create a strong unit capable of competing with the United States and Japan in the global market. To many Europeans, a unified European economy was a necessity, particularly in light of

Examining Photographs *The European Community's flag, showing a circle of 12 stars on a dark blue background, flies outside Community headquarters in Brussels, Belgium. In February 1992, the European flag was flown for the first time at an Olympics ceremony when the 16th Olympic Winter Games opened in Albertville, France.*

recent American, Canadian, and Mexican moves toward a free trade area in North America, as well as Japanese efforts to strengthen trading links with the rest of the Pacific region.

WORLD UPDATE FOCUS

1. World History Why did the Soviet coup fail? How did it affect the Soviet Union?

2. Government & Civics How is the Commonwealth of Independent States politically organized?

3. Geography Which Commonwealth republic is the largest in land area?

4. Economics What problems did the economies of the Commonwealth republics face in early 1992? What steps did Commonwealth leaders take toward free market systems?

5. U.S. History How has the United States responded to the economic crisis in the Commonwealth republics? How do you think the breakup of the Soviet Union and the end of the cold war will affect the United States?

6. World History Why did Croatia and Slovenia declare their independence from Yugoslavia? What role have the United Nations and the European Community played in the Yugoslav civil war?

7. Geography Where are Croatia and Slovenia located?

8. Economics How are economies changing in the nations of eastern Europe?

9. Government & Civics What agreements were reached by European Community members at their recent summit conference? How did Britain's position differ from that of other members?

10. World History Based on current trends, what kind of world order do you think might emerge by the year 2000?

Photo Credits

G82267.01